The **Rough Guide** to

Oregon and Washington

written and researched by

JD Dickey and Phil Lee

ROUGH
GUIDES

NEW YORK · LONDON · DELHI

www.roughguides.com

Contents

Beervana color section
following p.88

Scenic hikes color
section following p.440

◄◄ Haystack Rock at Cannon Beach, Oregon ◄ Ski tracks at Mount Bachelor, Oregon

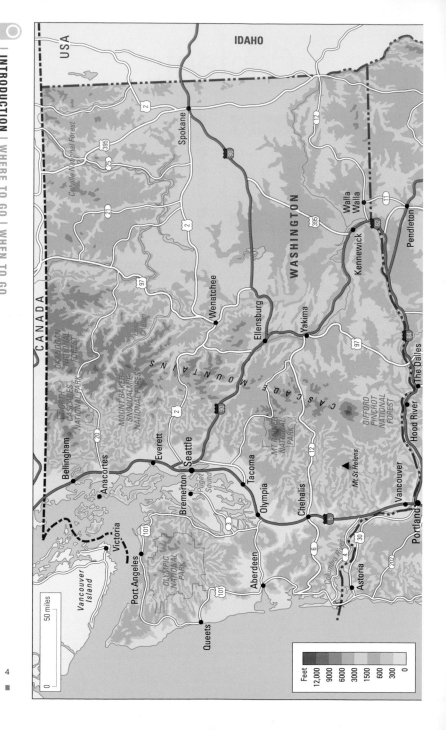

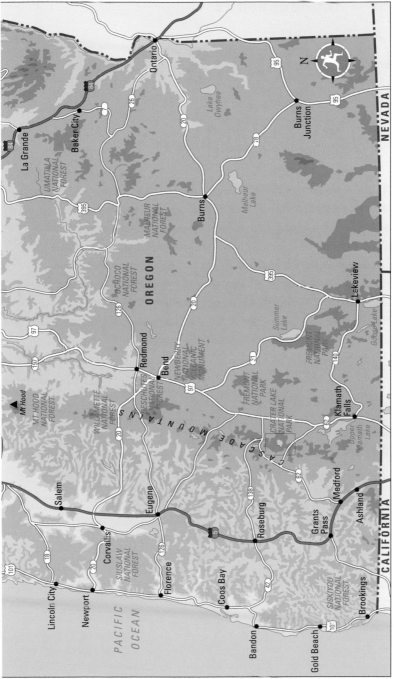

Introduction to

Oregon and Washington

Nestled up in the far northwestern corner of the continental United States, Oregon and Washington together make up one of North America's scenic gems, a highly varied realm of striking forests, beaches, and mountains, where the outdoors in all its rugged glory is always close at hand. Here you can find abundant fauna and flora – from wolves and whales to wildflowers and western hemlocks – and a formidable landscape of active volcanoes, lava beds, sheer cliffs, towering waterfalls, and untouched wilderness.

It's also a place of historical riches, thick with Native American, pioneer and cowboy legend and lore, elegantly preserved Victorian buildings, abandoned military forts, and romantic ghost towns. Beyond the compelling displays of nature and history, though, the region really hums with contemporary activity, with excellent seafood and Northwest Cuisine, state-of-the-art museums, and some of the continent's most urbane cities and evocative hamlets.

In the mid-nineteenth century, the Pacific Northwest was a distant land accessed mainly by a network of stark, rutted wagon trails. Most of these trails were carved in the 1840s and 1850s during the **Great Migration**, the massive exodus of farmers and prospective settlers from the Midwest to the edge of the continent – an unprecedented shift encouraged by the promise of cheap land, good soil, and a fresh start. Since those hallowed days – partly mythical, partly genuine – the region has grown in fits and starts, boosted by a gold rush here or bountiful fishing there but all too susceptible to the boom-and-bust cycles of resource-based economies: overfishing, timber clear-cutting, gold-scouring, and so on. Only in the past few decades have the old agricultural and manufacturing staples given way to an economy based on tourism, real estate, and the service sector, reflecting the major cities' flexibility to adapt to changing conditions. For one, **Seattle**, the Northwest's economic powerhouse, started out as a mill town, burgeoned as a trading post for the Alaska Gold Rush, hit an economic downturn before being revived by the defense industries of World War II, declined in the 1970s, then exploded as a high-tech center in the 1990s. The same varying pattern is true for **Portland**, and, to a lesser degree, the smaller towns that sit at the edge of forests, rivers, or the ocean.

Washington and Oregon do, however, differ in their attitudes toward **change** and **development**. With the notable exception of Seattle, the major cities and towns of **Washington** are fairly relaxed and unassuming, from pleasant mountain hamlets like Winthrop to quirky burgs like Oysterville. The more conservative of the two states, Washington heartily embraces the defense establishment, resulting in a slew of military bases and defense contractors like Boeing, and has little doubt that business development is the proper way to advance civic goals and make "progress." In these ways and others, **Oregon** couldn't be more different. Perhaps the most proudly provincial place in the country, the state is well known for its hostile attitudes toward unencumbered development and population growth. "You are welcome to visit Oregon, but please don't stay," Governor Tom McCall (in)famously said in 1971 – for some residents, still the prevailing view. For that and other reasons, the state has sometimes suffered economically, but such provincialism,

Fact file

• Seattle is the 23rd largest city in the US and Portland the 30th, each with around half a million people in its city limits, though the metro region of Seattle is about twice as large as that of Portland.

• Ethnically, Oregon and Washington are about 80 percent Anglo, 10–12 percent Latino, 3–5 percent Asian, 2–3 percent black, and less than 2 percent Native American.

• Mount Rainier is the region's tallest peak, at 14,411ft; Crater Lake is the deepest lake in North America, at 1932ft at its lowest point; and the Columbia River, at 1214 miles, is the second-longest river in the Western Hemisphere flowing into the Pacific Ocean.

• The name Oregon was derived either from the French word for hurricane, *ouragan*, or from a cartographical error, while Washington is named after the first American president. Seattle is widely known as the Emerald City, and Portland is variously called the Rose City, PDX, or Stumptown.

• Quillayute, Washington, is the rainiest place in the Pacific Northwest, getting 105 inches per year on the coast of Olympic National Park. Oregon's leader, Astoria, is a distant second, receiving 66 inches at the mouth of the Columbia River.

Volcanoes

The **Cascades** are the only active volcanoes in the contiguous United States. They run from southern British Columbia to Northern California but are most visible as the mountainous spine that crosses central Oregon and Washington. Although the geologic history of these mountains is impressive

enough (see box, p.223), what really grabs you about traveling through this alpine landscape is what a varied terrain it is – though one continually shaped and violently rearranged by geothermal and climatic forces. Encompassing chilly lava-tube caves, great expanses of rocky basalt, majestic icy summits, assorted hot springs and waterfalls, cinder-cone buttes, blown-out craters, and huge hills of black volcanic glass, the Cascades provide vivid testimony to the power of the earth's dynamic forces. There are countless opportunities to go wandering through this volcanic land as well, whether gliding through it on skis or a snowboard, plunging down its river canyons on a kayak or raft, using crampons to climb up its glaciers, or simply hiking around in a sturdy pair of boots. For some journeys you may need a detailed forest map, especially if exploring an official wilderness area, but for most trips the major highways should suffice. In fact, just off the road you may find some of the region's best settings, paths, and views of this scenic topography, without having to resort to an endless slog through the outback.

combined with big-city liberalism, has also helped it conserve its heritage, as well as countless parks and natural reserves.

Where to go

The one Pacific Northwest city that everyone knows, **Seattle** is as frenetic and freewheeling a place as you're likely to find on the West Coast outside of California, and is packed with scenic hills and winding streets and an appealing array of public artworks and outdoor markets. In Oregon, straddling the Willamette River, **Portland** boasts excellent bars, clubs, and restaurants, and features some of the best parks, gardens, and wilderness of any urban area in America. Portland is a national leader in promoting that elusive commodity known as "**quality**

of life," providing clean air, plenty of rustic parks, and abundant bus routes and bicycle lanes. Of the Northwest's smaller cities, **Tacoma** is an increasingly popular spot for viewing contemporary art and historic preservation; **Eugene** has a broad appeal for its laid-back leftist attitudes, lovely college setting, and licit (urban trails) and illicit (marijuana) pleasures; and hamlets such as **Ashland**, **Walla Walla**, and **Port Townsend** draw most of their fans for a single reason – a Shakespeare festival, an array of wineries, and Victorian architecture, respectively.

Beyond these cities, though, there can be no mistaking the Pacific Northwest's real attraction: its eye-popping array of gorgeous **landscapes and seascapes**, brimming with majestic peaks that soar over wooded valleys, expansive glaciers on the edge of volcanoes, stark lava fields and craters, thundering whitewater rivers, rainbow-hued fossil beds, colossal sand dunes, sun-dappled rain forests, cowboy vistas right out of the Wild West, and serpentine beaches peppered with giant rocky sea stacks. Much of this topography remains wild, empty, and fairly untouched by modern hands yet at the same time is rendered accessible by a network of superbly run national, state, and local parks.

A trip through the Northwest is best organized by terrain, starting east of Portland with the massive, geological oddity of the **Columbia River Gorge**, where historic roads pass by high waterfalls, charming burgs like Hood River, great imposing structures like the Bonneville Dam, and some of the best windsurfing spots in the country. West of Portland, the beautiful **Oregon Coast** is a well-protected strip of beaches, sand dunes, and rocky cliffs punctuated by excellent state parks and hiking trails, and a few interesting towns like the old nautical redoubt of Astoria and the pleasant port and aquarium of Newport. South of Portland, I-5 leads you through the **Willamette and Rogue River valleys**, which are rich with pioneer and religious enclaves, old-time country lanes, and covered bridges – not to mention a burgeoning, nationally acclaimed wine industry. In the

▼ Hikers in Columbia River Gorge – Eagle Creek

▲ Oregon Shakespeare Festival, Ashland

Willamette Valley, the state capital of Salem is mildly interesting for its museums and architecture, but less enticing than the thumping college town of Eugene. The Rogue River Valley is mainly worthwhile for the historic preserve of Jacksonville, the Bard-centric Ashland, and a short distance away, the eerie Oregon Caves.

Due east of the valleys, the great volcanic spine of the **Oregon Cascades** holds some of the region's most dramatic landscapes – craggy peaks and lava fields, fields of wildflowers, hidden caves and hot springs, looming glaciers, and glittering lakes and rivers – which you can explore on hikes, cycling trips, and scenic drives. The area's urban center is the outdoor-sports and microbrewing nexus of Bend, while its scenic focus is the dazzling blue oasis of **Crater Lake**, the nation's deepest lake, occupying the bowl of an ancient volcano. Farther east, in the rain shadow of the Cascades, **Eastern Oregon** is desert and lava-bed country, where prehistoric creatures became entombed as fossils and legendary ranchers once ran huge acreages teeming with cattle; today Western relics serve as reminders of the good old days of gold rushes, stagecoach lines, and mining camps, while fossil excavation sites throw a light on the far more distant past. On the very edge of the state is one of its essential sights – the wide, deep chasm of **Hells Canyon**, marking Oregon's eastern boundary with Idaho.

Washington's landscapes are no less appealing. Branching out from the Emerald City of Seattle, **Puget Sound** is for many the state's recreational highlight, a huge inlet bounded by engaging cities like Bellingham and

Olympia at either end, but best for its collection of sparkling islands and fetching waterside scenery, where hamlets like Port Gamble preserve the splendor of the past while bastions like Fort Ebey and the American and English camps are historically evocative treasures. For many visitors, though, the highlight of the Sound is a trip to the **San Juan Islands**, isolated spots of rustic beauty and small-town quaintness on the ferry route from Anacortes.

Continuing west from Puget Sound, the **Olympic Peninsula** is notable for the nineteenth-century Victoriana of Port Townsend and the native culture of Neah Bay but is best known as the site of the huge **Olympic National Park**, an eclectic wonderland of glacial peaks, winding trails, temperate rain forests, towering ridges, and remote beaches, crowned by the dramatic presence of **Mount Olympus**. South of the peninsula, Southwest Washington has few sights except for cranberry bogs, oyster beds, the rugged headlands of state parks at the mouth of the Columbia River, and

Sounds of the Pacific Northwest

The Pacific Northwest is one of the few regions outside of New York, California, and the South to invent its own subcategory of popular **music** – grunge. This blend of 1980s indie rock with punk and metal was set to its own gloomy, introspective beat and offered lyrics that nicely matched the region's  dark winter climate. It was also enormously influential in the 1990s and changed the music business, at least at the independent level, for the better. It may have died more than a decade ago, but its do-it-yourself – "DIY" – spirit continues to enliven the music scene throughout the Northwest in a variety of genres. Seattle, former grunge nexus, still has it all, from jazz and blues to punk and pop, while Portland is more of an upstart in recent years, attracting indie rockers from around the country — from the Shins to Modest Mouse to the Decemberists — for its hip image and unpretentious vibe. Folk, alt-country, and rock are mainstays in the cities, as they are in the college settings of Eugene and Olympia. Being in a band in the urban Northwest is the equivalent to writing a screenplay in Los Angeles, *de rigueur* for any would-be artist. When walking around the groovier parts of town — from East Portland to Seattle's Capitol Hill and U District — you'll be able to hear the echo of countless electric guitarists, bassists, and drummers practicing behind garage doors, in the ongoing quest to make it big on their own terms, trying to become the next Nirvana, Soundgarden, or Pearl Jam.

the historical site of Fort Vancouver. East of Puget Sound, the **Washington –Cascades** stretch northeast-southwest, separating the state's wet western half from its drier eastern counterpart. The explosive giant of **Mount St Helens** is the most famous member of this lengthy mountain range; other major peaks include scenic **Mount Rainier** – the tallest of the Cascades in the Northwest – and the winter playground of **Mount Baker**. The best driving concourse in these mountains is the massive circuit of the **Cascade Loop**, which navigates the high slopes of North Cascades National Park and passes such compelling sights as the thin finger of Lake Chelan and oddball theme towns like the faux-Bavaria of Leavenworth. As the mountains descend to foothills and parched valleys, **Eastern Washington** emerges as a fascinating, geologically scarred terrain of massive dry waterfalls, towering mesas of volcanic rock, and the hydroelectric colossus of the Grand Coulee Dam. Its towns, too, are worth a look, from the engaging Western spirit of Ellensburg to the winery hubs of Walla Walla and the Yakima Valley to the diverting city of **Spokane** at the eastern border.

Scenic drives

For many, the best way to experience the Pacific Northwest is to take a **scenic drive** on any of several unmissable routes. In Washington the most prominent is the huge **Cascade Loop** (see p.418) through the north-central part of the state, a 350-mile circuit leading over mountain slopes and valleys

and past quirky small towns and attractive waterfalls. Also worthwhile is the section of **Highway 101** around Olympic National Park (see p.399), bringing you close to the park's various beaches, rain forests, canyons, and mountain peaks. The section of this highway in Oregon is perhaps even better, lining the Oregon Coast and its eye-catching ports, beaches, sand dunes, and lighthouses – most of them linked by an interconnected string of state parks. The best known of the state's various scenic drives, though, is the **Historic Columbia River Gorge Highway** (see p.121), an early auto route from the 1910s that leads past some of the gorge's most stunning scenery – waterfalls, rocky cliffs, and wildflower meadows – and has been converted in some places to a hiking and biking zone. Finally, Oregon's main section of the Cascades has many excellent drives, the finest of which may be the seasonally open **Highway 242** (see p.245), which passes volcanic peaks, beautiful alpine lakes, and a massive lava field crowned by a jagged stone observatory.

When to go

▲ Farmers market, Eugene

Although wary attitudes toward the larger world are most apparent in Oregon, they're not absent from the rest of the region, either. One handy way of keeping out interlopers, and thereby managing growth, is to encourage the most exaggerated stories of the area's overcast **weather** and **rain**. Instead of downplaying the moist climate – or mentioning that the region is far from a national precipitation leader, and it's only in **winter** that storms are constant – Northwesterners enjoy frightening outsiders by tales of gale-force winds, unending weeks of rain, permanently gloomy skies, and occasional bouts of thick hail and snow. Of course, you can get quite drenched here from November to March, but the **summers** are typically lovely and free of storm clouds, and most residents have long since learned to deal with the elements by bundling up and wearing stocking caps – umbrellas are an uncommon sight, held only by newcomers and tourists. Keep in mind that during the **spring** and **fall**, the weather can get quite **erratic**, and no one day may be purely sunny, rainy,

▼ Edmonds-Kingston ferry, Washington

or windy – indeed, sometimes the climate can turn from chilly and rainy to bright and sunny within a single hour or less. It's not unheard of, either, to go sunbathing just a short time after it's been hailing.

In planning your trip, keep in mind that **midsummer** may be the most crowded time of the year, but it's also undeniably the most enjoyable, both for the good weather and the numerous festivals in the large and small towns. **Accommodation** can get scarce, especially on the Oregon Coast and the Puget Sound islands, but with enough advance planning you should be fine. If you want a bit more elbow room, **May**, **June**, and **September** are all recommended, although the weather won't be quite as warm, or as dry. Outside of these parameters, you risk getting caught in one of the region's wet spells – though even in **winter** there's still plenty going on to keep you occupied, especially throughout the Cascades, where the ski resorts and lodges are a huge draw; with this in mind, you should reserve accordingly well in advance. The exceptions to the climate rules are the eastern expanses of Oregon and Washington, semi-arid regions that can get too toasty during the summer but are most agreeable in the spring and fall; winter, instead of bringing rain, features punishing wind and ice-cold temperatures that would seem to defy the dry scrubland of the setting.

Average temperatures and rainfall

	Jan	Feb	Mar	Apr	May	Jun	Jul	Aug	Sep	Oct	Nov	Dec
Portland												
Av high °F	46	50	56	61	67	73	79	79	74	63	51	46
Av low °F	37	39	41	44	49	53	57	58	55	48	42	37
Rainfall (in)	6.2	5.0	4.5	3.1	2.5	1.6	0.7	1.0	1.9	3.4	6.4	6.8
Seattle												
Av high °F	46	50	53	58	64	70	75	76	70	60	51	46
Av low °F	36	37	39	42	47	52	55	56	52	46	40	36
Rainfall (in)	5.1	4.1	3.8	2.6	1.8	1.5	0.8	1.0	1.6	3.2	5.9	5.6

To convert Fahrenheit (°F) to Celsius, subtract 32 and multiply by 5/9.
To convert inches (in) to millimeters, multiply by 25.4.

26

things not to miss

It's not possible to see everything that Oregon and Washington have to offer in one trip – and we don't suggest you try. What follows, in no particular order, is a selective taste of the region's highlights: hip cafés, breathtaking outdoor scenery, charming towns, enchanting festivals, and more. They're arranged in five color-coded categories, which you can browse through to find the very best to see and experience. All highlights have a page reference to take you straight into the Guide, where you can find out more.

01 Olympic National Park Page **398** • A wonderfully varied natural treasure occupying much of Washington's Olympic Peninsula, where you can wander through rainforests, cross deserted beaches, and rise up to high mountain ridges and looming glaciers.

03 Northwest Cuisine

Page **321** • Chefs in Oregon and Washington have taken the style of California and French nouvelle cuisines, added their own fresh, local ingredients and creative interpretations, and created a delightful hybrid that makes the region's finest restaurants among the best in the West.

02 Bumbershoot Page **334** •

Seattle's most freewheeling festival, encompassing music, food, theater, dance, and countless other things, all taking place at venues across the city but with their focus at Seattle Center.

04 River rafting Page **211** •

If you're the outdoors type, the first place you should head for is whitewater country – from the Rogue to the Snake to the Yakima rivers and beyond – with classes of rapids to suit any skill level.

05 **Mount St Helens** Page **439** • The thermoblasted ruin of what was once a quaint snowy peak, now transformed into a colossal emblem of volcanic fury and natural destruction – and, not surprisingly, one of the region's chief tourist draws.

06 **Pike Place Market** Page **294** • Seattle's best contribution to American urban culture, a frenetic scene loaded with fish vendors, produce stalls, fancy restaurants, underground book and record stores, and just about anything else you can think of.

07 **Driving the historic Columbia River Highway** Page **121** • An official national treasure built in the 1910s, this evocative driving route travels over narrow bridges past canyons, parks, and waysides.

09 **Rodeos** Page **258** • Whether it's watching cowboys rustle up steers in Ellensburg and Pendleton, or mules in Enterprise, few events evoke the spirit of the Wild West more than these summertime spectacles full of homespun parades, spirited events, and tasty barbecue.

08 **Multnomah Falls** Page **124** • Always a favorite attraction for Portland visitors, this tower of water plunges 612 feet into two pools and is spanned by a pleasant little old-fashioned bridge.

10 Lake Chelan Page **423** •
Nestled snugly between forested hills and mountains, Washington's serpentine Lake Chelan is a glacially carved gem, with countless fine hiking trails striking out from its shores.

11 Port Townsend Page **387** •
On the Olympic Peninsula, a nicely preserved Victorian hamlet from the late nineteenth century, loaded with elegant mansions and quaint restaurants and boutiques.

12 Hells Canyon Page **268** •
Though not the steep-walled satanic chasm you might expect from the name, this striking gorge is still one of the Northwest's scenic wonders, its 130-mile depth making it the deepest canyon on the planet.

13 Oregon beaches Page **171** • Beautiful, interconnected strips of sandy beaches and dunes, rocky shores, and basalt cliffs that can be crossed by bicycle or on foot (as well as Highway 101), and which have been almost completely preserved as state parks and wildlife refuges.

14 **Rose Festival** Page **98** • Portland's one big yearly shindig, a flower fête celebrated with two parades across town, an explosion of blooms in the Rose Test Garden, the arrival of giant warships on the river, and a chaotic "Fun Center" on Waterfront Park.

15 **Snoqualmie Falls** Page **432** • Familiar from the TV show *Twin Peaks*, a 270-foot waterfall that flows from the heights of a solid bedrock gorge, and located outside Seattle near the grand wooden *Salish Lodge*, another favorite for David Lynch fans.

16 **Seafood** Page **44** •
Salmon, tuna, bass, sturgeon, and freshwater trout are but a few of the fishy delights that appeal to the Northwest palate, much of it caught locally.

17 **Wine tours** Page **191** • Whether you're exploring the vintages of the Yakima Valley, Walla Walla, or the upper Willamette Valley, there are plenty of good opportunities to sample the region's increasingly popular wines – highlighted by cabernet and pinot noir.

18 **John Day Fossil Beds** Page **273** • A quirk of geologic history created these colorful rock formations of painted hills and towering palisades, in the process entombing countless animals that are on view as intricate fossils today.

19 **Snowboarding** Pages **131**, **230** & **433** • The Cascade Mountains are some of the country's best places to hit the slopes, especially on a 'board – whether you want to shred on a halfpipe at Hood, boost off a lip at Bachelor, or slide a rail at Snoqualmie.

20 **Crater Lake** Page **233** • Oregon's only national park, and one of the region's top sights, a huge, dark-blue expanse of freshwater covering the pit of the blown-out volcano Mount Mazama, which has since become the country's deepest lake.

21 **Windsurfing** Page **128** • Cruising over whitecaps and troughs, windsurfers can find plenty of good places to ride the waves in Oregon, from the beautiful Columbia River Gorge near Hood River to the remote beaches and seastacks of Pistol River State Park.

22 Café culture Pages **108** & **326** • Not only places to sip a latte, but also bonafide bastions of high and low culture where you can check out homegrown art, listen to a music jam or poetry slam, access the Internet, or order a pastrami sandwich.

23 Fremont public art Page **311** • A handful of Seattle's most colorful and bizarre public artworks, scattered around one of its most bohemian and free-spirited districts, highlighted by this menacing troll under the Aurora Bridge.

24 Oregon Caves Page **217** • Strange and elaborate limestone formations, echoing dark caverns, and narrowly winding rock passages, together preserved in a national monument not far from the California border.

25 Walking the Wildwood Trail Page **97** • This winding, thirty-mile concourse through thick trees and over creek beds feels more like a trek through an isolated mountain slope than an urban hike, and is the highlight of Portland's supreme Forest Park preserve.

26 Oregon Shakespeare Festival Page **215** • An unexpected treat in the little southern Oregon town of Ashland, where three stages play host to the work of the Bard and other playwrights from February to October.

Basics

Basics

Getting there

Unless you live on the West Coast, the quickest and easiest way of getting to Oregon and Washington is by air. Approaches by rail are possible, too. The cheapest way to the region is by bus – though you'll pay a heavy price in comfort and length of travel. Coming here by car may also take time but will allow you to be far more flexible once you arrive.

Airfares always depend on the season, with the highest fares being charged from June into September and over the winter holidays, when seats are at a premium; you'll get the best prices during the **low season**, generally mid-January to the end of February, and October to early December; **shoulder seasons**, when prices hover between the low- and high-season averages, cover the rest of the year.

Flights from the US and Canada

The best means of getting to Oregon and Washington from most places in North America is to **fly**, as many airlines offer daily services – both nonstop and connecting – from points across the US and Canada to the region's hubs in Seattle and Portland. Another plus is that if you book your ticket in advance, flying is often not much more expensive than **rail** or **bus**.

Oregon's principal **airport** is in **Portland**, and Washington's is near **Seattle**. Major US air carriers regularly fly to these cities from other places in the region, though services to Seattle tend to be both more direct and more frequent. Air Canada is a good choice for frequent service from major cities in Canada.

As airlines tend to match one another's prices, there's not a huge difference in their quoted fares. However, week-to-week prices can vary dramatically, with many airlines now reducing their flight schedules to book planes more fully and tacking on fees for meal service and nonstop routes.

What make more difference than your choice of carrier are the conditions governing the ticket: whether it is fully refundable, the time and day you travel, and, most important, the time of year you travel. Least expensive is a low-season midweek flight with a weekend stay-over, booked and purchased at least three weeks in advance. Some no-frills carriers can often provide good value as well, notably Southwest, JetBlue, Frontier, and Air Canada's subsidiary, Jazz.

For Portland and Seattle, the cheapest round-trip prices generally start at around $250 from New York, $180 from Chicago (on Southwest), $300 from Miami, $220 from Los Angeles or San Francisco, US$210/CAN$240 from Vancouver, British Columbia, and US$380/CAN$440 from Toronto or Montreal.

Flights from the UK and Ireland

Flying **from the UK** to the Pacific Northwest, you'll most likely have to stop over in one of the major hubs – Chicago, New York, or Atlanta – and expect about 14–16hr of travel time. Seattle is accessible on a daily nonstop from Heathrow, taking 9–11hr for the trip. Because of the time difference between Britain and the West Coast (8hr most of the year), flights usually leave the UK mid-morning and arrive in the Northwest in the late afternoon or early evening of the same day.

There are no nonstop direct flights **from Ireland** to Seattle and Portland, but two airlines do operate nonstop scheduled services to other parts of the US. From both Dublin and Shannon airports, Aer Lingus (UK ☎0870/876 5000, Republic of Ireland ☎0818/365 000, ⓦwww.aerlingus .com) flies to New York, Chicago, Los Angeles, and Boston and can arrange onward flights to Seattle and Portland, often offering good-value specials.

Britain is one of the best places in Europe to obtain bargain flights, though **fares** vary widely according to season, availability, and the current level of inter-airline competition. Return tickets start at £380 in low season and £550 in high-. Prices are for departures from London and Manchester and do not include a UK airport tax of £40–50. British Airways and Aer Lingus offer service from Dublin (12–15hr), usually with a stopover in London and possibly another in the US, for £350–400 in low season and £500–600 in high season. KLM/Northwest offers similarly priced service, with one stopover in Amsterdam and possibly another in the US. In addition, other airlines – primarily British Airways and Air Canada – can quote you through-fares from Dublin to Seattle and Portland via major gateway cities. Otherwise, the cheapest flights to North America – if you are under 26 or a student – are available from UsitNOW (see p.32).

For an overview of the various offers and unofficially discounted tickets from the UK and Ireland, go straight to agents specializing in low-cost flights. The same agents also offer cut-price seats on **charter flights**. These are particularly good value if you're traveling from a UK city other than London, although they tend to be limited to the summer season and restricted to so-called "holiday destinations," with fixed departure and return dates. Brochures are available in most high-street travel agents; otherwise, contact the specialists directly.

Flights from Australia, New Zealand and South Africa

Getting to Seattle or Portland from **Australia** or **New Zealand** will most likely require a stopover in Los Angeles or San Francisco. **Travel agents** offer the best deals on fares and have the latest information on special offers, such as free stopovers – a brief, unbilled stay for a day or two – and fly-drive-accommodation packages. Flight Centre and STA Travel (which offer fare reductions for ISIC card holders and under-26 travelers) generally offer the lowest fares. Seat availability on most international flights out of Australia and New Zealand is often limited, so it's best to book at least several weeks ahead.

The travel time between Auckland or Sydney and the Pacific Northwest is 17–22hr. **From Australia**, there are daily flights from Sydney on American, United, Air New Zealand, and Qantas for around A$1650 in low season (or A$300 more in high season); options for connecting flights via LA and San Francisco to Seattle and Portland average around A$325 in low season, and $40–60 more in the high. Similar rates apply for stopping over in Auckland, Honolulu, Fiji, Tonga, or Papeete.

From New Zealand, the best deals are out of Auckland on Qantas, United, or Air New Zealand, with low-season deals around NZ$1800 (or NZ$2500 in high), all three with stopovers in LA. Japan Airlines offers the best fares via Asia, starting at NZ$1800/2150 for low and high seasons, with a transfer or stopover in Tokyo, while Korean Air (via Seoul) fares start at NZ$2000.

From major cities in **South Africa** such as Johannesburg, you'll have to make at least one stop, and possibly two, to reach Portland or Seattle. South Africa Airways will get you as far as Washington, DC, in most cases, and from there carriers such as United, Northwest, US Airways, Alaska and Delta provide the second leg of service. Alternately, Amsterdam, Frankfurt, or even Dakar, Senegal, may act as stops along the way. It will take at least a full 24hr day to arrive, and costs begin at US$2100/R$15000 in the high season, and at US$1800/R$12500 in the low.

Cars

Road links to Oregon and Washington make access by car convenient for those who live within striking distance of the region. The freeway choices are straightforward: from the east, I-90 in Washington or I-84 in Oregon; and I-5 from the south or north. In recent years, however, connecting to the southbound I-5 from Canada has become a rather tedious process, often resulting in hours of traffic at the border while drivers are grilled about drugs, weapons, and the like. At other, more obscure entry points the border patrol officers can be even more rigid.

Driving your own car (or renting one) may maximize your freedom and flexibility, but if you're traveling cross-country you'll need to

Fly less – stay longer! Travel and climate change

Climate change is a serious threat to the ecosystems that humans rely on, and air travel is among the fastest-growing contributors to the problem. Rough Guides regards travel, overall, as a global benefit, and feels strongly that the advantages to developing economies are important, as is the opportunity of greater contact and awareness among peoples. But we all have a responsibility to limit our personal impact on global warming, and that means giving thought to how often we fly, and what we can do to redress the harm that our trips create.

Flying and climate change

Pretty much every form of motorized travel generates CO_2 – the main cause of human-induced climate change – but planes also generate climate-warming contrails and cirrus clouds and emit oxides of nitrogen, which create ozone (another greenhouse gas) at flight levels. Furthermore, flying simply allows us to travel much farther than we otherwise would do. The figures are frightening: one person taking a round-trip flight between Europe and California produces the equivalent impact of 2.5 tons of CO_2 – similar to the yearly output of the average UK car.

Fuel-cell and other less harmful types of plane may emerge eventually. But until then, there are really just two options for concerned travelers: to reduce the amount we travel by air (take fewer trips and stay longer!) and to make the trips we do take "climate neutral" via a carbon offset scheme.

Carbon offset schemes

Offset schemes run by ⓦwww.climatecare.org, ⓦwww.carbonneutral.com, and others allow you to make up for some or all of the greenhouse gases that you are responsible for releasing. To do this, they provide "carbon calculators" for working out the global-warming contribution of a specific flight (or even your entire existence), and then let you contribute an appropriate amount of money to fund offsetting measures. These include rain-forest reforestation and initiatives to reduce future energy demand – often run in conjunction with sustainable development schemes.

Rough Guides, together with Lonely Planet and other concerned partners in the mass-travel industry, is supporting a **carbon offset scheme** run by climatecare.org. Please take the time to view our website and see how you can make your trip climate neutral.

ⓦ**www.roughguides.com/climatechange**

allow plenty of time. If you do use your own car, make sure your insurance is up to date and that you are completely covered. General advice and help with route planning is available from the American Automobile Association (AAA), which has offices in most US cities (☎1-800/AAA-HELP for roadside help; ☎212/757-2000 for general information; ⓦwww.aaa.com).

If you don't have a car or don't trust the one you have, one option worth considering is a **driveaway**. Certain automobile transit companies, operating in most major cities, are paid to find drivers to take a customer's car from one place to another. The company will normally pay for your insurance and one tank of gas; after that, you'll be expected to drive along the most direct route and to average 400 miles a day. Companies are keen to hire overseas travelers, but you'll need to be at least 23 and be willing to put down a $350 deposit, which you can get back once you've returned the car in good condition. Look under "Automobile transporters and driveaways" in the Yellow Pages for more information, or contact Auto Driveaway, with offices throughout the US (☎1-800/346-2277, ⓦwww.autodriveaway.com).

Other options include **renting a car** (see box, p.30 for major companies) or buying a **fly-drive package**, which includes bargain-rate and sometimes free car rental with

Car rental companies

Advantage ☎1-800/777-5500, ⓦwww.arac.com
Alamo ☎1-800/462-5266, ⓦwww.alamo.com
Avis ☎1-800-230-4898, ⓦwww.avis.com
Budget ☎1-800/527-0700, ⓦwww.budget.com
Dollar ☎1-800/800-3665, ⓦwww.dollar.com
Enterprise ☎1-800/261-7331, ⓦwww.enterprise.com
Hertz ☎1-800/654-3131, ⓦwww.hertz.com
National ☎1-800/CAR-RENT, ⓦwww.nationalcar.com
Payless ☎1-800/PAYLESS, ⓦwww.paylesscarrental.com
Thrifty ☎1-800/847-4389, ⓦwww.thrifty.com

purchase of airline ticket. Fly-drive deals usually work out to be less than renting on the spot and are especially good value if you intend to do a lot of driving.

Trains

The only reason to consider traveling to the Pacific Northwest **by train** from elsewhere in North America is if you think the rail journey itself would be a fun part of your vacation, as services can be infrequent and fares are not necessarily any cheaper than flying.

The national passenger rail line – **Amtrak** (☎1-800/USA-RAIL, ⓦwww.amtrak.com) – is a leisurely but expensive option. Although financially precarious for years, the company has managed to keep running, though rarely ever on time. The trains themselves vary in style, amenities, and speed, so it's worth checking ahead to see what type of train services your route.

Amtrak's **Cascades** line runs four times per day north to Seattle from Eugene, Oregon, and the daily **Empire Builder** travels west from Chicago to Seattle and Portland (with the split at Spokane, Washington). The most memorable route, however, is the daily

Coast Starlight, which runs between Los Angeles and Seattle, passing by and through some of the most appealing scenery anywhere, from rugged coastline to towering mountains to thick forest.

One-way cross-country fares can be as low as $150 during the off-season and as high as $300 during peak periods. Keep in mind, however, that those are base fares, and the cost rises quickly if you want to travel more comfortably: sleeping compartments, which include small toilets and showers, can be as low as $300 for one or two people but can climb as high as $730, depending on the class of compartment, number of nights, season, and so on. Basic one-way fares between Portland and Seattle start at $28 in the off-season.

Amtrak also offers package deals combining hotels, rental cars, and other services for American travelers, as well as rail passes. The **Explore North America** 30-day rail pass includes Canadian routes on VIA Rail and costs $999 for summer travel and $709 during the off-season.

Overseas travelers can choose from two **rail passes** that include the Pacific Northwest, each valid for fifteen or thirty days: the **West**, which covers roughly everything west of the Mississippi River, and the **National**, for the whole country. Passes must be purchased before your trip at travel agents, or at Amtrak stations in the US, on production of a passport issued outside the US.

Buses

Bus travel is a slow, often agonizing way to get to the Pacific Northwest, and in the end you won't really save that much money. Still, if your budget's tight, it's an option worth considering.

Greyhound (☎1-800/231-2222, ⓦwww.greyhound.com) is the sole long-distance operator servicing Seattle and Portland ($25 one-way between them) and will cost you at least $200 round-trip, paid at least seven days in advance, from major cities like New York, Chicago, and Miami. The main reason to take Greyhound is if you're planning to visit other places en route; the company's **Discovery Pass** is good for unlimited travel within a set time; seven days of travel costs

Amtrak rail passes for international visitors

	15 day (June–Aug)	15 day (Sept–May)	30 day (June–Aug)	30 day (Sept–May)
West	$335	$215	$415	$280
National	$455	$305	$565	$395

Outside the US, Amtrak rail passes are available at the following locations:

Australia Asia Pacific Travel Marketing, St David's Hall, 17 Arthur St, Surry Hills, Sydney ☏612/9319 6624, ⓦwww.aptms.com.au

Ireland USIT, 19/21 Aston Quay, O'Connell Bridge, Dublin ☏01/602-1094, ⓦwww.usit.ie

New Zealand Walshes World, Ding Wall Building, 87 Queen St, Auckland ☏09/379-3708

UK Trailfinders, 194 Kensington High St, London W8 7RG ☏020/7938 3939, ⓦwww.trailfinders.com

$283; 15 days, $415; 30 days, $522; and 60 days, $645. Passes are valid from the date of purchase, so it's a bad idea to buy them in advance.

Airlines, agents and operators

Online booking

ⓦwww.expedia.co.uk (in UK), ⓦwww.expedia.com (in US), ⓦwww.expedia.ca (in Canada)
ⓦwww.lastminute.com (in UK)
ⓦwww.opodo.co.uk (in UK)
ⓦwww.orbitz.com (in US)
ⓦwww.travelocity.co.uk (in UK), ⓦwww.travelocity.com (in US) ⓦwww.travelocity.ca (in Canada)
ⓦwww.zuji.com.au (in Australia) ⓦwww.zuji.co.nz (in New Zealand)

Airlines

These carriers all directly serve Portland and Seattle, except where stated.

Air Canada US and Canada ☏1-888-247-2262, UK ☏0871/220 1111, Republic of Ireland ☏01/679 3958, Australia ☏1300/655 767, New Zealand ☏0508/747 767, ⓦwww.aircanada.com

Air Canada Jazz US and Canada ☏1-888/247-2262, ⓦwww.flyjazz.ca

Alaska US ☏1-800/252-7522, ⓦwww.alaskaair.com

American US ☏1-800-433-7300, UK ☏0845/7789 789, Republic of Ireland ☏01/602 0550, Australia ☏1300/650 747, New Zealand ☏0800/887 997, ⓦwww.aa.com

Big Sky ☏1-800/237-7788, ⓦwww.bigskyair.com (Portland only)

British Airways UK ☏0870/850 9850, Republic of Ireland ☏1890/626 747, ⓦwww.ba.com

Cathay Pacific Australia ☏13 17 47, New Zealand ☏09/379 0861, ⓦwww.cathaypacific.com

Continental US and Canada ☏1-800-523-3273, UK ☏0845/607 6760, Republic of Ireland ☏1890/925 252, Australia ☏02/9244 2242, New Zealand ☏09/308 3350, international ☏1800/231 0856, ⓦwww.continental.com

Delta US and Canada ☏1-800-221-1212, UK ☏0845/600 0950, Republic of Ireland ☏1850/882 031 or 01/407 3165, Australia ☏1300/302 849, New Zealand ☏09/379 3370, ⓦwww.delta.com

Frontier US ☏1-800-432-1359, ⓦwww.flyfrontier.com

Hawaiian US ☏1-800-367-5320, Australia ☏02/9244 2377, ⓦwww.hawaiianair.com

JetBlue US ☏1-800/JETBLUE, ⓦwww.jetblue.com

KLM/Northwest US and Canada ☏1-800-225-2525, UK ☏0870/507 4074, Republic of Ireland ☏1850/747 400, Australia ☏1-300-767-310, New Zealand ☏09/921 6040, ⓦwww.nwa.com or ⓦwww.klmuk.com

Lufthansa US ☏1-800-645-3880, UK ☏0870/837 7747, Republic of Ireland ☏01/844 5544, Australia ☏1300/655 727, ⓦwww.lufthansa.com (Portland only)

Mexicana US ☏1-800-531-7921, UK ☏020/8492 0000, Australia ☏03/9699 9355, New Zealand ☏09/914 2573, ⓦwww.mexicana.com (Portland only)

Qantas Australia ☏13 13 13, New Zealand ☏0800/808 767 or 09/357 8900, ⓦwww.qantas.com

Scandinavian US ☎1-800-221-2350, UK ☎0870/6072 7727, Republic of Ireland ☎01/844 5440, Australia ☎1300/727 707, ⓦwww.scandinavian.net (Seattle only)

South Africa Airways US and Canada ☎1-800-722-9675, UK ☎0870/747 1111, Australia ☎1800/221 699, New Zealand ☎09/977 2237, SA ☎11/978 1111, ⓦwww.flysaa.com (connections through Washington, DC)

Southwest US ☎1-800/435-9792, ⓦwww.southwest.com

United US ☎1-800-UNITED-1, UK ☎0845/844 4777, Australia ☎13 17 77, New Zealand ☎09/379 3800, ⓦwww.united.com

US Airways US and Canada ☎1-800-428-4322, UK ☎0845/600 3300, Ireland ☎1890/925 065, ⓦwww.usair.com

Virgin Atlantic US ☎1-800-821-5438, UK ☎0870/380 2007, Australia ☎1300/727 340, New Zealand ☎09/308 3377, SA ☎11/340 3400, ⓦwww.virgin-atlantic.com

Travel agents

Airtreks.com US ☎1-877-AIRTREKS, ⓦwww.airtreks.com. Interactive database that lets you build and price your own round-the-world itinerary.

ebookers UK ☎0800/082 3000, Republic of Ireland ☎01/488 3507, ⓦwww.ebookers.com. Low fares on an extensive selection of scheduled flights and package deals.

Flight Centre Australia ☎13 31 33 or 02/9235 3522, ⓦwww.flightcentre.com.au, New Zealand ☎0800 243 544 or 09/358 4310, ⓦwww.flightcentre.co.nz. Rock-bottom fares worldwide.

STA Travel US ☎1-800/781-4040, UK ☎0870/1630 026, Australia ☎1300/733 035, New Zealand ☎0508/782 872, ⓦwww.sta-travel.com. Worldwide specialists in independent travel; also sells student IDs, travel insurance, car rental, rail passes, etc.

TFI Tours US ☎1-800/745-8000, ⓦtfitours.com. Consolidator.

Trailfinders UK ☎0845/054 6060, Australia ☎02/9247 7666 or 1300/780 212, ⓦwww.trailfinders.com. One of the best-informed and most efficient agents for independent travelers; produces a very useful quarterly magazine worth scrutinizing for round-the-world routes.

Travel.com.au Australia ☎02/9249 5444 or 1300/130 483, ⓦwww.travel.com.au. Comprehensive online travel company, with discounted fares.

Travel Cuts Canada Canada ☎1-866/246-9762 or ☎1-800/592-CUTS, ⓦwww.travelcuts.com. Canadian student-travel organization.

UsitNOW Republic of Ireland ☎01/602 1904, Northern Ireland ☎028/9032 7111, ⓦwww.usitnow.ie. Student and youth specialists for flights and trains.

Worldtek Travel US ☎1-800/243-1723, ⓦwww.worldtek.com. Discount travel agency for worldwide travel.

Tour operators

Adventure World Australia ☎02/8913 0755, ⓦwww.adventureworld.com.au, New Zealand ☎09/524 5118, ⓦwww.adventureworld.co.nz. Agents for a vast array of international adventure travel companies that operate trips to every continent.

Airtours UK ☎0870/238 7788, ⓦwww.uk.mytravel.com. Large tour company offering trips worldwide.

AmeriCan Adventures/TrekAmerica US ☎1-800/221-0596, UK ☎0870/444 8735, ⓦwww.americanadventures.com, ⓦwww.trekamerica.com. Seven- to twenty-eight-day sports and sightseeing trips along the West Coast and beyond.

American Holidays Belfast ☎028/9031 0000, Dublin ☎01/673 3840, ⓦwww.american-holidays.com. Specialists in travel to the US and Canada.

Amtrak Vacations US ☎1-800/AMTRAK-2, ⓦwww.amtrakvacations.com. Rail/hotel customized packages to Seattle and Portland.

Australian Pacific Touring Australia ☎1800/675 222 or 03/9277 8555, New Zealand ☎09/279 6077, ⓦwww.aptours.com. Package tours and independent US travel.

Backroads US ☎1-800/GO-ACTIVE, ⓦwww.backroads.com. A mix of cycling/walking and hiking/multisport packages, including trips to national parks and stays in luxury accommodation.

British Airways Holidays UK ☎0870/442 3820, ⓦwww.baholidays.co.uk. The airline offers a wide range of package and tailor-made vacations around the world.

Canada & America Travel Specialists Australia ☎02/9922 4600, ⓦwww.canam.com.au. Wholesalers of Greyhound Ameripasses, plus flights and accommodation in North America.

Collette Vacations US ☎1-800/340-5158, ⓦwww.collettevacations.com. Anything from short jaunts to lengthy trips up and down the West Coast.

Contiki Holidays US ☎1-866/CONTIKI, ⓦwww.contiki.com. Youth-oriented sightseeing and national parks trips.

Cosmos/Globus Gateway US ☎1-866/755-8581, ⓦwww.globusandcosmos.com. A variety of coach tours bookable through travel agents.

Gray Line of Seattle US ☎1-800/426-7505, ⓦwww.graylineofseattle.com. Extensive range of day tours, overnight packages, and longer trips in the region.
Maupintour US ☎1-800/255-4266 or 913/843-1211, ⓦwww.maupintour.com. Multi-day land trips of the region, as well as other international destinations.
Premier Holidays UK ☎0870/889 0833, ⓦwww.premierholidays.co.uk. Flight-plus-accommodation deals.

Suntrek US ☎1-800/SUNTREK or 707/523-1800, ⓦwww.suntrek.com. One- to nine-week journeys around the West Coast and the rest of the US.
Sydney Travel ☎02/8270 4888, ⓦwww.sydneytravel.com.au. US flights, accommodation, and car rental.
Thomas Cook UK ☎0870/750 5711; Australia: Sydney ☎02/9231 2877, Melbourne ☎03/9282 0222; New Zealand ☎09/307 0555, ⓦwww.thomascook.com. Packages or scheduled flights, with travelers' checks, travel insurance, and car rental.

Arrival

Unless you are coming from nearby, you will most likely *arrive* in the Northwest at one of its airports. However, there are other points of entry for train and bus riders, as well as for freeway travelers.

By air

The handiest air terminal for Washington, **Seattle Tacoma International Airport**, almost always known as Sea-Tac (☎206/433-5388 or 1-800/544-1965, ⓦwww.portseattle.org/seatac), is fourteen miles south of Downtown near the I-5 freeway. Several car rental firms (see p.30 for contact information) have counters in the baggage claim area, with pickup and dropoff on the first floor of the garage across from the main terminal; other companies with off-airport branches provide courtesy van service to their pickup points. Buses to Seattle leave from the north end of the baggage claim area. The cheapest option is Metro bus #194 ($1.25, $2 during peak hours Mon–Fri 6–9am & 3–6pm), a 30min trip that deposits you Downtown at the Convention Center (7th Ave and Pike St); bus #174 plies a similar route for the same cost, but takes an extra 15min. Taxis charge $35–40 for the Downtown route and leave from the third floor of the parking garage; call ☎206/246-9999 for pickup once you arrive. (See "Arrival" section of Chapter 7, p.285, for more information.) Outside of Seattle, the only real alternative is **Spokane International Airport**, 9000 W Airport Drive

(☎509/455-6445 or 455-6457, ⓦwww.spokaneairports.net), located southwest of town off Hwy 2 at Exit 277. It is best for its immediate access to eastern Washington and Idaho, and hosts airlines such as Alaska, Horizon, and Southwest, as well as Delta, United, and American (see p.31 for contact information).

Portland International Airport (☎503/460-4234 or 1-877/739-4636, ⓦwww.flypdx.com) is the entry to Oregon for most travelers, and is also good for Vancouver, Washington, and southwest Washington. It's twelve miles northeast of Downtown, beside the Columbia River. From Terminal C, the MAX Red Line light rail (every 5–15min, 5am–midnight; $2) shuttles passengers on a 40min journey downtown. Local hotels may operate free or inexpensive shuttles from the airport; taxis cost around $30 (see "Portland Arrival," p.77, for more information). Unlike Washington, Oregon has no sizable gateway to its eastern side, though Medford's **Rogue Valley International Airport** (☎541/776-7222) is fine for accessing Ashland, southern Oregon, and the southern Cascades, and many visitors come straight to the **Eugene Airport** (☎541/682-5430, ⓦwww.eugeneairport.com) for its access to central

Oregon and the Cascades. Airlines such as Alaska and Horizon have the most extensive schedules for the Northwest's smaller communities.

By train

In Seattle, **trains** arrive at the Amtrak terminal (☎206/382-4125 or 1-800/872-7245, ⓦwww.amtrak.com) in unlovely King Street Station at Third Avenue and Jackson Street, near the International District. It's about a dozen blocks from here to the city center; just to the east along Jackson Street, the International District Station is a hub for frequent Metro buses going Downtown. Portland's Amtrak station is at Union Station, 800 NW Sixth Ave (☎503/273-4865 or 1-800/872-7245, ⓦwww.amtrak.com). From here, it's about a 10min walk south to the city center. Both cities are connected on the short **Cascades** line, which also stops in Tacoma, Olympia, Salem, and Eugene, and a few small towns. The **Coast Starlight** line, which links Seattle with Los Angeles, stops in the Northwest at Tacoma, Olympia, Salem, Eugene, Klamath Falls, and a few smaller towns (see each city for respective train station details). You can get to points in the Columbia River Gorge, the Washington Cascades, and eastern Washington – including Wenatchee, Spokane, Pasco, and the outskirts of Hood River – on the **Empire Builder**, which goes on to Idaho, Montana, and eventually Chicago.

By bus and car

Greyhound **buses** (ⓦwww.greyhound.com) arrive in Seattle at Eighth Avenue and Stewart Street (☎206/628-5526 or 1-800/231-2222), on the eastern edge of Downtown, just a 15–20min walk from most Downtown accommodation, as well as at King Street Station, at Third Avenue and Jackson Street (☎206/382-4124) – convenient if you need to connect to an Amtrak train. Near Downtown Portland, the station is at 550 NW Sixth Ave at Glisan (☎503/243-2361 or 1-800/231-2222). Greyhound also travels the major interstates such as I-5, I-84, I-90, and I-82, with limited access to the central Oregon coast on Hwy 101. See each region's introductory section for more information on specific routes, and individual cities for bus station locations.

The interstates mentioned above are also, for most people, the main entry points into the Northwest **by car**, though I-97 is a prominent alternative into the region from the south via California and from the north via Canada. I-95 is one of the few highways that provide direct access from Nevada, in this case Reno, while visitors to and from Idaho may use Hwy 2 or Hwy 12 instead of I-90.

Getting around

The days when you could fully explore Oregon and Washington by train are long gone; Amtrak now provides only skeletal service, though it does link the major cities and has several particularly scenic routes. Greyhound buses offer a more extensive network of services, while in Puget Sound, the boats of Washington State Ferries are frequent, fast, and efficient. Flying is a key way – sometimes the only way – of reaching some destinations in the Northwest. It is more expensive than other means of travel, but competition in the skies can lead to some decent bargains.

On most forms of public transport there are **discounted fares** for children under 12, youths between 13 and 21, and seniors. Nevertheless, things are always easier if you have a **car**. Many of the most spectacular and memorable destinations in the Pacific Northwest are far removed from the cities and unreachable by public transport. Even if a bus or train could take you to the vicinity of a national park, it would prove impossible to explore the interior without your own vehicle.

By train

Amtrak services in most parts of the Northwest are generally restricted to one or two trains a day, except on the busier Seattle–Portland corridor. Details of the **Amtrak** (℗1-800/USA-RAIL, ⓦwww.amtrak.com) routes that connect Washington and Oregon with the rest of the United States, together with information on Amtrak's pricing and reservation policies, can be found in the box, p.31. Within the Pacific Northwest, the most appealing route is the **Coast Starlight**, which meanders up the coast from Los Angeles to cross the Oregon border near Klamath Falls, then links to the Willamette Valley before traveling to Seattle and connecting with buses going on to Vancouver, BC. The other major regional trains include the **Empire Builder**, which originates in Chicago and crosses eastern Washington to terminate in either Portland or Seattle, and the **Cascades**, a shorter route linking Eugene with Seattle.

Always **reserve** as far in advance as possible; all passengers must have seats, and some trains, especially between major cities, are booked solid prior to departure. There is an extra charge for **sleeping compartments** (around $100–300 extra per night for one or two people, including three full meals). However, even standard Amtrak trains are surprisingly spacious, and there are additional dining cars and lounge cars, some with full bars and glass-domed 360-degree viewing compartments.

For any one specific journey, the train can be more expensive than taking a Greyhound or even a plane, though special deals, especially in the off-peak season (Sept–May), bring the costs down considerably. Visitors can further reduce costs by buying an Amtrak rail pass (see box, p.31): the **Explore North America** pass (summer $999, off-season $709) is issued in conjunction with Canada's VIA Rail and is valid for thirty consecutive days of travel up to one year from the date of purchase, and you may travel up to four times, one way, over any given route segment. The pass is valid for

coach (second-class) travel but can be upgraded for an additional charge. Many trains fill quickly, so it's worth making reservations.

By bus

Buses are by far the least expensive way to get around by public transit. The main long-distance service is **Greyhound** (℗1-800/231-2222, ⓦwww.greyhound.com), which links all major cities and many smaller towns in the Northwest. However, out in the countryside and in the smaller towns, buses are fairly scarce, sometimes appearing only once a day, and here you'll need to plot your route with care. But along the **main highways**, buses run around the clock to a fairly full timetable, stopping only for meal breaks (almost always fast-food dives) and driver changeovers. Greyhound buses are nonsmoking, have toilets, and are more comfortable than you might expect. It's feasible to save on a night's accommodation by traveling overnight and sleeping on the bus – though you may not feel up for doing much the next day. To avoid possible hassle, lone female travelers in particular should take care to sit as near to the driver as possible and to board during daylight hours, since bus stations are often in fairly dodgy areas. (Don't assume any given bus stop to be anywhere near the town center.) Seats can be **reserved** either in person at a bus station or on the toll-free number, but this is rarely necessary – if all seats on a bus are sold, additional buses will be employed to take on overflow passengers.

Bus **fares** are relatively inexpensive but may not be considerably cheaper than a train or plane ticket. For example, it costs $25 one-way between Portland and Seattle on the bus, but only $28 in low season for the train, which is far more comfortable. However, the bus is the best deal if you plan to visit a lot of places: the **Discovery Pass** is good for unlimited travel nationwide, from a week to two months ($283–645; see "Getting There," p.30, for more information). Discounts are available for children under 12, seniors over 62, and students enrolled in a college or university. To buy online, you must purchase your pass no fewer than seven days prior to the start of travel. Otherwise you can

Bus companies

Clallam Transit ☎360/452-4511 or 1-800/858-3747, ⓦ www.clallamtransit.com. Washington's Olympic Peninsula.

Greyhound ☎1-800/231-2222, ⓦ www.greyhound.com. Washington, Oregon, and the rest of the US.

Jefferson Transit ☎360/385-4777 or 1-800/371-0497, ⓦ www.jeffersontransit.com. Washington's Olympic Peninsula.

Kitsap Transit ☎360/373-2877 or 1-800/501-RIDE, ⓦ www.kitsaptransit.org. Washington's Kitsap Peninsula and Bainbridge Island.

Quick Shuttle ☎1-800/665-2122, ⓦ www.quickcoach.com. Sea-Tac Airport, Seattle, Bellingham, Vancouver, BC.

Sunset Empire Transit ☎503/861-RIDE or ☎1-800/776-6406, ⓦ www.ridethebus .org. Northern Oregon coast from Astoria to Cannon Beach.

purchase a pass at any participating Greyhound terminal or agency.

By plane

Taking a **plane** is the quickest way to get about Oregon and Washington. Across the region, the big international airlines compete with a plethora of smaller, regional companies. One of these, **Kenmore Air**, schedules six to eight **seaplane** flights daily between downtown Seattle (on Lake Union) and the San Juan islands ($99 one-way, $198 round-trip; ☎866/435-9524, ⓦ www.kenmoreair.com).

By ferry

Ferries play an important role in transportation in Washington State – indeed, some of the islands on its long and fretted coastline can be reached only by boat. Around Seattle, ferries transport thousands of commuters a day to and from work, but for visitors, they're a novelty: an exhilarating way to experience the scenic splendor of the area. Ferry travel can be expensive, however, when you bring a car along.

Washington State Ferries (☎206/464-6400 or 1-800/84-FERRY, ⓦ www.wsdot .wa.gov/ferries), with a commuter-oriented fleet of some 25 ferries, handles more than 25 million passengers per year. Ferries run between Anacortes, Washington, to Sidney, BC (for Victoria and Vancouver Island) and the San Juan Islands; from Port Townsend to Keystone on Whidbey Island; and between Seattle and points on the Kitsap

Peninsula and Vashon and Bainbridge islands. Reservations are not accepted – except on cross-border services – and you should try to avoid peak commuter travel times. **Tickets** are available from Pier 52, Colman Dock, in Seattle, and schedules are available on the piers and at many places throughout town, usually at the same locations that carry racks of bus schedules. Timetables and fares vary by season, and sailing times vary between weekdays and weekends, so it's best to pick up sailing/fare schedules before making plans. See box, p.356, for more information.

Other Washington ferry companies include **Black Ball Transport** (☎360/457-4491, ⓦ www.cohoferry.com), which runs ferries from Port Angeles to Victoria, BC (2–4 daily, except in Jan), and charges $11.50 for a walk-on one-way ticket and $44 for a car and driver (other passengers $11.50 each), with a crossing time of 90min and no reservations; **Victoria Express** (☎360/452-8088, ⓦ www.victoriaexpress.com), operating a faster, 1hr trip on the same route, for passengers only (1–3 daily; $20–35 round-trip); and the passenger-only **Victoria Clipper** (summer three daily, winter one daily; $71–89 one-way, $117–140 round-trip; ☎206/448-5000, ⓦ www.victoriaclipper.com), which runs high-speed catamarans between Seattle's Pier 69 and Victoria, BC, in 2–3hr.

By car

Although the weather may not always be ideal and parking in Seattle and Portland can

Driving distances in Oregon and Washington

Driving distances in miles and kilometers (miles/km)

	Eugene			
Eugene	–	Portland		
Portland	88 /142	–	Seattle	
Seattle	258/416	170/274	Spokane	
Spokane	460/740	353/568	279/449	

be a pain, traveling **by car** is the best way to experience the entirety of the region. Apart from anything else, a car makes it possible to choose your own itinerary and to explore the wide-open landscapes that may well provide your most enduring memories of Washington and Oregon.

The two states holds some of the continent's greatest **highways**, notably Washington's North Cascades Loop, penetrating the glaciated heart of the spectacular Cascade Mountains; Oregon's Historic Columbia River Highway, with views of dramatic bluffs and waterfalls along; and Oregon's beautiful coastal route. On a more practical note, many Northwestern towns sprawl for so many miles in all directions that your hotel may be miles from the sights you came to see, or perhaps simply on the other side of a freeway that provides no pedestrian crossing.

Most vehicles – and almost all rental cars – run on unleaded gas, which is sold by the gallon in the US; prices have been rising steeply in recent years, but gas is still much cheaper than it is in Europe because of the lower taxes – prices run around $2.50–3.00 per gallon. **Fuel** is readily available, though gas stations thin out markedly in the more remote regions.

The main **border crossing** between the US and Canada, by car, is on Interstate 5 (I-5) at Blaine, Washington, 100 miles north of Seattle. Make sure you bring an up-to-date passport (see p.60 for requirements) and prepare for a considerable wait, as the border inspection process can be time consuming.

Backcountry driving

Oregon and Washington possess an extensive network of **roads**. Every major and

almost all minor towns and villages are reachable on a paved road, but for some of the scenic highlights you're likely to have to use rougher **forest roads** and **logging routes** – marked by a number, if at all – and even gravel and dirt roads. These roads are often in poor condition and can be treacherous when wet. Dust and flying stones represent major **hazards**, as does subsidence caused by ice and the thundering "big rig" trucks that use such routes with little regard for automobiles. **Weather** is another potential danger, with severe snowfalls possible in some areas even in summer, and dense fog plaguing the coast of Washington and Oregon. If you're planning to do a significant amount of driving along gravel and dirt roads, then radiators and headlights should be protected from stones and insects with a wire screen and headlight covers. Always carry a spare tire, fan belt, and gas can (preferably full), fill up at every opportunity, and check where the next gas station is available (on remote stretches, it could be literally hundreds of miles away). It goes without saying that your car should be in excellent shape: it's also a good idea to carry flares, tire jacks, and a set of tools and wrenches. If you're planning to do a lot of dirt-road driving, you'd be well advised to rent a four-wheel-drive vehicle or a pickup truck.

Roads, rules, and regulations

The best **roads** for covering long distances quickly are the straight and fast multilane freeways that radiate out from major cities. These have anywhere from four to ten lanes divided by a median and are marked on maps with thick lines and shields that contain the highway or US interstate number. Outside populated areas and off the principal arteries, highways go down to one lane each way and, though paved, the hard shoulder consists of gravel. The principal highways are the **interstates**. Across the region, lesser roads go by a variety of names – county roads, rural roads, or forest roads.

Americans drive on the **right-hand** side of the road, and streets in most urban areas are on a **grid system**. The first one or two digits of a specific address refer to the block, which will be numbered in sequence from a central point, usually downtown. For example, 620 S Cedar Avenue will be six blocks south of downtown. It is crucial, therefore, to take note of components such as "NW" or "SE" in addresses, as 3620 SW Washington Blvd will be a very long way indeed from 3620 NE Washington Blvd.

Out of town, exits on multilane highways are numbered by the distance from the beginning of the highway, as opposed to sequentially – thus Exit 55 is 10 miles after Exit 45. Junctions close together may carry the same number supplemented by "A" or "B," etc. Rural **hazards** include deer, bears, and other large animals lumbering onto the road – this is especially frequent in the summer, at dawn and dusk, and in spring, when they are attracted to the salt on the roads. Warning signs are posted in the more dangerous areas. Car lights can dazzle wild animals and render them temporarily immobile–"a deer in the headlights," so to speak.

The uniform maximum **speed limit** on major highways is 65 miles per hour in Oregon and 70mph in Washington. Although you can go for many miles without seeing a highway traffic cop in Oregon, Washingtonians have a justifiable paranoia about speed traps and the traffic-control planes that hover above to catch offenders. In both states, on-the-spot **fines** are standard for speeding violations, for failing to carry your license with you, and for having anyone on board who isn't wearing a seat belt. Needless to say, **drunk driving** is punished severely (keep any alcohol in the trunk of the car) as is traveling about carrying narcotics or a gun. On the road, spot checks are frequently carried out, and the police only need a thin excuse to stop and search your vehicle.

If you're using your own vehicle – or borrowing a friend's – get the appropriate insurance and make sure you're covered for **breakdown service**. Your home motoring organization – in the UK, the RAC and AA – will issue an appropriate insurance and breakdown policy with all the appropriate documentation. The American Automobile Association, or **AAA** (☎1-800/AAA-HELP or 1-800/222-4357, ⓦwww.aaa.com), has offices in most major cities.

Car rental

Most Americans, Canadians, and UK nationals over 21 with a driving license are eligible for **renting a car** (see box in "Getting there," p.30, for the major firms) in the Northwest, though rental companies may refuse to rent to a driver who has held a license for less than one year, and under-25s will get socked with a higher insurance premium, if they aren't barred from renting altogether. Car-rental companies will also expect you to have a credit card; if you don't have one, they may let you leave a hefty **deposit** (at least $300), but don't count on it. The driving licenses of other countries are recognized throughout the Pacific Northwest – check with your home motoring organization. Many companies prohibit travel on dirt or gravel roads or other potentially hazardous terrain; as an alternative, you may be able to sign a damage waiver, pay an additional premium, or rent a pickup truck or four-wheel-drive vehicle more suitable for such travel. If you're renting a car in winter, check if and where tire chains and other equipment are required or advised.

Often the least expensive way to rent a car is to book in advance with a major rental company. If you take a transatlantic flight, check to see if your airline offers discounted car rental for its passengers. At the height of the season in the more popular tourist areas, it's by no means uncommon to find that you can't locate an available vehicle at any price – another reason to book ahead. **Special deals** are more commonplace in the shoulder seasons and low season, though rates are consistently higher on the islands and in the wilderness than they are in the city. At a bare minimum it will likely **cost** you $150 a week to rent a basic subcompact car with unlimited mileage, more if you want a larger vehicle or more features. **Taxes** and other fees can add another 25 percent to the cost, but the biggest hidden surcharge is often the **drop-off charge**, levied when you leave your car in a different place from where you picked it up. This charge is usually equivalent to a full week's rental and can go as high as $500 or more. As for **driving insurance**, if you aren't already covered by your own policy or your credit card, a **Loss Damage Waiver** – sometimes called a Collision Damage Waiver (CDW) – may be well worth the expense. At around $15 a day, it can add substantially to the total cost of the rental, but without it you're liable for every scratch to the car, even if it wasn't your fault.

By bicycle

Cycling is an affordable and healthy way to get around Oregon and Washington, whether it's in the parks, many of which have rental outlets and designated bike trails, or in the big **cities**, which have cycle lanes. Portland, in fact, has been repeatedly named by *Bicycling* magazine as the best US city for two-wheeling. In the **country**, roads are usually well maintained, and many have wide shoulders. For casual riding, bikes can be **rented** by the hour, half-day, full day or sometimes by the week. Rates vary

Hitchhiking

Although it's the cheapest alternative for traveling the region's roads, **hitchhiking** is almost always a bad idea – both dangerous and illegal.

considerably depending on the type of bike you rent: reckon on $15–40 per day. Outlets are usually found close to beaches, parks, university campuses, or simply in areas that are good for cycling. Greyhound buses will take bikes aboard (so long as they're in a box), and Amtrak has a small charge for their transportation (often $5), as does Washington State Ferries ($1–6). A number of companies across the region organize multi-day cycle tours, either camping out or staying in country inns, and we've mentioned local firms where appropriate. Oregon, in particular, excels with its cycling routes and boasts the outstandingly scenic and well-maintained **Oregon Coast Bike Route**, which runs right along the state's 360-mile shoreline; a detailed brochure is available from the Oregon tourist office. All the region's state tourist offices provide general cycling information as well.

Accommodation

Oregon and Washington both maintain a high standard of accommodation, and in the cities it is priced accordingly. At the bottom of the accommodation price heap are campsites and hostel dorm beds, though be warned that both are heavily used in the Northwest's major cities and resorts – you may need to reserve months in advance for the more popular spots. Campsite rates range from free to around $30, and typically $15–21 in the state parks. Dorm beds in a hostel usually cost between $15 and $25 for non-members, with private rooms for $35–55. Many hotels will set up a third single bed for around $10 on top of the regular price, reducing costs for three people sharing.

Since inexpensive beds in tourist areas tend to be taken up quickly, always **reserve in advance** and take note of when prominent local events and festivals take place, as beds will be even harder to find during those times.

If you get stuck, try dropping by the local **visitor center**, where staff will often give you free advice, book accommodation for you, or perhaps provide a "courtesy phone" so you can call round after vacancies.

Accommodation price codes

Throughout this book, accommodation has been price-coded according to the cost, including tax, of the least expensive double room in high season; we have given individual prices for hostels and campgrounds.

Expect prices in most places to jump into the next highest category on Friday and Saturday nights and also when a major event is going on in town.

❶ up to $40 Basic double room either sharing a bathroom in an old hotel or en suite in a motel that's well off the beaten track.

❷ $40–55 No-frills motel room – double room with bathroom, TV, and phone – but with no amenities and probably in an unpopular location.

❸ $55–70 Standard rate for the most basic highway chain motel; rooms should be adequately comfortable and there's typically access to a pool.

❹ $70–90 Mid-priced motels in reasonable locations with more than just the very basic facilities. The room and its fittings will be bigger and more luxurious than in the highway chains – there's probably access to a hot tub, laundromat, and maybe even a coffee and doughnut for breakfast.

❺ $90–120 Well-located motels, or those with good fitness facilities and other amenities, will charge in this

bracket. Rooms in many of the least expensive bed-and-breakfasts begin at this price.

❻ $120–150 Exceptionally well-located motels and some basic hotels fall into this bracket. Most B&Bs will charge around these prices, too.

❼ $150–200 At this price you can expect to be staying in a good-quality hotel with nice facilities in a convenient location or one of the fancier antique-decorated B&Bs, where you start the day with gourmet breakfasts. Bathrooms at both may well contain an en-suite hot tub.

❽ $200–250 High standard hotels with concierge services and great facilities.

❾ $250+ Extraordinary accommodations, with outstanding service, exceptional location, and facilities, but also a little extra – like being a local historic landmark – that drives up the price.

Reservations can be made over the phone by credit card; wherever possible, take advantage of **toll-free numbers**, but note that almost all are accessible only in a single state, and if you call them from abroad you'll either pay international call rates or find the number unavailable. Reservations are held only until 6pm unless you've informed the hotel you'll be arriving late.

Checkout times are generally between 11am and 1pm; at hotels in popular areas, you may not be able to check in until late afternoon. At most places you have to give 24 hours' notice to **cancel your reservation** without a penalty, though a few big resorts require 48 hours' advance notice. You may be expected to **pay in advance**, at least for the first night, particularly if it's high season and the hotel's expecting to be busy. Payment can be in cash or travelers' checks, though it's more common to use a credit card and sign for everything when you leave.

Hotels

Hotels can include anything from high-class establishments and major resorts to mid-range chains and restored boutique properties to grim, shambling dives above a bar or diner.

Upper-end hotels can be very grand indeed, catering to a mix of rich tourists and business travelers, with high-season rooms anywhere from $150 to $500 – though $250 will get you a first-class double in most cases. It's always worth inquiring about midweek reductions and out-of-season discounts, as these can reduce rates to as low as $100 per night. **Mid-range** hotels offer standard-issue modern facilities, often in a downtown location. High-season doubles in this price bracket go for around $100. **Bottom-end** hotels, costing $40–50, are mostly holdovers from the days when liquor laws made it difficult to run a bar without an adjoining restaurant or hotel. Needless to say, for their battered units with little more than a basic bed, washroom, and TV, they're among the last options you should choose. For the same money, it's better to seek out a cheap motel or hostel, if possible.

Motels

As with the rest of the country, it is consistently easy to find a basic **motel** in most of the Northwest. In most places mentioned in the guide we've recommended particular establishments for reasons of value or uniqueness, but there are often many more choices around that are clean and cheap – check the Yellow Pages for the full gamut. The cheapest properties tend to be family-run, independent businesses, with the national chains costing $10–15 more for similar facilities.

Whether called inns, lodges, or motor hotels, most of these establishments amount to much the same thing: mostly doubles with bathroom, TV, and phone. For more than $60, the rooms get a bit bigger and better, and may even offer a swimming pool and in-room coffeemaker, iron and ironing board, and complimentary newspaper.

During **off-peak periods** (usually Oct–April) many motels struggle to fill their rooms; staying in the same place for more than one night may bring further reductions. Some places have cheap triple- or quadruple-berth rooms, and most are fairly relaxed about introducing an extra bed into a double. Many establishments also offer a **family plan**, whereby kids sharing their parents' room stay free. Prices tend to drop in the larger towns and cities the farther you move from downtown, and in more remote areas, with the exception of ski resorts, many motels are likely to be closed in the off-season.

Bed-and-breakfasts

In recent decades, **bed-and-breakfasts** have become popular as comfortable and less expensive alternatives to conventional hotels. Sometimes B&Bs – also known as **guesthouses** and **inns** – are just a couple of furnished rooms in someone's home, and even the larger establishments tend to have no more than ten units, often laden with flowers, stuffed cushions, and an atmosphere of contrived quaintness. The range of quality is considerable, from Gilded Age "heritage houses" of great charm to postwar ranch houses dolled up in chintz and ersatz Victoriana.

Prices vary from as little as $50 a night to more than $150, and may include a huge and wholesome breakfast, though the trend is increasingly to provide only a skimpy "Continental" meal (toast, coffee, and perhaps cereal). The other cost factor is whether each room has an en-suite bathroom; those that do tend to charge $20–30 more per unit. Another issue to consider is whether the establishment has a private **guest entrance**, useful if you're likely to be staggering in late or simply don't want to mix with your hosts. Avoid those places that have an explicit **curfew** for their guests – as in "all doors bolted at 10pm" – often a red flag for rigid, pedantic innkeepers. Also take careful note of an establishment's **location**: in cities and larger towns they may be out in the suburbs and inconvenient for transport and downtown sights, though some hosts will pick you up from the airport or bus station on your arrival.

Youth hostels

Youth hostels are not as plentiful in the US as in Europe. Moreover, unless you're alone, most work out to be little cheaper than motels, so the only real point of using them is if you like their youthful ambience and sociability.

Most of the region's hostels are affiliated to the American Youth Hostel (AYH) network, which is, in turn, affiliated to Hostelling International (HI). There are also privately run hostels in the Northwest, and additionally there are YMCAs and YWCAs that sometimes offer dormitories or, in a few cases, women-only accommodation. In Washington and Oregon, most hostels are located either in cities or in coastal towns, though a smattering can be found in good hiking country. In both states, hostels may still observe the old hosteling niceties – a limited check-in time (usually 5–8pm) and strict daytime lockouts (9.30am–5pm).

To stay in a hostel, you're supposed to be, in theory, a **HI member**, but in practice

Youth hostel organizations

Australia Australian Youth Hostels Association ☎02/9565 1699, ⓦwww.yha.com.au
Canada Hostelling International–Canada ☎613/237-7884 or 1-800/663-5777,
ⓦwww.hihostels.ca
England Youth Hostel Association (YHA) ☎0870/870 8868, ⓦwww.yha.org.uk
Ireland An Oige, Irish Youth Hostel Association ☎01/830 4555, ⓦwww.irelandyha.org
New Zealand New Zealand Youth Hostels Association ☎0800/278 299 or 03/379
9970, ⓦwww.yha.co.nz
Northern Ireland Hostelling International Northern Ireland ☎028/9032 4733,
ⓦwww.hini.org.uk
Scotland Scottish Youth Hostels ☎01786/891 400, ⓦwww.syha.org.uk
USA Hostelling International American Youth Hostels (HI-AYH) ☎202/783-6161,
ⓦwww.hiayh.org

you can join the HI on the spot or pay a slightly higher charge for a bunk without joining. Be warned that members are usually given priority when it comes to booking, an important consideration in some of the more popular locations. Most places offer communal recreational and cooking facilities, plus pillows and blankets, though in simpler places you're expected to provide your own **sleeping bag** and towels. Especially in high season, it's advisable to **reserve ahead**.

The invaluable *Hostel Handbook for the USA and Canada*, produced each May, lists more than four hundred HI and private hostels and is available for $6 by writing to Hostel Handbook, Dept. HHB, 730 St Nicholas Ave, New York, NY, 10031 (☎212/926-7030), or by logging on to ⓦwww.hostelhandbook.com.

YMCAs and YWCAs

Both the **YMCA** and **YWCA** – known as Y's – have establishments in the Pacific Northwest's bigger cities. The quality of accommodation is usually excellent, invariably exceeding that of most hostels, with cafeterias, sports facilities, gyms, and swimming pools for guest use. Though you can sometimes find bunks in shared dorms from $20, the trend is for single, double, and family units (with optional private bathrooms) ranging from $30 to $70. Credit-card **reservations** in advance are virtually essential to secure private singles and doubles in the high season. Most places,

however, keep a few rooms and dorm bunks available for walk-in customers.

Camping

Few areas of North America offer as much scope for **camping** as Oregon and Washington, and all national parks and many state parks have outstanding sites. If you're tent camping, be sure to confirm that the campground you're interested in has pitch sites, as many places cater chiefly to recreational vehicles (RVs), providing them with full or partial hookups for water and electricity ("serviced sites"). It might also be worth checking to see how many tent sites are available: there's a big difference between a cozy 20-pitch campground and a 500-site tent village. Statewide campsite details are available from the major tourist offices and the tourist boards listed on pp.68–69.

Take special care plotting your route if you're camping during **public holidays** or the high season (June–Aug), or hoping to stay at some of the big campgrounds near lake or river resorts, or in any of the national parks. Either aim to arrive early in the morning or book ahead. **Reservations** can be made at private campgrounds and at many national and state parks, though most tent sites are available on a first-come, first-served basis. Oregon and Washington state parks share the same campground reservation line, Reserve America (☎1-800/452-5687, ⓦwww.reserveamerica.com). Check that your chosen site is open – many campgrounds are open only from April to October.

Campground types

Private campgrounds run the gamut from basic facilities to huge outdoor complexes with shops, restaurants, laundries, swimming pools, tennis courts, even saunas and Jacuzzis. Best-known among the latter is the familiar Kampgrounds of America (KOA) network, with campgrounds across the Northwest (information at ☏406/248-7444, ⓦwww.koa.com). Some private campgrounds **charge** by the vehicle, others per couple, comparatively few on a tent or per-person basis. Two people sharing a tent might pay anything between $3 and $28 each, though an average price would be nearer $8–14. Where we've given a price it's invariably for two people sharing a tent.

National park campgrounds tend to be immaculately turned out and available year-round, though key facilities are offered and fees collected only in the summer: off-season you may be expected to leave fees in a box. You'll usually find at least one campground serviced for winter camping in the bigger national parks. **Prices** vary from $8 to $21 per tent, depending on location, services, and the time of year – prices may be higher between June and August.

Sites in the major parks, especially close to towns, usually offer a full range of **amenities** for both tents and RVs, and often have separate sites for each. As a rule, though, remote park campgrounds tend to favor tents and offer only water, stores of firewood (for an additional charge), and pit toilets. Hot showers, in particular, are rare. Alternatively, a number of state parks offer novel accommodation in the form of **cabins** and **yurts** – Mongolian style domed circular tents – both of which may have wooden floors, electricity, and lockable doors, as well as bunk beds and a futon ($27–40 per night).

Food and drink

Although Oregon and Washington have the same generic fast-food chains as others states in the US, the region has really become a hot spot for fine dining in recent years, with top-notch chefs from California, New York, Europe, and Asia relocating here for a variety of reasons – the great outdoors, the quality of life, the presence of other top-notch chefs and restaurants. Some of the best spots in the cities tend to be ethnic fusion restaurants and places that specialize in seafood and "Northwest Cuisine," a variant of California Cuisine that employs fresh, locally available ingredients in novel combinations with a nod to nouvelle French dining. Even out in the country – the domain of often grim family-run diners – you'll find the odd seafood or upscale boutique restaurant to save the day. Also not to be missed are the region's excellent wineries and microbreweries, which are nationally renowned for their artisan techniques and high quality. Of the wines, pinot noir is among the best choices, while favored beers include handcrafted ales, stouts, and porters.

Breakfast

Breakfast is taken very seriously all over the region, and with prices averaging between $5 and $15 it can be very good value. Whether you go to a cafe, coffee shop, or hotel snack bar, the breakfast menu is typically on offer until around noon. Eggs are the staple ingredient; many urban diners can draw as big a crowd for their signature omelet (some with shrimp, spinach, and the like) at 9am on a Saturday or Sunday as for a great steak or burger for dinner. The region's top breakfast joints are in Seattle's Capitol Hill and Portland's Northwest and Eastside neighborhoods.

Whatever you eat, you can wash it down with as much **coffee** as you can stomach: for the price of a cup, waiters will provide free refills until you beg them to stop. Diner coffee used to be fairly dismal, but with the rise of coffeehouse culture in the region, the better breakfast spots wouldn't be caught dead without their Caffe Vita or Stumptown brands (in Seattle and Portland, respectively). The better coffeehouses create their complex brews from a wide mix of savory beans. **Tea**, with or without lemon or milk, is also drunk at breakfast, and some places emphasize the English connection by using imported brands, or local varieties such as Tazo. **Chai** is an increasingly popular Indian-derived brew made from black tea, milk, and spices, served hot or cold.

Lunch and snacks

From around 11.30am to around 3pm many restaurants offer **lunch specials** that are generally excellent value. In Chinese and Vietnamese establishments, for example, you'll frequently find rice and noodles, or dim sum feasts for $5–10, and many Japanese restaurants give you a chance to eat sushi for $10–15, far cheaper than at dinner. **Pizza** is also widely available both from chain and family-owned restaurants and from pavement stalls. Some **cafes** feature whole foods and vegetarian foods, though few are nutritionally dogmatic, serving traditional seafood and meat dishes and sandwiches too; most have an excellent selection of daily lunch specials for around $8–12.

For quick **snacks** many **delis** do ready-cooked meals from $6, as well as a range of sandwiches and bagels. Regional snacks are all things nautical – from salmon and halibut to clams and shrimp, all of them potentially delicious. By contrast, the fare at shopping-mall **food courts** and **fast-food joints** is insipid, highly caloric, and best avoided unless you're near starving.

Some city **bars** lay out free **bar food** between 5pm and 7pm weekdays in an attempt to grab commuters on their way home. For the price of a drink you can stuff yourself with the likes of chicken wings, mozzarella sticks, burgers, and deep-fried shrimp. That apart, old-style urban dive bars are on the defensive here, replaced by **cafe-bars**, many of which serve up regional and European wines and bistro-style food.

Dinner and specialties

While the predictable burgers, piles of ribs, and rotisserie chickens – served up with salads, vegetables, and bread – are found everywhere, you should aim to explore the diverse regional cuisines of the Pacific Northwest when it comes to eating **dinner**. As you'd expect, **fish** and **shellfish** – anything from salmon and lobster to king crab, oysters, and shrimp – dominate the menus of just about all the coastal areas.

Vegetarian and vegan options

Being a **vegetarian** in the big cities of the Northwest presents few problems. Cholesterol-fearing North Americans are increasingly turning to health food, and most towns of any size boast a vegetarian café. Most Mexican, Asian, and Indian restaurants have at least one vegetarian item, often more, on their menu as well. However, don't be too surprised if in rural areas you find yourself restricted to a diet of eggs, peanut butter sandwiches, salads, and cheese pizza, and keep in mind that some ostensibly "safe" foods such as the nutritious-sounding red beans and rice often contain bits of diced pork, and even french fries may be cooked in beef fat. **Vegans** will find it even tougher going, though there are dedicated vegan cafes in Portland and Seattle, some of them holding somewhat militant attitudes that may prohibit anything from leavened bread to sugar and gluten. Not surprisingly, many travelers may find the idea of confining their diets to soy brownies and wheatgrass smoothies somewhat unpalatable.

Tipping

Almost everywhere you eat or drink, the service will be fast and friendly – thanks to the practice of **tipping**. Waiters and bartenders depend on tips for the bulk of their earnings, and unless the service is dreadful you should top up your bill by at least fifteen to twenty percent. A refusal to tip is considered rude and insulting in equal measure. If you're paying by credit card, there's a space on the payment slip where you can add the appropriate tip – though most servers prefer to be tipped in cash, with the implicit reason that it's easier to hide such gratuities from the watchful eye of the taxman.

Salmon, especially, is predominant, either served grilled or stuffed, or sometimes in pasta – though you're increasingly likely to be served blander, farm-raised salmon rather than the sharper wild variety, unless a restaurant identifies the wild version as such (with a correspondingly higher price tag). Of the shellfish, the more notable are **clams** and **oysters** (taken from places like Willapa Bay and, yes, Oysterville); Washington's highly rated **Dungeness crab** (smoother and creamier than the average kind); and most strikingly, **geoduck** (pronounced "gooey-duck") – a huge mollusk of intensely phallic appearance that is often served chopped up.

There is an endless variety of **ethnic** cuisine, especially in the major cities. Chinese food is ubiquitous and often inexpensive, though its quality is variable. Japanese is generally tastier, with an array of options from high-priced yuppie enclaves to cheap and tasty **sushi bars**. As Pacific Rim immigration continues apace, other **East Asian** imports, such as Thai, Indonesian, and, especially, Vietnamese cuisine, are making headway. **Italian** food is popular in excess of the number of quality establishments serving it, but it can be cheap and good – with the Northern variety typically being pricier and better. **French** food, too, is available, though almost always expensive,

and **Northwest Cuisine** borrows many of its techniques, in combination with exotic ingredients and artful design. **Mexican** food is one of the cheapest types of food to eat, and even a full dinner with a drink will not often be over $10 – though the cuisine is closer to Tex-Mex than authentic south-of-the-border dining. Other interesting and occasionally worthwhile ethnic fare includes **Indian**, with meat and veggie options; **Mediterranean**, best for its Arabic and Lebanese eateries, and somewhat weaker for Greek diners; **German**, delivered with a heavy, gut-busting punch in a few places; and best of all, Spanish **tapas bars**, which have become all the rage in recent years, with moderate to expensive prices. However tempting, faux **British pubs** are usually best avoided, their bangers and mash and fish 'n' chips only a pale imitation of the real thing.

Drinking

According to stereotype, American **bars** are long, dimly lit counters with a few lost souls perched on stools and the rest of the clientele occupying the murky tables and booths. In practice, bars in the Northwest vary enormously, from male-dominated, rough-edged drinking holes concentrated in blue-collar zones to fashionable establishments that provide food, live entertainment, and an inspiring range of cocktails. Indeed, it's often impossible to separate cafes from bars.

To **buy** and consume alcohol in almost every US state, you must be 21, and you may be asked for ID even if you look 30 or older. Wine and beer are sold by most supermarkets and groceries. Hard liquor, however, attracts tighter regulation, and in both Washington and Oregon can be purchased only from a state liquor store. Across the Pacific Northwest, bars usually stay open until 2am.

Microbreweries

Although most mainstream American **beer** tends to be limited to the fizzy and insipid lagers of the national brands, in the last two decades countless **microbreweries** and **brewpubs** have sprung up all over the Northwest, making the region the nation's undisputed king of "craft brewing." These are usually friendly and welcoming places, too, and almost all serve a wide range of good-value, hearty **food** to help soak up the drink. Brands to look out for include Pyramid, Elysian, and Hale's Ales in Seattle; Black Butte Porter in Bend, Rogue Ales in Newport and Full Sail Ale in Hood River (all in Oregon); and the most famous, Widmer Hefeweizen in Portland, a city that also boasts such local (and national) faves as Bridgeport and Hair of the Dog. You can find good microbrews and European imports in any decent grocery, especially Whole Foods and New Seasons markets. True microbrew fanatics can hunt down their favorite suds in specialized **beer stores** with racks of fancy bottles and oddball draughts arrayed on the walls; the names to watch for are **Bottleworks**, 1710 N 45th St, #3, in Seattle's Wallingford district (☎206/633-BIER, ⓦwww.bottleworks.com), with more than four hundred brews from twenty countries; **Liquid Solutions**, in the Portland suburb of Oregon City, 275 Beavercreek Rd, #C149 (☎503-496-1942, ⓦwww.liquidsolutions.biz); and **Belmont Station**, 4500 SE Stark St, Portland (☎503/232-8538, ⓦwww.belmont-station .com). For most people, Portland's best (smoking) pub for microbrews and international drafts is the Horse Brass, 4534 SE Belmont St (☎503/232-2202).

Drinking bottled beer in a bar works is much more expensive than drinking draught beer, which is usually served by the 170ml glass or by the pint; even cheaper is a **pitcher**, which contains six to seven glasses, or four pints.

Wine and spirits

Washington and Oregon produce large quantities of **wine**. In Washington, the main wine-producing area is along the Yakima Valley in central Washington, though there are also vineyards on Puget Sound and in the Columbia River Gorge; in Oregon, the vineyards are concentrated in the Willamette Valley. Both states have their own appellations, and the quality of production is closely regulated. Largely as a result, the general standard is high, with the best vintages receiving international plaudits.

Local wines are readily available in the region's cafes, restaurants, and bars and are identified by grape type as much as by vineyard; some of the best-known and best-regarded kinds include rich, complex varieties of **pinot noir**, **pinot gris**, and **cabernet sauvignon**. Prominent vintner names include Columbia Winery, Archery Summit, and Rex Hill, among many others. Needless to say, the industry takes itself very seriously, and most of the region's wineries offer free **tours** and **tastings**. Every local visitor center can provide opening times and directions. For an overview – and a glossy brochure – contact the **Washington Wine Center**, 1000 2nd Ave, Suite 1700, Seattle (☎206/667-9463, ⓦwww.washingtonwine .org), or the **Oregon Wine Advisory Board**, 1200 NW Naito Parkway, Suite 400, Portland, OR 97209 (☎1-800/242-2363, ⓦwww.oregonwine.org).

Wine may have made some inroads, but Northwest bars really excel with their

Smoking

As with most regions of the US, in Oregon and Washington **smoking** is severely frowned upon in the vast majority of public places. Cinemas are nonsmoking; restaurants, if they aren't completely nonsmoking, are divided into nonsmoking and smoking sections; and smoking is universally forbidden on public transport – including all domestic airline flights. If puffing away is really important to you, you may want to spend more of your time in Oregon, where smoking is regulated by municipality, not the state: Portland allows smoking in bars and truck stops, while Eugene and Corvallis have enacted only partial bans, requiring bars to provide ample ventilation, for instance. Washington has some of the most stringent anti-smoking laws in the world – smoking is outlawed in all workplaces, including restaurants, bars, bowling alleys, and (non-tribal) casinos, as well as anywhere within 25 feet of an open door or window.

spirits. Even in run-of-the-mill places there are startling arrays of gins, rums, and vodkas, as well as a good selection of both imported and domestic whiskeys. Also worth looking for is Portland's own **Clear Creek Brandy**, whose genuine fruit brandy (also known as eau de vie) uses locally grown apples, pears, and other fruits – be warned, though: this innocuous-looking clear liquid is one of the most potent drinks made in the region. Finally, in the smarter bars, you can experiment with all sorts of **cocktails**, anything from a dry martini and creamy Brandy Alexander to a sweet Singapore Sling or the dreaded Pink Squirrel.

The media

In terms of the media, the Pacific Northwest is not much different from anywhere else in the US: corporate control predominates in a slew of TV and radio stations owned by the gargantuan Clear Channel and Infinity networks, among a few other national heavyweights. This hegemony is challenged only by a handful of independent newspapers and alternative radio stations found in the major urban areas of Washington and Oregon.

Newspapers

Some of the more familiar national American **newspapers** include the *New York Times*, *Wall Street Journal*, *Washington Post*, and *USA Today*. The most prominent papers in the region are the *Seattle Post-Intelligencer* (Ⓦseattlepi.nwsource.com), simply called "the *P-I*" by locals, the *Seattle Times* (Ⓦseattletimes.nwsource.com), and Portland's *Oregonian* (Ⓦwww.oregonlive.com); all are published in the mornings. Every large town has at least one morning and/or evening paper, generally at least adequate at covering its own area but relying on agencies for foreign – and even national – reports.

Every community of any size has at least one **free newspaper**, found in street distribution bins or in shops and cafes. These can be handy sources for bar, restaurant, nightlife, and other listings; by far the biggest names are Seattle's *The Stranger* (Ⓦwww.thestranger.com) and *Seattle Weekly* (Ⓦwww.seattleweekly.com), and Portland's *Willamette Week* (Ⓦwww.wweek.com).

Radio

Radio stations are even more abundant than TV channels, but most are even more rigidly programmed, owned by a handful of megacompanies that care little about the needs or interests of their local listeners. Except for news, sports, and chat, stations on the AM band are best avoided in favor of FM, in particular the nationally funded **public** and **college stations** found between 88 and 95 FM. These provide diverse and listenable programming, be it bizarre underground rock or obscure theater, and they're also good sources for local nightlife news. Seattle's top choices are KUOW (94.9 FM; Ⓦwww.kuow.washington.edu), the local National Public Radio affiliate, for its excellent public affairs and news programming; KPLU (88.5 FM; Ⓦwww.kplu.org), which is strong on news, jazz, and blues; KEXP (90.3 FM; Ⓦwww.kexp.org), for all sorts of alternative and independent sounds; and KBCS (91.3 FM; Ⓦkbcs.fm), best for its jazz and folk, as well as some blues and world music. The choices are slimmer in Portland, basically a

Videos and DVDs

The standard format of VHS cassettes in North America is different from that in Britain, Australia, and New Zealand, and you cannot buy videos in the US compatible with video cameras or players bought in those places. The same is true for locally bought DVDs, which will work only in North American players, marked "Region 1." Such DVDs may be playable on your computer, however, depending on the model.

pair of inspired NPR affiliates next to each other on the dial: the solidly liberal KOPB (91.5 FM; ⓦwww.opb.org) and the more leftist and alternative KBOO (90.7 FM; ⓦwww.kboo.fm).

Beyond the larger cities, you're out of luck – except for the lone public-broadcasting affiliate in each town – and will probably have to resort to aimlessly scanning the frequencies, where you'll find a grab bag of soft-rock "classics," modern country-and-western crooners, fire-and-brimstone Bible thumpers, and various crazed phone-in shows. The best solution may be to make sure your car has a built-in CD player.

Television

Except for local stations, the **television** of the Pacific Northwest is effectively the TV of mainstream America. As an alternative, Seattle's KCTS (channel 9; ⓦwww.kcts .org) and Portland's OPB (channel 10; ⓦwww.opb.org) are **public broadcasting** affiliates that provide in-depth political and social documentaries, assorted nature and science programming, and a smattering of light history along the lines of Ken Burns's miniseries on baseball and jazz.

Most motel and hotel rooms are hooked up to some form of **cable TV**, though the number of channels available to guests depends on where you stay. See the daily papers for channels, schedules, and times. Most cable stations are actually no better than the big broadcast networks, though some of the specialized channels are interesting: CNN and CNN Headline News both have round-the-clock news, with Fox News providing a right-wing take on the day's events. ESPN is your best bet for all kinds of sports, MTV for youth-oriented music videos and programming, and VH-1 for easy listening and adult contemporary. HBO and Showtime present big-budget Hollywood flicks and excellent shows such as *The Sopranos* and *The Wire*, while Turner Classic Movies (TCM) takes its programming from the golden age of cinema.

Many major **sporting events** are transmitted on a pay-per-view basis, and watching an event like a heavyweight boxing match will set you back at least $50, billed directly to your motel room. Most hotels and motels also offer a choice of **recent movies** that have just finished their theatrical runs, at around $8–10 per film.

Festivals

Someone is always celebrating something in the Pacific Northwest, giving rise to a multitude of festivals: art and craft shows, county fairs, ethnic celebrations, music festivals, rodeos, sandcastle-building competitions, and many others of almost every variety.

January

Chinese New Year (late Jan) ⓦ www.cidbia
.org. Seattle's International District and Portland's Chinatown are at their most colorful around late January to early February, when parades are staged and dragon costumes come out in full force.

February

Tét in Seattle (early Feb) ⓦ www.tetinseattle
.org. The Vietnamese lunar new year, celebrated with scrumptious food, traditional music, dance programs, and film screenings, with many events at the Center House in Seattle Center.
Oregon Shakespeare Festival ⓦ www.orshakes
.org. Premier Bard-fest from mid-Feb to Oct in the charming small town of Ashland, OR.

March

Irish Week (mid-March) ⓦ www.irishclub.org. A Seattle salute to the Emerald Isle with food, drink, and dance, centered around St Patrick's Day; the holiday is celebrated almost as colorfully – if only for one night – in Portland.
Moisture Festival (late March) ⓦ www
.moisturefestival.com. Another one of those only-in-Seattle events, held over several weeks and presenting comedy and "variety" acts that range from neo-vaudeville shenanigans to outrageous burlesque and alternative-circus performers.

April

Hood River Valley Blossom Festival (mid-April)
ⓦ www.hoodriver.org. Oregon's hamlet in the Columbia River Gorge hosts an explosion of blooming orchards in the lush valleys that surround the town in an idyllic setting at the foothills of Mount Hood.
Seattle Poetry Festival (mid- to late April)
ⓦ www.poetryfestival.org. A week of poetry readings at various venues throughout the city, culminating in the Seattle Grand Slam, the ultimate poetry smackdown.

May

Seattle Maritime Festival (early May) ⓦ www
.boatsafloat.com. Port tours, tugboat races, a boat-building competition, and a chowder cook-off are on the bill at this free three-day Seattle event.
Maifest (mid-May) ⓦ www.leavenworth.org.
Community parades, marching bands, loads of food and drink, and more Bavarian kitsch than you can imagine at the spirited event held in Leavenworth, WA.
Northwest Folklife Festival (late May) ⓦ www
.nwfolklife.org. Memorial Day bash in Seattle attracting 200,000 visitors and thousands of participants, for all types of traditional music, including bluegrass, Celtic, roots, and world music, along with crafts, food, dance, and storytelling.

June

Portland Rose Festival (early June) ⓦ www
.rosefestival.org. Portland's grand Sunday parade has copious displays of roses and visiting US Navy boats, highlighted by an evening procession, the Starlight Parade, and a raucous waterfront "Fun Center."
Fremont Fair & Solstice Parade (mid-June)
ⓦ www.fremontfair.com. The most enjoyable and bizarre Seattle celebration, with hundreds of arts vendors, plus a parade allowing only human-powered floats and costumes, including nude bicyclists.
Pride Parade and Freedom Rally (mid-June)
ⓦ www.seattlepride.org, ⓦ www.pridenw
.org. Occurring in the major cities in the region, a celebration of tolerance and diversity, with zany costumes, outlandish floats, and various musical acts.
Sandcastle Contest (late June) ⓦ www
.cannon-beach.net/cbsandcastle.html. An annual summertime eruption of seaside sculpture and local color in Cannon Beach, OR.

July

Festival of American Fiddle Tunes (early July)
ⓦ www.centrum.org. Fascinating Port Townsend, WA, music event with big and prestigious names in

bluegrass, folk, and roots music, plus workshops if you want to learn how to rosin up the bow yourself.

Independence Day (4th). Fourth of July fireworks light up almost every city or town in Oregon and Washington: along the Seattle waterfronts at Elliott Bay, Lake Washington, and Lake Union, and Portland's Willamette River, among many other locations.

Seafair (early to late July) @ www.seafair.com. Intermittent three-week celebration of maritime culture in Seattle, featuring vendors selling seafood and events at various locations all over town. Includes a marathon and torchlight parade, hydroplane races on Lake Washington, and milk-carton races on Green Lake.

Oregon Country Fair (mid-July) @ www .oregoncountryfair.org. Huge fair and live-music shindig in Veneta, OR, outside Eugene, once the province of hordes of zoned-out hippies but now more a family-friendly event.

Oregon Brewers Festival (late July) @ www .oregonbrewfest.com. Unbelievably popular Portland festival celebrating the glories of suds-making and -drinking, spread over four days with countless regional and national craft brewers and beer lovers of every kind.

August

Britt Festival (early to mid-Aug) @ www.brittfest .org. Down in the perfectly preserved small town of Jacksonville, OR, an unexpected two-week music fest featuring the big names in mainstream jazz, classical, and pop music.

Astoria Regatta (mid-Aug) @ www .astoriaregatta.org. A week full of community parades, yacht and other sailboat races, fireworks, and a carnival atmosphere – with a "pirates' den" to boot – in this quaint town at the northernmost edge of the Oregon coast.

Chief Seattle Days (mid-Aug) @ www.suquamish .nsn.us. In Suquamish, WA, just over the bridge from Bainbridge Island, the Suquamish tribe celebrates this weekend festival with Native American food, culture, and canoe races.

Highland Games and Clan Gathering (late Aug) @ www.hypertype.com/highlandgames. Get out the bagpipes and tartan for a two-day celebration of all things Scottish (and Irish, too), with Celtic-flavored food and music and events like the caber-tossing, axe-throwing, and kilt-clad wrestling. In Sweet Home, OR.

September

Bandon Cranberry Festival (early Sept) @ www .bandon.com. Head down to this hamlet on the southern Oregon coast to wallow in the area's signature berry – celebrated with a fun fair, parade,

pageant, barbecue, sporting events, and loads of cranberry snacks, desserts, and drinks.

Bumbershoot (early Sept) @ www.bumbershoot .org. Mammoth multi-event extravaganza that's one of Seattle's best parties. Musical acts range from the famous to the obscure, with plenty of film, comedy, and theater thrown in for good measure. All in all, some five hundred acts perform at twenty different venues around town.

Puyallup Fair (early to mid-Sept) @ www.thefair .com. Western Washington's biggest country fair, in the burg of Puyallup, with livestock and home-made craft displays sharing space with a rodeo, rides, food, and mainstream country music.

Pendleton Round-Up (mid-Sept) @ www .pendletonroundup.com. Eastern Oregon hoedown combining traditional rodeo with extravagant pageantry, plus plenty of good old-fashioned barbecue, pony tricks, cowboy music, and flashy belt buckles.

Mount Angel Oktoberfest (mid-Sept) @ www .oktoberfest.org. Also known for its monastery, this little Oregon town is most famous for serving up the beer, lederhosen, and Tyrolean hats when the summer ends – a bit kitschy, but also one of the region's most enjoyable and intoxicating events.

October

Yachats Mushroom Fest (mid-Oct) @ www .yachats.org. Mycophiles will rejoice at this weekend festival in the central Oregon coast town of Yachats, where you can get your fill of mushroom-themed music, storytelling, and guided walks – and feast on plenty of good fungi, too.

Earshot Jazz Festival (mid-Oct to early Nov) @ www.earshot.org. Daily Seattle concerts spread out over several weeks and featuring some 150 performers at a dozen venues. The focus is on progressive contemporary jazz notables with an international reputation.

November

Cultural Crossroads (early Nov) @ www .crossroadsbellevue.com. Three-day multicultural music show on two stages (held around a major mall in Bellevue, WA), plus a wide-ranging food and crafts fair, representing more than one hundred different performers and groups.

December

Winter Worldfest @ www.seattlecenter.com. A month-long Seattle Center event that celebrates the holidays with the usual Christmas-related food, pageantry, and festivities including ice-skating, tree decoration, and so on.

Outdoor pursuits

Oregon and Washington are known for their fabulous backcountry and wilderness areas, swathed in dense forests, scoured by mighty whitewater rivers, and capped by majestic mountains and vast glaciers. Opportunities for outdoor pursuits are almost limitless, and the facilities to indulge them some of the best on the continent. The most popular activities are hiking, skiing and snowboarding, and fishing; other activities such as whale-watching, horseback riding, and rafting are covered where appropriate in the main guide. Once you're in the Northwest you can rely on finding outfitters, equipment rental shops, charter companies, tour operators, and guides to help you in most areas: tourist offices invariably carry full details or contact numbers. Most local bookstores also have a separate outdoor pursuits section with a variety of specialist guides.

Hiking

The Pacific Northwest boasts some of North America's finest **hiking**, and you don't need wilderness training or hiking experience to tackle most trails. All major parks have well-marked and -maintained trails, and any park center or local tourist office will furnish you with adequate **maps**. If you're entering into the backcountry, it's especially important to obtain the appropriately detailed maps. Be sure to consult park staff on the better hikes, or pick up the **trail guides** that are widely available in local bookshops for most of the region's prime hiking areas.

Some of Washington's best hiking areas are in its national parks, most dramatically among the glacial summits of the **North Cascades** and around high peaks like **Mount Rainier** and the scorched earth around **Mount St Helens**. In Oregon, **Crater Lake** presents some of the region's most stunning scenery, **Mount Hood** is a forbidding favorite for glacial climbers, and the other, smaller peaks in the **Oregon Cascades** have their own charm. Excellent **long-distance** trails include the **Oregon Coast Trail**, hugging the 360 miles of coastline from the Columbia River to the California border, and the **Pacific Crest Trail**, a 2620-mile path from Mexico to the Canadian border.

Wherever you go, and at whatever altitude, make sure you're properly **prepared** and **equipped**: good boots, a waterproof jacket, warm clothing, and spare food and drink to cover emergencies are essential. On longer walks, be sure to tell the park center of your intentions, so if something goes wrong there's a chance someone will come and hunt for you. Be prepared for sudden changes of weather, encounters with wildlife of all kinds, and potential dangers to your health (see box, p.52). Outdoor clothing can be bought easily in most towns, and in most mountain areas there's a good chance of being able to rent tents and specialized cold-weather gear.

Skiing and snowboarding

Wherever there's hiking in the Northwest, there's also usually **skiing**. Washington has sixteen ski areas, mostly in the **Cascades**, and many within easy striking distance of Seattle. Oregon boasts **Mount Bachelor** (see p.230), offering some of North America's finest skiing, and **Mount Hood** (see p.131), where you can sometimes ski throughout the summer. Despite the expense involved, **heli-skiing** is also taking off – the sport involves a helicopter drop deep into the backcountry (or to the actual summits of mountains) followed by some of the wildest and most exhilarating skiing you're ever likely to experience; contact visitor centers for details of packages and outfitters. For many locals, though, **night skiing** is the most invigorating option, tooling down an ice field in the evening,

Outdoor health tips

When it comes to protecting your **health** in the backcountry, camping or hiking at lower elevations should present few problems, though you may encounter a thick swarm of **insects** near any body of water; candles or bug repellents with allethrin or citronella can help deter the little beasts. If you develop a rash and flulike symptoms in the backcountry, you may have been bitten by a **tick** carrying **Lyme disease**, which is prevalent in wooded country. The condition is easily curable, but if left untreated it can lead to nasty complications. Get advice from a park ranger or warden if you've been bitten; otherwise buy a strong tick repellent and wear long socks, trousers, and sleeved shirts when hiking.

One serious backcountry problem is **giardia**, waterborne bacteria causing an intestinal disease characterized by chronic diarrhea, abdominal cramps, fatigue, and weight loss. To prevent it, never drink from rivers, streams, or glaciers, however clear and inviting they may look; boil water that doesn't come from a tap for at least ten minutes and filter it with an iodine-based or giardia-rated filter, available from any camping or sports store. Neither ordinary filters nor standard water-purification tablets will remove the bacteria.

Beware, too, of **poison oak**, which grows all over the region, usually among oak trees, and comes in leaf groups of three distinguished by prominent veins and shiny surfaces (waxy green in spring, rich red and orange in autumn). It causes open blisters and lumpy sores up to ten days after contact. If you come into contact with it, wash your skin and clothes as soon as possible, and don't scratch: the only way to ease the itching is to smother yourself in calamine lotion or take regular dips in the sea.

There's also the occasional danger of being bitten or stung by various **poisonous creatures** – spiders, rattlers, and the like. If bitten, apply a cold compress to the wound, constrict the area with a tourniquet to prevent the spread of venom, drink lots of water, and bring your temperature down by resting in a shady area. Stay as calm as possible and seek medical help immediately.

Hiking at higher elevations demands special care: late snows are common, even into July, and in spring there's a real danger of **avalanches**, not to mention meltwater making otherwise simple stream crossings hazardous. **Altitude sickness**, brought on by the depletion of oxygen in the atmosphere, can affect even the fittest of athletes. Take it easy for the first few days you go above seven thousand feet, drink lots of water, avoid alcohol, eat plenty of carbohydrates, and protect yourself from the increased radiation of the sun. Watch out for signs of **exposure** to the sun – mild delirium, exhaustion, an inability to get warm – and use a good sunblock if spending time outdoors, especially in the high country in summer and the snow in winter.

illuminated only by distant floodlights or moonlight. Even better, nocturnal lift tickets are half the price of day tickets in most resorts. As an alternative, **snowboarding** has become just as popular as skiing, if not even more so, and most of the same routes and lifts are available to 'boarders as to skiers. Some resorts may even have special snow parks or other facilities for snowboarders to take air without having to worry about getting run into by hard-charging downhillers; check each resort's home page for details.

Ski packages are available from most foreign travel agents, while companies and hotels in many Northwest cities organize their own mini-packages to nearby resorts. Visitor centers in ski areas open up in the winter to help with practicalities, and most towns have ski shops that sell or rent equipment. The price for lift tickets averages $50, and equipment may cost another $25–35 more but can be much cheaper if included in a **package deal** with a lift ticket. A cheaper option is **cross-country skiing**, or ski-touring. Backcountry ski lodges dot

Saving money on the slopes

Oregon and Washington feature some of the best ski terrain in the country, but without careful planning a **ski vacation** can be horribly expensive. In addition to the tips listed below, phone or write in advance to resorts for brochures, and when you get there, scan local newspapers for money-saving offers.

- Visit early or late in the season to take advantage of lower accommodation and lift-ticket rates.
- The more people in your party, the more money you save on lodgings. For groups of four to six, a condo rental unit costs much less than a motel.
- Before setting a date, ask the resort about package deals with flights, rooms, and lift tickets. This can be a very economical way to book a ski vacation.
- Shop around for the best boot and ski rentals – prices often vary significantly.
- If you have to buy lift tickets at the resort, save money by purchasing multi-day tickets.
- If you're a novice, look out for resorts that offer free beginners' lessons with the purchase of a lift ticket.
- Finish your day's skiing in time to take advantage of happy hours and dining specials, which usually last from 4pm to 7pm.

mountainous areas, offering rustic accommodation, equipment rental, and lessons from as little as $15 a day for skis, boots, and poles, up to $150–200 for an all-inclusive weekend tour.

Truly gung-ho skiers may wish to opt for a combination **hike-and-ski** trek, carrying their equipment as they ascend a peak such as Mount Adams, then schussing down or across the slopes in a burst of winter glory – only to trudge back up the mountain once more. Although you'll obviously save money on lift tickets this way (and such peaks as Adams are not equipped with c hairlifts in any case), this rather extreme approach to skiing should be considered only by the most vigorous athletes and hardcore outdoor enthusiasts. Another, more accessible option is summertime **ski-slope hiking**, wherein many ski resorts offer steeply discounted lift fares to take you down the mountain after a vigorous climb up the slopes; check each resort for details.

Fishing

The Pacific Northwest is nirvana for people who love **fishing**. While each area has its dream catches, such as Pacific salmon, excellent fishing can be found in most of the region's abundant lakes, rivers, and coastal waters. Most towns have a fishing shop for equipment, and any spot with fishing possibilities is likely to have companies running boats and charters. As with every other type of outdoor activity, states publish detailed booklets on outfitters and everything that swims within the area of their jurisdiction.

Fishing is governed by a medley of **regulations** that vary from state to state. These are baffling at first glance but usually boil down to the need for a nonresident permit for freshwater fishing, and another for saltwater. These are obtainable from most local fishing or sports shops (Oregon $61, Washington $40–44) and are valid for a year. Short-term (one- to six-day, $14–34) licenses are also available in some areas. In a few places you may have to pay a premium to go after particular fish, and there may also be quotas or a closed season on certain fish. Shops and visitor centers always have the most current regulations and fishing conditions. Alternatively, if your fancy runs toward digging for clams, geoducks, mussels, and other bivalves, you might also consider getting a **shellfish license** (Oregon $16, Washington $26).

National and state parks

Protected backcountry areas in the Northwest include national parks, large, federally controlled areas of great natural beauty or historical significance, and state parks, often of similar size and splendor but run by local or regional governments; national monuments, offering outstanding geological or historical features covering smaller areas than national parks; national seashores, protecting seafront geography and its attendant wildlife; and national forests, which often surround national parks and are also federally administered but are usually much less protected than national parks, allowing some logging and industries such as ski resorts and mining operations. Regulations common to all parks may include prohibitions against firearms, hunting, snowmobiles or off-road vehicles, the feeding of wildlife, and the removal or damaging of any natural objects or features.

National parks are usually supervised locally by a ranger based at a park office or a park **information center**, which can provide the lowdown on hiking and activities such as fishing, camping, or rock-climbing – pursuits that often require a **permit**. Most centers have information and audiovisual displays on flora, fauna, and outdoor activities, and virtually all employ experienced staff who can provide firsthand advice on your chosen trail or pursuit. For up-to-the-minute **online information** on the national park system, access the official website at ⑩www.nps.gov, which features full details of the main attractions of the national parks, plus opening hours, the best times to visit, admission fees, hiking trails, and visitor facilities.

Keep in mind that in many remote areas proper **planning** is essential, even if it's just making sure you have enough fuel in the tank of your car to get you to the next gas station or, more important, enough water to keep you alive in a parched backcountry environment. Weather can also turn, even in summer, and knowing the lay of the land can be important if you wish to avoid getting lost, being trapped in an isolated site after dark, or stumbling into a mountain lion's den.

Entrance fees

National park **entrance fees** range from $5 to $25, which covers a vehicle and all its occupants, or $5–10 for pedestrians or bikers. Fees are always collected at roadside entrance kiosks. If you plan to visit more than a couple of national parks, buy an **America the Beautiful** passport ($80), which gives a named driver and all passengers in the same vehicle unlimited access to all national parks and national monuments, as well as all federal parks managed by the US Fish and Wildlife Service, Forest Service, and Bureau of Land Management, for one year. Free passes are available for travelers with disabilities (see p.69), and for seniors over 62, who have to pay only $10 to get a lifetime pass. As for US **state parks**, the days when most were free have unfortunately passed, due to budget cuts, and you may be charged $5–10 for vehicle entry, or $3–5 for pedestrians and bicyclists.

Camping in the parks

If your time and money are limited or you want to get a feel for the wilderness – or both – one of the best options is **camping** out at night and cooking your own meals on a portable stove (if local regulations allow). If you don't fancy roughing it, there are usually also a wide array of public and commercially run campgrounds: **primitive**, a flat piece of ground that may or may not have a water tap, and that may be free; **semi-primitive**, usually with running water and pit toilets, where "self-registration" is the norm and a small fee ($5–15) is charged; and **full**, offering a broader mix of amenities, including restrooms and showers and sometimes shops, restaurants, and washing facilities, for

$12–30. An additional fee of $3–5 may be charged for firewood. **Yurts**, **cabins**, and **tepees** are also available at some campgrounds, usually for $27–45 per night.

Campgrounds in national parks are bound by special rules, with some sites for tents, others for RVs only; most national parks have at least one campground that remains open for basic **winter camping**, though this isn't the case for most state parks and commercial campgrounds; check opening times carefully. As for **fees**, some campgrounds may be free on a first-come, first-served basis but charge $20 or so for reservations.

Primitive camping

Official permission and registration, including a statement of your itinerary and planned return time, are required for **backcountry camping**, whether you're rough camping on your own chosen spot in the wilderness or using designated primitive or semi-primitive sites. This enables the authorities to know if you've run into trouble.

While registration and permits are obligatory, other regulations for rough camping vary enormously. Some parks allow backcountry camping only in tightly defined areas; others have a special **primitive wildland** zone where you can pitch a tent within a designated distance of the nearest road or trailhead. Throughout national parks, though, a quota system operates in the more popular areas: no permits will be issued once a set number have been allocated for a particular trail or backcountry campsite.

When camping in the outback – particularly in the dry tinder lands of central and southern Oregon – check that **fires** are permitted before you start one; even if they are, try to use a camp stove – in some places firewood is scarce, although you may be allowed to use deadwood. In wilderness areas, try to camp on **previously used** sites. Where there are no toilets, bury human waste at least 8in underground and 200ft from the nearest water supply and campsite. Never wash in rivers and lakes – use a container at least fifty feet from either, and try to use a biodegradable soap. It is unacceptable to burn any rubbish; the preferred practice is to **pack out**, or carry away all garbage, the ideal being to leave no trace of your presence whatsoever.

Spectator sports

Few occasions provide better opportunities for mixing with the locals than catching a baseball game on a summer afternoon or joining in with the screaming throngs at a football or ice hockey game. Professional sports teams almost always put on the most spectacular shows, but big games between college rivals and minor-league baseball games provide an easy and enjoyable way to get on closer terms with a community.

Baseball

Because its teams play so many games – 162 in all, usually five or six a week throughout the summer – **Major League Baseball** is probably the easiest sport to catch in the United States, and it's also among the cheapest to watch (as little as $7 a seat), with a season running from April to October.

In the early 1970s, after the short-lived presence of the Seattle Pilots, the **Seattle Mariners** arrived and faced many years of hardship on the field, finally establishing a winning record in the mid- to late 1990s and setting an all-time record for American League wins in 2001. Though it has still failed to get to the World Series, much less win a division championship, the team has endeared itself enough to the city to gain the public funds for an open-air stadium, Safeco Field (see p.302). **Tickets** are $7 for the cheapest seats, in the center-field bleachers, and $60 for the most expensive, in the lower box section; there's a whole range of prices and seats in between (call ℡206/622-HITS or visit Ⓦseattle.mariners.mlb.com to buy tickets). You can also buy tickets in person (and avoid the surcharge levied on telephone and online ticket purchases) at the Safeco Field box office and at the Mariners' team shops in Westlake Center (p.297) and Bellevue Square (p.318).

Minor league baseball can be found elsewhere in the region: in Washington, Tacoma's triple-A-level **Rainiers** play at Cheney Stadium (April–Sept; ℡253/752-7700 or 1-800/281-3834, Ⓦwww.tacomarainiers.com); while Everett's single-A **Aquasox** play at Everett Memorial Stadium (June–Sept; ℡1-800/GO-FROGS, Ⓦwww.aquasox.com); tickets run $7–15 at both stadiums. Oregon's triple-A-level **Portland Beavers** (April–Sept; $8–13; ℡503/553-5555, Ⓦwww.portlandbeavers.com) are a somewhat woeful franchise best known for their overpriced stadium, PGE Park, and indifferent fan base. Eugene's single-A **Emeralds** (June–Sept; $5–9; ℡503/DIAL-EMS, Ⓦwww.go-ems.com), along with their fans, are an altogether more spirited bunch.

Football

Professional football can be quite the opposite of baseball – tickets are expensive and difficult to get, particularly if the team is successful, which the **Seattle Seahawks** have been as of late. Additional interest in the team stems from their new home, Qwest Field (see p.302), which opened in 2002 next to Safeco Field. As you might expect, **tickets** are far from cheap, ranging from $25 to $300 (Sept–Jan; call ℡1-888/NFL-HAWK or visit Ⓦwww.seahawks.com to purchase).

Not surprisingly, then, **college football** has become much bigger in the Northwest than the pro leagues; the season runs from September to December or, if one of the teams is in a big bowl game, early January. In contrast to most of their history, Washington's pigskin squads haven't fared as well in recent years as Oregon's. The long-standing powerhouse in the region, the University of Washington **Huskies** play at the 72,000-seat Husky Stadium on the edge of the campus, near Lake Washington. **Tickets** are $25–35 for general admission to the bleachers and $35–60 for reserved seats (call ℡206/543-2200 or visit Ⓦwww.gohuskies.cstv.com). Their rivals, the Washington State **Cougars**, from the sticks of Pullman in Eastern Washington ($15–60; ℡1-800/GO-COUGS, Ⓦwsucougars.cstv.com), typically roll into town to stage a yearly upset. The Oregon **Ducks**, based out of Eugene ($16–60; ℡1-800/WEBFOOT, Ⓦwww.goducks.com), are known for their garish outfits and expensive renovated stadium with $3-million locker rooms, while the region's historically worst team, the Oregon State **Beavers** ($36–60; ℡1-800/GO-BEAVS, Ⓦwww.osubeavers.com), playing in the burg of Corvallis, was the only one of the four to finish in the national Top 25 in 2007.

Basketball

The two major **professional basketball** teams in Oregon and Washington have both achieved about the same level of success since their inception in the 1970s – one championship, a few more attempts at a title, and mediocrity or worse in recent years. The **Portland Trailblazers**, who play at the Rose Garden on the Eastside ($10–130; Nov–June; ℡503/797-9600, Ⓦwww.nba.com/blazers), have by far the worst reputation, widely known as the "Jail Blazers" for their public violation of drug laws and assorted acts of violence; they're currently rebuilding, though, with exciting young players like Brandon Roy, and tickets are pretty cheap. The **Seattle Supersonics**, based at Key Arena in the Seattle Center ($10–150; ℡206/283-DUNK, Ⓦwww.nba.com/sonics), are a bit less exciting all around – to the degree that they are likely to move elsewhere (possibly Oklahoma City) for the 2010 season. **Women's basketball** has experienced difficulties getting off the ground here, with teams often changing pricing plans, schedules, and marketing efforts from season to season, leaving potential fans bewildered; the local representative in the WNBA, the **Seattle Storm** ($8–75; ☎206/217-WNBA, ⓦwww.wnba.com), plays at Key Arena along with the Supersonics and, being under the same ownership, will probably also move along with them.

Other spectator sports

There are no major-league **professional hockey** teams in Oregon and Washington, but the **Seattle Thunderbirds** (Sept–March; tickets $12–20; ☎206/448-PUCK, ⓦwww.seattle-thunderbirds.com), of the minor Junior A Western Hockey League, play in Key Arena, and their counterparts the **Portland Winterhawks** ($10–24; ☎503/224-4400, ⓦwww.winterhawks.com) play at Memorial Coliseum near the Rose Garden arena. Tickets for all but the biggest games are usually available, though

it's always a good idea to try and obtain seats in advance.

Soccer enthusiasts can watch local squads in the USL First Division, the highest US pro soccer level other than major league soccer. The **Sounders** play at Memorial Stadium in the Seattle Center ($13–18; April–Sept; ☎206/622-3415 or 1-800/796-KICK, ⓦwww.seattlesounders.net), while the **Timbers** can be seen at Portland's PGE Park ($10–27; ☎503/553-5555, ⓦwww.pgepark.com/timbers).

Finally, **horse racing** is held at **Emerald Downs**, in the Tacoma suburb of Auburn (☎253/288-7000, ⓦwww.emdowns.com), and **Portland Meadows**, just off I-5 north of Downtown (☎503/285-9144, ⓦwww.portlandmeadows.com). The racing season runs from mid-April through mid-September, Thursdays to Sundays (Wed–Sun from mid-July through August).

Traveling with children

Traveling with children in the more populous parts of the Pacific Northwest is relatively problem-free: children are readily accepted in public places across the region, most state and national parks organize children's activities, and virtually every town or city has clean and safe playgrounds.

Restaurants often try hard to lure parents in with their kids. Most of the national chains offer high chairs and a special menu, packed with huge, excellent-value (if not necessarily healthy) meals like mini-burgers and macaroni and cheese. Virtually all **museums** and tourist attractions offer reduced rates for kids, and most large cities have kid-friendly natural history museums or aquariums, and quite a few have hands-on children's museums and, in the case of Seattle, even a children's theater (see p.307). State and city tourist offices can provide specific information and ideas on activities or sights that are likely to appeal to children; a huge range of books and guides is also available.

Transportation

Children under 2 **fly free** on domestic routes and usually for ten percent of the adult fare on international flights – though that doesn't mean they necessarily get a seat; on a full flight they will have to sit on your lap. Kids aged from 2 to 12 may be entitled to half-price tickets, though recent airline-industry economic troubles have reduced perks like these in some measure.

Traveling **by bus** may be the cheapest way to go, but it's also the most uncom-fortable for kids. Babies and toddlers can travel (on your lap) for free, whereas youth aged 2 to 4 are charged ten to fifty percent of the adult fare (depending on the distance), as are any toddlers who take up a seat. Children 5–12 are charged about sixty percent of the standard fare.

Even if you discount the romance of the rails, **train travel** is by far the best option for long journeys – not only does everyone get to enjoy the scenery, but you can get up and walk around, relieving pent-up energy. Most cross-country trains have sleeping compartments, which may be quite expensive but are a great adventure. Children's discounts are slightly better than for bus or plane travel, with babies and toddlers riding free and kids from 2 to 15 receiving half-price fares.

Most families choose to travel **by car**, but if you're hoping to enjoy a driving holiday with your kids, it's essential to plan ahead. Pack plenty of sensible snacks and drinks, plan to stop (don't make your kids make you stop) every couple of hours, arrive at your destination well before sunset, and avoid traveling through big cities during rush hour. If you're taking a fly-drive vacation, note that when **renting a car** the company is legally obliged to provide free car seats for kids.

Travel essentials

Costs

Thanks to the historic weakness of the US dollar, international visitors can find numerous options for cheap amenities and amusements, along with many bargains and affordable **costs** for goods and services. Beyond this, most Western European visitors find virtually everything – accommodation, food, gas, cameras, clothes, and more – to be better value in the US than it is at home.

Generally, if you're sticking to a very tight **budget** – camping and buying groceries from shops – you could squeeze by on $30–40 per person a day. You're not going to last long living like this, though, and a more comfortable average daily budget, covering a motel room, bus travel, a museum or two, and a restaurant meal, would work out at around $75–90 per person. Naturally, once you upgrade your accommodation, eat out two or three times a day, and take in the city nightlife, this figure can easily double or triple.

Accommodation is likely to be your biggest single expense. Few decent hotel or motel rooms in the cities cost under $50, and even a marginally decent room will run anywhere from $75 to $100,

with fancier hotels costing much, much more – upwards of $300 in some cases. Unless otherwise stated, the hotel price codes (see p.40) are for the cheapest double room in high season, exclusive of any local taxes and special deals. **Hostels** offering dorm beds – usually for $15–25 – are one alternative (with private rooms $35–55), and camping is also cheap, ranging from free to $30 per night. Accommodation prices may often be higher from June to September and throughout the more touristy areas of the region.

Unlike accommodation, prices for good **food** range widely, from espresso carts to chic restaurants. You could get by on as little as $20 a day, but realistically you should aim for around $50 – and remember, too, that the area has plenty of great spots for a splurge.

Traveling around on buses and trains is reasonably economical, too, though if you're traveling in a group of two or more, renting a car (around $150 a week) can be very good value, not least because it will enable you to stay in the ubiquitous budget motels along the interstates. Finally, you should figure in costs for **tipping** into your travel budget. Expect to tip about fifteen to twenty percent

Emergency numbers for lost cards and checks

American Express cards ☎1-800/528-4800, ⓦwww.americanexpress.com
American Express checks ☎1-800/221-7282
Citicorp checks ☎1-800/645-6556, ⓦwww.citicorp.com
Diners Club ☎1-800/234-6377, ⓦwww.dinersclub.com
Discover ☎1-800/DISCOVER, ⓦwww.discovercard.com
MasterCard ☎1-800/826-2181, ⓦwww.mastercard.com
Thomas Cook/MasterCard checks ☎1-800/223-9920, ⓦwww.travelex.com or ⓦwww.thomascook.co.uk
Visa cards ☎1-800/847-2911, ⓦwww.visa.com
Visa checks ☎1-800/227-6811

of the bill (before tax) to waiters in most restaurants unless the service is truly wretched, in which case tip no less than ten percent to avoid ripping off the busboys, dishwashers, and hosts/hostesses, who also take a cut of the tip. About fifteen percent should also be added to taxi fares; round up to the nearest 50¢ or dollar. A hotel porter should get $1–2 per bag, chambermaids $1–2 a day, and valet attendants $2.

Oregon is one of the few US states without a **sales tax**, making shopping there very enticing. In Washington the rate is 6.5 to 9.3 percent (depending on the area), and the tax is added to virtually everything you buy in shops. Towns and cities in both states may levy **hotel taxes** – the rate ranges from fourteen to sixteen percent in the cities to five to ten percent (or, occasionally, nothing) in more rural areas.

Crime and personal safety

Although Oregon and Washington are hardly free of crime, the region is much safer than other parts of North America. Away from the major centers, crime is low-key but for the odd bar brawl and car theft in a rough-and-ready small town. By being careful, planning ahead, and taking good care of your possessions, you should have few problems. Foreign visitors tend to report that the police are helpful and obliging when things go wrong, although they'll be less sympathetic if they think you brought the trouble on yourself through carelessness.

Mugging and theft

If you're unlucky enough to get **mugged**, just hand over your money; resistance is generally not a good idea. After the crime occurs, immediately report it to the police so you can later attempt to recover your loss from an insurance provider – unlikely, but worth a try. Also, keep **emergency numbers** for credit cards and travelers' checks handy, so they can be canceled after the crime occurs (see above). One prime spot to be mugged is at an **ATM** outside the tourist areas, where you're likely to be told to make the maximum withdrawal and hand it over. Needless to say, you should treat ATM use with the strictest caution.

If your passport is stolen (or if you lose it), call your country's consulate (see list on p.62), and pick up or have sent to you an application form for a new one; you must submit the form with a notarized photocopy of your ID and pay a reissuing fee, often around $30.

To avoid being the victim of a **hotel room theft** – a more frequent problem for lower-end establishments, though even the elite hotels are not immune to it – lock your valuables in the room **safe** when you leave, and always keep doors locked when you're in the room. Don't open the door to suspicious individuals, and if a questionable visitor claims to be a hotel representative, phone the front desk before opening the door to make sure of it.

Finally, a few **simple rules** to keep yourself safe are worth remembering: don't flash money around, don't leave your wallet open or count money in public, and don't look panicked, even if you are.

Car crime and safety

Crimes committed against tourists driving **rental cars** have made headlines in the past decade, but there are precautions you can take to keep yourself safe. In urban areas, any car you rent should have nothing on it – such as a special license plate – to distinguish it as a rental car. When driving, under no circumstances should you stop if you are "accidentally" rammed by the driver behind you; instead, drive on to the nearest well-lit and busy spot and phone the police at ☏911. Keep doors locked and hide valuables out of sight, either in the trunk or the glove compartment, and leave any valuables you don't need for your journey back in your hotel safe. Should a relatively uncommon "**carjacking**" occur, in which you're told to hand over your car at gunpoint, you should flee the vehicle as quickly as possible, get away from the scene, and then call the police.

If your car **breaks down** at night while on a major street, activate the emergency flashers to signal a police officer for assistance; if it happens during the day, first contact your rental-car company or auto organization such as AAA (see p.38), or find the nearest phone book and call for a tow truck. Should you be forced to stop your car on a **freeway**, pull over to the right shoulder of the highway – never the left – and activate your flashers. Wait for assistance either in your vehicle while strapped in by a seat belt or on a safe embankment nearby.

Electricity

Electricity outlets run on 110V AC in the US. Many plugs are still two-pronged and rather flimsy. Some European-made travel plug adapters don't fit American sockets.

Entry requirements

Keeping up with the constant changes to US entry requirements since September 11, 2001, can sometimes feel like a hopeless task. At least once a year the American government announces new, often harsher restrictions on foreign entry into the country, adding considerably to the red tape involved in visiting it. Nonetheless, there are several basic rules that apply, which are detailed (and should be frequently checked for updates) on the US State Department website ⊛ travel.state.gov.

Under the **Visa Waiver Program**, if you're a citizen of the UK, Ireland, Australia, New Zealand, most Western European states, or other selected countries like Singapore, Japan, and Brunei (27 in all), and visiting the United States for fewer than ninety days, at a minimum you'll need an onward or return ticket, a visa waiver form, and a Machine Readable Passport (MRP). The MRP requirement is a recent manifestation of America's security clampdown. MRPs issued before October 2005 are acceptable to use on their own; those issued from October 2005 to October 2006 must include a digital photograph of the passport holder; and those issued after October 2006 require a high-tech security chip built into the passport. It is up to the various countries covered by the Visa Waiver Program to provide such passports to their citizens; for more information, inquire at American embassies or consulates. The Nonimmigrant Visa Waiver Arrival/Departure Form, Form I-94W, will be provided either by your travel agency or embassy or when you get on the plane, and must be presented to Immigration on arrival. The same form covers entry across the US borders with Canada and Mexico (for non-Canadian and non-Mexican citizens). If you're in the Visa Waiver Program and intend to work, study, or stay in the country for more than ninety days, you must apply for a regular visa through your local US embassy or consulate. You will not be admitted under the VWP if you have ever been arrested (not just convicted), have a criminal record, or have been previously deported from or refused entry to the US. Under no circumstances are visitors who have been admitted under the Visa Waiver Program allowed to extend their stays beyond ninety days. Doing so will bar you from future use of the program.

Canadian citizens, who have not always needed a passport to get into the US, should have their passports on them when entering the country, as should Mexican citizens. If you're planning to stay for more than ninety days, you'll need a visa, which can be applied for by mail through the US embassy or nearest US consulate. If you cross the US border by car, be prepared for US Customs officials to search your vehicle. Remember, too, that without the proper paperwork, Canadians are barred from working in the US.

Citizens of all other countries should contact their local US embassy or consulate for details of current entry requirements, as they are often required to have both a valid passport and a non-immigrant visitor's visa. To obtain such a visa, complete the application form available through your local American embassy or consulate and send it to the embassy with the appropriate fee, two photographs, and your passport.

US Customs

Customs officers upon entry to the US will relieve you of your customs declaration form, which you receive with your waiver form when it is handed out on incoming planes, on ferries, and at border crossing points. It asks if you're carrying any fresh foods and if you've visited a farm in the last month.

As well as food and anything agricultural, it's prohibited to carry into the country any articles from such places as North Korea, Iran, Syria, or Cuba, as well as obvious no-no's like protected wildlife species and ancient artifacts. Anyone caught sneaking drugs into the country will not only face prosecution but be entered in the records as an undesirable and probably denied entry for all time. For **duty-free allowances** and other information regarding customs, call ☎202/354-1000 or visit ⊚www.customs.gov.

US embassies and consulates abroad

For a more complete list around the world, check ⊚usembassy.state.gov.

In Australia

Embassy

Canberra 21 Moonah Place, Yarralumla ACT 2600 ☎02/6214 5600, ⊚canberra.usembassy.gov

Consulates

Melbourne 553 St Kilda Rd, VIC 3004 ☎03/9526 5900
Perth 16 St George's Terrace, 13th floor, WA 6000 ☎08/9202 1224
Sydney MLC Centre, Level 10, 19–29 Martin Place, NSW 2000 ☎02/9373 9200
Visa hotline ☎1902/941 641 (prerecorded information, AU$1.05 per minute) or 1800/687 844 (live operators, A$2.75 per minute)

In Canada

Embassy

Ottawa 490 Sussex Drive, ON K1N 1G8 ☎613/238-5335, ⊚canada.usembassy.gov

Consulates

Calgary 615 Macleod Trail SE, Room 1000, AB T2G 4T8 ☎403/266-8962
Halifax Wharf Tower II, 1969 Upper Water St, Suite 904, NS B3J 3R7 ☎902/429-2480
Montréal 1155 St Alexandre St, QC H3B 1Z1 ☎514/398-9695, ⊚montreal.usconsulate.gov
Québec City 2 Place Terrasse Dufferin, QC G1R 4T9 ☎418/692-2095, ⊚quebec.usconsulate.gov
Toronto 360 University Ave, ON M5G 1S4 ☎416/595-1700, ⊚toronto.usconsulate.gov
Vancouver 1095 W Pender St, 21st floor, BC V6E 2M6 ☎604/685-4311, ⊚vancouver.usconsulate.gov
Winnipeg 201 Portage Ave, Suite 860, MB R3B 3K6 ☎204/940-1800, ⊚www.usconsulatewinnipeg.ca

In Ireland

Embassy

Dublin 42 Elgin Rd, Ballsbridge, Dublin 4 ☎01/668 8777, ⊚dublin.usembassy.gov

In New Zealand

Embassy

Wellington 29 Fitzherbert Terrace, Thorndon, ☎04/462 6000, ⊚newzealand.usembassy.gov

Consulate

Auckland 3rd floor, Citibank Building, 23 Customs St ☎09/303 2724
Address for visa applications Non-Immigrant Visas, Private Bag 92022, Auckland

In the UK

Embassy

London 24 Grosvenor Square, W1A 1AE
℡ 020/7499 9000, visa hotline ℡ 09042-450100,
Ⓦ london.usembassy.gov

Consulates

Belfast Danesfort House, 223 Stranmillis Road,
Belfast BT9 5GR ℡ 028/9038 6100
Edinburgh 3 Regent Terrace, EH7 5BW
℡ 0131/556 8315

Foreign consulates in Oregon and Washington

Australia 401 Andover Park East, Seattle, WA
98188 ℡ 206/575-7446 (honorary consul: by
appointment only)
Canada 1501 4th Ave, Suite 600, Seattle, WA
98101 Ⓕ 206/443-1777, Ⓦ geo.international
.gc.ca/can-am/seattle
New Zealand 10649 North Beach Road, Bow, WA
98232 ℡ 360/766-8002
United Kingdom Inquiries on Oregon and
Washington are handled by the San Francisco
consulate: 1 Sansome St, Suite 850, 94104
℡ 415/617-1300, Ⓦ www.britainusa.com

Gay and lesbian travelers

The big cities of the Pacific Northwest are progressive bastions for gays and lesbians, who, drawn to the area's liberalism and increasingly cosmopolitan character, have moved in large numbers to the region from other parts of the US. Although mostly integrated into their respective cities, gays and lesbians are most prominent in Seattle at Capitol Hill and in Portland in Eastside districts like Hawthorne and Irvington. Most hotels will provide at least the appearance of tolerance, and it's only when you get away from the urban areas that finding gay-friendly lodging becomes more of a problem. In the same way, most restaurants cater to gay customers without issue.

By marked contrast, **rural areas** of the Northwest can still be rather unwelcoming, with residents at best shunning open displays of same-sex affection and at worst reacting with harassment or even violence. There are notable exceptions, however: in Washington, Olympia has a well-regarded progressive and alternative scene welcoming to gays and lesbians, as do Tacoma and Bellingham; in Oregon progressive smaller towns include Eugene, Corvallis, and Ashland – all having passed anti-discriminatory municipal policies in recent years. Throughout the guide gay and lesbian **social centers**, **bars**, and **clubs** are listed for the more welcoming cities.

In June, gay and lesbian **pride parades and events** take place over a dozen blocks on Capitol Hill's main strip, Broadway, in Seattle and in Portland's Waterfront Park. They're among the region's most exuberant events, drawing tens of thousands of participants and spectators.

One good source for **information** is the **International Gay & Lesbian Travel Association** (℡ 1-800/448-8550, Ⓦ www .iglta.com), a trade group providing lists of gay-owned or gay-friendly travel agents, accommodations, and other travel businesses. **Publications** specific to the region include the biannual *Lesbian & Gay Pink Pages Northwest* (free; Ⓦ www .lesgaypinkpages.com), available at various cafes and shops throughout the area, which lists companies supportive of the gay and lesbian community and includes a comprehensive resource directory. In progressive coffee houses and other businesses you'll find numerous free **magazines** with weekly listings for gay-oriented bars, clubs, and cultural venues.

Health

If you have a serious accident or **health** condition while in the US, emergency medical services will get to you quickly and charge you later. For emergencies or ambulances, dial ℡ 911. If you have medical or dental problems that don't require an ambulance, most hospitals will have a walk-in emergency room: for your nearest hospital, check with your hotel or dial ℡ 411. The same is true for dental work.

Should you need to see a **doctor**, lists can be found in the Yellow Pages under "Clinics" or "Physicians and Surgeons." A basic consultation fee is around $75–110, payable in advance. Medications aren't cheap, either – keep all your receipts for later claims on

Rough Guides travel insurance

Rough Guides has teamed up with Columbus Direct to offer **travel insurance** that can be tailored to your needs. Products include a low-cost **backpacker** option for long stays, a **short break** option for city getaways, a **holiday package** option, and others. There are also annual **multi-trip** policies for those who travel regularly. Different sports and activities (trekking, skiing, etc.) can be covered if required. See our website (ⓦwww.roughguides.com/website/shop) for eligibility and purchasing options. Alternatively, US residents can call ☏1-800/749-4922 (provided through Travelex), UK residents ☏0870/033 9988, Australians ☏1300/669 999, New Zealanders ☏0800/55 9911, and all other nationalities ☏+44 870/890 2843.

your insurance policy. Good information on health can be found through the **Centers for Disease Control** (☏1-877-394-8747, ⓦwww.cdc.gov/travel), the official US government travel health site, and the **International Society for Travel Medicine** (☏1-770-736-7060, ⓦwww.istm.org), which has a full list of travel health clinics.

Many minor ailments can be remedied using the array of potions and lotions available in **drugstores**. Foreign visitors should bear in mind that many pills available over the counter at home are available only with a prescription in the US, and that local brand names can be confusing; ask for advice at the pharmacy in any drugstore. Finally, travelers from Europe do not require **inoculations** to enter the US.

Insurance

Although not compulsory, travelers from abroad should have some form of travel **insurance**: the US has no national health system, and it can cost an arm and a leg (so to speak) having even minor medical treatment. Before paying for a new policy, however, it's worth checking whether you are already covered; this is recommended for US residents as well. Holders of official student/teacher/youth cards in the US are entitled to meager accident coverage and hospital in-patient benefits. Students will often find that their student health coverage extends during the vacations and for one term beyond the date of last enrollment.

You might want to contact a **specialist travel insurance** company or consider the travel insurance deal we offer (see box above). A typical travel insurance policy usually provides cover for the loss of baggage, tickets, and – up to a certain limit – cash or checks, as well as cancellation or curtailment of your journey. Most of them exclude so-called dangerous sports unless an extra premium is paid: this can mean rock-climbing, whitewater rafting, and windsurfing, though probably not kayaking or hiking. Many policies can be changed to exclude coverage you don't need – for example, sickness and accident benefits can often be excluded or included at will. If you do take medical coverage, ascertain whether benefits will be paid as treatment proceeds or only after your return home, and whether there is a 24hr medical emergency number. When securing baggage insurance, make sure that the per-article limit – typically under $800 – will cover your most valuable possessions. If you need to make a claim, you should keep receipts for medicines and medical treatment, and in the event you have anything stolen, you must obtain an official statement from the police.

Internet

You can obtain plenty of information about Oregon and Washington from the **Internet**. The various sites include information on the area's history, lore, and quirks, and offer information on city hotels, restaurants, and clubs, along with pages devoted to art and architecture and the like. Some of these sites are listed below, but don't forget to visit our own site at ⓦtravel.roughguides .com for other suggestions for the Northwest and beyond.

Email is often the cheapest and most convenient way to keep in touch with people back home. **Cybercafes** are found throughout major cities (especially Seattle), either as a part of a regular cafe or as a place specifically devoted to coffee drinking and computer access, often for around $6 per hour. Additionally, many public libraries have computers that provide free Internet access, usually for Web surfing or for accessing the library database. Certain towns may even have their own WiFi "clouds" for free Net access anywhere in the immediate vicinity.

If none of these options fits the bill, or if you just need a fast machine with assorted peripherals, then find a commercial photocopying and printing shop (look under "Copying" in the Yellow Pages). They'll charge around 25¢ a minute for use of their computers – pricey, but you're guaranteed fast access. Most upscale hotels also offer email and Internet access – though at a steep price unless free WiFi is expressly offered. By far the easiest way to collect and send email on the road is to sign up with one of the advertisement-funded **free email** accounts – such as yahoo.com and hotmail .com – which can be accessed from any Net-linked computer.

Websites

Although a few simple clicks will get you plenty of information on a search engine or via Wikipedia, some **websites** seem to come up repeatedly no matter where you travel. Two of these are **nps.gov**, run by the National Park Service, and Ⓦ**www.fs.fed .us**, run by the US Forest Service, which are both great gateways for park information; **citysearch.com**, **tripadvisor.com**, and similar websites, whose city information may not be the most current but whose user comments can sometimes be valuable for lesser-known spots; and major **newspaper sites** such as Ⓦwww.oregonlive.com and Ⓦseattlepi.nwsource.com. **Alternative news sites**, such as Ⓦwww.wweek.com and Ⓦwww.thestranger.com, often offer an edgier, more unexpected angle on a given city's strengths (and weaknesses).

Other good sites include **PDX History** (Ⓦpdxhistory.com), displaying the glory of old-time Portland in photographs, postcards, and general lore; the **Portland Visitors Association** (Ⓦwww.travelportland.com), the official city tourism website, which has a

lengthy, if typical, array of hotel, restaurant, and shopping listings; the **City of Seattle** (Ⓦwww.cityofseattle.net), the official guide to Seattle, loaded with information on everything from local politics to sightseeing and entertainment to road conditions; and **HistoryLink** (Ⓦwww.historylink.org), an encyclopedia of Seattle and King County history, with more than 1500 searchable essays, cybertours of historic areas, copious links, and many fascinating old photos and documents.

Mail

Post offices are usually open Monday to Friday from 9am until 5pm, and Saturday from 9am to noon or 1pm. Stamps can also be bought from automatic vending machines, the lobbies of larger hotels, airports, train stations, bus terminals, and many retail outlets and newsstands. Ordinary mail sent within the US costs 39¢ for letters weighing up to an ounce, while standard postcards cost 24¢. For anywhere outside the US, **airmail** letters weighing up to an ounce cost 84¢; postcards and aerogrammes 75¢. Airmail between the US and Europe generally takes about a week.

The last line of US addresses is made up of an abbreviation denoting the state (Washington is "WA," Oregon is "OR") and a five-digit number – the **zip code** – denoting the local post office. Letters that don't carry a zip code are liable to get lost or at least delayed; to find the proper zip code for an address, consult a local phone book, go to the post office, or log on to Ⓦwww.usps.com.

You can have letters sent to you c/o **General Delivery** (what's known elsewhere as **poste restante**) to the most central post office to your accommodation in each town or city, but they must include the zip code and will usually be held only for thirty days before being returned to sender – so make sure there's a return address on the envelope. If you're receiving mail at someone else's address, it should include "c/o" and the regular occupant's name; otherwise it, too, is likely to be returned. In Seattle, letters will end up at the main post office downtown at 301 Union St, zip code 98101 (Mon–Fri 7.30am–5.30pm;

☎206/748-5417 or 1-800/275-8777), and in Portland at 715 NW Hoyt St, 97208 (Mon–Fri 7am–6.30pm, Sat 8.30am–5pm; ☎1-800/275-8777) Letters will also be held at **hotels** – mark such mail "Guest Mail, Hold For Arrival."

If you want to send **packages** overseas from the US, check the front of a telephone directory for packaging requirements. Bear in mind that you can't just drop a package in a mailbox, even with the proper postage; you'll need to fill in a green **customs declaration form**, available at post offices. International parcel **rates** for items weighing less than a pound run from $14 to $23 or more, depending on the package's size and destination, and how quickly you want it to arrive.

Maps

The free **maps** issued by each state or local tourist office are usually fine for general driving and route planning and can be used in conjunction with the maps provided in this guide. But if you're venturing into the more remote edges of town, especially in cities with confusing layouts, such as Seattle, it's highly advisable to get a more detailed map. If you're a member, you can get free maps from the local office of the **American Automobile Association**, in Seattle at 1523 15th Ave W (Mon–Fri 8.30am–5.30pm; ☎206/218-1222, ⓦwww .aaawa.com), or in Portland at 600 SW Market St (Mon–Fri 8am–5.30pm; ☎503/AAA-6734).

An even better choice may be to invest in an all-inclusive map-book like the excellent *2007 Thomas Guide to King County* ($21.95) or the same company's *2006 Portland Guide* ($24.95). Specialized **hiking** and **trail** guides are carried by most bookstores and camping/ outdoors shops as well. **Park, wilderness**, and **topographical maps** are available through the Bureau of Land Management for the West (ⓦblm.gov) and for the entire country through the Forest Service (ⓦwww.fs.fed.us/maps), which allows you to print out detailed maps as PDF files and provides information on ordering conventional paper versions as well. The best supplier of detailed, large-format map books for travel through the outback is **Benchmark Maps**, whose elegantly designed atlases of Oregon

and Washington (each $22.95) are easy to follow and make even the most remote dirt roads look appealing.

Money

Most cash-dispensing cards issued by **foreign banks** are accepted, as long as they are linked to international networks such as Amex ☎1-800/CASH-NOW, Cirrus ☎1-800/4-CIRRUS, The Exchange ☎1-800/237-ATMS, or Plus ☎1-800/843-7587 – check before you set off. Overseas visitors should also bear in mind that fluctuating exchange rates may result in spending more (or less) than expected when the item eventually shows up on a statement.

Financial emergencies

If you run out of money abroad, or there is some kind of **emergency**, the quickest way to get money sent out is to contact your bank at home and have it wire cash to the nearest bank. You can also have someone back home take cash to the nearest American Express Moneygram office (call ☎1-800/543-4080 for locations; also available at participating Travelex branches) and have it instantaneously wired to you – the entire process should take no longer than ten minutes, but the service will cost you ten percent of the amount sent. For similar, if slightly pricier, services, Western Union also has offices throughout the world (information at ☎1-800/325-6000 in the US; ☎0800/833 833 in the UK; and ☎1800/649 565 in Australia; ⓦwww.westernunion.com), with credit-card payments subject to an additional $10 fee.

If you have a few days' leeway, you can ask friends or family back home to send you an **international money order**, available through the post office. If worse comes to worst, you can throw yourself at the mercy of your nearest national **consulate** (see p.62), which will – in dire cases only – repatriate you, but will never under any circumstances lend you money.

Opening hours and public holidays

No matter how carefully you've planned your trip to Oregon and Washington, you may find

National holidays

New Year's Day Jan 1
Martin Luther King Jr's Birthday third Mon in Jan
Presidents' Day third Mon in Feb
Memorial Day last Mon in May
Independence Day July 4
Labor Day first Mon in Sept
Columbus Day second Mon in Oct
Veterans Day Nov 11
Thanksgiving fourth Thurs in Nov
Christmas Dec 25

the gates of your favorite park or museum closed if you don't check in advance about the various **public holidays** and festivals taking place throughout the year, which may shut down certain businesses altogether and otherwise throw a wrench into your well-laid plans. Beyond this, regular **opening hours** are somewhat more predictable.

Opening hours

As a general rule, most **museums** are open Tuesday through Saturday (occasionally Sun, too), from 10am until 5 or 6pm, with somewhat shorter hours on the weekends. Many museums will also stay open late one evening a week – usually Thursday, when ticket prices are sometimes reduced. (Hours for museums discussed in this guide accompany their respective entries.) Government **offices**, including post offices, are open during regular business hours, typically 8 or 9am until 5pm, Monday through Friday (some post offices are open Sat morning until noon or 1pm as well). Most stores are open daily from 10am and close at 5 or 6pm, while specialty stores can be more erratic, usually opening and closing later in the day, from noon to 2pm until 8 or 9pm, and remaining shuttered for two days of the week. **Malls** tend to be open from 10am until 7 or 8pm daily, though individual stores may close before the mall does.

While some diners stay open 24hr, **restaurants** typically open daily around 11am or noon for lunch and close as early as 8pm in rural areas and as late as 11pm in urban ones. Places that serve breakfast usually open early, between 6 and 8am, serve lunch later, and close in the early or mid-afternoon. Dance and live-music **clubs** often won't open until 9 or 10pm, and many will serve liquor until 2am and then either close for the night or stay open until dawn without serving booze. **Bars** that close at 2am may reopen as early as 6am to grab bleary-eyed regulars in need of a liquid breakfast.

Public holidays

The biggest and most all-American of the US **public holidays** is **Independence Day**, on July 4. **Halloween** (Oct 31) is not a public holiday, despite being one of the most popular yearly celebrations. More sedate is **Thanksgiving**, on the fourth Thursday in November.

On the **national holidays** listed in the box above, banks, government offices, and many museums are liable to be closed all day. Small stores, as well as some restaurants and clubs, are usually closed as well, but shopping malls, supermarkets, and department and chain stores increasingly remain open, regardless of the holiday. Most parks, beaches, and cemeteries stay open during holidays, too. The traditional season for **tourism** runs from Memorial Day to Labor Day, and some tourist attractions, information centers, motels, and campsites are only open during that period.

Phones

Even more than most parts of North America, Oregon and Washington has an excellent communications infrastructure.

Useful numbers

Directory information ☎411

Directory inquiries for toll-free numbers ☎1-800/555-1212

Emergencies ☎911; ask for the appropriate emergency service: fire, police, or ambulance

International operator ☎00

Long-distance directory information ☎1-(area code)/555-1212

Operator ☎0

Calling Oregon and Washington from abroad

From Australia 0011 + 1 + area code

From Canada 011 + 1 + area code

From New Zealand 00 +1 + area code

From Republic of Ireland 00 +1 + area code

From the UK and Northern Ireland 00 + 1 + area code

Calling home from Oregon and Washington

Australia 011 + 61 + city code

Canada 011 + 1 + province code

New Zealand 011 + 64 + city code

Republic of Ireland 011 + 353 + city code

UK and Northern Ireland 011 + 44 + city code

Public telephones invariably work and can be found on street corners and in railway and bus stations, hotel lobbies, bars, and restaurants. They take 25¢, 10¢, and 5¢ coins. The cost of a local call from a public phone (within a limited radius) is 50¢. Oregon and Washington have different area codes – three-digit numbers that must precede the seven-figure number if you're calling from abroad or from a region with a different code; in Oregon, you need to use an area code with all phone numbers dialed, regardless of where you are. Billing depends on whether you're using a LAN line (in which local calls may be unlimited and long-distance calls steeply priced) or a cell phone (in which all domestic calls may be billed at a flat rate).

Calling from your **hotel room** will cost considerably more than if you use a pay phone; hotels often charge a connection fee of at least $1 for all calls, even if they're local or toll-free, and international calls will cost a small fortune. **Long-distance** and **international calls** dialed direct are most expensive during daylight hours (6am–6pm), with charges slightly reduced in the evening

(6–11pm) and cheapest of all late at night and early in the morning (11pm–6am).

Many major hotels, government agencies, and car rental firms have **toll-free numbers** that are recognizable by their ☎1-800, ☎1-877, or ☎1-888 prefixes. Some of these numbers are meant to be accessed nationally, others only within a given state – dialing is the only way to find out. Numbers with a ☎1-900 prefix are **toll calls**, typically psychic hotlines and phone-sex centers, and will cost you a high fee for just a few minutes of use. Even worse, swiping a regular **credit card** at a public phone at, say, the airport can incur astronomical charges for long-distance service, including a mysteriously high "connection fee" – with the total amount as much as $7 a minute.

If you are visiting Seattle **from overseas**, your mobile phone probably won't work, unless you have one of the **tri-band** variety. For details on which types of phones work in the US and which don't, contact your service provider. Should you have a phone that works in the US, you'll probably have to ask your service provider before going abroad to get international access switched on; be sure to inquire about the charge for doing so and the rate for calls when you're overseas, as fees can be astronomically expensive.

Senior travelers

Seniors are defined broadly in the US as anyone older than 55 to 65 years of age. Traveling seniors can regularly find discounts of anywhere from ten to fifty percent at movie theaters, museums, hotels, restaurants, performing-arts venues, and the occasional shop.

On Amtrak, they can get a fifteen percent discount on most regular fares, and ten percent off the purchase of a North America Rail Pass. On Greyhound the discount is smaller, in the range of five to ten percent, but on Washington State Ferries it's roughly half the amount of regular adult fares – the best deal for **transportation** in the region. If heading to a **national park**, don't miss the **America the Beautiful Senior Pass**, which, when bought at a park for a mere $10, provides a lifetime of free entry to federally operated recreation sites, as well as half-price discounts on concessions such as boat launches and camping. For state parks, Washington has a free **annual pass** for low-income seniors that's good for half off camping and moorage fees, while all seniors can get the same services for free during the off-season by paying $50. Unfortunately, Oregon doesn't have a similar discount program for seniors, unless they're disabled veterans. At all state and national parks, seniors are defined as anyone over 62.

Time

Pacific Standard Time (PST) includes Washington and most of Oregon. The region is three hours behind New York, eight hours behind the UK, and eighteen hours behind eastern Australia. Mountain Standard Time, which in the Northwest covers only a small chunk of southeastern Oregon, is an hour ahead of PST.

Tourist information

National and state tourist offices are the most useful source of **tourist information** on Oregon and Washington, providing an enormous range of free maps, leaflets, and brochures. The offices are particularly helpful if you're able to specify a particular interest – skiing in the Cascades, for example – in which case they'll be able to save you time and trouble by sending you the latest rules, regulations, equipment rental shops, tour operators, and so forth regarding your request.

Visitor centers go under a variety of names throughout the Northwest, but they all provide detailed information about the local area. Typically they're open Mon–Fri 9am–5pm, Sat 9am–1pm, except in summer, when they may be open seven days a week from 8am or 9am until 6pm or later. In smaller towns many offices will close for the winter (from about mid-Sept to mid-May). In many US cities, visitor centers are run by the Convention and Visitors Bureau (CVB), while in smaller towns they many operate under the auspices of the **Chamber of Commerce**, which promotes local business interests. You'll also find small visitor centers in the region's airports, and there's usually a free phone system there connecting to leading hotels, too.

Park visitor centers should be your first destination in any national or state park. Staff are usually outdoors experts and can offer invaluable advice on trails, current conditions, and the full range of outfitting or adventure specialists. These are also the places to go to obtain national park permits and, where applicable, permits for fishing or backcountry camping.

State tourist offices

Oregon

Central Oregon Visitors Association 661 SW Powerhouse Dr, Suite 1301, Bend, OR 97702 ☎541/389-8799 or 1-800/800-8334, ⓦwww.visitcentraloregon.com

Eastern Oregon Visitors Association 15477 Sky Ranch Lane, Haines, OR 97833 ☎541/523-9200 or 1-800/332-1843 ⓦwww.eova.com

Oregon Coast Visitors Association PO Box 74, 137 NE First St, Newport, OR 97365 ☎541-574-2679 or 1-888/628-2101 ⓦwww.visittheoregoncoast.com

Oregon Tourism Commission 775 Summer St NE, Salem, OR 97301 ☎1-800/547-7842, ⓦwww.traveloregon.com

Southern Oregon Visitors Association PO Box 1645, Medford, OR 97501 ☎541/779-4691 or 1-800/448-4856, ⊛www.sova.org

Washington

North Olympic Peninsula CVB 338 W 1st St, Suite 104, PO Box 670, Port Angeles, WA 98362 ☎360/452-8552 or 1-800/942-4042 ⊛www.olympicpeninsula.org
Northwest Washington Tourism Association ☎1-800/382-5417, ⊛www.travel-in-wa.com
Southwest Washington CVB 110 E 8th St, Vancouver, WA 98660 ☎360/750-1553 or 1-877/600-0800, ⊛www.southwestwashington.com
Washington State Tourism 101 General Administration Building, PO Box 42500, Olympia, WA 98504-2500 ☎1-800/544-1800, ⊛www.experiencewashington.com

Travelers with disabilities

The US is extremely accommodating to travelers with mobility problems or other physical disabilities. All public buildings have to be wheelchair accessible and provide suitable toilet facilities, almost all street corners have dropped curbs, public telephones are specially equipped for hearing-aid users, and most public transport systems have such facilities as subways with elevators, and buses that "kneel" to let riders board. Even movie theaters – that last holdout for equal access – have been forced by courts to allow people in wheelchairs to have a reasonable, unimpeded view of the screen.

Washington's Alliance of People with disAbilities, 4649 Sunnyside Ave N, Suite 100, Seattle, WA 98103 (☎206/545-7055, ⊛www.disabilitypride.org), offers useful information and services to the disabled. *Easy Access to National Parks*, by Wendy Roth and Michael Tompane, is a Sierra Club publication that explores every national park from the point of view of people with disabilities, senior citizens, and families with children, and *Disabled Outdoors* is a quarterly magazine specializing in facilities for disabled travelers who wish to get into the outdoors.

The major hotel and motel chains are your best bet for accessible **accommodation**. At the higher end of the scale, Embassy Suites

has been working to comply with new standards of access that meet or, in some cases, exceed ADA (Americans with Disabilities Act) requirements, involving building new facilities, retrofitting older hotels, and providing special training to all employees. To a somewhat lesser degree, the same is true of Hyatt Hotels and the other big chains such as Hilton, Best Western, and Radisson.

The National Park Service offers a **free pass** to US citizens with permanent disabilities (⊛www.nps.gov/fees_passes) to federally operated parks, monuments, historic sites, and recreation areas that charge admission fees. Furthermore, the Washington State Parks and Recreation Commission offers a free annual **Disability Pass** that allows for half-price camping and boat-launching fees (⊛www.parks.wa.gov/ada-rec), while Oregon has a similar program for disabled veterans (⊛www.oregonstateparks.org).

Transportation

Major **car rental** firms can provide vehicles with hand controls for drivers with leg or spinal disabilities, though these are typically available only on the pricier models. **Parking regulations** for disabled motorists are now uniform: license plates for the disabled must carry a three-inch-square international access symbol, and a placard bearing this symbol must be hung from the car's rearview mirror. A good resource, the *Handicapped Driver's Mobility Guide*, is published by the American Automobile Association (☎212/757-2000, ⊛www.aaa.com).

American **airlines** must by law accommodate those with disabilities, and some even allow attendants of those with serious conditions to accompany them on the trip for a reduced fare. Almost every **Amtrak train** includes one or more cars with accommodation for disabled passengers, along with wheelchair assistance at train platforms, adapted on-board seating, free travel for guide dogs, and discounts on fares (24hr advance notice required). Passengers with hearing impairment can get information by calling ☎1-800/523-6590 (TTY) or checking out ⊛www.amtrak.com. By contrast, traveling by **Greyhound** and **Amtrak Thruway** bus connections is often problematic. Buses are not equipped with platforms for wheelchairs, though intercity carriers are required by law to provide assistance with boarding, and disabled passengers may be able to get priority seating. Call Greyhound's ADA customer assistance line for more information (℡1-800/752-4841, ⊛www.greyhound.com).

Finally, passengers with disabilities can travel on Washington State Ferries (⊛www.wsdot.wa.gov/ferries) for half to two-thirds of the regular fare by presenting a Regional Reduced Fare Permit ($3) or other proof of disability; contact WSF for information in acquiring a permit.

Women travelers

As one of the more socially liberal and progressive areas of North America, the Pacific Northwest has a good amount of resources for **women travelers**, especially in the major cities. Most of the time, a woman traveling alone in the Northwest, especially in places like Portland and Seattle, is not made to feel conspicuous or likely to attract unwelcome attention. The **National Organization for Women** (NOW) has done much to effect positive legislation, and its branches can provide referrals for rape crisis centers and counseling services, feminist bookstores, and lesbian and women-friendly bars. Seattle's chapter is at 1424 4th Ave, Suite 912 (℡206/632-8547, ⊛www.nowseattle.org), and Portland's is at 8700 SW 26th Ave (℡503/452-0272).

Going into **bars** and **clubs** should pose no problems, as women's privacy is usually respected, even in dance and rock clubs. If in doubt, gay and lesbian bars are generally trouble-free places. Sexual harassment is more common for lone women in country-and-western clubs and in working-class taverns and rural bars. If your vehicle **breaks down** in a country area without cell phone service, walk to the nearest house or town for help; on interstate highways or heavily traveled roads, wait in the car for a police or highway patrol car to arrive. On **Greyhound** buses, sit as near to the front – and the driver – as possible. Should disaster strike, all big cities and the larger towns have some kind of rape counseling service; if not, the local sheriff's office should arrange for you to get help and counseling and, if necessary, transport home.

As a rule, women (or men, for that matter) should **never hitchhike** anywhere alone. Also on the danger list is **walking** through desolate, unlit streets at night; you're better off taking a cab to your destination, even it's just a few blocks away. If you don't appear confused, scared, or drunk, and instead project a serious countenance and remain aware of your surroundings, your chances of attack may be lessened.

One option for women travelers to the US that's unavailable in most European countries and Canada is **pepper spray** or **mace**, which comes in a small canister that you can carry in a purse or pocket, and is typically purchased at gun shops. Upon contact with an attacker's eyes, the spray causes terrible, temporary pain – giving you the opportunity to flee the scene and alert the police. You should never enter an airport with the spray, and always get rid of it before you attempt to board a plane home.

Guide

Guide

1

Portland

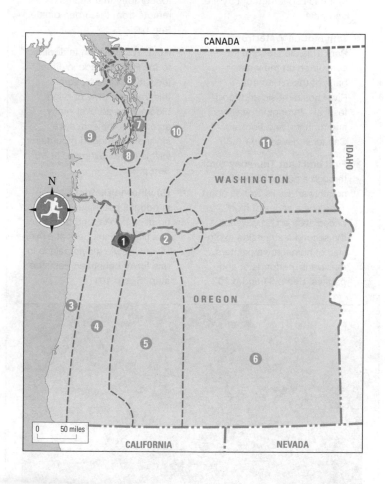

CHAPTER 1 # Highlights

✻ **Pioneer Courthouse Square** Portland's indisputable core built around a set of concentric brick terraces, and home to the full spectrum of city life. See p.84

✻ **Tom McCall Waterfront Park** This elegant grassy concourse on the west bank of the Willamette River hosts music and food festivals, throngs of walkers and runners, and flocks of Canadian geese. See p.88

✻ **First and Last Thursday** Stroll through a pair of compelling monthly art walks worlds apart – the first a series of high-priced abstract art galleries, the second a streetside explosion of homegrown painters, musicians, performers, and partiers. See p.94 and p.103

✻ **Forest Park** A huge natural preserve with countless hiking paths and striking views, and a thickly wooded topography that seems remote from the urban bustle. See p.95

✻ **Rose Test Garden** In addition to the Rose Parade in June, the City of Roses offers this fragrant array of bright blooms spread over many acres, with the evocative skyline and rugged mountains visible in the distance. See p.98

✻ **Hawthorne District** Browse in oddball boutiques, pick up used books, and take in a film or drink beer at a Moorish-style movie palace in this funky bohemian Eastside strip. See p.101

△ Washington Park International Rose Test Garden

Portland

aving been spared Seattle's aggressive, remorseless development, **PORTLAND** retains a pleasant, small-city feel, known for its well-preserved Beaux Arts architecture and walkable urban core, as well as for its easygoing atmosphere. Indeed, most of the city's handful of major attractions are located within close walking distance of one another on the short city blocks (they're half the size of those in most American cities). While Portland's unpretentious bohemian flavor may be lost on more gung-ho travelers, the city remains an excellent spot for casual visitors to while away weeks at a time, with a wealth of good diners, microbreweries, clubs, bookstores, and coffee houses to keep you occupied and intrigued.

Sometimes called the most "unchurched" city in the nation, with fewer adherents to mainstream religion than practically anywhere else in the US, Portland prides itself on having a certain free-thinking, freewheeling character, with all kinds of liberal policies, including a relaxed attitude toward marijuana, almost blanket protection for free speech (including pornography), and a generally hostile climate toward big business and overdevelopment. Although it is far from economically dynamic when it comes to the standard measurements of manufacturing and industrial capacity, Portland has succeeded in attracting a "creative class" of small-scale entrepreneurs with its welcoming spirit, unpretentious vibe, and bevy of good bars, coffee houses, and restaurants. Still, as befits a city full of leftists and libertarians, its residents are ambivalent about the praise: while some bask in Portland's reputation as one of the nation's most livable places, others ignore the attention entirely.

Some history

The city was founded in 1843 and named after Portland, Maine, following a coin toss between its two East Coast founders, **Asa Lovejoy** and **Francis Pettygrove**, in 1845 ("Boston" was the other option). It was then no more than a clearing in the woods, but its location on a deep part of the Willamette River, near the Columbia River just eighty-odd miles from the Pacific, and surrounded by fertile valleys, made it a perfect trading port. It grew rapidly, supplying lumber to San Francisco and the California gold fields. As the money poured in, Portland's elite built themselves elegant mansions and a suitably opulent business district, replacing the initial clapboard buildings with impressive Neo-Gothic, Florentine, and Second Empire piles.

Not everyone benefited from the boom. Away from the richer parts of town lurked the seamier side of Portland – the "North End" (along the waterfront north of Burnside Street), a violent, bawdy district, notorious for gambling,

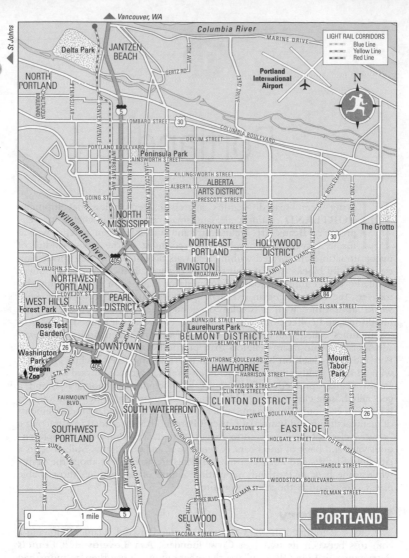

liquor, prostitution, and opium dens. At its peak, toward the end of the nineteenth century, the North End's vice industry was so well entrenched, and the police so heavily bribed, that its ringleaders were even able to run a large-scale shanghaiing operation (see box, p.92), in which scores of unwitting men were drugged, drunk, or beaten unconscious only to wake up as members of a ship's crew out on the Pacific. To encourage local laborers to guzzle a liquid other than alcohol, Simon Benson, one of the area's timber magnates, even paid

The area code for Portland is ⊤503.

for the installation of numerous "**Benson Bubblers**" around town. It is doubtful that this plan had any effect, but these constantly flowing, four-headed drinking fountains remain one of the prime fixtures on Downtown streets – just lean over for a gulp.

In the 1920s, with the regional ascendancy of the new ports of Washington's Puget Sound, which offered a more direct route to inland markets, Portland declined, leaving behind huge swaths of derelict riverside warehouses and rail yards. The city muddled along as a minor port and lumber center in later decades but nationally was more known for its endemic municipal corruption in the 1950s than anything else. As a consequence of this and a later downturn in the timber industry, along with the white flight and decentralization affecting the rest of the country, city planners in the 1970s faced a downtown in tatters, its historic buildings decayed or sacrificed to make way for parking lots and expressways. Under the leadership of mayor **Neil Goldschmidt**, Portland salvaged what was left of its past, killing several planned freeways that would have gutted its historic neighborhoods and removing a riverside highway to create the lovely Tom McCall Waterfront Park. In the past few decades, it has continued to replace concrete with red brick, introducing folksy statues and murals and a number of innovative mass-transit programs, including an old-fashioned streetcar line.

While the city's rehabilitation, along with its "**urban growth boundary**" to limit development (see box, p.89), has done much for its image nationwide, it has also made the city more conservative than most of its West Coast peers when it comes to groundbreaking architecture and urban design. Notwithstanding the odd splash of postmodernist color added in the 1970s, almost all of its notable buildings date before 1950. Still, the slow-growth attitudes and friendly liberal atmosphere are more than enough for the city to serve as a beacon to the young and artsy from San Francisco to New York and everywhere in between. While skilled college graduates may not find the ideal job when they arrive – they're sometimes reduced to pulling espresso shots or selling hot dogs – that hasn't kept them from coming. And so Portland – fueled by its reputation as a center for outdoor activities, microbrewing, indie rock, smart municipal growth, urban parks, and cycling – has become identified as one of the nation's most livable cities. This elusive quality has been hard-earned, especially after so many decades in the economic doldrums, and leads most residents to have sunny attitudes about their hometown, no matter how much it rains.

Arrival and information

Strangely enough, **PDX**, the abbreviation for **Portland International Airport**, is also shorthand for the city itself – so don't get confused if you hear a local praising "the great club scene in PDX." The airport proper is located twelve miles northeast of Downtown, beside the Columbia River. From Terminal C, the **MAX Red Line** light rail (every 5–15min, 5am–midnight; $2) shuttles passengers on a 40min journey along interstates 205 and 84 before heading downtown along SW First Avenue and SW Morrison Street (for more about MAX, see "City transportation" below). Local hotels may operate free or inexpensive **shuttles** from the airport (call each property for details). A **taxi** from the airport into town costs $30.

In Downtown Portland, the Greyhound **bus station** is at 550 NW 6th Ave at Glisan (☎503/243-2361 or 1-800/231-2222, ⊛www.greyhound.com). The

Amtrak **train station** is adjacent at Union Station, 800 NW 6th Ave
(☎503/273-4865 or 1-800/872-7245, ⓦwww.amtrak.com). From here, it's
about a ten-minute walk south to the city center, but if you arrive at either
terminal at night take a taxi – this part of town is not safe after dark. If you are
arriving by **car**, I-5 will bring you into the city from the north or south: heading
south, take the City Center/Morrison Bridge exit 300B (fork to the right after
the exit); northbound use the Naito Parkway/Front Avenue exit 299B. From the
east: I-84 joins I-5 just east of Downtown – merge south to Exit 300B. If you're
arriving from the west via Highway 26 (Sunset Hwy) or coming from the coast,
note that the road splits into three exits after the West Hills tunnel. The left exit
leads to Northwest Portland and the Pearl District, the center goes Downtown,
and the right connects to I-5 southbound to Salem.

Portland's **visitor center** is located Downtown in Pioneer Square, at 701
SW 6th Ave (Mon–Fri 8.30am–5.30pm, Sat 10am–4pm; ☎503/275-8355 or
1-877/678-5263, ⓦwww.travelportland.com). It issues free city maps, bus
timetables, event calendars, and a glossy city brochure, which includes
accommodation listings. The center also has plenty of information on the rest
of the state, with details on state parks, bicycle routes, bus services, and the
like. For more information, contact **Oregon Tourism** (☎1-800/547-7842,
ⓦwww.traveloregon.com).

City transportation

Portland's **transportation** infrastructure – its vast network of buses, streetcars,
and light-rail lines – has earned the city national renown as a center of
thoughtful urban planning and mass-transit solutions. Even today, the system
continues to grow, with the light rail extending east from Downtown and the
streetcar reaching points ever farther south, where there's even an aerial tram
running. Indeed, practically all major city sights are within easy access of bus
or light-rail stops.

Buses

Portland's comprehensive **bus** system is operated by **Tri-Met**. Each bus shelter is
labeled with a colored symbol – brown beaver, purple rain, blue snowflake, etc. –
which serves as a code for a route in a particular area of the city. Although
designed for simplicity, the system can still be pretty confusing, with different lines
often sharing the same number: visit the **Tri-Met Ticket Office**, sharing space
with the visitor center in Pioneer Courthouse Square (Mon–Fri
8.30am–5.30pm, Sat 10am–4pm; ☎503/238-7433, for disabled customers
☎503/238-4952, ⓦwww.trimet.org), to get a free transit map and route-planning
advice. The system is based on "zones" – one zone covers much of Downtown
outside Fareless Square (see below), two zones cover the inner west and east sides,
and three zones cover the suburbs. A two-zone ticket (good for both light rail and
bus service) will probably suffice for most visitors, except when getting to and
from the airport and Washington Park, which requires a three-zone ticket ($2).
One- and two-zone prices are nearly identical in any case: $1.70 per ticket (which
includes any transfers made within 2hr), $17 per ten-ticket, two-zone book
($16.50 for one zone), seven-day pass $16.50, and monthly pass $63. Both buses
and light rail are **free** in central Downtown – "**Fareless Square**" is edged by the
Willamette River to the east, Irving Street to the north, and I-405 to the south
and west, with a narrow extension across the river to the Lloyd Center mall. For

Major bus routes and symbols

Listed are the numbers and names of major **bus routes**, followed by their destinations. Bus kiosk **symbols** (beaver, fish, etc.) are marked for stops along Portland Transit Mall (on 3rd and 4th avenues until 2009). Downtown routes without symbols cross perpendicular to the Transit Mall at various points (see each route map for details).

From Downtown

#4 Division – Division St, Eastside (beaver)

#4 Fessenden – Mississippi District, St Johns, North Portland (fish)

#6 MLK – Northeast Portland via Grand Ave and MLK Blvd

#9 Broadway – East and West Broadway, Alberta St, Eastside (rain)

#9 Powell – East Powell Blvd (beaver)

#10 NE 33rd Ave – Irvington, Lloyd Center, Eastside (rain)

#10 Harold – Clinton St, Eastside (leaf)

#12 Sandy Blvd – Hollywood District, The Grotto, Eastside (rain)

#14 Hawthorne Blvd – Eastside (beaver)

#15 Belmont – Belmont Ave, Eastside, Mount Tabor

#15 NW 23rd Ave – Northwest Portland

#17 NW 21st Ave/St Helens – Northwest Portland, St Johns, Sauvie Island (fish)

#18 Hillside – Forest Park

#19 Woodstock – Sellwood (leaf)

#19 Glisan – East Burnside St and Glisan St (rain)

#20 Burnside/Stark – Burnside St, east and west

#32 Oatfield – Oregon City (rain)

#33 McLoughlin – Oregon City (rain)

#41 Tacoma – Sellwood

#63 Washington Park – Rose Garden, Oregon Zoo, Japanese Garden

#77 Broadway/Halsey – Troutdale

Major Eastside routes

#70 12th Ave – Sellwood to Lloyd District

#72 Killingsworth St/82nd Avenue – Eastside, including Alberta St

#75 39th Ave/Lombard – Southeast to Northeast Portland and St Johns

special fares, the disabled can ride in all zones for $1.65 per ride with a "LIFT" ticket, students for $1.35, and seniors for 85¢.

Note that the Transit Mall along Fifth and Sixth avenues Downtown has temporarily relocated to Third and Fourth avenues until 2009, as the mall is being torn up to make way for a light-rail extension.

MAX light rail

Operated by Tri-Met, **MAX** (Metropolitan Area Express), Portland's light railway, offers rides for the same price as a bus fare; tickets must be purchased before you start your journey. There are ticket machines at every stop, and these issue new tickets and validate unused ones purchased ahead of time.

The system takes passengers around Downtown, traveling east along SW Yamhill Street and west along SW Morrison Street, between SW 18th and SW

First avenues. On SW First Avenue, MAX travels in both directions, its **Red Line** passing through Old Town on its way to the Steel Bridge over to the northeast quadrant and the airport, with another line to the northeastern suburbs. West from SW 18th Avenue, the **Blue Line** tunnels under Washington Park (and the zoo) bound for the western suburbs. The **Yellow Line** heads from Downtown to the Expo Center along Interstate Avenue (following I-5 a few blocks east), while the planned **Green Line** will link Downtown with the far southeastern suburbs along I-205. Note that both of the latter two lines will operate downtown along Fifth and Sixth avenues when the Transit Mall is reconstructed and opened in late 2009 to accommodate them.

Other transportation options

Tri-Met's comprehensive system should cover almost all your transit needs, but there are a few touristy alternatives. Vintage **trolley cars** (every 30min; Mar–Dec, Sun noon–6.30pm; free) use the more central of the MAX lines, connecting the Lloyd Center mall to SW 11th Avenue – the entire route lies within Fareless Square. As an alternative, the brightly colored cars of the **Portland Streetcar** (every 15–20min; Mon–Fri 5.30am–11.30pm, Sat 7.15am–11.45pm, Sun 7.15am–10.30pm; @www.portlandstreetcar.org) ply a separate route from Northwest Portland and the Pearl District down to the South Waterfront District south of the Ross Island Bridge, covering most Downtown sights on NW and SW 10th and 11th streets. Fares are free inside Fareless Square, otherwise $1.70, and a bus or MAX ticket will suffice as payment. At the streetcar's southern terminus, at SW Moody Avenue and Gibbs Street, you can hop on the brand-new $57 million **Aerial Tram** (every 10min, same hours as streetcar; $2–4; @www.portlandtram.org) that connects the South Waterfront's expansive, upscale real-estate zone with the OHSU hospital 500ft up on Marquam Hill. The 3min ride itself is the draw: as the sleekly modern cab – painted to resemble a "bubble" in the sky – makes its steep ascent you can view the beautiful landscape of trees, skyscrapers, and, on a clear day, Mount Hood.

Portland's **taxis** don't stop in the street; you'll have to either get one at a hotel or call Broadway Cab (☏503/227-1234) or Portland Taxi Co (☏503/256-5400). Finally, there are countless firms throughout the city from which you can **rent a car** (see "Basics," p.30); you can also pick one up at the airport from the major chains, which are based on the ground level of the parking structure, across the concourse from the hotel-van and bus-transit pickup zones.

Cruises

Few would claim Portland's stretch of the Willamette River is much to look at, but **Portland Spirit River Cruises** gamely makes an effort, offering **dinner cruises** (nightly 7–9.30pm; $64 per person; ☏503/224-3900 or 1-800/224-3901, @www .portlandspirit.com) and **two-hour sightseeing trips** (1–2 daily; $25), departing from the jetty at the foot of Salmon Street. Another prominent cruise line you'll see along the river is **Willamette Jetboats**, 1945 SE Water Ave (☏1-888/538-2628 or 503/231-1532, @www.willamettejet.com), which runs small, open-top blue vehicles on short, tourist-oriented routes during the summer. The two main options include a basic one-hour city tour, as seen from the river (June–Aug daily 4.30pm; $20), and a two-hour jaunt that takes you down to Oregon City and back (April–Sept, 2–3 trips daily; $30). Both trips depart from the Blueback submarine site at the Oregon Museum of Science and Industry (see p.100).

Accommodation

Dozens of inexpensive **motels** line the main roads into Portland, but for most visitors the **Downtown** area provides more than enough choices for mid- to upper-end lodging, from refurbished classic **hotels** to stylish modern high-rises – all of them less than $180 per night in the off-season – with a hotel tax of 12.5 percent. Other than a few decent chain motels, you won't find much in the way of budget rooms here (unless you want to settle for one of the frightful fleabags around Old Town), so you may have to venture farther afield. Other than the suburbs – too far away from the main action and too dull, as well – there are only two decent choices outside Downtown: **Northwest Portland**, for a **B&B** here and a hotel there, and the **Eastside**, which has a range of appealing choices (mostly in the McMenamins brewpub–hotel chain) scattered across its main boulevards – though it's best to avoid seedy motel corridors like Sandy Boulevard and 82nd Avenue. The city also has two reputable **hostels** – one each in the southeast and northwest quadrants, and both a quick bus ride from Downtown.

Hotels, motels, and bed-and-breakfasts

Downtown

Ace 1022 SW Stark St ☏ 503/228-2277, ⊛ www.acehotel.com. New local outpost of Seattle's original budget boutique hotel, offering rooms for less than $100, amenities like flat-screen TVs, in-room murals and other art, WiFi Internet access, and convenient location between the core of Downtown and the Pearl District (and two blocks from Powell's Books). ❺

Benson 309 SW Broadway ☏ 503/228-2000 or 1-888/523-6766, ⊛ www.bensonhotel.com. The usual spot for visiting dignitaries and celebs, this classy hotel has a superb walnut-paneled 1912 lobby, swank bedrooms with modern appointments, suites, and even penthouses. Facilities include a health club and two restaurants. ❼

Days Inn City Center 1414 SW 6th Ave at Columbia St ☏ 503/221-1611, ⊛ www.daysinn.com. Great Downtown location and excellent value with well-tended, motel-style rooms. ❸

DeLuxe 729 SW 15th Ave at Yamhill ☏ 1-866/895-2094, ⊛ www.hoteldeluxeportland.com. Stylish old favorite now refurbished into a chic luxury item, with smart decor and onsite gym, plus in-room iPod docks and HDTVs. Well placed along the MAX tracks, just west of Downtown. ❻

Embassy Suites 319 SW Pine St ☏ 503/279-9000, ⊛ www.embassyportland.com. Grand complex spread out over a full city block just north of the main Downtown sights (and a few blocks from Old Town), boasting spacious suites, an indoor pool and fitness center, and a fine restaurant and bar, *Portland Steak and Chophouse*, on the ground floor. ❼

Four Points by Sheraton 50 SW Morrison St at Naito Pkwy ☏ 503/221-0711 or 1-800/899-0247, ⊛ www.starwoodhotels.com. This modern hotel has a modern gym and superb location across Front Avenue from the Willamette River, right by the MAX light rail. The front rooms overlook the river but don't have balconies, whereas those at the side do. The rooms themselves are large and comfortable. ❻

Governor 611 SW 10th Ave at Alder ☏ 503/224-3400 or 1-800/554-3456, ⊛ www.govhotel.com. Elegant rooms and suites with fireplaces, spas, plush sofas, and stylish decor (including carved woodwork), plus an onsite pool and fitness center. Mostly housed in a stylish Italian Renaissance 1923 office building, the lobby holds a striking sepia-toned mural inspired by the Lewis and Clark expedition. A block from MAX light rail and streetcar lines. ❼

Heathman 1001 SW Broadway at Salmon ☏ 503/241-4100 or 1-800/551-0011, ⊛ www.heathmanhotel.com. Occupies a finely restored Neoclassical building, with an elegant, teak-paneled interior and much marble and brass. Splendid rooms and suites, top-notch restaurant, and popular lobby lounge where you can swill among the swells. ❼

Lucía 400 SW Broadway ☏ 503/225-1717, ⊛ www.hotellucia.com. Minimalist, Asian-influenced lobby, arty B&W photos in the hallways and chic decor throughout make this one of the city's more prominent boutique hotels – though the rooms can be quite cramped. ❻

Mark Spencer 409 SW 11th Ave at Stark ☏ 503/224-3293 or 1-800/548-3934,

Ⓦ www.markspencer.com. Old but renovated 1907 pile with large, modern, and fairly comfortable rooms with kitchenettes; located in a central, if somewhat dodgy, location. ⑤

Paramount 808 SW Taylor St at Park Ave ☎ 503/223-9900 or 1-800/426-0670, Ⓦ www .portlandparamount.com. Neo–Art Deco high-rise in a central location, boasting more than 150 rooms, each decorated in modern style. The hotel has a fitness center, and some rooms have Jacuzzis. Most popular for its ground-floor *Dragonfish* pan-Asian bar and eatery (see p.105). ⑦

Vintage Plaza 422 SW Broadway at Washington ☎ 503/228-1212 or 1-800/263-2305, Ⓦ www .vintageplaza.com. An intimate boutique hotel in a handsome old building complete with imaginative settings and decor, oversize rooms, and a calm, relaxed atmosphere. Wine is offered in the afternoons in the lobby. One of the city's few dog-friendly hotels. ⑦

Westin 750 SW Alder St at Park Ave ☎ 503/294-9000, Ⓦ www.westin.com. Top-notch luxury hotel a block from Broadway. Chic and modern, the spacious rooms and suites are replete with full amenities, and the onsite restaurant and fitness center make this a favorite for business travelers. The only downside is the drab, uninspired postmodern facade. ⑦

Northwest Portland

Heron Haus 2545 NW Westover Rd ☎ 503/274-1846, Ⓦ www.heronhaus.com. Stylish 1904 Tudor B&B, with some large suites featuring fireplaces, spas, and cozy sitting areas. Excellent continental breakfast and close hiking access to Portland's expansive Forest Park. ⑥

Inn at Northrup Station 2025 NW Northrup St ☎ 503/224-0543, Ⓦ www .northrupstation.com. Poised right on the streetcar line (thus the name) in Northwest Portland, the inn offers a range of colorful suites with splashy retro designs, some with kitchens, patios, and wet bars. Excellent value for the area. ⑤

MacMaster House 1041 SW Vista Ave ☎ 503/223-7362 or 1-800/774-9523, Ⓦ www .macmaster.com. Grand, opulent 1895 mansion sporting a mix of Queen Anne and Colonial Revival styles, with eight rooms and suites arrayed over three levels. Decor is tasteful retro-Victorian, and the striking location – perched on King's Hill overlooking the city – is minutes from the main action on NW 23rd Ave. Rooms come with free wireless Internet. ⑤

Portland International Guesthouse 2185 NW Flanders St ☎ 503/224-0500 or 1-877/228-0500 Ⓦ www.pdxguesthouse.com. Excellent value in the heart of Northwest Portland, though there are only five cozy units, featuring shared bath and wireless Internet. Perfectly located between NW 21st and 23rd avenues. ②

Silver Cloud Inn 2426 NW Vaughan St at NW 25th Ave ☎ 503/242-2400 or 1-800/205-6939, Ⓦ www .silvercloud.com. Smart, well-kept motel with eighty rooms on the edge of Northwest Portland by the I-405 freeway. Some units are suites, and some regular rooms have Jacuzzis, for an extra $30. ⑥

Eastside

Edgefield 2126 SW Halsey St ☎ 503/669-8610 or 1-800/669-8610, Ⓦ www .mcmenamins.com/edge. Fifteen minutes east of the airport in the drab suburb of Troutdale (take bus #77), this unique brewery-resort features restaurants, bars, a winery and tasting room, a distillery, a movie theater, gardens, and an 18-hole golf course. With plenty of onsite drinking, the facility can be quite fun, if loud. Also with its own hostel, at $30 per dorm bed. Rooms $50, add $25 for private bath. ②

Jupiter 800 E Burnside St ☎ 503/230-9200, Ⓦ www.jupiterhotel.com. If you're too hip for your own good, you will be irresistibly drawn to this converted chain motel (on a dicey stretch of East Burnside) that's now flush with arty minimalism, a party atmosphere, and the über-cool presence of the adjoining *Doug Fir Lounge* (see p.112). ⑤

Kennedy School 5736 NE 33rd Ave ☎ 503/249-3983 or 1-888/249-3983, Ⓦ www.mcmenamins .com/kennedy. Thirty-five B&B rooms, in a refurbished 1915 schoolhouse with chalkboards and cloakrooms, plus modern conveniences. Excellent breakfast, multiple brewpubs, movie theater, outdoor bathing pool, and "detention bar." ⑤

Lion & the Rose 1810 NE 15th Ave ☎ 503/287-9245 or 1-800/955-1647, Ⓦ www.lionrose.com. Six rooms in a late-Victorian 1906 mansion near the Irvington neighborhood. Offers spacious beds, private baths, some units with Jacuzzis, and fairly precious period decor. ⑥

White Eagle 836 N Russell St ☎ 503/282-6810, Ⓦ www.mcmenamins.com/eagle. Hands-down Portland's best bargain, a refurbished old hotel now boasting a hip brewpub and great live-music club in an industrial-bohemian neighborhood. Rooms are clean and simple, and surprisingly cheap at $50–60, with shared baths. Bunk beds $30. ②

Hostels

HI-Portland Hawthorne 3031 SE Hawthorne Blvd ☎503/236-3380 or 1-866/447-3031, ⓦwww .portlandhostel.com. Hostel facilities in a cheery Victorian house, well located on the western edge of the Hawthorne District. Offers Internet access, van tours of local sights, bike rental, and occasional live music. $20–25 dorms, $43–51 private rooms. Take bus #14 (Hawthorne Blvd, beaver symbol) from the Transit Mall. Reservations recommended.

HI-Portland Northwest 425 NW 18th Ave ☎503/241-2783 or 1-888/777-0067, ⓦwww .nwportlandhostel.com. Located in a nineteenth-century home in Northwest Portland, just east of the main action on NW 21st and 23rd streets. Contains an espresso bar, kitchen and fireplace. Dorms $20–25, private rooms $39–52. Take bus #17 (NW 21st St, fish symbol) from Downtown.

The City

Portland has a straightforward layout: the **Willamette** ("wah-LAM-it") **River** divides the city into east and west, **Burnside Street** into north and south, and each street address describes its relation to these dividers – NE, SE, NW, and SW. The exception is North Portland, defined as everything roughly west of I-5 (more specifically, Williams Ave) and east of the river. The **Downtown** core lies between the river's west bank and the I-405 freeway, in the city's southwest section. Engagingly laid-back, the area boasts a harmonious mix of old and new architectural styles, where fading plasterwork and terracotta reliefs face seamless steel and glass, all punctuated by small grassy parks and whimsical street sculptures.

Downtown's pleasant air fades a bit, however, as it stretches north into **Old Town**, along West Burnside Street from Eighth Avenue to the river. Where the city's first merchants and loggers set up shop, today restored nineteenth century buildings are occupied by busy restaurants and bars – in unhappy contrast to the dejected street people crowded around the adjacent soup kitchens and shelters. Just a few blocks north and west, though, beyond small **Chinatown**, the continually rising condos of the **Pearl District** have become the city's unquestioned economic bright spot – and an undeniable yuppie magnet, filled with pricey boutiques and chic restaurants. Older money is found farther west, in **Northwest Portland** along 21st and 23rd avenues, where surviving Victorian

The perils of Portland driving

If you're used to the wide-open thoroughfares of other West Coast cities like LA and Seattle, **driving in Portland** will doubtless be one of the most unnerving experiences you're likely to have, due to the special, **non-automotive hazards** of city driving. Foremost are the aggressive cyclists who take advantage of the local bike-friendly climate to run red lights and stop signs, dart in between cars, and verbally (and sometimes physically) challenge drivers who don't offer them enough space. Also unsettling is Portland's widespread **jaywalking**, an infraction rarely enforced by police, resulting in swarms of people scurrying – and sometimes sauntering – across the roadway directly in front of vehicles. Luckily, Portland drivers are much less prone to speeding and tailgating, at least Downtown, than those of other major cities, and chronic horn-honking is generally not a problem in such a laid-back place. The best alternative, though, may be **taking a bus**, as countless city residents do, saving gas money and sparing yourself the hassle of navigating the narrow Downtown streets and hunting for a hard-to-find parking spot.

architecture adds a more relaxed, semi-bohemian air in places. Beyond this, the pick of the outlying attractions are among the **West Hills** – notably the ornate **Pittock Mansion**, the leafy trails and formal gardens of sprawling **Washington Park**, and the hiking paradise of **Forest Park**.

For many visitors, the **Eastside** across the river is unknown territory – though it shouldn't be. Along major routes such as **Hawthorne Boulevard**, **Belmont Avenue**, and **Broadway** you can find excellent vintage clothiers, novelty shops, fine ethnic diners, and all kinds of eccentric boutiques. From the antique dealers of **Sellwood** in the south up to the rough-and-ready bars of **St Johns** in the north, the Eastside has plenty of districts with their own quirky character, some a bit more charming than others.

Downtown

In true West Coast style, you can mill about the **Downtown** core for hours, sipping lattes and listening to street musicians, wandering into vintage boutiques, and browsing in book- and record stores. The unquestioned center is **Pioneer Courthouse Square**, from where cultural life in the city spills out in all directions, particularly along the splashy stretch of **Broadway**, home to many of the city's leading stores, restaurants, and theaters. Farther west, the linear green strip of the **South Park Blocks** hosts several decent museums, while to the east the riverside stretch of **Tom McCall Waterfront Park** is rivaled only by Pioneer Courthouse Square for cultural activity. As you head north and get closer to Old Town, Downtown's main highlights are mostly architectural – ornamental old office blocks that easily put the city's postmodern pile, the **Portland Building**, to shame.

Pioneer Courthouse Square and around

Sitting in a space once occupied by the legendary Portland Hotel – until it was unceremoniously razed in the 1950s to make way for a department-store parking lot – **Pioneer Courthouse Square** more than lives up to its

△ Pioneer Courthouse Square

ACCOMMODATION		RESTAURANTS & CAFÉS					
Ace	C	Abou Karim	20	Ruth's Chris Steak House	22	Kells	19
Benson	E	Bijou Café	18	Southpark	31	Portland City Grill	5
Days Inn		Dragonfish	30	Stumptown Roasters	15	Ringlers Annex	2
City Center	M	Great Harvest Bread		Three Lions Bakery	21	Rock Bottom	
DeLuxe	A	Company	33	Voodoo Doughnut	6	Brewery	32
Embassy Suites	D	Higgins	35			Roseland Theater	1
Four Points by		Jake's Famous Crawfish	12	**BARS & CLUBS**		Saucebox	14
Sheraton	K	Jake's Grill	25	Ash Street Saloon	10	Shanghai Tunnel	11
Governor	F	Karam	28	Aura	8	Tugboat Brewing Co.	13
Heathman	L	McCormick and Schmick's	24	Berbati's Pan	9	Voleur	17
Lucia	G	New York City Sub Shop	27	Dante's	4	XV	7
Mark Spencer	B	Pazzo	23	Fernando's Hideaway	34		
Paramount	J	Peet's Coffee and Tea	26	Fez Ballroom	3		
Vintage Plaza	H	Portland Steak and		Huber's	29		
Westin	I	Chophouse	16				

historic predecessor as a true urban hub of social and cultural activity, and even boasts a few of the hotel's original wrought-iron gates and fixtures at its margins. Hosting a broad range of types – everyone from pinstriped bankers to pierced-and-tattooed street kids – the square and its red-bricked, curving terraces and modest waterfalls are wedged directly between the eastbound and westbound light-rail tracks, and adjacent to Downtown's main strip of Broadway.

Lunchtime rock concerts and fashion shows take place during the summer; Christmas events, including the presence and lighting of a huge tree, during the holiday season; and periodic book and antique sales throughout the year. Near the southwest corner, a folksy, life-size bronze of a man with an open umbrella (*Allow Me*, by Seward Johnson) personifies the area's easygoing character. Equally iconic, the stylish **weathervane**, in the center of the square, reflects the climate: on warm days a churlish sun appears, on dark stormy days a growling dragon, and during plain old wet, overcast weather, a placid blue heron – naturally, the most common omen of all.

While major department stores (Nordstrom and Macy's) dot the square to the west and northeast, you can also visit the square to sip coffee or stock up on tourist brochures and bus schedules from the visitor center (see p.78) underneath the waterfalls.

Across the square, at the corner of Yamhill Street, is **Jackson Tower**, one of Portland's many historic terracotta office blocks, a splendid 1912 concoction faced with white-glazed panels and crowned with a looming clock. To the east, completed in 1868, is the domed, Renaissance Revival **Pioneer Courthouse**, the first major federal building constructed in the Pacific Northwest and now the Portland quarters for the US Ninth Circuit Court of Appeals.

From the square, you can take a two-and-a-half-hour **walking tour** of the city's highlights (March–Dec daily 10am; $15; ⓦ www.portlandwalkingtours .com), a good introduction to Portland for first-time visitors.

SW Broadway

Serving as the square's western border, **SW Broadway** is where Portland's old grandeur and contemporary style most successfully coalesce. To the north are the exuberantly Neoclassical **US National Bank** at Broadway and Stark Street; a few blocks east from the bank, the **US Bancorp Tower**, at Fifth Avenue and Pine Street, a magenta-colored block with a mirrored-glass top; and, two blocks south, the 1948 **Equitable Building** (now the "Commonwealth"). Clad in aluminum and glass, it was the first truly modern office building built west of the Mississippi River; Pietro Belluschi, better known for creating the Portland Art Museum (see opposite), designed it.

South of Pioneer Courthouse Square on Broadway are movie theaters, clothing chains, and assorted boutiques, dominated by the convex glass curtain wall of the **Fox Tower**, catercorner to the southwest of Pioneer Courthouse Square, and **1000 Broadway**, two blocks farther south, a shiny pink dome that's been compared to a roll-on deodorant stick.

Across the street, at Broadway and Main Street, is the striking **Portland Center for the Performing Arts**, 1111 SW Broadway (ⓣ 503/248-4335 or 224-4000, ⓦ www.pcpa.com), with two main buildings – the **Arlene Schnitzer Concert Hall** and the **Antoinette Hatfield Hall**, containing the Dolores Winningstad Theater and Newmark Theater. The "Schnitz" is a sumptuously restored 1928 vaudeville theater and movie house that presents musical extravaganzas, dance, and drama, while the Antoinette Hatfield is a flashy construction of brick and dark glass, whose cherrywood-paneled lobby is topped with a spectral dome that changes color with the light of the sky.

The South Park Blocks and around

Immediately west of the Center for the Performing Arts, the **South Park Blocks**, a block-wide strip of elm-shaded park, stretches eleven blocks from the university campus up to Main Street. This green belt is another favorite urbanite hangout, where retirees commingle with teen slackers and the homeless, all under the gaze of a gloomy-looking **Abraham Lincoln** with his head lowered in quiet anguish and a militaristic **Theodore Roosevelt** shown as a "Rough Rider" from his days as a cavalry leader in the Spanish-American War of 1898.

Farther south, around the university campus, the park hosts a very popular seasonal **farmers market** (May–Oct Wed 10am–2pm, May–Dec Sat 8.30am–2pm; ⓦ www.portlandfarmersmarket.org) that draws fruit and vegetable growers from around the region, as well as local vendors of bread, pastries, beeswax candles, and handicrafts. On Saturdays you might also take in a cooking demonstration, hear music from live bands – anything from rock to folk to polka – and encounter a bevy of petitioners, supporting a range of liberal causes from equal rights to veganism.

Looming near the market is the marvelously refurbished **Simon Benson House**, adjacent to the park at Montgomery Street (Mon–Fri 9am–5pm; donation; ☎ 503/725-4948, ⓦ www.alumni.pdx.edu/benson). As the former home of one of the city's most famous timber barons, responsible for the eponymous hotel and the constantly flowing "Benson Bubblers" (drinking fountains) on street corners, the Queen Anne mansion features rooms paneled in different types of regional wood, graceful moon windows and horseshoe arches, and a lovely wraparound veranda.

Oregon Historical Society

Also adjacent to the Park Blocks, the **Oregon Historical Society**, 1200 SW Park Ave (Mon–Sat 10am–5pm; $10; ☎ 503/222-1741, ⓦ www.ohs.org), has some imaginative exhibits exploring different facets of the state's history. The society's collections encompass photographs, artifacts, and mementos from a span of hundreds of years. These include art and crafts of native tribes, early coins minted before Oregon became a state, an early version of a streetcar, then-and-now photos of notable city boulevards, and assorted twentieth-century trinkets and souvenirs. Among the highlights of the latter are vintage matchbooks from forgotten hotels, cheeky advertising for state products, and campaign buttons for local politicians.

The society is also well known for its towering trompe l'oeil murals, by Richard Haas, which grace the south and west walls of the center. The **south mural**, a vision of the Oregon Trail crawling up the building, more resembles a pioneer pyramid than a trek to the horizon, while the **west mural** showcases the Lewis and Clark expedition, its members wedged uncomfortably into the complex painted architecture.

Portland Art Museum

Across the Park Blocks from the historical society lies the long, low facade of the **Portland Art Museum** (Tues, Wed & Sat 10am–5pm, Thurs & Fri 10am–8pm, Sun noon–5pm; $10; ☎ 503/226-2811, ⓦ www.pam.org). Architect Pietro Belluschi's early modern design is limited to the south building, but the museum now incorporates the adjacent Masonic Temple, dramatically refurbished and modernized into the Mark Building. In the Belluschi building, the museum prides itself on its temporary exhibitions, but it also possesses a large permanent collection – too large, in fact, to show at any one time, which means that exhibits are regularly rotated. On the **ground floor**, the **Asian Art Galleries** have one room each for Korean, Japanese, and Chinese pieces, highlighted by tomb artifacts from the Han and Tang dynasties. The **lower level** holds prints and a modest sample of African applied art – masks, figurines, and so forth – but is best known for its temporary photography and print exhibits, everything from Japanese scrolls to woodcuts from the European avant-garde.

On the **top floor** are the **European Galleries**, which trace the evolution of European fine art, beginning with medieval painted wooden panels and Italian Renaissance paintings and running through to modernism. Best represented here are the Impressionists and post-Impressionists, with minor examples by Cézanne, Monet, Pissarro, Renoir, and Degas on display.

Continuing on from the European Galleries, the **Hirsch Wing** focuses on American painters from the eighteenth century to modern times, and contains a good sample of nineteenth-century landscape painters who moved to or frequently visited the Pacific Northwest. In particular look out for **Cleveland Rockwell** (1836–1907), a New Yorker who came to Oregon in 1868 to survey the coast for the US government and painted soft and warmly hued land- and seascapes in his spare time.

The real reason to visit the museum, though, is the **Mark Building**, which, with its underground entrance (accessed via the old wing) and six floors, holds a fine array of modern and postmodern works in various media, with part of the top floor reserved for temporary shows. The highlights here are more notable than those of the other building, among them George Segal's *Helen with Apples*, one of his monochromatic figures set against a blue door frame; several of Anthony Caro's angular steel sculptures, as well as Dale Chihuly's garish glass pieces; Brancusi's *A Muse*, its elemental bronze form still clearly human; Chaim Soutine's swirling red grotesque of *Le Petit Patissier* ("The Little Pastry Chef"); a large, eerily "breathing" water bottle created by Claes Oldenburg; and, out front, a grand sculpted brushstroke of Roy Lichtenstein.

The Portland Building and around

A couple of minutes' walk east, at the junction of Madison and Fifth, is architect Michael Graves's **Portland Building**, a boxy concoction of concrete and glass, adorned with dark-red and blue-green tiling with pale blue ribbons to match – lauded as a herald of the postmodern movement on completion in 1982, it's now mostly ignored, gaining attention mainly for the huge *Portlandia* sculpture looming over the façade.

To the east, at Main Street and Third Avenue, in pleasant little **Lownsdale Square**, the **Soldiers' Monument** commemorates those Oregon volunteers who died in the Spanish-American War of 1898. Between this and neighboring **Chapman Square**, and smack in the middle of Main Street, is a **bronze elk**. One of the city's earliest street sculptures, it was plonked in 1900 on top of the granite horse trough that still sits beneath it. It's not a very successful piece – the poor animal looks strangely lopsided – but it did prompt major municipal rows on several occasions when plans were announced to move it to speed traffic.

Along with hosting various sculptures, Lownsdale and Chapman squares are also some of Portland's earliest green spaces, and while nothing much happens in them on most days, they're occasionally commandeered for fervent political protests and rallies, as well as serving as the start and finish line for the Portland Marathon.

Tom McCall Waterfront Park

A few blocks east of the squares lies the **riverfront**, whose beauty was eclipsed for more than a century with wharves, warehouses, and, in the 1970s, an express highway. Now the mile-long grassy strip along the west bank of the Willamette, reborn as **Tom McCall Waterfront Park**, accommodates a popular walking and cycling path and offers excellent views of the city's stylish old bridges, while in the distance you can spot the snow capped hump

Beervana

When it comes to beverages in the Northwest, coffee gets the national headlines and wine the glory, but to many residents what really makes the region unique is its beer. Oregon and Washington lead the nation in microbreweries per capita, Portland has more than any other US city, and any respectable small town has at least one independent business brewing up its own handcrafted ales. The quirky moniker "Beervana" aptly suits the region's sensibilities, blending the allure of a beer drinker's paradise with the earthy attitude of the grunge group that made the Northwest famous.

The history mash

Although the Northwest can claim to be the home of the first **brewpub** opened since Prohibition – the now-defunct *Grant's Pub* in Yakima, in 1982 – it was Northern California's Anchor Brewing Company, with its signature Anchor Steam beer, that proved that a small-batch brewery (one producing fewer than 15,000 annual barrels) could effectively distribute a quality beverage to a national market.

▲ Perfect pints at Portland Brewing Co.

Northwest brewers followed suit, developing signature labels like Bridgeport, Widmer, Rogue, Deschutes, Full Sail, and Portland Brewing. In fact, much of the early thrust of the movement was from brewers in Portland, though Seattle producers like Pyramid, Hale's, and Red Hook got in on the trend, too. It couldn't have come at a better time, either, since throughout the 1980s and 90s the old-line "macro"-brewers like Henry Weinhard's and Olympia were either dying or being absorbed by the major industrial brewers.

▲ Local beers

Type, style, and variety

What follows is a list of the more familiar **beer styles** you're apt to find in the region's taps and on its shelves, though it's by no means comprehensive.

Ale – Technically, refers to beer made with top-fermenting yeasts, though more synonymous with "good" in the Northwest, especially when opposed to the more industrially produced lagers. Covers a wide range of types and styles.

Amber – Darker, copper-colored type of pale ale.

Barley Wine – Dark, strong ale that isn't technically a wine, but does echo its alcohol content – up to twenty percent in some cases; rarely served in a pint glass.

Belgian – Catchall term referring to strong but light beverages, often made with herbs and spices in the Belgian abbey way, with subtypes like dubbel, trippel, and so on, based on potency.

Bitter – Type of pale ale with less alcohol than IPAs and often using British hops.

Blonde – Light, sometimes fruity ale with pale-yellow or straw color and low bitterness and alcohol.

Bock – Any of various types of strong German lagers, with names like Weizenbock, Doppelbock, etc.

Brown Ale – Dark-malted ales with mild flavors often derived from nuts, especially hazelnuts.

Cream Ale – Smooth, light ale with the taste of a lager, though still top-fermented like an ale.

Hoppy – A strong flavor of hops, from bright and herbal to bitter and astringent.

Hybrid – A blanket term that covers everything that doesn't fit into another category: bourbon-barrel-aged beers, smoky brews, steam beers, fruit and flower infusions, and anything not made with hops.

India Pale Ale (IPA) – Though not well known in most of the world, a dominant style in the Northwest; a strong pale ale with solid alcohol and hops content often freshly harvested from local farmers.

Lager – Beer made with bottom-fermenting yeasts. A word that makes beer purists cringe, especially when it refers to the yellow, fizzy American varieties made from rice or corn mash.

The land and water

While the microbrewing phenomenon has now spread across the country, Northwest brewers still have unique advantages over their competitors. The Pacific Northwest's **water** – the most important ingredient in beer – is clean and clear, lacking the fluoride, chlorine, and hard mineral content that can taint the flavor of

▲ Hops, beer's flavor source

a top-notch brew. Second, the region's **hops**, the green catkin of the climbing vine *Humulus lupulus*, are an essential flavoring agent and preservative in any good beer, and the Willamette Valley is perhaps the nation's premier producer of it. Hops come in many styles and flavors, and most of them tend to be dried after harvesting, making for the familiar bitter taste of many microbrews. More distinctive are **fresh-hopped** beers,

The quality German model has little in common with these aside from the name.

Malt Liquor – Type of basic lager with an alcohol content of six to nine percent; identified with industrial brewers, though occasionally made by microbrewers with a taste for irony.

On Nitro – Manner in which a beer is occasionally served on draft, containing nitrogen instead of carbon dioxide, resulting in a creamier beverage with a thicker head.

Pale Ale – Beer made with pale-colored malt, with a wide scope of subvarieties, though it tends to be hoppy in the Northwest.

Pilsner – The most common type of American lager, usually weak and fizzy, though microbrewers make occasional attempts to perfect the style based on the preferred Czech and German original.

Porter – Beer made with very dark malt having a typically dark-brown or black color, sizable head, and rich, complex flavor.

Rye Beer – Brew containing some portion of rye as a base, for a dry, spicy character.

Scotch Ale – Type of pale ale with strong, lightly sweet taste, with overtones of whisky in some cases, and higher alcohol content than other such ales.

Steam Beer – A lager and ale hybrid – mixing bottom-fermenting yeast in a top-fermenting process – made by few breweries other than Anchor Steam; named for an archaic means of cooling the wort on the brewery roof, creating a steam effect when the cool air hit it.

Stout – Heavy, potent brew made with the darkest malt; often black in color with a thick head, it can come in even stronger subtypes such as Imperial, Russian Imperial, and Oatmeal, or nicely flavored with coffee and chocolate.

Strong Ale – British-style beer with an alcohol content of at least seven percent, sometimes much more; related to English old ales and other potent types aged at least a year.

Wheat Beer – Brew made with a large amount of malted wheat; the signature Northwest type is Hefeweizen, referring to the unfiltered wheat yeasts that give the beer its cloudy appearance and pale yellow color.

For more information, any of beer writer Michael Jackson's books will do, as will historian Fred Eckhart's seminal *Essentials of Beer Style*.

▼ Pioneer Square Saloon, Portland

Beer tourism

Simply put, the Northwest is an essential stop on the **worldwide tour** of any lover of international beer. Although Portland and Seattle are the regular first stops on the junket, there are also many great small-town craft brewers — from Pelican Ale in Pacific City, to Rogue in Newport, to Terminal Gravity way out in Enterprise. If you don't have

▲ Belmont Station, Portland

the time for a lengthy expedition, drop by the chain McMenamins, which operates combination hotel-brewpub-theater-distilleries out of historic digs; and expansive shops like Seattle's Bottleworks, 1710 N 45th St, #3, Wallingford (☎206/633-2437), and Portland's Belmont Station, 4500 SE Stark St, Laurelhurst (☎503/232-8538). Even in the most run-of-the-mill urban bar, you can still find a half-dozen excellent microbrews on tap and a spirited mix of people who either know the nuances of ales, porters, and stouts or are just glad to drinking one, or many, of them.

which feature the little buds in their moist, ripe condition right off the vine. If made correctly, such a beer will have a bright, floral, and herbal flavor. However, only residents of the Northwest are usually able to sample these, since neither fresh-hopped beers nor fresh hops travel well. This has only encouraged true beer aficionados to make their own special journeys to Beervana.

The local flavor

Few, if any, Northwest brewers would claim to have invented a new style of beer, and most use the **British** and **German models** as their base. What sets many microbrews apart is that their makers often add locally available ingredients (such as fruits like marionberry and apricot) to their beers, tweak traditional formulas, or revive long-forgotten historical recipes. Naturally, the biggest exports from the region are the cloudy Hefeweizens, fruit-infused ales, and hoppy pale ales that gave the region its reputation, but locals know the full range of potables that are commonly on offer – or not. Indeed, some acclaimed brewers, such as Hair of the Dog, may regularly produce only a few select

▼ Oregon Brewers Festival, Portland

beverages, keeping their fans waiting in line at dock sales for **limited batches** of beers with names like "Doggie Claws" that quickly sell out and just as quickly become legendary. Some of the best beer-related events include Portland's huge **Oregon Brewers Festival** in July, supposedly North America's largest festival of craft brewers; the smaller-scale International Beer Festival in Seattle and Portland in June and July; and December's Holiday Ale Festival in both cities.

Smart growth and Tom McCall

Oregon, and Portland in particular, is nationally renowned as a leader in **"smart growth"** policies. These include stringent land-use rules, reuse of historic structures, and regulations to control billboards and other visual blight – as well as **"urban growth boundaries,"** which establish massive, multi-county bureaucracies to protect farmland and rural areas on the edge of the city from untrammeled development. In few other places in the US do you find the same degree of antipathy for population growth: locals seem to exaggerate stories of constant rainfall and gray skies to keep interlopers away.

Some claim this tradition of proud provincialism dates back to the days of the Oregon Trail. Pioneering governor Oswald West famously put it into practice when he fought to protect most of the state's beaches from development in the 1910s. Governor **Tom McCall** was even more influential, helping to pass groundbreaking environmental laws, including the influential **"bottle bill,"** and a host of anti-sprawl regulations in the 1960s and 1970s, as well as overseeing what may have been the nation's only state-sponsored rock festival, Vortex 1. A larger-than-life figure, McCall even placed signs at the border stating, "You are welcome to visit Oregon, but please don't stay." Still today McCall's legacy looms large over the state among partisans of all political stripes, and Oregon politicians are as loath to criticize the legendary governor as Bible Belt pols are to denounce Jesus.

of Mount Hood (see p.131). The park is named after liberal Republican governor McCall, a key figure in the late 1960s and 1970s movement to improve the state and the prime mover behind dozens of environmental measures (see box above).

Waterfront Park runs south from the Burnside Bridge to the marina at the foot of Clay Street. During early June's **Rose Festival** (see p.98), the docks along the northern part of the park feature the presence of all manner of colossal US Navy destroyers and cruisers (usually from West Coast ports), which sometimes allow tours, depending on the national level of terrorism fears. In the middle of the park, opposite Salmon Street, you'll find the Portland Spirit River Cruises jetty (see p.80 for cruise details) and the playful, gushing fountains of **Salmon Street Springs**, which spurt forth from ground level and attract children and the odd adult to caper around in their waters. The southern end of the park has the most expansive greenery and hosts countless summertime festivals and concerts, the **Blues Festival** (see Ⓦ www.waterfrontbluesfest.com) and **Oregon Brewers Festival** (see Ⓦ www.oregonbrewfest.com) being two of the highlights. The visual interest peters out around the RiverPlace district to the south, but the rather antiseptic waterside strip mall here is a good spot to hop aboard the Portland Streetcar.

Ira Keller Auditorium and Fountain

Three blocks inland from the park, Downtown's last major sights of note can be found at SW Third Avenue and Clay Street, where the homely **Ira Keller Auditorium** (☎503/274-6560) is home to traveling musicals, occasional rock shows, and the **Portland Opera** (☎503/241-1407, Ⓦ www.portlandopera.org). More eye-catching is the **Ira Keller Fountain** across the street, an array of concrete blocks, staircases, alcoves, and troughs, which provides locals with an outlet for wading and splashing in the warmer months. While some prefer to take it easy on the terraced concrete slabs away from the water, others perch perilously – and get soaked – atop the sheer walls above, where the torrents flow in a thick mist. North of the auditorium is the

△ Ira Keller Fountain

KOIN Building, which, looking like a brick-red rocket, is an essential part of a picture-postcard view of Portland's cityscape.

Old Town

From the Willamette River to Sixth Avenue, between the Morrison and Burnside bridges, **Old Town** was the site where Portland was founded in 1843, and it still retains a handsome Victorian atmosphere. By the 1850s, wealthy Portland merchants were edging the streets with grand, cast-iron-frame buildings, which were less expensive and faster to build than their stone and brick predecessors. In 1889 iron was abruptly replaced by steel, mostly with terracotta embellishments (a fashion that lasted until the 1930s). The area tended to flood, though, and when the railroad came in 1883 the town center started to shift away from the river, a gradual process that eventually pushed Old Town right down the social scale. This process was accelerated in the 1920s, when Portland was displaced as the Northwest's premier port by Seattle and other Puget Sound cities; the addition of a high seawall in the 1930s put an end to Old Town's crusty, old-fashioned nautical atmosphere and sent it on a path toward becoming one of the city's perennially troubled districts, home to all manner of drug addicts, homeless people, prostitutes, and petty criminals.

While recent attempts at **rejuvenation** have resulted in an attractive patchwork of restored old buildings, many of which house bistros and boutiques, Old Town is still a dicey area after dark, especially between Second and Fifth avenues. Nevertheless, if you're a clubgoer, you won't be able to escape the area, for the stretch around Third Avenue (north and south) and Burnside is home to the city's most exciting and frenetic concert halls and dance clubs (see p.113).

OLD TOWN, PEARL DISTRICT & NW PORTLAND

ACCOMMODATION		RESTAURANTS & CAFÉS						BARS & CLUBS	
Heron Haus	A	Anna Bannanas	7	In Good Taste	30	Papa Haydn	19	Bridgeport Brewing	10
HI-Portland		Besaw's Café	2	Justa Pasta	5	Paragon	23	Embers Avenue	37
Northwest	D	Bluehour	29	Le Happy	12	Pearl Bakery	35	The Gypsy	21
Inn at Northrup		DF	9	Ken's Artisan		Silk	25	Hobo's	34
Station	C	Escape from		Bakery	27	Sungari Pearl	13	Jimmy Mak's	28
MacMaster		NY Pizza	22	Kornblatt's		Sushiville	1	New Old Lompoc	4
House	F	Fenouil	15	Delicatessen	20	Swagat	14	Ringlers	40
Portland Intl.		Filbert's	3	Marrakesh	8	Vegetarian		Ringlers Annex	39
Guesthouse	F	Golden Horse	33	Mio Gelato	38	House	36	Rogue Ales	
Silver Cloud Inn	B	Hot Lips Pizza	18	Mio Sushi	16	Via Delizia	11	Public House	26
				Oba	24	Wildwood	6	Tiger Bar	31
				Old Town Pizza	32	World Cup	17		

Skidmore Fountain and New Market Theater

One of the best excuses for a visit to Old Town, the **Saturday Market** (March–Dec Sat 10am–5pm, Sun 11am–4.30pm; ⓦ www.portlandsaturdaymarket.com) packs the area south of and underneath the Burnside Bridge with arts and crafts stalls, eclectic street musicians, spicy foods, and lively crowds, all crammed cheek by jowl along the MAX tracks.

In the middle of the market area, at First Avenue and Ankeny Street, stands the **Skidmore Fountain**, a bronze basin raised by caryatids above a granite pool, designed to provide European elegance for Portland's citizens and water for the city's hard-worked "men, dogs and horses," as the opening ceremony had it. Across the MAX tracks from the fountain is the **New Market Theater**, whose interior, with its Venetian-style arcades and cast-iron trimmings, dates from 1872. Built by Alexander Ankeny, who made a fortune in the California gold fields, it was designed to house a vegetable market downstairs and a theater upstairs. It served its function well over the years but soon declined with the rest of the neighborhood – its north-side cast-iron columns were removed in the 1950s and it was threatened with demolition a decade later. In the 1980s, however, after years of neglect, it was restored to its something like its original layout (minus the theater), and now hosts restaurants, shops, and offices.

Second and Third avenues

Old Town's other architectural highlights begin with the 1889 **Rodney Glisan Building**, 112 SW 2nd Ave at Ash Street, which cleverly incorporates several

Shanghaiing

Until the end of the nineteenth century, international trade depended on wooden sailing ships, requiring large, docile **crews** and sailing times that varied enormously depending on the weather. The result was that ships could lie empty in harbor for weeks, if not months. To keep costs down, captains habitually dismissed most of the ship's crew when they reached their destination, but this created difficulties when they were ready to leave – low wages and poor conditions never attracted enough volunteers. Into the breach stepped dozens of waterfront hoodlums, or **crimps**, who were hired to supply the crews with no questions asked. **Shanghaiing**, as it became known in the US (as China was the principal destination), was big business, nowhere more so than in Portland, where thugs like Jim Turk, described by his contemporaries as "225 pounds of florid-faced, beef-fed Britisher," and Joseph "Bunco" Kelly worked the scam. As boardinghouse owners, they could select their victims from among their own residents with all the violent aplomb of a press gang. And if this failed, they simply roamed the waterfront brothels and bars, descending on their victims when their pants or inhibitions were down.

Although it was the steamship rather than the law that polished off Portland's crimps, this grim period in city history lives on in the **Shanghai Tunnels Tours** ($16, by reservation only at ☏503/622-4798), which depart on periodic evenings from Hobo's bar in Old Town at 120 NW 3rd Ave. They take you on an eye-opening 90min journey through the corridors and cellars beneath the streets, where shanghaiing victims were supposedly held in tiny, dank cells and would-be rebels were "managed" with a clunk to the skull with a brick or blackjack.

styles, its cast-iron columns, Gothic pediment and Neoclassical entrance presently home to *Kells Irish Restaurant & Pub* (see p.110). Further south along **Second Avenue** at Oak Street is the old **Portland Police Headquarters**, a heavyweight 1912 Renaissance Revival edifice that served as police headquarters until the 1980s, and the place where George Baker, the belligerent mayor of Portland from 1917 to 1924, installed a special police detail, the "red squad," to hunt down every socialist and labor activist in sight.

Not far away, the 1891 **Concord Building**, 208 SW 2nd Ave at Stark Street, features elegant brick and sandstone-trimmed lines, while opposite, in striking contrast, the Gothic Revival **Bishop's House** is a brick, cast-iron, and stucco structure built in 1879 for the city's Catholic archbishop and subsequently home to a Prohibition speakeasy and several restaurants. Around the corner, at Third Avenue and Washington Street, are two of the city's finest buildings, the **Postal Building** of 1900, whose Renaissance Revival order is adorned by frilly terracotta panels and a delightfully intricate cornice, and opposite, the 1892 **Dekum Building**, whose brick and terracotta upper levels perch on rough-hewn red sandstone in an outstanding example of the Romanesque Revival.

Chinatown

North of West Burnside from Old Town, the several blocks immediately adjacent were in the nineteenth century known as the **North End**, an area where all kinds of vice and sordid doings flourished, perpetually vexing the Portland bourgeoisie. Writer Dean Collins described the conflict as "the Puritan soldiers of the Lord vs. the Adversary Satan's City," a battle handily won by the latter, as the commerce generated from the shipping trade made the area's vice lords – who ran the flophouses and bordellos, controlled the underworld, and operated shanghaiing schemes – too formidable to control.

Around the same time, beginning in the 1860s, the **Chinese** population of the area began to grow, from a mere two hundred at the end of the Civil War to almost eight thousand by the turn of the century. Most were concentrated in **Chinatown**, which in the late nineteenth century was the second-largest such community on the West Coast, after San Francisco. Today the **ornamental gate** at Fourth Avenue marks the entrance to the neighborhood, which is interesting enough but still a shadow of its historic peak a century ago, due to emigration from the area and the adjacent blight of Old Town. Still, there's enough of a community here to support a range of cheap ethnic restaurants and dive bars, along with a smattering of fun dance clubs and rock venues. Otherwise, Chinatown's main attraction is the **Classical Chinese Garden**, on NW Third Avenue at Everett (daily: April–Oct 9am–6pm; Nov–March 10am–5pm; $7; Ⓦ www.portlandchinesegarden.org), a Suzhou-style garden with traditional vegetation, ponds, and walkways, with evocative "picture windows" framing some of the garden's more interesting views.

If you want to find out more about this fascinating area, Portland Walking Tours hosts the **Underground Portland** jaunt (March–Dec daily 2pm; $15; Ⓦ www .portlandwalkingtours.com), covering the tumultuous history of Chinatown and Old Town, both above and below ground, on a two-and-a-half-hour tour.

The Pearl District

The concept of the **Pearl District**, due north and west of Chinatown, is a recent phenomenon. Much like Seattle's Belltown, this was for many decades considered an irredeemable dead zone by politicians and developers – known throughout most of its history as **Slabtown**, it was home to workaday garages, warehouses, rail tracks, and a few artists' lofts. The district's proximity to Downtown, however, proved too enticing to ignore. To kick-start the makeover, the area was given a fanciful name by developers in the 1980s, and the city later provided countless tax breaks to developers. Nowadays, snappy public art and the sleek Portland Streetcar mark a new "urban village" – at least according to the ad copy. High-rise condos sell for around $1 million per unit, and where greasy spoons once drew a loyal working-class clientele, stylish bistros and smart cafés now draw the swells.

Loosely bounded by NW Broadway, Naito Parkway, and the I-405 freeway, "the Pearl," as residents call it, has a rather amorphous shape, and it seems always to be growing in new directions. Where maps only a year or two old show railroad tracks, there are likely now condos or office towers. Amid the new chain retailers, the swanky galleries, and the usual rash of *Starbucks* coffee houses, a handful of sights stand out for your attention.

The Ecotrust Building and around

The **Ecotrust Building**, at NW Tenth Avenue at Johnson (Ⓦ www.ecotrust .org/ncc), is a good starting point to an excursion into the Pearl District. An 1895 brick-and-timber warehouse now remodeled into the sleek new Jean Vollum Natural Capital Center, it hosts a range of environmental organizations, along with what is arguably the city's best pizza joint, *Hot Lips* (see p.106). Across Tenth Avenue is another neighborhood bright spot, **Jamison Park**, best known for its delightfully terraced **fountain**. It is popular with countless children, who frolic and leap in the puddled water below while adult visitors sit and sunbathe or read books on the stone slabs above.

Lining the west side of the park is the **Portland Streetcar** line (see p.80), which connects west to Northwest Portland and south to Downtown. A few blocks north, **Tanner Springs Park** is one of the city's most distinctive green spaces, with a western wall of metal girders, a geometric path bordering a small pond, and sloping, marshy turf peppered with benches and indigenous plants.

PICA and First Thursday

The Pearl District is well known for its **gallery** scene, and the main institution in the area is the **Portland Institute for Contemporary Art**, almost always known as **PICA** (office at 224 NW 13th Ave, Suite 305; ☎503/242-1419, Ⓦ www.pica.org), which organizes periodic festivals, theatrical performances, and film screenings, all of them with a heavy experimental and conceptual bent but still quite popular. The biggest is **Time-Based Art**, a ten-day September event with theater, film, and multimedia presentations at different venues in the Pearl (tickets free to $50 per show; show pass $75–150).

While many of the countless galleries in the Pearl District serve as mere excuses for wine bars and boutiques, there are a few decent art galleries in the neighborhood. Most of them are covered in the district's **First Thursday** event (6–9pm; free; Ⓦ www.firstthursday.org), in which a collection of upper-end establishments keep their doors open late on the initial Thursday of each month. The walk draws yuppies, tourists, and serious art lovers alike for its mostly abstract or conceptual paintings and drawings, with a sprinkling of Pop Art and mixed media thrown in.

Powell's City of Books and the Brewery Blocks

On the southern edge of the Pearl is the district's biggest attraction, **Powell's City of Books**, at West Burnside Street and 10th Avenue (daily 9am–11pm; ☎503/228-4651, Ⓦ www.powells.com), which claims to be the largest bookstore in America. The "City" occupies an entire block and spreads over four floors, issuing free maps so customers can find their way around. There's a huge selection of used, out-of-print, and discounted titles here, which you may bring into the adjoining coffee shop to browse before you buy. The rooms are color-coded by topic, with most of the new books and magazines at the entrance on Burnside. An alternate entrance, at 11th Avenue and Couch Street, sits directly across from the high-rise behemoth known as the **Brewery Blocks** (Ⓦ www.breweryblocks.com). Occupying the site (and in one case the actual structure) of the former Blitz-Weinhard Brewery, the five-block development is home to coffee shops, organic groceries, condos, and upscale restaurants. One of the Blocks, the former **Portland Armory**, 128 NW 11th Ave, is particularly worth seeing. It was recently renovated and is now the main facility for **Portland Center Stage** (☎503/445-3702, Ⓦ www.pcs.org), whose rusticated stone facade and stately exposed timbers within provide a dramatic setting for the troupe's modern and classic works staged throughout the year.

Northwest Portland

Due west of the Pearl District, across the recessed channel of the I-405 freeway, lies the district most residents call **Northwest Portland** (even though the Pearl District and Chinatown also sport NW street prefixes). The neighborhood, however, was originally known as **Nob Hill**, its name imported by a San Francisco grocer who hoped the area would become as fashionable as the Nob Hill neighborhood back home. The district does, like its San Francisco counterpart, feature a number of beautifully refurbished Victorian townhouses and mansions, along with a charming number of renovated churches, historic-revival buildings, the city's main Jewish temple, and, along **21st and 23rd avenues**, some of the city's smarter boutiques and restaurants. One of the key architectural highlights – of which there are many – is the **Mackenzie House**, 615 NW 20th Ave; it looks like a medieval hunting lodge with its prominent cast-iron stag's head, rough stone arches, and fortress-like design.

NW 21st and 23rd avenues

Despite the quality of its historic architecture, Northwest Portland is best known to locals for its two main strips of NW 21st and 23rd avenues, which together feature many of the city's best restaurants, coffee houses, and boutiques. The more modest of the two, **NW 21st Avenue**, is at its liveliest around NW Hoyt St, where **Cinema 21** (℡503/223-4515, ⓦwww.cinema21.com) draws crowds with a steady supply of art films and independent releases. In the same area there are a number of old-time bars and clubs that attract a loyal following. Farther north, around Overton Street, are some of Portland's swankiest restaurants. Although these eateries offer valet parking, if you want to visit the less expensive diners or other establishments, you'll be forced to contend with what some call the **worst parking** in Oregon, with drivers often forced to hunt for twenty minutes or more to find a space. To escape the congestion, take a bus here (#15 NW 23rd St and #17 NW 21st St lines) or, better yet, hop on the **Portland Streetcar** (see p.80) from Downtown, which runs here along Lovejoy and Northrup streets.

Two blocks west, **NW 23rd Avenue** is much more chic and upscale, with snooty attitudes and well-heeled shoppers to match. Decades ago, the road used to be one of the neighborhood's grungier stretches, but like the Pearl District, this area's seedy past has since been sanitized by a welter of fancy clothing boutiques and pricey restaurants. The renovated blocks stretch all the way from Burnside to Vaughn streets, almost the full gamut of the district's alphabetically ordered east–west roads. Fans of *The Simpsons* will recognize street names like Flanders, Kearney, Lovejoy, and Quimby from the TV show: the series' creator and Portland native son Matt Groening named many of his characters after them.

From Vaughn Street, you can immediately access the I-5 and 405 freeways to the east. If you head west along Thurman, you can enter into the vast urban greenery of Forest Park (see p.95).

The West Hills

The long line of wooded bluffs that make up the **West Hills** has long restricted Portland's capacity to expand westward. Although a good slice now accommodates the homes of the wealthy, the terrain is also home to several of the city's top attractions, from museums and zoos to nature preserves. There remain large chunks of dark and dense forest as well, which far-sighted city planners and conservationists have long fought to keep free of development. Because of this, the road connections to the west are quite limited and very circuitous; they include the winding slope of **West Burnside** as it rises over the crest of the hills, and the hairpin turns and tunnels of **Cornell Road**, which links to Lovejoy Street in Northwest Portland.

Forest Park

Forest Park (#18 Hillside bus from Downtown) is one of the best – and largest – nature preserves contained within the boundaries of any US city. It sprawls many miles to the northwest from Portland's west side and has myriad points of entry and possibilities for hiking, biking, and exploring. You're best

△ Forest Park

off focusing on one of two main routes into the park, both accessible from Northwest Portland (with less inviting spots off Cornell Road). The first, the thirty-mile **Wildwood Trail**, can be accessed around NW 31st Avenue and Upshur Street and is best for casual walkers and hikers who really want to explore the scenery and get a feel for the plants and topography of the park. It's not necessary to travel the full distance (which is a one-way route, in any case), but unless you have a trail **map** (available from entry kiosks or from Ⓦwww.friendsofforestpark.org), you may well get lost unless you retrace your steps back to the beginning.

The second route, **Leif Erickson Drive**, accessible from where NW Thurman Street comes to a dead end, is a graveled, partially paved concourse that wends some fifteen miles into the park and attracts some of the city's more gung-ho mountain bikers and long-distance runners. With that in mind, stay alert and steer well clear of the cyclists, who have been known to tumble downhill around the sharp curves and take out a few unwitting hikers as they go – a daunting thought considering the wooded precipices at the edge of the trail.

Pittock Mansion

Justifiably one of the first sights mentioned in any tourist brochure to Portland, the **Pittock Mansion**, 3229 NW Pittock Drive (daily: Jun–Aug 11am–4pm; Sept–Dec & Feb–May noon–4pm; closed Jan; $7; ☎503/823-3623, Ⓦwww .pittockmansion.com), is a luxurious estate located off – and up in the hills from – West Burnside Street, a couple of miles from Downtown. Perched on a ridge with great views of the city, the 1914 mansion was built for *Oregonian* newspaper publisher Henry Pittock and took five years to complete. It's broadly French Renaissance in style, and its 22 rooms are a perfect illustration of the energetic, ostentatious character of the American tycoon. The house is stuffed with antique furnishings, and there's a mind-boggling mix of styles: the library is English Jacobean, the smoking room Turkish, and the drawing room Renaissance Revival. The house sports the latest inventions of its time: a room-to-room telephone system, showers with multiple showerheads, and an ambitious central vacuum-cleaning system. It's a delightful mishmash in any case, and when you've finished looking around, you can stroll the carefully manicured gardens and check out some of the city's best views from the expansive front lawn – which has the added benefit of being admission-free.

To get to the Pittock Mansion by **bus** from Downtown, take bus #20 west along West Burnside Street and you'll be dropped at the start of the steep, signed, half-mile side road that winds up to the entrance.

Washington Park

Cutting through the West Hills from the south side of downtown Portland (via Clay Street), Highway 26 serves as the main approach to **Washington Park**, a green and hilly expanse that holds many of the city's biggest-name attractions. The most popular is the **Oregon Zoo** (daily: April–Sept 9am–6pm; Oct–March 9am–4pm; $9.75; ☎503/226-1561, Ⓦwww.oregonzoo .org), on the park's southern perimeter. Although the zoo has the requisite primates, penguins, and, this being the Northwest, beavers, the facility's real stars are its Asian elephants, now a herd of seven that in 1962 produced the first birth of an Asian elephant in the Western Hemisphere. The zoo's most unusual feature is the Elephant Museum, detailing the biological and cultural history of pachyderms – and decorated with a giant mastodon skeleton. The zoo also puts on an excellent program of live music in the warmer months (June–Aug; tickets $9.50–26; ☎503/226-1561).

Back at the zoo entrance, it's a few minutes' walk over to the **World Forestry Center** (daily 10am–5pm; $7; T 503/228-1367, W www .worldforestry.org), which largely celebrates the glories of the timber industry using lots of interactive exhibits. Among several displays, the most diverting concerns the life cycle of a forest, which charts trees' beginnings as seedlings, growth to larger, more stately forms of life, and death by bulldozer, to end up in houses and pulp mills.

A miniature train connects the zoo and the Forestry Center with two formal gardens farther north in the park. The first, the five-acre **Washington Park International Rose Test Garden** (daily 7.30am–9pm; free), is justifiably one of the city's highlights, an explosion of enticing colors set on a hillside overlooking the fetching cityscape. The garden is at its best in early summer, when eight thousand rose bushes cover layered terraces with a gaudy range of blooms, which are labeled by each bush's year of vintage – some date back almost to the nineteenth century. The place earns its name by testing new varieties of rose sent here by growers: the flowers are checked for two years and are judged on their color, fragrance, and form. Also look out for the **Royal Rosarian** and **Shakespearean gardens**, the former home to some stately, old-fashioned blooms with historic pedigrees, and the latter a display of the roses mentioned in the works of the Bard, including the sprightly Angel's Trumpet – mentioned in three separate tragedies.

On the hill above the roses, the **Japanese Garden** (daily: April–Sept 10am–7pm; Oct–March 10am–4pm; $8; T 503/223-1321, W www .japanesegarden.com) is actually a collection of five traditional gardens with

---

Seeing roses in the City of Roses

The Rose Test Garden is the obvious first stop if you're interested in discovering why Portland lays claim to the title **"City of Roses,"** unless you can visit during the crowded and colorful **Rose Festival** (W www.rosefestival.org) held in early June. For the event, a rose festival **Queen** and **Court** are selected from local high school girls, and thousands flock to Burnside Street to watch a massive parade with multicolored floats, marching bands, and the whole works. The weekend **Starlight Parade** takes a Downtown route to showcase bands, local bigwigs, and other marchers, while the ongoing **Fun Center** spreads out along Waterfront Park to offer a blinding array of carnival rides and fast-food stands, thronged by families and youthful hedonists. Looming above the Fun Center are the silhouettes of **US Navy warships**, which make this their port of call for a week or two but allow public tours only sporadically in the wake of terrorism fears.

If you have no interest in parades but still want to sample the city's fine blooms, there are a few places around town that are good choices during the growing season. Well off the beaten track, one such place is **Peninsula Park** in Northeast Portland, three blocks east of the Portland Boulevard exit on I-5. Spread over eight blocks, the park presents a wide array of blossoms amid a tranquil setting with copious paths and trees. The Eastside's other top area for roses is **Ladd's Addition**, north of Division Street and south of Hawthorne Boulevard, between 12th and 20th avenues. However, instead of the usual grid, the district's roads and alleys – built in the 1890s – are laid out in an **axial form**, meaning they radiate out from a central circle and lead in all kinds of odd directions. It's well worth plunging into this maze to see the four striking rose gardens here, which have many of the same classic blooms as the Rose Test Garden and only a fraction of the crowds. Rich with appealing architecture, this neighborhood is one of Portland's great little treasures – just be sure to bring a map.

ponds, bridges, foliage, and sand designs. It's a tranquil spot, with cool, green shrubs reflected in pools, and abstract sand-and-stone patterns making minimal use of color. Surprisingly enough, it has been named in several reviews as one the most authentic Japanese gardens outside of Japan. Finally, a bit further west in the park, **Hoyt Arboretum**, 4000 Fairview Blvd (daily 6am–10pm; free; ☎503/865-8733, ⓦwww.hoytarboretum.org), rewards a leisurely walk with views of its collection of ten thousand trees and plants from throughout the region and the world. Other sites worth a look include two very different memorials: on the park's southern side, a chronological procession of names listed on a winding hillside concourse honors local soldiers who died in the **Vietnam War**, while on the northeast side, influential local Communist **John Reed** is remembered with a commemorative bench and plaque – though he's actually buried inside the Kremlin walls.

In terms of access, side roads weave through Washington Park connecting all of its (clearly signposted) attractions. Most sights have convenient access to MAX **light rail** ($1.70 from Downtown), whose station is buried deep underground and accessible only by elevator. Once you get here, you can hop on a summertime **shuttle** (every 15min daily: June–Sept 10am–7pm) and access all the park's attractions on a cheap day pass. To go straight to the Japanese Gardens or the International Rose Test Garden from Downtown, take the Washington Park **bus** #63 (elk symbol) from the Transit Mall at Main Street.

The Eastside

While the west side of the Willamette River provided an agreeably deep port, the east side was too shallow for shipping and the area remained undeveloped for the first fifty years of Portland's life. Even before the Hawthorne, Steel, and Broadway bridges crept across the river in the early nineteenth century (they've since been rebuilt several times), residential neighborhoods were rapidly spreading east, stretching out toward the forested foothills that approach Mount Hood. These extensive former suburbs – **the Eastside**, for short – now accommodate most of Greater Portland's population of two million, and you can find a number of stretches here popular with young hipsters and aging bohemians for their cheap ethnic diners, quirky boutiques, and vintage clothiers.

Keep in mind that the Eastside's **main drags** – Sandy and Powell boulevards and 82nd and Grand avenues – are uniformly unappealing. It's easy enough, however, to stay clear of these dismal stretches and explore the area's interesting districts on less traveled side streets.

The Eastbank Esplanade and OMSI

While the **east bank of the Willamette** is still filled with plenty of gritty stretches – storage facilities, grim warehouses, and looming overhead freeways – the **Eastbank Esplanade** that runs alongside them is still worth a visit, especially for its near-perfect view of the city skyline to the west across the river. A $30-million concourse that runs across floating walkways and cantilevered footpaths, it forms a three-mile loop connecting to Waterfront Park on the south end and the vicinity of the train station on the north. The Esplanade attracts a good number of runners, strollers, and cyclists, even on rainy days, and on summer weekends you can see Portland's fitness obsession in full flower.

From the faded red-and-green towers of the 1910 **Hawthorne Bridge** (the city's oldest), the pathway leads under the deafening traffic of the less appealing

ACCOMMODATION

HI-Portland Hawthorne	E
Jupiter	D
Kennedy School	A
Lion & the Rose	B
White Eagle	C

RESTAURANTS & CAFÉS

Bombay Cricket Club	25	Lauro Kitchen	30	Tao of Tea	21	The Goodfoot	14
Bread and Ink Café	28	Le Pigeon	10	Whiskey Soda Lounge	34	Holocene	16
Cadillac Café	1	Milo's City Café	2			Horse Brass Pub	22
Clay's Smokehouse Grill	33	Navarre	9	**BARS & CLUBS**		Laurelthirst Public House	7
Colosso	5	Pambiche	6	ACME Food and Drink	23	Lucky Labrador	24
Crema	12	Pied Cow	20	Blue Monk	18	Produce Row	13
Esparza's	11	Pix Patisserie	35	Crush	17	Roots Organic Brewing	27
Genie's	29	Rimsky-Korsakoffee		Dot's Café	32	White Eagle	4
Genoa	19	House	15	Doug Fir Lounge	D	Widmer Gasthaus	3
Kalga Kafe	31	Taqueria Nueve	8	The Egyptian	26		

Morrison and Burnside bridges, drops down to river level on bobbing concrete slabs, then crosses under the double-decked **Steel Bridge**, itself almost as old as the Hawthorne, just a few (well-protected) feet away from where Amtrak and freight trains roar by.

On the south and east end of the Esplanade, at 1945 SE Water St at Clay, the large and lavish **Oregon Museum of Science and Industry**, known as **OMSI** (daily: June–Aug 9.30am–7pm; Sept–May 9.30am–5.30pm; $9, kids $7; ☎503/797-OMSI, ⍟www.omsi.edu), offers splashy exhibits primarily geared toward children, with hundreds of interactive booths, toys, and kiosks that will also appeal to adults with only a sketchy knowledge of science. In the Space

Science hall, for example, you can check your weight on Mars and clamber into a space capsule. In addition, there's separate admission for the OMNIMAX theater ($8.50, or $6.50 for seniors and kids), planetarium ($5.50), and USS *Blueback* submarine (45min tours; daily 10am–4.10pm; $5) docked in the Willamette River and named after a type of trout. To save money, you can buy a package deal covering all OMSI's attractions for $19 ($15 for seniors and kids), though you have to choose between the planetarium and the submarine. Although there's no longer direct bus service, OMSI is an easy walk across the Hawthorne Bridge from Downtown.

Sellwood

Going south to north, the first Eastside district of any consequence is **Sellwood**, which isn't exactly close to the rest of the city, and to get there you'll have to take a lengthy bus ride; even so, it's worth a trip if you're hunting for affordable **antiques**. Indeed, while the district's commercial center is at SE 17th Avenue and Bybee Boulevard (#19 Woodstock bus) – where you can find a number of decent coffee houses, fancy eateries, and the area's signature Moreland moviehouse – its hub for "antiquing" is a little over a mile away, at SE 13th Avenue north of Tacoma Street (#41 Tacoma bus). This popular strip hosts numerous sellers of all kinds of castoffs, from authentic Victorian furniture to Pop Art novelties to worthless junk that both looks and smells bad. If you're lucky you may find, wedged into some alcove or stuck in a mezzanine, that essential black-velvet painting or pair of 1960s go-go boots you've been trying to find for several decades.

Clinton Street and the Hawthorne District

Several miles north of Sellwood there's a small pocket of interest on Clinton Street near where it intersects with SE 26th Avenue (#10 Harold bus). This two-block-long array of businesses features coffee houses and ethnic diners (Mexican to Hawaiian), vintage clothiers (including one of the city's best, Xtabay, at no. 2515), and hipster bars and clubs – foremost being the ever popular *Dot's Café*, no. 2521 (see p.111) – along with a few alternative galleries. And don't miss Portland's signature, oddball **Clinton Street Theater**, on the corner of SE 26th Avenue (℡503/238-5588, Ⓦwww.clintonsttheater.com), best known for its midnight Saturday showings of *The Rocky Horror Picture Show* and all kinds of bizarre, alternative, and underground fare.

If you're still hungry for a taste of local bohemian culture, drift a little over a half-mile north to the **Hawthorne District** (#14 Hawthorne bus), along the eponymous boulevard – this is *the* alternative shopping district for Portland, thick with boutiques, antique dealers, music- and bookstores, and novelty shops. The crux of the district is the neon spectacle of the historic **Bagdad Theater**, at SE 37th Avenue (℡503/236-9234, Ⓦwww.mcmenamins .com), a second-run moviehouse and brewpub with a stunning 1927 Moorish Revival interior, complete with ornamental columns and dark mood lighting; it's part of the local McMenamins chain. Across the street you can find a good, sizable branch of **Powell's Books** (℡503/238-1668, Ⓦwww.powells.com), while farther west club kids and costume-partygoers won't be able to resist a stop at **Red Light**, 3590 Hawthorne Blvd (℡503/963-8888), a secondhand clothing merchant that's best for its irreverent **window displays**, featuring anything from Dick and Jane dissecting a corpse to a drag-king Elvis shooting out a TV screen.

As you continue eastward on Hawthorne, you rise up the slopes of **Mount Tabor**, the only (dormant) volcano contained within the bounds of a major US city. Attracting a constant flow of hikers and dog-walkers, the small mountain makes for a robust morning trek, with the Downtown towers visible three miles away and the city's more fervent exercisers going through their paces. Enter by foot on SE Salmon Street east of 60th Avenue, or take the #15 Belmont bus to SE 69th Avenue (or the #14 Hawthorne, with a half-mile extra walk east from SE 50th Avenue).

Belmont Street to 28th Avenue

A third of a mile north of Hawthorne is **Belmont Street** (#15 Belmont bus), which runs through a truly old part of town whose most vibrant section lies from SE 30th to 37th avenues. Here you can see the type of early-twentieth-century storefronts (almost flush with the road) and neon signs that have long since disappeared from other neighborhoods. However, the district itself is far from shambling, and boasts all manner of chic, up-to-date businesses in these historic digs, from swanky café-clubs like the *Blue Monk*, no. 3341 (see p.112), to elegant teahouses like the *Tao of Tea*, no. 3430 (see p.110), to some of the region's best coffee at *Stumptown* (see p.108). As with so many other Eastside districts, this one too is built around a classic theater, the **Avalon**, no. 3451 (℡503/238-1617), which still shows movies and offers a video arcade to boot.

A few blocks north, **Laurelhurst Park** is one of the city's most attractive green spaces, a sloping concourse of hills built around a small lake, which draws myriad dog owners as well as children. The park itself was designed by the **Olmsted brothers** (sons of Frederick Law Olmsted, the landscaper of New York's Central Park). Five blocks north along SE 39th Avenue, another unmissable sight sits in the middle of a giant, European-style traffic circle – the stalwart figure of **Joan of Arc** riding her horse, carrying a banner, and swathed in blinding gold leaf.

Finally, a half-mile farther north, the area around **28th Avenue** has emerged as a destination only in the last few years, when a group of swanky restaurants, clothing boutiques, and salons set up shop here, north and south of East Burnside Street – take the #19 Glisan or #20 Burnside/Stark bus. Sure enough, this district has an anchor theater, too, the **Laurelhurst**, 2735 E Burnside St (℡503/232-5511), a remodeled mid-century gem showing second-run movies and selling microbrews and pizza.

Northeast Portland

Historically, **Northeast Portland** – east Portland north of Burnside Street – has been home to a more racially mixed population than that found in the rest of this mostly white city. In particular, many African Americans came here after redlining practices prevented them from buying homes in white enclaves. But recently the neighborhoods along what is now Martin Luther King Jr Boulevard and farther east have become some of the hippest in the city, and the spectre of gentrification looms.

The latest hot spot is **North Mississippi Avenue** (#4 Fessenden bus), which, while technically in the north part of town, is more contiguous with the districts of the northeast, given its position on the east side of the I-5 freeway. The center of the area runs from Shaver to Fremont streets and sports a lively mix of chic bars and clubs, alternative galleries, and homespun businesses that have been there for decades or longer. The scene really comes to life with the **Second Thursday Music Walk** (the neighborhood's answer to the Pearl District's First Thursday and Alberta Street's Last Thursday art events), in which local musicians entertain visitors along the sidewalk or inside shops and restaurants. A good place to relax and check out the vibe is *Amnesia Brewing*, 832 N Beech St (☎503/281-7708), one of the city's best microbrewers, offering a nice summer beer garden for outdoor people watching.

A similar, if more spread out, scene can be found on **Alberta Street**, whose axis of primary interest runs from NE 15th to 30th avenues, where upscale galleries and boutiques stand next to storefront churches, diners, and barbershops. You're bound to find an interesting mix of classes and cultures here – along with some fairly good bargains in the antique stores, junk emporia, and trinket shops. Make sure to take in the district's eye-opening gallery walk known as **Last Thursday** – a reaction to the Pearl District's stodgier First Thursday event (see p.94) – which takes place the last such day of every month from about 6pm to 10pm. It's a fervent bustle of noise, color, and chaos, in which self-taught painters and sculptors spread their work across the pavement, wild rock bands and hip-hop DJs play at every other corner, oddball galleries display all kinds of curiosities, and a thick mass of people mills about – almost to the point of claustrophobia in the summer. To get here from Downtown, take the #9 Broadway bus and get off when it crosses Alberta.

Farther south and west, and closer to the I-84 freeway, the other main attraction of Northeast Portland is the section of **NE Broadway** that runs through the charming old precinct of **Irvington**, from NE 20th to 12th avenues, with tasteful bistros and boutiques, a number of decent breakfast spots, and stately homes – from Colonial Revival to Craftsman – dating from the early twentieth century (mostly located on the several blocks north of Broadway). The adjacent **Lloyd Center** mall (Ⓦwww.lloydcenter.com), two blocks south of Broadway, offers the usual rash of chain stores, with the added draw of an ice rink. You can take the #8 NE 15th Avenue or #9 Broadway buses to get here, or hop on the MAX light rail – the mall zone itself is considered a part of **Fareless Square** and thus free for all riders from Downtown. While Irvington, unlike other old city districts, doesn't have a classic moviehouse, if you head a little over a mile west, the **Hollywood Theatre**, at NE Sandy Boulevard and 42nd Avenue (#12 Sandy bus; Ⓦwww .hollywoodtheatre.org), is well worth a look, with a flamboyant Baroque facade and steady diet of art films and foreign releases.

Finally, only sports fans should bother to visit the overhyped **Rose Quarter** (Ⓦwww.rosequarter.com), whose basketball stadium is the sole point of interest amid a clutch of overpriced restaurants and dreary chain motels. Wine lovers, however, will find a tasting room in the neighboring **Oregon Convention Center**, 777 NE MLK Blvd (Wed–Sat noon–6pm; ☎503/226-9797), where for $7 you can try the vino of fifteen of the top state wineries.

North Portland

There aren't too many reasons to travel any more than a few miles beyond Downtown to reach **North Portland**, primarily residential and industrial turf roughly west of the northern section of I-5 and best known for the **Jantzen Beach** outlet mall, which lies almost exactly between the downtown zones of Portland and Vancouver, Washington, on the south bank of the Columbia River off of I-5.

Several miles west of Jantzen Beach off of Columbia Boulevard (or Lombard Street west from I-5) sits St Johns, a small historic neighborhood that used to be its own city. It has a low-slung, working-class (former) downtown on **North Lombard Street** and some handsome old architecture amid good, unpretentious bars, theaters, and diners. Just west, the Willamette River is crossed by what is easily the city's most beautiful span, the **St Johns Bridge**, a towering green structure with lofty spires and Gothic Revival arches underneath, best viewed from below in the pleasant confines of **Cathedral Park**, off North Edison Street, which offers jazz, pop, and folk music concerts through the summer. Finally, from downtown St Johns you can hop on the #17 NW 21st Street/St Helens bus line (from Downtown) and head north to **Sauvie Island**, many residents' favorite weekend getaway. Almost completely undeveloped, the island features a pleasant, if chilly, beach on its eastern side and many miles of country lanes, seasonal fruit sellers, and evocative riverside views. It's also great for jogging and cycling, and has its own simple B&B, *River's Edge*, on the island's east side at 22502 NW Gillihan Rd (℡503/621-9856, Ⓦwww.riversedge-bb.com; ❺), with a pleasant location and a pair of basic rooms.

The Grotto

Farther out in Northeast Portland is **The Grotto** (daily 9am–5.30pm; free; ℡503/254-7371, Ⓦwww.thegrotto.org), a Roman Catholic complex located in its own wooded setting and isolated from a dismal stretch of NE Sandy Boulevard (take the #12 Sandy bus, get off around 82nd Ave, and follow the signs). The Grotto itself, officially known as the **National Sanctuary of Our Sorrowful Mother**, is a strange and quiet spot, spread out over some twenty square blocks, or sixty acres. As a religious shrine and sanctuary first established by the Servite order of monks, it offers a serene, contemplative environment, and not just for Catholics. Highlights include the **Moyer Meditation Chapel**, whose curving steel-and-glass wall perches out over a heart-stopping rock cliff; several pleasant gardens with symbolic foliage and statues; and a series of carved wooden panels depicting the Stations of the Cross. If you're not feeling overly pious, the whole effect can be a bit much, but for the spiritually inclined the Grotto is one of Portland's more notable, if anomalous, attractions.

Eating

Portland is a great place to **eat** and **drink**, with a good range of cuisines, prices, and attitudes. Your best bet may be to sample the city's **Northwest Cuisine**, which, as in Seattle, brings together fresh regional produce, organic meats, artisanal cheese, and the like with international flavors. **Seafood**, too, features prominently, with salmon a particular favorite, either grilled, seared, or baked, or incorporated into elaborate pasta dishes. **Asian** cooking can be an excellent choice: there are good, affordable sushi bars all over Portland, as well as a number of Vietnamese, Thai, and Chinese spots serving up cheap and delicious meals. All-American food like **burgers** and **steaks** is ubiquitous, with the occasional standout restaurant. For more traditional cuisines – **Italian**, **French**, and so forth – you may have to look a little harder for truly inspired fare, but you can still find it at a handful of establishments. **Indian**, **Middle Eastern**, and **Caribbean** cuisines are also a bit thin on the ground, but there are serviceable eateries if you know where to look. Lastly, **vegetarian** and **vegan** cooking is increasingly popular, especially when mixed with international cuisines (Mexican to Middle Eastern), with the best being a delicious takeoff on Northwest Cuisine and the worst being the sort of flavorless sprouts-on-spelt sandwiches and tofu casseroles that make carnivores cringe.

Restaurants

When it comes to **restaurants**, twenty years ago Downtown was pretty much it for fine dining. These days, though, it's just another neighborhood, and if anything the pulse and spirit of the best dining have moved to the Pearl District and Northwest Portland, which together offer a lively mix of bistros, bakeries, and Asian fusion and vegetarian restaurants. Also not to be overlooked is the Eastside, which has many of the city's most inventive restaurants, typically at affordable prices. Otherwise, Downtown has numerous **food carts** that dole out Mexican food, Italian panini, Indian cuisine, and *bentos* (rice and meat in a bowl); they're concentrated in parking lots at SW 5th Avenue and Oak Street and at SW 9th Avenue and Alder Street.

Downtown

Dragonfish 909 SW Park Ave ☎ 503/243-5991. Solid pan-Asian restaurant on the ground floor of the *Paramount* hotel (see p.82), with dishes such as yakisoba noodles marinated in a spicy Korean red-bean paste, ginger chicken, and sesame prawns. Popular hangout for the late-night and post-theater crowds, with a great bar-food menu.

Heathman 1009 SW Broadway ☎ 503/241-4100. One of the ritziest restaurants in town, offering outstanding Northwest Cuisine for dinner – the seared salmon is especially delicious. After your meal head to the swank lobby lounge for light jazz, desserts, and spirits.

Higgins 1239 SW Broadway at Jefferson ☎ 503/222-9070. Nationally recognized Northwest Cuisine restaurant, where fresh local ingredients and scrumptious desserts are served in cozy quarters just south of the city's main attractions. Menu rotates, but watch for the cider-glazed pork loin and winter squash lasagna. Main courses around $20–30.

Jake's Famous Crawfish 401 SW 12th Ave ☎ 503/226-1419. A landmark restaurant for more than a hundred years, with a staggering choice of fresh fish like Columbia River sturgeon, Depot Bay Dungeness crab, and spicy crawfish cakes, as well as novel combinations like salmon stuffed with crab and shrimp. Terrific desserts, too. Lunch specials under $10.

Jake's Grill 611 SW 10th Ave at Alder ☎ 503/220-1850. A superb restaurant, sister to *Jake's Famous Crawfish*, that occupies a tastefully converted 1910s building, complete with mosaic floors, glass domes, and thick wooden paneling. Check out the savory steaks, pan-fried oysters, pot roast, and salmon linguine.

Karam 316 SW Stark St ☎ 503/223-0830. Some of the city's best Lebanese fare (from $10 to $15 per entree), including a tasty lamb couscous, kofta and other kebabs, and sauteed goat *bil tfeen*. Also good are the casseroles and veggie dishes like pumpkin kibbee, with onions and walnuts. Plus, cheap lunches and breakfasts under $10.

New York City Sub Shop 725 SE Alder St ☎ 503/525-4414. Usually having a name like this outside Manhattan is a bad sign, but this sandwich joint is an exception. Hot, deliciously greasy subs, packed crowds at lunchtime, and curt, finger-snapping service give this place an air of the Big Apple. The pastrami-laden Park Avenue sub is tops.

Pazzo 627 SW Washington St, in the *Hotel Vintage Plaza* ☎ 503/228-1515. One of the city's best Italian restaurants, known for its traditional pastas, pancetta, and veal and salmon dishes – and one of the few places in town you can get decent gnocchi. Just as popular is the bar, a hot spot for networking and carousing for the Downtown elite.

Portland Steak and Chophouse 121 SW 3rd Ave, in the *Embassy Suites Hotel* ☎ 503/223-6200. Located off the hotel's chic lobby, a swanky steak-and-seafood spot offering the likes of crab cakes, crab-stuffed prawns, and wood-oven pizzas for around $15–20 per entree. There are excellent burgers, salads, and seafood on the happy-hour bar menu, for only $2–4 per item.

Ruth's Chris Steak House 309 SW 3rd Ave at Oak ☎ 503/221-4518. Fine chain steakhouse providing juicy steaks in a cheerfully upscale atmosphere. A quality range of Northwest wines and microbrews are also on offer.

Southpark Seafood Grill and Wine Bar 901 SW Salmon St at 9th Ave ☎ 503/326-1300. Bistro-style restaurant specializing in seafood accompanied by a good selection of beers and wines. It's a popular spot, appropriately looking toward the South Park Blocks. Main courses $20–25.

Old Town and Chinatown

Abou Karim 221 SW Pine St ☎ 503/223-5058. The pick of Old Town's Lebanese restaurants, quite fine for its roasted lamb, traditional stews, and *baba ghanoush* (eggplant spread). Lunch is what really draws people here, when entrée prices are $5–10 cheaper than the still affordable dinner fare.

Golden Horse 238 NW 4th Ave ☏503/228-1688. Most of the better Chinese eateries in Chinatown are located within three blocks north of Burnside on NW 4th and 5th avenues, and this is one of them, despite the spotty service. Salt-and-pepper shrimp, fresh crab, and wontons are but a few of the highlights, and most of the prices are affordable.

McCormick and Schmick's 235 SW 1st Ave at Oak ☏503/224-7522. The first location of what's become a national chain of fine seafood restaurants, offering fresh nightly specials and a lively oyster bar with a happening singles' scene. Located right off the light-rail tracks. There's another outpost at the marina at 0309 SW Montgomery, River Place district (☏503/220-1865).

Old Town Pizza 226 NW Davis St ☏503/222-9999. One of those places with as many passionate believers as dismissive detractors – the fat, gooey slices and generous portions may not be for New Yorkers, but the fans love the piles of toppings, chewy crust, and cheap prices.

Vegetarian House 22 NW 4th Ave ☏503/274-0160. One of the city's top Chinese and vegetarian restaurants, with decent prices for straightforward veggie fare including a solid wonton soup and imitation-meat dishes like mu shu beef and orange chicken. Watch the dicey neighborhood, though.

Pearl District

Bluehour 250 NW 13th Ave ☏503/226-3394. If you can handle all the pretension and "conceptual" decor, you'll find the upscale Northwest Cuisine fare to be some of the city's best – red snapper, osso buco, veal chops, and nouveau spins on traditional diner items like pot pie and chicken and dumplings. Lunch burgers and sandwiches around $10–15.

DF 1139 NW 11th Ave ☏503/243-4222. Known as "day-EFF-ay," the Spanish short form of Mexico City's Federal District, this is Portland's best Mexican food, which can match up with almost any such restaurant in the region – the delicious moles, pork and goat tacos, and wild boar carnitas are supreme, and the strong, spicy cocktails are also worth a sip.

Fenouil 900 NW 11th Ave ☏503/525-2225. If you have the money, this is a fine place to get your fill of foie gras, seared scallops and other seafood, rack of lamb, and French onion soup – pricey Continental fare that attracts a smart, black-clad crowd.

Hot Lips Pizza 721 NW 10th Ave ☏503/595-2342. Located inside the Ecotrust Building (see p.93), a pizza joint serving what may be the city's best pies – complex, delicious concoctions that use organic, locally grown ingredients.

Oba 555 NW 12th Ave ☏503/228-6161. Flashy eatery that fuses flavors from all over Latin America to create food you won't find anywhere else in town – especially during happy hour in the bar, when the tasty entrees, including coconut shrimp and *queso fundido* dip, are $3–5.

Paragon 605 NW 13th Ave ☏503/833-5060. You'll find a mix of all-American fare and Northwest Cuisine at this ever popular staple – savory pot roast with fancy herbs, well-cooked salmon and trout entrees, plus inventive desserts.

Silk 1012 NW Glisan St ☏503/248-2172. Vietnamese bistro that's been converted into a showplace for stylish, upmarket pan-Asian cuisine. The inventive curries, noodle dishes, and *pho* soups are among the highlights, and some swear by the colorful, potent cocktails.

Sungari Pearl 1105 NW Lovejoy St ☏971/222-7327. In a town not known for top-end Chinese fare, this dapper gem easily outshines its competitors, with a strong array of complex flavors in dishes such as Peking duck and General Tso's chicken. Although prices aren't cheap, the lunch specials can be a bargain.

Northwest Portland

Escape from New York Pizza 622 NW 23rd Ave ☏503/227-5423. While the service is erratic and the attitudes are just this side of scornful, this pizza joint lives up to its name with hot, flat pies that might just past muster in the Big Apple.

Filbert's 1937 NW 23rd Place ☏503/222-2130. Nothing too surprising at this upscale Northwest Cuisine restaurant – mainly staples like crab cakes, risotto, and pork chops, along with pork dumplings – but the food is still excellent and the atmosphere warm and tastefully modern.

Justa Pasta 1326 NW 19th Ave ☏503/243-2249. Unassuming hole-in-the-wall serving some of the city's best and most affordable fine Italian fare, including savory soups, delicious pastas, and locally grown Painted Hills beef. The coconut cake and assorted ice creams are also a treat.

Le Happy 1011 NW 16th Ave ☏503/226-1258. Crepes galore at this cozy bistro, sited in the shadow of a freeway ramp, with modern interpretations of French classics – Le Trash Blanc, with bacon and cheddar; chorizo and curry offerings; and many fine, berry-filled dessert crepes.

Marrakesh 1201 NW 21st Ave ☏ 503/248-9442. Plop down on the ground or into an overstuffed cushion, watch belly dancers gyrate, and partake of some truly tempting Moroccan cuisine, such as traditional stews, pitas, and desserts.

Mio Sushi 2271 NW Johnson St ☏ 503/221-1469. Fine sushi, sashimi, and combo meals, plus solid and inexpensive *bentos* (rice and meat in a bowl). There's a second location at 3962 SE Hawthorne Blvd, on the Eastside (☏ 503/230-6981).

Papa Haydn 701 NW 23rd Ave ☏ 503/223-7317. Classic French eatery whose entrees aren't what they used to be – but the place is still worth it for a taste of the delicious, fifty-odd desserts on offer, from chocolate truffle cake to baked Alaska.

Sushiville 1514 NW 23rd Ave ☏ 503/226-4710. Bright, modern, somewhat plastic-looking place, where you grab plates of ultra-cheap sushi and combo rolls off of a two-way conveyor belt moving through the restaurant. It's all a bit goofy, but the food is good and fairly authentic.

Swagat 2074 NW Lovejoy St ☏ 503/227-4300. Nothing fancy here, just cheap and straightforward Indian fare – the usual vindaloos, tandooris, and curries – prepared with just the right spiciness and served in heaping portions. Good lunch buffet, too.

Wildwood 1221 NW 21st Ave at Overton ☏ 503/248-9663. Top-shelf Northwest Cuisine restaurant with a warm interior and imaginative food like bacon-wrapped pork loin and rack of lamb. Fresh local ingredients are the rule, served up by perennial big-name chef Corey Schreiber. The downside: erratic, sometimes dreadful, service.

Eastside

Bombay Cricket Club 1925 SE Hawthorne Blvd ☏ 503/231-0740. Terrific mid-level restaurant a mile west of the main Hawthorne scene, with the town's best Indian food. Dive right into the delicious vindaloos and tandooris.

Clay's Smokehouse Grill 2932 SE Division St ☏ 503/235-4755. Among the top barbecue houses in town, serving up rich and hearty fare like ribs and pork sandwiches, spicy and delicious hot wings, and super-sweet, old-fashioned desserts like pineapple upside-down cake.

Colosso 1932 NE Broadway ☏ 503/288-3333. Dark, brooding design and low lighting give this tapas joint big hipster credentials, and the food's not bad, either. A variety of rotating, Spanish-inspired "little plates" and a smoky bar that really brings out the black-clad crowd.

Esparza's 2725 SE Ankeny St ☏ 503/234-7909. The height of Tex-Mex in the Pacific Northwest, a cheery place loaded with bric-a-brac and offering big plates of traditional fare like burritos with lamb or pork, as well as unconventional entrees like ostrich and alligator.

Genoa 2832 SE Belmont St 503/238-1464. Arguably the region's best, and certainly most expensive, Italian food; its three- to seven-course rotating seasonal menu ($45–80) offers a sumptuous taste of northern Italy.

Lauro Kitchen 3377 SE Division St ☏ 503/239-7000 The kind of local favorite that doesn't need any publicity – even the mayor has to wait for a table on weekends. If you don't mind the delay, come for some of the city's best and most affordable Northwest Cuisine.

🏃 **Le Pigeon** 738 E Burnside St ☏ 503/546-8796. Puzzling how one of the city's top restaurants has been plunked down next to a strip club on a grim Eastside stretch, but here it is: a small, expensive, but unassuming spot serving up wonderfully prepared entrees of pork medallions, filet mignon with foie gras butter (!) and squab (the titular pigeon) in a cozy modern atmosphere.

Navarre 10 NE 28th Ave ☏ 503/232-3555. Moderately priced Northwest Cuisine eatery in the heart of the Eastside. Offers tapas with local ingredients, along with some Italian and French dishes, as well as good home-made bread and desserts.

Pambiche 2811 NE Glisan St ☏ 503/233-0511. Cuban and Caribbean food served up for surprisingly low prices, including excellent plantains, shredded beef and pork, and fine desserts. The only downside is the cramped seating.

Siam Society 2703 NE Alberta St ☏ 503/922-3675. While there are plenty of excellent, affordable Thai diners around town, this mid-level entry is a welcome newcomer, doling out inventive versions of Southeast Asian fare – delicious seafood, curries, noodles, and desserts – in a moody modern setting.

Taqueria Nueve 28 NE 28th Ave ☏ 503/236-6195. Supreme *nuevo* Latino cuisine on a two-block stretch of fine restaurants north of Burnside on 28th Avenue – this one's excellent for its savory seafood, innovative takes on Mexican staples, and rich and tasty desserts.

Whiskey Soda Lounge 3226 SE Division St ☏ 503/232-1387. Popping up unexpectedly in 2006, this has suddenly become one of the city's best spots for Thai food – scrumptious curry noodles, green papaya salad, and pad Thai – though portions can be small. The adjoining takeout shack, *Pok Pok*, has much cheaper, but still excellent, food.

Cafes and coffee houses

△ Sidewalk café culture

Local **cafes** are a good bet for noshing at all hours, and coffee, too, is a predictably big deal in Portland, as it is in most urban areas of the Northwest. Specialist **coffee houses** mostly take the form of a takeaway bar with a few stools where a bewildering variety of coffees are on offer, together with cakes and snacks. Cafes often resemble informal restaurants, with arty decor and an emphasis on coffee, tea, and breakfast. Cafes and coffee houses are scattered all over the city but are at their best on the **Eastside**, where you'll find everything from the most familiar chain java merchants to the quirkiest holes-in-the-wall serving meticulously prepared coffee drinks. Rarely will you find coffee mixed up with musical performances or poetry readings; in Portland, such activities are typically relegated to brewpubs.

Downtown

Bijou Café 132 SW 3rd Ave ☎503/222-3187. Laid-back Downtown café that uses local organic ingredients in its wide-ranging menu. Lunches are especially good with meat and fish dishes as well as French toast, oyster hash, and vegetarian-friendly offerings like quesadillas and tofu.

Great Harvest Bread Company 810 SW 2nd Ave at Yamhill ☎503/224-8583. Sells a wonderful range of breads with different types featured every day. Elephantine cinnamon buns and the city's best muffins, too.

Peet's Coffee & Tea 508 SW Broadway ☎503/973-5540. Smarter than many of its corporate rivals, this cheerfully decorated coffee house offers teas as an added bonus. Just north of Pioneer Courthouse Square. There's another popular branch in the Pearl District, at 1114 NW Couch St (☎971/244-0452).

Stumptown Roasters 128 SW 3rd Ave ☎503/295-6144. Easily the best coffee in town, perhaps in the entire region, Stumptown uses seven different types of beans in its "Hair Bender" espresso blend and attracts a fervent crowd of coffee fanatics for its various gourmet drinks, including a mean chai. Two other branches at 4525 SE Division St (☎503/230-7702) and 3356 SE Belmont St (☎503/232-8889), both on the Eastside.

Three Lions Bakery 506 SW 6th Ave ☎503/224-9255. A nice selection of hearty but healthy breakfast meals (especially the tasty omelets) and lunchtime sandwiches (mix and match your own ingredients), as well as cheese- and chocolate cakes.

Voodoo Doughnut 22 SW 3rd Ave ☎503/241-4704. The apotheosis of cult bakeries in the Northwest, serving up a range of tasty, bizarre selections to late-night partygoers (open 22hr a day) – including doughnuts covered with Cocoa Puffs, stuffed with peanut butter, "bleeding" cherry jelly, or made in the alarming shape of a cream-filled "Cock & Balls." You can even get married here.

Pearl District

In Good Taste 231 NW 11th Ave ☎ 503/248-2015. A combination cooking school, kitchen-utensil store, and lunchtime cafe that has the best food you're ever likely to get under $10. The budding chefs here are in training, but they rarely make mistakes with their tasty salads, pastas, and desserts.

Mio Gelato 25 NW 11th Ave ☎ 503/226-8002. Some of the best gelato in the Pacific Northwest, located in one of the Brewery Blocks. Fruit flavors like lime, grapefruit, and kiwi are enough to make your taste buds dance. Also serves scrumptious sandwiches, soups, and espresso.

Pearl Bakery 102 NW 9th Ave ☎ 503/827-0910. A favorite lunchtime hangout for its French breads, sweet rolls, desserts, and sandwiches. Due to the weekday lunch crowds, you may have to eat standing up.

Via Delizia 1105 NW Marshall St ☎ 503/225-9300. Another solid choice for gelato, and also good for its panini, coffee drinks, and comfortable setting just off Tanner Springs Park.

World Cup 721 NW 9th Ave ☎ 503/546-7377. A reliable spot for gourmet coffee drinks, tea, and pastries in a central Pearl location across from Jamison Square Park. It's part of a chain, but much tastier than that *other* one.

Northwest Portland

Anna Bannanas 1214 NW 21st Ave ☎ 503/274-2559. The type of place that never makes the tourist brochures but that locals adore. A very laid-back coffee house serving inventive java concoctions, with a popular deck and overstuffed chairs for inspired slacking.

Besaw's Café 2301 NW Savier St at 23rd Ave ☎ 503/228-2619. One of the most long-standing cafés in Portland, dating back about a century, this old-fashioned bar and grill serves good-sized burgers, steaks, and sandwiches, plus solid, inexpensive breakfasts.

Ken's Artisan Bakery 338 NW 21st Ave ☎ 503/248-2202. Delicious sandwiches and savory coffees are on offer at this comfortable spot, just south of the busy part of 21st Avenue, but the undeniable highlight is the bread – rich, complex, and handcrafted with local ingredients.

Kornblatt's Delicatessen and Bagel Bakery 628 NW 23rd Ave ☎ 503/242-0055. Portland's version of an East Coast deli – not quite authentic, but the mouthwatering bagels, breads, and smoked meats are unbeatable if you're cruising the boutiques on 23rd Avenue.

St Honore 2335 NW Thurman St ☎ 503/445-4352. It's all about dessert at this top-of-the-line French patisserie, tempting you with fine croissants, berry-laden tarts, chocolate confections, and good coffee, sandwiches, and bread, too.

Eastside

Bread and Ink Café 3610 SE Hawthorne Blvd ☎ 503/239-4756. Busy, spacious café on the Eastside that puts together a varied menu of bagels, burritos, and Mediterranean food. The dessert selection is often excellent.

Cadillac Café 1801 NE Broadway ☎ 503/287-4750. Great, popular place for breakfast and lunch, with "French custard waffles" (encrusted with crumbled hazelnuts) that are among the finest in the city. Its name comes from a pink Cadillac on view inside behind glass.

Crema 2728 SE Ankeny St ☎ 503/234-0206. Prime espresso and other gourmet coffee drinks, solid sandwiches, and a range of tasty cookies and other baked goods make this quiet spot a good choice for dropping in; it's just south of the main action on 28th Ave.

Genie's 1101 SE Division St ☎ 503/445-9777. If you want to visit here on a weekend morning, be prepared to wait on a bench outside (in the rain, wind, cold) – it's worth it for some of the most flavorful and inexpensive omelets, scrambles, and cocktails in southeast Portland.

Kalga Kafé 4147 SE Division St ☎ 503/236-4770. Dark, mysterious Indian-vegetarian hangout where you can munch on green curry, potato pastries, sushi, and assorted finger foods while listening to the hypnotic sound of Bhangra DJs on weekend nights.

Milo's City Café 1325 NE Broadway ☎ 503/288-6456. Easily one of the city's most crowded and tempting spots for breakfast. Nothing too fancy here, just straightforward waffles, eggs, and omelets served in a variety of ways, along with some supreme Dungeness crab cakes.

Pied Cow 3244 SE Belmont Ave ☎ 503/230-4866. Long-standing favorite for coffee, tea, and dessert in a stately Victorian house, with late-night hours, lush garden seating, and the option to puff fruit-flavored tobacco from a hookah.

Pix Patisserie 3402 SE Division ☎ 503/232-4407. Hot spot with a range of inventive French desserts prepared by a Parisian-trained chef known as the "Pixie." The cafe's Belgian beers are also worth a quaff, and its bright red walls are unmistakable.

Rimsky-Korsakoffee House 707 SE 12th Ave ⓣ503/232-2640. Despite having an awful name and truly glacial service, this is an excellent place to linger for hours on end over dessert and coffee. Immensely popular with bohemians and slackers.

Tao of Tea 3430 SE Belmont St ⓣ503/736-0119. More than 120 kinds of tea are served in an exquisite room with zen-like decor and a somewhat pretentious air, in the heart of the Belmont scene.

Nightlife

Portland has a surprising number of **nightlife** offerings for a city its size – far more good choices, in fact, than can be listed below. The comprehensive *Willamette Week* (Ⓦ www.wweek.com) and the slimmer *Portland Mercury* (Ⓦ www.portlandmercury.com) carry up-to-the-minute weekly **listings** and reviews of what's on and where. They're available free in the self-service stands on many street corners and at leading bookshops. The Friday edition of the *Oregonian*, the main local newspaper, has a useful listings in its A&E (arts and entertainment) section.

Bars and microbreweries

The Northwest's proud brewing traditions have been revived in Portland's many large and small **microbreweries**, where you can enjoy porters, ales, stouts, and other beers made on the premises – the Eastside is the center of this grassroots activity. The local **McMenamins** chain operates many such places, often in combination with hotels and movie theaters – specific venues are mentioned throughout this chapter and in the Accommodation listings; for a full list, see Ⓦ www.mcmenamins.com. Many of Portland's **bars** operate till two in the morning, and some open up again as early as 7am. You're apt to find almost anything in them, from the most obscure oatmeal-chocolate porter to big-name industrial brews like the redoubtable Pabst Blue Ribbon, supposedly more popular here than anywhere else in the US – locals just call it by its acronym, PBR.

Downtown

Goose Hollow Inn and Tavern 1927 SW Jefferson St ⓣ503/228-7010. Great microbrews, the city's best Reuben sandwich, and a convenient location near the MAX tracks, a mile west of Downtown. Watch for owner Bud Clark, the colorful city mayor in the 1980s, known for his signature slogan, "Whoop whoop!"

Huber's 411 SW 3rd Ave ⓣ503/228-5686. Hands-down the most historic bar around, an 1879 marvel with a stained-glass skylight, classic brass fixtures, terrazzo flooring, and mahogany paneling. Also famed for its roast turkey sandwiches and Spanish coffee – hot or iced – and a fine array of beers, wines, and cocktails.

Portland City Grill 111 SW 5th Ave, 30th floor of the US Bancorp Tower ⓣ503/450-0030. Skip the pricey meals and head straight for happy hour in the lounge, which offers not only copious booze and delicious and cheap appetizers but also one of the best views of the city. Beware the late-night

hours, though, when the place becomes a teeming meat market.

Rock Bottom Brewery 206 SW Morrison St at 2nd Ave ⓣ503/796-2739. Fairly conventional, but popular, chain microbrewery. The bar food here is filling and tasty, but it's probably best to spend your time knocking back ales and porters.

Tugboat Brewing Company 711 SW Ankeny St ⓣ503/226-2508. Although this place is basically a hole in the wall in a dingy location, make no mistake – some people claim these ales are among the city's best, and with live jazz and cheap bar food to boot, it's hard to go wrong.

Old Town and Chinatown

Kells 112 SW 2nd Ave ⓣ503/227-4057. Long-standing favorite Irish bar, with fine authentic cuisine (Irish stews, soda bread) and a range of microbrews, imported beers, and of course, Irish (and Scotch) whiskey.

Shanghai Tunnel 211 SW Ankeny St ☏503/220-4001. Located just off Burnside Street, a subterranean bar popular with hipsters and offering Asian-style soul food.

Tiger Bar 317 NW Broadway ☏503/467-4111. Über-hip lounge with a tiger-striped bar and long banquettes. Dark, sultry, and smoker-friendly, with late-night food and guest DJs.

Voleur 111 SW Ash St ☏503/227-3764. Right by the MAX tracks, with terrific drink specials and a super, cheap bar menu of ribs, crab cakes, and fries with spicy blackberry sauce.

Pearl District

Bridgeport Brewing 1313 NW Marshall St ☏503/241-3621. The huge warehouse that's home to Oregon's oldest microbrewery (1984) has recently been extensively remodeled into a sleeker space. Its tasty pizzas and bar food make for good ballast when quaffing pints of primo Bridgeport Ale.

Ringlers Annex 1223 SW Stark St ☏503/525-0520. Great people watching in the sizable basement of the ornate wedge-shaped 1917 Flatiron Building. Companion bar *Ringlers* is two blocks away at 1332 W Burnside St (☏503/225-0627). Both are good for a swig before a show at the Crystal Ballroom (see p.112).

Rogue Ales Public House 1339 NW Flanders St ☏503/222-5910. One of the top choices for microbrew-guzzling in the Pearl District, with an eye-popping range of brews – from Yellow Snow Ale to a jalapeño beer – but best for its scrumptious Chocolate Stout. Also has solid burgers and BBQ fare.

Northwest Portland

The Gypsy 625 NW 21st Ave ☏503/796-1859. Purple-colored joint located across from the Cinema 21 theater, doling out decent diner food and potent classic cocktails, with rollicking Tues-night karaoke, too.

MacTarnahan's Brewing Company 2730 NW 31st Ave ☏503/226-7623. Beers like BlackWatch Cream Porter and Mac's Ale on tap have made this one of the city's more esteemed microbreweries. The menu features reliable fare with burgers, soups, and grilled meats, either indoors or on the outdoor patio.

New Old Lompoc 1616 NW 23rd Ave ☏503/225-1855. Great, creaky old space with a sizable back patio that draws beer lovers for its broad range of suds – try the "LSD" brew for a kick or the seasonal, fresh-hopped IPAs – and good burgers, pasta, and sandwiches at cheap prices.

Eastside

ACME Food and Drink 1305 SE 8th Ave ☏503/230-9020. Though located on a charmless industrial side street in inner SE Portland, this hip and lively bar and club still draws those in the know with its funky DJ nights, movie screenings, range of beer and spirits, and savory bar menu.

The Alibi 4024 N Interstate Ave ☏503/287-5335. The pinnacle of Polynesian tiki bars, a fun and divey joint in North Portland that has cheap, powerful drinks, a spirited atmosphere, and a Thurs–Sun karaoke scene that's among the city's best.

Amnesia Brewing 832 N Beech St ☏503/281-7700. Terrific summertime people watching in this microbrewer's beer garden, set on a happening stretch of the North Mississippi District. Quaff a flavorful brew or sample a burger or a banger from the pub menu.

Dot's Café 2521 SE Clinton St ☏503/235-0203. In the center of the Clinton District, a cheap late-night spot with stiff booze and solid music. Decked out in garage-sale decor, it also offers a classic bacon cheeseburger, vegan burritos, and a mean grilled-cheese sandwich.

Horse Brass Pub 4534 SE Belmont St ☏503/232-2202. The voluminous beer list loaded with micro- and Eurobrews – considered one of the best in the region – isn't the only reason people flock here, nor is the savory British pub menu of Scotch eggs, bangers and mash, and the like. It's also one of the rare smoke-friendly (and -heavy) places in Portland.

Lucky Labrador 915 SE Hawthorne Blvd ☏503/236-3555. Just a mile and a half west of the main Hawthorne action, this unpretentious, dog-friendly brewpub occupies a large warehouse space with an outdoor patio. Fresh ales, great sandwiches, and BBQ specials.

Produce Row 204 SE Oak St ☏503/232-8355. Be one of the rare tourists at this local favorite. It's stuck in an unglamorous location by the railroad tracks but is a paradise for beer lovers, with nearly thirty taps and countless bottled brews. Also has a nice range of live music from country to rock and a colorful clientele of hard-bitten regulars and even a few newbies.

Roots Organic Brewing 1520 SE 7th Ave ☏503/235-7668. The epitome of Portland "Beervana": this upstart microbrewer has won a large and devoted following for its selection of inspired, handcrafted concoctions on tap – the Woody IPA, EXXX Calibur Imperial Stout, Heather Ale, and Island Red, to name a few.

Widmer Gasthaus 929 N Russell St ☎ 503/281-3333. The flagship bar and restaurant of this increasingly popular brewer, known not only for its Hefeweizen but also for its Broken Halo IPA and Snowplow Milk Stout; also serves tasty burgers and sandwiches and heavy German pub food.

Live music venues

For **live music**, Portland is a small but vital presence on the national map, with countless alternative and punk bands relocating here in the last few years. To get a sense of the scene, head to East and West Burnside streets, where the coolest venues are located. In addition, there is a reasonable range of folk, rock, jazz, and blues spots in Old Town, the Pearl District, Northwest Portland, and the Eastside. Except for big-name bands, cover charges – where they exist at all – are minimal or at least affordable.

Rock and pop

Ash Street Saloon 225 SW Ash St ☎ 503/226-0430. Popular Old Town club featuring a wide range of bands, many of them playing blues, rock, or metal. A place to spot up-and-coming local talent, with solid microbrews on tap.

Berbati's Pan 10 SW 3rd Ave ☎ 503/248-4579. Features a reconstructed nineteenth-century European bar and a nightly selection of eclectic bands – local to international – usually for $15 or less. The downside is the oversize, sometimes empty space.

Crystal Ballroom 1332 W Burnside St ☎ 503/778-5625. On the top story of the building housing the *Ringlers* bar (see p.111) there's a nineteenth-century dance hall with a "floating" floor on springs. Bands range from hippie to hip-hop, and the site features good DJs in "Lola's Room" on the second floor.

Dante's 1 SW 3rd Ave ☎ 503/226-6630. Perhaps the city's hippest nightspot. Cabaret acts and live music mix with the club's signature "Sinferno" Sunday strip shows and "Karaoke from Hell" Mondays. Wed showcase the lounge-punk stylings of Storm and the Balls, whose lead singer made a memorable appearance on TV's *Rock Star: Supernova*.

Doug Fir 830 E Burnside St ☎ 503/231-WOOD. One of the city's prime venues for alt-country, dance, and indie rock despite its cramped underground space with limited room to groove.

Rose Garden Arena 1401 N Wheeler Ave ☎ 503/224-4400. Where the big touring rock and pop acts appear. On the east side of the Willamette River, just north of Downtown, the arena seats 21,000 and is part of a large, bland shopping complex.

Roseland Theater 8 NW 6th Ave ☎ 503/224-2038. Located in one of the city's dicier areas, but a top spot for rock and alternative acts on the verge of touring the bigger concert halls with higher-priced tickets.

Towne Lounge 714 SW 20th Place ☎ 503/241-8696. You won't have heard of any of the underground acts that experiment here with psychedelia, metal, punk, avant-garde, jazz, and countless other styles, but this spot is a great, inexpensive venue to find out what's bubbling under the surface of the local music scene.

Wonder Ballroom 128 NE Russell St ☎ 503/284-8686. A specially renovated old ballroom that now plays host to some of the more intriguing national and international acts in indie rock and other alternative styles. Just off a gritty stretch of MLK Blvd, so drive or take a cab.

Jazz and blues

Benson Hotel 309 SW Broadway ☎ 503/228-2000. Live jazz in one of the city's smartest Downtown hotels. Mostly local acts in mainstream styles, but occasional touring stars, too.

Blue Monk 3341 SE Belmont St ☎ 503/595-0575. A hip little spot along a rejuvenated Eastside stretch, where you can devour serviceable Italian food upstairs and hear the sounds of local jazz performers downstairs. Music Tues–Sat.

Green Room 2280 NW Thurman St ☎ 503/228-6178. A tiny, unassuming club on the northern edge of Northwest Portland that offers some of the better folk, blues, and soul acts in town.

Jimmy Mak's 300 NW 10th Ave ☎ 503/295-6542. One of the few choices for nightly jazz in a town not known to swing. Come by to hear local Mel Brown or visiting name acts.

Country and folk

Alberta Street Pub 1036 NE Alberta St ☎ 503/284-7665. Combination Irish bar and music venue that appeals for its regular shows of earnest, skilled bluegrass and folk performers.

Laurelthirst Public House 2958 NE Glisan St ☎503/232-1504. A smoky, relaxed lounge for listening to roots and folk performers strum and fiddle through traditional tunes and modern takes on bluegrass, Cajun, and other Americana styles.

White Eagle 836 N Russell St ☎503/282-6810. In the McMenamins chain of bar/hotels, this is the only one devoted to roots, folk, and country music, with a little jazz and rock thrown in for good measure, in a long brick-walled space that attracts attentive music lovers.

Clubs

The **clubs** in town often feature a revolving cast of DJs and musical styles, though some present dance music in the salsa and reggae vein. **Gay**-oriented clubs are generally located around SW Stark Street, paralleling West Burnside a block south, from 10th to 13th avenues.

XV 15 SW 2nd Ave ☎503/790-9090. Known as Fifteen, this darkly lit, brick-walled place has solid cocktails, comfortable seating, and a regular array of DJs (Mon, Thurs, Sat) spinning your favorite techno, house, and other electronica. Near the heart of Skid Row, though.

Aura 1022 W Burnside St ☎503/597-2872. If you've got to spend a night out in a trendy bar, this chic, minimalist scene will suffice, with fine cocktails and Northwest Cuisine, and a rotating selection of DJs who provide old-school hip-hop, funk, and soul for your aural needs.

Crush 1400 SE Morrison St ☎503/235-8150. Trendy but not torturous, this sleek modern spot has novel drinks, a smoke-friendly room, and a savory selection of DJs delving into techno and other electronica on Thurs–Sun evenings.

Embers Avenue 11 NW Broadway ☎503/222-3082. An often-crowded club with drag shows in the gay-oriented back room and high-energy dancing, frenetic DJs, and go-go cages in the straight-leaning room in front.

Fernando's Hideaway 824 SW 1st Ave at Yamhill ☎503/248-4709. Popular Spanish place in a handsome old building with a restaurant and bar serving wonderful and authentic tapas. Also offers salsa lessons Thurs–Sat night, and thumping salsa music on the busy dancefloor.

Fez Ballroom 316 SW 11th Ave, 3rd floor ☎503/226-4171. Has interesting shows with a variety of DJs and live-music acts – rock, folk, electronica, and hip-hop, among other styles – plus occasional theme nights and costume parties.

Goodfoot 2845 SE Stark St ☎503/239-9292. Frenetic live-music joint and dance club decorated in mildly retro decor and always sweaty, smoky, and crammed on weekends – but still worth it to hear top-notch DJs spinning and scratching the lights out, plus the occasional live band.

Holocene 1001 SE Morrison St ☎503/239-7639. Though packed with would-be hipsters posing at point-blank range, an essential spot on the local DJ scene, offering a broad range of cocktails and even broader spectrum of nightly electronica.

Saucebox 214 SW Broadway ☎503/241-3393. Fine restaurant and bar that features great pan-Asian cuisine, colorful cocktails, and eclectic DJ music (Wed–Sat) that attracts both black-clad poseurs and serious hipsters.

Performing arts and film

Portland's **performing arts** scene revolves around the Portland Center for the Performing Arts (PCPA) at 1111 SW Broadway (☎503/248-4335 or 224-4000, ⓦwww.pcpa.com; see p.86) – though confusingly the center often includes the Keller Auditorium on SW 3rd Avenue and Clay Street, too (☎503/274-6560; see p.89). Broadway's PCPA is where you'll find much of the city's best **theater**, though the refurbished Portland Armory (see p.94) is also worth a visit, and several good-quality companies perform elsewhere in smaller digs. PCPA is the place to go for **classical music** and home to the prestigious Oregon Symphony Orchestra. During the summer, **free concerts** are held at Pioneer Courthouse Square, Tom McCall Waterfront Park, the zoo, and the amphitheater at the International Rose Test Garden in Washington Park. For arts listings, see the *Oregonian*'s Friday A&E (arts and entertainment) section or the alternative *Willamette Week* and *Portland Mercury*, both available free from street racks or online at ⓦwww.wweek.com and ⓦwww.portland mercury.com, respectively.

Classical music, dance, and opera

With some exceptions, **classical music** and **opera** are predictably the most cautious in their programming, generally focusing on light pops fare and the traditional warhorses of the canon, though the **dance** scene has been a bit more adventurous in recent years. As for venues, these can vary widely, with **prices** depending largely on the prominence of the institution – anywhere from $5 for an alternative dance show in an art gallery to $100 for a big-name concert at one of the major venues. As always, check arts listings (see above) for the best options.

Chamber Music Northwest ☏503/294-6400, ⓦwww.cmnw.org. Presents affordable chamber music in rotating venues around town, often at Reed College, and appreciated for its wide-ranging repertoire – from the spiritual odes of Palestrina to the modern stylings of Shostakovich, with plenty of Bach and Haydn in between.

Keller Auditorium SW 3rd Ave and Clay St ☏503/274-6560. Large, ungainly venue for concerts, operas, and big touring theatrical productions – typically familiar musicals.

Oregon Ballet Theater 1120 SW 10th Ave ☏503/222-5538, ⓦwww.obt.org. Oregon's premier ballet company has a core repertoire of the classics, but they do modern and experimental pieces, too. The company offers performances at the Keller Auditorium.

Oregon Symphony Orchestra 921 SW Washington St ☏503/228-1353, ⓦwww.orsymphony.org. A first-rate orchestra that performs at the Arlene Schnitzer Concert Hall between Sept and May. The orchestra's Teutonically oriented program, led by Carlos Kalmar, is beefed up with special events and guest performers.

PICA (Portland Institute for Contemporary Art) office at 224 NW 13th Ave ☏503/242-1419, ⓦwww.pica.org. Mixes art, music, dance, and even opera into a variety of hard-to-classify performances, often in festivals, throughout the year. One of the prime performance-art entities in the city.

Portland Center for the Performing Arts (PCPA) 1111 SW Broadway at Main ☏503/248-4335 or 224-4000, ⓦwww.pcpa.com. Offers a varied program of performing arts from theater to chamber music, opera and ballet. Comprises the Arlene Schnitzer Concert Hall and the Antoinette Hatfield Hall, the latter of which is divided into the Dolores Winningstad Theater and the Newmark Theater.

Portland Opera 1515 SW Morrison St ☏503/241-1407, ⓦwww.portlandopera.org. Puts on five annual productions, mixing the usual operatic warhorses with a sprinkling of more modern works. The season runs from Sept to July, with performances at the Keller Auditorium.

Theater

Theater in Portland has many devoted adherents, and you're apt to see almost anything on its variety of stages, from canonical works by Shakespeare, Ibsen, and Shaw to quirky shows that straddle the border between drama and performance art. The PCPA is the centerpiece of the major venues (and usually draws the tourists and suburbanites) but is far from the only worthwhile facility, especially with the remodelling of the Portland Armory (see p.94). Smaller venues can be found throughout the Pearl District and the Eastside, usually for much cheaper **prices** – around $5–15 per ticket, compared to $25 or more at the PCPA. You're well advised to scour the weekly arts listings for the full range of shows and venues.

Artists Repertory Theater 1516 SW Alder St ☏503/241-1278, ⓦwww.artistsrep.org. The emphasis here is on modern plays and modern adaptations of classic works, with imaginative scripts, striking settings, and strong acting.

Back Door Theater 4319 SE Hawthorne Blvd
☎503/993-9062. A good spot to catch modern
plays – both avant-garde and classics – performed
by some of the city's most talented theater groups.

Imago 17 SE 8th Ave ☎503/231-9581,
🖥www.imagotheatre.com. Portland's one
essential theater troupe, and its only nationally
known ensemble. The inventive, often bizarre group
puts on shows drawn from modern and classic
texts, mixing different acting styles, creative
staging and lighting, and puppets and multimedia
to achieve inexplicable, wonderful results.

Liminal 403 NW 5th Ave ☎503/890-2993, 🖥www
.liminalgroup.org. Anything conceptual, minimal, and
experimental is fodder for this daring company,
which is willing to tinker with time, space, and
audience endurance in pursuit of artistic perfection.
Performance schedule is somewhat irregular.

Portland Center Stage at the Portland Armory,
128 NW 11th Ave, ☎503/248-6309, 🖥www.pcs
.org. Portland's premier professional theater troupe
offers contemporary and classical works in the
stylish new-old space of a former armory
converted into the Gerding Theater.

Theater! Theatre! 3430 SE Belmont St
☎503/239-5919, 🖥www.tripro.org. Quirky,
comic, sometimes melodramatic plays and
musicals written and performed by some of the
city's more unheralded thespians. Compelling,
entertaining work.

Third Rail Repertory 5340 N Interstate Ave
☎503/235-1101. Performing at the Interstate
Firehouse Cultural Center, this troupe serves up a
hefty helping of postmodern angst and political
Sturm und Drang, with the odd comedy to
lighten the mood.

Film

If you're interested in watching a **film**, it's hard to avoid the monolithic Regal chain, which owns most of the town's theaters. Decent alternatives include Cinema 21, 616 NW 21st Ave (☎503/223-4515, 🖥www.cinema21.com), for foreign and independent movies; the Clinton, 26th Avenue at Clinton Street (☎503/238-5588, 🖥www.clintonsttheater.com), for art-house, cult, and underground cinema; the Living Room Theater, SW 10th Avenue at Stark (☎971/222-2010), with a Northwest Cuisine eatery and screening rooms for modern indie works; and the grand Hollywood, 4122 NE Sandy Blvd (☎503/281-4215, 🖥www.hollywoodtheatre.org), for all of the above kinds of movies. The **Northwest Film Center**, at the Portland Art Museum, 1219 SW Park Ave (☎503/221-1156, 🖥www.nwfilm.org), shows art-house, foreign-language, and classic movies. The selection is adventurous and often obscure, and be sure to look out for the themed evenings and frequent festivals. There are also many good historic neighborhood **moviehouses** on the Eastside that show art films, second runs, and classics; these are listed in the respective sections on each district.

Listings

Banks Major branches Downtown include Bank of
America, 1001 SW 5th Ave (☎503/279-3445);
Washington Mutual, 1239 NW Couch St
(☎503/295-7827); Wells Fargo, 1300 SW 5th Ave
(☎503/886-3340); and US Bank, 1040 NW Lovejoy
St (☎503/412-3420). ATMs are located at the
airport and across town.

Bike rental Bike Central, 113 SW Naito Pkwy
☎503/227-4439; Citybikes, 734 SE Ankeny St
☎503/239-6951; Fat Tire Farm, 2714 NW
Thurman St ☎503/222-3276; Waterfront Bicycle
Rental ☎503/227-1719.

Bookstores Powell's City of Books, 1005 W
Burnside St (daily 9am–11pm; ☎503/228-4651,
🖥www.powells.com; see p.94), is a huge labyrinth
of new and secondhand books. Other good
branches include Powell's Hawthorne, 3723 SE
Hawthorne Blvd (☎503/238-1668), and Powell's
PDX, inside the airport (☎503/249-1950).

Emergencies Police and medical emergencies
☎911.

Gay and lesbian *Just Out* (🖥www.justout.com),
a free, twice-monthly news sheet, has articles on
gay issues and provides cultural and social

listings. The best place to pick it up is at Powell's City of Books, 1005 W Burnside St (see above). Most of Portland's clubs are gay- and lesbian-friendly. Otherwise, many gay-male bars and clubs can be found on SW Stark Street between 10th and 13th avenues; the main, perhaps the only, lesbian bar is *The Egyptian*, 3701 SE Division St (T503/236-8689).

Hospital The most convenient: Legacy Good Samaritan Hospital and Medical Center, 1015 NW 22nd Ave T503/413-7711, Wwww.legacyhealth.org; and Providence Medical Center, 4805 NE Glisan St T503/215-1111, Wwww.providence.org/oregon.

Internet access Downtown at FedEx Kinko's (6am–11pm), 221 SW Alder St (T503/224-6550); many free terminals at the Downtown library, with a short waiting time.

Library Downtown's grand Central Library 801 SW 10th Ave (T503/988-5123, Wwww.multcolib.org), is a Renaissance Revival jewel with a sizable collection spread over three floors and a reading room for books and magazines. Annual circulation is 16 million, making for an average of 24 books checked out per year for each county resident.

Parks Information on Portland city parks at 1120 SW 5th Ave, Suite 1302 (T503/823-PLAY, Wwww.portlandonline.com/parks).

Pharmacy 24hr pharmacy at Walgreen's, 940 SE 39th Ave at Belmont Street (T503/238-6053).

Police Central Precinct, 1111 SW 2nd Ave T503/823-0097.

Post office The main city post office, and by far the best, is in the Pearl District, 715 NW Hoyt St, zip code 97208 (Mon–Fri 7am–6.30pm, Sat 8.30am–5pm; T1-800/275-8777). Letters can be sent c/o General Delivery and picked up during public hours; if you're receiving mail at someone else's address, it should include "c/o" and the regular occupant's name.

Road conditions T503/222-6721.

Tax Oregon has no sales tax, but hotel taxes in the city are currently 12.5 percent.

Weather T503/261-9246, Wwww.wrh.noaa.gov/portland.

Women's Crisis and Rape Hotline T503/235-5333.

2

The Columbia River Gorge

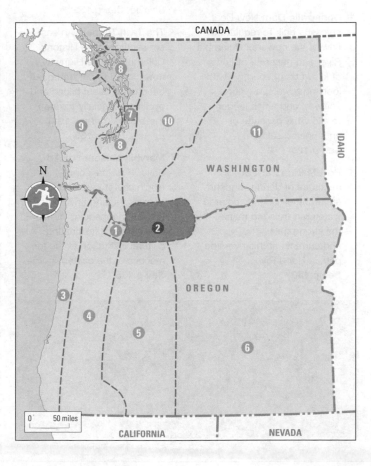

CHAPTER 2 # Highlights

✳ **Multnomah Falls** One of the most popular of Oregon's many scenic attractions, this thin torrent of water topples over a high basaltic ledge and crashes down dramatically into two pools surrounded by thick forest. See p.123

✳ **Bonneville Dam** New Deal colossus built to regulate the flow of the powerful Columbia River and generate millions of kilowatts of energy – with looming towers, a giant spillway, and a fish ladder to allow the passage of endangered salmon. See p.125

✳ **Port Marina Park** See a multitude of daring windsurfers and their brightly colored watercraft trying to manage the strong gales and currents at this riverside park in Hood River. See p.130

✳ **Timberline Lodge** The epitome of a classic mountain lodge – a rough-hewn stone-and-timber edifice sitting on an upper slope of Mount Hood, with a classic 1930s design and a forbidding, rugged presence in *The Shining*. See p.132

✳ **The Twin Tunnels** An eastern section of the Historic Columbia Gorge Highway, now closed to car traffic but offering excellent hiking and cycling, especially through these stark, narrow 1917 tunnels. See p.133

✳ **Maryhill Museum of Art** Savor Russian icons, Rodin sculptures, oddball chess sets, and tiny French fashion mannequins at this unexpectedly fascinating cultural institution at the far reaches of the eastern gorge. See p.135

△ Windsurfing in the Columbia River Gorge

The Columbia River Gorge

he mighty **Columbia River** rises in Canada's Rocky Mountains and takes a circuitous path through eastern Washington before heading west toward the Pacific, defining much of the border between Washington and Oregon along the way. The **Columbia River Gorge** is the most scenic part of the river's course, a spectacular eighty-mile corridor of forest, cliffs, and waterfalls that stretches from Corbett, Oregon – which lies 22 miles east of Portland – to Maryhill, Washington.

Though I-84 runs along the river all the way from Portland east to Boardman, the best way to view the trees and waterfalls at the western end of the gorge is by taking the delightful 22-mile **Historic Columbia River Highway**, roughly paralleling the freeway to the south. It connects the two biggest sights within easy reach of Portland – **Multnomah Falls**, a strikingly beautiful tower of mist that is the state's top natural attraction, and **Bonneville Dam**, the New Deal colossus immortalized by folk singer Woody Guthrie, and one of many such titans that now control the river's flow.

Farther east, roughly halfway along the gorge, pocket-size **Hood River** is a lively little town with several good places to stay and a laid-back vibe that attracts sports enthusiasts from around the region. For many, there's nothing better than windsurfing on the river, whose waves blow through with nice intensity as they're channeled in the natural wind tunnel of the gorge, and then biking around the orchard country of the Hood River Valley south of town. Skiing is predictably a big wintertime draw at nearby Mount Hood (it's just 55 miles from Portland), but the peak is also excellent for its biking and hiking terrain and for the stately Timberline Lodge, whose New Deal grandeur was put to menacing use as an outdoor location in Stanley Kubrick's cinematic take on Stephen King's novel *The Shining*.

To the northeast, in Washington, the verdant forests are left behind for bare, sweeping steppes, where you can find the art collection of the eccentric tycoon Sam Hill, displayed in the singular **Maryhill Museum of Art**, and the workaday town of **The Dalles**. Along the way are some unexpectedly good places to hike, including the restored **Twin Tunnels**, hinting at a distant age of early-twentieth-century motor transport.

Apart from hiking, the best way to see the gorge is by **car** – there's no public transit along the Historic Columbia River Highway, though Greyhound **buses**

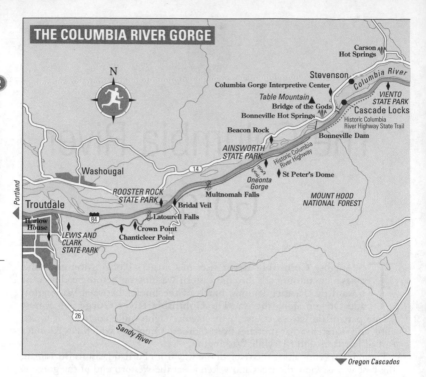

THE COLUMBIA RIVER GORGE

N

Carson
Hot Springs

Stevenson

Columbia River

Columbia Gorge Interpretive Center

Table Mountain

VIENTO
STATE PARK

Bridge of the Gods

Cascade Locks

Bonneville Hot Springs

Historic Columbia
River Highway State Trail

Beacon Rock

Bonneville Dam

AINSWORTH
STATE PARK

Historic Columbia
River Highway

St Peter's Dome

Washougal

14

Oneonta
Gorge

MOUNT HOOD
NATIONAL FOREST

ROOSTER ROCK
STATE PARK

Multnomah Falls

Portland

Bridal Veil

Troutdale

84

Latourell Falls

Harlow
House

Crown Point

LEWIS AND
CLARK
STATE PARK

Chanticleer Point

26

Sandy River

▼ Oregon Cascados

do stop at Hood River and The Dalles as they whiz along I-84 to and from
Portland. Another alternative is Gray Line (☎503/684-3322, ext. 21, or
1-888/684-3322, ext. 2, Ⓦ www.grayline.com), which offers **day tours** (April–
Oct; 4 weekly; 4hr 30min; $47) of the gorge from Portland, leaving from
Pioneer Courthouse Square (see p.84). While the scenery is pleasant enough on
such a tour, it's only when you take one of the many trails dotted along the
historic highway that the real charm of this lushly forested ravine becomes
apparent – which means it's a good idea to spend the night locally, preferably at
Hood River.

Some history

Native tribes such as the Yakima and Klickitat had fished and transported
goods along the Columbia River for centuries by the time the exhausted pair
Meriwether Lewis and William Clark reached "**The Great River of the
West**," as it came to be known, in 1806. Less than forty years after their 28-
month trek across the continent, the gorge was the site of the perilous final
leg of the **Oregon Trail** (see p.188), negotiated by pioneer families on
precarious rafts, which were known to buckle and capsize in the tumultuous
currents of the fast-flowing water. Years later when **gold** was discovered in
eastern Oregon in 1861, the river turned into a lifeline for pioneering
miners and farmers. By the 1880s the river's steamboats were already
carrying tourists and because of their size were managing the currents much
better than the flimsy rafts of decades past.

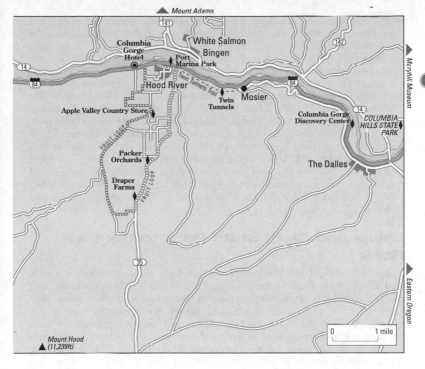

By the twentieth century, the biggest events in the Columbia Gorge have been the construction of a series of massive hydroelectric **dams**, such as Bonneville (see p.125), starting in the 1930s and continuing apace until the 1960s. Not only generating energy for a wide swath of the West in today's world, these dams (along with Washington's Grand Coulee and Nevada's Hoover) played a large role in creating the hydropower necessary for the energy- and water-intensive **aluminum** industry, which reached its peak during World War II in the creation of military supplies and war material. The dams' more recent effects have been much more deleterious, though: not only have they cut off the migration routes of **salmon**, the region's signature fish, but they've decimated the native tribes that once depended on them: legendary spearfishing sites like Celilo Falls are now submerged under many feet of water.

Historic Columbia River Highway

The advent of automotive tourism in the early twentieth century prompted the construction in 1915 of what's now known as the **Historic Columbia River Highway**. Although this 22-mile stretch of road, now bypassed by Interstate 84, offers the area's prettiest views and most striking landscapes, it was not always regarded so fondly. With its narrow lanes and hairpin curves, the road could be a nightmare to travel, especially when the weather got bad; in later decades big-rig trucking threatened not only commuter traffic but commuters themselves. The construction of I-84 in the 1960s relieved the strain and gave the highway a historic, rosy glow. Most visitors come from Portland via I-84, getting off at Corbett (Exit 22), but there are several other access points, including one at Multnomah Falls (Exit 31).

If you're interested in taking the route for its entirety, you should start at the uneventful burg of **Troutdale**, where the *Edgefield*, 2126 SW Halsey St (see "Accommodation," p.82), a fun brewpub-hotel that was formerly mental asylum and old folks' home, provides a good base. A little over a mile west, near where the highway officially starts, the stately **Harlow House**, 726 E Columbia River Hwy (June–Sept Tues–Sun 1–4pm; Oct–May Sat & Sun 1–4pm; donation; ☎503/661-2164, ⓦwww.troutdalehistory.org), is a 1900 structure that was the home of the city's founder, a former sea captain, and displays late-Victorian antiques and relics. Both sites are accessible off I-84's Exit 17 and can provide further information on the historic highway and Columbia Gorge in general.

Lewis and Clark State Park to Rooster Rock

A few miles east of Troutdale, the first major sight along the highway, **Lewis and Clark State Park** (dawn–dusk; free; ☎1-800/551-6949), marks the spot where the explorers set up camp on their westward journey in November 1805. Clark tried to wade across the **Sandy River** but feared its bottom was quicksand; today's outdoor lovers know better, and you can see hordes of them bobbing and swimming here at the height of summer. Otherwise, the park mainly acts as the gateway to the **Columbia River Gorge National Scenic Area**. In this federally protected zone of more than a quarter million acres, development is strictly controlled and state parks are plentiful (check out

△ Vista House on Crown Point

www.oregonstateparks.org for full descriptions). One of these is named for the **Portland Women's Forum** (which has worked for gorge preservation), nine miles farther east, and marks the spot of **Chanticleer Point**, site of an old inn where the highway's developers first met in 1913 to plot the course of the road. The views from here are some of the best in the gorge, with sweeping vistas over the basalt cliffs to the winding river on the horizon. If you get here at the right time in the spring or fall, the sight can be awe-inspiring, with the sun breaking through thick clouds and morning mist to illuminate the river valley in all its rugged beauty.

One of the major sights visible from Chanticleer Point is the striking promontory of **Crown Point**. Located at milepost 24 and reachable from I-84 at Exit 22, the point is perched 733ft above the sheer dark walls of the gorge and best known for its octagonal, tile-roofed ✈ **Vista House** (May–Oct daily 9am–6pm; free; ⓦ www.vistahouse.com) – an essential image of the Columbia Gorge. This sandstone-faced 1916 concrete structure was designed by Edgar Lazarus – brother of Emma Lazarus, who wrote "The New Colossus," the poem inscribed at the base of the Statue of Liberty – to provide views in which "the Columbia could be viewed in silent communication with the infinite." Beyond its stylish architecture and some historic displays, there's not much to see inside, but the recently renovated site is a handsome place to stop and easily merits a visit for its eye-opening views alone.

Shortly after leaving Crown Point, about a mile east, you enter a handsome patch of forest that is crossed by the unnerving **Figure Eight Loops**, a sequence of five hairpin turns with tight curves built around a formidable slope – no doubt one of the prime reasons why I-84 was built as a bypass. Once you leave the loops, you reach **Guy W. Talbot State Park**, where a few pleasant hiking trails surround **Latourell Falls**, a fetching, 250ft spire of water. Finally, just to the north off I-84 (Exit 25), down on the Columbia River itself, is **Rooster Rock State Park** ($3; ☎503/695-2261 or 1-800/551-6949), named for a prominent chunk of basalt and popular with windsurfers for its agreeable winds (average 25–40mph). However, it's best known for offering one of the few nude, or clothing-optional, beaches in the region (there is a clothing-required section as well) – with peeping strongly discouraged by interlopers.

Bridal Veil Falls, Multnomah Falls, and Ainsworth State Park

Moving east from Latourell Falls, the Historic Columbia River Highway begins to run much closer to I-84, until both routes are more or less parallel at **Bridal Veil Falls**, at milepost 29. Here a big-time lumber operation once used the site for logging and planing stacks of timber. Nowadays the timber company is gone and the falls are once again open to public view in a state park (free; ☎1-800/551-6949). A lower-level trail offers a good taste of the site, wending around the base of the falls, but the upper-level trail is more appealing, taking you to the precipice over which the waters plunge. The upper hike also features some splendid gorge flora and a close view of the **Pillars of Hercules**, massive basalt columns left exposed by the Bretz Floods (see box, p.124), one of which is 120ft tall and a predictably popular spot for rock climbers in training.

Beyond Bridal Veil the highway reaches the base of 242ft **Wahkeena Falls**, the starting point for a number of trails into the backcountry of the **Mount Hood National Forest**. In particular, the two-mile **Perdition Trail** is a stiff hike that takes you high above Wahkeena through thick groves of cottonwood and maple. At the end of Perdition Trail is the junction with Larch Mountain

The Bretz Floods

Despite a sequence of dams that have turned what was once a raging torrent into a comparatively docile current, the **Columbia River**'s width and majesty still impresses. Although the river once fed more directly into the Pacific across central Washington, massive **lava flows** some fifteen million years ago altered its course to today's more southerly route. The resultant river valley then assumed a fairly conventional, gently sloping V-shape, which it maintained until fairly recently in geologic time. This changed after a mind-bending sequence of events near the end of the last **Ice Age**.

Oddly enough, the current topography of the gorge owes much to the existence of an ancient lake in western Montana. Hemmed in by an advancing ice sheet some 18,000 years ago, **Glacial Lake Missoula** once held around five hundred cubic miles of water – more than lakes Erie and Ontario combined – and was kept in its icy lair only by a single dam around what is now Pend Oreille, Idaho. Although two thousand feet high, this giant **ice dam** failed and drained the entire lake in as little as 48 hours. A gargantuan wall of water thousands of feet tall broke through the chasm and rushed into eastern Washington with ten times the force of all modern rivers put together, tearing loose trees, stripping away the topsoil, and uncovering the earth down to the level of basalt from the ancient lava flows; these desolate stretches of rock are now aptly referred to as the **Channeled Scablands**. The glacial flood channels surged and crossed in huge flows and tributaries, creating monstrous **waterfalls** – seen in desiccated form today in places like Dry Falls and Upper Coulee – hundreds of feet high and many miles across.

By the time the torrent reached the Columbia River Valley, it was a murky brown stew of topsoil, tree limbs, boulders, and icebergs, demolishing anything in its path at a speed of up to 200mph. The flood eventually tore away the river bottom and hillsides entirely, exposing the stark, jagged columns of basalt that are now visible throughout the area. And what was a sylvan, V-shaped valley became a sprawling, **U-shaped gorge**, its sides miles apart in places and the softer terrain of the valley's lower slopes swept away, making for high precipices where waterfalls – formerly gentle streams – tumbled down from the edges of gaping cliffs. The water reached its final destinations at both the mouth of the Columbia River, near present-day Astoria, and in the Willamette Valley, where the transplanted soil and rocks of eastern Washington created farmland that's still rich today.

Perhaps the most amazing thing about this geologic spectacle is that it occurred repeatedly (perhaps fifty or more times) over the course of thousands of years as the lake kept refilling behind new ice dams and breaking through when the dams failed – dramatic events that may have occurred as recently as 12,000 years ago, when native tribes were probably living in the region. Only the end of the Ice Age, and the retreat of North American ice sheets, put a halt to these **Bretz Floods** – named after their University of Washington discoverer – but by that time the millennia of glacial turmoil had permanently altered the landscape, from western Montana all the way to the Pacific Ocean.

Trail, which you can follow for the mile-long descent to the tallest and most famous of the gorge's waterfalls, the two-tiered **Multnomah Falls** (reachable off I-84 via a sudden left-lane exit, in both directions). This dramatic waterfall plummets 542ft down a mossy rock face, collects in a pool, then tumbles another 70ft and collects in another – adding up to the second-tallest waterfall in the US with a year-round flow. The best place to watch the natural spectacle is the quaint stone **Benson Bridge**, spanning the rocks above the lower waterfall and named after the lumber baron who deeded the land to the state. At the foot of the falls, the appealing rustic stone and timber *Multnomah Falls Lodge* (daily 8am–9pm; Ⓦ www.multnomahfallslodge.com) has been catering to tourists since 1925, though unfortunately you can't stay overnight anymore. The food is inexpensive, but pretty standard tourist fare – stick to the home-made bread and soups. The **visitor center** (daily 9am–5pm; ☎503/695-2372) next door issues free maps of the historic highway's hiking routes – though for the longer routes you'll need to buy one of their more detailed maps. If you want to **stay** in the area, head three miles back west to *Bridal Veil Lodge*, across from the eponymous park on the historic highway (☎503/695-2333, ⓦwww.bridalveillodge.com; ⑤), a B&B that offers agreeable lodge rooms and a guest cottage.

Alternatively, you can stay four miles east of Multnomah Falls at **Ainsworth State Park**, at milepost 35, which offers seasonal **campgrounds** (Mar–Oct; $10–16; ☎503/695-2301 or 1-800/551-6949) and some tremendous scenery to rival that of Multnomah Falls. The park is best explored on a 2.7-mile loop starting at **Horsetail Falls**, a powerful torrent that comes crashing down close to the road, and from there taking the Horsetail Falls Trail, which climbs the short distance to the quieter **Ponytail Falls** before pushing on to **Oneonta Falls**, just over a mile from the trailhead. It's a lovely hike, and rather than returning the way you came, you can scramble back to the road just west of Horsetail Falls beside **Oneonta Gorge**, a starkly evocative site with towering rock walls, and alive with countless floral treasures in its own botanical reserve, among them endemic trees, flowers, and shrubs. Also looming near the park site, and best seen on Nesmith Point Trail, is the massive **St Peter's Dome**, a huge, rounded basalt tower that is, at 2000ft, every bit the geological equivalent of its architectural namesake.

Bonneville Dam

At the east end of the motorized section of the historic highway, it's a few minutes' drive to **Bonneville Dam**, across I-84 at Exit 40 (daily 9am–5pm; free; ☎541/374-8820, ⓦwww.nwp.usace.army.mil/op/b), named after Benjamin Bonneville, the mid-nineteenth-century commander of Fort Vancouver (see p.411), who later became a general in the Union Army. As the first in a chain of WPA dams that made the Columbia River the biggest producer of hydroelectric power in the world (immortalized by Woody Guthrie's lyrical paean "Roll On, Columbia," in which the folk poet sang, "Your power is turning our darkness to dawn, so roll on Columbia, roll on"), the 1937 structure is an engineering marvel that has also done much to damage the ecosystem of this part of the Columbia River. Here native tribes once fished in abundance at various river falls along the way and explorers like Lewis and Clark and pioneers on the Oregon Trail experienced a white-knuckle ride down a series of plunging flumes. However, these and countless other natural attractions were summarily buried underwater with the construction of the dam, which also had the effect of backing up the river for many miles eastward and turning its once-fearsome stretches into little more than a placid, slow-moving lake.

Designed to process more than 700 million gallons of water per minute through its huge turbines, the dam is built over one of the river's steepest stretches to generate a colossal amount of energy. To see its monumental architecture up close, you can drive along its western wall and over its giant spillway to reach the **visitor center**. Inside, there are a few interpretative displays that mostly soft-pedal the dam's environmental impact, glossing over the fact that the dam, like others in the region, has had a dismal effect on native salmon, which used to swim in abundance upstream – nowadays, their flow has been reduced to three percent of what it was during pioneer days. Through viewing windows in the center, you can see a few salmon bravely navigating the dam's **fish ladders** to migrate upstream. Few of them will be headed to the dinner table, though. Most salmon from Washington and Oregon are now raised in aquacultural farms, their meat needing to be dyed red (from gray) to effect the look of healthy, muscular fish.

Historic Columbia River Highway State Trail

Beyond the turnoff for Bonneville Dam, most drivers heading east abandon the historic highway and rejoin I-84 at Exit 40. However, the route actually continues as the **Historic Columbia River Highway State Trail** ($3 day-use fee). Here the old highway has been converted to use by cyclists and hikers, who now have to themselves the road's commanding views of the gorge and its lovely bridges, narrow tunnels, and decorative railings (there's a second section of the trail around the Twin Tunnels; see p.133). Running a little over five miles until its junction with Cascade Locks (under the Bridge of the Gods), the trail begins from the west at **Tooth Rock**, where a parking lot allows you to deposit your automobile during daylight hours. The first major sight is the **Eagle Creek Bridge**, designed in 1915 from concrete, though its rough-hewn stone facing, low archway, and rustic guardrails are supposed to call to mind the antique bridges of old Europe. Just beyond, in the vicinity of Eagle Creek State Park, you'll have access to the 25-mile-long **Gorge Trail** – a striking overview of the area's scenery that leads back to Bridal Veil – and a short trail to the **Punchbowl**, a low basaltic chamber into which a short waterfall drops – a good spot for lounging in crisp, bubbling pools amid verdant scenery in the summer months. Finally, closer to the state trail's eastern end, near Exit 44 on I-84, the area around **Ruckel Creek** offers a steeply sloping trail along the gorge's high rock walls and past fetching collections of native trees and flowers.

Cascade Locks, the Bridge of the Gods, and points farther east

Sleepy little **CASCADE LOCKS**, off I-84 at Exit 44, was long ago the site of yet another harrowing spot on the pioneer river route, where the water level dropped twenty feet in the space of 1200ft – a daunting prospect for wagons traveling on flimsy rafts, which often had to be portaged around the riparian hazard. The site gets its present name from the 1896 locks that were built here to protect river traffic from the dangerous rapids, though the backwaters of Bonneville Dam submerged these by the end of the 1930s. Around the old spot where the locks operated, a **historical museum** (May–Oct daily noon–5pm; free) provides details on the perils of this stretch of the river, along with pioneer and native relics. Try to check out the replica stern-wheeler the **Columbia Gorge** (☎1-800/224-3901, ⓦwww .sternwheeler.com) in surrounding Marine Park, an old-fashioned ship that goes on two-hour sightseeing trips along the Columbia River (June–Oct; 1–2 daily; $25) and also provides romantic dinner cruises (June–Oct daily 6.30–9pm; $64). You can **stay** in Cascade Locks in a few chain motels or **camp** in Marine Park ($15–25 per night), though you're better off pushing on to Hood River or camping in one of the nearby state parks.

Toward the west end of town, a toll bridge ($2 fee) marks the fabled site of the Native Americans' **Bridge of the Gods**. Legend has it that a natural stone bridge once crossed the water here, but the sons of the Great Spirit, who had been sent to earth as snow mountains, quarreled and belched out so much fire, ash, and stone that the sun was hidden and the bridge was destroyed. There's some truth in the story: about a thousand years ago, the gigantic **Bonneville Slide** blocked the river here, creating an inland sea that eventually tunneled through the barrier, leaving a natural stone bridge suspended above.

Although you'll see no trace of any such span today, you can't miss the colossal 1925 **steel bridge** named after the native legend, crossing over to Washington a few miles west of the town of Stevenson (see below). Farther east in Oregon, at Exit 54 along I-84, **Starvation Creek State Park** is a small, isolated spot poised at the base of the gorge's towering basaltic walls that provides a nice jumping-off point for trails up the slopes and a few crumbling sections of the Historic Columbia Gorge Highway. There's a charming waterfall here and a trailhead that leads two miles east to the last major campground before Hood River, **Viento State Park**, at Exit 56. This park has first-come, first-served **camping** ($10–16; ☎541/374-8811) on a site wedged in between the highway and the railway – the noise from passing trains can be very loud at night, so bring earplugs. However, the campsites are near the water's edge, making for an easy transition from pajamas to wetsuit when you're ready to go windsurfing. Although not as blustery as Hood River, it's still an excellent spot to catch the whitecaps when the beaches around the town are overflowing with summer surfers.

Stevenson and around

If you cross the Bridge of the Gods, you will be on the main drag on the north (Washington State) side of the gorge, State Route 14 (also officially known as the Lewis and Clark Highway), which more or less parallels I-84 on the Oregon side. A few miles east of the bridge, look out for the **Columbia Gorge Interpretive Center** (daily 10am–5pm; $6; ☎509/427-8211 or 1-800/991-2238, ⊛www.columbiagorge.org), a new, modern facility that compiles the legend, history, and lore of the gorge into a series of informative exhibits. Among these are vividly portrayed native tales, carvings, sculptures, and petroglyphs; a restored steam engine and replica "fishwheel" used for hauling salmon out of the river by the bushel; and an overview of the river as Lewis and Clark saw it and the way it was remade for the hydroelectric age. After you're done, the town of **STEVENSON**, just east, provides one major attraction – one of the region's best **microbreweries**, ☀ *Walking Man Brewing*, off SR-14 at 240 SW First St (☎509/427-5520), offering a full range of taste-bud-tingling delights like Black Cherry Stout and Walking Man IPA. East of town, you can **stay** at century-old *Carson Mineral Hot Springs*, 372 St Martin Rd (☎1-800/607-3678, ⊛www.carsonhotspringresort.com; ❺–❻), a small-time resort that offers rooms with fireplaces, kitchenettes, and Jacuzzis; a golf course; and access to bubbling tubs full of natural mineral water. If you go back to the Bridge of the Gods and head three miles west of it, *Bonneville Hot Springs Resort*, 1252 E Cascade Dr, North Bonneville (☎866/459-1678, ⊛www .bonnevilleresort.com; ❼), is also well worth a stop, offering rooms with private balconies and an onsite pool, sauna, and Jacuzzis (or in-room hot tubs for an additional $50) whose bubbling water is taken from a natural spring.

This immediate area provides access to the Washington side of Bonneville Dam (see p.125), and the largest peak in the vicinity is just four miles north of the dam, the 600ft **Table Mountain**, whose spikier higher levels feature basaltic columns, remnants of the region's lava flows from fifteen million years ago. Nowadays the blockier terrain around the mountain is due to the accumulated debris of the Bonneville Slide, which sheared away the south side of the mountain three hundred years ago; even today, winter slides occur with some frequency, including several small events in 2007. The chunky landscape can make hiking a bit of a challenge, but the views can be quite striking with their mix of thick forest, sheer cliff walls, and rocky spires. Just as eye-opening, four miles west of North Bonneville, the 900ft-tall monolith of **Beacon Rock** sits in its own state park (℡509/427-8265) and was once a simple tall plug of volcanic rock surrounded by looser sedimentary soils. These were, of course, summarily wiped out when the Bretz Floods charged through the river, and only this oddly shaped haystack of basalt remains. On a mile-long trail full of catwalks and switchbacks, you can hike up to the summit of the rock and peer down at fine views of the river and the gorge. If sufficiently inspired, you can even **camp** here (first-come, first-served; $16–21) – though note that the rock can be a popular retreat for horseback riders and mountain cyclists during the summer.

Hood River

Back along I-84, just seven miles east of Viento State Park at Exit 63, the charming town of **HOOD RIVER** is small, with only 6600 full-time residents, but is still one of the best spots in the region for **mountain biking** and in the country for **windsurfing**. Windsurfers are especially drawn by an unusual but reliable phenomenon: in summertime the heat of the eastern steppes draws cooler air in from the west at a rate too great to be smoothly absorbed within the narrows of the Columbia Gorge. By around noon, the pressure has built up to such an extent that it has to be released – in great gusts of air that rip along the gorge, with the windsurfers ready and waiting to "catch the blow." Since they appeared on the scene in the early 1980s, the windsurfers have effectively reinvented Hood River, turning what was once a workaday agricultural burg into a modern hillside community complete with laid-back cafes and restaurants and all manner of outdoor-sports equipment stores.

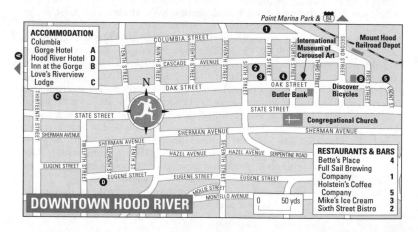

Arrival and information

Long-distance Greyhound **buses** pull in at 600 E Marina Way (☎541/386-1212, ⓦwww.greyhound.com), in Port Marina Park, near I-84's Exit 64. From here, it's a five- to ten-minute walk southwest to the town center. Amtrak **trains** on the *Empire Builder* route don't stop in Hood River, but do right across the river in Bingen, Washington, at SR-14 and Walnut St – almost within walking distance (3–4 miles); if you don't want to hoof it, call a cab (Gorge Yellow Cab; $5–6; ☎1-800/981-7543) or reserve public transit in advance (Columbia Area Transit; tickets $1.25–2; Mon–Fri 8.30am–4pm; ☎503/386-4202).

The **visitor center** (☎541/386-2000 or 1-800/366-3530, ⓦwww.hoodriver .org) is located down by the river, a good 10min walk from the town center. The center has free maps, accommodation listings, and details of recommended sports outfitters. Some of these include **bike rental** companies like Discover Bicycles, 116 Oak St ($5–8 per hour, $25–45 per day; ☎541/386-4820, ⓦwww.discoverbicycles.com), which has a good selection of mountain bikes and recommends cycling trails; you can rent **windsurfers** ($49 per day) from Hood River WaterPlay, 100 Port Marina Way (daily: mid-May to early Sept; ☎541/386-9463, ⓦwww.hoodriverwaterplay.com), which also provides lessons and even rents out kites and kayaks.

Accommodation

The town has a reasonable supply of motels, hotels, and B&Bs, but finding a **place to stay** can still get a little difficult in the summer, when advance reservations are advised and prices jump by about $20–30 per night. A handful of medium-priced **B&Bs** sit west of the town center, while sitting a few blocks south is the *Inn at the Gorge*, 1113 Eugene St (☎541/386-4429, ⓦwww.innatthegorge.com; ❺), a stately 1908 Colonial Revival home that has been transformed into a tasteful, elegant B&B with minimal Victorian kitsch. Rooms and suites are well decorated, and the house features a wraparound veranda and pleasant rear terrace. Also centrally located, *Love's Riverview Lodge*, 1505 Oak St (☎541/386-8719 or 1-800/789-9568, ⓦwww.riverviewforyou.com; ❸), is a basic but clean motel within walking distance of town center. The ⚲ *Columbia Gorge Hotel*, 4000 Westcliff Drive, a mile west of town, at Exit 62 off I-84 (☎541/386-5566 or 1-800/345-1921, ⓦwww.columbiagorgehotel.com; ❼), is perched on a cliff right above the gorge. Developed by the lumber king Simon Benson in 1921, the hotel has exquisite gardens with their own waterfalls, and the forty rooms are lavish and relaxing. Less expensive hotel accommodation can be found at *Hood River Hotel*, 102 Oak St (☎541/386-1900 or 1-800/386-1859, ⓦwww.hoodriverhotel.com; ❹). Built in 1913 and featuring a serviceable Italian restaurant, this pleasantly renovated establishment offers simple, tasteful rooms as well as more elaborate suites with river views. If all else fails, you can **camp** by the river at **Memaloose State Park**, twelve miles east of Hood River off I-84 (campsites $12–20; ☎541/478-3008 or 1-800/452-5687).

The Town

With its abundance of leisure pursuits and homegrown industries (gourmet jellies, beeswax candles), Hood River can feel like a **boutique town**, its prominent attractions geared primarily to the tourist trade. Even the setting itself – perched quaintly on a hillside above a gorge landscape of undeniable beauty – makes it seem like no one here does anything but shop for kites, eat bistro food, drink microbrews, and go windsurfing. This impression is, of course, just a façade – Hood River is as much an agricultural center for the neighboring Hood River Valley as anything else – but few small towns in Oregon have such a relaxed, engaging atmosphere, despite the relative paucity of conventional attractions.

Port Marina Park

The first stop is obvious: **Port Marina Park**, immediately north of I-84 at Exit 64. The main windsurfers' hot spot, it sits amid a wide landscape of sweeping riverside scenery and stark, rocky vistas – the whole of it enlivened by strong gorge winds and dappled sunlight in the summer. Take a seat on the sloping grass or the gravelly beach and watch the seasoned windsurfers go through their paces, managing the whitecapped currents, finessing the gales, and dodging novices who can barely stay upright. Other than the visitor center (see above), there's little else to do here and hardly anything in the way of food or facilities, but the park nonetheless offers a good introduction to the town – and a ready explanation for its popularity.

Downtown

From the park, make your way back over the freeway to ascend the slope on which **downtown** sits. Arrayed from First to Sixth streets, there are in theory three main drags in town – Cascade Avenue and Oak and State streets – though you can easily see most of the historic highlights with a simple stroll on Oak. From First Street, climb the hill past some of Hood River's more stately architectural gems, passing grand hotels such as the *Hood River* (see p.129) and various eateries along the way. The old **Butler Bank**, at Third and Oak streets, is worth a look for its spartan design and Egyptian Revival columns. Two blocks away, at Fifth and State, the former **Congregational Church** is a massive 1912 stone pile that dominates the streets below it. Beyond the architecture itself, it's hard to say that there are any truly essential sights downtown, amid all the diners, windsurfer dealers, and antique stores. One exception may be the incongruous **International Museum of Carousel Art**, 304 Oak St (Mon–Sat 11am–3pm, Sunday noon–4pm; $5; ☎541/387-4622, ⓦwww.carouselmuseum.com), basically an excuse to display 120 quaint old carousel horses from old-time carnivals – a visual treat for fans of the ornamental wooden creatures.

The Mount Hood Railroad and the Fruit Loop

Between downtown and the I-84 freeway, hop on the charming, antique blue-and-red trains of the **Mount Hood Railroad** (☎541/386-3556 or 1-800/872-4661, ⓦwww.mthoodrr.com), for a twenty-mile sightseeing trip down along the Hood River Valley south of town. The railroad was built in 1906 to service the valley's agricultural communities, but today the ride (4hr 15min) is just a fun tourist junket. Trains depart from the old railway station at 110 Railroad Ave, just off Second Street (April–Dec; 2–6 weekly; $23; departures at 10am and/or 3pm). The railroad also offers alternate trips throughout the year on the same route, focusing on brunch ($58), dinner ($70), or – in the case of the special "murder mystery" trains ($80) – an onboard whodunit.

A different kind of experience can be had by taking the **Fruit Loop** (ⓦwww.hoodriverfruitloop.com), a 35-mile driving concourse around the county that connects to growers of cheap and delicious apples, pears, cherries, and peaches, depending on the season. Amid the roadside stands and vineyards are a few standout orchards. On the east side of the loop, **Packer Orchards**, 3900 Hwy 35 (☎541/490-3684, ⓦwww.packerorchardsand-bakery.com), is a bakery and fruit stand with prime cherries, apples, peaches, and pears, and **Draper Farms**, 6200 Hwy 35 (☎541/352-6625), is excellent for its wide variety of just-picked fruit and vegetables; the highlight of the west loop is the **Apple Valley Country Store**, 2363 Tucker Rd (☎541/386-1971, ⓦwww.applevalleystore.com), packed with local jams and jellies and a gut-busting array of fresh-fruit milkshakes, pies, candies, and cobblers. Most loopside farms and stores are open at least from April to October, with a few managing to stay open all year round.

Eating and drinking

Good places to **eat** downtown include the easygoing *Holstein's Coffee Company*, 811 E 3rd St (☎541/298-2326), which serves up tasty light meals, with great coffees and sandwiches, and *Bette's Place*, 416 Oak St (☎541/386-1880), which offers more traditional burgers and soups. Alternatively, the *Sixth Street Bistro*, 509 Cascade Ave (☎541/386-5737), has microbrews, seafood, and pasta at affordable prices. The busiest **bar** in town is the ☀ *Full Sail Brewing Company*, 506 Columbia St (☎541/386-2247), a fine microbrewery, making some of the region's finest craft beers, that also offers limited free tours of its facility. To cool down, *Mike's Ice Cream*, 504 Oak St (☎541/386-6260), sells a great range of ice creams, highlighted by its legendary huckleberry milkshakes.

Moving on from Hood River

Along with being an attractive little place, Hood River is also a **crossroads** for the Columbia Gorge. To the **west** are most of the scenic riverside attractions along the Historic Columbia Gorge Highway (see p.121). To the **south**, and unmistakable as it looms over the Hood River Valley, **Mount Hood** is a top-notch spot for skiing, hiking, and hanging out in mountainside lodges. To the **east**, the remaining section of the historic highway is now a striking **scenic trail** (see p.133), while The Dalles is bigger and blander than Hood River. Finally, on the Washington side to the **north**, the little towns of **Bingen** and **White Salmon** offer access to Mount Adams (see p.445) on Hwy 141. Moreover, this side of the gorge has a handful of decent **wineries** that, while not quite on the level with those farther north around Yakima (see p.456), nonetheless are beginning to make a name for themselves. Contact the **Klickitat Wine Alliance** (☎1-800/785-1718) for details on locations, tastings, and tours.

Mount Hood

From Hood River, Hwy 35 heads south through verdant orchards toward the snowcapped monolith of **Mount Hood**. At 11,235ft, the peak is the tallest of the Oregon Cascades, dominating the surrounding landscape. The road begins by running through the Hood River Valley before climbing to skirt the mountain's heavily forested southern flank. Eventually, after about forty miles, the road reaches its highest point, **Barlow Pass**. Take note, though, that in late 2006 the road was repeatedly damaged by rock- and snowslides, and may be

The Barlow Road

Since the Columbia River Gorge was impassable by wagon, when the early pioneers reached The Dalles, they were forced to change means of transport, which meant floating precariously down the river with their wagons on rafts, their horses abandoned or left to make their own way downstream by bobbing or swimming. Knowing how much the pioneers dreaded battling the turbulent waters, **Samuel Barlow**, a wagon-train leader, led a party off to forge a land route around the south side of Mount Hood in 1845. Unfortunately, they were trapped by snow while chopping their way through the thick forests and had to leave their wagons behind in the struggle to reach the Willamette Valley, for fear that they would starve or freeze to death. Barlow returned a year later, however, and this time he oversaw the completion of the **Barlow Road**, the upper reaches of which are still followed by highways 35 and 26). Not surprisingly, many migrants chose to brave its steep ridges – where wagons frequently skidded out of control and had to be lowered by ropes in places – rather than face the wrathful Columbia, though many echoed the feeling of pioneer leader Ralph Geer, who recalled that "the road was just horrible, a description of it is impossible by me." To the irritation of many pioneers, Barlow grew rich on his endeavors, charging them a crunching $5-per-wagon fee to use his road – the new final leg of the Oregon Trail – while his partner completed the rip-off at the end of the trail by opening the one and only general store in the area, with predictably steep prices.

irregularly open during the winter months; contact the Mount Hood Information Center (see opposite) for updates.

Beyond Barlow Pass, Hwy 35 meets Hwy 26, which leads either west to Portland or southeast to Madras and Bend (see p.226). It's about a mile west from the crossroads to the signposted turnoff to the six-mile-long road that weaves up the mountainside to 🏂 **Timberline Lodge** (☎503/272-3311 or 1-800/547-1406, Ⓦwww.timberlinelodge.com; shared-bath chalet rooms ❺, otherwise ❼), rightfully one of Oregon's most celebrated hotels and well worth a visit even if you're not staying here or skiing. Constructed in the 1930s as part of a New Deal jobs program, the hotel is a grand and handsome affair, solidly built in rough-hewn stone and timber with an interior loaded with Arts and Crafts–style wooden furniture and antique fittings. Note the main staircase, decorated with finely carved animals, and the expansive atrium with wooden galleries and a huge stone fireplace. Most people know the lodge as the exterior location for Stanley Kubrick's *The Shining* – though the film's interiors were shot on a British soundstage and the grounds lack that movie's fiendish hedge maze.

At 6000ft, *Timberline Lodge* is also at the center of a busy year-round **ski resort** (lift tickets $45; ☎503/622-0717) – one of three (and undoubtedly the best) on the mountain – with six chairlifts and 35 runs to suit all abilities, though the majority are aimed at experienced skiers and snowboarders. The highest chairlift, **Palmer**, climbs to 8540ft, with an average snowfall of 350 inches per year. You can also **rent ski equipment** (skis, boots, and poles $25 per day; snowboards and boots $35) and learn how to ski (☎503/231-5402) here. Along with Timberline, two other downhill ski areas – Mount Hood Meadows ($49; Ⓦwww.skihood.com) and Mount Hood SkiBowl ($38; Ⓦwww.skibowl.com) – offer nighttime **skiing** from November to April (around $25). There are also many miles of cross-country skiing trails and summer hiking trails throughout the **Mount Hood National Forest**. For more information on mountain activities, contact the Mount Hood Information Center (daily 8am–4pm; ☏503/622-4822 or 1-888-622-4822, ⓦwww.mthood.info). To check **snow conditions**, call ☏503/222-2211 or 1-877/754-6734; also check if tire chains are required for the last leg of the journey up to the lodge – they are often necessary until well into June.

Finally, if you're up for **climbing** the mountain, contact the information center, which can put you in touch with outfitters, guides, and other essentials for ascending to the summit. Keep in mind, though, that despite its popularity, climbing the mountain is not for novices, and you can expect to face numerous hazards including sudden blizzards and whiteouts, deep and hard-to-spot ravines, and the looming threat of avalanches. As TV watchers know, each year at least one climbing party gets trapped on the mountain and has to be airlifted out, or faces the death or disappearance of some of its members.

The eastern gorge

Heading east from Hood River along I-84, you enter the strikingly different terrain of the **eastern gorge** – instead of verdant forests and mossy glades, there are bare cliffs and rocky shelves; instead of damp forest trails home to countless wildflowers and native plants, dusty scrubland and parched earth; and instead of beautiful vistas clouded with mist and fog, bleak Wild West horizons on the edge of unforgiving plains. In few other places is the landscape devastated by the Bretz Floods (see box, p.124) quite so desolate or wind-blasted. Even the gorge itself resembles less a deep emerald ravine than a gaping brown chasm.

The Twin Tunnels

Despite the dry landscape, the eastern gorge can be quite evocative in places, and nowhere more so than along the hiking route of the **Twin Tunnels** between Hood River and the small burg of Mosier. This five-mile pedestrianized route is actually the course of the old **Historic Columbia Gorge Highway** (see p.126), which, east of Cascade Locks, exists only in fragments. Here it's a well-preserved delight, a restored stretch of roadway that state engineers labored over for many years. The centerpiece is, of course, the pair of classic old tunnels on the eastern approach to the trail, which were finished around 1919 but had to be closed decades later because of falling rocks. After that they were summarily filled in and practically ruined until the state undertook the laborious process of unsealing them, reinforcing their failing structure, and opening them once more to traffic – this time walkers and cyclists.

To access the route you can either approach from the west at the **Hatfield Trailhead**, where Hwy 30 ends motorized access east of Hwy 35, or from the east at **Rock Creek Road** in Mosier (Exit 69 off I-84). The day-use **fee** is $3 (information at ☏1-800/551-6949), and unless someone's willing to pick you up, you'll have to make a ten-mile round-trip if you want to see the whole route. Still, for those with the stamina, it's a great hike through varying terrain, full of stunning vistas of the arid gorge, towering basalt monoliths, and the historic highway's restored fixtures and passages, on a sloping, sometimes winding trek that makes for an excellent workout. Inside the narrow, somewhat eerie tunnels themselves, it's hard to imagine how mid-twentieth-century traffic could have ever fit through; in fact, drivers could become snowbound within them if the weather suddenly turned bad – which explains the stray pieces of graffiti here and there on the walls, some of which date back to the 1920s.

The adventures of Sam Hill

The **Maryhill Museum** was the singular creation of idiosyncratic tycoon **Samuel Hill**, who was born into a Quaker family in North Carolina in 1857. Nothing if not ambitious, Hill moved to Seattle in the early 1900s and married the daughter of a railroad owner before skillfully amassing a fortune by manipulating the stock market. With money matters out of the way, he threw himself into all manner of projects – some, like road construction, eminently sensible, others downright nutty.

In the latter category came his plan for the Maryhill site – named after his wife and daughter – which he discovered through his highway work and acquired as part of a 6000-acre parcel in 1907. Convinced it was a Garden of Eden, he planned to establish a Quaker farmers' colony here but failed to convince the Quakers of the bleak, windswept area's agricultural potential. Instead, Hill ended up building an extravagant three-story home on the site; made of concrete and steel, it was rendered in a vaguely penitentiary style. Not content with this, Hill turned to his trusty concrete again and built a miniature copy of **Stonehenge** (daily 7am–dusk; free) on a hill overlooking the Columbia, four miles upstream from his mansion. In its "unruined," idealized form, it's a pacifist's tribute to those who died in World War I, for Hill believed Stonehenge to be a sacrificial site, its faithful reproduction appropriate as "humanity is still being sacrificed to the god of war."

Despite Hill's best endeavors, however, no one, and least of all his family, showed the slightest interest in living at Maryhill, and the house stood neglected for years. Then in the 1920s – in another strange twist – two of Hill's European chums, **Queen Marie of Romania** and the well-connected Folies Bergere dancer and Auguste Rodin model **Loie Fuller**, saved the whole enterprise. First, they persuaded Hill to turn the house into an art museum and then they helped by donating a generous sample of fine and applied art. Not surprisingly, their intriguing gifts remain the kernel of the collection and the main reason to visit the museum.

The Dalles

Thirteen miles east of Mosier on I-84 is the grim industrial township of **THE DALLES**, an old military outpost where many of the pioneers transferred to rafts for the perilous journey down the last stretch of the Columbia River. Before then, it had been a meeting place for French Canadian trappers, who named it after the basalt rocks that line this stretch of the river, looking like flagstones (*les dalles*). A mile or two upstream, the river once tumbled over a series of rocky shelves called **Celilo Falls**, long used by Native Americans as fishing grounds and the source of much folklore – "the great fishing place of the Columbia," wrote Washington Irving. However, when the Dalles Dam was completed in 1957, the backed-up waters soon drowned these native legends and traditions.

One sight in the vicinity is the **Columbia Gorge Discovery Center** (daily 9am–5pm; $8; @www.gorgediscovery.org), on the riverbank at the western edge of The Dalles, at 5000 Discovery Drive (Exit 82 off I-84). It provides a broad informative overview of the history of the region – from ancient lava flows and Ice Age floods to nineteenth-century explorers to more contemporary pursuits like hydroelectricity and windsurfing – and features antique relics from early state history, assorted rocks and geologic specimens, and various dioramas and walk-through exhibits. One of these, a small-town street from over a century ago, is a bit sentimental but nonetheless more enticing than the dour modern townscape beyond the museum.

Seventeen miles east of The Dalles, and just south on Hwy 206, **Deschutes River State Recreation Area** is a pleasant getaway set beside the bubbling currents of the Deschutes River, with opportunities for mountain biking, hiking, camping (sites $12–16; reserve at ☏1-800/452-5687), and especially fishing for trout and steelhead. You can launch a fishing boat here or a take a raft and brave the lower rapids of the deep canyons of north-central Oregon.

Beyond The Dalles, I-84 leaves the official Columbia Gorge National Scenic Area and continues on into the desert heart of eastern Oregon, while heading south US-197 skirts the eastern side of the Oregon Cascades on the way down to Madras and Bend (see p.226). North on US-97, you can cross over into Washington and then head east toward the Maryhill Museum.

The Maryhill Museum of Art

Lying east of The Dalles and over the bridge into Washington on US-97, the extraordinary **Maryhill Museum of Art** (mid-March to mid-Nov daily 9am–5pm; $7; ☏509/773-3733, ⓦ www.maryhillmuseum.org) is awash in all manner of unexpected displays and exhibits, acquired over the years by the museum's eccentric founder, Sam Hill (see box opposite). The highlights are the assorted baubles and trinkets given by Queen Marie of Romania, including a small but delightful collection of Russian icons, Marie's Fabergé coronation crown, and an imposing corner throne carved in Byzantine style in 1908. Just as interesting, the **Theatre de la Mode** presents a small selection of 1940s French wire-frame mannequins clothed by some of the leading fashion houses of the day. There was a desperate shortage of fabric in postwar Europe and these miniatures were an ingenious way around the problem of how to advertise new designs. Downstairs, there's a fine sample of the sculptures of **Rodin**, a gift from dancer-model Loie Fuller, and a bizarre collection of **chess sets** – including a *Nixon v McGovern* edition.

△ Maryhill Museum of Art

There's also a Native American gallery, at its best in the sections devoted to the bands of the Columbia River Valley and its environs – with everything from small totemic figures and arrow straighteners through to petroglyphs and pile drivers. The museum's only real downside is its spotty collection of European artworks and a rather kitschy array of American "classical realism" pieces – apparently meaning garishly painted saints, grotesque crucifixions, and the like. There's a **cafe** on this floor, too (10am–4pm), while the uppermost floor is largely given over to temporary exhibitions.

Columbia Hills State Park

Twelve miles west of the museum on SR-14, a few miles east of the US-197 junction, **Columbia Hills State Park** ($5 day-use fee) is based around **Horsethief Lake**, a ninety-acre body of freshwater created during the backfill of the Dalles Dam; it's serviceable enough for day use and has agreeable basaltic scenery and first-come, first-served **camping** ($16–21), but it's mostly notable as the site for preserved native **petroglyphs**. These mysterious-looking designs, from jagged and angular icons to more rounded, anthropomorphic forms, were created many centuries ago, and are strange and compelling even if you know little about the subject. Tours run seasonally and must be reserved well in advance (April–Oct Fri & Sat 10am; free; ℡509/767-1159).

3

The Oregon Coast

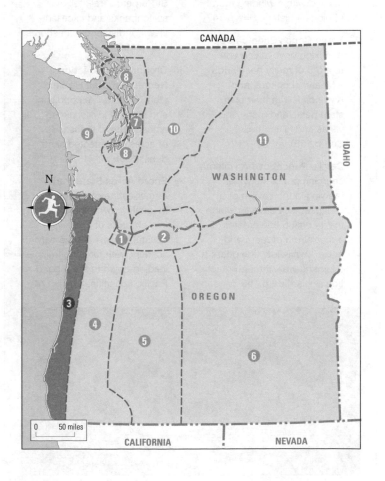

CHAPTER 3 # Highlights

* **Astoria Column** Look out over the stunning vastness of the Columbia River as it merges with the Pacific Ocean from this towering pillar painted with a winding mural of pioneer history. See p.147

* **Three Capes Scenic Loop** A striking drive taking you to a trio of rocky headlands – Meares, Lookout, and Kiwanda – with their own state parks and many fine vistas and hiking trails. See p.156

* **Devil's Punchbowl** A violently churning pot of saltwater brewing in the cavern of a collapsed sea cave, in which the incoming tide creates a maelstrom of foam and noise – while low tide offers a charming walk through quiet tide pools. See p.159

* **Cape Perpetua** One of the more colossal promontories on the coast, a great mound of rock and forest you can hike up on the challenging St Perpetua Trail, full of switchbacks and excellent views of distant ocean shores. See p.166

* **Oregon Dunes National Recreation Area** Hike in stark, Sahara-like conditions and swim in idyllic lakes among tens of thousands of acres of protected sand dunes. See p.171

* **Shore Acres State Park** A former estate of a lumber magnate, now transformed into an oasis of sparkling coastal blooms and verdant scenery, with fetching trails leading down to the rugged Pacific coastline. See p.174

△ Devil's Punchbowl

The Oregon Coast

A ninety-minute drive west from Portland and the Willamette Valley, the **OREGON COAST** is a magnificent, 350-mile stretch of undeveloped beaches and parks, scenic hills and forests, and rugged coves and cliffs. Amid this sparkling terrain are also more unexpected sights like craggy headlands jutting out at strange angles, Sahara-like sand dunes, and unusual **sea**

Exploring the Oregon Coast

The best way to explore the coast is via the main route of **Highway 101**, a winding concourse that closely follows the contours of the seaboard and takes you past many eye-opening vistas, including clifftop perches, deep ravines, and expansive tidal flats. The road was completed in the 1930s under a Work Projects Administration program orchestrated by inventive engineer **Conde McCullough**, who was responsible for the string of beautifully designed **bridges** that remain a highlight of the coastal drive. If you plan to spend a good amount of time on the coast, note that many state and federal parks sell an **annual pass** ($35) that covers entrance and day-use fees and parking for all park sites on the coast, as well as a **five-day pass** ($10) that covers the same things.

For those traveling by **bus**, Greyhound (☎1-800/229-9424, ⍵www.greyhound.com) provides service only to the central coast between Coos Bay and Newport, also stopping at Florence and Reedsport. Don't expect Greyhound to drop you in the middle of any of these towns – you're just as likely to be left beside the main road, which can be a long haul from the center. North of Lincoln City, you're dependent on intermittent local buses, the most significant of which is the **Sunset Empire** service ($1.25; ☎503/325-0563, ⍵www.ridethebus.org) linking Astoria, Cannon Beach, and Seaside.

The popular **Oregon Coast Bike Route** follows, for the most part, reasonably wide, cyclist-only shoulder lanes (about 3ft wide) on either side of the highway, though small sections do run along quiet country roads. You have to be fairly fit to manage the hills, and the occasional logging truck may put the wind to you, but for the most part it's a delightful and comparatively straightforward bike ride that takes six to eight days to complete. It's best attempted between May and October when the prevailing winds pretty much dictate a north-to-south itinerary. Oregon Tourism produces a detailed brochure (☎1-800/547-7842, ⍵www.traveloregon.com) on the route.

Most **hikers** are more than satisfied with the hundreds of walking trails that crisscross the coast's forests and wilderness areas – anything from short afternoon strolls to full-scale expeditions into the outback. One such long-distance hiking route, the **Oregon Coast Trail**, weaves through some of Oregon's finest coastal landscapes and is aimed at outdoor adventurers. Information is available from Oregon State Parks, 1115 Commercial St NE, Salem, OR 97301-1002 (☎503/378-4168, ⍵www.oregonstateparks.com).

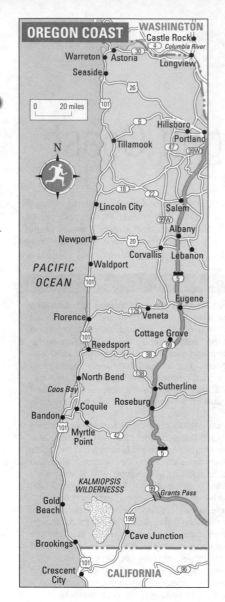

OREGON COAST

WASHINGTON
Castle Rock
Columbia River
Warreton · Astoria
Longview
Seaside

0   20 miles

N

Hillsboro
Tillamook
Portland

Lincoln City   Salem
Albany
Newport
Corvallis   Lebanon
PACIFIC   Waldport
OCEAN
Eugene
Florence   Veneta
Cottage Grove
Reedsport
North Bend   Sutherline
Coos Bay
Coquile   Roseburg
Bandon
Myrtle
Point

KALMIOPSIS
WILDERNESSS
Grants Pass
Gold
Beach
Brookings   Cave Junction

Crescent
City   CALIFORNIA

stacks – great chunks of basalt that, through millennia of erosion and land changes, now sit as isolated monoliths in the shallow sea, home only to the likes of seagulls and mussels. On a sunny day the trip along the coast is wonderfully exhilarating, though some claim stormy days are even better. This superb scenery is often best appreciated from the string of state parks – and their campgrounds – that form what amounts to a preserved oceanside parkway running the length of the state. Though crass development that has engulfed small sections here and there, several of the coast's towns are appealing too, including the diverse charms of **Newport** and its relaxing Nye Beach, the grand old mansions and nautical relics of **Astoria**, and the subtle beauty of **Bandon**. Each of these makes for a nice one- or two-night stay; **Lincoln City** and **Seaside**, on the other hand, have well-established reputations as tourist traps. Overall, the **North Coast** is a bit more commercialized and much more visitor-oriented than the **South Coast**, which is best known for its largely unspoiled views and remote, evocative landscapes.

The coast's high degree of protection results largely from the pioneering work of citizen-activists over the decades like **William Tugman** and **Samuel Boardman**, both of whom have excellent parks named after them (see p.173 and p.181), and the conservationist Republican governor **Oswald West**, who was in office for only four short years in the 1910s but managed to politically engineer much of this preservation. His name and reputation are enshrined in several places around the state, including at the state park named after him (see p.153), a rugged stretch of coastal hills and lowlands with few facilities.

The North Coast

The Oregon coast is as beautiful as any stretch of American coastline and for much of the year is largely untrammeled, its sands explored by a few locals and spare visitors from Portland and other Willamette Valley cities. Nonetheless, when summer comes tourists arrive en masse, and the prime destination for many is the **North Coast**, a strip of coastline stretching roughly from Astoria to Heceta Head that is home to the coast's more developed towns as well as a handful of tourist traps. Apart from such places, extensive and sometimes isolated beaches offer many free activities throughout the year, ranging from beachcombing and shell-fishing to whale watching and, in winter, storm watching – but rarely swimming: the currents are too strong and dangerous and floating logs are too common a hazard to make this practicable. That said, some adventurers do surf amid the potential hazards, but you'll need a wet- or drysuit at a minimum and plenty of knowledge about the topography and experience avoiding the marine perils.

Even with its many legal protections, the North Coast has not escaped commercialism and sports a series of resorts for golf, tennis, and other outdoor activities. Luckily, most of these are not garish high-rises, so the broad sweep of oceanside beauty remains inviolate. From the upper edge of the Oregon coast and heading south, the first prominent town is **Astoria**, a stately old industrial burg that's reinvented itself as a boutique community, located a few miles inland near the mouth of the Columbia River. Starting south on **Highway 101**, the popular confines of **Cannon Beach** and **Seaside** are often the first, though rarely the best, choices for coastal visitors, while places like **Manzanita** and **Tillamook** are known for vacationing urbanites in rented condos and tourable cheese companies, respectively. Sizable **Lincoln City** is laid out like a low-rent oceanside suburb, but the fishing village of **Newport** is a fetching attraction with a historic bayfront, pleasant series of lighthouses and beaches, and notable state aquarium.

Throughout this area, the offshore islands, rocks, and reefs are incorporated in the **Oregon Islands National Wildlife Refuge**, and in the summer you can expect to see elephant seals, harbor seals, and Steller sea lions as well as herons, cormorants, oystercatchers, puffins, and other sea birds. There's considerable variety in the flora, too, with hemlock, Sitka spruce, cedar, and Douglas fir common in the north, and madrone, redwood, ash, and myrtle more prevalent in the south.

Astoria and around

Set on a hilly tongue of land adjacent to the mouth of the Columbia River, about a hundred miles northwest of Portland, **ASTORIA** is a modest port operating in the shadow of the huge **Astoria Bridge**, spanning the river over to Cape Disappointment in the southwest corner of Washington State (see p.409). Activity along the harbor is not especially busy these days – Astoria's heyday as a seaport and cannery town was at the end of the nineteenth century, boom times recalled by a string of ornate **Victorian mansions** that have since become private middle-class homes or charming bed-and-breakfasts. They

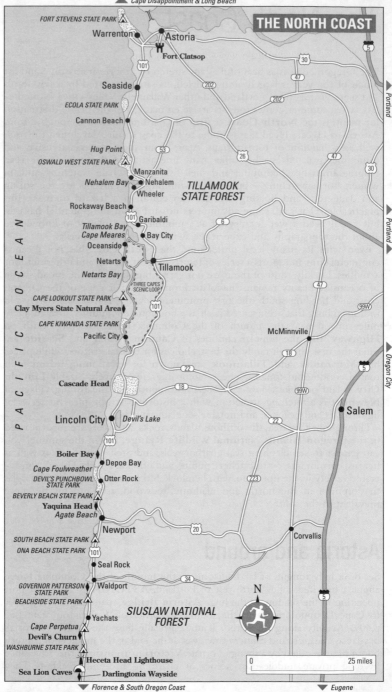

▲ Cape Disappointment & Long Beach

THE NORTH COAST

FORT STEVENS STATE PARK

Warrenton   Astoria
Fort Clatsop

30

47

5 ▶ Portland

Seaside

202

ECOLA STATE PARK

Cannon Beach

202

Hug Point
OSWALD WEST STATE PARK   Manzanita
Nehalem Bay   Nehalem
Wheeler

53

26

47

30 ▶ Portland

**TILLAMOOK
STATE FOREST**

Rockaway Beach   Garibaldi

101

Tillamook Bay
Cape Meares   Bay City
Oceanside
Netarts   Tillamook

6

THREE CAPES
SCENIC LOOP

Netarts Bay

CAPE LOOKOUT STATE PARK
Clay Myers State Natural Area

CAPE KIWANDA STATE PARK

Pacific City

101

47

McMinnville

18

5 ▶ Oregon City

Cascade Head

22

99W

Lincoln City   Devil's Lake

18

Salem

101

22

Boiler Bay   Depoe Bay
Cape Foulweather
DEVIL'S PUNCHBOWL   Otter Rock
STATE PARK
BEVERLY BEACH STATE PARK
Yaquina Head
Agate Beach

223

Newport

20

Corvallis

SOUTH BEACH STATE PARK
ONA BEACH STATE PARK

101

Seal Rock

34

GOVERNOR PATTERSON
STATE PARK   Waldport
BEACHSIDE STATE PARK

**SIUSLAW NATIONAL
FOREST**

N

Yachats
Cape Perpetua
Devil's Churn
WASHBURNE STATE PARK
Heceta Head Lighthouse
Sea Lion Caves   Darlingtonia Wayside

0   25 miles

▼ Florence & South Oregon Coast

▼ Eugene

P A C I F I C   O C E A N

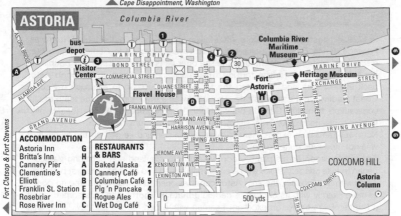

make perfect romantic perches from which to view the striking hillside scenery and watch the region's current economic lifeline out in the Columbia channel – huge oil tankers, container ships, and barges passing through the icy waters, with the odd bellow of their horns to announce their presence.

With its combination of strong currents, shifting sandbars, breakers, frequent fog, and stormy weather, the mouth of the Columbia can be very difficult to negotiate, and around two thousand ships are known to have sunk there. Dredgers, automated buoys, and a pair of gigantic moles have made navigation much easier today, but ships still require the services of Astoria's pilots, whose powerful little boats are often to be seen bobbing about the river.

Given that the town is probably the most historic along the coast of the Pacific Northwest, it's encouraging that recent attempts to spruce up its waterfront have worked well, with boutiques, restaurants, and a nautical museum complementing the long line of low-slung sheds and piers that hark back to the old port and cannery days. Also reminiscent of olden times are the old sites of **Fort Clatsop** and **Fort Stevens**, just west of town, the former once the winter quarters for the Lewis and Clark Expedition and the latter a military installation turned state park.

Some history

First settled by native tribes like the Chinook, the Astoria area was briefly famous when Lewis and Clark camped here in 1806. In 1811 millionaire fur tycoon **John Jacob Astor** (see box, p.144) founded the town itself as a private trading post – the first, abortive American attempt at colonizing the West Coast. By the time new colonists began arriving via the sea and the Oregon Trail in the 1840s, little was left of the outpost from the old days. Its port grew rapidly, and by 1847 it had the first US post office on the West Coast. Within twenty years Astoria began to make a name for itself as a **salmon-canning** town and an outlet for the timber trade.

At the turn of the last century it was one of the more rough-and-ready ports in the Northwest, home to the type of vice and corruption usually associated with the Wild West – rampant prostitution, random violence, and occasional clashes between races and nationalities, all of it fueled by alcohol and class tensions. Chinese, Swedish, and Finnish laborers were but a few

The price of fur

In 1779, exhausted British sailors, after failing in their search of the fabled Northwest Passage during Captain Cook's long final voyage, docked in Canton. There they discovered, quite by accident, that the sea otter pelts they had traded for baubles in the Northwest were worth a fortune. The intelligence reached **John Jacob Astor** back in New York and prompted the fur tycoon's decision to establish a **Pacific Coast trading post** called Astoria. Though it was a bold gamble in the teeth of stiff competition from the Canada-based North West Company, Astor's idea behind founding his namesake was simple enough: gather furs here from all over the Northwest and then export them to Asia, where demand verged on the feverish. It was not, however, quite so simple.

Almost as soon as his plans – comprising both overland and seafaring parties – began to take shape, Astor's whole enterprise turned into a fiasco. The first problems arose with the *Tonquin*, the ship Astor commissioned to establish the trading post – or more exactly with its captain, a certain **Jonathan Thorn**, who cuts something of a Captain Bligh figure: an excellent seaman with a bad temper and few leadership skills. The ship left New York in September 1810, and trouble broke out in the Falklands when Thorn intemperately set sail without his landing party, who were abandoned just because they were late returning to the ship. Thorn was persuaded to go back for the men only when one of the fur traders held a pistol to his temple – as you might expect, relations remained strained thereafter. Indeed, when the *Tonquin* reached the mouth of the Columbia River, Thorn dumped the fur traders off as quickly as possible and sailed north – to his death at the hands of the Nootka of British Columbia, one of whose chieftains he hit in the face with a roll of furs in an unwise fit of pique.

Meanwhile, Astor's **overland party**, which had left St Louis in March 1811, was in trouble too. First there were endless delays and then the party argued so bitterly that it broke up into separate groups, each of which endured extraordinary hardships in the struggle to press on west in the depths of winter. Perhaps no one endured quite as much as **John Day**, who caught fever and lay at death's door for weeks; got hopelessly lost in the mountains; lived for days by eating moccasins, beaver skins, and roots; and finally, just when he began to get his bearings, was robbed and stripped by hostile natives on the banks of the Columbia River, forcing him to wander around naked before friendlier natives took pity on him. Day's sufferings, including his own severe bouts of dementia, soon acquired almost mythical status, and a string of towns and a valley in eastern Oregon now bear his name. Remarkably, most of Astor's overland party managed to dribble into "Fort Astoria" early in 1812, but, exhausted and sick, they were more of a liability than a reinforcement, and the dispirited Americans were only too willing to sell out to the Canadians at the onset of the War of 1812. Washington Irving made the best of the saga in his chunky novel *Astoria*, published just twenty years later.

types of the international workers in the port, as each community established its own cultural celebrations, rituals, and meeting halls. Almost inevitably, Astoria became notorious for **shanghaiing** (see p.92), whereby drunken revelers had more than a passing chance of waking up halfway across the Pacific, having been knocked unconscious and sold to an unscrupulous captain to complement his crew. The situation got so bad at one point that workers at quayside canneries carried guns to get themselves safely to the night shift.

In 1920 much of the town burned down in a cataclysmic **fire** that engulfed the port's shambling old wooden-frame buildings; another fire took place two years later. More catastrophic were the structural **economic changes** over the next fifty years, which led to the demise of many canneries and a depression in the wood-products industry – a double blow for the resource-based economy. Only by the 1980s did residents see that a change was necessary, so like just about every place else along the coast, Astoria has embraced **tourism**. It's worked, perhaps too well: the chic hotels and restaurants have predictably arrived, but so too have a clutch of expat Portlanders and other urbanites, whose cookie-cutter condos now pepper the landscape east of town where once the only development was a lonely railroad line.

Arrival and information

Astoria is located a hundred miles from Portland along US-26 connecting to northbound Hwy 101, or via the more interesting, slightly longer Columbia River drive along Hwy 30. Local **bus** service is provided by Sunset Limited ($1.25; ☎503/325-0563, ⓦwww.ridethebus.org), which principally runs along Marine Drive but can also connect you with the center of town (route #10), within range of Fort Stevens (#15), and farther south on to Seaside (#101 express; $2.50). Astoria's clearly signposted and well-stocked **visitor center**, 111 W Marine Drive (summer daily 8am–6pm; rest of the year Mon–Fri 9am–5pm; ☎503/325-6311, ⓦwww.oldoregon.com), is located near the base of the massive Highway 101 bridge over the Columbia River and issues a free and extremely detailed brochure on the town and its surroundings. For a leisurely trip along the waterfront, hop aboard the **Astoria Trolley** (summer Mon–Thurs 3–9pm, Fri–Sun noon–9pm; rest of year Fri–Sun 1–4pm; $2), historic railcars that ply a tourist-oriented route.

Accommodation

Astoria prides itself on its **B&Bs**, mostly housed in the splendid old mansions uptown. If you're on a tighter budget, note that there are a number of more routine modern **motels** on Marine Drive. You can also **camp** – in yurts or traditional campsites – in **Fort Stevens State Park** (sites $13–22, yurts $30; ☎1-800/452-5687; see p.149).

Astoria Inn 3391 Irving Ave ☎503/325-8153 or 1-800/718-8153, ⓦwww.astoriainnbb.com. An 1890s farmhouse-turned-B&B offering sweeping views across the Columbia from its location high up on the bluff, a mile or so east of the town center. The four guest rooms are nice, if unsurprising. ❹
Britta's Inn 1237 Kensington Ave ☎503/325-4940, ⓦwww.brittasinn.com. Handsome 1914 Craftsman home offering good, savory breakfasts and two tasteful modern rooms (sans Victoriana) with DVD players and wireless Internet access. ❻
Cannery Pier 10 Basin St, near the Astoria Bridge ☎503/325-4996 or 1-888/325-4996, ⓦwww .cannerypierhotel.com. The upper end of lodging in town, a swank boutique property housed on a waterfront pier, whose sleek modern rooms have high-speed Net access, fireplaces, and balconies. There's also an onsite gym and sauna. ❼
Clementine's 847 Exchange St ☎503/325-2005 or 1-800/521-6801, ⓦwww.clementines-bb.com.

Five pleasant bedrooms in a handsome 1888 villa, which provides delicious breakfasts and has agreeable period decor. Unexpectedly, the B&B also operates two expansive suites in an adjoining former "Moose Lodge" with more modern furnishings and not so much chintz. Rooms ❹, suites ❻
Elliott 357 12th St ☎1-877/EST-1924, ⓦwww.hotelelliott.com. Historic 1924 charmer that's been refurbished in grand style. Located in the heart of downtown, this chic affair offers upscale amenities in its rooms and suites, some with fireplaces and Jacuzzis and all with tasteful modern furnishings. The rooms are cheapest in winter; add about $60 per unit in the summer high season. ❻
Franklin St Station 1140 Franklin St ☎503/325-4314 or 1-800/448-1098, ⓦwww.franklin -st-station-bb.com. Comfortable spot constructed by a local shipbuilder for his son at the end of the nineteenth century, with six rooms and suites and a potpourri of period furnishings. ❺

The Town

The main road into Astoria from the south, **Marine Drive**, runs parallel with the **waterfront**, whose assorted piers and warehouses give little indication of the Victorian-era debauchery that once spawned dozens of harborside saloons and brothels. In a different form, the waterfront continues to be the town's cultural and historic centerpiece, and Marine Drive is the axis for most activity. The (mostly) restored, charming old buildings of **Downtown** lie a few blocks inland, and although the rest of Astoria stretches some distance farther south along the peninsula, the only major highlight therein is the **Astoria Column**, unmissable on the highest hill in the center of town.

The Columbia River Maritime Museum

The waterfront's prime attraction is the expansive **Columbia River Maritime Museum**, 1792 Marine Dr at 17th Street (daily 9.30am–5pm; $8; ☎ 503/325-2323, ⊛ www.crmm.org), whose several galleries illustrate facets of the region's nautical history. The collection begins in the large main hall, which contains models and mock-ups of old boats, either sitting on the floor or perched against the wall with careful rigging. Of the galleries that follow, one of the more interesting is the "Sailing Vessels" section, with its melodramatic ships' figureheads and fancy sideboard retrieved from the nearby wreck of a British ship, the *Peter Iredale*, slowly sinking into the sand near Fort Stevens (see p.149). The "Fishing, Tanneries and Whaling" display holds a fascinating collection of old Astoria photographs, as well as several walrus-tusk Inuit sculptures – notably that of a cribbage board – sold as scrimshaw souvenirs to visiting sailors. "Navigation and Marine Safety" focuses on the treacherous sandbar that broke the back of many a ship as it pushed into the Columbia River from the Pacific. Buoys were installed in 1979, replacing the red-hulled *Columbia* lightship, which is now part of – and moored outside – the museum, though its cramped interior quarters don't really allow for ease of visitation.

Flavel House and the uptown mansions

The most impressive of Astoria's **mansions**, the 1880s **Flavel House**, at 441 8th St and Duane (daily: summer 11am–4pm; rest of the year 10am–5pm; $5; ☎ 503/325-2203), is a fine example of the Queen Anne style with its cresting balconies, shingles, angular tower, wraparound verandas, and hipped roofs. Its first owner, Captain **George Flavel** (1823–93), began by piloting ships across the Columbia River sandbar, but he grew rich as a ship owner and razor-sharp entrepreneur who trained a beady eye on his vessels from the telescope he placed in his mansion's tower. The main rooms are set up as dioramas featuring period furniture and decor, and the newly constructed annex has a hodgepodge of interesting items, including relics from the nautical era and photographs of old Astoria.

The town's other historic sites – the **Heritage Museum**, 1618 Exchange St (daily: summer 11am–4pm; rest of the year 10am–5pm; $3; ☎ 503/325-2203), and **Uppertown Firefighters Museum**, Marine Drive at 30th Street (Wed–Sat 11am–2pm; $3; same phone as Heritage Museum) – provide more background on local history with all of its rowdy port antics and social violence, commercial canning and logging, multiethnic workers, and various fires.

From Marine Drive, numbered streets climb toward the uptown area, where the wealthy of the late nineteenth century built their elegant mansions well away from the noise of the port. Handsomely restored, with contrasting pastel shades picking up the delicacy of the carving, these appealing timber homes are distinguished by their fanciful verandas, attractive bay windows, and high gables; some of the most enjoyable are concentrated on Exchange, Franklin, and Grand avenues between 11th and 17th streets. Here also, at 15th Street and Exchange Avenue, you'll find a replica timber bastion of **Fort Astoria**, a modest tribute to the travails of John Jacob Astor's unhappy group.

Coxcomb Hill and the Astoria Column

Beyond Astoria's fancy Victorian mansions, you ascend toward the center of town and its geographic focus, **Coxcomb Hill**, by following signs and painted street emblems up 16th Street and then Coxcomb Drive. On top of the hill stands the grand **Astoria Column** (daily dawn–dusk; donation), painted with a circular, winding mural depicting the region's early pioneer history and offering superb views over the Columbia River and its surroundings. The column was patterned after Trajan's Column in Rome and erected in 1926 by John Jacob Astor's great-grandson Vincent to commemorate a rather thin slice of early nineteenth-century history. Sure enough, six of the fourteen scenes (from the middle to the top) involve the establishment and travails of Fort Astoria, stopping at 1818 with the fort's sale to the British and subsequent return to the US. Four of the other, lower scenes involve Lewis and Clark's challenges in staking and managing their 1805–06 wilderness camp.

Most visitors don't gape at the column images, though, and instead make for the **observation platform** at the top – the place to take in some stunning, windswept views of the region. You do, however, have to be willing to climb its 164 gloomy spiral stairs and contend with gawking children and rowdy teens during the summer months – everyone perched on a high, narrow platform behind a small railing.

Also on top of the hill is a concrete replica of a Native American **burial canoe**, which serves as a memorial to **Chief Comcomly** of the Chinook. He was on good terms with the first white settlers, one of whom married his daughter, until he caught his son-in-law hoeing potatoes (women's work in the chief's opinion). Comcomly's son, on the other hand, is said to have proposed to **Jane Barnes**, a barmaid from Portsmouth who arrived on an English ship in 1814 to become, Astorians claim, the first white woman in the Northwest. Jane turned him down, which wreaked havoc on local race relations. There's nothing inside today's concrete canoe, but the original would have been crammed with tools and weapons to help the spirit of the body in the afterlife.

Eating and drinking

Downtown has several good places to **eat**. *Columbian Café*, 1114 Marine Drive (☏503/325-2233), has gourmet seafood and vegetarian meals, and offers tasty pizzas and weekend musical jams in its attached *Voodoo Room*; the *Cannery Cafe*, at the end of 6th Street on the pier (☏503/325-8642), has upscale Northwest cuisine and seafood in a nice, romantic location; and the swank and modern ⅍ *Baked Alaska*, 1 12th St (☎503/325-3554), has fine entrées like Columbia River sturgeon, Dungeness crab, and a coffee-dusted "thundermuck" tuna, as well as the delicious eponymous dessert. If all else fails, make like the locals and head to *Pig 'n Pancake*, unavoidable at 146 W Bond St (☎503/325-3144), where you can get your fill of good 'n' greasy, gut-busting breakfasts. For **drinking**, the *Wet Dog Café*, on the waterfront at 144 11th St (☎503/325-6975), is a prominent hangout with reasonable bar food, decent microbrews, and live music; and a new branch of Newport-based *Rogue Ales*, 100 39th St (☎503/325-5964), serves up its signature microbrews and burgers and seafood right on the water a bit east of town.

Fort Clatsop National Memorial

Less than ten miles south of Astoria, reached by a turnoff on Hwy 101, **Fort Clatsop National Memorial** (daily: summer 8am–6pm; rest of the year 9am–5pm; $5; ⓦwww.nps.gov/lewi) is the main historic highlight of the North Coast, the centerpiece of a bevy of Lewis-and-Clark-related sites (see website) in this part of Oregon and Washington. While it's only a replica of the explorers' winter camp, the various exhibits, reconstructions, and activities make it well worth seeking out – though the place can get congested during summer months. For that reason, spring and fall may be the best times to visit, the rain only adding to the authenticity of the expedition's wet and troublesome lodging.

The gist of the story is that, having finally arrived at the mouth of the Columbia River in November 1805, the explorers **Meriwether Lewis** and **William Clark** needed a winter base before the long trudge back east. Beside a tributary a few miles south and across the bay from current Astoria, they built Fort Clatsop and had a thoroughly miserable time there. It rained on all but 12 of their 106 days, and most of the party was infested with fleas. Morale must also have been deflated by the leaders' insistence that the men keep away from native women – no matter how Lewis dressed it up in his *Journals*: "[A group of Chinook women] have formed a camp near the fort and seem determined to lay close siege to us, but … the men have preserved their constancy to their vow of celibacy."

Lewis and Clark's winter fort, a log stockade, was reconstructed in 1955 in a somewhat idealized fashion – the lines clean and parallel, the logs smooth and regular. In 2005, though, the site mysteriously burned, and it has since been re-reconstructed in a more historically accurate manner, with a much rougher, more unfinished look, lacking any hint of coziness or perfect right angles. The setting is, by contrast, delightful – deep in the forest not far from the water's edge. The **visitor center** has an outstanding display on the expedition, explaining its background as well as providing details of the journey itself. In the summer, docents in pioneer costumes give exhibitions on shooting flintlock muskets, pouring molten bullets, and making beef-tallow candles. From the center you can take two good trails, the **Clatsop Ridge** route, which provides a four-mile loop to a scenic overlook above the site, or the **Fort to Sea Trail**, which leads 6.5 miles one-way to Sunset Beach on the Pacific coast. The latter trail is one of the more impressive on the Oregon coast; for more information, visit ⓦwww.forttosea.org.

To get here from downtown Astoria just follow the highway over Youngs Bay Bridge and watch for the signs. The fort is about three miles east of Highway 101. In the summer, the site does not allow parking in the visitor center lot. Instead, you'll have to head down to the water launch at Netul Landing, a mile south of the site off Fort Clatsop Road, park there, and ride a **shuttle** back to the center.

Fort Stevens State Park

Ten miles west of Astoria, and also signposted from Highway 101 beyond Youngs Bay Bridge, is **Fort Stevens State Park**, a sizable recreational area that occupies the tapering sand spit that nudges into the mouth of the Columbia River. Hundreds come here to wander the bike and hiking trails, go freshwater swimming, and stroll miles of beach before **camping** (sites $13–22, yurts $30; ☎1-800/452-5687) for the night. There's also some historical interest a mile to the west of the campground in the beached and rusting wreck of the **Peter Iredale**, a British schooner that got caught out by high winds in 1906; it is slowly sinking into the sand but remains enough of a curiosity to clamber over at low tide. In the historical area to the north of the campground, an array of **military ruins** spreads out over the park. Fortifications were first constructed here to guard against Confederate raiders during the Civil War, and the army continued to use the site until the end of World War II. Fort Stevens was shelled one night by a passing Japanese submarine, which makes it, incredibly, the only military installation on the US mainland to have been fired on by a foreign government since 1812. A self-guided walking tour leaflet is available to help you navigate the ruins, though they probably won't be of much interest to you unless you're already into this kind of thing.

South to Oswald West State Park

Lying sixteen and twenty-five miles south of Astoria along Highway 101, Seaside and Cannon Beach are the most prominent towns on the North Coast. They're also overrun by tourists and urban day-trippers, particularly in the summer, when street after street is lined with vendors selling souvenirs, saltwater taffy, and T-shirts. Amid this teeming scene are a few decent attractions, mostly in Cannon Beach, and some decent stretches of beach, though they can almost get as crowded as the towns themselves. If this is a bit much for you, seek out the more deserted and idyllic state parks found in abundance farther south, namely **Hug Point** and **Oswald West**.

Seaside

Seventeen miles down the coast from Astoria, **SEASIDE** is a seedy resort, a mix of crude carnival rides and chain motels, that seems to maintain its popularity despite a rather checkered reputation. Even if you don't want to visit, it's pretty much unavoidable as you slowly head south on Highway 101. Long before the town came into existence, this was the place where every member of the Lewis and Clark expedition had to take a tedious turn boiling down seawater to make salt – vital to preserve meat for the return journey – a process that produced three and a half bushels of the "excellent, fine, strong & white" mineral over two winter months. The reconstructed **Salt Cairn** – a few boulders and pans – is located toward the south end of the town's main drag, The Prom (short for "promenade"), and there's a commemorative statue of Lewis and Clark halfway along The Prom at the traffic circle. Twice in the summer, near Avenue U on the beach, costumed docents reenact the historical drudgery over the course of 48 hours and answer visitors' questions with a proper 1805 perspective; contact ℡503/861-2471, ext. 214, for details.

The **visitor center**, at the junction of Hwy 101 – here Roosevelt Drive – and Broadway (℡503/738-6391 or 1-800/444-6740, ⊛www.seasidechamber .com), can provide more information on the town's carnival attractions and minor points of interest. Seaside isn't an ideal place to **stay**, with Astoria and Cannon Beach in the vicinity, but you can try the ten comely Victorian rooms of the 1893 *Gilbert Inn*, 341 Beach Drive (℡1-800/410-9770, ⊛www .gilbertinn.com; ❺, summer ❻), or the *HI-Seaside Hostel*, 930 N Holladay Drive (℡503/738-7911, ⊛2oregonhostels.com; dorms $22–25, private rooms $47–59), which rents canoes and kayaks and is located a few blocks north of Broadway and a stone's throw from the Necanicum River, which runs parallel to – and a few blocks from – the beach. Sunset Empire Transit (℡503/325-0563, ⊛www.ridethebus.org) operates a limited daily **bus** service between Seaside and Cannon Beach ($1.25) and Seaside and Astoria ($2.50), running along Marine Drive in Astoria and Highway 101 through the other two towns. For **food**, the town has sired some surprisingly decent restaurants lately, among them *Taste of Tuscany*, 1815 S Roosevelt Dr (℡503/738-5377), which turns out solid versions of pasta, chicken parmesan, and other staples; and the *Lil' Bayou*, 20 N Holladay Drive (℡503/717-0624), with its unexpectedly spicy and flavorful catfish, jambalaya, and crawfish *étouffée*.

Cannon Beach

Nine miles south of Seaside, **CANNON BEACH** is a somewhat more upmarket place. The town, which takes its name from several cannons washed onto the beach from the wreck of a warship, the USS *Shark*, in 1846, is a low-slung place whose atmosphere is a mix of authentic oceanside charm and tourist kitsch. On the plus side, skillful painters sell their work from weathered cedar-shingled studios and you can wander from bookshop to bistro, dropping in at kite shops, clothing boutiques, and microbreweries along the way. On the other hand, plenty of stores sell the usual beach bric-a-brac, galleries peddle the likes of marble seagulls and driftwood elves, and there are a good number of mediocre seafood diners. The town's one big attraction is its annual **Sand Castle Contest** (ⓦ www.cannon-beach.net), a free one-day event in mid-June where you're apt to see anything from dinosaurs and sphinxes to mermaids and monkeys to Elvis and Jesus rising from the sand as soon as the tide permits.

Beyond the town, the **beaches** are some of the most beautiful on the Oregon coast, beginning with the wide strip of sand that backs onto the town

△ Haystack Rock

center at the mouth of Ecola Creek. They continue – about a mile to the south – with a narrower strand that's dominated by the 240ft **Haystack Rock**, a craggy and imposing monolith with nesting seagulls on top and starfish, mussels, and other shellfish in the rock pools at the bottom – although it's accessible at low tide, it's definitely not climbable. More remote and less visited beaches are within a few miles of Cannon Beach, too – the highlight being **Ecola State Park** ($3 day-use fee), a couple of miles north of town, where dense conifer forests decorate the basaltic cliffs of Tillamook Head with beaches studded with sea stacks down below. The newly developed **Clatsop Loop Trail** (2.5mi round-trip) runs north over a stark headland and details the area's natural and human history, passing a viewpoint for the disused **Tillamook Rock Lighthouse**, which sits twelve miles out to sea on a lonely rock. No visitors are allowed, at least if they're alive – the site is now a columbarium for storage of cremated ashes.

A useful alternative when the crowds on Ecola get thick, the smaller **Arcadia Beach** on the south side of Cannon Beach is a good choice for picnicking or strolling, with fewer tourists than elsewhere in the area.

Practicalities

Sunset Empire Transit offers limited daily **bus** service to and from Seaside ($1.25; ℡503/325-0563, ⊛www.ridethebus.org); the stop is right in the center of town, within 50ft of the **visitor center** (℡503/436-2623, ⊛www .cannonbeach.org) at Second and Spruce streets. The best way to see Cannon Beach is on **foot**, but if you're after exploring the local coastline it's a good idea to rent a **bike** from Mike's Bike Shop, downtown at 248 N Spruce St (℡503/436-1266).

There's a wide range of **accommodation** to choose from, but things still get very tight over the summer and impossible during the Sand Castle Contest. Excellent oceanfront options include the modern, cedar-shingled *Schooners Cove Inn*, 188 N Larch St (℡503/436-2300 or 1-800/843-0128, ⊛www .schoonerscove.com; ❺, summer ❽), whose rooms and suites have microwaves, fridges, and DVD players (some have fireplaces, kitchens, and seafront balconies, too); the *Waves Motel*, 188 W 2nd St (℡503/436-2205 or 1-800/822-2468, ⊛www.thewavesmotel.com; ❺, summer ❼–❾), another dapper, modern place right on the ocean, with a wide range of studios and suites spread across several buildings; and the equally well-sited *Webb's Scenic Surf Motel*, 255 N Larch St (℡503/436-2706 or 1-800/374-9322, ⊛www.webbsscenicsurf.com; ❺, summer ❽), with oceanfront studios and suites, some with kitchenettes and fireplaces. There are cheaper alternatives south of the town center near Haystack Rock – the *Cannon Beach Hotel*, 1116 S Hemlock St (℡503/436-1392, ⊛www .cannonbeachhotel.com; ❹–❼ by season), for one, is newly refurbished with smart, modern furnishings and tasteful appointments.

For **food**, the town center is the best bet, with a string of reasonable choices dotted along the main drag, North Hemlock Street. Among them, the informal *Lazy Susan Café* (℡503/436-2816), next to the Coaster Theater at no. 126, does excellent health food and inexpensive breakfasts; the *Wayfarer*, 1190 Pacific Ave (℡503/436-1108), is the choice for upscale seafood – razor clams to pan-fried oysters – as well as filet mignon; and arguably the town's top restaurant, ⅍ *Newman's at 988*, 988 S Hemlock (℡503/436-1151), provides pricey Continental fare that's fresh and succulent, from duck breast and the catch of the day to beef medallions and seafood pasta. *Bill's Tavern & Brewhouse*, 188 N Hemlock St (℡503/436-2202), is the town's busiest **bar**, offering bar food along with its own handcrafted brews.

Food foraging along the coast

With patience, the region's beaches can yield a **hearty meal**, though there are limits on the numbers of shellfish and crabs you're allowed to catch, so check for local restrictions – staffers at town visitor centers can usually tell you. Be aware also that pollution has made it unsafe to catch anything at all on certain parts of the coast – again, ask locally or call the Oregon State Department of Agriculture (☏503/986-4720). There are several sorts of **clams**: razor clams are the hardest to catch, moving through the sand remarkably quickly, but others are easier game. **Gapers**, found at a depth of fourteen to sixteen inches, and **softshells**, found at a depth of eight to fourteen inches in firmer mud flats, both have meaty and rather phallic-looking "necks"; **cockles** don't have these (a decided advantage if you're squeamish) and are also the easiest to dig, lying just below the surface. The **geoduck** ("gooey-duck") is a giant, long-necked specimen that acts as the holy grail for local clam-diggers and is notoriously difficult to catch. Arm yourself with bucket and spade and find a beach where other people are already digging – obviously a promising spot.

Cleaning and cooking gapers and softshells is not for the fainthearted. To do so, immerse them in fresh warm water until the neck lengthens so the outer skin will slip off easily. Then pry the entire clam out of its shell with a sharp knife, peel off the outer skin from the neck, and slit lengthwise. Split open the stomach, remove all the cark material and gelatinous rod, and cook as preferred – they can be steamed, fried, battered, or dunked into a chunky chowder soup. Cockles are much less messy; you just steam them in fresh- or saltwater until their shells open – some people prefer them almost raw.

For **crabbing**, you'll need to get hold of a crab ring (often rentable) and scrounge a piece of fish for bait. Lower the ring to the bottom of the bay from a boat, pier, or dock – and wait. The best time to crab is an hour before or an hour after low and high tides; you're not allowed to keep babies (less than 5.75 inches across) or females, identified by a broad round flap on the underside (the male flap is narrow). To cook a crab, boil it in water for twenty minutes, then crack it, holding its base in one hand, putting your other thumb under the shell at midpoint, and pulling off its back. Turn the crab over to remove the leaflike gills and "butter" from its center – then pick the meat from its limbs and body.

Hug Point and Oswald West state parks

South of Cannon Beach, Highway 101 threads through the wooded hills that overlook the ocean and provides some very eye-opening views of the rocky headlands and majestic sweep of the landscape. Many tourists simply blow through this part of 101 on their way down to the cheese factories in Tillamook, but if you're interested in good hiking, there are a number of fine spots in the vicinity. Just a few miles south of Ecola State Park – and accessible via the beach if you've got the legs for it – is the turnoff for **Hug Point State Park**. This romantic-sounding place is nice for sunsets and such, but the name derives from the late-nineteenth-century reaction to the narrow road built around the promontory near beach level. The coach route literally "hugged" the base of the cliff as it made its away around it, no doubt a rather nauseating trip for those facing hours of such transport. Impressively enough, a small stretch of this road is still visible at the place marked **Hug Point**, on a trail leading a half-mile north from the parking lot, and even today you can see the wagon-wheel ruts that were deeply cut into the rock surface, and journey around the point on foot at low tide.

A few miles further south is **Oswald West State Park**, named after the pioneering governor responsible for protecting much of the state's shoreline in the 1910s. The park is easily accessible from both sides of the highway and offers a rugged and densely forested chunk of seashore that incorporates two headlands. The first is **Cape Falcon**, the second the 1660ft **Neah-Kah-Nie Mountain**, meaning "place of fire" in reference to the local Tillamook tribe's habit of burning the mountain forest to provide better grazing for the deer and elk it relied on. Neah-Kah-Nie has also been linked with buried treasure ever since white settlers first heard a Tillamook tale of an enormous canoe – presumed to be a Spanish galleon – swept onto the shore with its great white wings flapping in the wind. The Spaniards, so the story went, stashed their valuables in a hole in the mountainside and rounded off the enterprise by slitting the throat of a crew member before burying his body on top of the treasure – which, if nothing else, should have given the Tillamook a clue as to the treatment they might expect from Europeans. Some support has been given to the legend by the discovery hereabouts of a handful of Spanish artifacts and several tons of beeswax – a favorite Spanish trade item – but despite much searching and digging, the treasure itself has never been found.

In between the two headlands at the mouth of Short Sand Creek, Oswald West State Park has a beach that's good for surfing, a picnic area, and a small and simple **campground** (Oct–April $10; May–Sept $14) with tables, fireplaces, drinking water, and flush toilets. It is a wonderful spot, popular with young surfers with wetsuits and others willing to hike the third of a mile down the hillside from Highway 101 to get to it; one of the parking lots is for campers only, with plastic wheelbarrows provided to help lug equipment. From the campground, there's a choice of two short **hikes**: either the stiff, four-mile climb south to a vantage point near the top of Neah-Kah-Nie Mountain, or the easier two-and-a-half-mile hike north to the tip of Cape Falcon, weaving through patches of old-growth Sitka spruce before reaching some superb coastal views.

Nehalem Bay to Tillamook Bay

Just past Neah-Kah-Nie Mountain, Highway 101 begins a circuitous section that encompasses a string of small beach- or bayside communities that continues down to **Tillamook**. Weaving around the bays of **Nehalem** and Tillamook, with a run past the ocean in between, the road has a number of good stopping points where ocean cliffs tumble down to rocky shores, rusty skiffs bob at the waterside, and seagulls perch on dock pilings. It's a compelling landscape, with its mix of natural wonders and antique hamlets, but there's not much to do here beyond hiking and beach strolling – which can be magnificent in places.

Nehalem Bay and around

A mile or two south of Neah-Kah-Nie Mountain, the highway takes a sweeping turn inland toward a trio of small towns built around the pleasant inlet of **Nehalem Bay**. At the north end of the bay, the first place of any size is the burg of **MANZANITA**, rarely a major sight on the coastal tour route but a big draw for vacationing Portlanders, who set up shop here in the summer months and while away the days. Although the locals tout their **seven-mile beach** as something special, the sands here aren't anything you haven't seen before. Still, the overall atmosphere is nice and low-key, and the place does have a few **restaurants** worth a visit if you're famished for decent chow. *Marzano's*, a block from the beach at 60 Laneda Ave (☎503/368-3663), has better pizzas and calzones than you'd expect to find at the beach, while the *Seafood and Chowder House*, 519 Laneda Ave (℡503/368-2722), doles out serviceable fish and chips, clam chowder, and other seafood. You can **stay** at the *Inn at Manzanita*, 67 Laneda Ave (℡503/368-6754, Ⓦwww .innatmanzanita.com; ⑥), which has clean, modern units with jetted spas, fridges, fireplaces, and microwaves; while *Zen Garden B&B*, near the end of Carey Road (℡503/368.6697, Ⓦwww.neahkahnie.net/zengarden; ⑥), sports two modest but agreeable rooms and is pleasantly isolated from the main part of town. This B&B is conveniently adjacent to **Nehalem Bay State Park** (day-use fee $3), which occupies the tip of the spit covering the bay entrance and provides good **camping** (tent sites $16–20, yurts $27; reserve at ℡1-800/452-5687). With its prime ocean views and relaxing nature strolls, the park is a quiet highlight of the journey around the bay, also offering canoeing, fishing, clamming, and horseback riding – though it does put you at some remove from the rest of town farther east along Highway 101.

Returning to the route from Manzanita will send you twisting around the flanks of the coastal mountains before reaching the village of **NEHALEM**, offering some mildly interesting antique stores and knickknack shops, as well as *Currents*, 35815 Highway 101 (℡503/368-5557), an unexpectedly chic yet casual eatery serving up expensive Northwest Cuisine dishes like game hen and crab cakes and strawberry-avocado salad. Indeed, the Oregon coast sports many such towns, which have almost no conventional sights but do offer a fine restaurant or two, often run by a chef fleeing the hubbub of the big city. The next town around the Nehalem Bay bend, **WHEELER**, is another such example – its *Nehalem River Inn*, a mile east off Highway 101 at 34910 Hwy 53 (℡1-800/368-6499), presents rotating gourmet offerings of duck, lamb, steak, and seafood with color and dash.

Tillamook Bay and around

Highway 101 leaves Nehalem Bay with an abrupt ninety-degree turn to the south and makes a beeline for the dull linear sprawl of Rockaway Beach, about twenty miles south of Cannon Beach. At its southern end, the highway veers east round **Tillamook Bay**, once called "Murderer's Harbor" after natives killed a sailor from Captain Robert Gray's expedition here in 1788. On the north side of the bay, **GARIBALDI**, named after the 1870 unifier of Italy, is one of the most strangely fetching of the state's declining industrial towns. With a huge disused smokestack announcing the former mill town's presence, Garibaldi has a smattering of evocative ruins, though increasingly these are disappearing as development encroaches on the hamlet's old character. For a whiff of the good old days, drop by the modest confines of **Lumberman's Park**, right off Highway 101, and poke around an old steam engine and various industrial-age odds and ends. At the park you can hop also aboard the **Oregon Coast Scenic Railroad** (mid-May to mid-Sept Sat & Sun, sometimes Fri, noon, 2pm, 4pm; $13, kids $7; ℡503/842-7972, Ⓦwww.ocsr.net), which provides an old-fashioned 1910 locomotive experience, chugging along the rocky oceanside on a 90min trip between here and Rockaway Beach; it's especially good for the kids, and if you pay an extra $3, you can even ride in the caboose.

A few miles south, Highway 101 rounds the northeast end of the bay to travel its broad eastern side. The bay and its tidal flats offer some good opportunities for beachcombing, clam-digging, and crabbing; the small town of **BAY CITY**, along the way, has few sights but a pair of good restaurants: in the *Artspace*

Restaurant and Gallery, Hwy 101 at 5th Street (☎503/377-2782), you can dine on tasty soups, salads, and seafood while taking a peek at the work of regional artists. The *Pacific Oyster Company*, 5150 Oyster Dr (☎503/377-2320), is a diner with ultra-fresh, hand-shucked shellfish and crabs, and savory items like cioppino, crab Louie, and good ol' clam chowder.

From here the highway suddenly veers inland away from the bay and across the wide, green valley that announces **TILLAMOOK**. This workaday dairy town is best known for its two cheese-making factories, among the region's most popular tourist attractions. In a bright and cheerful building on the north side of town beside Highway 101 is the **Tillamook Cheese Factory** (daily: summer 8am–8pm; rest of the year 8am–6pm; free; ⊚ www.tillamookcheese .com), where the self-guided tour provides glimpses of hair-netted workers beside conveyor belts and bent over large, milky vats of cheddar and Monterey Jack. But the factory plays second fiddle to the gift shop, which sells every type of bovine souvenir imaginable, and its ice cream counters, where the company's oversize scoops are devoured by equally oversize customers. The other factory, the **Blue Heron French Cheese Company** (daily: summer 8am–8pm; rest of the year 9am–6pm; free; ⊚ www.blueheronoregon.com), signposted off Highway 101 less than a mile south, specializes in locally produced French-style cheeses and has a tasting area featuring both cheese and Oregon wine. Here you can sample the company's savory pepper-encrusted brie, among others, before heading out back to have a close encounter with a goat, mule, or rooster in the quasi-petting zoo.

Cape Meares to Otter Rock

Heading south from Tillamook on Highway 101, it's a humdrum 45-mile trip along a series of inland valleys to get back to the sea – but there's a much more enjoyable, and time-consuming, coastal alternative: the **Three Capes Scenic Loop**, which leads you southward on a lengthy, circuitous trip, lurching around long bays and jagged promontories, across lowlands and around hillsides, until the road merges with Highway 101 west of the coastal **Siuslaw National Forest**. After dealing with **Lincoln City**, you once again find yourself edging a long, straight stretch of Oregon coastline and a variety of natural features and state parks leading to the little town of **Otter Rock**.

The short route to reach the loop begins on Bayocean Road northwest from central Tillamook, where you meander through dairy country and bucolic farmsteads until you reach the southern spit of **Bayocean**, which guards Tillamook Bay. A century ago this was a notable real-estate colony and amusement zone; the resort literally fell into the sea due to unexpected erosion, and the spit became an island. It's now been reconnected with a causeway, and provides a good place for a rugged hike over its hilly interior or a gentle beach-front walk.

Three Capes Scenic Loop

Named after capes Meares, Lookout, and Kiwanda, the clearly signposted **Three Capes Scenic Loop** is a 38-mile detour from Highway 101 that begins where Bayocean Road crosses from Tillamook Bay over to the Pacific Ocean. From here it's just a few miles to reach the short approach to **Cape Meares Lighthouse** (April–Oct daily 11am–4pm; free; ⊚ www.capemeareslighthouse .org), a late-nineteenth-century structure of brick faced with sheet iron; it is a mere 38ft tall but boasts gorgeous views out along the rough and rocky shoreline. While you're here, take a look also at the nearby "**octopus tree**," an oddly shaped Sitka spruce – its branching trunk forms a 60ft-wide base – that may be up to 2000 years old. The cape is also a good place to take your binoculars and peer out at the expanse of the **Oregon Islands National Wildlife Refuge** (Ⓦwww.fws.gov/oregoncoast/oregonislands), off-limits to human interlopers but fascinating for its puffins, murres, and cormorants in the spring, pelicans and terns in the summer and autumn, and loons and grebes in the winter. Amid all the winged creatures is also a smattering of mammals, which you can see throughout the coastal zone, among them seals and sea lions, dolphins, and whales.

Two and a half miles farther along the Cape Meares Scenic Loop, **OCEANSIDE** is an agreeable little place that spreads along the seashore and up the steep, wooded hill behind. There are fine views of the offshore **Three Arch Rocks**, a favorite with nesting sea birds, especially the tufted puffin, and a long sandy beach. There are also a couple of places to **stay**. Down near the seashore is the simple modern motel *Oceanside Inn*, 1440 Pacific St NW (Ⓣ503/842-2961 or 1-800/347-2972; ❸), and up above, high on the hill with great views, is the more appealing *House on the Hill Motel*, 1816 Maxwell Mountain Rd (Ⓣ503/842-6030, Ⓦwww.houseonthehillmotel.com; ❺), a comfortable spot where all the rooms have seaside views, and some have decks or balconies and fridges or full kitchens.

Pushing on down the coast from Oceanside, the shallows of **Netarts Bay** are almost entirely enclosed by a sand spit that protrudes from the bay's south shore. At the base of the spit behind the beach, **Cape Lookout State Park** is named after – and also incorporates – the forested headland immediately to the south. It offers a picnic area, **campground**, and **yurts** (pitch sites $16–20, yurts $27; Ⓣ503/842-4981 or 1-800/452-6949), as well as the uncommon **deluxe cabins** ($45–66 by season) that include fridges, microwaves, and hot showers. From the campground area, you can stroll out onto the spit and go clamming and crabbing in the sheltered waters of the bay, or hunt for glass fishing floats that have bobbed here all the way from Asia – an obsessive pursuit for some Northwesterners, who prize them for their antique value and scarcity since they've been out of use for decades. Around where Jackson Creek and the entry road meet the sand, the beach is built along a series of **sand dunes**, and around these dunes lies a helter-skelter array of huge spruce logs. To the south, it's a brief drive – or a stiff two-and-a-half-mile walk – from the campground to the trailhead and parking lot (day-use fee $3) of the Cape Lookout Trail. This is a mildly strenuous and very popular two-and-a-half-mile jaunt to the tip of **Cape Lookout** as it pokes a precipitous finger out into the Pacific.

From the base of Cape Lookout the road jockeys around the small inlet of Sand Lake, around where the **Clay Myers Natural Area** protects an estuary home to many sea birds, salmon, deer, and otter. Just south of here, the road reaches the third and final cape on the scenic loop, **Cape Kiwanda**, a sandstone promontory that's trimmed by sand dunes and partly protected by a monolithic mound of basalt, **Haystack Rock** (not to be confused with the same-named rock in Cannon Beach).

Pacific City

The Kiwanda headland is near the tiny town of **PACIFIC CITY**, which is hidden away near the mouth of the Nestucca River and sheltered from the sea by another sand spit. The fishermen here are known for their ability to launch their fishing dories straight from the seashore into the oncoming surf – a real skill even though outboard motors long ago replaced oars.

If you'd like to **stay** in this romantic environment, the best choice is the *Inn at Cape Kiwanda*, 33105 Cape Kiwanda Drive (☎1-888/965-7001, ⓦwww.innatcapekiwanda.com; ➐), which has rooms with plush amenities like fireplaces, Jacuzzis, CD and DVD players, and oceanfront decks, as well as a day spa and espresso bar. Just a few miles outside town are the B&Bs the *Eagle's View*, 37975 Brooten Rd (☎1-888/846-3292, ⓦwww .eaglesviewbb.com; ➏), a friendly modern place amid unspoiled terrain, featuring five smart units with separate baths and an outdoor porch and hot tub; and, a bit farther inland off Highway 101 in the town of Cloverdale, the *Sandlake Country Inn*, 8505 Galloway Rd (☎503/965-6745, ⓦwww .sandlakecountryinn.com; ➏), a century-old farmhouse with one modest room and two suites decorated in Victorian furnishings, with private baths and Jacuzzis; there's also a cottage on the grounds.

For **eating** and **drinking** in Pacific City, the *Delicate Palate Bistro*, 35280 Brooten Rd (☎1-866/567-3466), has seafood from halibut to salmon, plus steak and ribs and decent cocktails. Even more well known and well regarded is the ⅄ *Pacific Pub & Brewery*, 33180 Cape Kiwanda Drive (☎503/965-7007), which serves a decent blend of gourmet pizzas, steak, and seafood but really shines for its award-winning microbrews, among them such delectables as India Pelican Ale, Tsunami Stout, and Doryman's Dark Ale.

Cascade Head, Lincoln City and Devil's Lake

From Pacific City, it's about four miles back to Highway 101 and then around fifteen miles south to the enticing natural preserve of **CASCADE HEAD**, protecting nearly ten thousand acres on a coastal promontory rising to 1800ft. Although there are ample opportunities for exploration here, the area's varying topography and stunning views are best taken in on a five-and-a-half-mile loop trail that's aimed at hardy outdoor adventurers. To reach it, travel south on 101 a little over three miles past the tiny town of **Neskowin** and take a gravel road west four miles until it ends. As you hike past ravines and over hillsides, you'll pass an intriguing display of rugged natural beauty, from a stand of old-growth Sitka spruce to the craggy, watery reaches of Hart's Cove to one of the last remaining sections of coastal grasslands in the state.

South of Cascade Head the highway reaches what is one of the less appealing towns on the Oregon coast, **LINCOLN CITY**, actually the merged version of five small beach towns, run together in 1965. The amalgamation rattles along for seven congested miles on Highway 101, with precious little to get you to stop. Still, despite the visual clutter, the beach can be enticing in places and there are plenty of inexpensive **motels** to choose from – the **visitor center**, 801 SW Hwy 101 (☎541/996-2152, ⓦwww.lincolncity.org), has the complete list. The one top-of-the-line place to stay locally is the *Inn at Spanish Head*, 4009 SW Hwy 101 (☎1-800/452-8127, ⓦwww.spanishhead.com; ➏–➒), an ocean-facing resort clinging to a coastal hillside that provides a range of elegant rooms and suites, as well as a good upper-end **restaurant** known as *Fathoms*, best for its surf 'n' turf. It's also worth dropping in on the ⅄ *Blackfish Cafe*, 2733 NW Hwy 101 (☎541/996-1007), which is one of the coast's better eateries, serving up local rockfish 'n' chips, duck breast, and smoked Chinook salmon for cheaper prices than you might expect. Just as fine is the top-notch *Bay House*, 5911 SW Hwy 101 (☎541/996-3222), which features supreme Northwest

Cuisine like pheasant, rack of lamb, and a full range of locally caught seafood. South of town, the *Side Door Cafe*, 6675 Glendenen Beach Rd (☎541/764-3826), makes a mean seafood chowder and also has salmon cakes and good desserts for inexpensive prices. The adjacent *Eden Hall* (☎541/764-3826) is a solid choice for **music** in the area, serving up regionally known artists in blues, folk, and country.

It may be worth staying a few miles east of town in a **campground** at **Devil's Lake**. As the first of four Satan-themed natural areas along the coast, Devil's Lake is by far the most benign, a fetching summer playground on the eastern edge of Lincoln City that has tent and hookup sites and yurts (sites $13–22, yurts $29; reserve at ☎1-800/452-5687), with opportunities for boating and fishing, too. Conveniently, its main access route, Devil's Lake Road, also provides an alternate route around the heavy traffic of Lincoln City, which you must otherwise traverse at a glacial pace for up to a half-hour by car.

Boiler Bay to Otter Rock

Beyond Lincoln City, Highway 101 skirts Siletz Bay before slicing down a few miles south to **Boiler Bay**, a heaving basalt inlet where the surf pounds relentlessly and makes for a dramatic sight during winter storms. Named after the boiler of a ship that crashed here in 1910, the nautical relic can actually, some claim, be spotted the at low tide – though it's usually more fruitful to explore the accessible tide pools along here, which are as rich and diverse as any place along the coast. Immediately to the south, **DEPOE BAY** is an unassuming coastal settlement straddling the tiniest of harbors. The town basically lies along the highway itself, and most of what you'll see are simple diners and trinket shops. One worthwhile exception is the **Whale Watching Center**, 119 SW Hwy 101 (May–Sept daily 9am–5pm; Oct–April Wed–Sun 9am–4pm; free; ⓦwww.whalespoken.org), where you can learn about the gentle cetaceans and view the migration of gray whales in December and March. Good for **dining** are *Tidal Raves*, 279 NW Hwy 101 (☎541/765-2995), which as you might expect from the name is known for its seafood, including Dungeness crab and cioppino; and the *Surfrider*, 3115 NW Hwy 101 (☎541/764-2311), worth a stop for its prime rib, crab cakes, and razor clams. The latter is part of the *Surfrider Resort* (☎1-800/662-2378, ⓦwww.surfriderresort.com; ④–⑤), whose **rooms** and suites offer hot tubs, kitchens, fireplaces, and DVD players, with an onsite pool and sauna.

South of here the highway climbs up toward the forested mass of **Cape Foulweather**, discovered and named by a jaded Captain Cook, whose historic expedition up the Pacific Coast had nearly been dispatched to a watery grave by a sudden Northwest storm – the winds hereabouts can gust at 100mph. A short and narrow side road leads off Highway 101 to the cape's lookout, from which there are stirring coastal views – but be prepared to negotiate some hair-raising switchbacks on the way.

Returning to Highway 101, it's just a couple of miles farther south to an easier turnoff at **OTTER ROCK**, a tiny town at a bend in the highway that nonetheless hosts one of the coast's most impressive sights, less than a mile west on the coast. Here, **Devil's Punchbowl** is a sandstone cave whose roof has fallen in, and is now a well-named cauldron during the winter months, when the sea heaves and churns at high tide, throwing up huge dollops of sea spray and thunderous waves. Luckily, at low tide the waters recede to reveal a lattice of rock pools, which you can explore on a pleasant beachside trail. Directly on the upper lip of the Punchbowl, you can **eat** at *Mo's Otter Rock* (May–Oct;

@541/765-2442), part of a chain of seaside diners. The one here is little more than a oceanside shack, but it does dole out the thick and delicious seafood slurry known as "slumgullion." A bit further south along Highway 101, you can **stay** at the elongated sands of **Beverly Beach**, part of which is designated a state park with picnic facilities, yurts, and a large and well-equipped **campground** ($13–21, yurts $29; @1-800/452-5687 or 541/265-9278).

Newport

With a population of just nine thousand, **NEWPORT** occupies the seashore at the mouth of Yaquina Bay, about 25 miles south of Lincoln City. It's one of several Oregon fishing ports that has at least partially turned itself into a resort, with bits and pieces of the old fishing port decorated by the occasional mural and some decent restaurants and microbreweries moving in. Don't be deterred by the first view of the town; there are plenty of homely motels and strip malls along this stretch of Highway 101, but other areas offer more than enough sights and scenery to hold your interest for a day or two.

Arrival and information

Newport's **Greyhound** depot is at 956 SW 10th St, just north of the Yaquina Bay Bridge, off the main drag of Highway 101 (@541/265-2253). The **visitor center**, nearby at 555 SW Coast Hwy (Mon–Fri 9am–5pm; @541/265-8801 or 1-800/262-7844, @www.newportchamber.org), issues maps and brochures on the town and its environs, advises about agate hunting, and has complete motel and campground listings. There are no buses within the town limits, which can be a bit of a pain if you don't have a vehicle – the visitor center is a good mile from both the harbor to the south and Nye Beach to the north.

Accommodation

Newport offers a wide range of **accommodation**, including distinctive **B&Bs** around Nye Beach and fairly modern **hotels**, which line the bluff above the beach on Elizabeth Street. Less appealing, drab **motels** are dotted along Highway 101. There's also a popular **campground** (and yurts) in Beverly Beach State Park seven miles north of town (see above), and another – not as well appointed – in **South Beach State Park** (pitch sites $17–22, yurts $29; @541/867-4715), a mile or so south of the Yaquina Bay Bridge. There is good crabbing and windsurfing at South Beach, though, along with the opportunity to go on a kayak tour (@541/867-6590 for details).

Elizabeth Street Inn 232 Elizabeth St @541/265-9400 or 1-877/265-9400, @www .elizabethstreetinn.com. Particularly large and modern, with sizable rooms having kitchenettes, microwaves, fireplaces, and sea-facing balconies, with an onsite spa, gym, and pool. **❼**

Newport Belle moored off South Beach @541/867-6290 or 1-800/348-1922, @www .newportbelle.com. Within view of the town marina and the Yaquina Bay Bridge, a fetching, recently built sternwheeler converted into a B&B, with five cozy rooms that provide the requisite dash of romance, as well as private bathrooms. **❺–❻**

Oar House 520 SW 2nd St @541/265-9571 or 1-800/252-2538, @www.oarhouse-bed-breakfast.com. Five plush, en-suite rooms in a handsome old house that comes complete with a lovely garden and a tower offering sea views; the gourmet breakfasts here are first rate, too. **❻**

Sylvia Beach 267 NW Cliff St @541/265-5428 or 1-888/795-8422, @www.sylviabeachhotel.com. Overlooking Nye Beach, a renowned three-story

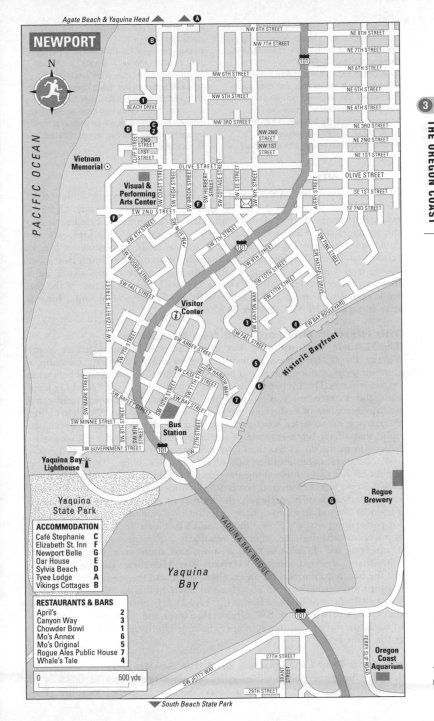

Agate Beach & Yaquina Head ▲ ▲ Ⓐ

NEWPORT

N

NW 8TH STREET
NE 8TH STREET
Ⓑ
NW 7TH STREET
NE 7TH STREET
101
NW 6TH STREET
NE 6TH STREET
NW 5TH STREET
NE 5TH STREET
NE 4TH STREET
❶
BEACH DRIVE
NW 3RD STREET
NE 3RD STREET
NW 2ND STREET
Ⓓ Ⓒ
NW 1ST STREET
NE 2ND STREET
❷
NE 1ST STREET
2ND STREET
1ST STREET
OLIVE STREET
OLIVE STREET

Vietnam Memorial ⊙

SE 1ST STREET

Visual & Performing Arts Center
Ⓕ
SW 2ND STREET
SE 2ND STREET

PACIFIC OCEAN

Ⓕ
SW 4TH STREET
SW WOODS STREET
SW FALL STREET
SW 7TH STREET

SW 7TH STREET
101
SW 9TH STREET
SW 10TH STREET
SW 11TH STREET

SW PINE STREET
SW HATFIELD DRIVE

SW ELIZABETH STREET

Visitor Center ⓘ
SW ABBEY STREET
SW FALL STREET
❸ SW CANYON WAY
❹ SW BAY BOULEVARD

Historic Bayfront
❺
❻
SW CASE STREET
SW HARBOR WAY
❼

SW MARK STREET
SW BAYLEY STREET
SW MINNIE STREET
SW 8TH STREET
SW 9TH STREET
SW GOVERNMENT STREET
SW 10TH STREET
SW 11TH STREET
SW BAY STREET

Bus Station
101
SW 27TH STREET

Yaquina Bay Lighthouse ⚓

Yaquina State Park

Rogue Brewery
Ⓖ

YAQUINA BAY BRIDGE

Yaquina Bay

101

Oregon Coast Aquarium

FERRY SLIP ROAD

27TH STREET
BRANT STREET
SW JETTY WAY
29TH STREET

ACCOMMODATION
Café Stephanie **C**
Elizabeth St. Inn **F**
Newport Belle **G**
Oar House **E**
Sylvia Beach **D**
Tyee Lodge **A**
Vikings Cottages **B**

RESTAURANTS & BARS
April's **2**
Canyon Way **3**
Chowder Bowl **1**
Mo's Annex **6**
Mo's Original **5**
Rogue Ales Public House **7**
Whale's Tale **4**

0 ————— 500 yds

▼ South Beach State Park

hotel with a literary character – each of the twenty rooms is named after a famous writer. Among the best are the Mark Twain and the Herman Melville. Excellent eats, too. ⑤–⑦
Tyee Lodge 4925 NW Woody Way ☎1-888/553-8933, ⓦwww.tyeelodge.com. Five comfortable and modern B&B units with expansive oceanfront views near Agate Beach. There's also B&B accommodation in the adjacent *Ocean House* (same phone, ⓦwww.oceanhouse.com), owned by the same people, with eight, more

Victorian-styled units with all the charm and chintz. Both ⑦
Vikings Cottages 729 NW Coast St ☎541/265-2477 or 1-800/480-2477, ⓦwww .vikingsoregoncoast.com. A pleasingly old-fashioned option on Nye Beach, there are renovated 1920s units with simple furnishings and private baths, along with more modern, less romantic condominiums. Bigger units also have fireplaces, fridges, and microwaves. Cottages ⑤, condos ⑥

The Town

Most of Newport lies on the grand curve of **Yaquina Bay**, the outlet of the Yaquina River, with the majority of sights on the bay's north side. Unfortunately, the three main areas of town – the Historic Bayfront and Nye Beach near the center, Yaquina Head and Agate Beach to the north, and the Oregon Coast Aquarium across the bay to the south – are not readily accessible on foot in relation to one another. Even the town's main campground at South Beach (see above) is in a less than inviting location on the far side of two jetties and a highway bridge. Luckily, you can **rent a car** with Enterprise, one of the few name brands in town, at 533 E Olive St (☎541/574-1999), or rent a **bike** at Bike Newport, 125 NE 6th St (☎541/265-9917).

The Historic Bayfront and Nye Beach

The **Historic Bayfront** along Bay Boulevard, just to the northeast of the Yaquina Bay Bridge, is the obvious first stop for many – a breezy collection of souvenir shops, seafood diners, and hordes of sea lions wallowing and bellowing on the wharves. This lively mixture can be seen in a quick half-hour-long jaunt along the docks, where you can peek at the rusty trawlers floating nearby and perhaps get a bite of fresh clam chowder in a bayside setting. Worth avoiding, though, are the scattered tourist traps such as "Undersea Gardens," outmoded sights that offer a 1960s-era view of the deep blue sea in creaky old confines.

Away from the docks less than two miles to the west, and across Highway 101, Newport reveals another side of its character among the old, peeling timber houses that ramble along the oceanfront north of Yaquina Bay. From NW Second Street to around Tenth Street, immediately behind the long and uncrowded sands of **Nye Beach**, the hippies of yesteryear have bequeathed a friendly air and arty atmosphere, manifest in a pair of **arts centers** – one for performing arts, at 777 W Olive St and SW Coast St (☎541/265-ARTS, ⓦwww.coastarts.org), the other for visual arts, at the same address (Tues–Sun 11am–5pm; ☎541/265-6540). Apart from this, there are few official sights other than a deserted, modern **Vietnam War Memorial** on a nearby bluff, but the beach itself makes for an excellent stroll, and the seaside development is a bit more restrained than elsewhere in town. South of SW Second Street – but still north of Yaquina Bay – the Nye Beach district gives way to the shiny oceanfront hotels of **SW Elizabeth Street** and the commercial center of town, an uninspiring modern sprawl along Highway 101, which doubles as the main drag.

Yaquina Bay Lighthouse and the South Bay

Standing amid the manicured greenery of a tiny state park at the foot of Elizabeth Street, near the bridge over Yaquina Bay, the **Yaquina Bay**

Lighthouse (daily: summer 11am–5pm; rest of the year noon–4pm; donation) is one of the coast's more interesting late-nineteenth-century lighthouses. Far from huge, the 40ft tower sits attached to the old keeper's house, a quaint timber building constructed in the Cape Cod style. Actually, it's surprising the lighthouse has survived: it was in operation for only three years during the 1870s while the Yaquina Head Lighthouse – a much larger edition – was built. You can wander around upstairs in the stately old quarters where the keeper and his family stayed; period furnishings provide an antique glimmer of their brief tenure there.

To cross to the south side of the bay, you traverse the majestic span of the **Yaquina Bay Bridge**, perhaps the finest bridge on the coast among several contenders, its huge, sweeping steel arches reminding one of the heroic days of public architecture – it was completed in 1931. The south side of the bay is considerably removed from its counterpart and holds only two sights of any prominence. The first is the large and impressive **Oregon Coast Aquarium** (daily: summer 9am–6pm; rest of year 10am–5pm; $12; ☎541/867-3474, ⓦwww.aquarium.org), at 2820 SE Ferry Slip Rd, signposted off Highway 101. The facility is home to marine mammals like the sea otter and seal, sea birds like the tufted puffin, and a whopping octopus in a glass-framed sea grotto, but its highlight is Passages of the Deep, a shark-surrounded underwater tunnel. There are also mock-ups of rocky and sandy shores, wetlands, and coastal waters where the jellyfish steal the show. The other major sight holds a very different, though still aqueous, sort of appeal: the **Rogue Brewery**, near the south end of the bridge at 2320 OSU Drive (☎541/867-3660, ⓦwww.rogue.com), easily identifiable with its red, walk-through silo out front. Every day at 4pm, the site gives free tours in which you can wander around the massive "micro"-brewery works, with its huge brew kettles and heavy bags of hops and flavorings like chocolate and herbs, and get a free sample or two while you're at it. Rogue also operates its own pub in town (see Eating and Drinking).

Yaquina Head and Agate Beach

Built on a basalt headland three miles north of town off Hwy 101, the stately white column of the **Yaquina Head Lighthouse** (tours daily: summer 9am–4pm; rest of the year noon–4pm) has been incorporated into the **Yaquina Head Outstanding Natural Area** (daily dawn to dusk; $5 entry), an appropriately named centerpiece of environmental protection – one of the best on the coast. The area's **visitor center** (daily: June–Sept 9am–5pm; rest of year 10am–4pm) has displays on local flora and fauna and the geology of this rocky cape, but even better are the unsurpassed views of the coastline, especially from a high path leading over the bluffs, and of whales migrating out at sea during the winter. Other sights include seals, otters, and sea birds gathered on the offshore rocks. Descend a wooden stairway below the lighthouse bluffs to a **beach** of rounded (and slippery) dark rocks, and you can get a closer view of these creatures than practically anywhere else they exist in their natural environment. Farther east, accessed by a short turnoff, **Quarry Cove** sits in an oceanside depression formed by a rock quarry that's now a series of **tide pools** inhabited by purple sea urchins, sea stars, hermit crabs, and anemones.

Between Yaquina Head and Nye Beach on the way back to Newport lies the wide sweep of **Agate Beach**, where winter storms toss up agates from gravelly beds under the sea. Rock hounds search for them here and at Seal Rock State Park – locals' preferred spot – ten miles south of Newport on Highway 101. If you walk along either beach toward the sun on an outgoing tide, the agates (after a winter storm, at least) sparkle up at you: moonstone agates are clear, carnelians are bright red and transparent, and ribbon agates have colored layers. Newport's visitor center (see p.160) provides further information.

Eating and drinking

Seafood cafes and other **restaurants** line the Historic Bayfront's SW Bay Boulevard, the first choice for dining. There are also some agreeable options around Nye Beach, both on the bluff above the sands and in the little commercial strip just to the north.

△ Yaquina Head Lighthouse

Ocean adventures around Newport

Newport is a good place to try your hand at **deep-sea fishing**: Newport Tradewinds, down by the harbor at 653 SW Bay Blvd (℡541/265-2101 or 1-800/676-7819, ⓦwww.newporttradewinds.com), offers a variety of trips from year-round halibut and sea-bottom fishing – for sea bass, rock cod, sea trout, and other species – to seasonal salmon and tuna fishing. A five-hour excursion costs $65 per person, $175 for twelve hours of halibut fishing. From March to October, **whale-watching** excursions are possible here, too, with two-hour cruises offered by Marine Discovery Tours, 345 SW Bay Blvd ($30; ℡541/265-6200 or 1-800/903-2628, ⓦwww.marinediscovery.com). You can also stay at the company's *Anchor Pier* (℡541/265-7829; ◑), adjacent to the boat slip; the hotel has five clean, modern rooms with fireplaces, Net access, and hot tubs.

April's 749 NW 3rd St ℡541/265-6855. Near the major hotels on Nye Beach, a spot that offers fine Continental and Northwest cuisines with inventive pasta and seafood entrees on a changing menu – the town's best restaurant.

Cafe Stephanie 411 NW Coast St ℡541/265-8082. Just north of Nye Beach, a good place to go for sandwiches, fish tacos, and solid salmon chowder, with solid breakfasts, too.

Canyon Way Restaurant and Bookstore 1216 SW Canyon Way ℡541/265-8319. Just up from the harbor, a pleasant, pink-painted spot with a decent selection of books, an art gallery, and a wide range of seafood. Dungeness crabs are the specialty, though it's hard to beat the oysters and prawns.

Chowder Bowl 728 NW Beach Dr ℡541/265-7477. Creaky-looking type of place you see up and down the coast, except the seafood – and especially the chowder – is exceptional, and the prices are, naturally, nice and cheap.

Mo's Original 622 SW Bay Blvd ℡541/265-2979. Along with *Mo's Annex*, no. 657 (℡541/265-7512),

two decent seafood restaurants in a local chain, specializing in gut-stuffing favorites (clam chowder, fish 'n' chips, and so on) and always thick with tourist families. Conveniently located right on the bayfront.

Oregon Oyster Farms 6878 Yaquina Bay Rd ℡541/265-5078. Seafood dealer six miles east of the Bayfront, but well worth seeking out to stock up on fresh oysters galore, with a medium pint of bivalves going for less than $6.

Rogue Ales Public House 748 SW Bay Blvd ℡541/265-3188. Local brewer serving up the best microbrews in town, everything from light ales like Oregon Golden to the dark and tangy oatmeal Shakespeare Stout. Also with serviceable pizzas, fish 'n' chips, and the like, and one- and two-bedroom "bed and beer" motel units (d-e, plus two complimentary bottles) so you don't have to risk driving drunk.

Whale's Tale 452 SW Bay Blvd ℡541/265-8660. The top choice along the Historic Bayfront, offering delicious seafood at affordable prices in cozy, vaguely nautical surroundings.

Seal Rock to Heceta Head

Highway 101 sticks close to the seashore south of Newport, past a series of state park beaches such as **Ona Beach** – lying at the mouth of a pretty little creek with places to swim and fish – until it reaches **Seal Rock**, a small, unassuming town that was once the terminus of the first coastal stage route linked to the Willamette Valley in the 1860s. Nowadays it's not much, but the eponymous state park here is an attractive spot with dramatic basalt and sandstone sea stacks framing a sandy beach. Western gulls, black oystercatchers, and guillemots are among the many types of sea birds that gather here, and there are also sea lions and seals to be spotted. There are also tide pools, and it's a good spot for clam-digging. Looming over the entire scene is the gnarled dark mass of **Elephant Rock**, a pile of basalt that vaguely resembles a pachyderm; it was stranded in the ocean when the surrounding softer rock eroded away over the course of millions of years. The highway works its way southward to **Heceta Head**, offering as many inspiring seaward vistas and compelling parks as found farther north, but with fewer tourists – making the striking surroundings that much more evocative.

Waldport to Yachats

From Seal Rock, it's five miles south to the unexciting little town of **WALDPORT**, which straddles the mouth of **Alsea Bay** with the aid of the grand **Alsea Bay Bridge**, whose main arch is frequently photographed in picture postcards of the coast, and is a striking modern replica of an outmoded 1936 span. On the south side of the bridge, below the road bed, you can learn more about the heroic days of creating the coastal bridges and highway at the **Historic Interpretive Center** (Tues–Sat 9am–4pm; information at ℡541/563-2002). A mile down the road, **Governor Patterson State Park** is a good place for a relaxing walk along the sands and shoals at the mouth of the bay. Two miles south of here on Highway 101, the appropriately named **Beachside State Park** is one of only two coastal parks in Oregon (with Cape Lookout; see p.157) where (along with the requisite hiking, crabbing, and clamming) you can literally **camp** on the sands. This feature, alas, makes the place very popular throughout the year, so you'll have to reserve long in advance ($13–21; yurts $29; reserve at ℡1-800/452-5687).

Continuing south, the green flanks of the Siuslaw National Forest close in around the highway as it zips down to **YACHATS** – pronounced YAH-hots – a low-slung seaside village whose ribbon of cottages and town lanes is at its prettiest around the mouth of the Yachats River. It's a humble sort of place, but the next few miles of coast are startlingly beautiful and the town is a good base if you're keen to explore its nooks and crannies. The pretty and well-tended *Rock Park Cottages*, 431 W 2nd St (℡541/547-3214; ❸), are enticing places to **stay**; though spartan, many units nonetheless have kitchenettes. Another good choice, *Shamrock Lodgettes*, south of town at 105 Hwy 101 (℡541/547-3312 or 1-800/845-5028; ❺), offers comfortable and pleasantly old-fashioned log cabins with fireplaces and kitchenettes (some with Jacuzzis), along with more conventional motel accommodation. The *Adobe Resort*, 1555 Hwy 101 (℡541/547-3141, ⓦwww.adoberesort.com; ❹–❼ by season), exemplifies the new standard of lodging in town, with ocean-view rooms and suites that have fridges and microwaves; some also have balconies, hot tubs, and fireplaces. For **food** in Yachats, the restaurant of the *Adobe Resort* has upscale steak and seafood, as well as a Sunday brunch; *La Serre* (℡541/547-3420), by the river at Second and Beach streets, serves good, somewhat cheaper surf 'n' turf; and the *Drift Inn*, 124 Hwy 101 (℡541/547-4477), has decent fish tacos, burritos, and burgers, plus serviceable seafood crepes, pasta, and stews.

Cape Perpetua and Devil's Churn

Heading out of Yachats, Highway 101 winds its way up the densely forested edge of **Cape Perpetua** (day-use fee $5), a colossal mound formed by volcanic action that, at 800ft, is one of the most scenic peaks on the coast. It is latticed by hiking trails, described on maps given out at the tiny **interpretive center** (daily: summer 9am–5pm; rest of year 10am–4pm; ℡541/547-3289), two and a half miles from Yachats. Of the ten **hikes** to choose from, perhaps the most impressive is the strenuous three-mile return trip along the **St Perpetua Trail**, a thickly wooded trek from the interpretive center to the cape's summit, with plenty of steep switchbacks providing eye-popping views of the coastal scenery along the way. Once you reach the top, the views over the coast are even better. If you feel like avoiding the hike but still want the view, take Highway 101 north from the interpretive center, turn down Forest Road 55 and then take Forest Road 5553. This climbs up to the parking lot, and from here you can take a straightforward, ten-minute stroll on the **Whispering Spruce Trail** to the viewpoint. Other short but steep trails beginning at the interpretive center snake down to the seashore – either to tide pools or the beach.

Along the oceanside, the **Devil's Churn** may in many ways be the most compelling, dramatic, and frightening of all the various "Devil" formations on the coast – a deep and narrow basalt gash on the shore, where the ocean relentlessly comes in, pounding the rocks hard and sending columns of salt spray and tumultuous waves high in the air. You can see it on the mile-long **Restless Waters Trail**, but if you get too close, you can easily get pelted, and at worst might well get swept into the whirlpool and crushed on the rocks. Unnervingly, there are no rails or barriers to keep you from meeting this grim fate. In a much safer location, the US Forest Service operates the small **Cape Perpetua Campground** (May to mid-Sept; $20; reserve at ☎1-877/444-6777) beside a creek in the shadow of the cape: it's signposted from Highway 101 just north of the interpretive center, down Forest Road 55. Note also that in the summertime the cape's parking lots fill up fast, so try to arrive early.

Heceta Head and around

Beyond Cape Perpetua, the drive along Highway 101 is incredibly scenic, with thick forests climbing above and the anything-but-pacific surf crashing against the rocks below. After eleven miles, you reach the idyllic **Heceta Head Lighthouse State Park** (daily: May–Sept 11am–5pm; March, April & Oct 11am–3pm; entry $3), where the slender arc of **Devil's Elbow** beach – much less wicked than its neighbor to the north – lies at the back of a charming cove. This quiet beachside spot is surprisingly photogenic, with a rocky promontory curving up to the north, while the elegant **Cape Creek Bridge** – designed by Oregon bridge master-builder Conde McCullough in 1932 – crosses a little stream to the south with great style.

From the beach, it's a short and easy walk to the old lighthouse keeper's house, **Heceta House**, an 1893 Queen Anne-style structure that has been converted into a graceful **B&B** (☎541/547-3696, ⓦwww.hecetalighthouse.com; ⑥), offering six rooms (four with private bath), a solid seven-course breakfast, and nighttime visits to the nearby **lighthouse**. You can also tour the lighthouse (same entry and fee as park) without staying at the B&B, getting a close-up view of its classic 1894 beacon, old-time Fresnel lens and all, and from there go wandering on some of the scenic trails that wind around the cape. To **stay** in the area without paying a bundle, drop in at **Washburne State Park**, three miles north of – and accessible by loop trail from – Heceta Head, a spot that offers tide pools, fishing and hiking opportunities, as well as **camping** ($13–22, yurts $29; reserve at ☎1-800/452-5687).

A mile south of Heceta Head, the overly hyped and privately owned **Sea Lion Caves** (daily 9am–dusk; $9; ⓦwww.sealioncaves.com) are reached by an elevator that shoots down through the sea cliffs and a winding path that leads farther down the cliffside to an observation point. From there, you can look into a dark, cavernous sea cave, but the Steller sea lions – when they are present – are too far away to see well and seem to spend a fair bit of time asleep.

Finally, less than four miles south of the caves comes one of the coast's most bizarre and fascinating attractions, **Darlingtonia Wayside** (daily dawn–dusk; free), right off Highway 101 and accessed by a short trail. This officially protected natural site – laden with explanatory signs – harbors a small collection of unusual **cobra lilies**, carnivorous plants that devour insects by luring them into their gaping leaves, slick with hairs pointing down into their digestive chambers. The curious, boggy landscape and rare plants make for a rather unexpected scene, yet one well worth examining in May and June, when the hungry and deadly lilies are in full bloom.

The South Coast

In any number of ways, the **South Coast** of Oregon is considerably different from its northern counterpart, even though both have large stretches of protected natural habitat, countless state parks, and the linear presence of Highway 101. The most obvious distinction is that this part of the coast, starting south of **Florence** and continuing to the California border, is much less developed and more rugged than the northern section, with far fewer visitors and a sizable number of beauteous parks strung together almost without interruption. The scenery, too, is a bit different, with an abundance of sand dunes, beach grass, and especially colossal sea stacks. Indeed, these geological castaways – isolated from the rest of the coastal cliffs – do much to give the area its distinctive topography, and in some places make the edge of the shoreline look as though it were breaking apart into huge earthen chunks.

The highway provides immediate access to all the beaches and coastal parks, and rarely strays inland as it does farther north. The towns along the route, such as workaday and industrial **Coos Bay** and **North Bend**, are for the most part little more than way stations, not destinations in themselves. If much of the South Coast, then, is not exactly ready for prime-time tourism, it's all for the better: the rocky beachside scenery, proudly working-class small towns, and paucity of out-of-towners give the place a palpable authenticity, one not likely to be forgotten by anyone interested in exploring sights and having experiences off the beaten path.

Florence and around

On the north bank of the Siuslaw River, **FLORENCE** was founded in the 1850s as a timber port but is best known today for its proximity to the Oregon Dunes National Recreation Area (see p.171). The town's main drag (Hwy 101) has an unlovely string of motels; to the east off the highway, more appealing is **Old Town**, a small-scale affair whose sturdy early twentieth-century architecture has been revamped to accommodate cafes, boutiques, and gift shops. With the exception of its striking 1930s Art Deco **Siuslaw River Bridge**, Florence has no formal sights as such, but it makes a good stopover on your way to the dunes.

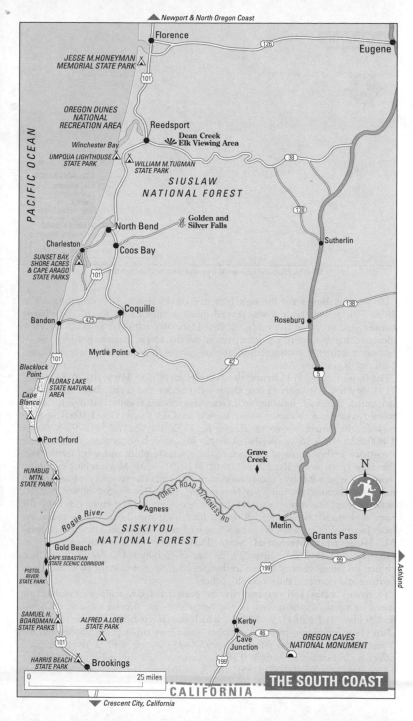

Newport & North Oregon Coast

Florence

126

Eugene

JESSE M.HONEYMAN
MEMORIAL STATE PARK

101

OREGON DUNES
NATIONAL
RECREATION AREA

Reedsport

Dean Creek
Elk Viewing Area

38

Winchester Bay

UMPQUA LIGHTHOUSE
STATE PARK

WILLIAM M.TUGMAN
STATE PARK

SIUSLAW
NATIONAL FOREST

PACIFIC OCEAN

138

North Bend

Golden and
Silver Falls

Charleston

Coos Bay

Sutherlin

SUNSET BAY,
SHORE ACRES
& CAPE ARAGO
STATE PARKS

101

Bandon

425

Coquille

138

Roseburg

Myrtle Point

42

Blacklock
Point

FLORAS LAKE
STATE NATURAL
AREA

Cape
Blanco

101

5

Port Orford

HUMBUG
MTN.
STATE PARK

Grave
Creek

N

FOREST ROAD 33 / AGNESS RD

Rogue River

Agness

Merlin

SISKIYOU
NATIONAL FOREST

Grants Pass

Gold Beach

CAPE SEBASTIAN
STATE SCENIC CORRIDOR

199

99

PISTOL
RIVER
STATE PARK

Ashland

SAMUEL H.
BOARDMAN
STATE PARKS

ALFRED A.LOEB
STATE PARK

Kerby

46

Cave
Junction

OREGON CAVES
NATIONAL MONUMENT

HARRIS BEACH
STATE PARK

101

Brookings

199

0   25 miles

THE SOUTH COAST

CALIFORNIA

Crescent City, California

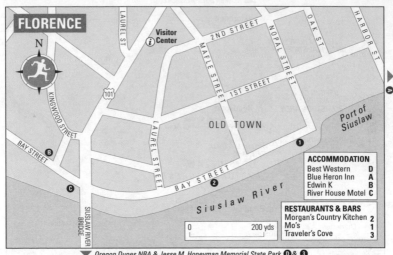

Oregon Dunes NRA & Jesse M. Honeyman Memorial State Park, &

Greyhound **buses** zip through Florence on Highway 101, dropping off at 1856 37th St, off the highway several miles north of Old Town. The **visitor center**, just north of the bridge at 290 Hwy 101 (☎541/997-3128, ⓦwww .florencechamber.com), has information on the town, including a long list of (mostly routine) accommodation. It also carries flyers on the Oregon Dunes National Recreation Area.

For those staying in Florence, the *Best Western*, 85625 Hwy 101 (☎541/997-7191, ⓦwww.bestwestern.com; ❺), is a cut above the usual chain fare, with a spa, sauna, and pool, and the usual clean and modest rooms. But if you can, it's worth paying a few dollars more to stay in Old Town. Good **B&B** options include the smart, six-room *Edwin K*, 1155 Bay St (☎541/997-8360 or 1-800/833-9465, ⓦwww.edwink.com; ❻), which occupies an attractive two-story timber house at the foot of the riverside bluff, and, a bit farther out, the *Blue Heron Inn*, 6563 Hwy 126 (☎541/997-4091, ⓦwww.blue-heroninn .com; ❺), which has five old-fashioned rooms with river views and some with hot tubs. Alternatively, the *River House Motel*, 1202 Bay St (☎1-888/824-2750, ⓦwww.riverhousemotel.com; ❺), has an appealing setting right down by the river underneath the bridge; all rooms have high-speed Net access and a few have Jacuzzis (extra $30). With two hundred **tent sites** and a few yurts, **Jesse M. Honeyman Memorial State Park**, three miles south of town on Highway 101 ($13–22, yurts $29; reserve at ☎1-800/452-5687), is the first choice for many visitors, with a freshwater lake on one side for swimming and boating and dramatic dunes on the other.

Florence's **cafes** and **restaurants** are geared for day-trippers, emphasizing speed rather than quality. Two of the better ones are *Morgan's Country Kitchen*, 85020 Hwy 101 (☎541/997-6991), which has down-home biscuits and gravy, clam chowder, plump pies and cobblers, and other rib-sticking staples, and the *Traveler's Cove*, 1362 Bay St (☎541/997-6845), a cafe with a riverside patio offering sandwiches and salads. If all else fails, you can always hit good old *Mo's*, 1436 Bay St (☎541/997-2185), the local branch of the coast's signature seafood-and-chowder eatery.

Oregon Dunes National Recreation Area

Beginning at Florence, **sand dunes** dominate the coast as far south as Coos Bay, a distance of 45 miles. Lying along the Pacific shoreline and up to two and a half miles inland, they are punctuated with pockets of forest and lake, cover 32,000 acres, and rise up to an incredible 180ft high but are infrequently visible from Highway 101. About half of them, however, are accessible to the public in the **OREGON DUNES NATIONAL RECREATION AREA**, part of the Siuslaw National Forest ($5 day-use fee; ⓦ www.fs.fed.us/r6/siuslaw).

Park practicalities

Florence and North Bend bracket the dunes on the north and south respectively. You can reach the dunes from the I-5 freeway in the southern Willamette Valley via highways 126 and 38 – there's no other access over the coastal mountains. The dunes themselves have suffered from the ill effects of ATVs (all-terrain vehicles) and ORVs (off-road vehicles), whose use is now confined to three specific areas that cover about half the acreage of the park. The US Forest Service, which manages the dunes, maintains seventeen **hiking trails** that are, for the most part, free of motor vehicles. These are described on the USFS website (see above) or in a free booklet, *Hiking Trails in the Oregon Dunes*, available from local visitor centers and the **Oregon Dunes National Recreation Area Visitor Center**, 855 Highway Ave (summer daily 8am–4.30pm, rest of the year Mon–Fri same hours; ☏ 541/271-6000), at the junction of Highway 101 and Hwy 38, twenty miles south of Florence in Reedsport.

Of the hiking trails, one of the most enjoyable is the mile-long **Oregon Dunes Overlook trail**, ten miles south of Florence on Highway 101; an

---

A history in sand

The amazing expanse of the **Oregon sand dunes** were formed by the crumbling of sandstone some twelve million years ago, when plate tectonics pushed up a section of seafloor and the wind and water above ground began eroding it. The resulting sand deposits were supplemented by others washed up here from rockier parts of the coast, and the whole lot dried out on the shore before being picked up and blown into dunes by the prevailing winds. The result today is an almost surreal landscape where the colossal size of the dunes belies the complex delicacy of the ecosystem, which was changed somewhat within the last hundred years by the introduction of marram grass, or beach grass, to stabilize the shifting, blowing sand grains.

The dunes can be divided into a succession of distinctive zones, beginning closest to the ocean with the **beach** and, running behind it, 20–30ft high **foredunes**. Behind them is the **deflation plain**, an irregular terrain of sandy hummocks held together by plants such as beach grass and shore pine, and then come the largest of the sandhills, the **oblique dunes**. These are named after the slanted angle at which the prevailing winds hit them, creating a constantly shifting mass that makes it impossible for vegetation to take root. Behind these dunes are **tree islands**, where small stands of trees are floating in sand, followed by both the **transition forest**, where the ocean-based ecosystem gives way to that of the land, and the freshwater **coastal lakes**, mostly formed when either ocean inlets became cut off or sand dammed a stream. One cautionary note is that in wet winters the water table rises to create patches of swamp and, more ominously, **quicksand** – watch out for pools of water on the sand in low, unvegetated areas between the dunes.

observation platform along the trail offers smashing views over the dunes to the sea and acts as the trailhead for the two-and-a-half-mile **Tahkenitch Creek Loop**. There are longer trails (two to four miles each) a mile to the south on Highway 101 at **Tahkenitch Creek**, where you can also **camp** at any one of thirteen USFS campgrounds in the area ($17–20; reserve at ℡1-877/444-6777, ⓦwww.reserveusa.com).You can rent an ATV or ORV from a long list of rental companies. Rides typically cover about twenty square miles' worth of dunes. Sandland Adventures, about a mile south of Florence on Highway 101 ($40 per hour; ℡541/997-8087, ⓦwww.sandland.com), offers guided "long-buggy" tours of the area, while Sand Dunes Frontier ($45 per hour; ℡541/997-5363, ⓦwww.sanddunesfrontier.com), about three miles farther south on US-101, has individual ATVs for rent.

Reedsport to Cape Arago State Park

It's easy to get distracted by the dunes and pay attention to little else as you zip down to North Bend and Coos Bay, and beyond them the pleasant resort of Bandon. However, there are a number of good spots worth exploring in the vicinity if you have the time. Roughly in the middle of the dunes, the little burg of **REEDSPORT** is a spot that built its existence on the fishing and lumber trades.Although the Greyhound **bus** makes one of its few stops on the Oregon coast here, along Highway 101, there's not much to it for visitors.You can, however, visit the **Umpqua Discovery Center**, 409 Riverfront Way (daily: summer 9am–5pm, rest of the year 10am–4pm; $8; ⓦwww.umpqua discoverycenter.com), for a quick gloss of the area's natural history and human endeavors, and visit the **Pathways to Discovery** wing to learn more about the region's assorted ecological zones. The charming neighboring port of **Winchester Bay**, also known as Salmon Harbor, is supposedly the largest public harbor in Oregon and a good spot to watch the old-time trawlers and more modern fishing vessels drift by or, if you have the equipment, to go fishing, clamming, or crabbing yourself. Three miles east of Reedsport on Highway 138, wildlife enthusiasts won't want to miss the **Dean Creek Elk Viewing Area** (℡503/947-6000), where you can spot a herd of up to a hundred Roosevelt elk eating, playing, and rutting; the majestic beasts are most visible during the summer mating season, especially around September. Reedsport is hardly a place to **stay**, unless you have a fondness for RV "resorts" and roadside motels; one exception to this is the *Rose Wood Cottage*, 140 Westwood Court (℡541/271-2436, ⓦwww.rosewoodcottagebb.com; ❺), a pleasant and homey B&B with three quaint rooms. For **food**, the *Schooner Inn Cafe*, 423 River Front Way (℡541/271-3945), has river views and serves decent seafood and sandwiches.

Just south of Winchester Bay, off Salmon Harbor Drive, lighthouse enthusiasts will enjoy a stop at **Umpqua Lighthouse State Park**, whose main feature, along with a relaxing lakeside trail, is its squat red-and-white beacon (tours May–Sept Wed–Sat 10am–4pm, Sun 1–5pm; free; ℡541/271-4631), located on a small bluff.The park also has great **camping** for beach and dune trekkers with a full complement of tent sites ($12–20), a pair of cabins ($35), and yurts ($27) – even including a few deluxe models with bathrooms and kitchenettes ($45–66); reserve any of these at ℡1-800/452-5687. A few miles south and on the east side of Highway 101, **William Tugman State Park** – named after another champion of the state parks system – is another camping alternative

△ Golden and Silver Falls

(pitch sites $12–16, yurts $27). Built around freshwater **Eel Lake**, the park offers fine opportunities for bass, trout, and salmon fishing, and for spotting birds like eagles, osprey, and hawks, and mammals like bear, elk, otters, and even cougars. For twelve miles south of here it's all dunes along Highway 101 until you reach the huge, curving mouth of the Coos River.

At the end of the dunes, another fine Conde McCullough bridge spans Coos Bay, a deep natural harbor that gathers around its shabby shoreline the merged industrial towns of **North Bend** and **Coos Bay**. There's no mistaking the main activity here, with the main road lined by wood-chip mountains and stacks of cut timber. The obvious thing to do is to drive straight through on Hwy 101 and head directly to Bandon, about 25 miles to the south, but if you've a couple of hours to spare, there are two enjoyable detours you can take. The first leads you 24 miles northeast of Coos Bay along the winding concourse of Coos River Hwy (accessible from Hwy 101 at the southern end of the town and Coos Bay itself), up to the gorgeous surroundings of **Golden and Silver Falls State Natural Area** (T1-800/551-6949) – one of the best attractions in the coastal mountains. Not to be confused with the equally appealing Silver Falls near Salem (see p.196), this park features a pair of striking waterfalls that cascade a hundred feet over basalt cliffs onto wet, rounded boulders. You can explore the sheer rock walls and rugged trees of the forest setting on a number of hiking trails leading up to the heights of the falls and past excellent vistas of the mountains and fauna such as hawks and herons.

The other detour from Coos Bay takes you southwest along the coast to a trio of state parks within a mile or so of each other. To get to them from Highway 101 in North Bend/Coos Bay, follow the signs for **Charleston**, a small, workaday sportfishing town about nine miles away. From here, it's about three miles farther to **Sunset Bay State Park**, a popular spot on account of its pretty sheltered bay, sandy beach, opportunities for swimming, clamming and crabbing, and **campground** (pitch $12–20, yurts $27; reserve at T1-800/452-5687).

The next park along, **Shore Acres** (daily 8am–dusk; $3), is green and lush and was once the estate of shipping tycoon and lumber magnate Louis Simpson. Although his palatial mansion was demolished in the 1940s, the formal gardens have survived, planted with exotic species as well as azaleas, rhododendrons, roses, and dahlias. The park also offers seasonal displays of brightly colored lights and evergreen trees and bushes during the winter holidays and at other times of the year. Perched on a bluff above the jagged rocks of the seashore, an observation shelter has been erected where the mansion once stood, and a footpath leads down through the woods to a secluded cove. It's one of the most delightful parks on the coast, and it's also just a mile from **Cape Arago State Park**, a wild and windswept headland where, on the South Cove Trail (closed March–June), you'll be able to spy Steller sea lions, elephant seals, and harbor seals on the offshore rocks in their protected habitat.

The cape is at the end of the road. On the return journey, rather than going all the way back to Highway 101 in Coos Bay, you can – in Charleston – turn onto signposted **Seven Devils Road**. This is a meandering country road that slowly and pleasingly twists its way south to Highway 101 near Bandon.

Bandon to Brookings

The most southerly section of the Oregon coast – from **Bandon** to **Brookings** – has close beach access from Highway 101, striking scenery of beachside hills and monumental sea stacks, and small working-class towns that don't merit more than a stopover. Keep in mind that once you drive south of Bandon you cannot easily cross over to the Oregon interior and I-5 until you reach Crescent City, California. For much of the journey there are almost no roads (other than the occasional logging route) that breach the impressively rugged, undeveloped topography of the Klamath Mountains, and from Gold Beach onward the interior is inviolate, comprising such huge preserves as the Kalmiopsis Wilderness that barely even have hiking trails, let alone driving routes. If you do decide to make the trip, consider picking up Hwy 199 in Crescent City and coming back through the Rogue River Valley (see p.208) via the Oregon Caves. If you're coming by public transit, the closest you can get is the Greyhound **bus station** in Coos Bay, at 275 N Broadway (☎541/269-7183). From the town you can pick up the **Coastal Express** (☎1-800/921-2871), a South Coast transit service that runs from North Bend to Brookings, stopping at various small towns in between for $4 per segment.

Bandon

The one appealing little town on this stretch, easygoing and likable **BANDON**, lies 25 miles from Coos Bay at the mouth of the Coquille River. Known as Bandon-by-the-Sea in tourist brochures, the place boasts a beguiling combination of old-town restoration and New Age style. It's one of the nicest places to stay on the whole of the coast, having shed its blue-collar roots as a logging and fishing port to become something of an arts and crafts center, only to reemerge in recent years as a hot spot for golf and resort travelers.

Bandon was originally a Native American settlement, and when the local Coquille were swept aside in the middle of the nineteenth century, they are supposed to have cursed the town to burn down three times. It's happened twice so far, in 1914 and 1936, and the superstitious are still waiting for the curse to run its course. Memories of these troubled times stirred when townsfolk dynamited **Tupper Rock**, a sacred tribal site on Jetty Road, to improve the sea wall, much to the anger of the remaining Coquille.

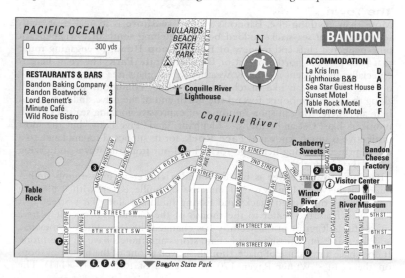

Arrival and accommodation

The **visitor center** is located at 300 2nd St and Chicago St (daily: June–Sept 9am–5pm; Oct–May 10am–4pm; ☏541/347-9616, ⓦwww.bandon.com). As for **accommodation**, there are a number of solid **B&B** and **hostel** options, but if rooms are tight – as they often are in the summer – try the assorted **motels** dotted south of the center along Highway 101, which runs inland from – and parallel to – Beach Loop Road. **Camping** at Bullards Beach State Park (sites $16–20, yurts $27; ☏541/347-2209, reserve at ☏1-800/452-5687), north of the town center and across the river, is another option.

La Kris Inn 940 Oregon Ave ☏541-347-3610 or 1-888/496-3610, ⓦwww.lakrisinn.com. The least expensive, but still more than adequate, accommodation in town, with twelve nicely decorated motel rooms with microwaves, fridges, and DVD players. ❸–❹

Lighthouse B&B 650 Jetty Rd ☏541-347-9316, ⓦwww.lighthouselodging.com. Just west of the town center, along 1st Street, this comfortable, five-room establishment occupies an old and attractive timber building overlooking the harbor and lighthouse. The most expensive rooms also have hot tubs. ❻

🏃 **Sea Star Guest House** 370 1st St ☏541/347-9632, ⓦwww.eastarbandon.com. A lively and agreeable spot that has just five rooms (❹), some with kitchenettes and fireplaces, and a wonderful, three-level penthouse (❻) with DVD player, kitchen, and expansive views. Advance booking recommended.

Sunset Motel about a mile from town at 1865 Beach Loop Rd ☏541/347-2453 or

1-800/842-2407, ⓦwww.sunsetmotel.com. Outstanding waterside option that comprises motel rooms, condos, and, best of all, several older seafront cabins with fabulous views along the coast – it's well worth paying the extra money for them. Most units ❺, though some of the cabins ❼–❽, and a handful of basic units as low as ❸

Table Rock Motel 840 Beach Loop Rd ☏541/347-2700, ⓦtablerockmotel.com. Another good and distinctive choice for cheap lodging in town, with a nice range of rooms from economy cottages (❸) to cottages with ocean views (❹) to larger suites with Internet access, and some with kitchenettes and balconies with beach views (❺–❻).

Windermere Motel 3250 Beach Loop Rd ☏541/347-3710, ⓦwww.windermerebythesea.com. Modest choice two miles from town that has small but affordable chalet-huts, with fireplaces and kitchenettes in many units. Some units have fabulous views almost right on the beach. ❹–❺ by season

The Town

More than anything else, Bandon's rugged **seashore** is its real treat, with several miles of sea-stack-studded beach stretching south of town beneath pine-peppered cliffs and in view of **Beach Loop Road**, an engaging route that runs past the northern end of **Bandon State Park**. The coast here is especially magnificent in stormy weather, when giant tree stumps are tossed up out of the ocean like matchsticks; in calmer conditions you can stroll along the beach for hours. Toward the north end of the drive, and signposted here and there, you can spot a number of expressive-looking sea stacks with monikers like "Cat and Kittens," "Elephant," and "Five Foot," but the most distinctive is simply known as **Face Rock**, for its supposed resemblance to a native princess poking her huge rocky head out from the waves and gazing at the sky longingly.

Bandon's **town center** is based around a cluster of unassuming timber buildings between Highway 101 and the Coquille River, with a pleasing hodgepodge of wooden shacks and fishing buildings along First Street as it runs west from the center to the mouth of the Coquille. In recent years a successful golf resort in the vicinity has changed the atmosphere somewhat, and the usual souvenir shops and chain stores and motels have all taken root. It does have a real sense of place, though, as well as one of the best bookshops on the coast – Winter River, 170 SE Second St (☏541/347-4111). The

△ Face Rock

town's history is on display at the **Coquille River Museum**, 270 Fillmore St and Hwy 101 (Mon–Sat 10am–4pm; $2; ⓦbandonhistoricalmuseum.org), which has a good section on the fire of 1936 and a large sample of old photographs.

On the other (north) side of the river, whose mouth is bracketed by a pair of jetties, the **Coquille River Lighthouse** (May & Oct daily 10am–4pm; June–Sept Mon 10am–4pm & Tues–Sun 9am-6pm; donation) is a squat white cylinder that cuts a romantic silhouette even though its beacon has been extinguished since the 1930s. However, its keeper's quarters – almost two-thirds as tall as the lighthouse itself – are now used for a mildly interesting **museum** (same hours) laying out the story of the building and its past. The lighthouse marks the start of **Bullards Beach State Park**, a long stretch of pristine beach and sand dunes knee-deep in contorted piles of driftwood. To get there, take Highway 101 north over the river and watch for the turnoff on the left. And, as if all that weren't enough, the mudflats of the Coquille estuary are perfect for **clamming** and **crabbing** from the town's jetties.

The town's biggest shindig is the **Cranberry Festival**, held over three days in the middle of September. Going strong for nearly sixty years now, it includes a parade, live music, and all sorts of food stalls. Cranberries are big business in Bandon, and there are even tours of the bogs where they grow. Located a few miles east of town off Hwy 42, **Faber Farms** offers such visits during the autumn harvest season and sells the fruit for inexpensive prices (information at ☏1-866-347-1166, ⓦwww.oregoncranberry.com). You can also pick up these famously tangy treats – mixed with nuts, chocolate, and the like – at Cranberry Sweets, First St at Chicago Ave SE (☎1-800/527-5748); if cranberries aren't your thing, there are alternatives. Bandon is also well known for its Bandon Cheese Factory, 680 E Second St (☎541/347-2456), a good spot to sample various types of cheese and curds – though the facility is now owned by the Tillamook Cheese company, located on the North Coast (see p.156).

Eating

In addition to cranberries and cheese, Bandon has a fair supply of good **cafes** and **restaurants**. The *Wild Rose Bistro*, 130 Chicago Ave SE (☎541/347-4428), has reliable pasta, steak, and seafood, as well as good home-made bread and desserts, and the *Minute Cafe*, 125 2nd St (☎541/347-2707), is a local favorite, with omelets, crepes, and pancakes for breakfast and chili and chowder for lunch. More upmarket options include two restaurants noted for their seafood, *Bandon Boatworks*, 275 Lincoln Ave SW (☎541/347-2111), known for its steaks, clam chowder, and Sunday brunch, and the smart *Lord Bennett's*, by the *Sunset Motel*, at 1695 Beach Loop Rd (☎541/347-3663), which also has good desserts and views of the ocean, including the more prominent sea stacks. Finally, the *Bandon Baking Company*, 160 2nd St (☎541/347-9440), is the spot to stock up on tasty handmade cookies, pastries, and croissants.

Floras Lake State Natural Area

Towns become fewer and farther between as you travel south from Bandon, with Highway 101 staying a few miles inland as it careers through forested hills. After about twenty miles, the highway reaches the unmarked turnoff for **Floras Lake State Natural Area**, which, though it has stunning basalt columns, limestone walls, rugged trails through native trees and foliage, native cranberry bogs, and eye-opening views of the coast, has hardly been developed by the state – indeed, the lake itself isn't even in the park. Nonetheless, it can be reached, more or less, by taking Airport Road (three miles north of the turnoff for Cape Blanco, or five miles south of the village of Langlois) west almost three miles until it ends. From here the runway of a small state airport – no more than a minor airstrip – leads north, beyond which are a pair of rough trails. One of these leads to the jagged, striking **Blacklock Point**, littered with broken volcanic columns and huge chunks of driftwood, which used to sit near a sandstone mining site, and you can still see the odd fragmentary ruin of the narrow gauge railway that carted the stone to a nearby dock. The other trail heads toward some chillingly steep **limestone cliffs** that fall away sharply to the sea, carved by millennia of waves and forming one of the most unforgettable spots on the coast. Although these sights are some of the indisputable jewels anywhere in the state, they're also rather difficult to get to without a detailed hiking map (available from any decent outdoors or travel bookshop, or by calling Oregon State Parks at ☎503/378-4168). Lacking this, you're risking getting lost by venturing too far out here and could find yourself tumbling down a cliff face if you're not careful.

Cape Blanco State Park

Much more user-friendly, and almost as visually appealing, **Cape Blanco State Park** lies a short distance south of Floras Lake State Natural Area (but isn't accessible from it) and fills out a bumpy, triangular headland marked by a

Victorian **lighthouse** (April–Oct Thurs–Mon 10am–3.30pm; donation), perched high on a cliff some five miles west of Highway 101. Signs of the early homesteaders who colonized the coast are rare, but here in the park, in a lovely tranquil spot overlooking the river, is the solitary, shingle-clad **Hughes House** (same hours as lighthouse; donation), a sturdy two-story structure built in the 1890s and now refurnished in period style. The surrounding farmland has been left pretty much untouched, too, and nearby are the scant remnants of a pioneer cemetery. Among several **hikes**, one short trail leads to the coast from the boat ramp near the house, while another winds down from the lighthouse promontory to the craggy beachhead. The **campground**, with its excellent set of cabins (pitch sites $12–16, cabins $35; ☎541/332-6774, reserve at 1-800/452-5687), sits in the woods on a bluff behind the seashore.

Port Orford

Back on Highway 101, it's four miles more to **PORT ORFORD**, a casual little fishing port whose main attraction is **Battle Rock**. This large, chunky outcrop was the site of an 1851 struggle between white settlers, in the form of the crew of the steamship *Sea Gull*, and a band of local Rogue natives, who tried to resist the landing of the whites – with predictably disastrous consequences. The rock pokes up above the seashore beside Hwy 101 on the south side of town and is climbable if you have good hiking boots; a handful of nineteenth-century graves sit on the wooded crest, from which there are fine views of the sea and the town – as well as a precipitous drop from the north face. Next to the rock is a seasonal **visitor center** (June–Aug Mon–Fri 10am–5pm; ☎541/332-8055, ⓦwww.portorfordoregon.com). More appealing than the rock is the **port** itself (signposted throughout town), which unlike most coastal harbors is actually a **dry dock** – a crane hoists every boat from the water and deposits it on the wharves. Walking amid these crusty trawlers is an intriguing experience, given that you rarely get to see the underside of such craft or their full size. If sufficiently impressed, you can have **lunch** here at *Dock Tackle* (☎541/332-8985), whose ultra-fresh crab meat and fish 'n' chips are as good as any meal in town. Also worth a visit is the *Crazy Norwegian's Fish and Chips*, 259 Hwy 101 (☎541/332-8601), doling out good, old-fashioned clam chowder and solid fish 'n' chips, as well as homemade pies.

If you break your journey here, you can choose from the cozy **B&B** *Home by the Sea*, 444 Jackson at 5th St (☎541/332-2855, ⓦwww.homebythesea .com; ❺), which offers pleasant views over the coast and has just two guest rooms, and *Castaway by the Sea*, 545 W 5th St (☎541/332-4502, ⓦwww .castawaybythesea.com), a decent **motel** with units ranging from economy rooms (❸) to two-level condo suites (❺–❻) – overall, though, the property is best for its fine ocean views.

Gold Beach and around

Five miles south of Port Orford, Highway 101 makes a rare and brief turn inland to loop around **Humbug Mountain State Park**, centered around a mighty coastal headland whose 1756ft summit is reached from the highway along a three-mile switchback-laden hiking trail – making for a strenuous six-mile round-trip. The first-come, first-served **campground** ($12–16; information at ☎541/332-6774) is down by the river, beside the main road beneath the mountain.

Beyond the park, Highway 101 sticks close to the coastline in the shadow of forested mountains that sweep smoothly down to the sea. These mountains mark the western limit of the **Siskiyou National Forest**, a vast slab of remote wilderness that is most easily explored by boat along the turbulent **Rogue River** from **GOLD BEACH**, at the river mouth 23 miles from Humbug Mountain. In the 1850s the town prospered from the gold the river had washed into its dark sands; later, the Rogue fed its salmon canneries. Now the workaday town is largely devoted to packing visitors off on **jet boats**, up canyons and through the Rogue's roaring rapids. Among several boat operators, the best of the lot are Mail Boat Hydro-Jets (May–Oct; $42 for 64-mile trip; ☎541/247-7033 or 1-800/458-3511, ⓦwww.mailboat.com), whose wharf is on the north side of the river, and Jerry's Rogue Jets ($42–84 for 64- to 104-mile trip; ☎541/247-4571 or 1-800/451-3645, ⓦwww.roguejets.com), on the south bank. There's a two-hour break for lunch at a riverside lodge, but food isn't included in the price; reservations are strongly advised.

There are many modern **motels** south of the river along Hwy 101; one of the more appealing is the well-kept ⚘ *Ireland's Rustic Lodges*, 29330 Ellensburg Ave at 11th St (☎541/247-7718, ⓦwww.irelandsrusticlodges.com; ❸), which has a number of quaint wooden chalets (❺), cabins (❺), and condos (❻), as well as oceanfront spa units (❻). The *Gold Beach Resort*, 29232 Ellensburg Ave, off Hwy 101 (☎1-800/541-0947 or 541/247-7066, ⓦwww.gbresort.com), has basic motel units with microwaves and fridges (❹) and a pair of condos with kitchens, fireplaces, balconies, and laundry facilities (❻). Although you'll probably not want to linger in town for a fancy **meal**, the *Indian Creek Cafe*, sited where that creek meets the Rogue River, at 94682 Jerry's Flat Rd (☎541/247-0680), has solid omelets, pancakes, and sandwiches.

Rogue River National Recreation Trail

If you want to explore the scenery around the Rogue River on foot, you'll want to hike at least a portion of the forty-mile **Rogue River National Recreation Trail** (also see p.210). It begins at Grave Creek, thirty-odd miles to the northwest of Grants Pass, but you cannot get there from the coast by road without taking a huge, day-long detour around the mountains. So your best bet is to travel upriver by boat and then hike downriver and downhill. None of the Gold Beach boats get anywhere near Grave Creek, but they do travel far enough upriver to provide a good long hike on the journey back. There are regular first-come, first-served campgrounds ($12–20) along the trail, as well as a series of strategically placed lodges on its lower half, each a day's hike from the other. For detailed advice, visit Gold Beach's **Siskiyou National Forest Ranger Station**, just south of the Rogue River on Hwy 101 at 29279 Ellensburg Ave (Mon–Fri 8am–5pm; ☎541/247-3600, ⓦwww.fs.fed.us/r6/rogue-siskiyou). The adjacent **visitor center** (☎541/247-7526 or 1-800/525-2334, ⓦwww.goldbeach.org) has details of all the local jet-boat operators.

South to Brookings

Down toward the California border is Oregon's "banana belt," so named because of its unusually warm and sunny weather (it's often over 60°F in January), a result of drifting thermal troughs from the north California coast. Though popular with retirees, it's largely undiscovered by others. Starting seven miles south of Gold Beach are a trio of very appealing state parks. The first, **Cape Sebastian**, has a fine viewpoint perched two hundred feet above the surging waves, as well as trails through flowery meadows and ocean bluffs;

Exploring the redwoods

The quickest way to reach the Rogue River Valley from Brookings is to continue south on **US-101** into California. Twenty miles beyond the border, US-101 meets **US-199**, which weaves northeast through the Siskiyou Mountains toward Cave Junction (see p.218), negotiating inhospitable mountain passes and curving around plunging gorges, key features of the landscape's forbidding beauty. A few miles east of the juncture on US-199 lies **Jedediah Smith Redwoods State Park**, where mighty **redwoods**, colossal trees up to 350ft tall, crowd in on the highway as it wriggles up toward Oregon, passing the trailhead for the Simpson-Reed Trail, a short and easy stroll through some of the grandest trees. Just past the park, the **Redwood National Park Information Center** (☎707/464-6101, ⓦwww.nps .gov/redw) supplies maps and has cycling and hiking trail details for the series of parks that stretch forty miles along the California coast, protecting groves of the ancient redwoods.

the second, just south, **Pistol River**, is set among sprawling sand dunes but is best known for its fabulous collection of sea stacks – monstrous, gnarled behemoths scattered amid the waters, providing a dramatic backdrop for the summer **windsurfing** competitions held here. Just a few miles beyond Pistol River, the third, **Samuel H. Boardman**, is a twelve-mile coastal strip whose various viewpoints, picnic areas, and paths – from the bluffs down to the beach – are all accessed via Highway 101. Among several sandy coves, **Whalehead Cove** is one of the most scenic spots, and there are plenty of other striking landscapes, too – sheer cliff walls, chunky basalt monoliths, old mining sites, and 300-year-old stands of Sitka spruce. Especially memorable is the sizable Native American **midden** – a huge pile of ancient discarded seashells and animal bones that's an officially protected artifact.

   BROOKINGS, 29 miles south of Gold Beach, is the place where most of North America's Easter lilies are grown, and some of the local azaleas are over twenty feet high and three hundred years old, inspiring the annual **Azalea Festival** on Memorial Day weekend at the end of May. There's a **visitor center** (Mon–Fri 9am–5pm; ☎541/469-3181, ⓦwww.brookingsor .com) down by the harbor to tell you more about it. There are a few good choices of places to **stay** in the area, like *Lowden's Beachfront B&B*, 14626 Wollam Rd (☎541/469-7045 or 1-800/453-4768, ⓦwww.beachfrontbb .com; ❺), whose comfortable suites are right above the ocean, with microwaves, fridges, and fireplaces; and the *Ocean Suites Motel*, 16045 Lower Harbor Rd (☎541/468-4004, ⓦwww.oceansuitesmotel.com; ❹), which has clean and comfortable suites with kitchens. On the north end of town is **Harris Beach State Park**, right off Hwy 101 (campsites $13–21, yurts $29; information at ☎1-800/551-6949, reserve at ☎1-800/452-5687), which has much of the same compelling scenery found in the above parks but with the added draw of a national wildlife sanctuary, **Goat Island**, harboring tufted puffins. Alternatively, if you head ten miles northeast of town along North Bank Road, you can swim, boat, and camp at **Loeb State Park** (campsites $12–16, cabins $35; reserve as above), whose major attractions are its stately groves of redwood and myrtle trees. Brookings isn't exactly a hot spot for fine **dining**, but it does have one of the area's better microbreweries in *Wild River Brewing*, 16279 Hwy 101 (☎541/469-7454), which makes a mean English-style Snug Harbor Old Ale, Blackberry Porter, and Double Eagle Imperial Stout, as well as decent pizzas, sandwiches, and fried chicken.

There isn't anything to detain you between Brookings and California, but just over the border lie the mighty redwoods of **Redwood National Park** and **Jedediah Smith Redwoods State Park** (see p.181) and beyond this you can take US-199 over the Siskiyou Mountains to make the loop to the Oregon Caves and Grants Pass (see p.210) – the first highway back to the Oregon interior after more than a hundred miles.

The Willamette and
Rogue River valleys

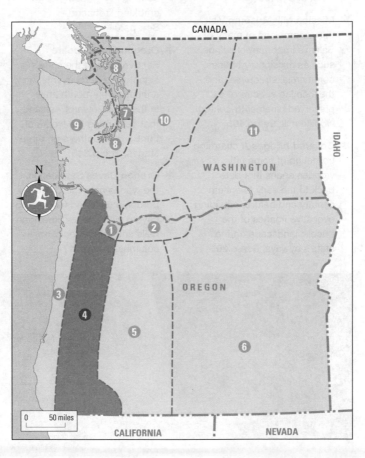

CHAPTER 4

Highlights

❋ **Silver Falls State Park**
Justifiably the most popular
park in the state, a beautiful
assortment of waterfalls you
can traverse on a leafy loop,
the highlight of which is the
towering cascade of South
Falls. See p.196

❋ **Mission Mill Museum** Visit
this assemblage of many of
Salem's important buildings,
such as missionary houses,
commercial structures, and
the looming spectre of a
preserved nineteenth-century
woolen mill. See p.199

❋ **Covered bridges** A charming
collection of some fifty
wooden spans that date
back to the early twentieth
century and before, providing
evocative images of the
bucolic landscape on the
state's byways. See p.201

❋ **Eugene Saturday Market** A
colorful and frenetic weekly
festival of hippie-flavored
arts and crafts, buzzing
with all kinds of visitors and
vendors peddling the likes
of beeswax candles, herb
soaps, and glass pipes for
smoking "tobacco."
See p.204

❋ **Oregon Shakespeare
Festival** One of the state's
signature cultural events, an
annual seven-month affair
in the small town of Ashland
that celebrates the works of
the Bard and others on three
stages. See p.213

❋ **Oregon Caves** Set deep in
the woods near the California
border, a dark and fascinating
cavern with echoey limestone
halls and drippy rock
columns. See p.217

△ Silver Falls State Park

The Willamette and Rogue River valleys

Running north-south from Portland almost to the California border, the **Willamette** and **Rogue River valleys** are home to the majority of Oregonians, encompassing the state's four largest cities (along with Portland and its suburbs). The valleys may not have quite the natural appeal of the Cascades or the coast, but they make up for it with interesting cultural attractions, historic sites, and colorful festivals and fairs. More important, the valleys are easily accessible along the busy four- to six-lane route of Interstate 5, which leads many to dub the entire area the **I-5 Corridor** – a fast and generally straight route within the valleys, but a hilly, winding concourse in between them. This mountainous middle section – roughly from **Cottage Grove** to **Grants Pass** – is a bridge between the mighty Cascades and the coastal Klamath Mountains, and offers fine views of rugged landscapes and a few appealing small towns, but not much else.

As with Portland, the most engaging towns along the route – such as **Eugene**, **Ashland**, and **Jacksonville** – either have **urban–growth boundaries** or stringent planning and development guidelines, keeping them small and well preserved. Moreover, their downtown cores typically lie some distance from the freeway, built around historic structures or train depots more than off-ramps and overpasses. Those cities that do little to control development – mainly **Medford** and **Roseburg** – are uninspiring amalgamations of strip malls and office complexes built up along the highway, with hardly any attractions. **Highway 99** – the main route up and down the state before the freeway was finished in the 1960s – provides a slower-paced alternative to the interstate. In some places split into two highways marked East and West (in relation to I-5), these two-lane roads have many outstanding parks, viewpoints, and historic sites scattered along their length, and anyone interested in traveling the back roads will become familiar with them rather quickly.

Geographically the valleys lie roughly an equal distance from the Oregon Cascades and the coast, and numerous two-lane roads provide access to both. You will, of course, find immediate **Greyhound** and **Amtrak** access along I-5 (see "Basics," p.35). In the case of the latter, the **Coast Starlight** line to California runs from Portland to Eugene before darting in to the southern mountains away from the valleys, while the **Cascades** line travels from Seattle down through the Willamette Valley to Eugene.

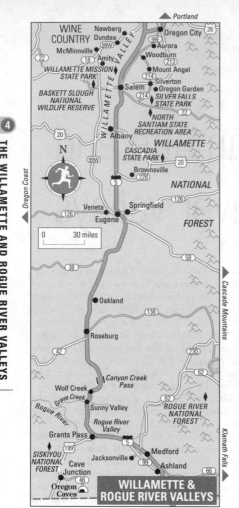

Some history

The **Willamette Valley's** even terrain and agricultural richness are largely a result of the Ice Age–era Bretz Floods (see box, p.124) that stripped away the topsoil of much of eastern Washington and deposited it here, hundreds of miles away. Native tribes recognized the valley's potential (and may have been present to witness the last of the floods), making their homes around the northward-flowing **Willamette River**, the odd glacial boulder adding a surreal touch on the landscape. The **Rogue River**, by contrast, is the prototypical mountain stream, draining the higher ground near Crater Lake to wend westward to the sea at Gold Beach. What's unusual is that the river crosses the mostly north-south **Rogue River Valley** at a perpendicular angle, becoming its namesake perhaps by convenience more than anything else.

It wasn't until the rise of the **Oregon Trail** (see box, p.188) that both areas experienced major settlement. The main route of the trail ended in the Willamette Valley, but the Rogue River Valley, too, attracted migrants on the alternate **Applegate Trail** (p.210). These heady pioneer days are still recalled in the minds of many old-time Oregonians with a memorable tall tale: a legendary **fork** on the trail once showed two routes – the one to California was marked by a cairn of shimmering quartz, the other by a marker stating "To Oregon." The pioneers who could read came to Oregon; everybody else went south.

Oregon City, Salem, and Portland became bustling trading centers, as newcomers began farming the fertile soil and cutting and selling timber. The lack of safe anchorage along the storm-battered coast furthered the success of Portland, from where ships left for Europe and the East Coast laden with raw materials, and through its docks the other Willamette Valley towns gained access to the Pacific via the Columbia River. In 1852, **gold** was unearthed on the Rogue River, and during the subsequent gold rush the prospectors' colony of Jacksonville was even touted as the state capital. However, the gold gave out in the 1880s, and the region resumed its more pedestrian agricultural progress.

For the next eighty years the commerce from agriculture and timber largely defined the valleys. By the 1970s, though, the rise of the **environmental**

movement and the demise of many old-growth forests limited the activities of the major logging companies, and by 2000 no significant timber enterprises were based in the state. That said, logging still occurs erratically throughout the western forests, and agriculture remains strong. With help from environmentalists, farmers have led Oregon to pass some of the nation's strictest and most tightly enforced **land-use planning** codes, which have kept most of the land in the valleys, at least outside the cities, green and rural, with seed growers, farmers of produce and grain, and winemakers all finding comfortable niches here. The minimal roadside billboards and many state parks and natural preserves in the region give it the feel of a charming anachronism: rural and small-town America largely free of the excesses of modern development, and kept that way by law.

The Willamette Valley

Running 120 miles parallel to and an hour's drive from the coast, the flat, green **Willamette Valley** was the home of Oregon's first settlements and towns, and the valley (pronounced "wah-LAM-it") is still at the heart of the state's social, political, and cultural existence. Most of Oregon's population is concentrated here, either in the cities strung along the **Willamette River** or in rural towns, and many remain dependent on agriculture even today. Among the more diverting of the small cities are **Oregon City**, of historic interest as the settlement at the end of the Oregon Trail; the state capital, **Salem**, which has a handful of historic curiosities, along with its legislative campus; and fun and friendly **Eugene**, a lively college town with a New Age feel. Other scattered points of interest include the pleasant **vineyards** on the northwest side of the valley, Howard Hughes' giant airplane the **Spruce Goose** in **McMinnville**, and the intriguing ethnic and religious enclaves of **Aurora** and **Mount Angel**.

Public transportation along the Willamette Valley is excellent, with regular Greyhound **buses** running from Portland to Eugene and beyond, and Amtrak operating two **train** lines. Portland's transit system, Tri-Met, covers Oregon City. Beyond the I-5 corridor, you may have more trouble accessing the various towns and parks, though some city bus systems – notably Eugene's LTD – are extensive and can take you all over their areas.

Oregon City

Set beside the confluence of the Willamette and Clackamas rivers, about thirteen miles south of downtown Portland, **OREGON CITY** is where the state began. This was the end of the Oregon Trail and the **first capital** of the Oregon Territory – though ironically, it was founded by the British-owned Hudson's Bay Company. The company's local agent, **John McLoughlin**, built a lumber mill here in 1829, when American settlement of the region was minimal and the term "Northwest" referred to places like Ohio and Michigan, not Oregon. Today,

The Great Migration

Perhaps more than any other early American leader, **Thomas Jefferson** realized the opportunities presented by the vast lands west of the Mississippi, and after he became president in 1801, he was in a position to act on his expansionist vision – though with caution. The French held the **Louisiana Territory** between the Mississippi and the Rockies, and the British claimed the land from the Rockies to the Pacific – a vast wilderness known as the **Oregon Country**, buffered by Russian Alaska and Spanish California. Consequently, when Jefferson began organizing an American overland expedition to the Pacific he was careful to define its purpose solely in terms of trade and commerce.

Luckily, the European powers were embroiled in the Napoleonic Wars, the expense of which led Napoleon to sell the Louisiana Territory to the Americans in 1803. And so, when the **Lewis and Clark Expedition** left St Louis for the Pacific in 1804, it had as much to do with taking stock of the country's new possessions as with the long-term strategy of contesting British influence. Indeed, Anglo–American territorial rivalry dragged on until 1846, but by this time the British claim to the region south of the 49th Parallel (present-day Washington and Oregon) had been swept away by the rising tide of overland immigration launched by pioneer farmers, the majority of whom came from just east of the Mississippi.

The detailed reports emanating from the Lewis and Clark Expedition catalyzed the migration west, but the migrants – or **movers**, as they're often called – were much more inspired by the missionaries who went west to Christianize the "heathen" native tribes in the 1830s. After all, Lewis and Clark traveled by canoe, but the missionaries headed out in simple covered wagons encumbered by farming equipment and livestock. The missionaries also sent back glowing and widely circulated reports of the Oregon Country's mild climate, fertile soil, and absence of malaria and confirmed crucially that the lands of the West Coast were well forested. Mid-nineteenth-century American farmers judged the fertility of land by the size of the trees it supported. This was quite wrong from a modern agricultural view, but it explains why they passed up the treeless prairie just beyond the Mississippi – what they referred to as the "Great American Desert" – and pushed west.

In the spring of 1843, one thousand movers gathered at Independence and Westport on the banks of the Missouri River to prepare for the **Great Migration**.

the core of the town sits along Highway 99E and consists of a bland modern section down by the river and an uptown area of old wooden houses set on a bluff, which you can ascend via steep roads and stairways. There's also a free, space-age-style **elevator** at 7th Street and Railroad Avenue (Mon–Sat 6.45am–7pm, Sun 11am–7pm) whose top observation deck provides good views of the area and the town's signature **Willamette Falls** watercourse.

Among a series of nineteenth-century clapboard houses located on the compact, gridiron upper level is the restored **McLoughlin House**, 713 Center St (Wed–Sat 10am–4pm, Sun 1–4pm; free; ⓦ www.mcloughlinhouse.org), which was moved up from the riverfront and saved from destruction in 1909. It was once the home of John McLoughlin, who ignored both political antagonisms and the instructions of his employers in providing the Americans who survived the Oregon Trail with food, seed, and periodic rescue from hostile native tribes. His main base was north of here in Vancouver on the Columbia River, but he retired to Oregon City in 1846 confident that his cordial relationship with – and generosity to – the pioneers would put him in good stead. He was wrong. Despite becoming an American citizen and being elected mayor of the growing town, McLoughlin was stripped of his local landholdings by his

The pioneers were a remarkably homogeneous bunch, nearly all experienced farmers, traveling in family groups with ordinary ox pulled farm wagons with flimsy canvas roofs, often walking alongside their vehicles instead of riding and adding extra weight to them. Only too aware of the difficulties of the journey, the movers voted in wagon-train leaders after the first hundred miles and established camp rules to govern everything from the grazing of livestock to the collection of fuel (usually buffalo dung).

Traversing almost two thousand miles of modern-day Kansas, Nebraska, Wyoming, and Idaho, they cajoled their wagons across rivers, struggled over mountain passes, endured the burning heat of the plains, chopped their way through forests, and paused at the occasional frontier fort or missionary station to recuperate. They also bartered supplies with various tribes in return for rafts and knowledge of the outback. Finally, after six months on the trail, they arrived at what is now **The Dalles** (see p.134). Here the group faced a difficult choice: either build rafts and risk the treacherous currents of the Columbia River, or take the Barlow Road (see box, p.132) around Mount Hood, notorious for its inclement weather and steep hills, many of which required the use of heavy ropes to lower the wagons down the slopes. Either way, most of the migrants made it to the Willamette Valley despite their travails, founding Oregon City and making it the capital of the new Oregon Territory from 1848 to 1851, when it was displaced by another valley town, Salem. The pioneers' arrival doubled Oregon's American population and led to Oregon's being the second Western state after California to join the Union, in 1859.

Over the next thirty years, further waves of settlers followed the Oregon Trail, along with an offshoot that populated the Rogue River Valley, the **Applegate Trail** (see p.210). Other amateur adventurers whittled away at the time it took by blazing shortcuts across the mountains and finding hitherto unfamiliar passages. Overall, these pioneers swelled the population of the Willamette Valley by some 53,000, and only with the coming of the railroad in the 1880s did the trails fall into disuse. Precious little survives today to remember the pioneers by, but out in eastern Oregon a few scattered hillsides still show the deep ruts made by the wheels of their wagons, and there are several interpretive centers along the way.

political enemies, and he died an embittered man in 1857. His two-story house has been refurnished in period style, with a good scattering of McLoughlin's own possessions.

Another relocated historic home, the 1845 **Ermatinger House**, 619 6th St (Thurs & Fri 11am–4pm; $3; ☎503/650-1851), was where the name of neighboring Portland was chosen on the flip of a coin – with "Boston" as the alternative. Call about the house's "living history" teas, in which you can sip and stir with docents in period garb putting on the airs of old-time pioneers. Just down the street at no. 603, the **Stevens Crawford House** (Feb–Dec Wed–Sat noon–4pm; $4) is a historic 1908 home, restored to something of its original appearance, with various antiques and decor from the town's founding families of the Victorian era.

The Stevens Crawford House is associated with **Museum of the Oregon Territory**, right off Hwy 99E at 211 Tumwater Drive (daily 11am–4pm; $7; ☎503/655-5574, ⊛www.orcity.com/museum), which has mildly interesting town relics and native artifacts, as well as a replica pioneer schoolroom and pharmacy. Pride of place goes to the 1850 **land plat** for the brand-new city of San Francisco, which had to be filed in Oregon City when the town had the main federal court and land office serving the entire West Coast. For a more engaging, if not quite as authentic, taste of local history, head to the **End of the Oregon Trail Interpretive Center**, 1726 Washington St (March–Oct: Mon–Sat 9.30am–5pm, Sun 10.30am–5pm; Nov–Feb: Tues–Sat 11am–4pm; $7; ℡503/657-9336, ⊛www.endoftheoregontrail.org), on the northern edge of the lower part of town. In a gallant attempt to give the flavor of the pioneer's difficult and dangerous trek westward, the center is housed in a trio of giant buildings resembling covered wagons, full of interactive, user-friendly displays – dioramas, replica antiques, and documentary films – that can appeal to all ages. Although the actual artifacts are thin on the ground, the costumed staff gives the lowdown with great gusto as you tour the facility.

Oregon City has little in the way of hotels or restaurants worth seeking out, though the reliable McMenamins **microbrewery** chain does have a solid outlet at 102 9th St (℡503/655-8032), where you can knock back a Terminator Stout or a Black Rabbit Porter. Your best bet is to visit on a day-trip from Portland. Tri-Met **buses** (Oatfield line #32 and McLoughlin #33; rain symbol), run from Portland's Transit Mall (see p.78) to various points in Oregon City, including the upper town.

The northern valley

South and west of Oregon City, the bucolic **northern section** of the Willamette Valley has rolling green hills, small farmsteads, and rippling creeks that you can explore on two-lane roads that often trace the routes of nineteenth-century trails. There are fine **wineries** in the area, little European **ethnic** and **religious colonies**, and assorted **architectural curiosities** like a monastery library built by the modernist Finnish architect Alvar Aalto and a tourable modern house designed by Frank Lloyd Wright. Keep in mind, though, that you'll probably need a **car** to access these sites and, even with one, may find yourself stymied by the lack of bridges across the Willamette River (there's even a ferry here and there). Thus, it's best to choose one side of the valley at a time to explore unless you plan on crossing the river near Newberg or Salem.

West of the river

On the opposite side of I-5 from Oregon City, the land **west** of the Willamette River is a lovely terrain of low valleys and stands of second-growth trees, crossed by narrow two-lane roads that lead by flowing streams, old barns, and plots set aside for growing berries, grasses, and grapes.

Accommodation

Amid the region's various small towns, there are several possibilities for **accommodation** if you're really into the rural vineyard scene – mainly B&Bs, though a new luxury resort near Dundee is slated for construction in the coming years. The only state campground in the area is at **Champoeg State Park**, seven miles east of Newberg off Hwy 99W (sites $16–20, yurts $27, rustic cabins $35; reserve at ℡1-800/452-5687), though inconveniently on the other side of the Willamette River.

Best Western Newberg Inn 2211 Portland Rd, Newberg ℡503/537-3000, ⊛www.bestwestern .com. Nothing fancy, just a clean and reliable motel with microwaves and fridges in each room, and a fine central location in town, within easy reach of the wineries. ④

Grand Lodge 3505 Pacific Ave, just north of wine country in Forest Grove ☎ 877/992-9533, 🌐 www.mcmenamins.com. Grand, palatial building that used to be a (rather colossal) Masonic retreat and has since been converted to a hotel-microbrewery-retreat, with multiple onsite watering holes and inexpensive, often sizable rooms and suites, as well as a movie theater and soaking pool. ❷–❻
Hotel Oregon 310 Evans St, McMinnville ☎ 1-888/472-8427, 🌐 www.hoteloregon.com. A stately 1905 pile in this town's smallish downtown core, the Hotel Oregon used to be a lodge, dance hall, telegraph office, and bus depot. It now features a pub with a good selection of micro-brews, blues and folk concerts, quirky artwork, and nicely renovated, economical suites and rooms (cheaper with shared bath). ❸–❺
Lobenhaus 6975 NE Abbey Rd near Lafayette ☎ 1-888/339-3375, 🌐 www.lobenhaus.com. Smart and comfortable lodgings in a leafy setting, with three levels holding six modern rooms, some with views of the gardens, pond, and woods. Located almost right in the center of the main vineyard zone. Two-night minimum stay April–Nov. ❻
Springbrook Hazelnut Farm 30295 N Hwy 99W, Newberg ☎ 1-800/793-8528 or 503/538-4606, 🌐 www.nutfarm.com. Grand old 1912 estate built around a restored farmhouse with a cottage and carriage house that make for a fine stay among orchards and vineyards; the rooms are thick with modern furniture and copious antiques. ❽
Youngberg Hill Inn 10660 SW Youngberg Hill Rd, McMinnville ☎ 1-888/657-8668, 🌐 www.youngberghill.com. Perched on a romantic hill overlooking lovely hills and valleys, this elegant complex offers seven tasteful and comfortable rooms and suites with sweeping views. The estate is part of a winery where, naturally, you can taste the merchandise. ❼

Wine country

Grapes are particularly abundant in the center of Oregon's **wine country**, where the hillsides are blanketed with vineyards and many wineries are open to the public for tours and tastings. The region runs from as far north as Gaston down to Salem, with a particular concentration in the triangle between McMinnville, Yamhill, and Newberg, surrounded by highways 99W, 47, and 240. The most direct route into the area is along **Highway 99 West**. There are six different American Viticultural Areas (AVA) here, encompassing more than a hundred wineries, many of which pour superb pinot noirs, pinot grigios, Chardonnays, and Rieslings. Notable and top-rated brands here include Archery

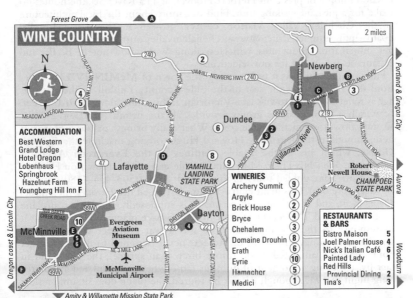

Summit, Domaine Drouhin, Eyrie, Erath, Hamacher, Bryce, Medici, Chehalem, Brick House, and Argyle. However, don't come expecting the type of multimedia shows put on by the big wineries in California's Napa and Sonoma valleys; most Oregon wineries are very much homegrown businesses, with a tasting room and gift shop, warehouse, and vineyard on view, and in some cases a few extra frills like attached hotels, swank restaurants, and golf courses. This no doubt underlines the charm of the region, which is only beginning to give way to the prospect of larger, more capitalized operations.

Most wineries are open daily from between 10am and noon to 5pm or so. Pick up a wine-country tour **map** from any local visitor center (or from ⓦwww.oregonwine.org, which has a comprehensive list of all facilities, locations, and websites), and expect the odd traffic delay in little burgs like **Dundee**, which is swamped by summer wine enthusiasts. If you want to sample before you go, stop by the official state wine-tasting room in Portland; it's inside the Oregon Convention Center at 777 NE MLK Blvd (Wed–Sat noon–6pm; ⓣ503/226-9797), and for $7 you can try the vino of fifteen of the top state wineries, most from this region. If you'd prefer to be in the hands of a capable **wine tour guide**, try Grape Escape Winery Tours (ⓣ503/283-3380, ⓦwww .grapeescapetours.com), which offers a range of group trips around the valley, from afternoon junkets (four people for $500) to full-scale evening sojourns with exquisite dinner and drink ($880 for four). A cheaper alternative is offered by Eco Tours of Oregon, 3127 SE 23rd Ave, Portland (ⓣ503/245-1428, ⓦwww.ecotours-of-oregon.com), which, along with offering a number of appealing treks around the region, provides day tours of the wine country ($55), hitting at least four wineries and including a nice picnic lunch.

Newberg, McMinnville, and Amity

Forty minutes southwest of Portland along Hwy 99W, the historic crossroads of **NEWBERG** boasts a number of fine old structures, some dating to pioneer days. Although none is particularly distinctive (except for the boyhood home of president Herbert Hoover, at 115 River St), the homes do make for a pleasant walking tour. Find out more about the local architecture at the Chehalem Valley **visitor center** at 415 E Sheridan (Mon–Fri 10am–3pm, summer daily; ⓦwww.chehalemvalley.org), where you can also get information about area wineries, along with good hotels, B&Bs, and restaurants (see p.194 for our selections).

Fifteen miles southwest of Newberg, the town of **McMINNVILLE** dates from the 1840s and is the seat of the oldest county, Yamhill, in the state. Its age is reflected in the town's late-Victorian architecture along **Third Street**, of which a local business group provides all the details (ⓣ503/472-3605, ⓦwww.downtownmcminnville.com). What really brings curious visitors out here, though, is the legendary Howard Hughes flying machine the **Spruce Goose**, which sits in the sizable confines of the **Evergreen Aviation Museum**, 3685 NE Three Mile Lane, a mile east of downtown on Hwy 18 (daily 9am–5pm, guided tours 11am & 2pm; $12; ⓣ503/434-4180, ⓦwww .sprucegoose.org). This giant craft – variously named the *Hercules*, the *Hughes Flying Boat*, and the *Flying Lumberyard* – is supposedly the largest airplane ever constructed. The eccentric, later mad aerospace magnate Hughes built it in response to those who claimed he was a war profiteer who pocketed government money in pursuit of projects never designed to fly or even get built. Made of laminated wood (more birch than spruce), the *Goose* did in fact fly, achieving a moment of dubious fame when it completed a minute-long flight in 1947. Though it can't be toured, the plane does sit amid a slew

△ The *Spruce Goose*

of fighters, passenger crafts, spy planes, and other aircraft, making the museum an essential stop for aviation buffs.

About seven miles south of McMinnville on Hwy 99W lies the small village of **AMITY**, home to a **monastery** of Brigittine monks, at 23300 Walker Lane (☎503/835-8080, Ⓦ www.brigittine.org). The facility itself is very basic, but what draws most people out here (call or see the website for directions) is the stunning quality of the monks' home-made **fudge** – amazingly decadent slabs of amaretto fudge and "cherry nut fudge royale," all freshly prepared on the premises.

Baskett Slough National Wildlife Refuge and Willamette Mission State Park

Ten miles south from Amity on Hwy 99W is the striking **Baskett Slough National Wildlife Refuge** (May–Sept dawn–dusk; ☎503/623-2749), which occupies nearly 2500 acres and provides winter habitat for a variety of birds, particularly waterfowl. Although you can't visit during their winter migration here (visitors disturb the flocks), at other times you can spot such majestic creatures as herons, hawks, and Canadian geese, along with many types of mammals and reptiles, from viewing platforms scattered around the refuge.

Another enjoyable natural attraction, **Willamette Mission State Park** ($3 day-use fee), can be found about seven miles east of Amity, on a bend in the Willamette River just past Hwy 221. The park commemorates the site where Methodist preacher Jason Lee founded a mission in 1834 to try to convert the native tribes. He wasn't terribly successful in this endeavor (his efforts are also examined in Salem's Mission Mill Museum; see p.194), but there is a memorial here to him, with outlines representing the places where the original buildings stood, along with countless trails for horseback riding, hiking, and cycling, plus a summer **campground** (group sites $40–61). Even better, the park contains the region's first river ferry for covered wagons, the **Wheatland Ferry**, which began running in 1844 and is amazingly still in operation, though in a more modern form designed for automobiles (daily 5.30am–9.45pm; vehicles $1.35, bicycles free; ☎503/588-7979, ⊛www.wheatlandferry.com). So along with its historic value, the park is also a convenient place to cross the river.

Eating

While the valley certainly has its share of run-of-the-mill diners, the main reason to come out here to **eat** is to partake in its top-notch **Northwest Cuisine**, which is even more influenced by French nouvelle cuisine here than it is in comparable restaurants in Portland. Indeed, since many Oregon pinot noir grapes are transplanted French varieties, so too are many of the elite dishes, using fresh local ingredients and seasonal, rotating menus. Keep in mind that while some restaurants have a relaxed and friendly environment, their prices can match those of the best Portland restaurants. All are located on or near Highway 99W.

Bistro Maison 729 NE 3rd St, McMinnville ☎503/474-1888. Highly regarded Continental cuisine spot that offers favorites like coq au vin and braised-lamb cassoulet, plus a fine French onion soup and desserts like profiteroles and crème caramel.

🏃 **Joel Palmer House** 600 Ferry St, Dayton ☎503/864-2995. Grand, historic 1853 Colonial Revival estate is a nationally renowned restaurant to which urbanites make special trips for its delicious and chic Northwest Cuisine – the likes of wild-mushroom Stroganoff and black-bean-rubbed duckling – so make sure to reserve well ahead.

Nick's Italian Café 521 NE 3rd St McMinnville ☎503/434-4471. A local favorite for local fare with a Continental twist, presented in sumptuous five-course dinners that may last hours and feature the likes of Dungeness crab, baby lamb chops, and

braised rabbit – though this is only a hint of what you might find, as the menu changes regularly.
Painted Lady 201 S College St, Newberg ☎503/538-3830. Well-regarded Northwest Cuisine with a wide range of fresh and local flavors and elements, from roasted duck breast to black tiger prawns to huckleberry tarts.
Red Hills Provincial Dining 276 N Hwy 99W, Dundee ☎503/538-8224. Terrific Northwest Cuisine restaurant that presents long, leisurely meals that may include salmon, filet mignon, wild mushrooms, and lamb, all inventively and stylishly prepared.
Tina's 760 Hwy 99W, Dundee ☎503/538-8880. Excellent, straightforward regional fare in the center of wine country that features savory selections of locally raised or caught salmon, halibut, duck and lamb, along with crab cakes and oysters.

East of the river

To reach the area **east** of the river, you'll soon find that bridges are in very short supply between Oregon City and Salem, potentially leaving you driving around in circles as you hunt for a crossing point. Other than a single overpass on I-5 at the Portland suburb of Wilsonville and the Wheatland Ferry (see p.193), the sole way to traverse the river is a highway bridge a mile south of Newberg on Hwy 219.

Robert Newell House

After you cross the river, your first (eastbound) left will take you to the agreeable, if uneventful, grounds of **Champoeg State Park** (locally pronounced CHAM-poo-ey) and the **Robert Newell House** (Feb–Nov Fri–Sun 1–5pm; $2). This 1959 reconstruction of an early Oregon pioneer's house is loaded with antiques from different periods in US history. It also houses a second-floor display of the gowns of the wives of Oregon governors – more interesting than it sounds – providing a colorful look at the changing styles of provincial fashion, as well as six rooms decorated in various historical styles and a selection of native baskets. The most compelling part of the house is the depiction of Newell himself, who, unlike the typical stoic Protestant pioneer, was a true "mountain man" – an explorer of the West, local town founder, and larger-than-life character who operated an assortment of businesses here until an 1861 flood wiped out his enterprises. A friend of the native tribes, Newell spent his last years on land given him by the Nez Percé in Idaho, acting as their interpreter and liaison to the federal government.

Aurora

From Champoeg, it's just a few miles farther east along well-signposted country lanes to the German colony of **AURORA**. After relocating from Bethel, Missouri, the immigrants who started the town in 1857 founded it as a odd mix of Christian spiritual refuge and Marxist commune, with residents sharing goods among themselves and subsisting on the fruits of their farm labor. Although the former part of the equation lasted longer than the latter, Aurora nonetheless held on as an ethnic enclave until well into the twentieth century. Even today there's a historic pocket that sports a number of **antiques stores** and quaint clapboard houses dating from the nineteenth century, giving a good impression of what the place may have been like in the old days. You can find out more about all these things, and pick up a walking-tour brochure of the town's dwellings, at the engaging **Old Aurora Colony Museum**, 2nd St at Liberty (Feb–Dec Tues–Sat 11am–4pm, Sun noon–4pm; $4.50; ☏503/678-5754, ⓦwww .auroracolonymuseum.com), which is stuffed with the furniture, quilts, farm tools, books, and bric-a-brac of the colony, including some articles of the simple clothing worn by the residents – many garments sport hook-and-eye closures, as the villagers considered buttons to be a cheap and frivolous adornment.

If the idea of **staying** in these historic digs appeals, try *Willamette Gables B&B*, 10323 Schuler Rd (☏503/678-2195, ⓦwww.willamettegables.com; ⑥), some of whose rooms have fireplaces, claw-foot tubs, and riverside views; or *Anna Becke House*, 14892 Bobs Ave (☏503/678-6979 or 1-866/383-2662, ⓦwww.annabeckehouse.com; ⑤), with less expensive, if a bit smaller and more precious, units with antique styling.

Woodburn and Mount Angel

The town of **WOODBURN**, about five miles south of Aurora on Hwy 99E, is mainly known for its dreary outlet mall, though away from the highway you can find the grand **Settlemier House**, Settlemier Ave at Garfield (first Sun of month 1–4pm, or by appointment at ☏503/982-1897; $3). As one of the valley's most prominent dwellings, this 1892 Queen Anne mansion features a wraparound veranda, conical tower, and assorted antiques inside. The stylish manor gives a hint of the aspirations of its owner, the town founder and an early horticulturist in the valley, and though it's open only once a month, it is well worth touring by appointment at other times.

Looping six miles to the southeast on Hwy 214, you come across the small burg of **MOUNT ANGEL**, associated with one thing in the minds of many Oregonians – **Oktoberfest**. This annual month-long spectacle is celebrated here with sprightly ethnic displays of lederhosen and Tyrolean hats, copious beer, and the usual gut-busting German cuisine. More historically authentic than Washington's Bavarian theme town of Leavenworth (see p.428), Mount Angel has been home to German immigrants since the 1880s. The town's founder named the place after the Benedictine **Mount Angel Abbey**, which itself was named after Engelberg, the Swiss city where he received his religious education. The abbey and its seminary sit atop one of the local hills, and the abbey is open to the public. Late July is a good time to show up because it's when the monks put on a compelling **Bach Festival** (tickets at ☏503-845-3321, ⓦwww.mtangel.edu), employing a grand pipe organ and including a dinner meal in the ticket. Additionally, fans of high-modern architecture won't want to miss the abbey's striking **library**, designed in 1970 by legendary Finnish architect Alvar Aalto and freely tourable with the aid of a helpful brochure. One of Oregon's few architectural treasures outside of Portland, the library has a curving, asymmetrical design spread over two floors, with light flooding through hillside windows and skylights, and light-wood paneling, giving the space a warm, inviting feel. The town's other claim to fame is as the site of the country's biggest **glockenspiel**, completed in 2006. It plays music four times a day (at 11am, 1pm, 4pm & 7pm) at Charles and Garfield streets, accompanied by seven carved figures like a tuba player, abbey prior, nun, tribal chief, and two apple-cheeked Alpine children who pop out on a swing warbling "Edelweiss."

For representative **dining** in town during the festival or any time of the year, check out *Angel's Table*, 415 S Main St (℡503/845-9289), which has flavorful Teutonic selections like breaded pork Wiener schnitzel and savory chicken breast with spinach and blue cheese.

The Gordon House and Silver Falls State Park

Although it has its advocates, the **Oregon Garden**, five miles south of Mount Angel in **Silverton** at 879 W Main St (May–Sept 10am–6pm; Oct–April 10am–4pm; $10; ⓦwww.oregongarden.org), is one of the more disappointing sites in the state, advertised heavily in tourist brochures but strangely uninvolving, despite its copious selection of native foliage. The main, perhaps the only, reason to visit is to tour Frank Lloyd Wright's elegant **Gordon House** (May–Oct 10am–5pm; Nov–April noon–4pm; tours $5; reserve at ℡503/874-6006), which was moved here from its original location, 25 miles north along the banks of the Willamette, after being threatened with demolition. Intended as mass housing for the middle class, Wright's "Usonian" homes feature canti-levered roofs, horizontal layouts, and narrow windows. This model is particularly interesting as its displays a number of idiosyncratic Wright experiments – hot water piped through a concrete floor for internal heating, a towering skylight over the kitchen, an absence of 90-degree angles throughout, and a frame built of concrete block and western red cedar.

In a more remote section of the valley, ten miles to the southeast, lush, green **Silver Falls State Park** (℡503/873-8681, ⓦwww.oregonstateparks.org), with its array of large and small **waterfalls**, is the state's most popular park, and its **Trail of Ten Falls**, which you can pick up at the North or South Falls, is one of the best hikes in the state. The trail takes you past huge stands of trees and verdant native foliage, over hills and across ravines, and along the banks of gently flowing Silver Creek. The undeniable highlights, though, are the two waterfalls that bracket the park – **North Falls**, a precipitous spray of mist you can approach on a narrow trail, and **South Falls**, a huge and spellbinding tower of crashing water that you can actually walk behind on a rocky basaltic ledge, hearing its thundering roar from just a few feet away.

While in the area, you can **stay** at the *Water Street Inn*, 421 N Water St in Silverton (℡1-866/873-3344 or 503/873-3344, ⓦwww.thewaterstreetinn .com; ❺), a pleasant 1890 Victorian manor whose five lovely rooms and suites offer tasteful decor with minimal chintz. Another option is **camping** at Silver Falls (sites $16–20, rustic cabins $35), but you'll have to reserve weeks or months in advance to have a chance at getting a spot. Beyond the inn or the park, you're best off trying accommodations in Salem, 26 miles west of Silver Falls via highways 22 and 214. Outside of Oktoberfest and the German diners in Mount Angel, you'll find few distinctive eateries in the immediate area. Either head into Salem or cross over the Willamette River for a meal.

Salem

Despite being the second-most-populous city in Oregon, **SALEM**, located fifty miles south of Portland, has always often proven an elusive attraction. Not only does the modern sprawl of the town defy a sense of cohesion (and the visitor's navigation skills), but the buildup of motels and fast-food chains that greet you off the I-5 freeway give the place a strong air of dreariness. There are plenty of valid historical attractions here (some among the best in the state), but the city itself doesn't yet have the feeling of a true destination, and after poking around for a day or so, you'll probably be itching to move on to Eugene or Portland.

Arrival and accommodation

Easy to reach along the I-5 corridor, Salem can be visited on a day-trip from Portland or, better, on the way south toward Eugene and Ashland. The Greyhound **bus** station is located conveniently downtown at 450 Church St NE and Center Street, and so is the Amtrak station, at 13th St SE and Oak Street, whose **trains** run five times daily between Portland and Eugene. The **visitor center** is part of the Mission Mill Museum, off 12th Street at 1313 Mill St SE (℡503/581-4325 or 1-800/874-7012, Ⓦwww.travelsalem.com).

DOWNTOWN SALEM

ACCOMMODATION
A Creekside Garden Inn   B
Phoenix Inn Suites   C
Red Lion   A

RESTAURANTS & BARS
Arbor Café   2
Boon's Treasury   1
Court Street
Dairy Lunch   3
Da Vinci's   6
Jonathan's Oyster
Bar   4
Wild Pear   5

Salem has more than its share of modern budget **motels**, but most of the more enticing places are a little way out from the center. Among them, one good option is the comfortable *Phoenix Inn Suites*, south of downtown at 4370 Commercial St SE (℡503/588-9220, ⊛www.phoenixinn.com; ❺), which has around ninety spacious rooms, plus a pool and Jacuzzi. A bit more central is the serviceable chain lodging at the *Red Lion*, northeast of the capitol at 3301 Market Street NE (℡503/370-7888 or 1-800/RED-LION, ⊛www.redlion.com; ❹), while *A Creekside Garden Inn*, 333 Wyatt Court NE (℡503/391-0837 or 1-800/949-0837, ⊛www.salembandb.com; ❹), is a stately Colonial Revival estate close to downtown, with five rooms elegantly furnished with antiques and fetching gardens surrounding the place. About ten miles from downtown, *Bethel Heights Farm,* 6055 Bethel Heights Rd NW (℡503/364-7688, ⊛www.oregon-b-and-b.com; ❺), has modest pair of modern rooms in the Eola Hills, on the twenty-acre grounds of one of the region's best vineyards.

The City

Salem is not a very user-friendly place for newcomers, and unless you have a state map with a wide, sprawling view of the city, you may well get lost (our map covers the downtown area, the main area worth seeing). Perhaps the easiest and most predictable access to downtown is to go westbound on Highway 22 to 17th Street. Turn right (north) and go six blocks to State Street. Take a left on State and it will lead you directly to the capitol.

The capitol campus and Willamette University

Lying along State Street is the **state capitol campus** and the city's unmistakable centerpiece, the tall, white, Vermont-marble **State Capitol**, whose tower is topped by a large gold-leaf pioneer, axe in hand, eyes to the West. Finished in 1938 in a vaguely Moderne style, the building sports a marble carving at its entrance, at 900 Court St NE (Mon–Fri 7.30am–5.30pm; free; ℡503-986-1388, ⊛www.leg.state.or.us), of Lewis and Clark processing regally towards (presumably) the Willamette Valley. Inside murals celebrate the state's beginnings and on the floor there's a large bronze take on the state seal, in which wheat, a covered wagon, and trading ships symbolize Oregon's entry into the Union in 1859. There are also historical **tours** of the building (free; by reservation at ℡503/986-1388) and tours just of the tower itself (Mon–Fri on the hour 9am–4pm; free), beginning at the information desk inside the rotunda. Outside, manicured gardens surround the building, with statues of Salem founder Jason Lee and Oregon City founder John McLoughlin on the east side.

Next to the capitol, south across State Street, leafy **Willamette University** is the oldest university in the West, originally a mission school set up by Lee. Its only real highlight for visitors is the **Hallie Ford Museum of Art**, 700 State St (Tues–Sat 10am–5pm, Sun 1–5pm; $3; ℡503/370-6855, ⊛www.willamette.edu/museum_of_art), which features compelling native baskets and handicrafts, plus assorted antiquities like ancient Greek vases and Egyptian funeral masks, and a handful of original prints by William Hogarth and Auguste Rodin.

The historic downtown core

Downtown Salem has a compact collection of nineteenth-century, low-slung red-brick commercial buildings, which were declared a National Historic District in 2001. Lying just west of the capitol on State Street, with most of its key structures concentrated on Liberty and Commercial streets between Chemeketa and Ferry, the district has as its showpiece the 1869 **Reed Opera House**, Court St at Liberty (Ⓦ www.reedoperahouse.com), an Italianate 1869 structure that was once the nexus of local cultural activity and is now a trim little shopping mall with bars and diners, plus ballrooms and a theater. Opera houses like this sprang up all over the Northwest in the second half of the nineteenth century – performances were not genteel affairs, but boisterous spectacles of anything that was touring, from Sophocles to dancing dogs.

The old operatic and vaudeville entertainment, though, gave way in the early twentieth century to sparkling movie palaces; the town's best remaining example, the grand **Elsinore Theatre**, three blocks away at 170 High St, is a charming 1926 Neo-Gothic gem that is now a performing arts center (Ⓣ503/375-3574 or Ⓦ www.elsinoretheatre.com for details). It also shows monthly classic and silent movies (Oct–May Wed 7pm; $5) and employs a Wurlitzer organ to add period atmosphere. Built in a medieval English style and named after Hamlet's castle, the theater has ornate decoration throughout and stained-glass windows showcasing some the Bard's most famous *dramatis personae*.

Mission Mill Museum and Marion County Historical Society

Methodist missionary Jason Lee's wooden, two-story former dwelling now sits on the grounds of **Mission Mill Museum**, just east of the downtown core and Willamette University at 1313 Mill St SE (Mon–Sat 10am–5pm; $8; Ⓣ503/585-7012, Ⓦ www.missionmill.org), along with other restored pioneer structures and the old mill, a looming industrial relic. Volunteers recount the complicated history (see box, below) of Lee's endeavors in great detail as they lead tours of the village, taking you from the simple old houses of Lee and his followers to the huge, somewhat ominous mill facility nearby. As you poke around the array of giant picking, carding, weaving, and drying machines (some of which creak to life at the press of a button), you get a sense of the dangerous, repetitive work required to produce woolen wear in the high American industrial age. In any case, by the later twentieth century the factory was antiquated by modern standards and closed its doors – though its owner's descendants did go on to found the mighty, and still active, Pendleton Woolen Mills out in eastern Oregon (see p.259).

Around the back, the separate **Marion County Historical Society museum**, 260 12th St SE (Tues–Sat noon–4pm; $3; ☏503/364-2128, Ⓦ www.marionhistory.org), is a modest institution in the course of expanding its facility. It's worth checking out its exhibit on the Kalapuyan, who lived in the Willamette Valley until white settlers, the Klickitat tribe, and disease drove them out. As much as ninety percent of the native population were killed by a nineteenth-century malaria epidemic. The museum's pride and joy is a rickety and rare 125-year-old **canoe**, hollowed out, in the traditional manner, by hot coals.

Deepwood Estate and Bush House

About seven blocks south of the capitol campus are two historic residences that are worth touring if you're spending more than a day in town. The first, **Deepwood Estate**, 1116 Mission St SE (May–Sept Sun–Fri noon–5pm; Oct–April Tues–Sat noon–5pm; $4; ☏503/363-1825, Ⓦ www.oregonlink .com/deepwood), is a spacious, three-level Queen Anne home from 1894 with pleasant English-style gardens, handsome oak-paneled walls, stained-glass windows, and an original adjoining carriage house – along with a quaint gazebo first used in Portland's Lewis and Clark Exposition in 1905 and relocated here 44 years later.

Five blocks west, the **Bush House**, 600 Mission St SE (May–Sept Tues–Sun noon–5pm; Oct–April Tues–Sun 1–4pm; $4; ☏503/363-4714, Ⓦ www .salemart.org), isn't one of the homes of Dubya but was the residence of an early newspaper publisher who had a hand in crafting the state constitution. The 1878 house is a tasteful affair, with a reserved mid-Victorian-era facade and rooms decorated with period furnishings and minor nineteenth-century art. The highlight is the collection of ten Italian **marble fireplaces**, beautiful and ornate creations that seem too elegant to have ever housed burning logs and falling ash. Elsewhere on the grounds, the **pasture park** has a nice selection of rose gardens, orchards, flowerbeds, and a conservatory, while an **art center** sits in the estate's former barn and displays a decent array of modern artworks from regional artists.

Eating and drinking

For **food**, you're best off downtown, where the *Court Street Dairy Lunch*, 347 Court St (☏503/363-6433), is a classic 1960s diner with primo burgers; *Jonathan's Oyster Bar*, 445 State St (☏503/362-7219), serves fresh seafood and cajun and southwestern cuisine; the pleasant *Arbor Café*, 380 High St NE (☏503/588-2353), has a nice range of pasta, sandwiches, and salads; *Da Vinci's*, 180 High St SE (☏503/399-1413), offers Italian cuisine and pizzas fired in a wood-burning oven; and *Wild Pear*, 372 State St (☏503/378-7515), is a good place for lunch, with salmon cakes, ham-and-brie sandwiches, and pasta salad.

The **drinking** scene is highlighted by the terrific ♫ *Boon's Treasury*, 888 Liberty St NE (☏503/399-9062), which offers rock, roots and blues jams (Wed–Sat) and a wide array of burgers and microbrews. Even better, the bar is located in a classic old building from 1860, which once housed the state's first treasury.

Covered bridges

Homesteaders in the Willamette Valley put roofs over their **bridges** to protect the wooden trusses from the Oregon rain, lengthening a bridge's life span from ten to up to eighty years or so – a tradition that continued until fairly recently. The privacy they afforded earned them the nickname of "kissing bridges." There are no fewer than fifty covered bridges in the state, many of them preserved by state law, and although it's unlikely you'll want to see them all, a good cluster of them can be visited between Salem and Eugene, roughly on or around highways 20, 126, and 34. Since many of them look pretty similar, differing only by color, roof and side style (support walls or columns), and type of wood used, your best bet is to pick up or order the excellent brochure Oregon's Covered Bridges, which details the exact location of all the Willamette Valley's covered spans. It's available from any major visitor center hereabouts; you can also visit the Covered Bridges Directory at ⓦcoveredbridges .stateoforegon.com, which lists them by area, style, and detail.

Moving on from Salem

Mainline attractions are thin on the ground between Salem and Eugene. Highways 20 and 22 run west to the coast and east into the Cascades, but there's just a handful of interesting sights directly off I-5. The standout state parks include **North Santiam**, some twenty miles east of I-5 on Hwy 22, and **Cascadia**, about thirty miles east of I-5 on Hwy 20. Both offer excellent swimming, fishing, and hiking, and the latter has **camping** as well (May–Sept; $14; reserve at ⓣ1-800/452-5687).

If you're interested in antique architecture, the pulp-mill town of **Albany**, fifteen miles south of Salem, features three national historic districts, including its downtown core, where you're apt to see anything from Victorian banks to Craftsman bungalows. The Albany Visitors Association (ⓣ541/928-0911, ⓦwww.albanyvisitors.com) has information on the various districts and self-guided walking tours. Also diverting, the hamlet of **Brownsville** is seventeen miles south of Albany on I-5, then four miles east of the freeway on Hwy 228. Much of the townscape was used in the filming of the movie *Stand By Me*, convincingly doubling as a rural hamlet seen through the haze of twisted nostalgia, and you may recognize some of the old structures as you lope along Brownsville Road or Kirk Avenue. The **Linn County Historical Museum**, 101 Park Ave (Mon–Sat 11am–4pm, Sun 1–5pm; free; ⓣ541/466-3390, ⓦwww.co.linn.or.us/museum), can give you the lowdown on the town's history (it basically grew up around a woolen mill), but for a closer peek, check out the stately **Moyer House** one block south (same hours and website as museum; free). This two-story 1881 Italianate home has gingerbread detailing, finely carved eaves, and ornamental decor, and also sports a rooftop tower, considerable oak and walnut woodworking and panels, and hand-painted nature scenes above the interior windows.

Eugene

Some 65 miles south of Salem on I-5, **EUGENE** dominates the southern end of the Willamette Valley with a lively social mix of University of Oregon students, professionals, graying hippies, and blue-collar workers. The city takes its name from timber-cutter **Eugene Skinner**, the first person to build a

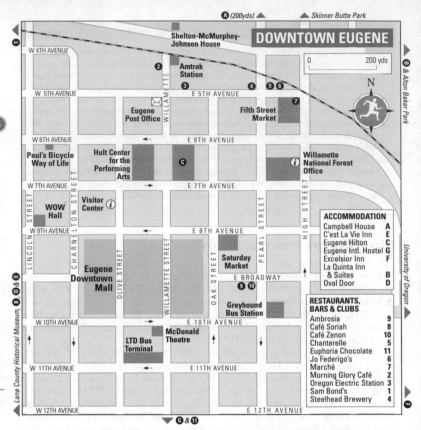

homestead here in 1846, whose success led other settlers to follow. Eugene soon developed as an agricultural supply center, and boomed when the California–Eugene–Portland railroad was completed in the 1870s. The city's role as a cultural hub began with the traveling theater groups that stopped here on their way between Portland and San Francisco in the late nineteenth century. More recently, in the late 1960s, *One Flew Over the Cuckoo's Nest* author Ken Kesey and some of the Merry Pranksters came to live in the woods here after tiring of the San Francisco Bay Area. The famous Nike running shoe, with its sole made on a waffle iron, was first invented by University of Oregon track coach Bill Bowerman and tested by his student-athletes. And in the late 1970s, much of the movie *Animal House* was filmed on campus.

Arrival, information, and city transportation

Eugene is easy to get to by public transit: Amtrak's Coast Starlight and Cascades **trains** connect Eugene to Los Angeles, Portland, and Seattle. Both the train and bus **terminals** are both handily located downtown, with Greyhound pulling in at 987 Pearl St at Tenth Avenue (℡541/344-6265), and Amtrak at Fourth Avenue and Willamette Street. For information, there's a useful **visitor center** at 754 Olive St (Mon–Fri 9am–5pm, Sat 10am–4pm;

①541/484-5307 or 1-800/547-5445, ⓦwww.visitlanecounty.org), which has brochures detailing driving tours of the area's covered bridges (see box, p.201) and regional wineries – many of which offer free tours and tastings. The visitor center also has myriad maps of **cycling** and **walking** trails, both in the city center and along leafy riverbanks. You can **rent** bikes from Paul's Bicycle Way of Life, 234 W 6th Ave (①541/344-4105, ⓦwww.bicycleway.com), starting at $20 per day, or at Blue Heron Bicycles, 877 E 13th Ave (①541/343-2488), for as little as $4 an hour. Hiking **maps** of the forested hills east of Eugene are available at the **Willamette National Forest Office**, in the Federal Building, downtown at 211 E 7th Ave at Pearl St (Mon–Fri 8am–4.30pm; ①541/465-6521, ⓦwww.fs.fed.us/r6/willamette).

Eugene is best explored on **foot** – it takes only about ten minutes to walk from one side of downtown to the other, or less than twenty minutes from downtown to the campus of the University of Oregon. Eugene also has a terrific **bus system**, the LTD ($1.25; ①541/687-5555, ⓦwww.ltd.org), offering day passes for $2.50, and 50¢ rides on the "Breeze" shuttle linking downtown, the university, and local malls. The **main bus station** is at Willamette St and Eleventh Ave (Mon–Fri 6am–8.30pm, Sat 9am–5pm), where free transit maps, timetables, and route-planning advice are available, along with tickets.

Accommodation

To get the flavor of Eugene, it's best to **stay** either downtown or in one of the **inns** or **B&Bs** located a short distance away. In addition, there is a cluster of reasonably priced chain **motels** on and around Franklin Boulevard, near the university off I-5 (Exit 192), and north of town beside I-5 (Exit 195A). **Campers** can access forested campgrounds in the Willamette National Forest (see p.242), the nearest being an hour's drive east of town on Highway 126.

Campbell House 252 Pearl St at E 3rd Ave ①541/343-1119 or 1-800/264-2519, ⓦwww.campbellhouse.com. A fine old B&B built in 1892 with lovely gardens, gracious public rooms, and a handsome veranda. Each of the eighteen guest rooms is decorated in period style – lots of tartans and warm colors – as are those in the adjacent carriage house. Well placed on the slopes of a wooded hill with Skinner Butte Park just a short, steep walk up above. ⑥

C'est la Vie Inn 1006 Taylor St ①866/302-3014, ⓦwww.cestlavieinn.com. Regal and elegant B&B in an 1891 Victorian that offers good value with its four stylish, painter-themed rooms, of which the Matisse is the smartest (though hardly Fauve) with claw-foot tubs, flat-screen TVs, and DVD players. Well located downtown just south of the major attractions. ⑤

Eugene Hilton 66 E 6th Ave ①541/342-2000 or 1-800/937-6660, ⓦwww.eugene.hilton.com. Right in the center of town, next door to the Hult Center for the Performing Arts, this is an excellent downtown option – a sturdy modern tower block with a tasteful interior and rooms with superb valley views. ⑦

Eugene International Hostel 2352 Willamette St ①541/349-0589, ⓦwww.eugenehostel.com. Offers twenty clean and comfortable dorm beds for $19 per person, or $30–40 for private rooms. A bit removed from the center, but still worth it for the price, and predictably thick with backpackers and other adventurers.

Excelsior Inn 754 E 13th Ave ①541/342-6963 or 1-800/321-6963, ⓦwww.excelsiorinn.com. In the middle of the university quarter, and handy for its cafes and bars, this small hotel has fourteen rooms and suites named after classical composers (though the modern decor undercuts any real connection). Some units offer Jacuzzis as well. ⑥

La Quinta Inn & Suites 155 Day Island Rd ①541/344-8335, ⓦwww.laquinta.com. Conveniently sited between the Willamette River and downtown, this clean and friendly chain motel is one of the cheaper options around, with a gym, pool, and spa and close access to trails and the Fifth Street Market. ⑤

The Oval Door 988 Lawrence St ①541/683-3160, ⓦwww.ovaldoor.com. Good-value B&B downtown with five tasteful rooms offering brass and wood-framed beds and one unit with a Jacuzzi. ⑤

The City

Eugene's classic homes and commercial architecture aren't quite up to the level of Salem, except in isolated pockets, but its local dining and cultural atmosphere is much more energetic and appealing. You can easily spend a week or more eating out, enjoying concerts, and touring the back roads and byways of the excellent surrounding mountain scenery. Although the downtown and campus core of Eugene is fairly centralized – roughly a one-by-two-mile grid – the larger city area sprawls, especially as the entire metropolitan area lies several miles west of I-5. Luckily, though, most of the key sights are close together, and there are only a few good reasons to go venturing out any farther – mainly Spencer's Butte and Mount Pisgah.

Downtown and around

Eugene's homely but centralized **downtown** of modern shopping malls and offices is clean and almost devoid of high-rise development. Clustered around the main north–south axis of **Willamette Street**, you'll find many of the town's best restaurants and cafes. Eugene puts on a vivid display at its fine **Saturday Market**, Eighth Ave and Oak St (April to early Nov 10am–5pm; free; Ⓦ www.eugenesaturdaymarket.org), a 37-year-old institution and still something of a neo-hippie carnival, with live folk music and street performers. Tie-dye and whole foods set the tone, but rastas, skateboarders, and students join in, too. **Fifth Street Market**, north at E 5th Ave and High St (most shops Mon–Sat 10am–8pm, Sun 10am–6pm; Ⓦ www.5stmarket.com), is actually a converted chicken-processing plant that now has three levels of cafes, restaurants, arts and crafts boutiques, and toy stores centered on a brick inner courtyard.

From here it's about six hundred yards up High Street – over the railway tracks – to **Skinner Butte Park**, whose grassy lower portion trails along the banks of the Willamette River. This was where Eugene Skinner had his initial landholding, as commemorated by a tiny **log cabin**. Up above you'll find the wooded butte that gives the park its name, and you can drive or walk to the top for views of the town and river. On the lower part of the south slope, though, and not to be missed, is the **Shelton–McMurphey–Johnson House**, 303 Willamette St (Tues–Fri 10am–1pm, Sat & Sun 1–4pm; $5; Ⓣ 541/484-0808, Ⓦ www.smjhouse.org), an intriguing 1888 Queen Anne mansion known as the "Castle on the Hill." Its lurching corner tower, red-and-green color scheme, and wraparound veranda are among its most striking features, giving it the odd, somewhat eerie appearance of a colorfully restored haunted house lurking in the woods.

The one noteworthy attraction a few blocks southwest of downtown is the **Lane County Historical Museum**, 740 W 13th Ave at Monroe (Tues–Sat 10am–4pm; $2; Ⓣ 541/682-4242, Ⓦ www.lchmuseum.org), hosting exhibits on logging and the Oregon Trail, including an original covered wagon – one of just a handful to survive.

The University of Oregon campus

The campus of the **University of Oregon**, a mile southeast of downtown, is the only college in the state that merits a visit for outsiders. Although much of its architecture epitomizes 1960s and 1980s High Modernism and Postmodernism, a few stately old buildings survive from the Victorian era. The two oldest, **Deady** and **Villard halls**, from 1876 and 1885, respectively, sit near the northwest corner of campus and anchored the original campus. Both are National Historic Landmarks built in the grand Second Empire style; since they're also both in use, you can wander around them almost any time you like.

A short distance south of here, the **quadrangle**, though dominated by the drab, quasi-corporate **PLC Tower**, is the social nexus of campus (just a block from its western edge). It's highlighted by Frisbee and hackysack players, summer sunbathers, and all manner of joggers and outdoor enthusiasts. It's also adjacent to two of the university's key sights. The first, the newly rechristened **Jordan Schnitzer Museum of Art** (Wed 11am–8pm, Thurs–Sun 11am–5pm; $5; ☎541/346-3027, Ⓦ uoma.uoregon.edu), recently reopened after a lengthy renovation and shows a broad selection of rotating contemporary shows and the jewels of its collection: Van Gogh's almost-Impressionist *Woman Walking in a Garden*, a Cezanne watercolor, Asian art and artifacts (among them Japanese ceramics, lacquerware, textiles, and gowns), and Russian Orthodox icons. The second, the **Philip Knight Library**, on the south end of the quadrangle (hours vary, generally weekdays 7.30am–midnight, weekends 11am–7pm; Ⓦ libweb .uoregon.edu), is nothing less than the state's largest library, renamed after the Nike founder and UO graduate, who gave a small fortune for its renovation. The slick results of the corporate largesse include a modern glass staircase, local artworks made of native wood and stone, and a high-tech computer system to inventory the giant selection of books available.

Just to the west, beyond the official campus boundary, **13th Street** is a several-block-long amalgamation of student-friendly bars, bike shops, book- and record stores, cafes, and boutiques. Although this isn't necessarily the best place to eat or drink in town, it's plenty vivacious, and offers a good opportunity for browsing. On the other side of campus, the university's estimable **Museum of Natural History**, 1680 E 15th Ave (Wed–Sun 11am–5pm; $3; ☎541/346-3024, Ⓦ natural-history.uoregon.edu), covers Oregon's geology, archaeology, and anthropology in an engaging style, with plenty of artifacts and relics from over the centuries and epochs. High points include the fossil discoveries of Thomas Condon (see p.274), as well as native baskets dating back to the nineteenth century, a replica of a coastal tribal plank house from 500 AD, and a 10,000-year-old pair of bark sandals – perhaps the oldest in existence. Also interesting, just a few blocks away, the **Maude Kerns Art Center**, 1910 E 15th Ave (Mon-Fri 10am–5.30pm, Sat noon–4pm; free; ☎541/345-1571, Ⓦ www.mkartcenter .org), provides a good overview of contemporary regional artwork through rotating exhibits in a variety of media.

Alton Baker Park

North of the Willamette River from downtown and the university is one of the city's natural gems, 400-acre **Alton Baker Park**, which was established here in 1959 but only in the last fifteen years has it really taken off as a destination for walking, biking, and other outdoor pursuits. The eastern side of the park is devoted to the **Whilamut Natural Area**, a lovely place for a stroll that has been the subject of an ecological experiment, replanting native trees and grasses and giving a sense of what the terrain might have looked like before white settlement. Encircling the natural area is **Pre's Trail**, named after legendary runner and University of Oregon alumnus Steve Prefontaine, who is commemorated by this four-mile running trail featuring terrific riparian views, three main loops, and a variety of surfaces including wood chips, asphalt, gravel, and dirt. The west part of the park is a bit less bucolic, but it's still attractive, with a boat launch, pleasant canal for canoeing, rock garden, and memorial garden showcasing the valley's indigenous trees. There's also a BMX track, amphitheatre for hosting seasonal events and concerts, and the **Science Factory Children's Museum and Planetarium** (museum Wed–Sun noon–4pm, planetarium shows Sat & Sun 1pm & 2pm; $4 per facility, $7 for both; ☎541/682-7888,

@www.sciencefactory.org), a fun and colorful facility hosting exhibits on human anatomy and biology, ecology and wildlife, and tot-friendly games like a Ping-Pong ball maze and an interactive puppet show.

You can get to the west part of the park from downtown by taking the riverfront walk past where Second Avenue ends and crossing over on the pedestrian **DeFazio Bridge**. You can get to the east part of the park from the university by crossing at **Knickerbocker Bike Bridge**, located where Agate Street turns into Riverfront Parkway. (There's also a span right in between at Hilyard Street.)

Spencer's Butte and Mount Pisgah

The highlight of Eugene's many urban hiking routes is the steep trip to the summit of 2000ft **Spencer's Butte**, a towering outcropping of basalt surrounded by trees and looming over the south part of town. Start from the parking lot off Willamette Street (LTD bus #73 can get you within a mile; ask driver for details) and hike two miles up the butte's winding concourse, past the lower stands of imposing trees to the thinner shrubbery of the middle slope, until you finally reach the craggy peaks and rocky boulders at the top. When it's not raining or foggy, the views from the crest of the butte are memorable.

A bit less jaw-dropping in height, but almost as appealing in views, are the slopes of **Mount Pisgah Arboretum**, fifteen miles south of Eugene at 34901 Frank Parrish Rd, east of I-5 and the Willamette River (dawn–dusk; ☎541/747-3817, @www.efn.org/~mtpisgah). The squat mountain features seven miles of trails spread over widely varied terrain, and a nature center providing background on the geology, flora, and fauna of the site. It helps to have a car to access this 200-acre arboretum, but you can also reach it by taking LTD bus #92 and getting off at Seavey Loop Road; it's a two-mile walk east, crossing the river and taking a right onto Parrish Road.

Eating and drinking

With thousands of students to feed and water, Eugene is well supplied with **bars**, **cafes**, and **restaurants**, the pick of which are clustered downtown, mostly between Broadway and Fifth Avenue in the vicinity of Willamette Street.

Ambrosia 174 E Broadway at Pearl St ☎541/342-4141. One of Eugene's best Italian restaurants with reasonably priced pizzas, baked in an oak-fired oven, and fresh pasta. Excellent range of Oregon wines and occasional live music, too.

Cafe Soriah 384 W 13th Ave ☎541/342-4410. Perhaps the only place south of Portland you can get decent Middle Eastern fare in the valley – and it's quite good, with staples like kebabs and chicken gaza, along with the more unexpected chili verde lamb stew, tournedos of beef, and duck confit salad.

Café Zenon 898 Pearl St at E Broadway ☎541/343-3005. An upbeat cafe-cum-bistro with marble-topped tables, tile floors, and a rotating, eclectic international menu with dishes ranging from pasta to curry.

Chanterelle 207 E Fifth Ave ☎541/484-4065. An intimate French bistro, one of the more expensive places to eat in town, and also one of the best. Good for its pasta and salmon but especially for its eponymous mushrooms, when in season.

Euphoria Chocolate 6 W 17th Ave ☎541/343-9223, @www.euphoriachocolate.com. Unbelievably delicious sweets and chocolate truffles – for many Oregonians, reason alone to make a trip to Eugene.

Marché 296 E Fifth Ave, ground floor of 5th Street Market ☎541/342-3612. Successful blend of French and Northwest Cuisine, with expensive but exquisite wild salmon, seared duck, and lamb tagine. The cafe on the market's upper story is also quite good, with savory tarts, delicious sandwiches, panini, and quiche for less than $7 each.

Morning Glory Café 450 Willamette St ☎541/687-0709. Footsteps from the train station, this simple cafe, with its unreconstructed hippie air, may not be to everyone's taste, but it does offer good and cheap vegetarian and vegan meals for breakfast or lunch.

Oregon Electric Station 27 E 5th Ave at Willamette ☎541/485-4444. Housed in a refurbished train station and railway cars, and featuring live music on weekends, this fashionable spot offers delicious, top-quality prime rib, seafood, and pasta.

Steelhead Brewery 199 E 5th Ave at Pearl ☎541/686-2739. Solid microbrewery with decent sandwiches, burgers, and pizzas. Look out for the delicious wheat beers, such as the Hairy Weasel Hefeweizen, and the award-winning Raging Rhino Red.

Nightlife and entertainment

For **nightlife**, countless cafes and bars have **live music** one or two nights a week, but the city's **entertainment** showpiece is the **Hult Center for the Performing Arts**, on Seventh Avenue at Willamette (☎541/682-5000, ⓦwww.hultcenter.org).This sleek complex showcases everything from opera to blues and musicals, with performances by touring companies of international standing as well as the city's symphony and ballet company.The center is also the prime venue for Eugene's prestigious annual Oregon Bach Festival in late July (see below). Also downtown, the converted 1928 **McDonald Theatre** moviehouse, 1010 Willamette Ave (☎541/345-4442, ⓦwww.mcdonaldtheatre .com), is a stylish performing-arts venue that hosts a range of shows and concerts. Elsewhere, **WOW Hall**, 291 W 8th Ave at Lincoln (☎541/687-2746, ⓦwww.wowhall.org), was once a meeting hall for the Industrial Workers of the World, but now features mid-level national acts, while more up-and-coming regional rockers take the stage at **Sam Bond's**, downtown at 407 Blair Blvd (☎541/431-6603, ⓦwww.sambonds.com). For different musical styles, *Jo Federigo's*, 259 E Fifth Ave (☎541/343-8488, ⓦwww.jofederigos.com), serves solid Italian cuisine and has nightly blues and jazz, and the *Oregon Electric Station* (see above) has jazz on the weekends.

To catch a **movie**, it's hard to beat the Bijou, four blocks from campus at 492 E 13th Ave (☎541/686-2458, ⓦwww.bijou-cinemas.com). Housed in a converted Spanish Mission-style church built in 1925, the art-house cinema often makes for a surreal scene, with the occasional sexually explicit or gratuitously violent images displayed on the walls of the former nave and rectory.

Summer festivals around Eugene

Eugene's biggest annual event is the **Oregon Country Fair**, a big hippie festival of music, arts, food, and dancing held during the second weekend in July in **Noti**, which is just west of Veneta, itself ten miles west of Eugene on US-126. Traffic is heavy, so if you have a ticket it's easier to travel there by free **shuttle bus**, leaving from downtown Eugene at 10th and Olive streets. Note that fair tickets must be purchased before you get there ($15 per day; ☎541/343-4298, ⓦwww.oregoncountryfair.org).

Held in late June and early July at the Hult Center, the **Oregon Bach Festival** draws musicians from all over the world (tickets $15–52; ☎1-800/457-1486, ⓦbachfest .uoregon.edu) to play the music of Johann Sebastian Bach, among a sprinkling of other classic composers. The artists and conductors are a varied and impressive lot, highlighted by the likes of Helmuth Rilling and Krzysztof Penderecki, and drawing plenty of adoring crowds.

Lastly, there's another big summer festival at **Cottage Grove**, twenty miles south of Eugene on I-5. This, the **Bohemia Mining Days** (ⓦwww.bohemiaminingdays.org), in the third week of July, recalls the nineteenth-century gold strike of one James Bohemia Johnson and involves a family-oriented carnival scene with gold-panning demonstrations, musical concerts, characters in period costume, and vendors selling food and mining-related trinkets.

South from Eugene: Oakland and Roseburg

If you're heading **south from Eugene** into southern Oregon, you can leave most of the traffic far behind by traveling southeast along **Highway 58** through the southern reaches of the Willamette National Forest and over the crest of Willamette Pass to Crater Lake (see p.233). An alternate route, for the Cascades or the coast, is **Highway 126**. The most obvious – and certainly the quickest – route south from Eugene is along I-5, which leaves the Willamette Valley to wind through vast tracts of mountain forest.

Fifty miles south from Eugene and two miles east of I-5, tiny **OAKLAND** was settled in the 1840s and soon became the center of a flourishing agricultural district, producing grain, hops, prunes, and eventually prize-winning turkeys. It was also a major stopping point on the stagecoach line from Sacramento to Portland, but a series of fires destroyed almost all the original wooden buildings. The townsfolk took the opportunity to replace the old with new stone and brick buildings graced by cast-iron trimmings. Today, it's a quiet rural hamlet whose halcyon days are recalled by the classic storefronts of **Locust Street**, the main drag, and a number of antique stores. Worth a look are the pioneer displays of the **Oakland Museum** (daily 12.30–3.30pm; donation), housed in the former grocery store and post office, while neighboring City Hall has street plans and walking-tour maps that point out what happened where and when among the various red-brick buildings (alternatively, you can check out ⓦwww.makewebs.com/oakland). While you're in town, don't miss a stop at *Tolly's*, 115 Locust St (☏541/459-3796), which features an old-fashioned ice-cream parlor, gift shop, and candy counter downstairs, and an acceptable restaurant up above.

Less than twenty miles farther south on I-5, **Roseburg** is a colorless, conservative enclave with few attractions to offer, though it can be a decent jumping-off point for trips into the Cascades or down the Umpqua River. You can get supplies here before you go camping or biking into the outback, but unfortunately the town has few distinctive hotels or B&Bs to keep you here.

The Rogue River Valley

A few hours' drive south of the Willamette Valley, the **Rogue River Valley** has plenty to offer, including nicely preserved nineteenth-century architecture and classic theater festivals. Its pocket of mostly small towns is hemmed in by three mountain ranges (the Coastal, Cascade, and Siskiyou ranges) and is accessible via the I-5 freeway as it makes its sixty-mile journey through the valley on a northwest-southeast route. The only big town in the area (and the one place definitely worth a miss), **Medford**, is a staunchly conservative sprawl of shopping malls, tract homes, and chain retailers, while just a few miles down the road, **Ashland** is a delightfully progressive little town best known for hosting the Oregon Shakespeare Festival. Between these cultural extremes are **Wolf Creek**, site of a historic tavern and stagecoach stop; workaday **Grants Pass**, a popular base for whitewater rafting along the Rogue River; and **Jacksonville**, a lovely preserved pioneer hamlet in the foothills. As one major alternative route, US-199 sneaks southwest through the remote and rugged **Siskiyou Mountains**, leading through the dark forests, deep ravines, and wild coastal mountains that span this part of the Oregon–California border, and past the strange and fascinating chambers of the **Oregon Caves**.

Traveling the I-5 by Greyhound **bus** is a straightforward affair, with daily services linking Eugene with, among other places, Grants Pass and Medford. There are also regular services from Eugene to Klamath Falls, but none to Crater Lake in the Cascades. Amtrak **trains** are not so useful, though you can debark from the Seattle-to-California service, the **Coast Starlight**, at Klamath Falls and make your way to the valley by bus.

Canyon Creek to Grants Pass

Some thirty miles south of Roseburg along I-5, the area around **Canyon Creek** tells one of the central parts of the story of the settling of Rogue River Valley (see box, p.210), even though it's located some 25 miles north of the valley itself. The first actual sight near the northern edge of the Rogue River Valley, about fifteen miles south of Canyon Creek Pass on I-5, is **WOLF CREEK**, a burg best known for its 🍴 **Wolf Creek Tavern**, which began as a stagecoach stop in the 1850s and emerged as a hotel within thirty years. The tavern was constructed of rough-hewn boards and planks cut from area trees but despite its simplicity managed to host presidents like Ulysses S. Grant and Rutherford B. Hayes, as well as writers such as Sinclair Lewis and Hollywood actors like Clark Gable. Its most important visitor, though, was the author and roustabout **Jack London**, who worked on one of his novels while residing here. Nowadays, the tavern-hotel is a protected state-park facility that still offers solid food and drink – mostly steak, seafood, ribs, and chicken – as well as cozy but quaint rooms, with some antique decor and a handful of larger suites (☎1-541/866-2474, ⓦ www.thewolfcreekinn.com; ❹).

Sunny Valley and around

As you make your way south toward the Rogue River Valley, five miles from Wolf Creek is the town of **SUNNY VALLEY**, which isn't much in itself but does sit near some sites relevant to nineteenth-century history. The first, **Grave Creek**, was originally the name of the town (the current version a bit of a euphemism) and the place where little Martha Crowley, a typhoid victim, was buried – literally, in this case, under the modern roadway. The creek is crossed by a **covered bridge** not far from I-5, on Sunny Valley Loop Road, that dates from 1920 and features small Neo-Gothic windows across its span. In close vicinity, the area saw the worst of the various wars in the 1850s between native tribes and federal soldiers, who were based nearby, and the long-gone Fort Leland. Historical exhibits dealing with this period are on display at the **Applegate Trail Interpretive Center**, 500 Sunny Valley Loop (10am–5pm: Mar–May Thurs–Sun, June–Oct daily, Nov–Feb Fri & Sat; donation; ☎541/472-8545, ⓦ www.rogueweb.com/interpretive), which itself resembles a two-story

The Applegate Trail

In 1843 the surveyor and abolitionist Jesse Applegate, author of a farm-oriented news column called "A Day with the Cow," made his way into the Willamette Valley via the Oregon Trail. An outspoken individualist who espoused all kinds of causes, Applegate was also a bit of a crank, and he took it upon himself to devise a new trail that would take a more southerly route to fill up the underpopulated Rogue River Valley. This pathway, known as the **Applegate Trail**, opened in 1846 and cut through land previously trekked by fur traders, native tribes, and few others. Applegate's surveying skills were put to the test, as he created a truly arduous, frequently precipitous circuit that ran up and down canyons, along steep cliffs, and across myriad streams and creeks. The most frightening part of the journey was along the gorge at **Canyon Creek**, a few miles beyond modern-day Canyonville, where the pioneer wagons were forced to make a sudden 1300ft descent, and their accompanying families were expected to keep them from rolling out of control and smashing down the hillsides.

Needless to say, many of these early trekkers met with disaster, leaving a different kind of trail – one of broken and battered wagons, dead livestock, and lost and abandoned belongings. On top of that, many newcomers were beset by hostile native tribes determined to keep white trespassers out of their land; some of the pioneers, such as 16-year-old Martha Crowley, died here and were buried in the vicinity. Ultimately, the Applegate Trail did bring a small but steady stream of migrants to the Rogue River Valley, though many other Oregon Trail pioneers figured their own slog was difficult enough as it was and stuck to the more established route.

wooden frontier outpost and hosts a museum stuffed with old Applegate Trail artifacts, photos, relics, and letters.

Rogue River National Recreation Trail

If you'd rather focus on the scenery of the Rogue River, you should explore at least part of the forty-mile **Rogue River National Recreation Trail** (W www.fs.fed.us/r6/rogue-siskiyou), which provides some wonderfully wild hiking. The trail begins at Grave Creek, nudging through dense groves of hemlock, Douglas fir, and oak and traversing bare canyon walls with the river far below. It's a sweaty walk in summer, and muddy to the point of impassability in winter, but in spring and fall it's an excellent trek for serious hikers, and there are first-come, first-served campsites sprinkled along the way. A series of strategically placed lodges on the lower half of the trail – each a day's hike from the other – makes a rather more comfortable option. To get the most out of the trail, your best bet is to start at Gold Beach (see p.180) on the coast, travel upriver by boat, and then hike down. If that sounds too daunting, Rogue Wilderness (see below) organizes four- and five-day guided hikes that include rafting and camping or lodge stays, starting at $749. The Grants Pass visitor center has a useful range of leaflets on the Rogue River, too.

Grants Pass

Ten miles south of Sunny Valley, **GRANTS PASS** is the first sizable community in the Rogue River Valley, an old sawmill town straddling the Rogue River as it tumbles from the Cascades to the Siskiyou National Forest. There's not much to the place, but it does have a fine, scenic setting and a tiny, central **historic district** of fetching late-nineteenth- and early-twentieth-century buildings, on

△ Whitewater kayaking on the Rogue River

and around G Street west of Sixth Street. To get to the center from I-5, it's easiest to take Exit 58 and then follow Sixth Street (Hwy 99) south. G Street is just beyond the railway tracks, and the Rogue River, with its assortment of logging mills, is a few blocks farther.

Grants Pass earns much of its living by packing visitors into rafts or jet boats to bounce over the Rogue's **whitewater rapids**. A half-day raft tour costs around $60, a full day $85, and $30 and $55 respectively for jet-boat trips; there are longer, overnight excursions, too, and the season lasts from May to October. Two of the more reliable operators are Hellgate Jetboat Excursions (☎541/479-7204 or 1-800/648-4874, ⓦwww.hellgate.com), whose river trips leave from the foot of Sixth Street, and the whitewater rafting and fishing-tour specialists Rogue Wilderness (☎541/479-9554 or 1-800/336-1647, ⓦwww.wildrogue.com), based in the hamlet of Merlin, about ten miles northwest of Grants Pass.

Practicalities

The **visitor center**, 1995 NW Vine St (Mon–Fri 9am–5pm, June–Sept also Sat & Sun; ☎541/476-7717 or 1-800/547-5927, ⓦwww.visitgrantspass.org), is both close to and clearly signed from I-5's Exit 58. Here you can get details on the many licensed companies operating river excursions. You'll find the bulk of the town's chain **motels** on Hwy 99 (Seventh St northbound and Sixth Street southbound) between the river and I-5 (Exit 58), though your best bet would be to stay at the agreeable *Motel del Rogue*, 2600 Rogue River Hwy (☎541/479-2111, ⓦwww.moteldelrogue.com; ❸–❺), which in addition to its close river access has sixteen clean and pleasant rooms with fridges and microwaves, and some with kitchenettes and exterior decks; or the *Buona Sera Inn*, 1001 NE 6th Ave (☎541/476-4260, ⓦwww.buonaserainn.com; ❸), which has prices as low as any roadside motel but unique, quirky rooms with cute, almost twee, decor and fridges and microwaves. There are a number of good **B&Bs** in the area, too, highlighted by the spacious and modern ⚘ *Flery Manor*, 2000 Jump Off Creek Rd (☎541/476-3591, ⊛www.flerymanor.com; ⊜), with its lush appointments, onsite gym, pool, and art studio, as well as smart rooms and suites with fireplaces, Jacuzzis, and balconies – not to mention tasty gourmet breakfasts.

The best **places to eat** are *The Laughing Clam*, 121 G St (☎541/479-1110), with primo seafood dishes and regional wines; *R-Haus*, 2140 Rogue River Hwy (☎541/474-3335), with its nice, mid-priced meals of pasta, seafood, and particularly steak; and *Wild River Brewing & Pizza Co*, 595 NE E St (☎541/471-7487), which specializes in wood-fired pizzas and terrific handcrafted beers.

From Grants Pass, US-199 leads southwest to the Oregon Caves and into the California redwoods (see p.181), while I-5 veers southeast for Medford, Jacksonville, and, best of all, Ashland.

Jacksonville and Ashland

Heading inland on I-5, it's a quick 25-mile journey from Grants Pass to **Medford**, the Rogue River Valley's urban center – an industrial sprawl squatting among huge paper mills. From here you can continue on to the more appealing **Jacksonville**, just five miles west of Medford on Hwy 238, or stay on I-5 a little longer until you get to **Ashland**, whose downtown core is a few miles west of I-5 on Hwy 99. These latter two towns are easily the most diverting south of Eugene on the freeway, and while Jacksonville makes for an interesting day-trip, Ashland can keep you going for two or three days with food and drink, nature trails, and, of course, Shakespearean plays.

Jacksonville

Once the largest of Oregon's gold rush towns, a flourishing and boisterous prospectors' supply center, **JACKSONVILLE** had its improbable beginnings after a gold-panner's mule kicked up a nugget here in 1851. No sooner had the miners arrived, however, than they were involved in the savage **Rogue River Indian Wars** of 1853–56, which saw the natives defeated and deported or confined to reservations (see also Grave Creek, p.209). The town's fortunes faded when the gold boom ended in the 1880s, after which it crumbled, quietly, until it was old enough to attract tourists.

It takes only an hour or two to fully explore Jacksonville's small **town center**, whose restored late-nineteenth-century buildings, all false-fronts and symmetrical brickwork, roughly cluster around the main intersection of California and Oregon streets. Highlights include the sturdy **US Hotel** of 1880, at California and Third streets, whose first guest was Rutherford B. Hayes and is now only open for special events, and the **C.C. Beekman House**, at California and Laurelwood streets (summer tours Wed–Sun 1–5pm; $5), now done up in period furnishings and shown by costumed actors portraying its former owner, an early-twentieth-century banker, and his family members.

The **Jacksonville Museum**, housed in the glum-looking County Courthouse of 1883, at 206 N 5th St and East C St (Wed–Sun 10am–5pm; $5; ⊛www.sohs .org), offers a straightforward presentation of the town's background, enlivened by a selection of compelling early photographs. They are the work of the talented **Peter Britt**, who came to Oregon on an ox cart in the 1850s and spent almost fifty years photographing it. Britt's house burnt down years ago, but the grounds, a short walk up California Street from Oregon Street, are now used for the **Britt Festival** (tickets $20–52; ☎541/773-6077 or 1-800/882-7488, www.brittfest.org), a major performing-arts shindig that takes place from June to August, with a strong bent toward classical, jazz, and pop music, some played by international names. The grounds hold 2200 people, and although the bench-style seats are often booked up months in advance, some of the lawn space is allocated on a first-come, first-served basis.

Practicalities

There are no long-distance **buses** to Jacksonville (the nearest you'll get is Medford), but the Rogue Valley Transportation District (RVTD) provides a bus service to the town from 200 S Main St in Medford roughly every 60–90 minutes (Route #30; Mon–Fri 7.30am–6pm; $2; ☎541/779-2877, ⓦwww .rvtd.org). Jacksonville's tiny **visitor center**, 185 N Oregon St (☎541/899-8118, ⓦwww.jacksonvilleoregon.org), can give you the lowdown on the main historic buildings and has a complete list of accommodation. Note that it's virtually impossible to find somewhere to stay in Jacksonville during the Britt Festival. If you plan to attend a concert, it's a good idea to contact the Southern Oregon Reservation Center (☎1-800/547-8052, ⓦwww.sorc.com), which sells festival tickets and books hotels.

The town has a limited supply of **B&Bs** in restored old houses. Two of the most appealing are the centrally located *Orth House*, 105 W Main St (☎541/899-8665 or 1-800/700-7301, ⓦwww.orthbnb.com; ⑤), a two-story brick Victorian manor from 1880, with three rooms with balconies and private baths; and the *TouVelle House*, 455 N Oregon St (☎541/899-8938, ⓦwww.touvellehouse.com; ⑥), whose six rooms and suites are a bit more refined and stylish than the usual Victorian-chintz inns and have antique touches, Net access, and CD players, with an onsite pool and sauna. The more formal 1861 *Jacksonville Inn*, 175 E California St (☎541/899-1900 or 1-800/321-9344, ⓦwww.jacksonvilleinn.com; ⑥ ⑧), has twelve stately rooms, some of which feature Jacuzzis and fireplaces, as well as pricier cottages. The latter inn provides a swanky **restaurant** where you can indulge in steak, lamb, or seafood, or imbibe various wines from the region. For a cheaper bite to eat, *MacLevin's*, in the center of town at 150 W California St (☎541/899-1251), bills itself as "The Unconventional Jewish Deli," with solid pancakes, frittatas, and latkes, and a tempting pastrami-and-eggs scramble. You can also have a sip at the *Collins Tea Room & Bakery*, 125 S 3rd St (☎541/899-1888), which offers a popular afternoon tea in a European setting with scones, tarts, and other pastries; reservations are recommended.

Ashland

Throughout Oregon, the small town of **ASHLAND**, twelve miles south of Medford on Hwy 99, is identified with William Shakespeare – a curious cultural anomaly among the workaday timber and farming towns straddling the California border. The idea of an **Oregon Shakespeare Festival** came to a local teacher, **Angus Bowmer**, fifty years ago, and now – from mid-February to the end of October – the town is dominated by all things theatrical. Its setting, between the Cascades and the Siskiyou Mountains, is magnificent, with good skiing in the winter and river-rafting in summer. What's more, performance standards are high and there's some excellent contemporary fringe theater – not to mention pleasant cafes and a young, lively atmosphere.

Ashland also has a reputation as a **spiritual refuge** for former urbanites and graying flower children, who consider the town a veritable "beacon of light." The bookshops are awash with New Age material and information about local retreats and workshops, including some organized by or featuring resident

luminaries such as Neale Donald Walsch and James Twyman. The cumulative effect of the emphasis on holistic religion, theatrical and visual arts, and chic eateries and B&Bs has been to take Ashland quite a ways from its bucolic roots, until it now scarcely resembles the homespun rural towns of the Rogue River Valley surrounding it.

Arrival, information, and outdoor activities

Ashland is on the Greyhound line from Portland to San Francisco, but **buses** pause on the outskirts of town, at I-5's Exit 19, leaving you a couple of miles northwest of the center (call ☎1-800/231-2222 for drop-off details). Otherwise, the RVTD Route #10 connects Medford's Front Street Station with Ashland, taking about 45–50 minutes to arrive (every 30min Mon–Fri 5am–6.30pm; $2; ☎541/779-2877, ⓦwww.rvtd.org). The **visitor center** is downtown, at 110 E Main St (Mon–Fri 9am–5pm; ☎541/482-3486, ⓦwww.ashlandchamber.com). It issues town maps and brochures and has details on lodging and the arts, as well as **whitewater rafting** companies, which lead trips up the Rogue, Klamath and Umpqua rivers. One reliable operator is Noah's River Adventures, on Ashland's main plaza at 53 N Main St (☎541/488-2811 or 1-800/858-2811, ⓦwww.noahsrafting.com), which runs half-day ($79), one-day ($129–139), and two-day camping ($399–445) rafting trips daily from March to October and a variety of fishing trips throughout the year for similar prices. There's also **skiing** and **snowboarding** at the **Mount Ashland Ski Area** (Nov–April; ☎541/482-2897, ⓦwww.mtashland.com), high in the Siskiyou Mountains some twenty miles south of town, featuring four chairlifts and 25 runs – many of them, sure enough, named after Shakespearean plays and characters. A one-day lift pass costs $39 (or $20 on Tues), with night skiing for $23; additionally, skis and snowboards ($25) can be rented on arrival. The ski area is located eight miles west of – and clearly signposted from – I-5 (Exit 6). For the latest snow report, telephone ☎541/482-2SKI. For details of special **buses** from Ashland to the ski area, ask at the Ashland visitor center.

Accommodation

Ashland has many plush **B&Bs**, but they are much in demand and advance booking is essential in the summer – either independently or via a reservation service such as Ashland B&B Network (☎1-800/944-0329, ⓦwww.abbnet.com). There is more chance of a vacancy at one of the town's basic **motels**, which are lined up along Siskiyou Boulevard east of the center.

Ashland Hostel 150 N Main St ☎541/482-9217, ⓦwww.theashlandhostel.com. Friendly, clean, and well-placed budget option near the center of the action, with dorm beds for $25 and private rooms for $55 for two (with extra people $15 each).

Ashland Springs 212 E Main St ☎541/488-1700, ⓦwww.ashlandspringshotel.com. The best and most prominent hotel downtown, a grand 1925 edifice visible for miles around. This renovated, centrally located hotel has a charming two-story lobby, day spa, afternoon tea, and nicely appointed rooms. ⑥

Coolidge House 137 N Main St ☎541/482-4721 or 1-800/655-5522, ⓦwww.coolidgehouse.com. Central B&B offering six luxurious en-suite rooms, some with Jacuzzis, and gourmet breakfasts from its attractively refurbished Victorian premises. ⑤–⑥ by season

Cowslip's Belle 159 N Main St ☎541/488-2901 or 1-800/888-6819, ⓦwww.cowslip.com. Five en-suite B&B rooms here in this overly precious, but wonderfully comfortable, early twentieth-century bungalow and carriage house. ⑥

Mount Ashland Inn 550 Mount Ashland Ski Rd ☎541/482-8707 or 1-800/830-8707, ⓦwww.mtashlandinn.com. Lovely log lodge, perched high up on the wooded slopes of Mount Ashland, with five well-decorated suites featuring antique furniture, fireplaces and spa tubs. It's just a short drive up to Mount Ashland Ski Area and about twenty minutes to Ashland in the valley below. Mountain bikes and, in winter, snowshoes are available at no extra charge. Inn is located six miles west of I-5 (Exit 6). ⑦

Palm Motel 1065 Siskiyou Blvd ☎541/482-2636 or 1-877/482-2635, ⓦwww.palmcottages.com. Unexpectedly lovely motel east of the town center, with thirteen pleasant rooms and onsite pool and gardens. Easily the best choice in this price category, so it's booked solid in the summer. ③–⑤ by season

Plaza Inn & Suites 98 Central Ave ☎1-888/488-0358, ⓦwww.plazainnashland.com. Just a block from the center, this property has a good range of well-decorated and spacious rooms and suites, which may come with microwaves, fridges, DVD players, and Jacuzzis. A reliable hotel choice in a land of B&Bs. ⑤–⑦ by season

Winchester Inn 35 S 2nd St ☎541/488-1113 or 1-800/972-4991, ⓦwww.winchesterinn.com. Attractive inn with attractive gardens and nineteen en-suite rooms, which variously come with fireplaces, CD players, hot tubs, and plenty of plush decor, in a pleasant setting three blocks from the main plaza. ⑦

The Town

The world-renowned **Oregon Shakespeare Festival** runs from February to October. The works of Shakespeare and other Elizabethan and Jacobean dramatists are performed at the **Elizabethan Theatre**, near Main and Oak streets, a delightful half-timbered replica of sixteenth-century London's Fortune Theatre. The adjacent **Angus Bowmer Theatre** stages both Shakespearean and more recent works, and the austere **New Theatre**, with seating in three-quarters around the stage or in the round, has a mostly modern repertoire. The trio of theaters share the same box office, at 15 S Pioneer St (☎541/482-4331,

△ Oregon Shakespeare Festival

Ⓦ www.orshakes.org), with **tickets** running $30–75 in the summer and $22–56 from February to May and also October. For a further helping of contemporary drama, the lively **Oregon Cabaret Theatre** performs in a renovated church at 1st and Hargadine streets (tickets $19–30; ☎ 541/488-2902, Ⓦ www .oregoncabaret.com), also showcasing mainstream musicals and comedies.

Just around the corner from the Elizabethan Theatre, the tiny, cafe-flanked **plaza** forms the heart of Ashland – a pleasant spot to loiter, especially as it's beside the entrance to leafy **Lithia Park**. This one-hundred-acre park was designed by John McLaren (of Golden Gate Park fame), its shrubs, trails, brooks, and spreading trees reminders of Ashland's pre-festival incarnation as a spa town, a project of New York advertising mogul Jesse Winburne. He overestimated the appeal of the nasty-tasting local Lithia Springs water, though, and the spa idea failed, but it did lodge the germ of Ashland's potential as a center for tourism.

One of the more prominent zones for tourism in recent years has been the **Historic Railroad District** (Ⓦwww.ashlandrrdistrict.com) three blocks north of Main Street. This six-block-long amalgamation, from Oak to Fifth streets along A Street, used to be a busy industrial strip home to railway-related businesses and supply centers, many a century or more old. Through renovation and gentrification it's now emerged as a hot spot for galleries, restaurants, and boutiques. Here you can watch performance art and grab a cocktail at *The Mobius*, 281 4th St (℡541/488-8894), search for sculpture and graphic art at Ashland Art Works, 291 Oak St (℡541/488-4735), pick up an old-fashioned quilt at Due Madri Quilt Gallery, 552 A St (℡541/552-1818), or enjoy the smart cafes and B&Bs occupying former banks, hotels, and offices.

Eating and drinking

With its ready supply of well-heeled tourists, not to mention its local college students at Southern Oregon University, Ashland has lots of appealing places to **eat** and **drink**. Conveniently, the best are clustered in and around the plaza, which is flanked – rather confusingly to newcomers – by both North and East Main streets. Be on the lookout for the town's nationally regarded *Dagoba Chocolate*, which offers some ultra-dark styles with a cacao content of more than eighty percent.

Alex's Plaza 35 N Main St ℡541/482-8818. Smart mid-priced restaurant offering traditional American dishes with a flourish. Worth a try for its duck-breast fettuccine, seafood stews, and New Zealand rack of lamb.

Amuse 15 N 1st St ℡541/488-9000. Upscale eatery known for its grilled prawns, but also good for its crab cakes, seared scallops, and pork chops, with a decent wine list to boot.

Ashland Bakery Café 38 E Main St. Laid-back, slightly arty cafe where the breakfasts, sandwiches, and pastries are delicious and inexpensive. Standouts include the potato pancakes and the lemon ricotta-stuffed French toast.

Chateaulin 50 E Main St ℡541/482-2264. One of the classiest restaurants in town, a formal, attractively decorated place serving up first-rate French cuisine, but only for dinner. Reckon on $35 per person, excluding wine, for the three-course menu.

Greenleaf 49 N Main St ℡541/482-2808. On the central plaza, this enjoyable, inexpensive eatery has tasty staples like pasta, burgers, salads, and seafood, nicely crafted with fresh local ingredients. Also with alfresco dining on a pleasant riverside terrace.

Larks Home Kitchen Cuisine 212 E Main St in the *Ashland Springs Hotel* ℡1-888/795-4545. One of the best Northwest eateries to emerge in recent years, offering fancy dinners showcasing delicious braised short ribs and steelhead filets, and cheaper lunches where you can get a succulent portobello sandwich or shrimp po' boy for less than $12.

Tabu 16 N Pioneer St ℡541/482-3900. A surprisingly solid choice for modern Latin cuisine, served in a smart atmosphere, with fish tacos, tamales, and mole dishes among the highlights – along with Thurs and Sat salsa nights.

Oregon Caves National Monument

Back at Grants Pass, US-199 leaves I-5 (Exit 55) to wander down the Illinois River Valley toward the Northern California coast; the road also provides the only practical access to the beach towns on Oregon's South Coast (see p.168). It's an enjoyable journey, with forested hills to either side, and after about thirty miles you reach the roadside burg of **Cave Junction**, where Hwy 46 branches off east for the narrow and twisting, twenty-mile trip to **Oregon Caves National Monument** (tours daily late March to Nov: hours vary, often 9am–5pm; ☎541/592-2100, ⓦwww.nps.gov/orca), tucked away in a canyon in the Siskiyou Mountains. The caves were discovered in 1874, when a deer hunter's dog chased a bear into a mountainside hole, but they became famous only when poet Joaquin Miller described "the marble halls of Oregon" on his 1909 visit.

Inside, the caves are actually one enormous cavern with smaller passages leading off from it. The marble walls were created by the centuries-long compression of lime, mud, and lava, then slowly carved out by subterranean water. Thereafter long years of steady dripping created elaborate formations from the limestone-laden water: clinging stalactites hang from the ceiling, some met by stalagmites to form columns, while rippled flows of rock run from the walls. The caves are wet and slippery, so good shoes or boots are required, as is warm clothing – underground it's a constant 42°F (6°C). You have to go in with the 90min **tour** ($8.50), and although these leave regularly, you can still face a long wait in the summer, when it's wise to turn up early in the day. The monument grounds also contain a couple of **hiking trails** into the surrounding mountains, with the three-mile loop of the Big Tree Trail giving sight of a whopping Douglas fir that's more than a thousand years old.

Easily the best **accommodation** hereabouts is the *Oregon Caves Chateau*, 2000 Caves Hwy (mid-May to Oct; ☎541/592-3400, ⓦwww.oregoncave .com; ⑤), an attractive, rustic affair of high gables and timber walls dating from the 1930s – and a stone's throw from the caves. The lodge, with its comfortable furnishings and fittings, has characterful rooms and suites, and its restaurant serves good food, too; it's not surprising, therefore, that reservations are pretty much essential. Alternatively, there are drab **motels** in Cave Junction or several **campgrounds** along Hwy 46, with *Grayback* and *Cave Creek* being the closest to the monument ($10–16; ☎541/592-2166 for reservations).

The Oregon Cascades

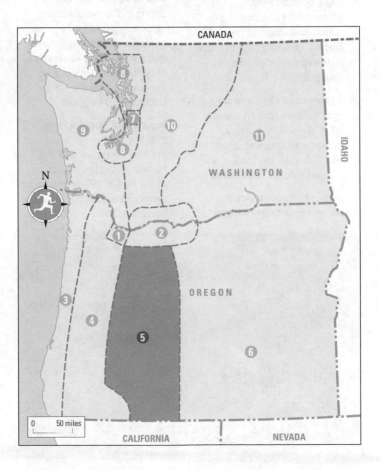

CHAPTER 5

Highlights

✱ **Smith Rock** Deep gashes in the lava rock in this fascinating state park have created a lovely gorge that's perfect for cycling, horseback riding, and hiking. See p.224

✱ **Big Obsidian Flow** Monumental outpouring of glassy lava that has formed a bizarre, glittering hillside made of the rare rock obsidian. See p.232

✱ **Crater Lake** Oregon's only national park, this freshwater pit of deep-blue water is the nation's deepest lake and occupies the shell of an ancient volcano. See p.233

✱ **Upper Klamath Lake** The second-largest natural lake west of the Rockies, its excellent National Wildlife Refuge is a seasonal stopover for countless birds, from pelicans to herons to swans. See p.238

✱ **Dee Wright Observatory** Sitting in the middle of an astounding 65 square miles of frozen lava, a rough-hewn, medieval-looking tower made of basalt that looks out at the grandest peaks in the Cascades. See p.246

✱ **Mount McLoughlin** Hike this, the southernmost of the Oregon peaks and the highest in the lower section of the range, offering fantastic views of the region's exquisite landscape. See p.250

△ Crater Lake

The Oregon Cascades

5

F or many outdoor adventurers, the **Oregon Cascades** are the highlight of any trip to the Pacific Northwest. Generally lower in elevation than Washington's five Cascade peaks, Oregon's section of the 700-mile-long volcanic chain comprises seventeen major peaks, running along a north–south axis from Mount Hood near the Columbia Gorge down to Mount McLoughlin near the California border. Most are undeniably stunning, a snowy necklace of radiant white jewels arrayed across the central Oregon landscape. They are varied in appearance, too, including archetypal volcanoes like mounts **Jefferson** and **Bachelor**, shallow calderas like **Newberry**, exploded-peaks-turned-freshwater-pits like **Crater Lake**, and strange and gnarled fragments like **Broken Top** and **Mount Thielsen**. Almost all of these major mountains reside in the swath known as the **High Cascades**, the prominent volcanic belt whose fringe abuts eastern Oregon. The much older **Western Cascades** are, after millennia of erosion, more like large, nubby hills and offer few name-brand attractions – they lie on the western edge of the High Cascades and act more like foothills to the bigger peaks.

There are several major routes to the Cascades from the cities of the west. **Highway 26** begins in Portland and skirts the southern foothills of Mount Hood (see p.131), continuing on to Madras; from there the major southbound route is **US-97**, which you take to reach the focus of the Cascades, the vibrant, fashionable town of **Bend**. Well worth a visit of a day or two, the town lies near the wonderful scenery of the ski resort of **Mount Bachelor**. Also south of Bend, US-97 passes by the volcanic landscape of **Newberry National Volcanic Monument**, where a sprinkling of cinder cones, lava fields, and a massive caldera are found not far from the highway. Perhaps the most extraordinary sight of all is **Crater Lake**, another hour south, the deep-blue remnant of an ancient volcano that is the state's only national park and merits a few days to explore its hiking trails or admire its glimmering surface up close on a boat ride. The lake is within an hour's drive of **Klamath Falls**, a curious little town with two enjoyable museums and access to the splendid **Upper Klamath National Wildlife Refuge**.

While US-97 is clearly the best way to explore the vastness of the Cascades, alternative routes are available from the Willamette and Rogue River valleys. From Salem, **Highway 22** leads east past such vacation centers as **Detroit**

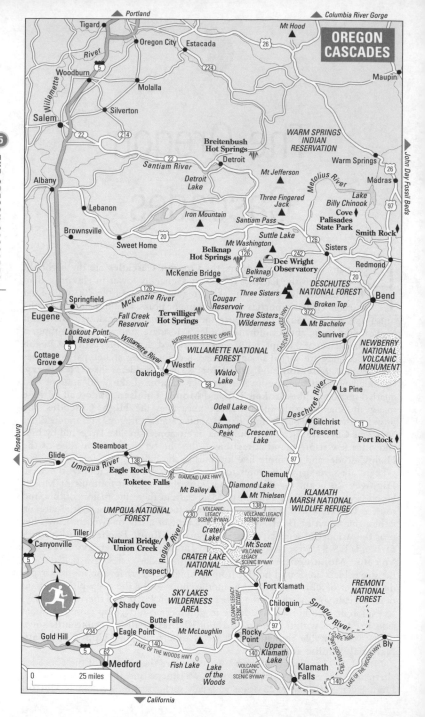

OREGON
CASCADES

Portland
Columbia River Gorge
Tigard
Mt Hood
Oregon City
Estacada
26
Maupin
Woodburn
Molalla
224
Salem
Silverton
John Day Fossil Beds
WARM SPRINGS
INDIAN
RESERVATION
22
Breitenbush
Hot Springs
214
Warm Springs
26
Santiam River
Detroit
Madras
Albany
Mt Jefferson
Lake
Billy Chinook
Detroit
Lake
97
Lebanon
Three Fingered
Jack
Cove
Palisades
State Park
Iron Mountain
Santiam Pass
Smith Rock
Brownsville
20
Suttle Lake
Sisters
Sweet Home
Mt Washington
126
Belknap
Hot Springs
126
Dee Wright
Observatory
Redmond
McKenzie Bridge
Belknap
Crater
242
20
DESCHUTES
NATIONAL FOREST
Three Sisters
Springfield
McKenzie River
Cougar
Reservoir
Bend
Broken Top
372
Fall Creek
Reservoir
Terwilliger
Hot Springs
Three Sisters
Wilderness
Mt Bachelor
Eugene
Sunriver
Lookout Point
Reservoir
Willamette River
AUFDERHEIDE SCENIC DRIVE
WILLAMETTE NATIONAL
FOREST
NEWBERRY
NATIONAL
VOLCANIC
MONUMENT
Cottage
Grove
Westfir
Waldo
Lake
La Pine
Oakridge
58
Deschutes River
Odell Lake
Diamond
Peak
Crescent
Lake
Gilchrist
Crescent
31
Steamboat
Fort Rock
Glide
Umpqua River
Eagle Rock
Chemult
97
Toketee Falls
DIAMOND LAKE HWY
Diamond Lake
KLAMATH
MARSH NATIONAL
WILDLIFE REFUGE
Mt Bailey
Mt Thielsen
138
UMPQUA NATIONAL
FOREST
230
VOLCANIC
LEGACY
SCENIC BYWAY
VOLCANIC LEGACY
SCENIC BYWAY
Tiller
Natural Bridge/
Union Creek
Rogue River
Crater
Lake
Mt Scott
Canyonville
227
VOLCANIC
LEGACY
SCENIC
BYWAY
FREMONT
NATIONAL
FOREST
N
CRATER
LAKE
NATIONAL
PARK
62
Prospect
Fort Klamath
Sprague River
SKY LAKES
WILDERNESS
AREA
Chiloquin
Shady Cove
97
VOLCANIC LEGACY
SCENIC BYWAY
STATE TRAIL
Butte Falls
234
Mt McLoughlin
Rocky
Point
Bly
Eagle Point
140
Gold Hill
5
62
LAKE OF THE WOODS HWY
Upper
Klamath
Lake
LAKE OF THE WOODS HWY
Medford
Fish Lake
Lake
of the
Woods
VOLCANIC LEGACY
SCENIC BYWAY
Klamath
Falls
140
0   25 miles
California

Roseburg

The rise of the Cascades

The only active volcanic chain in the continental US, the **Cascades** are a line of majestic peaks that runs from Mount Baker in Washington to Mount Lassen in California. Although Oregon has the greatest number of the larger-size mountains – seventeen of the twenty-seven – all three states have roughly the same number of recently active volcanoes, seven in Oregon's case. These mountains all experienced eruptions within the last several thousand years, with **Mount St. Helens** (see p.442) erupting in 1980, and Oregon's **Mount Hood** emitting a steam belch in 1865.

The peaks of the Cascades began their rise some forty million years ago when **continental drift** forced the oceanic Farallon, or Juan de Fuca, plate to crash into the North American plate, causing the uplift of the coastal mountains and propelling the Juan de Fuca into the magma below the earth's crust. At the point of melting, around 120 miles inland from the coast and far underground, boiling steam forced the layers of magma to rise, where it either sat below the surface in massive "plutons" or erupted as runny lava or explosive ash. However, this reaction – which occurred from forty million up to five million years ago – created only the first incarnation of the Cascades, known as the **Western Cascades**. These once-grand peaks are located roughly between the current volcanoes and the I-5 freeway, but if you go hunting for them, all you're likely to find are severely eroded stumps and rocky nubs, with the highest – **Iron Mountain** – only half the size of the tallest of the modern peaks.

Some three to four million years ago, the range of Cascade volcanic action mysteriously shifted thirty to fifty miles to the east. Dozens of new mountains, now known as the **High Cascades**, formed along a great arc; the tallest peaks are Mount Rainier (14,410ft) in Washington and Mount Shasta (14,162ft) in Northern California. As with most of the big-name peaks in the region, these are **strato volcanoes**, or the familiar conical peaks that dominate the landscape and conform to most people's idea of what a volcano is supposed to look like. However, another type of volcano, the flatter, rounder **shield** variety, can be just as explosive and dangerous.

Oregon's recently active volcanoes (within the last eight thousand years) include mounts Hood, Jefferson, and Bachelor; the South Sister; the craters of former mounts Mazama and Newberry; and the Belknap shield volcano (aka Belknap Crater). The state's ten other peaks have been inactive for much longer, and many of these have silhouettes that have been fractured, scoured, or split by glaciers. This is even more true of the Western Cascades. Although hard to imagine nowadays, the irregular rocky stumps and basaltic nubs of these forgotten giants dominated the landscape for 35 million years, producing six times the volcanic output of lava, ash, and rock as today's High Cascades – a sobering thought when exploring these invincible-looking titans.

Lake and the rocky, wooded **Western Cascades**. To the south, Eugene has several routes into the mountains: **Highway 126** heads due east into the forests and lava fields of the **High Cascades**, threading past the rugged hamlet of **Sisters** and a bevy of spiky peaks like **Broken Top** and **Three Sisters**, and **Highway 58** runs southeast over the verdant crest of Willamette Pass. In southern Oregon **highways 138** and **62** lead toward Crater Lake from Roseburg and Medford, but also compelling is Highway 140, or the **Lake of the Woods Highway**, branching off from Highway 62 and taking you to the graceful setting of **Mount McLoughlin**.

Getting around

If you're camping, a **car** is pretty much essential. Even just hopping from town to town by **public transit** in the Cascades can be difficult. Local bus services are negligible. Greyhound **buses** (☎1-800/231-2222, ⓦwww.greyhound.com) run east from Portland and dip through the mountains to Bend and Klamath Falls to the south. Amtrak **trains** (☎1-800/USA-RAIL or ⓦwww .amtrak.com) enter from California near Klamath Falls and proceed diagonally through the south side of the Cascades until they reach Eugene. Unfortunately, the only station in between them – and actually in the mountains itself – is the tiny burg of Chemult on US-97, a good distance from any major sights.

Northeast of the Cascades

Traveling on **US-26** southeast from Portland, many day-trippers make it only as far as the northern reaches of the Oregon Cascades and Mount Hood (see p.131). After the highway skirts the mountain's southern flank it begins a rather tedious trek through the desert-like scrublands and canyons **northeast** of the Cascades. The highlights are few and far between, though the Warm Springs Indian Reservation draws some for its touristy resort of **Kah-Nee-Tah** (☎1-800/554-4SUN, ⓦwww.kah-nee-taresort.com; ⑤), which in addition to golf and gambling offers some rather pricey, but compelling, packages ($200–300) for taking a dip in its toasty mineral waters and getting a Swedish massage. Beyond this, the dusty burgs of **Madras** and **Redmond** are two major crossroads into eastern Oregon, though not particularly appealing in themselves. However, Redmond does mark the start of an area much favored by "rock hounds," or amateur excavators, who come here to find such trophies as jasper thunder eggs, obsidian, and agates. Staff at the **visitor center**, 446 SW 7th St (☎541/923-5191, ⓦwww.redmondcofc.com), can tell you where to dig for the rocks as well as where to buy them.

The Cove Palisades and Smith Rock

About fifteen miles southwest of Madras off US-97, the **Cove Palisades** is perhaps the best state **campground** in the Cascades (day use $3, tent or electric sites $17–21, cabins $48–70; reserve at ☎1-800/452-5687), an ideal spot for hiking, as well as fishing, boating, and kayaking on **Lake Billy Chinook**, a 1960s manmade reservoir. The high rocky walls of the park are truly eye-opening with their towering rutted columns, as is the signature **Petroglyph Rock**, a huge boulder carved with mysterious designs.

The Cove Palisades makes a good day-trip with **Smith Rock**, a state park about fifteen miles southeast, or nine miles north of Redmond off US-97 (day use $3, primitive camping $4; ☎541/548-7501), whose towering basalt cliffs draw thousands of urbanites to practice their skills climbing and rappelling. These craggy, colorful giants were first formed some twelve million years ago when a great outpouring of lava – the Deschutes Formation – overwhelmed the ancient riverbed. Consequently the Crooked River took a new path that has cut a deep gorge in the park today, making perfect conditions for horseback riding, cycling, and hiking – though not all the trails are easy. In fact, **Asterisk Pass** is a so-called "rock scramble," meaning you get to scamper over piles of chunky lava rocks and try to avoid twisting your ankle. If you're interested in taking that initial climb, First Ascent, 1136 SW Deschutes Ave, Redmond (☎541/548-5137, ⓦwww .goclimbing.com), can teach you how to ascend the rocks with full-day instruction ($150 per person for two, $250 for one person).

A few miles west of the park across the highway, **Ogden Viewpoint** provides a striking view of a deep rocky gorge created in much the same manner as Smith Rock.

△ Smith Rock

Bend and around

Some 160 miles southeast of Portland, the area around **Bend** appeals for its splendid natural setting and access to some of the best attractions in the Cascades, while the city itself has a lively, easygoing air, with several fine restaurants, bars, and B&Bs. The surrounding region is excellent for its green, alpine scenery surrounding the Cascade peaks, among them the ski haven of **Mount Bachelor**, the stark cones and lava flows of **Newberry National Volcanic Monument**, the superb **High Desert Museum**, and the strange and austere sights of **Fort Rock** and **Hole-in-the-Ground**. Unfortunately, public transit in the region is almost nonexistent: there are no **trains** and the only town well served by Greyhound **bus** is Bend, which you can reach from Portland, Klamath Falls, and Seattle.

Bend

A booming resort town, **BEND** is one of the region's essential centers for outdoor pursuits, with cross-country and alpine skiers gathering here in the winter and spring, and hikers, rafters, and mountain bikers from spring to fall. An urbane mix belies its authentic frontier origins: early hunting trails led away from the Deschutes River here, and hunters came to know the place as "farewell bend" – a name that stuck until an impatient US post office made the abbreviation.

By emphasizing the area's potential for farming and ranching (and later, timber), an early-1900s East Coast entrepreneur, one Alexander Drake, and his development company transformed Bend from a ramshackle scattering of half-deserted ranches and dusty houses into a real town linked by the railroad. Its growth has since followed the rickety, uneven pattern of the Western frontier – cars came here before gaslights or even electricity. More recently, Bend has begun welcoming thousands of newcomers every year, drawn by the excellent outdoor activities, temperate climate (other than winter), low cost of living, and easygoing vibe. The influx has naturally pushed up property values and spurred new construction. As in the days of yore, however, public services have been slower in coming: though traffic had been worsening for years, a public bus system wasn't established until September 2006.

Arrival and information

For those arriving by **car**: US-97 slices right through Bend from north to south; US-20 comes in from the north, too, merging with US-97 just outside downtown, but soon forks off to eastern Oregon. The town center is west of US-97 along Franklin Avenue. Greyhound **buses** shoot along US-97, stopping at 20545 Builders St; call ☎541-382-2151 for schedules and drop-off details. The newly established **Bend Area Transit** (tickets $1, day passes $2; most routes Mon–Fri 6.15am–6pm, Sat 7.15am–5pm; ☎541/322-5870) has made getting around the city a bit easier, operating seven routes that branch out from the central Hawthorne Station between 3rd and 4th streets; routes #2, 3, and 11 run downtown.

The **Central Oregon Welcome Center**, 661 SW Powerhouse Drive, Suite 1301 (☎541/389-8799 or 1-800/800-8334, ⊛ www.covisitors.com), has brochures and accommodation listings, while the **visitor center**, 917 NW Harriman (☎541/382-8048 or 1-877/245-8484, ⊛ www.visitbend.com), has maps, hotel listings, and details of the many outfitters specializing in outdoor sports.

Accommodation

Finding **accommodation** in Bend in the summer – and especially on the weekend – can be a real headache, so it's best to book ahead. The town's budget chain **motels** are strung out along US-97, but there are more distinctive offerings, notably several charming **B&Bs**, in the town center. There are also several forest **campgrounds** with a good range of facilities.

Bend Riverside Motel 1565 NW Wall St ☎541/388-4000 or 1-800/284-2363, ⊛ www .bendriversidemotel.com. Down by the east bank of the Deschutes River, but north of downtown off US-97 at Revere Ave, this agreeable motel has a pleasant leafy setting, rooms with kitchenettes, as well as a pool, a sauna, and sports facilities. ⑤

La Pine State Park off US-97, 27 miles southwest of Bend ☎541/536-2071 or 1-800/551-6949,

reserve at ☎1-800-452-5687. On the Deschutes River, the park isn't as close to Bend as Tumalo State Park (see below), but it's well placed for exploring Newberry Crater and the southerly sites, and features good hiking and fishing and a range of campsites, including RV hookups and tent sites ($13–17) and cabins ($38–70).

Lara House 640 NW Congress St at Franklin Ave ☎541/388-4064 or 1-800/766-4064,

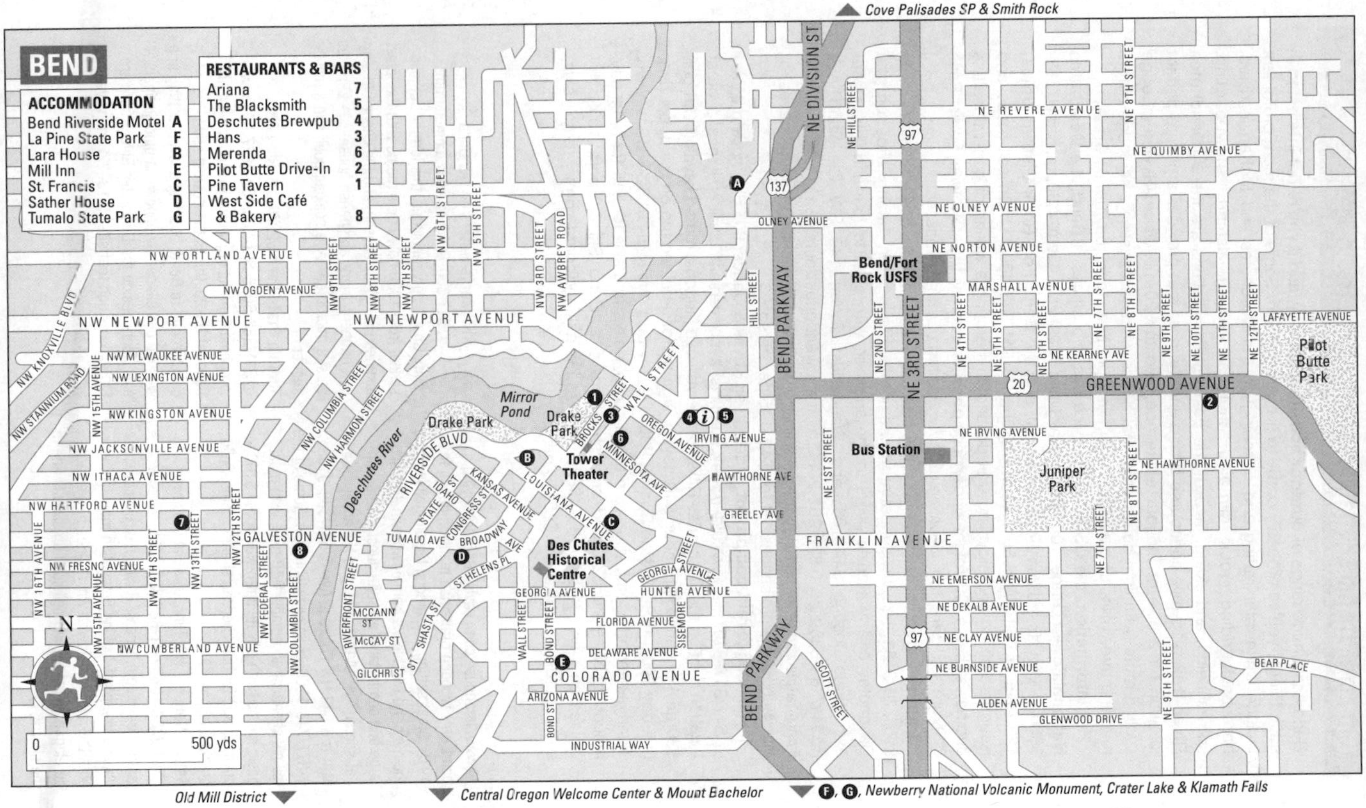
BEND
ACCOMMODATION
Bend Riverside Motel A
La Pine State Park F
Lara House B
Mill Inn E
St. Francis C
Sather House D
Tumalo State Park G
RESTAURANTS & BARS
Ariana 7
The Blacksmith 5
Deschutes Brewpub 4
Hans 3
Merenda 6
Pilot Butte Drive-In 2
Pine Tavern 1
West Side Café & Bakery 8
Cove Palisades SP & Smith Rock
Old Mill District
Central Oregon Welcome Center & Mount Bachelor
F, G, Newberry National Volcanic Monument, Crater Lake & Klamath Falls
0
500 yds
N
Bend/Fort Rock USFS
Bus Station
Juniper Park
Pilot Butte Park
Mirror Pond
Drake Park
Tower Theater
Des Chutes Historical Centre
Deschutes River
NE DIVISION ST
BEND PARKWAY
NE 3RD STREET
GREENWOOD AVENUE
FRANKLIN AVENUE
NW NEWPORT AVENUE
NW PORTLAND AVENUE
NW OGDEN AVENUE
GALVESTON AVENUE
RIVERSIDE BLVD
COLORADO AVENUE
WALL STREET
BOND STREET
OREGON AVENUE
MINNESOTA AVE
LOUISIANA AVENUE
KANSAS AVENUE
IRVING AVENUE
HAWTHORNE AVE
GREELEY AVE
OLNEY AVENUE
HILL STREET
NE REVERE AVENUE
NE QUIMBY AVENUE
NE OLNEY AVENUE
NE NORTON AVENUE
MARSHALL AVENUE
NE KEARNEY AVE
NE IRVING AVENUE
NE HAWTHORNE AVENUE
LAFAYETTE AVENUE
NE EMERSON AVENUE
NE DEKALB AVENUE
NE CLAY AVENUE
NE BURNSIDE AVENUE
ALDEN AVENUE
GLENWOOD DRIVE
BEAR PLACE
SCOTT STREET
INDUSTRIAL WAY
ARIZONA AVENUE
DELAWARE AVENUE
FLORIDA AVENUE
HUNTER AVENUE
GEORGIA AVENUE
SISEMORE
ST HELENS PL
BROADWAY AVE
TUMALO AVE
CONGRESS ST
STATE ST
IDAHO ST
SHASTA ST
MCCANN ST
McCAY ST
GILCHRIST ST
RIVERFRONT STREET
NW COLUMBIA STREET
NW FEDERAL STREET
NW HARMON STREET
NW CUMBERLAND AVENUE
NW FRESNO AVENUE
NW HARTFORD AVENUE
NW ITHACA AVENUE
NW JACKSONVILLE AVENUE
NW KINGSTON AVENUE
NW LEXINGTON AVENUE
NW MILWAUKEE AVENUE
NW KNOXVILLE BLVD
NW STANNIUM ROAD
NW AWBREY ROAD
NE HILLSTREET
97
137
20

Bend has a huge range of **outdoor activities** to enjoy, and if you're not interested in such things, you've probably come to the wrong town. Some of the more prominent include whitewater rafting and canoeing on the Deschutes and McKenzie rivers, horseback riding, rock climbing, mountain biking, fishing, snowboarding, snowshoeing, and skiing. Two of the best outdoor options are the 🎿 **Deschutes River Trail**, a 30-mile concourse built along the river that provides a picture-perfect location for a hike or mountain-bike ride, and the 20-mile **Bend-Skyliner Lodge** cycling route (with light auto traffic) that heads west and passes a ski lodge before reaching three miles of gravel to top out at a pretty waterfall on Tumalo Creek.

For **information**, the US Forest Service has two offices in Bend, the **Deschutes National Forest Office**, 1001 SW Emkay Drive (Mon–Fri 7.45am–4.30pm; ☎541/383-5300, 🌐www.fs.fed.us/r6/centraloregon), and the **Bend/Fort Rock District Office**, 1230 NE 3rd St (Mon–Fri 7.45am–4.30pm; ☎541/383-4000). Both sell maps and issue free hiking and bicycling trail descriptions among a wealth of general leaflets and news sheets. Overnight **wilderness permits**, such as the Northwest Forest Pass ($5), are sold here, too, or online at 🌐www.fs.fed.us/r6/mbs/passes.

Tour operators include Sun Country Tours, 531 SW 13th St (☎541/382-6277 or 1-800/770-2161, 🌐www.suncountrytours.com), offering fun rafting trips on the Deschutes and McKenzie rivers in the summer, with one- to four-and-a-half-hour excursions costing $44–108; and Wanderlust Tours, 143 SW Cleveland Ave (☎541/389-8359 or 1-800/962-2862, 🌐www.wanderlusttours.com), which has an imaginative range of half-day trips – summer canoeing, spelunking through caves, or clambering over volcanoes, all for $42–105 per person.

If you need to **rent equipment**, Alder Creek Kayak & Canoe, 805 SW Industrial Way (☎541/317-9407, 🌐www.aldercreek.com), is a convenient choice: it has a great location right on the Deschutes River where you can launch a rented kayak ($10/hour, $30/day) or canoe ($10/hour, $40/day) or sign up for a guided trip on the upper river (full-day $90). At Sunnyside Sports, 930 NW Newport Ave (☎541/382-8018, 🌐www .sunnysidesports.com), you can rent ski boots, poles, and skis for $15 for a full day, mountain bikes for $20, and snowshoes for $12. Bend Ski & Sport, 1009 NW Galveston Ave (☎541/389-4667, 🌐www.bendskiandboard.com), rents skis, snowboards, and bikes for $25–45 per day.

🌐www.larahouse.com. Lavish B&B occupying a handsome wooden Craftsman mansion dating from 1910. Great setting, too, among big old houses near the river and two blocks from downtown. Has six large and comfortable en-suite guest rooms with flat-screen TVs, DVD players, and Net access. ⑤

Mill Inn 642 NW Colorado Ave ☎541/389-9198 or 1-877/748-1200, 🌐www.millinn.com. Some of the town's cheapest acceptable B&B digs, with most basic rooms (with private bath) well under $100, or down to $30 for bunk beds in shared rooms. Solid breakfasts, too. ④

Sather House 7 NW Tumalo Ave at Broadway ☎541/388-1065 or 1-888/388-1065, 🌐www .satherhouse.com. Fine B&B with four guest rooms housed in a good-looking Edwardian mansion near both the river and downtown. Antique furnishings, an elegant veranda, and delicious breakfasts add to the charm. ⑥

🏃 **St Francis Hotel** 700 NW Bond St ☎541/330-8560, 🌐www.mcmenamins .com. Charmingly renovated, this former Catholic school from 1936 now offers rooms with the latest luxuries (⑤–⑥ by season) and the chance to stay in a nunnery, friary, and parish house (⑧–⑨), plus bars, a microbrewery, a soaking pool, and a movie theater.

Tumalo State Park 62976 O.B. Riley Rd ☎541/388-6055 or 1-800/452-5687, 🌐www .oregonstateparks.org. Five miles northwest of Bend off US-20, this is the nearest state campground to Bend, boasting a lovely setting in a wooded dell shaded by ponderosa pine, junipers, and alders beside the Deschutes River. There are RV hookups and tent sites ($13–22) and seven yurts ($29).

The Town

Bend has been undergoing some considerable renovation and revision in the last few years, bringing its old-time Central Oregon streets and atmosphere up to the standard of a 21st-century resort town. The **downtown** core lies right along the leafy banks of the Deschutes River. It only takes a few minutes to stroll from one end of it to the other – to get there, turn west off US-97 down Franklin Avenue.

Bracketing the west side of downtown along the river, **Drake Park** is a popular half-mile stretch with pleasant paths, an outdoor stage, and a setting near fetching **Mirror Pond**, widely acknowledged to be the most picturesque sight within the city.

Many of Bend's businesses are housed in appealing 1930–40s structures and include boutiques, restaurants, art galleries, salons, and book- and record stores. One of the best, the classic 1940 **Tower Theatre**, 835 NW Wall St (℡541/317-0700, ⊛www.towertheatre.org), a former moviehouse, has been remodeled into a neon-lit nexus of the performing arts. To get a look at an even older slice of Bend, drop by the **Des Chutes Historical Center**, on the southern edge of downtown at 129 NW Idaho Ave (Tues–Sat 10am–4.30pm; $5; ℡541/389-1813, ⊛www.deschuteshistory.org), which provides a glimpse of the distant days of native inhabitation, fur-trapping, and pioneer history through relics like old photos, cooking and agricultural artifacts, and a horse and buggy.

Serious shoppers and history buffs may want to take a look at the **Old Mill District**, less than a mile south of the downtown core off SW Bond St (most shops Mon–Sat 10am–8pm, Sun 11am–6pm; ⊛www.theoldmill.com). The brick powerhouse, outbuildings, and smokestacks of this large 1916 sawmill operation stood abandoned for a decade before making way for a new type of commerce in the 1990s, now evident in the chain stores, condos, diners, and knickknack shops that have taken over the site. More appealing is the opportunity to take a peek around one of Oregon's top microbreweries, located just across the river from the Old Mill. Almost as well known around here as skiing itself, the **Deschutes Brewery**, 901 SW Simpson Ave (tours Tues–Fri 1pm, 2.30pm & 4pm, Sat hours vary; free; ℡541/385-8606, ⊛www.deschutesbrewery.com), gives you a chance to see its massive brew kettles at work before sampling the merchandise, including such signature favorites as Black Butte Porter, Mirror Pond Ale, and Obsidian Stout, in the tasting room (Tues–Sat noon–5pm); if a sample isn't enough, drop by the company's brewpub for a pint or two (see below).

The one prominent sight on the far side of US-97 is the striking, 100-acre mound of **Pilot Butte**, along with Portland's Mount Tabor the only (dormant) volcano contained within the bounds of a continental American city. This towering landform is located a mile east of downtown off US-20; you can drive the winding concourse to the top or take a strenuous walk up the 500ft slope. Afterward you're rewarded with stunning views of downtown and the entire region, guided by interpretive displays that point out which snow-covered peak is which.

The High Desert Museum

The diverting **High Desert Museum**, 59800 US-97 (daily 9am–5pm; $12; ℡541/382-4754, ⊛www.highdesertmuseum.org), just four miles south of Bend on US-97, comprises a fascinating collection of artifacts from Native American and pioneer history, displays of regional flora and fauna, and a reconstructed pioneer homestead, tepee, and sawmill out back. As much a zoo as a museum, it describes life in the arid desert of southeast Oregon with exhibits arrayed along an outdoor path, where pens and pools of creatures – river otters, porcupines, and so forth – are interspersed with labeled trees and shrubs, as well as historical exhibits. A log cabin and a shepherd's wagon stand as testaments to an isolated nineteenth-century life spent guarding the animals against natural perils. Apart from animal predators, rustlers, and extreme weather conditions, there were poisonous weeds, scabies, liver flukes, and foot rot to contend with, prompting all manner of ingenious treatments, such as dipping the sheep in a solution of sulfur, hot water, and black leaf – nicotine squeezed from tobacco – to protect against parasites. Inside the museum are several well-organized display areas, including the **Spirit of the West Gallery**, which takes visitors through a sequence of historical scenes presented as dioramas, and the **Hall of Plateau Indians**, examining the culture of the region's indigenous population.

Eating and drinking

Bend is a great place to **eat** and **drink**. There are cafes with an easygoing feel, Western diners, brewpubs, chic restaurants, and everything in between – and keen competition keeps prices down to affordable levels. It's worth dropping a few more dollars to sample the delicious **Northwest Cuisine** offered by a handful of skillful chefs at selected elite restaurants – as good as any in the Northwest.

Ariana 1304 NW Galveston Ave ☎ 541/330-5539. On the west side of the river across from downtown, an upscale, stylish Mediterranean restaurant with a rotating menu, which may feature succulent steak with truffle fries, squash and ricotta cannelloni, and oysters with flying-fish roe aioli.

The Blacksmith 211 NW Greenwood Ave ☎ 541/318-0588. The cutting edge of dining in town, perhaps in Oregon, with pricey but successful experiments like lobster corn dogs, cider-brined pork chops, and sassafras-marinated chicken – not to mention a tremendous version of s'mores for dessert.

Deschutes Brewery and Public House 1044 NW Bond St ☎ 541/382-9242. Downtown brewpub offering good bar food and a wide selection of excellent handcrafted ales and stouts, made just south across the river at the brewery facility (see p.229).

Hans 915 NW Wall St ☎ 541/389-9700. Smart but informal restaurant with a wide-ranging menu, featuring Northwest Stroganoff with wild mushrooms, BBQ short ribs, and a nice rack of lamb – plus fine gourmet pizzas.

Merenda 900 NW Wall St ☎ 541/330-2304. Another of the top-name elite restaurants that's transforming Bend into a culinary haven, in this case with the aid of fresh chilled oysters, affordable wood-fired pizzas and zesty pastas, and entrees from wild salmon to elk sausage.

Pilot Butte Drive-In 917 NE Greenwood Ave/US-20 and 10th St ☎ 541/382-2972. Folksy, friendly diner that serves up the last word in hamburgers – the enormous 18-ounce version looks big enough to amble off the table. It also doles out cheeseburgers topped with the likes of roasted garlic and guacamole, among other offbeat choices.

Pine Tavern 967 NW Brooks St ☎ 541/382-5581. Chic, long-standing favorite in a pretty location overlooking Mirror Pond, and legendary for its delicious, locally raised prime rib, plus savory filet mignon, grilled prawns, and cheaper, but still tasty, ribs, pasta, and meatloaf.

West Side Café & Bakery 1005 NW Galveston Ave ☎ 541/382-3426. The apotheosis of the Bend breakfast, doling out tasty and filling all-American breakfasts and a solid range of baked goods, within walking distance of the downtown core.

Mount Bachelor and the Cascade Lakes Highway

Bend is perhaps most famous as the gateway to one of the Northwest's largest ski resorts, **Mount Bachelor**, centered on a 9060ft volcanic peak 22 miles west-southwest of town in the **Deschutes National Forest**. This great slab of forested wilderness occupies a one-hundred-mile strip on the western side of the High Cascades, tipped by brownish-black lava fields at its highest elevations to the south and west of Bend. The mountain is reached along a short spur road off the scenic, hundred-mile Cascade Lakes Highway (also known as Hwy 372 or, closer to Bend, Century Drive Highway). The skiing season runs from around mid-November to as late as June, snowfall permitting (snow reports on ☎541/382-7888), and you can rent cross-country and downhill skis as well as snowboards (packages starting at $30 per day), or attend a well-respected ski school (details at ☎541/382-2442 or 1-800/829-2442, Ⓦwww.mtbachelor .com). There are twelve ski lifts and no fewer than seventy runs for snowboarders and downhill skiers (one-day ski-lift pass $52) and groomed terrain for cross-country skiers (daily trail pass $13–16). There's a park-and-ride bus shuttle (mid-Dec to mid-April daily, rest of year Sat & Sun only; $5 each way) from Bend to the slopes in the winter season, leaving four times daily from the Park & Ride at Colorado and Simpson avenues, about half a mile west of the river.

Beyond Mount Bachelor, the **Cascade Lakes Highway** pushes on west before turning south to wind along the slopes of the Cascades, passing dense forests and deep-blue lakes, crumbly lava flows and craggy peaks. It's a pleasant enough drive – though the highway is closed beyond Mount Bachelor during the winter, opening again in April, May, or June depending on the weather – but the magnificence of the scenery is best appreciated along one of the many **hiking trails** that begin beside the highway. The US Forest Service offices in Bend (see p.228) have all the trail details. One of the most enjoyable is the 6.5-mile **Green Lakes Trail**, whose roadside trailhead is about 25 miles out from town. This moderately difficult trail climbs north up gurgling Fall Creek to reach the meadows and lava field beside the three little basin lakes, with the white-capped triple peaks of the **Three Sisters** stretching away to the north. From the lakes you can press on deeper into the wilderness or vary your return via either **Todd Lake**, where there's a backcountry **campground** (free with $5 Northwest Forest Pass; information on all Deschutes forest camping at ☎541/383-5300, Ⓦwww.fs.fed.us/r6/passespermits), or **Devils Lake**. Beyond this, the highway continues southward until it reaches a fork. The west branch leads to Highway 58, which leads back to Eugene over the Willamette Pass, while the east branch takes you to US-97, on which you can either return to Bend or go south to Crater Lake.

Newberry National Volcanic Monument

The so-called **lava lands** cover a huge area of central Oregon, stretching roughly from Redmond down south to Crater Lake, with the greatest concentration of sizable lava formations around Bend. Occupying a narrow slice of the Deschutes National Forest to either side of US-97 just a few miles south of Bend, the volcanic landscapes of **Newberry National Volcanic Monument** ($5 parking passes, valid for all of the monument for up to five days; Ⓦwww .fs.fed.us/r6/centraloregon) include neat conical cones, obsidian fields, ropy lava and pumice fields, craggy caves, and rocky molds of tree trunks, and date back more than seven thousand years to the eruptions of mounts Newberry and Mazama (today's Crater Lake; see p.233), which dumped enormous quantities of ash and pumice across the region. The newly renovated **Lava Lands Visitor Center**, just eleven miles from Bend on US-97 (April–Oct daily 9am–5pm; ☎541/593-2421), has various types of volcanic rock on display and is a useful source of maps and practical information on the Newberry monument. Of more immediate interest is the adjacent **Lava Butte**, a colossal, dark cinder cone side-breached by a gush of molten lava that spilled over the surrounding land. Two short trails lead from the visitor center through the cracked moonscape of the lava flow to the top of the butte, but the walk is an uncomfortable one up a steep, uneven rock slope, so you're better off driving the 1.5-mile road to the top, taking in a wide view of dark green pine forest interrupted by chocolate-colored lava. The butte is cratered at the top, the basinlike hole tinged red where steam once oxidized the iron in the rock; it's also the site of a forest **lookout station**, where distant mountains – sometimes ablaze with wildfires in late summer – are visible throughout the year.

A mile or so south of the visitor center, just east off US-97, the **Lava River Cave** (summer Wed–Sun 9am–5pm; $5 day pass, plus $3 for a lamp) leads down a subterranean passage into the chilly volcanic underworld. The cave was created during the last Ice Age by a rush of molten lava, most of which eventually cooled and hardened around the hottest, still-molten center of the flow. When this drained away, it left an empty lava tube over a mile long, discovered only when part of the roof fell in. There are supposedly all kinds of formations along the cave, but even with a lantern it's hard to see much beyond the next few steps, and it's cold at a constant 42°F (5°C) – wear extra clothes and sturdy shoes.

From the cave, it's about three miles south on US-97 and a further nine miles east along rough, unpaved Forest Road 9720 to the **Lava Cast Forest**. This contains the tree molds – easily seen on a one-mile loop trail from the parking lot – formed centuries ago when lava poured into a forest of ponderosa pines, leaving empty shells when the trees burned to charcoal and ash. The lava here came from what was once the volcano of Mount Newberry, whose multiple eruptions deluged its surroundings for hundreds of years. Finally, worn out by the effort, the mountain collapsed to create **Newberry Crater**, a five-mile-wide caldera that's approached along – and traversed by – a narrow and tortuous eighteen-mile side road that cuts east off US-97 about 24 miles south of Bend. (Note that this road is closed by snow in winter from about November to May.) The crater is a classic example of a volcanic landscape, featuring **Paulina Peak**, an 8000ft remnant of the original mountain, standing sentinel over two little lochs, **Paulina** and **East lakes**, whose deep, clear waters are popular with fishermen for their regularly stocked trout and salmon.

A puncture in the side of the crater provides an outlet for Paulina Lake in the form of the 80ft **Paulina Falls**, while the volcano's most recent eruption – about 1300 years ago – created the **Big Obsidian Flow**, huge hills of volcanic black glass that native tribes throughout the Northwest once quarried to make arrowheads. Beginning at the roadside, easy half-mile **hiking trails** reach both features. As you walk on the trail past the Obsidian Flow, giant mounds of the glassy dark material loom over you, in forms ranging from sheer walls to chunky blocks to glistening crumbs. The rock is still quite sharp and brittle – and especially rare – so you're strongly advised not to take home any geological souvenirs. Harder hikes include the strenuous haul up Paulina Peak. The crater is easily visited on a day-trip from Bend, but there are several seasonal **campgrounds** here, too, mostly around the lakes (generally May–Oct; $6–14; reservations from Lava Lands Visitor Center or the US Forest Service offices in Bend).

Fort Rock and Hole-in-the-Ground

A monumental plateau of volcanic tuff located some seventy miles south of Bend, off US-97 along Hwy 31, **Fort Rock** is an unusual geological formation created when billows of steam and rivers of molten rock came into contact with an Ice Age lake. Thousands of years later the huge solidified table rock stood in an expansive lake, whose various levels are still visible in horizontal "wave cuts" on the rock's exterior walls. Native tribes used to row canoes over these waters to decamp at the rock – their ancient presence later discovered in the 1930s with a pair of 9000-year-old moccasins (one of 75 pairs from the era found here). Although the lake has vanished, the rock's cliffs are still imposing, rising up to 325ft high and overlooking the sagebrush desert as it stretches toward the horizon in all its sun-scorched beauty. Less than a mile west sits the unmarked entrance to **Fort Rock Cave**, an eerie underground expanse you can only explore through an official 90min state-guided tour (April–Oct twice monthly; reserve at least three days in advance at ☎541/536-2428).

Head back to Bend on Hwy 31, just a few miles to the northwest, for the turnoff for **Hole-in-the-Ground**, accessed via an unimproved road over crumbly rockfall. One of the more bizarre and lesser-known geological oddities in the region, this mile-wide depression is about three hundred feet deep; geologists believe it formed during the last Ice Age when an ancient underground volcano erupted, causing magma to rise the surface, where it violently collided with groundwater along the shore of an ancient lake. This isn't the only curious sight in the area; less than two miles north, back along Hwy 31, lies another great void known as **Big Hole**, and beyond this the area is littered with rocky buttes and ice caves too numerous to mention. Contact the ranger stations in Bend if you want to explore them.

Crater Lake National Park

Farther south on US-97, sitting high up in the Cascades about 120 miles southwest from Bend, **CRATER LAKE NATIONAL PARK** ($10 seven-day access fee; ⊛www.nps.gov/crla) conserves the Pacific Northwest's grandest volcanic crater, where the jagged shell of **Mount Mazama** holds impossibly blue and resoundingly beautiful **Crater Lake**, the deepest in the US and seventh deepest in the world – and justifiably the image on Oregon's own "state quarter". The **Steel Visitor Center** (April–Oct 9am–5pm, rest of year 10am–4pm; ☎541/594-3100, ⊛www.crater.lake.national-park.com), located three miles south of Crater Lake on Hwy 62, is the park's main visitor center and headquarters, and can provide assorted maps, information, and details on guided walks. Its services are a little better than those at the **Rim Village Visitor Center** (June–Sept daily 9.30am–5pm), perched on the lake's southern rim.

Getting there

The **drive** from Bend to Crater Lake takes several hours and requires a westward turn onto highways 138 or 62. If traveling from Eugene, you can take Hwy 58 and then US-97 to either of these access roads. Of the two, the **northern entrance** off Hwy 138 is the more exciting, with a narrow park road emerging from the forests to cut across a bleak pumice desert before arriving at Crater Lake's precipitous northern rim. This road is, however, closed by snow from mid-October to late June, sometimes longer, and attracts more than its share of fog, which can turn what should be a magnificent drive into a white-knuckle ride. The **southern entrance**, off Hwy 62, is kept open all year. It's an easier route that creeps up Mazama's wooded flanks to reach the lake at its southern rim. The 33-mile **Rim Drive** wriggles around the crater's edge, linking the two access roads and providing the most magnificent of views – though it too is open only in summer.

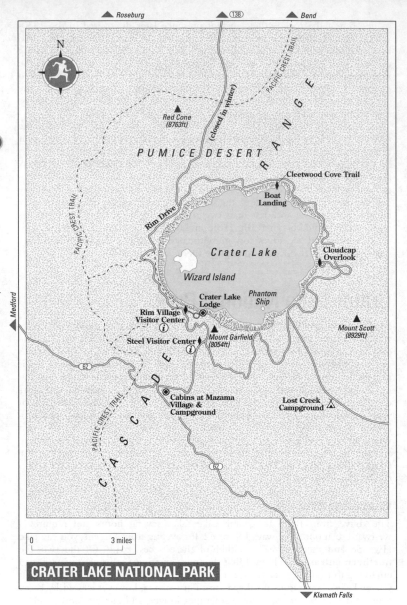

CRATER LAKE NATIONAL PARK

The park

For half a million years, Mount Mazama sent out periodic sprays of ash, cinders, and pumice. Eventually, the mountain burst, blowing its peak over eight states and three Canadian provinces in an explosion that was 62 times as powerful as the most recent Mount St Helens blast (see p.442). Conic mini-volcanoes soon began to sprout again within the hollowed-out mountain, but when it cooled and became dormant the basin was filled by springs and melted snow. This new lake eventually submerged all but two volcanic outcrops, a tree-covered cinder cone known as **Wizard Island**, which emerged hundreds of years after the eruption, and the so-called **Phantom Ship**, a jagged volcanic dike that, in dim light or fog, resembles a mysterious clipper on the water. In its splendid isolation, Crater Lake is awe-inspiring, especially in summer, when wildflowers bloom and wildlife (deer, squirrels, chipmunks, elks, foxes, porcupines) emerges from hibernation. The lake itself has a small population of rainbow trout and kokanee (landlocked) salmon, but these were introduced in the early 1900s.

There are a number of short **hiking trails** in the park, detailed at the Steel Visitor Center, most of which climb the mountainous slopes surrounding Crater Lake. The most popular, though still strenuous, hike is up **Garfield Peak**, an 8054ft mountain that offers a tremendous view of the lake and is particularly striking during winter. More intrepid hikers can explore the marginally better views offered by the park's tallest outcrop, **Mount Scott**, rising to almost nine thousand feet. One particularly good route travels along the lake's western rim, a wonderful hike with great views across the caldera. From this trail, two further trails climb up to the **Pacific Crest Trail** (see p.51), which runs right across the national park on its way from Mexico to Canada. The park's higher hiking trails are, of course, snow-covered for most of the year, when they are favored by cross-country skiers.

On the northern side of the lake, Rim Drive connects with the steep, mile-long **Cleetwood Cove Trail**, the only way to reach the lakeshore. From the bottom of the trail, pleasure boats make regular **cruises** of the lake (July–Sept daily 10am–4pm; 1hr 45min; $22); tickets are sold in the parking lot at the Cleetwood Cove trailhead and at the *Crater Lake Lodge* (see below). If you're hardy enough, you can also inquire at the visitor center about taking a **scuba dive** (June–Sept; free permits) into the depths of the deep blue lake, though you must bring your own equipment, as there are no rentals here; summer surface temperatures are around 55°F but plunge to 38°F below 260ft.

Practicalities

One of the man-made highlights in the park is the splendid ☆ **Crater Lake Lodge** (late-May to mid-Oct; ☎541/830-8700, ⓦwww.craterlakelodges .com; ❺), a fully refurbished 1915 hotel on the lake's south side. The lodge has a magnificent Great Hall, complete with Art Deco flourishes, and pleasant rooms – get either a corner room or one overlooking the lake. Advance reservations are essential, as are reservations at the lodge's **restaurant**, which has agreeable, if expensive, Northwest Cuisine. There are less-expensive lodgings in the modern, shingle-roofed chalets of the *Cabins at Mazama Village*, on the main access road seven miles south of the lodge (June to mid-Oct; ☎541/830-8700; ❺). Next door is the large *Mazama Village* **campground** (June to mid-Oct; sites $18–24; ☎541/830-8700) in a quiet wooded setting. The park's other campground is the tiny *Lost Creek* (July to early Oct; $10; ☎541/594-3100), down a spur road off Rim Drive southeast of Crater Lake, where there are sixteen basic plots. Beyond the *Crater Lake Lodge*, there's not much in the way of decent eats around, so you'll either have to bring your own grub or venture to Bend or Klamath Falls to stock up on supplies.

Klamath Falls and around

On the southern flank of the Cascades, sixty-odd miles from Crater Lake at the south end of Oregon's section of US-97, remote **KLAMATH FALLS** was once a bustling logging town and railway junction as well as a key staging point on the route to the Pacific Coast. Though less important these days, the town still manages to rustle up a couple of diverting sights – good enough even to justify a day-trip, particularly from Crater Lake if the wet and foggy weather proves inhospitable there. Indeed, warm and sunny "K Falls," as residents call it, is sited at the southern tip of enormous **Upper Klamath Lake**, the second-largest lake west of the Rockies and part of the pancake-flat **Klamath Basin**. With marshes and reedy lakes spread over the Oregon–California border, the basin is quite active geothermally – much of downtown Klamath Falls is heated by naturally hot water – and seismically unstable, prone to the odd earthquake.

The entire 500-mile route from Crater Lake, past Upper Klamath Lake and Klamath Falls, and south to the California lava beds and Mount Lassen is protected as the **Volcanic Legacy Scenic Byway**, in Oregon mostly following highways 62 and 140. It is deservedly considered one of the most visually stunning drives in the region, taking you past a variety of terrain, from mountain passes to crystal lakeshores to bleak fields of basalt and pumice. You can get more information from the route's California headquarters, at 300 Pine St, Mount Shasta (☎866/722-9929, ⓦ www.volcaniclegacybyway.org), or from any visitor center in Klamath Falls.

Arrival and accommodation

Connecting with Portland and Bend, the Greyhound **buses** drop off and pick up passengers at 445 S Spring St, off Hwy 39 (☎541/883-2609). Amtrak **trains** on the Coast Starlight route, which links Seattle with Los Angeles (and, closer to home, Eugene), pull in on the eastern edge of downtown at 1600 Oak St. The **visitor center**, 205 Riverside Drive (Mon–Sat 9am–4.30pm; ☎541/882-1501 or 1-800/445-6728, ⓦ www.travelklamath.com), issues free town maps and has details of local accommodation. The center stands across the street from

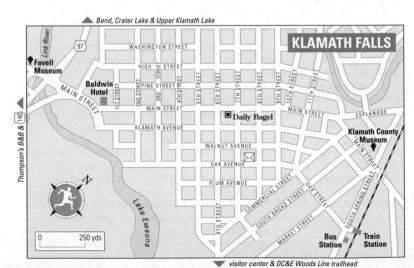

Bend, Crater Lake & Upper Klamath Lake

KLAMATH FALLS

WASHINGTON STREET

HIGH STREET

PINE STREET

MAIN STREET

Favell Museum

Baldwin Hotel

Thompson's B&B & (140)

1ST STREET
2ND STREET
3RD STREET
4TH STREET
5TH STREET
6TH STREET
7TH STREET
8TH STREET
9TH STREET
10TH STREET
11TH STREET

MAIN STREET

ESPLANADE

■ Daily Bagel

KLAMATH AVENUE

Klamath County Museum

WALNUT AVENUE

OAK AVENUE

PLUM AVENUE

Lake Ewauna

COMMERCIAL STREET
SOUTH BROAD STREET
OAK STREET
6TH STREET

MARKET STREET

SOUTH SPRING STREET

Bus Station

Train Station

0   250 yds

236

visitor center & OC&E Woods Line trailhead

THE OREGON CASCADES | Klamath Falls and around

Captain Jack and the Modoc War

When white settlers reached the Klamath Basin in considerable numbers in the 1850s, they rushed to drain the marshes for pastureland, dispossessing the local natives – the **Modoc**, from around Tule Lake on the Oregon–California border, and their traditional rivals, the **Klamath**, to the immediate north – with violent gusto. In 1864, keen to legitimize their new landholdings, they brought in federal treaty commissioners to persuade the Modoc to formally sign away their homeland in return for a reservation beside Upper Klamath Lake.

For the Modoc, signing the treaty brought no respite: they had endless problems with the rival Klamath, who shared the same reservation, and the Indian agent failed to provide the supplies that had been promised. In desperation, Modoc leader Kientpoos (aka **Captain Jack**) led three hundred of his people back to their old hunting grounds, precipitating the so-called **Modoc War**, whose pathetic finale of 1873 had Captain Jack and his remaining followers holed up in the mazelike lava beds south of Tule Lake. In the event, the US Army found it extremely difficult to smoke out the Modoc, despite their howitzers and a huge numerical advantage – 1000 against 150 – but smoke them out they did. The captured Modoc were then transferred to Oklahoma, with the exception of Captain Jack and three of his followers, who were hanged in Fort Klamath – though even that was not quite enough: Captain Jack's body was later dug up, embalmed, and taken East to be exhibited in a freak show.

The **Fort Klamath Museum**, between Crater Lake and Klamath Falls at 51400 Hwy 62 (June–Sept Wed–Sun 10am–6pm; donation; ☎541/381-2230), provides the full story of this bloody chapter, with a replica of the old guardhouse and the actual graves of four tribal leaders.

the stately Victorian **Goeller House**, one of several classic structures open to the public during late July's **Century Days**, when the town gets duded up in its best Wild West wear and celebrates the old days with chuckwagon dinners, high-steppin' folk music, and cowboy poetry.

Since isolated Klamath Falls is a natural stopover between Ashland and eastern Oregon, or between Portland and Reno, Nevada, you may want to **stay** the night, and there's a clutch of mundane motels strung out along 6th Street (Hwy 39) on the south side of town. The best choice for mainstream lodging is the *Best Western Olympic Inn* (not to be confused with the less appealing *Best Western Klamath Inn*), 2627 S Sixth St (☎541/882-9665, ⓦwww.bestwestern.com; ⑤), which has clean and comfortable rooms, pool, gym, Internet access, and solid complimentary breakfasts. *Thompson's B&B*, 1420 Wild Plum Ct (☎541/882-7938, ⓦwww.thompsonsbandb.com; ⑤), provides four basic bed-and-breakfast rooms near an expansive city park and the south shore of Upper Klamath Lake. The two rooms of the *Devonridge B&B*, 1403 Devonridge Drive (☎541/883-3172, ⓦwww.devonridge.com; ⑤), come with hot tubs, fireplaces, and Net access, and offer fine views of the city and lake.

The Town

The Modoc War (see box, above) is detailed at the **Klamath County Museum**, 1451 Main St at Spring (Wed–Sat 9am–5pm, Sun 1–5pm; $3), but it's the haunting photographs of the captured Modoc that are memorable rather than the military details. The museum has an austere character, and even though some of the displays hardly enhance the exhibits, there are several interesting sections on, for instance, the wildlife of the Klamath Basin, local pioneer life, and early steamship travel on Upper Klamath Lake. The museum stands on the northeast edge of the town center, a simple gridiron focused on Main Street and Klamath Avenue. With its fancy, if faded, early-twentieth-century red-brick facades, **Main Street** has an old-fashioned flavor best expressed by the **Baldwin Hotel**, 31 Main St (tours June–Sept Tues–Sat 10am–2.30pm, Sun noon–2.30pm; tours $6; reserve at ☏541/883-4207), which began life as a 1906 hardware store owned by Senator George Baldwin before he turned it into accommodation five years later. These days you can't stay here, but you can visit the renovated facility on guided two-hour tours and check out intriguing antiques and assorted castoffs from the decades, as well as the senator's daughter Maud's photo studio, where she assembled a compendium of area sights a century ago.

Main Street runs beyond the hotel past a US-97 slip road before reaching the Link River and the fascinating **Favell Museum**, 125 W Main St (Mon–Sat 9.30am–5.30pm; $6; ☏541/882-9996, ⓦwww.favellmuseum.com), stuffed with all manner of Native American artifacts, highlighted by a breathtaking collection of Columbia Gorge pieces, notably hundreds of agate gem points – or arrowheads – all sorts of tools, an intriguing assortment of trade goods, and a sample of the three-dimensional rock reliefs for which the gorge tribes are well known. Another display area concentrates on the Modoc and Klamath, whose stone sculptures feature animal and human figures imbued with spiritual significance – as in the *henwas*, small stone sculptures used in fertility rites. The museum also features a sizable collection of twentieth-century paintings about the West, though for the most part these epic canvases adopt a sort of latter-day Custer approach – wild, lean natives and tough, weather-beaten Bluecoats.

Eating

There are limited options for **food** in Klamath Falls, and the better restaurants are located some distance southeast from downtown, except for the *Daily Bagel*, 636 Main St (☏541/850-0744), a cafe selling tasty pastries, coffee, and snacks. If you're looking for something more substantial, try *Red's Backwoods BBQ*, 3435 Washburn Way (☏541/883-2175), which doles out slabs of hearty country ribs and chops, or the small *Pho Hoa & Hong*, 4023 S 6th St (☏541/850-9441), which has serviceable Vietnamese fare. Nearby, one of the few elite dining spots is *Mr. B's Steakhouse*, set in a converted Craftsman home at 3927 S 6th St (☏541/883-8719) and offering succulent seafood, lamb, duck, and of course, prime rib.

The Klamath Basin National Wildlife Refuges

Simply put, the **Klamath Basin National Wildlife Refuges** are among the most incredible sights in the region – though scarcely known to the great majority of Oregonians. Admittedly remote in this south-central part of the state, the refuges are six vast, blue oases on both sides of the Oregon–California border, and are memorably approached on the Volcanic Legacy Scenic Byway that lines their shores.

Whereas most of the Klamath Basin has been drained and turned into either cattle-grazing pasture or potato and onion farmland, the refuges continue to act as great preserves devoted to some 250 species of waterfowl – especially pelicans, cormorants, herons, osprey, ducks, geese, and swans – along with the raptors they attract and a substantial population of bald eagles, which swoop in around mid-February. Otherwise, the best seasons to visit are spring and fall, when hundreds of thousands of birds stop in the basin during their annual

△ Upper Klamath Lake

migration. The most accessible refuge is the **Upper Klamath Lake National Wildlife Refuge**, situated just north of Klamath Falls off US-97. Here, you can fish or take a canoe out on the placid lake surface or into its side marshes, or hike one of the many interpretive trails crossing the site.

For detailed advice about the best **bird-watching** sites and maps of the network of rough gravel roads that traverse this and the other refuges, see Ⓦ www.klamathbirdingtrails.com or contact the Klamath Falls visitor center (see p.236); the refuges' main visitor center near Tule Lake, four miles south of the Oregon border off Hwy 161 (Mon–Fri 8am–4.30pm, Sat & Sun 10am–4pm; Ⓦ www.fws.gov/klamathbasinrefuges); or the Klamath Wildlife Area Office, Oregon Department of Fish and Wildlife, 1850 Miller Island Rd, West Klamath Falls, OR 97603 (Ⓣ 541/883-5732).

If you want to **stay** in the vicinity, your best bet is the 🏃 *Rocky Point Resort*, a half-hour north of downtown Klamath Falls at 28121 Rocky Point Rd (Ⓣ 541/356-2287, Ⓦ www.rockypointoregon.com). With a lakeshore location that's good for taking a canoe trip and seeing the wildlife on Upper Klamath Lake, it has a range of accommodation, from tent sites ($18) to basic lodge guest rooms (❹) to private cabins with kitchens and barbecues. The seven basic B&B rooms of the *Crystalwood Lodge*, farther north at 38625 Westside Rd (Ⓣ 1-866/381-2322, Ⓦ www.crystalwoodlodge.com; ❹–❺ by season), are another option. Thirty miles north of Klamath Falls, **Collier Memorial State Park** (Ⓣ 541/783-2471) has a **campground** (April–Oct; first-come, first-served tent sites $11–17) and horse camp (April–Oct; $10–15). It also features an outstanding **outdoor logging museum** (daily dawn–dusk; donation) full of antique saws, wagons, train engines, and lots of other timber-related apparatuses, including perilous-looking gang saws and band mills for processing the wood and seventy other such relics, plus a "pioneer village" showcasing twelve relocated cabins and buildings like a general store, smokehouse, barn, and privy.

OC&E Woods Line State Trail

Klamath Falls is also an embarkation point for one of the best examples of recreational conservation in the state, the **OC&E Woods Line State Trail**, a hundred-mile-long former railway bed that has been converted into an excellent path for cycling, hiking, and horseback riding, with all manner of stunning vistas and varying topography. Beginning south of town, just before Washburne Way crosses Hwy 140, the trail follows the tracks of the old Oregon, California & Eastern (hence OC&E) Railroad – at one time a major carrier for the lumber industry – as they snake south and then to the far northeast of the **Winema** and **Fremont national forests**. Along the way the trail crosses from paved to gravel to dirt surfaces, parallels pristine streams, climbs over lava buttes and down forested valleys, and crosses hair-raising train trestles and archaic steel bridges before it ends in the tiny village of **Bly** – roughly halfway between Klamath Falls and Lakeview, Oregon, near Hwy 140. There are assorted waysides and campgrounds ($10–16) along the 200-mile path, though you'll need plenty of supplies and, should you want to quit mid-journey, a detailed map to find your way to the nearest town. For further details on making this fascinating expedition, or to request a brochure, contact the Klamath Rails-to-Trails Group (☎541/884-3050, ⓦwww.u-r-here.com/OCE) or the Oregon State Parks Department (☎1-800/551-6949, ⓦwww.oregonstateparks.org).

The trans-Cascade roads

Whereas US-97 leads you along a "greatest hits" collection of the High Cascades, from Smith Rock to Crater Lake to Upper Klamath Lake, the much lower-slung **Western Cascades** some thirty to fifty miles away are better explored on the several **trans-Cascade roads** that lead east across the peaks and valleys. Starting in cities along I-5 like Salem, Eugene, Roseburg, and Medford, these state highways frequently meander up hillsides, down switchbacks, alongside riverbeds, and below mountain flanks. Moreover, the peaks such roads pass are not the big names of the Cascades – such as Hood, Bachelor, and Newberry – but the lesser-known ones, each with its own distinctive silhouette and often accessible only on hiking trails. Venturing into the mountains this way will no doubt closely acquaint you with the area's lakes, hot springs, lava fields, forest glades, and waterfalls, but you may need a detailed hiking or topography map (available at bookstores or forest offices) to find your way through some of the thornier mountain passes and confusing geography. Keep in mind that a sturdy four-wheel-drive vehicle can be a necessity when venturing off the major roads, and make sure to equip yourself with the necessary supplies if embarking on a serious trek through the woods.

Salem to Santiam Junction

The most popular east-west route into the heart of the Cascades is **Highway 22** from Salem, which for the first forty miles east is fairly uneventful, though it does pass the fine North Santiam State Park (see p.201) about halfway along this first leg. Only when the highway reaches the recreational center of **Detroit Lake**, 45 miles from Salem (March–Nov; $3 day-use fee), does it really spring to life. This eponymous state park is unquestionably a favorite among Oregonians, primarily for its excellent boating, swimming, and fishing, though a walk along its shoreline is also rather pleasant. You can **camp** at its lakeshore sites

($12–20; reserve at ☎1-800/452-5687) or, if you feel up to it, take a boat and make the journey out to **Piety Island** in the middle of the lake to stay at one of its twelve free primitive campsites during the summer. Keep in mind there are no facilities on the island, though, including freshwater. For maps and information on how to best explore the lake, drop by the **Detroit Ranger Station**, two miles east of the lake in Mill City (year-round Mon–Fri 8am–4.30pm; ☎503/854-3366).

Ten miles north of Detroit Lake along Breitenbush Road are the enticing **Breitenbush Hot Springs** (☎503/854-3320, ⓦwww.breitenbush.com), a New Age resort boasting a collection of three toasty mineral pools, four hot tubs, massage therapists, and a sauna, along with an imitation Native American sweat lodge. There are both basic cabins (c) and tent sites ($50–56), but you'll have to stay here, and reserve in advance, to use the facilities. Travel another four miles along the road to reach Forest Road 4685, which, after a mile, leads to trailheads for the **South Breitenbush Gorge**, a National Scenic Trail that takes you on a five-mile trek along a river rushing through a steep-walled basalt canyon and back. A Northwest Forest Pass ($5; see p.228), available at area ranger stations, is required to park here. To embark on another brisk hike into the woods, continue north on Breitenbush Road for another eight miles and follow the signs for the **Olallie Lakes Scenic Area**, and you'll soon find yourself at a trailhead with access to dozens of appealingly isolated mountain lakes, best known for their fishing. *Olallie Lake Resort*, on the north shore off Forest Road 4220 (June–Oct; ☎541/504-1010, ⓦwww.olallielake.com), has a range of cabins (❸–❹), a renovated guard station (❺), yurts (❹), and campsites ($10–14), and you can rent a sizable rowboat for $6–9 per hour, or $25–35 per day. Weekday accommodation prices drop by up to half during the fall.

Back on Highway 22, twelve miles east of the town of Detroit, is the turnoff for Pamelia Road, which leads after three miles to a trailhead. From here, a path brings you through evocative groves of old-growth forest along a creek until you reach **Pamelia Lake**, another sparkling mountain jewel, which is also good for fishing and acts as a base for trips into the rugged landscape beyond. It's so popular that during the summer a free **wilderness permit**, available only at the Detroit Ranger Station (details at ⓦwww.fs.fed.us/r6/willamette), is required to visit the lake and its trails. Of immediate interest is the 2.8-mile one-way trek up **Grizzly Peak**, a nearly 6000ft mountain of the Western Cascades that affords excellent views of its High Cascades counterparts – Mount Jefferson, Three-Fingered Jack, and, in the distance, the Three Sisters. The 10,500ft **Mount Jefferson** is the closest of the peaks, and adventurous visitors with proper equipment can make a climb for the summit. There are nine primitive **campgrounds** ($5–10) in the area around the mountain, nearly two hundred miles of trails, five glaciers, and 150 lakes of varying size. Again, you'll need a detailed forest map and a wilderness permit from June to October; contact the Detroit Ranger Station or Willamette National Forest office in Eugene for more information and planning advice.

Also in the vicinity are a number of good fishing lakes, among them **Marion Lake** and **Lava Lake**. Some fifteen miles south of **Marion Forks** – noted mainly for its fish hatchery, though it also has camping nearby for $5–10 with a wilderness permit – highways 22 and 126 intersect at **Santiam Junction**, sitting in the center of a group of snow parks and winter recreation areas (see p.244).

From Santiam Junction, you can either continue eastbound on Hwy 126 (see p.242) or return west on Hwy 20 to the Willamette Valley towns of Sweet Home and Albany. Twelve miles west of the Hwy 126 junction, just past the Tombstone campground area, Forest Road 2000-035 leads a short distance north of the highway to the trailhead for **Iron Mountain**, around 5400ft high, which is one of many local remnants of the ancient Western Cascade chain – the predecessors of today's High Cascades. This two-mile one-way route leads to one of central Oregon's prime habitats for **wildflowers**, with roughly three hundred varieties visible in the spring and summer, and some excellent views of distant mountains and valleys. At the top is a fire lookout (open summer daily) built atop the mountain's spiky basaltic summit. Visit the **Sweet Home Ranger Station**, at 4431 Hwy 20 (Mon–Fri 8am–4.30pm; ☎541/367-5168), for maps and more information on exploring this and other peaks in the Western Cascades.

East from Eugene

Although all of the trans-Cascade routes have their own charm, for many the most inspiring attractions are to be found **east from Eugene** along a trio of state roads: **Highway 126**, which leads into the central core of the mountains and is one of Oregon's finest drives; **Highway 242**, a seasonal route that is unlike any stretch in the Pacific Northwest for its eerie and bizarre beauty; and **Highway 58**, heading southeast in the general direction of Crater Lake. Any of these roads must be regarded as a first option for those serious about exploring the Western or the High Cascades.

Practicalities

Most of the routes from Eugene lead into the **Willamette National Forest**, part of the larger **Deschutes National Forest**. For **information** on approaching this expansive terrain, contact the Willamette National Forest Office, in downtown Eugene at 211 E 7th Ave and Pearl (Mon–Fri 8am–4.30pm; ☎541/225-6300, ⓦwww.fs.fed.us/r6/willamette), which carries a full range of maps, trail details, and information, and can provide Northwest Forest Passes ($5) for many off-road areas. The office does not, however, provide the free limited-access permits that are designed to prevent overcrowding at key areas (such as Pamelia Lake, see p.241) in peak months; these you'll need to get from local ranger stations in each forest district. Within the national forest, parts of the McKenzie River offer excellent **whitewater rafting** and **boating**. Several Eugene- and Bend-based companies organize excursions – contact the nearest visitor center or try Rapid River Rafters, 500 SW Bond St #160, Bend ($65–85 per full-day trip; ☎541/382-1514 or 1-800/962-3327, ⓦwww.rapidriverrafters.com), or Oregon Whitewater Adventures Inc, 39620 Deerhorn Rd, just east of Eugene in Springfield ($85 per full-day trip; ☎541/746-5422 or 1-800/820-7238, ⓦwww.oregonwhitewater.com).

As far as public transit is concerned, Lane Transit District runs a regular #91 **bus** (Mon–Fri 4 daily, Sat & Sun 2 daily; $1.25) out of Eugene along Hwy 126 as far as the McKenzie Bridge Ranger Station – the journey takes about an hour and a half, and you'll be dropped close to the foot of the McKenzie River National Recreation Trail (see below).

Highway 126

Highway 126 can be considered the Main Street of the Cascades, a resplendent stretch that connects many of the region's iconic peaks and valleys into one eye-opening concourse, along the way passing glittering lakes, secret ice caves, stark lava beds, and countless rugged hiking trails – the latter some of the best treks in the state, from simple, lovely riverside routes to gut-wrenching trips past cliff walls and rock slides. The truly gung-ho can even take a chance scaling a mountain – though you'll need plenty of preparation and skill. Contact area ranger stations for details on maps, outfitters, and any permit or wilderness requirements.

McKenzie River Valley to Clear Lake

Heading east from Eugene into Willamette National Forest, Highway 126 tracks along the **McKenzie River Valley**, passing through miles of fruit and nut orchards before arriving at **Aufderheide Scenic Drive**, whose turnoff is 41 miles east of Eugene. This twisting, verdant concourse travels through thickly forested glades and around canyons and lakeshores, following the path of the south McKenzie and Willamette rivers. For 57 miles the drive snakes bewitchingly through this fetching topography, providing good opportunities for hiking and cycling as well, ultimately reaching Highway 58 near Oakridge. Initially, though, its most popular sight is **Cougar Reservoir**, a monumental dammed-up lake high in a mountain canyon that is best known for its **Terwilliger Hot Springs** (also known as Cougar Hot Springs; eleven miles south of the turnoff from Hwy 126), a free, day-use-only set of seven hot and warm pools, which range from scalding to tepid the farther you descend along the hillside; many visitors take the opportunity to enter them *au naturel*. They're located a half-mile from the parking lot, accessed by a narrow dirt path. About twenty miles farther along the Scenic Drive, just past Roaring River campground, you come to the highest point on the drive at **Box Canyon**, featuring a series of meadows grazed by deer and elk, along with the occasional bear or mountain lion. There's a horse camp nearby, along with stunning trails leading past waterfalls, mountain ridges, and the source of several state rivers.

Continuing east on Hwy 126 you soon come to the village of **McKenzie Bridge**, near the trailhead for what might be the best mountain bike course in Oregon, or at least the most scenic – the 🚶 **McKenzie River Trail**. This 25-mile one-way route passes a variety of eye-catching environs, from bucolic lakes to gushing rivers and waterfalls to thick forest cover, but the first ten miles are the most difficult as you try to navigate sharp and ropy lava fields without your tires getting punctured. Plan on taking at least eight hours to make a round-trip on the trail. Just beyond McKenzie Bridge are the McKenzie Bridge Ranger Station (8am–4.30pm: summer daily, rest of the year Mon–Fri only; ☎541/822-3381) and the medium-size and very popular **Paradise campground** (April–Oct; ☎541/822-3381; $14), pleasantly tucked away in the dense forest close to the river. One mile further on there's a fork in the road and Hwy 242 (see below) splits off to the east, leaving Hwy 126 to wend its way north, climbing steeply as it follows the course of the McKenzie River. The first major commercially developed sight after the fork is **Belknap Hot Springs** (☎541/822-3512, 🌐www.belknaphotsprings.com; ⑤), a simple motel with several pools of heated mineral water ($6.50 per hour/$10.50 per day for non-guests), eighteen lodge rooms, and seven cabins. Of course, the surrounding forest has several isolated sites hosting hot springs for no charge, but you'll have to do a bit of research through the ranger stations and have a detailed hiking map to find them. Seven miles north on Hwy 126 is the access road to **Koosah Falls**, a 70ft waterfall flowing off a lava ridge, which is connected by a short path to **Sahalie Falls**, a higher and grander version of the same thing.

Edged by lava flows another mile or so farther north, the delightful **Cold Water Cove campground** (May–Oct; ☎541/822-3381; $14) overlooks the beautiful blue-green **Clear Lake**, the source of the McKenzie River, which was dammed by onrushing lava some three thousand years ago. Even today, its glimmering waters cloak a submerged forest valley, and if you look hard enough you may even see the skeletons of ancient drowned trees. Two miles north is the eastern end of the **McKenzie River National Recreation Trail** (see p.243), though for mountain biking the route is best covered starting from the west.

The Santiam Pass to Black Butte

Highway 126 takes a turn to the east after two more miles and merges with Hwy 20. A short distance from here, Hwy 22 leads back to Salem (see p.197), while the Hwy 126/20 combination rises up to the **Santiam Pass**, crossing through the heart of the Cascades at nearly five thousand feet. Splendid mountain scenery dominates all vistas, with the gnarled rocky claws of **Three-Fingered Jack** rising to the north just a few thousand feet above the pass, and the spiky crest of **Mount Washington** looming over the road's southern flank. Not surprisingly, there is a wealth of fine hiking trails and outdoor adventures to be had in the area, whether boating on pristine lakes or scaling rocky cliffs; for more information, contact the Deschutes National Forest office in Bend, 1001 SW Emkay Drive (Mon–Fri 7.45am–4.30pm; ☎541/383-5300, ⓦwww .fs.fed.us/r6/centraloregon). More prominent, though, are the number of ski centers and "sno-parks" scattered along this portion of Hwy 126/20; you can give any of them a go – many offer options for downhill or cross-country skiing, snowboarding, and the like in winter and hiking and mountain biking the rest of the year. The biggest name is **Hoodoo Ski Bowl** (lift tickets $39–42; ☎541/822-3799, ⓦwww.hoodoo.com), unmissable just west of the Santiam Pass, with its two lodges, five chairlifts, and forty or so runs, some of them with oddball names like "Frank's Flight" and "Art's Alley."

Less than a mile from the ski bowl you pass over the high ridgeline that marks the north-south route of the **Pacific Crest Trail**, connecting a broad swath of the mountains along the West Coast (see ⓦwww.pcta.org for more details). Just beyond lie a pair of glacially carved lakes of very different character. **Suttle Lake** is a shallow, rectangular body of water popular for trout fishing, boating, and swimming, with a trio of nice summer campgrounds ($14; reserve at ☎1-877/444-6777) and the *Lodge at Suttle Lake* (☎541/595-2628, ⓦwww. thelodgeatsuttlelake.com), with rooms and suites set in a handsome wooden lodge (❽–❾), as well as large, plush cabins (❾) and six cheaper cabins with primitive facilities (❹).

A half-mile west, **Blue Lake** is a small, deep freshwater pit that has only a fifth the surface area of its neighbor but six times the depth. Indeed, this 300ft-deep bowl is richly blue in color, sitting serenely in the shadow of Mount Washington. It owes its origin to a massive geothermal blowout, which cut this deep chasm and gave meltwater the chance to fill it in – many appropriately refer to it as Crater Lake in miniature. A few miles beyond these lakes, the highway cruises past the idyllic headwaters of the **Metolius River** – another good area for fishing, hiking, and the like – flowing through the little recreational town of **Camp Sherman** and past the resort of **Black Butte** (☎1-800/452-7455, ⓦwww.blackbutteranch.com; ❺–❽ by season), whose basic condos for rent can be quite affordable if you arrive during the winter low season, though the warmer months are better for golf, tennis, and horseback riding. The similar *Metolius River Resort*, whose stylish modern cabins are just west of Black Butte at 25551 SW Forest Road 1419 (call for directions at ☎1-800/818-7688, ⓦwww.metoliusriverresort.com; ❼–❽ by season), hosts one of the best restaurants in the region, ⅄ the *Kokanee Café* (late April to Oct; ☎541/595-6420), which serves up terrific Northwest Cuisine, including braised short ribs, wild salmon, and lavender-honey-glazed duck breast.

Sisters

About eight miles southeast of Black Butte, Hwy 126 wends its way to the mountain hamlet of **SISTERS**, with US-97 less than twenty miles farther east. Featuring Wild West–style, false-fronted buildings, Sisters began as a military post and logging town in the shadow of looming Cascade Range and took its name from the Three Sisters peaks southwest of town. However, after several fires immolated the place and the timber trade met its demise, the town had to find a new purpose – drawing the overspill of summer visitors from nearby Bend.

These days it sports a few restored old buildings along **East Cascade Avenue**, around which you can find some interesting **restaurants**. These include *Bronco Billy's*, no. 190 (T541/549-0361), serving up solid steaks, seafood, and barbecue in the former Sisters Hotel, a renovated 1912 relic that is the town's most historic structure. The nearby *Sisters Bakery*, no. 251 (T541/549-0361), based in the shell of a 1925 general store, is good for its doughnuts, pastries, breads, and espresso. More surprisingly, a top regional restaurant is sited here, *Jen's Garden*, 403 E Hood Ave (Wed–Sun; T541/549-2699), a fine Southern French restaurant whose rotating menu may include items like grilled rack of lamb in a mixed-berry port wine reduction with au gratin potatoes.

There are a few decent places to **stay** in town. The best and nicest of the local B&Bs is the *Blue Spruce*, 444 S Spruce St (T541/549-9644 or 1-888/328-9644, Wwww.bluesprucebandb.com; ●), with fireplaces, fridges, and Jacuzzis, plus stylish room decor with wood-planked walls and Western antiques like log trunks and wagon wheels. A bit cheaper, the *Best Western Ponderosa Lodge*, 505 Hwy 20 W (T1-888/549-4321 or 541/549-1234, Wwww.bestwesternsisters.com; ●), has rooms and suites that have been recently renovated, with fridges and microwaves, and an onsite pool and hot tub. Finally, the most central, the *Grand Palace Hotel*, 101 E Cascade Ave (T541/549-2211, Wwww.grandpalacehotelsisters.com; ●), offers five Western-themed rooms with DVD players and kitchenettes.

Highway 242

Although appearing on maps as a handy, 36-mile shortcut from McKenzie Bridge west to Sisters, **HIGHWAY 242** is in reality one of the state's twistiest and slowest routes – but also one of its most austere and strangely beautiful. Not publicly accessible between November and June, when steady snowfall makes it impassable, the highway has countless waysides for rugged mountain hikes and awe-inspiring vistas of many of the peaks in the central Cascades. Up to just a few thousand years ago, this area was for millions of years the scene of violent geological upheavals. Nearby mountains belched up towers of smoke and ash, sent bombs of pumice and basalt hurtling through the air, and covered the landscape with rivers of free-flowing lava – which left many square miles of the terrain covered in jagged black hillocks and rutted craters. A trip along Hwy 242 almost demands a closer look on foot, and luckily there are plenty of places to go exploring.

Proxy Falls to the McKenzie Pass

Starting from the western junction where Hwy 126 turns north, Hwy 242 leads east seven miles toward the turnout for **Proxy Falls**. This pair of waterfalls, reached on an easy mile-and-a-half loop trail, is divided into upper and lower sections with drops of 125ft and 200ft, the water tumbling over the rocky ledge only to seemingly disappear at the bottom. This odd effect occurs as the water literally vanishes into thousands of tiny holes in the porous lava rock. Less than two miles east on Hwy 242 lies the striking and serene landscape of **Linton Lake**, where a mile-and-a-half one-way trail leads you to a curious mountain lake and its waterfall, sitting amid a forest and meadow into which chunks of broken lava have abruptly, but not completely, intruded. Less than five miles away, as the highway begins to turn sharply through dips and switchbacks, sometimes narrowing to sixteen feet or so, you reach **Scott Lake**, a pristine setting with a pleasant **campground** (July–Oct; free).

The stark lava terrain begins in earnest about three miles east at **Belknap Crater**, an ominous-looking cinder cone whose shield volcano was responsible in large part for the torrential flood of basalt you begin to see everywhere along the road, estimated to be less than three thousand years old. A few miles farther east is the 5300ft **McKenzie Pass**, the road's highest and most striking plateau, which leads into a 65-square-mile landscape of nothing but solidified lava, broken into its own strange jagged swirl of mounds, hills, troughs, and ridges. Undoubtedly the best place to view the dark lunar topography is at the **Dee Wright Observatory**, a 1930s tower just off Hwy 242, which is itself built of chunky lava rocks, making it look as if it simply rose up out of the ground. Inside the structure, crude windows offer startling views of the many peaks in the region, and just beyond it, a half-mile asphalt path leads you around this rough, jagged world, which 1960s astronauts used as an imitation moonscape to practice walking in their space suits. In the 1860s, pioneers on the **Deschutes Wagon Road** paid a toll of $2 for the privilege of crossing the dreadful surface with a wagon and pair of horses.

The Three Sisters Wilderness

As the road continues to the east you go deeper into the harsh land of the **Three Sisters Wilderness**, and the grand monuments of the **Three Sisters** and **Broken Top** make a clearer appearance to the south. The former peaks – also known as Faith, Hope, and Charity – are in various states of geological activity, with the South Sister being the most recently active. By contrast, Broken Top is clearly dormant, and looks as though it's fought a losing battle with the glaciers that have scoured and ruined its summit. It makes for an interesting hiking excursion if you have a good map to get there; contact the Deschutes National Forest office in Bend for more details (see p.228). There are many serious and worthy treks in the area, but if you pick only one, consider the 7.5-mile round-trip jaunt up **Black Crater** ($5 Northwest Forest Pass required), with its trailhead about four miles east of the observatory. While there are no facilities en route and the lengthy slog demands great stamina, the views from the crest of this 7300ft former volcano are truly awe-inspiring, with the craggy, glacier-damaged face of **North Sister** rising nearby and a panoply of mountain peaks stretching far into the distance. The crater itself atop the mountain – a dark, exploded remnant from which rivers of lava and columns of ash once issued mercilessly – is also bleakly fascinating.

Recently, in summer 2006, the **Black Crater Fire** in the general area burned some ten thousand acres of wilderness south of Highway 242 and nearly destroyed the town of Sisters in the process. While the burned acreage hardly makes the lava lands look any different, you may find extensive charred trees and immolated groundcover surrounding them for years to come.

The drama of Highway 242 lessens considerably on the last ten miles toward the town of Sisters (see p.245), as you return to alpine meadows, pleasant lakes, and an altogether less threatening landscape. Should you want to spend the night here, just off the roadside, the **Cold Springs Campground** ($12), four miles from town, provides 23 sites in the shadow of the mountains. Less than a mile east, a more unexpected attraction can be found at the edge of private

△ Dee Wright Observatory

Patterson Ranch, where crowds of llamas and elk can be observed firsthand from a wayside along the highway.

Highway 58

Heading southeast from Eugene to US-97 on the way to Crater Lake, **HIGHWAY 58** travels 86 miles and crosses the crest of the Cascades at the 5100ft **Willamette Pass**. Well before it gets there, it skirts a number of thin, angular lakes carved into shape by glaciers from the last Ice Age and earlier, as well as numerous campgrounds, hiking trails, and gorgeous mountain vistas.

Elijah Bristow State Park, seventeen miles from Eugene, is a great spot for horseback riding, fishing, and exploring the scenery on ten miles of trails, with the surrounding forests and wetlands featuring seasonal displays of bald eagles, osprey, and herons. For the next ten miles there are long, spindly reservoirs along the highway visible at **Dexter** and **Lookout Point**. For camping in the outback, try **Fall Creek**, 27 miles southeast of Eugene on Hwy 58 ($3 day-use fee, campsites May–Sept $15), which has a reservoir for boating and 47 primitive sites sitting at the western edge of **Willamette National Forest**. Back on the highway, it's just seven miles to the burg of **Westfir**, home to the **Office Covered Bridge**, which is the state's longest such span at 180ft and looks like a stretched-out red barn plunked across a river. From town you can take a sharp left northward to access Aufderheide Scenic Drive (see p.243) up to Hwy 126 or continue a few miles east to the workaday town of **Oakridge**, really just a place to gas up and get a snack.

Twenty-three miles past Oakridge, 286ft **Salt Creek Falls** ($5 day-use fee) is the second-highest waterfall in the state; an excellent 2.5-mile trek around its high basaltic cliffs provides good views of it (there are also other, smaller falls nearby worth a look). Eight miles farther along, just a few miles north of Hwy

58 and sitting on the east side of the Pacific Crest Trail, **Waldo Lake**, with a depth of 420ft, is the state's second-deepest undammed lake. The wonderfully pristine waters make a fine spot for canoeing; on its shores you can bicycle or ride horses, or **camp** in any of three Forest Service sites (July–Sept; $14). Especially good is the lakeside hiking circuit, which runs 21 miles through varying terrain from idyllic mountain meadows to jagged lava cliffs.

Back on Hwy 58 you soon cross over the Willamette Pass and approach the recreational heart of the area: striking **Odell** and **Crescent lakes**, which sit near the road and offer prime fishing (for salmon and trout), camping, and hiking opportunities. Immediately north of the road, the **Willamette Pass Ski Area** (Nov–April; lift tickets $38; ℡541/345-SNOW, Ⓦwww.willamettepass .com) draws winter adventurers for its four chairlifts and 25 or so runs.

From here, continue another five miles to the northbound turnoff for the **Cascade Lakes Highway** (see p.231) back up to Mount Bachelor and Bend, reach US-97 another ten miles past the turnoff, or venture south of Highway 58 to explore the wilderness around **Diamond Peak**, a dormant shield volcano that sits amid a cluster of smaller volcanoes and has been undergoing erosion for thousands of years. At 8700ft, it is one of the smaller of the High Cascades. Still, there are enough intact snow fields that **ski mountaineering** is possible, involving plenty of hiking and white-knuckle schussing across the uneven terrain; less daring outdoor lovers can be content with the good trails and **campgrounds** (most open April or May to Oct; contact the Deschutes National Forest office in Bend, at 1001 SW Emkay Drive (Mon–Fri 7.45am–4.30pm; ℡541/383-5300, Ⓦwww.fs.fed.us/r6/centraloregon).

The Diamond Lake Highway

Although the trans-Cascade routes from Salem and Eugene are deservedly the most popular access roads across the mountains, the southerly routes across the Cascades also have a number of nice options for exploring the forested outback. One of the best routes is the **DIAMOND LAKE HIGHWAY**, which links Roseburg to Mount Thielsen and, beyond that, Crater Lake (see p.233). Following the curving banks of the nationally recognized "Wild and Scenic" **Umpqua River**, this route, also known as **Highway 138**, provides a wonderful trip through beguiling forest and volcanic scenery, highlighted by waterfalls, whitewater rapids, hidden caves, rocky chasms, and even a few hot springs. To orient yourself with the area you should drop by the **Umpqua National Forest office**, in Roseburg at 2900 NW Stewart Pkwy (℡541/672-6601, Ⓦwww.fs.fed.us/r6/umpqua), or the **ranger stations** in Glide, 16 miles east at 18782 Hwy 138 (℡541/496-3532), or nearby Idleyld Park, 2020 Toketee Ranger Station Rd (℡541/498-2531), which can all provide more information on the many hiking trails and seasonal campgrounds (often $10–16) available in the area.

In tiny Glide, the North Umpqua and the Little rivers meet appropriately at **Colliding Rivers**, an excellent spot for a picnic in the face of the dramatic, onrushing waters. Just a few miles east of town, signs mark the beginning of the 77-mile **North Umpqua Trail**, which follows the river up to Lemolo Falls and for hikers or mountain bikers offers stunning views of lava flows, rocky cliffs, and violent river rapids, with numerous meadows, glades, and forests along the way. If you're interested in the full journey, make sure to pick up a trail map at the forest office and be prepared to **camp** ($10–16; $5 Northwest Forest Pass required) at the mostly primitive campgrounds en route.

Job's Garden Geological Area and its chunky columns of lava rock in gnarled formation lie eight miles farther east along the highway, while fifteen miles beyond this is a collection of basalt columns peppering the roadside. The most well known of these is **Eagle Rock**, a mottled rocky tower that developed long ago as a volcanic plug – a big knob of magma that has protruded upward and been stripped and revealed by erosion. Six and eight miles farther along short trails, you reach two of southern Oregon's best waterfalls – **Toketee**, a spire of water 135ft high falling from a curving notch in the rock, and **Watson**, twice as high and the tallest waterfall in the region. Between these lies the turnoff for the Toketee Reservoir, north of which Thorn Prairie Road leads to the pleasantly isolated setting of **Umpqua Hot Springs** (day-use only; free). Accessed by a half-mile hike, this small tub on a steep hillside has 106°F (41°C) water flowing through it.

Back on Hwy 138, over the next twenty miles the road takes a sharp turn to the south and eventually leads up toward the slopes of Crater Lake (see p.233). Just before the junction of Hwy 230, which leads southwest to Hwy 62 and the south side of Crater Lake, you pass the eastern edge of **Diamond Lake**, a recreational complex highlighted by the **Diamond Lake Resort** (☎1-800/733-7593, ⓦwww.diamondlake.net), which offers kayaking, boating, canoeing, cycling, skiing, and so forth, and **lodging** from basic motel rooms (❹) to suites with Jacuzzis (❼) to spacious cabins on the lake (❼–❽). There are also some four hundred Forest Service **campsites** ($12–16) around the lake.

Rising on opposite sides of the lake are two grand mountains. To the west, **Mount Bailey** looms 8300ft tall and is accessible on forest roads beginning southwest of the lake. From here you can take a strenuous, ten-mile jaunt up and down its slopes and check out the fractured ridge-rock around its summit. On the other side of the lake, across Hwy 138, lies the trailhead leading to **Mount Thielsen**, a 9200ft dormant volcano with a splintered silhouette, rising up to a jagged, razorlike peak that is only ten feet wide – the result of some 300,000 years of erosion. Nonetheless, experienced hikers and climbers can make it up the slope on an eight-mile round-trip, though for the last push to the pinnacle you're forced to scramble over spiky boulders and shattered chunks of lava rock. At the summit, rock hounds may be able to spot the rare mineral **fulgurite**, which has formed due to repeated lightning strikes on the mountain's narrow summit – keep away from here at any sign of a storm. For more information on climbing either of these mountains, contact the Umpqua National Forest office in Roseburg or the ranger stations east of town (see opposite).

Highway 62

The fast and direct route to Crater Lake from Medford, **HIGHWAY 62**, has many charms, beginning some thirty miles north from Medford alongside the upper reaches of the **Rogue River**, where you can access trailheads for the lovely and curving **Rogue River Trail**. Like other sights in this wilderness, you can find more about it at the Rogue River National Forest office, 333 W 8th St in Medford (Mon–Fri 8am–4.30pm; ☎541/858-2200, ⓦwww.fs.fed.us/r6 /rogue-siskiyou), or the High Cascade Ranger Station, 47201 Hwy 62 in Prospect (same hours; ☎541/560-3400). About ten miles before you get to the ranger station, though, you can **camp** at one of the better state parks in the region, **Joseph H. Stewart State Park** (☎1-800/551-6949; $10–16), located 35 miles north of Medford next to the Lost Creek Reservoir, with good angling and hiking. Less than ten miles east, at the little town of **Prospect**, there are two options: continue north toward Crater Lake on Hwy 62 or make a sharp turn to the southeast, following forest roads into the 113,000-acres **Sky Lakes Wilderness**. If you take the second route, you can explore no fewer than two hundred lakes of varying size, peppered throughout the forest, with only a network of rough trails (or the odd unimproved road) connecting them. The north part of the area is also riddled with pumice fields and volcanic debris deposited from the ancient eruption of Mount Mazama. Toward the southern part of the wilderness, the many pools, ponds, and lakes – cut into the rock during the last Ice Age by retreating glaciers – make a perfectly inviting setting for camping ($5 Northwest Forest Pass required; see p.228) amid a lovely and glistening landscape. You can find out much more about them by heading south from Prospect along Butte Falls–Prospect Road to the little town of **Butte Falls**, where staff at the ranger station, at 800 Laurel St (Mon–Fri 8am–4.30pm; ☏541/865-2700), can tell you everything you need to know.

Nine miles north of Prospect on Hwy 62, the **Natural Bridge** is a curious geological phenomenon in which the Rogue River is channeled along a narrow rocky gorge until it disappears into an ancient lava tube, over which stretches the striking bridge itself. A two-and-a-half-mile trek leads you around the area for a closer look at this odd sight, and you can also **camp** here (May–Oct; $8). A few miles north, **Union Creek** marks the place where Hwy 62 splits from Hwy 230, which leads 25 miles north through a seemingly unending stand of Douglas fir trees to reach Diamond Lake (see p.249). Hwy 62, however, takes a turn to the east and then the south as it passes by the lower edge of Crater Lake. Seventeen miles from the turnoff you reach **Fort Klamath**, the former federal military base dating from 1863, where Captain Jack and three other Modoc natives were hanged in one of the area's most shameful episodes (see box, p.237).

From here it's ten miles to the edge of the lakeshore of **Agency** and **Upper Klamath lakes**, huge and beautiful preserves lined by several National Wildlife Refuges (see p.238). After merging with US-97, you finally reach the town of Klamath Falls (see p.236) at the latter lake's southern edge.

Lake of the Woods Highway

Traversing the southern edge of the Oregon Cascades, almost to the northern flank of the Klamath Mountains, is **Highway 140**, or the **Lake of the Woods Highway**. A much more direct route between Medford and Klamath Falls than Hwy 62, this road still has plenty of scenic splendor along its 79 miles. In the Rogue River National Forest office in Medford (see p.249), or at the ranger station up in the village of Butte Falls (see above), you can get information on the highway and its various campgrounds, hiking trails, and so on. The really distinctive places along the way are right in the middle, about halfway between Klamath Falls and Medford. The first of these is attractive **Fish Lake**, at the junction of the road from Butte Falls 35 miles east of Medford, which, not surprisingly, offers excellent fishing ($3 day-use fee) for rainbow and brook trout, and ice fishing at the height of winter. You can also **camp** here (May to mid-Oct, $15), as you can a few miles east at **Lake of the Woods** (☏866/201-4194, ⓦwww.lakeofthewoodsresort.com), a high mountain resort with sparkling waters and plenty of recreational activities, as well as 26 **cabins** that are rentable for two nights or more in the summer (❻–❺), or a week at a time the rest of the year, starting at $260.

On the north side of the highway, though, lies the real reason for driving out this far – **Mount McLoughlin**. With a trailhead reached by Forest Road 3650, located between the two lakes, the mountain is the tallest in southern Oregon at 9500ft, cuts a dashing silhouette against the thick forests and volcanic scenery, and best of all is climbable. The mountain's summit is reached on an 11.5-mile loop trail, which crosses the Pacific Crest Trail near its base. Higher up, the mountain's frame gets more daunting, as you rise past the tree line to encounter rough blocks of andesite or basalt and the hardscrabble remnants of icy moraines. Near the summit it's necessary to scramble over the jagged terrain with nimble footwork, but the view from the top is well worth it – a stunning vista of magnificent snowy peaks stretching from California's Mount Shasta in the south to Mount Jefferson, more than one hundred miles north, just visible at the edge of this great volcanic horizon.

Eastern Oregon

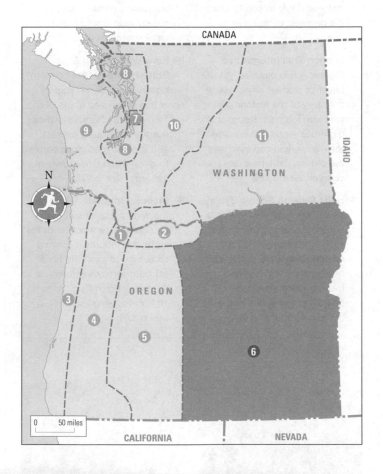

CHAPTER 6

Highlights

✳ **Pendleton Round-Up** A classic event that keeps the spirit of the Old West alive, with calf-roping, bronco-bucking, and plenty of cowboy chow and lore to satisfy even the greenest of greenhorns. See p.258

✳ **Oregon Trail Interpretive Center** A fine place to get the flavor of pioneer days, where the story of the historic trail is told with journals, relics, and dioramas – and just outside the center, you can even see the old wagon-wheel ruts yourself. See p.262

✳ **Hells Canyon Scenic Byway** This is the best way to experience the scenic glory of the yawning chasm: a 200-mile driving concourse that leads past many fine parks and trails, historic sites, and, of course, grand vistas of the canyon itself. See p.264

✳ **John Day Fossil Beds National Monument** This monument commemorates millennia of geological tumult that produced strange rock palisades, painted hills, and the curious fossils entombed within them. See p.272

✳ **Kam Wah Chung & Co State Heritage Site** Western history is vividly on display at this preserved home of a 19th-century herbalist, whose assorted antiques, trinkets, and archaic medicines testify to a forgotten Chinatown in the area. See p.275

✳ **Steens Mountain** Sitting in the windswept desert at the far southeastern corner of the state, the mountain offers a challenge to even the hardiest outdoors adventurers: a 30-mile-long trail up to the 10,000-foot-high summit. See p.279

△ Steens Mountain

Eastern Oregon

ast of the Cascades, Oregon's temperature rises, the drizzle stops, and green valleys give way to the scrubby sageland, bare hills, and stark rock formations of **Eastern Oregon**. Though it's nowhere near as popular a destination as the lush coastal areas, the austere beauty of the region is frequently eye-catching and there is a real sense of adventure in exploring this vast, sparsely populated land. Much of it is classic **cowboy country**, familiar from some Hollywood films not made in the Southwest. **Pendleton**, in the north along I-84, is the epitome of the cowboy town, where Stetsons and pickups rule the roost, especially during September's famous Pendleton Round-Up rodeo, and farther along the highway, **Baker City** has an attractive set of c.1900 architecture and pleasant small-town ambience. In the isolated northeast corner of the state is some spectacular scenery in the snowcapped **Eagle Cap Wilderness** of the Wallowa Mountains and the long deep slash of **Hells Canyon**, an immense gorge cut by the Snake River. Back in north-central Oregon, east of Bend, are the three sites that constitute the **John Day Fossil Beds**, whose remarkable geology – replete with reminders of a tumultuous volcanic past – features many prehistoric plant and animal fossils. Southeast Oregon is mostly barren and virtually uninhabited desert, but tiny **Burns** makes a useful stop for its proximity to the lakes and wetlands of the **Malheur National Wildlife Refuge** and imposing **Steens Mountain**.

Some history

The original inhabitants of Eastern (mostly northeastern) Oregon were tribes such as the Cayuse, Walla Walla, Umatilla, and, largest of all, Nez Percé, who occupied a prime slice of territory spreading across Washington, Oregon, and Idaho – making them a prime target for later white settlers. Initially, none of Eastern Oregon looked very promising to these American immigrants, though, and most hurried along the Oregon Trail to the farmland farther west. One bemoaned, "This barren, God-forsaken country is fit for nothing but to receive the footprints of the savage and his universal associate the coyote."

In the early 1860s, things changed rapidly when gold was discovered in Baker and Grant counties, prompting a short-lived **gold rush**. To feed the miners, herds of **cattle** were driven over the Cascades from the Willamette Valley, and thousands of animals were soon flourishing on the bunchgrass and meadowgrass of the interior. Neither the cattlemen nor the miners had much tolerance for the native population, which was displaced in a series of skirmishes that escalated into successive mini-wars that fizzled out only when the tribes were forced onto reservations – mostly in other states. Since

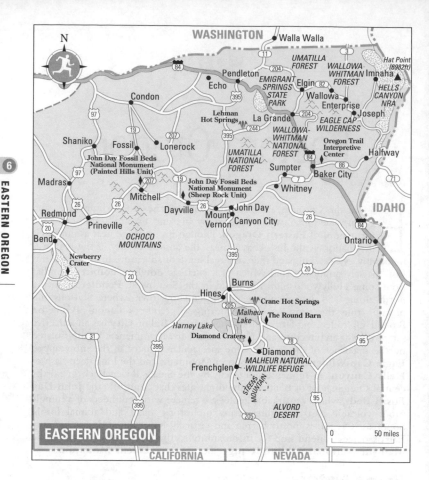

EASTERN OREGON

then, Eastern Oregon's main business has been agriculture, supplemented by forestry and tourism – though prosperity is patchy and the smaller places hang on by their economic fingertips.

Practicalities

All of Eastern Oregon's larger towns have a reasonable supply of **motels** and a few decent **hotels**, with **B&Bs** increasingly popular, too. If you're after exploring the wilderness, you should definitely consider camping. A dozen or so state parks in Eastern Oregon have **campgrounds**, many of which are open all year, with a good number bookable through a central reservation number (☎1-800/452-5687, ⍵www.reserveamerica.com). In addition, the US Forest Service operates a scattering of National Forest campgrounds. These are usually open from Memorial Day to Labor Day on a first-come, first-served basis, though a small percentage can be reserved (☎1-800/280-2267).

To get around, a **car** is essential if you're intending to do anything more than hop from town to town, and even that can be difficult by **public transportation**.

Greyhound **buses** (☎1-800/231-2222, ⓦwww.greyhound.com) connect Portland with Pendleton, La Grande, and Baker City on I-84 on the way to Boise, Idaho. A second route links Ontario with Burns and Bend. There are no Amtrak trains, and local bus services are negligible.

Northeast Oregon

Oregon's principal east-west highway, the speedy **I-84**, leaves The Dalles (see p.134) to track along a wide, parched section of the Columbia River Gorge before cutting southeast to a trio of small towns – **Pendleton, La Grande**, and **Baker City** – on its way to Ontario and the Idaho border. Much of I-84 follows the course of the **Oregon Trail** (see box, p.188), and wayside markers trace the pioneers' progress. Of particular interest are those that illuminate the problematic crossing of the **Blue Mountains**, a narrow band of peaks lying just east of Pendleton and now incorporated within the colossal **Umatilla** and **Wallowa-Whitman national forests**.

The most obvious detour from I-84 involves making a 200-mile loop to the east on the **Hells Canyon Scenic Byway**, which can be approached in either direction – though the central section is closed by snow from mid-October to June – but it's probably best to leave I-84 at La Grande to follow Hwy 82 to **Joseph**. This country town is the most agreeable base for exploring the nearby **Eagle Cap Wilderness**, the scenic highlight of the **Wallowa Mountains**, a mighty cluster of alpine peaks latticed with rugged hiking trails – again closed by snow till early summer. East of Joseph, the **Wallowa Mountain Loop Road** weaves up through the forested hills beside **Hells Canyon**, which marks part of the Oregon–Idaho border, and then meanders down to Hwy 86 near the sleepy hamlet of **Halfway**. The canyon is vast and the continent's deepest, but it has little of the high scenic drama of the Grand Canyon, as it is a low-relief gorge framed by ascending ridges rather than sheer cliffs. The canyon is best appreciated from the **Snake River**, which created it, and there are regular jet-boat and rafting excursions from the boat dock beyond the east end of Hwy 86.

Echo

About 165 miles from Portland, Interstate 84 leaves the Columbia River to cut across the undulating wheat fields of the Columbia Plateau, where the tiny settlement of **ECHO**, beside the banks of the Umatilla River just a mile or so off I-84, was once a halting point on the **Oregon Trail**. It was here that the pioneers faced a difficult choice. They could opt to travel over to the Columbia River and head west by native canoe or Hudson's Bay Company bateaux, but this was fraught with danger. So most went for the slower, overland route across the plateau, hurrying along from spring to stream in the hope that they would prove strong enough to survive the intense heat and suffocating dust or, if they arrived later, quick enough to beat the snows. This history is represented at a few sites around the little town. **Fort Henrietta Park** on the river used to be a stopover point on the trail, good for camping and doing laundry, and now has some old trail relics and a covered wagon on display. On and around **Main Street** there are also ten buildings on the National Historic Register, most dating from around 1900, though the only really eye-catching one is the 1920 terracotta and brick **Echo Bank**, 230 W Main St, which features some nice marble flooring and wrought-iron teller cages. It also houses the town **museum**

(April–Oct Sat & Sun 1.30–4.30pm; or by appointment at ☎541/376-8150), which has tribal and Oregon Trail artifacts; staff here can point out where the remains of the old wagon ruts are around town.

Pendleton

Set within a wide ring of rolling hills fifteen miles east of Echo, **PENDLETON** cultivates its cowboy reputation, and there's a great buildup to its immensely popular annual **Pendleton Round-Up**, in which traditional rodeo events such as bareback riding, steer roping, and bronco bucking are mixed with extravagant pageantry, parades, and cowboy barbecue and ranch food. All this takes places over four days in mid-September ($11–15 per rodeo event; ☎541/276-2553 or 1-800/45-RODEO, ⓦ www.pendletonroundup.com). At other times, you can see rodeo photos, costumes, saddles, and a onetime star horse, now stuffed, at the **Round-Up Hall of Fame**, under the arena grandstand on the Round-Up grounds, just west of the town center at 1205 SW Court Ave (June–Sept Mon–Sat 10am–5pm; free).

No trip to Pendleton is complete without dropping in on some of its historic **Western boutiques**. To dress the part, make your way downtown to **Red's Clothes**, 233 S Main St (☎541/278-1404), famous for its broad range of cowboy hats, from cheap $5 models to exquisite showpieces lined with mink and ermine that fetch up to $3000. Even more interesting, **Hamley & Co**, 30 SE Court Ave (☎541/278-1100), is a century-old saddler and leather merchant with plenty of Wild West duds, boots, and saddles; antique furnishings like a solid-oak bar in its upstairs *Slickfork Saloon*; and occasional fiddle, guitar, and poetry performances from cowboy troubadours.

When the rodeo isn't in town, the star turn is **Pendleton Underground**, 37 SW Emigrant Ave at 1st Street (Mar–Oct Mon–Sat 9.30am–3pm, rest of year varies; 90min; $10; ⓦ www.pendletonundergroundtours.org), regular guided tours exploring the town's extensive network of subterranean passageways. The tunnels were initially built to insulate citizens from the inclement climate, but they soon assumed other purposes and were used through Prohibition as saloons, card rooms, and brothels, as well as housing, laundries, and opium dens

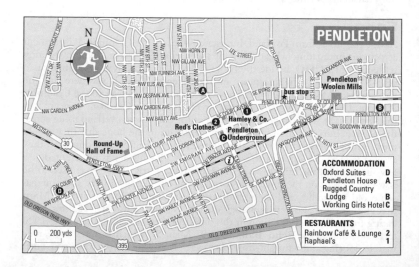

△ Pendleton Round-Up

for much-abused Chinese, who were the object of indiscriminate potshots from drunken cowboys when they walked the streets. The tour is brought to life not so much by the tunnels themselves but by a commentary full of insights into the life and times of early Pendleton, when the town had 32 saloons and 18 bordellos, including the famous "Cozy Rooms." Back outside, be sure to spend a little time strolling Pendleton's tiny **downtown**, centered on South Main Street between the river and Emigrant Avenue, the stately stone and brick buildings mostly dating to the early twentieth century.

As well as the Round-Up, Pendleton is known for its woolen goods: by the end of the nineteenth century, sheep-ranching had gained a firm hold on the local economy and, although cereal production takes pride of place today, sheep remain important. The renowned c.1900 **Pendleton Woolen Mills**, 1307 SE Court Place (guided tours Mon–Fri 9am–3pm; ℡541/276-6911, Ⓦwww .pendleton-usa.com), can initiate you into the assorted mysteries of carding, spinning, warp dressing, and weaving.

Practicalities

Greyhound **buses** pull in at 801 SE Court Ave, and the **visitor center** at 501 S Main St (Mon–Fri 9am–5pm; ℡541/276-7411 or 1-800/547-8911, Ⓦwww .pendleton-oregon.org) issues free town maps and has details of local attractions and accommodation. Pendleton has a good range of **accommodation** and prices are reasonable, though it can be nearly impossible to find anything during the Round-Up, when you should book as far in advance as possible. The clean and functional *Oxford Suites*, 2400 SW Court Place (℡1-877/545-7848, Ⓦwww.oxfordsuitespendleton.com; ❹), has rooms with fridges and microwaves, and an onsite pool and hot tub with complimentary breakfast, while the similarly inexpensive *Rugged Country Lodge*, 1807 SE Court Ave (℡541/966-6800, Ⓦwww.ruggedcountrylodge.com; ❹), has affordable suites and complimentary breakfast. More unusual is the *Working Girls Hotel*, 17 SW Emigrant Ave (June–Oct; ℡541/276-0730 or 1-800/226-6398; ❸), where four guest rooms and one suite are housed in what was once – until the 1950s, in fact – a brothel. The conversion of the premises is successful, if a little frugal, and the rooms – except for one – have shared bathrooms. As for **B&Bs**, the *Pendleton House*, pleasantly situated just across the river from downtown at 311 N Main St (☏541/276 8581 or 1-800/700-8581, ⓦ www.pendletonhousebnb .com; ⑤), occupies a handsome old villa of Italianate design and has five attractively furnished rooms, one en suite.

Pendleton's **cafes** and **restaurants** tend to have basic, all-American fare with burgers, steaks, baked potatoes, and huge breakfasts. The best of the lot is the *Rainbow Café and Lounge*, 209 S Main St (☏541/276-4120), an atmospheric place of wooden booths with intriguing Round-Up memorabilia plastered over the walls, doling out rib-stuffing burgers, sandwiches, and chicken-fried steak. Alternatively, ⚒ *Raphael's*, 233 SE 4th St (☏541/276-8500), offers a touch of upscale and innovative Northwest Cuisine, from crab legs and salmon to barbecued elk chops and glazed rattlesnake.

The La Grande area

Leaving Pendleton, it's just forty miles north to Washington's Walla Walla (see p.459) on Hwy 11, or you can continue southeast on I-84, slicing across the open range before climbing up into the **Blue Mountains**, divided between the Umatilla and Wallowa-Whitman national forests. It took the wagons of the early emigrants three or four days to cross this range; they would pause at what is now **Emigrant Springs State Park** – beside I-84 at Exit 234 – to wait for stragglers and prepare themselves for the descent into the valley below. For many, the "Blues" were a frightening place: the thick forest was confusing and the nocturnal cries of the cougars eerie and demoralizing. Nowadays, the state park is a lovely spot to break your journey, and there's a small **campground** (☏541/983-2277; $12–16) with a handful of cabins ($20–35) here, too. On the other side of the mountains, there's another, much smaller campground ($5–8) at **Hilgard Junction State Park** (I-84, Exit 252), where thousands of early emigrants once bedded down before tackling the steep climb ahead.

Beyond, on the east side of the Blue Mountains, is the large, flat and mountain-rimmed **Grande Ronde Valley**, now mostly drained to become farmland, but once a marsh and breeding ground for birds. It was also fatally boggy to the wheels of pioneer wagons, forcing the Oregon Trail to keep to the higher but tougher ground edging the hills. The economic center of the valley is **LA GRANDE**, a simple lumber, university, and trading town. La Grande's best-looking buildings line the long main drag, **Adams Avenue** (US-30), between about Greenwood and Fourth streets, an ensemble of early-twentieth-century shops with symmetrical brickwork and stone trim. Beyond the architecture, there's little in the way of conventional sights, though the **Eastern Oregon Fire Museum**, 102 Elm St (call for hours at ☏541/963-8588; $2), is diverting if you have an affection for antique fire engines, six of which from the early twentieth century are on display. To get there, leave I-84 at Exit 261 and follow Hwy 82 into town as far as Adams and turn right. The historic downtown is three blocks ahead. One of La Grande's most popular events is mid-July's **Oregon Trail Days** (ⓦ www.oregontraildays.com), with "pioneers" camped down by the riverside, carnival rides, a quilt show, a chili-cooking contest, craft stalls, and a fiddle contest.

On the outskirts of La Grande are several noteworthy attractions, beginning with the **Ladd Marsh Wildlife Area**, off I-84 at Exit 268 (☏541/963-4954), a preserved wetland of some four thousand acres four miles south of town.

More than two hundred species of bird either nest here or pass through on their spring and fall migrations, from geese and ducks, avocets, grebes, and cranes through to hawks and bald eagles. Footpaths explore parts of the wetland and there are several observation points.

A little further afield, about fourteen miles southeast of La Grande off I-84 (Exit 265) and along Hwy 203, amenable little **UNION** was the first white settlement hereabouts, founded as an agricultural center in 1862 and becoming a gold rush boomtown later on in. Its history has produced Main Street's attractive assortment of old buildings, among them one enjoyable hotel (see below) and the **Union County Museum**, 333 S Main St (May–Oct Mon–Sat 1–4pm; $3; ☎541/562-6003), where pride of place goes to the "Cowboys Then & Now" collection. This outlines the evolution of the cowboy supported by a good range of photographs and all sorts of artifacts, from antique branding irons and barbed wire to a tack room and a chuck wagon.

In the vicinity of Union are several thermal hot springs, notably the **Forest Cove Warm Springs Pool**, a bathing and picnic spot located in the hamlet of **COVE**, about eight miles north of Union via Hwy 237, which is open only in the summer (daily 1–5pm; $6; ☎541/568-4890). Cove is also on the western edge of the Wallowa Mountains, with gravel Forest Road 6220 sneaking up to trailheads and campgrounds in the range's Eagle Cap Wilderness (see p.267). The area's other major hot springs, **Lehman Hot Springs** (Wed–Fri 10am–8pm, Sat & Sun 9am–8pm; $7; ☎541/427-3015, ⓦwww .lehmanhotsprings.com), are 38 miles southwest of La Grande off Hwy 244; there are three enticing pools here ranging, depending on the season, from 85°F to 116°F (29° to 47°C).

Practicalities

Greyhound **buses** stop in La Grande at 63276 Hwy 203. The town's **visitor center** is in the Fire Museum at 102 Elm St (Mon–Fri 9am–5pm; ☎541/963-8588 or 1-800/848-9969, ⓦwww.visitlagrande.com), issuing town maps and flyers with details of the region's attractions and hiking in the Wallowa Mountains' Eagle Cap Wilderness. More hiking advice is available at the US Forest Service **ranger station**, 3502 Adams Ave (☎541/963-7186).

With regard to **accommodation**, the best place in town is the lavish, four-room *Stang Manor*, 1612 Walnut St and Spring (☎541/963-2400 or 1-888/286-9463, ⓦwww.stangmanor.com; ❺), a refurbished timber magnate's mansion located among well-kept gardens off Adams Street at the west end of town. The proficient *Best Western Rama Inn*, 1711 21st St (☎541/963-3100 or 1-800/726-2466,ⓦwww.lagranderamainnsuites.com;❹),has more conventional rooms and suites, with onsite pool, spa, and sauna. The cheapest option, the *Union Hotel*, 326 N Main St in the small town of Union, fourteen miles from La Grande (☎541/562-6135 or 1-888/441-8928, ⓦwww.theunionhotel .com;❸), is perhaps the most enjoyable, an attractively restored 1920s hotel with sixteen pleasant rooms and suites.

The height of local **dining** is ⚐ *Foley Station*, 1114 Adams Ave (☎541/963-7473), known for its excellent Belgian waffles for breakfast, as well as oyster stew, seafood, and tender, locally raised beef and lamb for lunch and dinner. Another solid choice is *Ten Depot Street*, at the same address (☎541/963-8766), which has good pasta and seafood, as well as a mean prime-rib sandwich and wide selection of microbrews. *Mamacita's*, 2003 4th St (☎541/963-6223), serves decent, inexpensive Mexican meals, while at *Sunflower Books*, 1114 Washington Ave (☎541/963-5242), you can get coffee and cake as you browse.

From La Grande you can head southeast on I-84, and it's a quick 44 miles to Baker City, the last worthwhile stop before Idaho, another seventy miles away. Alternatively, the 200-mile Hells Canyon Scenic Byway loops northeast, running to Joseph and the Wallowa Mountains' Eagle Cap Wilderness, Hells Canyon, and Halfway along Forest Road 39 (closed Oct–June) before returning to I-84 at Baker City. To hike the Wallowas, you can avoid the long drive by approaching the mountain range from La Grande. Several roads lead up to mountain trailheads – get directions, maps, and trail advice at the La Grande visitor center or ranger station before you start out.

Baker City

In full view of the Elkhorn Mountains, **BAKER CITY** is a substantial red-brick hamlet that outlived the gold-boom days of the 1860s to prosper from agriculture and ranching. From 1876 into the 1890s, enormous herds of cattle and sheep would be assembled here, headed for the dinner plates of the East. A modest monument in honor of the **American Cowboy** celebrates those busy years; it's located in the city park at Campbell and Grove streets, just east of and across the Powder River from Main Street. Also in the park are several rusty metal spikes, relics from nineteenth-century horseshoe-throwing contests.

Opposite the park, at 2480 Grove St, the **Oregon Trail Regional Museum** (late-March to Oct daily 9am–5pm; $5) is housed in the 1920s natatorium, a combined swimming pool, ballroom, and community center. The exhibits are a motley miscellany of Wild West bric-a-brac, from various historic cars to a scale model of the movie set for the locally filmed *Paint Your Wagon*, the 1968 bomb best known as the singing debut of Clint Eastwood. The museum's main highlight is its extraordinary collection of rocks: precious stones, agates, minerals, petrified wood, fossils, and shells crowd the shelves, and in a dark room, fluorescent crystals glow weirdly under ultraviolet light.

The grand old buildings of Baker City's **Main Street** are stylish structures mostly built of local stone in a potpourri of European styles – from Gothic through Renaissance revivals. In fact, there are enough here that the little town has the second-highest number of listings (a hundred or so) on the National Historic Register in the state, many of them slowly being restored. The Italianate **Geiser Grand Hotel**, 1996 Main St, is a Victorian delight, with its conical tower, mahogany interior columns, and stained-glass ceiling; the rugged stone **St Francis Cathedral**, 2000 Church St, like a lot of buildings around here, used local volcanic tuff in its construction; and the equally impressive **Baker Tower**, now offices and condos at 1700 Main St and Auburn Ave, is a nine-story 1929 pile built as a hotel, with an high observation tower and some eye-catching Art Deco details, from filigree panels to a whole flock of bald eagles. Get a hold of the *Historic Baker City Walking Tour* guide from the visitor center, or check out Ⓦwww.historicbakercity.com, and poke around all the classic structures.

Among the sagebrush foothills five miles east of town, at 22267 Hwy 86, the **Oregon Trail Interpretive Center** ambitiously attempts to re-create the early emigrants' life on the trail (daily: April–Oct 9am–6pm; Nov–March 9am–4pm; $5; Ⓣ541/523-1843, Ⓦwww.blm.gov/or/oregontrail), using extensive dioramas, replicas, and relics from the journey. Contemporary quotations with matching illustrations are well used, dealing with a wide variety of subjects – from marital strife to the pioneers' impact on Native Americans. Background sound tapes, as well as a short video, further set the scene. Outside, you can wander down and around the hill to examine wheel ruts left by the pioneers' wagons, and during special events the staff re-create a wagon camp.

Practicalities

Greyhound **buses** stop at 515 Campbell Street beside I-84 (Exit 304), about a twenty-minute walk from Main Street. The **visitor center** is across the street at 490 Campbell St (Mon–Fri 8am–5pm; ☎541/523-3356 or 1-800/523-1235, ⓦwww.visitbaker.com) and has a list of accommodation and information on sights in town, though to get the scoop on the Wallowa Mountains and Hells Canyon (see p.257 & p.268), you're better off visiting the **Wallowa-Whitman National Forest Headquarters**, 1550 Dewey Ave, at the southern extension of Main St (☎541/523-6391). It sells hiking maps and park passes ($5), which are required by visitors intending to park at any of the trailheads, and issues detailed descriptions of hiking trails and has a list of local outdoor tour operators for everything from hunting and fishing to horse, mule, and llama expeditions.

Main Street has the best **accommodation**, including the *Baer House*, no. 2333 (☎541/523-1055, ⓦwww .baerhouse.com; ❹), a fetching 1882 Victorian B&B with rooms awash in period antiques and charming Western-flavored decor, and the opulent ☆ *Geiser Grand*, no. 1996 (☎541/523-1889, ⓦwww.geisergrand.com; ❺), a classic 1889 hotel decked out with a stained-glass ceiling and mahogany fixtures as well as smart, refurbished rooms. The surrounding Wallowa-Whitman National Forest has many **campgrounds**; get details from the visitor center. Among the limited choices for **eating**, try *Barley Brown's Brewpub*, 2190 Main St (☎541/523-4266), for its dependable pub fare and good microbrews; the upscale *Geiser Grill* restaurant in the *Geiser Grand* hotel for its fresh regional cuisine; and the *Baker City Cafe*, 1840 Main St (☎541/523-6099), for its affordable pizza, pasta, and sandwiches.

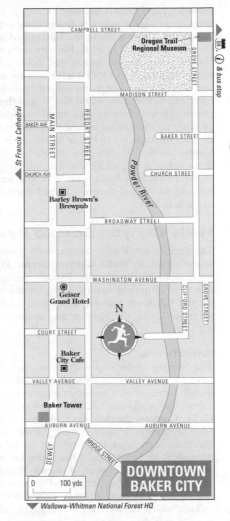

Wallowa-Whitman National Forest HQ

Moving on from Baker

Despite its distant location, Baker is something of a **crossroads**: from here, Hwy 7 pushes west across the Elkhorn Mountains for Hwy 26 and the John Day Valley (see p.274), while Hwy 86 is the first – or last – leg of the 200-mile Hells Canyon Scenic Byway (see below). Heading southeast, I-84 makes a long, dull passage to **ONTARIO**, seventy miles away, infamous as the former site of relocation centers for several thousand Japanese Americans who were stuck out here during World War II, and these days home to the state's largest prison. There's obviously no reason to linger, unless you want to find out more about the various people who have populated this parched terrain, from Basques to Hispanics to Paiute natives, at the extensive **Four Rivers Cultural Center**, 676 SW 5th Ave (Mon–Sat 10am–5pm; $4; ℡541/889-8191, Ⓦwww.4rcc.com), which also has involving displays and dioramas on the rise of the railroads, irrigation projects, and internment camps – with a replica barracks and actual testimonials and photos from that disgraceful episode in national history.

Hells Canyon Scenic Byway

The greatest patch of striking scenery, commanding views, and vivid flora is accessible on the **Hells Canyon Scenic Byway** (Ⓦwww.hellscanyonbyway .com), a nationally identified scenic circuit that connects many of the best and most inspiring natural sights in the state. It's a little over 200 miles for the full loop, but you'll want to take more than a day to explore it, so enticing are the state parks, assorted attractions, and historic sites of the area.

Enterprise

The first leg of the trip is the least engaging. Heading north and then east from La Grande, it's 65 uneventful miles to the burg of **ENTERPRISE**, which serves as the commercial center and county seat for the Wallowa Valley's farms and ranches. The big shindig here is a three-day blowout called **Hells Canyon Mule Days** (Ⓦwww.hellscanyonmuledays.com), held in early September. It features mule parades, mule rodeos, and such, celebrating the early settlers and prospectors hereabouts who were almost entirely dependent on the animal. Otherwise, the main reason to visit is to drop in on the US Forest Service's **Wallowa Mountains Visitor Center**, just west of town at 88401 Hwy 82 (June–Oct Mon–Sat 8am–5pm & Sun noon–5pm; rest of the year Mon–Fri 8am–5pm; ℡541/426-5546, Ⓦwww.fs.fed.us/r6 /w-w), which shows videos, sells hiking maps, and issues detailed descriptions of trails. You can also get information on hunting and fishing, mountain biking, and horse, mule, or llama expeditions up into the Eagle Cap Wilderness (see p.267) or down into Hells Canyon, where there are also jet-boat and raft trips (see p.268).

If you're using Enterprise as a base, you can **stay** in one of the two suites at *Barking Mad Farm*, 65156 Powers Rd (℡541/426-0360, Ⓦwww .barkingmadfarm.com; ❺), with nice valley views in an bucolic location; or the cheaper, cabin-style motel units of the *Country Inn*, 402 W North St (℡541/426-4986, Ⓦwww.neoregon.net/countryinn; ❸), with cozy country decor in its rooms and suites. Like a lot of small towns in Oregon, Enterprise has at least one great **microbrewery** – actually one of the top brews in the entire Northwest – ♣ *Terminal Gravity*, 803 School St (℡541/426-0158), where you can sample the goods (a hoppy but smooth pale ale) and eat some better-than-expected pub fare, too. For upscale **dining**, you'll have to head 35 miles north of Enterprise on Hwy 3 to the *RimRock Inn*, 83471 Lewiston Hwy (May–Oct; ☎541/828-7769), which serves pricey steaks and salmon and cheaper pasta and soups, with the added draw of three well-furnished **tepees** ($36) overlooking stunning Joseph Creek Canyon – bring along a sleeping bag.

Joseph

Six miles south of Enterprise is **JOSEPH**, whose wide and spacious Main Street slopes up the valley with the Wallowa Mountains as a backdrop. Joseph has become a popular tourist spot mainly because of its setting but also on account of resident sculptor David Manuel, who specializes in heroic **bronzes** depicting historical figures, visionary pioneers, frontier marshals, and noble natives – Main Street is dotted with examples of his work. They may not be to everyone's taste, but the **Manuel Museum**, 400 N Main St (March–Nov Mon–Sat 9am–8pm; Dec–Feb 10am–3pm; $6), is worth a visit for its collection of Nez Percé artifacts – among them basketry and clothing cabinets – as well as its military memorabilia, all tidily displayed alongside yet more Manuel statues. After visiting the museum, enthusiasts can tour Manuel's foundry and workshop at no extra cost (reserve at ☎541/432-7235).

Manuel is not the only sculptor in town – there are several other foundries that follow his stylistic lead, including **Valley Bronze**, 18 S Main St (☎541/432-7445), which offers foundry tours and displays finished works in its showroom. To some all this can get pretty kitschy, but keep in mind that local foundries are well regarded enough to have created the bronze wreaths and armatures for the National World War II Memorial in Washington, DC. Afterward, head for the **Wallowa County Museum**, inside an 1888 bank building at 110 S Main St (late May to late Sept daily 10am–5pm; $2), which has a good section devoted to the region's pioneers and a feature on the Nez Percé and Chief Joseph (see box, p.266), for whom the town is named. Appropriately, Joseph's main event is the five-day **Chief Joseph Days Rodeo** (☎541/432-1015, ⓦwww.chiefjosephdays.com), held over the last weekend in July – a boisterous event with bucking broncos, Western dancing, and cowboy parades.

Joseph's **visitor center** is located just off Main Street at 102 E 1st (Mon–Fri 9am–4.30pm; ☎541/432-1015). The town is easily the best base for exploring the nearby Eagle Cap Wilderness (see below), but the choice of **accommodation** is limited and reservations are advised throughout the summer. Options include *Belle Pepper's*, 101 S Mill St (☎541/432-0490, ⓦwww.bellepeppersbnb.com; ❹-❺ by season), whose three clean and modern B&B rooms are set in a stately manor, though the nicest B&B is the ⚘ *Bronze Antler*, 309 S Main St (☎541/432-0230, ⓦwww.bronzeantler .com; ❹-❻ by season), with antique European furniture in its three spacious Arts-and-Crafts-style rooms. Less expensive is the pleasant and agreeable *Chandlers' Inn*, 700 S Main St (☎541/432-9765 or 1-800/452-3781; ❹), a modern brick and shingle house with seven guest rooms and suites and a pretty garden. The cheapest decent option is the modern *Indian Lodge Motel*, 201 S Main St (☎541/432-2651, ⓦwww.indianlodgemotel.com; ❸). For **food**, the *Old Town Café*, 8 S Main St (☎541/432-9898), offers delicious sandwiches and soups, pies, and pancakes; *Wildflour Bakery*, 600 N Main St (☎541/432-7225), has fine pastries, bread, and coffee, and well as solid breakfasts and organic vegetarian cuisine; and *Embers Brewhouse*, 204 N Main St (☎541/432-2739), has serviceable pizza, calzone, and sandwiches but is best for its twenty or so regional microbrews.

The original inhabitants of the Wallowa Valley and Hells Canyon were the **Nez Percé**, so called by French Canadian trappers for their shell-pierced noses. Primarily hunter-gatherers, the Nez Percé were well disposed to white settlers, but relations soured after whites started moving into the Wallowa Valley in the 1850s. In 1855, the Nez Percé ceded a large chunk of their territory in the hope that this would allow for peaceful coexistence, but they were hopelessly optimistic. The federal government soon came back for more, and in 1863 the tribe was pressured into a second treaty that gave away yet more land – much to the disgust of **Chief Joseph**, who led a segment of the tribe that refused to sign.

With the land situation unresolved over the next fourteen years, escalating tension between the whites and the rebel faction of the Nez Percé prompted several violent incidents. Things came to a head in 1877, when the US government gave the holdouts thirty days' notice to quit their tribal lands, ordering them to move to a reservation in Idaho, as had other members of the tribe in the 1860s; if they refused, the army was to eject them. Accepting the inevitable, Chief Joseph agreed to move but asked for more time to round up livestock and avoid crossing the Snake River at a high and dangerous time. The government rejected his request, forcing the band to leave behind many of their cows and horses and negotiate a perilous river crossing, during which more animals were lost.

In the angry aftermath, three members of the tribe broke away and murdered four white settlers, turning the sad march to the reservation into a dramatic, three-month flight as Joseph tried to evade **General Oliver Howard**, who was brought in to fight the tribe and embodied a behavioral contradiction of some officers of the time: an inveterate foe of native peoples, he was also the commissioner of the Freeman's Bureau and third president and namesake of Howard University, one of the first universities in the nation open to blacks after the Civil War. Joseph proved extraordinarily adept at guerrilla warfare against the Union veteran, outmaneuvering army columns in a series of hair's-breadth escapes, but the odds were stacked against him. In October 1877 Gen. Nelson Miles finally cornered Joseph in Montana just fifty miles from the safety of the Canadian border. It was then that Chief Joseph (reportedly) made his much-quoted speech of surrender, "From where the sun now stands I will fight no more forever . . ."

The splinter band of Nez Percé were made to pay for their resistance. Instead of being moved to Idaho, they were taken to a marshy reservation in Kansas, where most died from malaria. Eventually, some survivors were carted back to Idaho to join the part of the tribe that had agreed to the relocation long before, though Chief Joseph and his remaining followers were taken separately to the Colville reservation in Washington – where they remain today. During the long years of exile, the chief petitioned the government ceaselessly, urging it to return his people to their tribal lands. Though some US newspapers praised Joseph as a "red Napoleon," one leading Oregon newspaper spoke of the "delightful repast of killing those unaccountable heathens who were brought into existence by a slight mistake." Chief Joseph died on the Colville reservation in 1904.

Wallowa Lake Village

Traveling south from Joseph, the main road passes a small but clearly signposted **cemetery** that contains the grave of – and an eloquent memorial to – Chief Joseph's father, Old Chief Joseph (1783–1872), of the Nez Percé. Thereafter, the road skirts glacially carved **Wallowa Lake**, which is supposedly inhabited by an Oregonian version of the Loch Ness monster, before slipping into **Wallowa Lake Village**, at the far end of the lake, six miles from Joseph. Much too popular for its own good, the village is crowded with lodges, cottages, and campgrounds, all packed in the narrow, forested space between the lake and the mountains. The lodges and cottages are mostly an undistinguished bunch, though the old-fashioned *Wallowa Lake Lodge*, 60060 Wallowa Lake Hwy (℡541/432-9821, ⓦwww.wallowalake.com), does have a lakeshore setting, with 22 bedrooms in the renovated 1920s lodge (❹–❻ by season) and eight pine cabins (❺–❼) close by; be sure to ask for a room with a lake view – otherwise you may end up overlooking the parking lot. Another option is *Eagle Cap Chalets*, 59879 Wallowa Lake Hwy (℡541/432-4704, ⓦeaglecapchalets .com), comprising timber chalets with motel-style rooms (❸–❹ by season) and nine modern cabins (❹–❻), with an onsite pool and spa. There's also a large and well-equipped seasonal **campground** (℡1-800/452-5687) – with yurts ($29), tent sites ($17–21), and a range of cabins ($58–70) – in the woods of **Wallowa Lake State Park**, good for its hiking, horseback riding, and canoeing. The best **restaurant** by far is ⅄ *Vali's Alpine Delicatessen*, 59811 Wallowa Lake Hwy (℡541/432-5691), just up the road from the cable car (see below), where the speciality is inexpensive, mouthwatering Hungarian food. Breakfast is served from 9 to 11am; dinner is by reservation only (no lunch). You can also get a bellyful of heavy German cuisine at late September's **Alpenfest** (℡541/432-4704), which takes place at the lake and involves lots of spirited folk dancing, yodeling, Teutonic crafts, and the inevitable Tyrolean hats and lederhosen.

Eagle Cap Wilderness

From the village, the **Wallowa Lake Tramway**, 59919 Wallowa Lake Hwy (hours vary, generally May–June 10am–4pm; July–Sept 10am–5pm; $20 return; ℡541/432 5331, ⓦwww.wallowalaketramway.com), takes fifteen minutes to hoist its passengers on an eye-opening trip with tremendous views to the top of **Mount Howard**, at 8256 feet, where short trails lead to equally magnificent overlooks. Mount Howard is on the edge of the Wallowa Mountains' 360,000-acre **Eagle Cap Wilderness** (ⓦwww.fs.fed.us/r6/w-w), which stretches away to the south and west, its granite peaks soaring above glaciated valleys, alpine lakes, and meadows. The higher slopes support spruce, white pine, larch, and mountain hemlock, and below are thick forests of ponderosa pine. This vast wilderness is crisscrossed by more than five hundred miles of **hiking trails** accessed via several dozen trailheads. For the most part, the terrain is extremely challenging, and on all but the shortest of hikes you'll need to come properly equipped – you're even advised to carry an axe or saw to clear downed trees that might block your path – and prepared for the likes of black bears and mountain lions. The trails are usually opened in early July when the snow clears, but the weather is notoriously changeable with summer temperatures ranging from 30°F to 90°F. There are some daylong hikes, but Eagle Cap is more the preserve of the **backcountry camper**. Part of the wilderness is managed by the US Forest Service, which maintains a handful of small and primitive, first-come, first-served **campgrounds** (free) in the Lostine River, Bear Creek, and Hurricane Creek areas and runs the Wallowa Mountains Visitor Center, back in Enterprise (see p.264).

At the top of Wallowa Lake Village, the **Wallowa Lake Trailhead** offers a choice of trails, some good for a short hike, others leading into the heart of the wilderness. One of the best takes you six miles up the East Fork Wallowa River to **Aneroid Lake**, flanked by towering mountains, where you can picnic before heading back. A longer, more arduous trek begins by ascending the west fork of the Wallowa River for six miles as far as **Six Mile Meadow**. Here you turn west for the short, but lung-wrenching, three-mile climb over to Horseshoe Lake, on the eastern edge of the **Lakes Basin**. Circled by mighty peaks and sprinkled with tiny lochs, this basin is the most hiked part of Eagle Cap, and a network of trails allows you to wander from lake to lake without too much difficulty – though on summer weekends the basin's popularity can make backcountry camping difficult. In all cases, get maps and trail advice at the Wallowa Mountains Visitor Center before you set out.

Highway 350 to Hells Canyon viewpoints

East from Joseph, Little Sheep Creek Road (**Highway 350**) wends across the valley to reach southbound Forest Road 39, the **Wallowa Mountain Loop Road**, which takes a surprisingly peaceable course through the forested hills to the west of Hells Canyon. The road emerges on Hwy 86 near Halfway and makes a useful shortcut but is closed by snow from October to June, sometimes later. In total, it's 62 miles from Joseph to Hwy 86, an easy drive that offers – after about 45 miles – a three-mile paved and signposted detour along Forest Road 3965 to the **Hells Canyon Overlook**. The view is stirring, with Idaho's Seven Devils mountain range rising above and the river glimmering below, its low-relief canyon edged by gradually ascending false peaks.

Alternately, instead of turning down Forest Road 39, you could continue northbound on Hwy 350 until you reach to little **Imnaha**, where over the course of 23 tough miles a narrow and vertiginous graveled Forest Road 4240 leads to Road 315 and another stunning view from **Hat Point**, site of a lookout tower. If you'd like to **stay** around here, six miles farther back on Road 4240 is the free **Saddle Creek campground**, with only four campsites available from July to November. If you're traveling anywhere in the area during the late summer or early autumn, get advice about road conditions from the Wallowa Mountains Visitor Center (see p.264) before you set out.

Hells Canyon

Marking the Idaho border, **Hells Canyon** is the deepest chasm on the continent, its 130-mile gorge a thousand feet deeper than the Grand Canyon and carved over millions of years by the **Snake River**. From the southern end of the Wallowa Mountain Loop Road, it's just six miles east on Hwy 86 to minuscule **Copperfield**, on the west side of the canyon.

Since prehistoric times, the canyon's hot and sheltered depths have provided a winter sanctuary for wildlife and local natives, and stone tools and rock carvings have been found at dozens of ancient clearings. The Nez Percé used the northern reaches of the canyon, the Shoshoni the south, but they were bitter enemies, and although they traded with each other, skirmishes were commonplace.

Both the Shoshoni and the Nez Percé were driven from the gorge in the late nineteenth century, around the time that an enterprising steamboat company keen to drum up trade gave it its provocative name. In 1974 legendary stuntman Evel Knievel almost made good on it when his attempt to cross the canyon on a motorcyle nearly ended in disaster (see box, above). Most of the canyon is now managed by the US Forest Service and preserved as **Hells Canyon National Recreation Area** (Ⓦ www.fs.fed.us/hellscanyon).

Deer, otters, mink, black bears, mountain lions, and whole herds of elk live here, along with rattlesnakes and black-widow spiders. Mechanical vehicles are banned above water level, so the most obvious ways to explore the canyon are by **boat** along the Snake River (see below) or by **hiking** – there are more than nine hundred miles of trails to choose from. The most difficult and dramatic trails zigzag down the canyon's sides – with two such trails weaving down from

Portrait of a daredevil

The archetypal stuntman **Robert Craig "Evel" Knievel** was famous both for risking his neck in death-defying stunts and for becoming a brand name applied to everything from toys and games to lunch boxes and TV shows. His record as a stuntman, however, was mixed at best.

A high-school dropout, Knievel might have endured a hardscrabble life as a **copper miner** in Butte, Montana, had he not been fired for popping a **"wheelie"** on an earth-moving machine. From this ignoble beginning, he began a wild ride in which he provoked and was frequently arrested by local police for racing his motorcycle, often crashing it in the process.

After a stint racing motocross and selling motorcycles, Knievel set to work as a stuntman in the 1960s, taking the name Evel after he rejected a promoter's initial attempt to name him after the more wicked-sounding homonym. He began with the relatively mild efforts like jumping over mountain lions and boxes of rattlesnakes, then proceeded to a series of increasingly jaw-dropping feats: bodily jumping over an oncoming motorcycle (causing a groin injury), wheeling his bike over a dozen cars and a van (broken arm and ribs), cycling over a panel truck (concussion), leaping cars in Las Vegas (broken pelvis, femur, hip, wrist, and ankles, plus a month-long coma), and jumping fifteen Mustang cars (broken leg and foot). Despite the injuries, Knievel kept it up until he was a nationally known commodity, hauling in $25,000 per jump and drawing a TV audience who waited for the next crash with breathless anticipation.

On September 8, 1974, Knievel set out to jump Hells Canyon near Twin Falls, Idaho, in one of the nation's first pay-per-view cable events. (He wanted to jump the Grand Canyon but was deterred by the authorities.) He initially planned to get a boost from his signature **"X-2 Skycycle"** rocket engines, but after they failed in two tests he decided to risk his neck without their aid. Technical difficulties bedeviled him anyway: Knievel started up the ramp to cross the canyon, but even before he was airborne the cycle's **parachute** deployed. The result was near-disaster, with the motorcycle and its rider plunging straight toward the Snake River before the wind came to the rescue and carried both to the bottom of the canyon slope.

Although the jump wasn't technically a success, it guaranteed Knievel's notoriety for the rest of the 1970s – and for once didn't cause him serious injury. He went on to do more jumps, sustain more broken bones, and tangle publicly with his family, the media, the police, and the IRS. Long retired, he has passed the daredevil baton to his son, who regularly stages death-defying leaps – though without his father's formidable celebrity.

the Hat Point and McGraw lookouts – but even hiking along the canyon bottom can be very tough going (and hot).

Hells Canyon activities

If you do decide to hike the canyon, it's essential to pick up detailed information before you set out. The **USFS visitor centers** in Enterprise (see p.264) and Baker City (see p.263) have maps, a complete list of hiking trails, and information on licensed companies offering jet-boat rides, whitewater rafting, and mule and horse expeditions. Also available is information on the USFS's twenty widely scattered primitive **campgrounds** (first-come, first-served; free or $5) – eleven in Oregon, nine in Idaho.

At Copperfield you can take the bridge over the Snake River and follow the minor road along the east (Idaho) side of the river for the 25-mile drive north to **Hells Canyon Dam**. From here, Hells Canyon Adventures (℡541/785-3352 or 1-800/422-3568, ⓦwww.hellscanyonadventures.com), one of several outfitters, runs sightseeing **jet-boat tours** (2–3hr; $35–45 per person) from late May to September, taking you skimming over whitewater rapids between the deceptively low, bare hills of the canyon. The same company also operates overnight jet-boat excursions ($285), staying in a motel in Lewiston, Idaho; one-day **whitewater rafting** trips ($170); and a "drop-off" service ($35 per person), taking you to hiking trails and fishing spots along the canyon and then picking you up later in the day or the week. For every type of boat trip, reservations are advised.

Halfway

Fifty miles east of Baker City, **HALFWAY** is no more than a scattering of old timber houses in the bowl of a valley just off Hwy 86, but it is a pleasant little place on southern end of the Hells Canyon Scenic Byway. It's worth dropping in to stay at the delightful *Clear Creek Farm B&B*, almost four miles north of town at 48212 Clear Creek Rd (ⓣ541/742-2238 or 1-800/742-4992, directions at ⓦ www.clearcreekfarm.biz; ❹). Framed by orchards and ponds and with gentle views out across the valley, the farmhouse is an immaculately restored building with a wraparound veranda, five crisply decorated, en-suite guest rooms, and a captain's quarters with its own entrance and balcony.

The Columbia Plateau

Covering nearly 200,000 square miles in north-central and northeast Oregon and eastern Washington, the **Columbia Plateau** is geologically one of the most distinctive terrains on the face of the earth. From 14 million to 17 million years ago, about 40,000 cubic miles of **molten lava** erupted from the earth and immersed the land in basaltic flows more than a mile deep – completely burying whatever topography previously existed. Scientists still don't know exactly what caused these flows – nearby Cascade mountain uplift or a meteor strike are possible candidates – but they were dramatic enough to force the Columbia River out of its old channel to occupy a new one much farther south. Today, the rolling wheat fields, country lanes, and romantic rural vistas of north-central Oregon don't give much indication of such unimaginable turmoil, though there are places where history's remnants – both human and geological – are on vivid display, making this area a great field trip if you have the time to explore.

Starting southbound from I-84 on Hwy 97, the state has marked out the region's most historically interesting route as the **Journey Through Time Scenic Byway**; most, if not all, of the area's compelling sights can be found along it, including a fine selection of photo-ready **ghost towns**. Whether they were agricultural hamlets, mining company towns, or stage stops, these semi- or fully deserted places have now become evocative emblems of the past, their clapboard schools, grange halls, and barns sitting in eerie silence. In some cases the remaining residents are aware of their towns' unique appeal and have renovated a hotel or opened a B&B, trying to draw at least a trickle of visitors from the more touristed circuit farther south near Bend.

Shaniko and Antelope

An hour's drive south of I-84, Oregon's signature ghost town is **SHANIKO**, an old railway hub and sheep-ranching center whose crumbling churches, school-house, water tower, laundry, and city hall have all been preserved in states of arrested decay, making for a strange and eye-catching setting that merits a hour's stroll amid the quiet, windswept townscape. Technically, Shaniko isn't a true ghost town – a few dozen people live here in nooks and crannies – and the few businesses that still operate include a post office and the **Shaniko Hotel**, 4th and E St (℡541/489-3441; ❹), a refurbished Western haunt whose exterior could be right out of a gunslinger movie, with wood-planked walkways, shaded veranda, and antique windows and signage. The rooms are clean and pleasant, and the proprietors should be able to tell you everything you need to know about the town and provide you with walking maps.

From Shaniko it's an eight-mile ride south on Hwy 18 to **Antelope**, even more deserted, which got national attention in the 1980s when it was briefly taken over by followers of Bhagwan Shree Rajneesh and renamed **Rajneesh** (see box below). The group's Big Muddy Ranch, found south of Hwy 218 along unimproved roads, has been turned into a Christian youth camp, Young Life, which has guest facilities (℡541/489-3100, ⓦsites.younglife.org/camps /wildhorse) if you want a closer look at the site where the bizarre spectacle played out.

Fossil

About twenty miles east of Antelope on Hwy 218 is the Clarno Unit of the John Day Fossil Beds (see p.272), and after another fifteen miles stands the

Antelope and the Bhagwan

In 1981, followers of the Indian guru **Bhagwan Shree Rajneesh** bought the **Big Muddy Ranch**, twenty miles southeast of Antelope, converting it into an agricultural commune. Dressed exclusively in shades of red – and thus sometimes known as "the orange people" – the Bhagwan's followers were a middle-class lot, mostly graduates in their 30s who came from all over the world. The commune's mishmash of Eastern philosophy and Western Growth Movement therapies raised great (and initially sympathetic) interest across Oregon – and eyebrows in conservative Antelope. The commune was an agricultural success, but despite this, relations between locals and the Rajneeshis disintegrated fast, especially when the latter took over the town council and the Bhagwan took to cruising the ranch in any one of the ninety Rolls Royces purchased for him by his acolytes. The appearance of Rajneeshi "peace patrols" clutching semi-automatic weapons did little to restore confidence in the guru's good intentions.

The Rajneeshis' hold on the community was, however, fairly short-lived. Just before the local county elections in 1984, the Rajneeshis began a "Share a Home" project that involved bussing in street people from across the US and registering them to vote here. Many vagrants later turned up in neighboring towns (without the promised bus ticket home), saying they'd been conned, drugged, or both, and creating big problems for the local authorities. Worse, an outbreak of salmonella poisoning in The Dalles turned out to have been part of a Rajneeshi strategy to lay their voting opponents low. When the law eventually moved in on the commune – by now, in early shades of Waco, an armed fortress – they discovered medical terrorism (more poisoning, the misdiagnosis of AIDS) had been used on Rajneeshi members themselves in an internal power struggle. The culprits were jailed and commune members dispersed. The Bhagwan, after a bungled attempt to flee the country, was deported to India and his fleet of cars sold off, along with the ranch, to pay debts. By 1986, embattled Antelope was quiet again and a plaque on a flagpole in the town center, dedicated to the triumph of the Antelope community over the "Rajneesh invasion," is the only sign that anything ever happened.

tiny burg of **FOSSIL**. True to its name, Fossil may not be the most lively place, but it does feature a handful of sights that provide a good introduction to the area, along with a few **B&Bs** that provide good comfort and a convenient base to access the fossil beds. The pick is the *Bridge Creek Flora Inn*, 828 Main St (☎541/763-2355, Ⓦwww.fossilinn.com; ❸), a three-story 1905 estate that's been converted into fetching accommodation, with pleasant rooms and suites and a good breakfast. The inn isn't far from the region's only **public fossil beds**, in a lot behind Wheeler High School, Main and B streets, where for $3 you can hunt for your own paleontology treasures and keep whatever you find, up to a limit of 25 pounds or so of rock per visit. It's not a scam, either: the flaky shale outcrops have numerous impressions of ancient leaves and plant matter, and with a little luck you might even take home a fossilized insect or reptile. For more recent history in town, the **Fossil Museum** (June–Aug daily 10am–2pm; donation; also by appointment at ☎541/763-2698) is located in the old schoolhouse and courthouse and has relics of local history, including church pews from the forgotten ghost town of Richmond, about 25 miles south. Indeed, despite its tiny size, Fossil has tried to make itself into a gateway for all kinds of historical exploration in recent years. At the **Paleo Lands Institute**, 401 W 4th St (☎541/763-4480, Ⓦwww.oregonpaleoproject.org), you can find out more about hikes and cycling rides that explore the area's rich geology and paleontology and go on adventure tours and activities during the summer, from two-day whitewater rafting trips down the John Day River ($350) to three-day poetry workshops in the shadow of the Painted Hills ($185), to a short guided trek on The Dalles Military Road ($45), whose construction opened up the full exploration of the fossil lands in the nineteenth century.

Condon to Hardman

Twenty miles north of Fossil on Hwy 19, **CONDON** has fewer diversions than Fossil but does boast the area's best hotel, the **Hotel Condon**, 202 S Main St (☎541/384-4624, Ⓦwww.hotelcondon.com; ❺). This historic 1920 gem has been refurbished with modern rooms and wireless Internet access, complimentary breakfast, and, in the dining room, some of the only good meals you're likely to find within a hundred miles – well-prepared Northwest Cuisine that includes short ribs, salmon, and grilled pork loin. Twenty and forty miles east of Condon off Hwy 206 are a pair of ghost towns that are worth a look if you have plenty of time to get to them. The first, **Lonerock**, is named for the huge, inexplicable boulder that sits next to its Methodist church, while the second, **Hardman**, is arguably the state's most beautiful abandoned site. Amid the grasslands and rolling hills of the landscape stands a strange collection of broken-down sheds, teetering wooden frames, and a creaky, decrepit city hall – the entire scene evoking the image of the perfect ghost town, with the whistling wind providing an appropriate soundtrack.

The John Day Fossil Beds

Simply put, the 14,000-acre **JOHN DAY FOSSIL BEDS NATIONAL MONUMENT** (Mon–Fri 9am–5pm; free; ☎541/987-2333, Ⓦwww.nps.gov/joda) is one of Oregon's essential sights, and any lengthy trip to the state should at least attempt a visit to these strangely colored rock formations, which have been carefully excavated to reveal an amazing assortment of fossils. Named after **John Day**, a member of the ill-fated Astor expedition of 1811 (see p.144), the fossil beds date from the period just after the extinction of the dinosaurs, from

△ John Day Fossil Beds

65 to 40 million years ago. Before the Cascade Mountains raised their rain-blocking peaks to the west, a subtropical rain forest covered this land in a dense jungle of palms, ferns, and tropical fruit trees. The forest was inhabited by creatures that predate the evolution of current species – *Hypertragulus*, a tiny, mouse-size deer, *Diceratherium*, a cow-size rhinoceros, and *Miohippus*, a small, three-toed horse, to name but three. As the Cascades sputtered into being, volcanic ash poured down on the forest, mixing with the rain to make a thick, muddy slurry, which fossilized bits of the leaves and fruit and then the bones and teeth of the animals. Consequently, paleontologists, who first visited the area in the 1860s, have been able to put together an epic of evolution and extinction. At the three official "units" of the monument, short **trails** wind through barren hills over crumbly textured earth, and information sheets or plaques are available at key trailheads to point out various geological and paleontological curiosities.

The Clarno Unit

Off Hwy 218 between the towns of Antelope and Fossil, the monument's **Clarno Unit** comprises a series of fossilized remnants of bark, leaves, and nuts from subtropical plants related to bananas, which flourished here 35 to 50 million years ago along with palm trees and other equatorial flora. Among the various animals that roamed through, which included crocodiles and tiny proto-horses, the most distinctive was the **brontothere**, a giant plant browser that stood more than eight feet tall and, late in its evolution, came equipped with two matching horns protruding from its skull. By taking the unit's **Trail of the Fossils**, one of three quarter-mile jaunts here, you can see up-close impressions of the plants and tiny creatures that lived in the junglelike forest conditions of those ancient days. Even more striking are the huge **palisades** that loom over the setting, massive pillars of rock created by volcanic mud flows some 44 million years ago. When these great lahars swept through the terrain, they buried scores of the hapless creatures in their wake, thus preserving them until they could be rediscovered in the modern era.

The Painted Hills Unit

South of Fossil on highways 19 and 207, the **Painted Hills Unit** is located 75 miles from Bend, alternately reached by way of Hwy 26 and the green band of the **Ochoco Mountains**, whose ponderosa and lodgepole pines are dusted over tightly bunched hills studded with canyons, meadows, and volcanic plugs. Unlike the other two units, the Painted Hills are famous for the color of the rocks rather than the relics embedded in them: striped in shades of red, gold, and brown, their smooth surface is quilted with rivulets worn by draining water. The colors become brighter when it rains and the pores in the dry, cracked earth close up, and are at their most mellifluent in the late afternoon. Mid-spring is the best time to visit here, when the **wildflowers** are in bloom and create eye-catching, almost blinding, contrast against the frail hills – with primrose, yellow bell, desert paintbrush, lilies, and purple sage among the more vivid varieties. There are several good trails, each a quarter-mile to a mile-and-a-half long, that provide more detailed views of the geology, along with the early leaf fossils discovered here in the 1920s.

The Sheep Rock Unit

A further 25 miles to the east off US-26 is the **Sheep Rock Unit**, which takes its name from the volcanic capstone that looms like the Matterhorn over the John Day River Valley. At the foot of the capstone, **Cant Ranch** (summer 9am–5.30pm, rest of the year daily 9am–4pm) is the monument's headquarters, a sheep rancher's house from 1917 that has displays and videos on the area's complex geology and fossils, as well as background on how the John Day River Valley was settled and its scientific discoveries made. The enterprising figure in this narrative is **Thomas Condon**, a Congregational minister and geologist who uncovered numerous fossils here starting in the 1860s (some of them on display at the University of Oregon's Natural History Museum; see p.205) and wrote of his adventures in several books. His namesake, the **Condon Paleontology Center** (same hours), has exhibits and multimedia presentations on the distinctive rocks and fossils of the monument. It's just two miles south of the **Blue Basin** canyon, where the clay-stone rock is a pale, greenish color, with occasional dark red flashes. The one-mile **Island in Time** trail leads into the Blue Basin – a rock-enclosed natural amphitheater – past fossil replicas, including a tortoise that hurtled to its death millions of years ago and a saber-toothed cat, while the three-mile **Blue Basin Overlook** offers a good workout and takes you past some striking, expansive vistas of the John Day River Valley.

Dayville to the Blue Mountains

Beyond the Sheep Rock turnoff, the Journey Through Time Scenic Byway continues eastward on US-26 for seven miles, along the John Day River Valley, to tiny **DAYVILLE**, easily the prettiest village hereabouts. Dayville also possesses a cozy **B&B**, the *Fish House Inn*, beside the main road (℡541/987-2124 or 1-888/286-3474, ⊛www.fishhouseinn.com; ❸), with five comfortable units on offer, as well as the entire ground floor of a 1908 guesthouse ($120) with kitchen, dining room, and three bedrooms. Moving on, it's thirty miles east through cattle-ranching country, past the valley's rambling homesteads, to **JOHN DAY**, which was originally a mining boomtown, founded when gold was discovered at nearby Canyon Creek in 1862. Along with the rush of hopeful white miners came several thousand Chinese immigrants, often to work sites abandoned as unprofitable by whites. Despite the racism that then characterized the Northwest, a Chinese herbalist **"Doc" Ing Hay** made quite a name for himself here, treating patients of both races, and his two-story home (also the local shop, temple, pharmacy, opium den, and gambling parlor) has survived. It has recently been restored as the **Kam Wah Chung & Co State Heritage Site** (daily 9am–5pm; $3), named after the Chinese labor-contracting company Hay and his partner Lung On bought in 1887. The rest of John Day's Chinatown, which once stretched down from the museum to the river, is long gone, but Hay's old home is literally stuffed with bygones – everything from old salmon tins and bootleg whiskey bottles from Prohibition days to antique herbs and medicines. The heavy steel doors and small windows are no stylistic nicety, but attest to nights when drunken cowpokes came to have "fun" at Hay's expense. Fortunately, they didn't know that by the time of his death in 1948 Ing Hay had $23,000 worth of uncashed checks under his bed.

In the vicinity, you can fish, hike, camp, or stay in a replica tepee at **Clyde Holliday State Park**, eight miles west of John Day off Hwy 26 (sites May–Nov $12–17, tepees $28), but there's little other worthwhile accommodation aside from the odd roadside motel. From here, lonely US-26 leaves the John Day Valley a few miles east of John Day, climbing over the southern reaches of the **Blue Mountains** to reach the arid buttes and plains that extend to the Idaho border.

In the middle of the mountains, just past Dixie Pass, the scenic byway continues as Hwy 7 branches off to travel northeast to Baker City (see p.262), wriggling past old gold-mining settlements and near a handful of **ghost towns** with good Western names like Bourne, Austin, Granite, and Greenhorn. With most, anywhere from two to twenty abandoned buildings are still standing (or in various stages of collapse) and you'll have to brave some dicey forest roads to get to them. A worthwhile exception is **Whitney**, just a half-mile south of Hwy 7 on County Road 529, whose weather-beaten homes and businesses are appropriately decrepit, none more so than the three-story wreck of a sawmill that used to be the town's primary employer. Amazingly enough, you can actually **stay** in Whitney at the *Antlers Guard Station*, a little over a mile south of town on County Road 529 (℡541/523-1400), a rustic cabin with two rooms, futon, kitchen, lights, and wood stove, which provides a good base ($40 per night) if you want to go mountain biking or cross-country skiing in the vicinity.

Sumpter

One of the area's more interesting stops is **SUMPTER**, just off Hwy 7 about twenty miles west of Baker City, a quasi-ghost town whose low population (around 175) doesn't keep it from hosting several museums devoted to mining and a few businesses aimed at the handful of tourists who pass through. There are two key points of interest. The first, the **Sumpter Valley Dredge** (dawn–dusk; free; ℡541/894-2486), sits in its own state park as a colossal relic of the Industrial Age. Launched in 1935 and in operation for twenty years, this huge gold dredge sat floating over its own flooded pit and scooped up piles of sand and gravel for their gold ore, depositing the castoff material, or tailings, in miles of long, ugly piles with little regard for the environment. Despite the menacing silhouette of this mechanical beast, it is strangely fascinating with its rotting superstructure and huge hull and boom, lined with 72 buckets that would grab the earth and send it back to be sluiced for its valuable ore. The other attraction, the **Sumpter Valley Railway** (℡541/894-2268, ⓦwww.svry.com), is a restored narrow-gauge railway that operated until 1961 and now, with its two engines and several cars, runs five miles between Sumpter and little McEwan during the summer (six daily 10am–4.30pm; round-trip $12.50), making for an evocative, old-fashioned trip through the mountains.

Though most people follow Hwy 7 to Baker City rather than staying the night, Sumpter does have a few facilities. You can get coffee and Internet access at *Java Net*, 215 Sumpter St (℡541/894-2412), or **stay** at the *Sumpter B&B*, 344 NE Columbia St (℡541/894-0048, ⓦwww.sumpterbb.com; ❹), a former hospital and Masonic temple that now hosts six agreeable rooms with an old-fashioned ambience.

Southeast Oregon

Despite occupying nearly a third of the state, Oregon's dry and hot **southeast** corner is mostly barren land, lined with sagebrush and punctuated with great flat-topped, cowboy-movie mountains and canyons. Early exploration of the area was mostly accidental: the best-known tale of desert wanderings is that of the **Blue Bucket Mine Party** of 1845, which left the Oregon Trail in search of a shortcut and got lost in the parched land with neither food nor water. Most of them were eventually rescued, and they caused great excitement with their account of a big nugget of gold discovered in the bottom of a blue bucket of water brought by children from a creek; members of the party went back to look for the lost gold mine, but it was never found. Unscrupulous promoters conned homesteaders into settling the land by painting rich pictures of the land's farming potential, yet those who came here faced a bleak, lonely country where water was scarce, dust blew in clouds, and gardens turned green in the spring only to wilt under the summer sun – a grim life, which few could endure for long. When World War I broke out, most homesteaders left to take jobs in the new war industries, and even today the area is barely populated.

The region's only major highway, **US-20**, runs 260 miles east from Bend to Ontario, on the Idaho border. This is the open road at its most empty, and especially on a hot summer's day, it's a long and arduous drive, whose brain-numbing tedium is interrupted only by the occasional battered hamlet, boasting a couple of fuel pumps and (maybe) a cafe: fill up with gas, pack extra water, and check your car before you set off.

Burns

The halfway point on US-20 is **BURNS** – named after the Scottish poet Robert Burns – the biggest settlement for miles. Indeed, it was the town's relative success as a commercial center in the 1920s that polished off many of its neighbors. Details of the town's pioneer past are displayed in the **Harney County Historical Museum**, 18 West D St (April–Sept Tues–Fri 10am–4pm, Sat 10am–3pm; $4; ℡541/573-5618, ⓦwww.burnsmuseum .com), but the prize exhibits are those salvaged from the ranch of **Pete French**, the greatest of the state's cattle barons, who in the 1870s first realized the great cattle-grazing potential of the meadows south of Burns. At the height of his success he had more than 200,000 acres of grazing land, but within ten years his empire was under threat as homesteaders began to arrive in droves. Although French kept them at bay, he became an increasingly isolated and unpopular figure, especially in the era of the range wars (see box below). A disgruntled homesteader murdered him in 1897, and the killer's subsequent acquittal by a jury of fellow settlers showed it was the end of the line for the cattle barons. After the museum, there's not much else to do in Burns – and the journey on to Ontario is a real yawn, but you can leave the barren spaces behind by heading north on US-395 for the seventy-mile trip to John Day (see p.274).

Practicalities

Burns's **visitor center**, 76 E Washington St (Mon–Fri 9am–5pm; ☎541/573-2636, ⓦ www.harneycounty.com), is located just off US-20 as it doglegs its way through the center of town. It has a useful range of leaflets including several good ones describing which birds can be seen in the Malheur National Wildlife Refuge (see below). Greyhound **buses** (☎1-800/231-2222) pull in at a pizza parlor at 63 N Buena Vista Ave three times a week. The town has a handful of modest **motels** on US-20, and a downtown **B&B**, too – the very pleasant *Sage Country Inn*, in a refurbished 1907 house at 351 W Monroe St/US-20 (☎541/573-7243, ⓦ www.sagecountryinn.com; ❹), with three comfortable rooms and a home-cooked breakfast. Most agree the family-run *Pine Room Café*, 543 W Monroe St/US-20 (☎541/573-6631), is the best place to eat for its steak and seafood. Alternately, you can head 25 miles southeast of Burns on Hwy 78 to reach the quiet and isolated **Crane Hot Springs** (☎541/493-2312, ⓦ www.cranehotsprings.com), which along with its inexpensive cabins ($40–50) and campsites ($12) offers a large hot-springs pool with a temperature of 90°–100°F and several private soaking tubs for $7.50 an hour.

Malheur National Wildlife Refuge

In the middle of the high desert, beginning about twenty miles south of Burns on Hwy 205, the **Malheur National Wildlife Refuge** is centered on two landlocked lakes, Malheur and Harney, and incorporates large sections of Pete French's old "P Ranch." The refuge is an important bird sanctuary: cranes,

Cattle vs sheep

Like many parts of the American West in the 1880s and 1890s, Oregon saw uneasy relations and occasionally open conflict between its **cattle ranchers** and **sheep ranchers**: whereas cattlemen once had virtually unlimited space for grazing and driving their herds, their huge tracts were parceled off into smaller ranches and homesteads as the land became more valuable. When sheep began to graze the rangelands – many raised by European immigrants with a strong tradition of sheep-herding in their native countries (the Basques, most notably, in central Oregon) – it became clear that the cattlemen couldn't compete. One shepherd and his dogs could keep several thousand sheep together with ease, moving them to better pasture at will. Cattle, on the other hand, wandered far and wide over the range and took ages to round up.

Cattlemen showed some initial resistance to the shepherds – some even formed themselves into **"Sheepshooter"** associations and attacked their rivals in the so-called **range wars** – but most gave up without a fight, either agreeing to share the rangeland or leaving the business altogether. In any case, the days of the open range were numbered, and by the mid-1890s there were deeded and leased sheep and cattle ranches from the Cascades to the Idaho border. Sheep and cows now safely graze side by side, and some small towns still celebrate their cowboy roots with annual rodeos, dances, and other Western-flavored events.

herons, hawks, swans, ducks, and geese, among more than three hundred other species, stop off in this giant, soggy marshland during their spring and fall migrations. The refuge has a network of gravel roads, some of which are much too treacherous without a four-wheel-drive vehicle, but you can drive an ordinary car on the most important, the **Center Patrol Road**, which runs north–south through the refuge for about 35 miles. There are also one or two short hiking trails, but this swampy, mosquito-infested terrain is tough going for hikers, especially under the burning sun of summer. In all cases, be sure to bring water, insect repellent, and binoculars – and keep an eye on your gas gauge, as the nearest pumps are back in Burns.

To get your bearings, stop first at the refuge **visitor center**, on the southern edge of Lake Malheur (Mon–Fri 8am–3.30pm plus weekends in spring and summer; ☏541/493-2612, ⓦwww.fws.gov/malheur), which provides maps, wildlife information, and advice on good vantage points. A free leaflet, *Watchable Wildlife*, lists all the birds and the seasons they can be seen here. To get to the center from Burns, drive south on Hwy 205 from the highway 78/205 intersection for 26 miles and then take the six-mile turnoff onto County Road 404 east toward Princeton. If you make reservations in advance, you can **stay** at the **Malheur Field Station**, a scientific research site at the refuge that has seasonal lodging for visitors, from dorms to apartments and trailers, for cheap prices (☏541/493-2629, ⓦwww.malheurfieldstation.org for details).

Diamond Craters and the Round Barn

Not to be missed by anyone with an interest in geology, the **Diamond Craters** lie southeast of the wildlife refuge on rough country roads between highways 205 and 78. Accessed on the forty-mile **Diamond Loop** driving route, the craters site is actually a compendium of all kinds of volcanic formations, created when a series of pyroclastic blasts nine million years ago covered the land in lava for countless acres around. Now you can see a variety of basalt and other rock in evidence, from reddish-brown tuff from ash flows to deep craters rich with pahoehoe lava (as with Hawaiian volcanoes) to all manner of tubes, spatter cones, spires, and natural bridges created when the hot basalt cooled and formed into unusual patterns. Other sights worth a look on the drive are the Graben Dome, a large hilly structure made of cooled magma, deep craters carved out by volcanic bombs, and the decomposing tephra that covers parts of the landscape in forms from ash to chunky lava bricks to great basalt boulders. Unexpectedly sited near the south end of the loop, the century-old *Diamond Hotel*, 10 Main St in tiny Diamond (☏541/493-1898; ❹), provides a good, historic place to **stay**, with eight pleasant B&B rooms and a restaurant that serves up the likes of black-bean chili and sour-cream lemon pie.

Farther north, just off Hwy 278, is the **Round Barn** (daily dawn–dusk; free), a National Historic Site built around 1880, where Peter French would break anywhere from 300 to 1000 horses per year. It's an iconic, curious structure on the landscape, 100ft in diameter, held up with a center truss and umbrella-like wooden ribs supporting its shallow, conical roof.

Frenchglen and Steens Mountain

Beyond the wildlife refuge and lava craters, Hwy 205 pushes south on its way to the end-of-the-world hamlet of **FRENCHGLEN**, sixty miles from Burns. There's not much to the place, but there is somewhere to stay – the state-park-owned 🪶 *Frenchglen Hotel* (mid-March to mid-Nov; ☏541/493-2825 or

△ The Round Barn

☎ 1-800/551-6949; ❹), a small, attractively restored frame house built as a stagecoach stop in the 1920s. The hotel has eight frugal guest rooms with shared bathrooms and without TVs or telephones; still, it is an extraordinarily remote and special place, alive to the nuances of the desert; room and dinner reservations are essential. Failing that, there are several **campgrounds** on the edge of the wildlife refuge – ask for details from the wildlife refuge visitor center (see above).

Frenchglen is also the starting point for the hair-raising Steens Loop Road, a 56-mile gravel track that negotiates **Steens Mountain**, a massive basaltic fault-block some 30 miles long and looming up to 10,000ft above the surrounding desert. Open only in the summer due to wet conditions the rest of the year – and even not suitable for ordinary vehicles – the road climbs the mountain's sloping west side to reach the sheer cliff face of the east, from which you can see the hard sands of the **Alvord Desert** sweeping away toward the horizon. Frenchglen's own Steens Mountain Packers (☎ 1-800/977-3995, ⓦ www.steensmountain.com) organizes horseback day trips ($95–130) into the wilderness on and around the mountain, and has **lodging** in its base camp, with four-person cabins (❺) and camp-style breakfasts and dinners.

Seattle

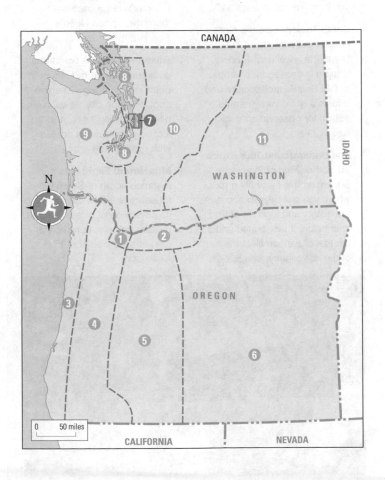

CHAPTER 7

Highlights

✳ **Pike Place Market** Check out this frenetic urban scene loaded with fish vendors, produce stalls, fancy restaurants, underground book and record stores, and just about anything else you can think of. See p.294

✳ **Smith Tower** Once the city's highest building, this 1914 terracotta jewel near Pioneer Square is an elegant example of Old Seattle architecture and boasts a great view from its 35th-floor observation deck. See p.299

✳ **The Underground Tour** Explore the netherworld of Pioneer Square on this fascinating tour, where you can hear all about the history and legends of the area before it was buried under ten feet of earthen fill at the turn of the last century. See p.299

✳ **Seattle Center** The former site of the 1962 World's Fair is now home to museums, athletic arenas, concert stages, a newly reconstructed opera house, and of course, the city's redoubtable icon, the Space Needle. See p.305

✳ **Gasworks Park** A wondrous conversion of an old industrial plant into a strangely serene spot with fine city views, rolling hills, kids flying kites, and looming gas towers riddled with graffiti. See p.312

✳ **Museum of Flight** A fair distance south of Seattle, the museum is worth the trip for its collection of classic aircraft, military fighters, commercial jets, and dark spy craft. See p.319

△ Pike Place Market

Seattle

The commercial and cultural capital of the state of Washington, **SEATTLE** sits along the curving shore of Elliott Bay, with Lake Washington behind and the snowy peak of Mount Rainier hovering in the distance. The beautiful natural setting plays host to shimmering glass skyscrapers, scenic winding streets, excellent restaurants, colorful nightlife, and a flourishing performing-arts scene, all making for a compelling urban experience.

For all its arriviste character, though, Seattle is not an overly dynamic place or a 24-hour party zone. While its museums are respectable, its theater scene vibrant, and its cafe culture unmatched in the US – offering social centers where coffee-drinking, avant-garde decor, and lively performance meld in one artsy pot – the overall mood of the city is decidedly low-key, and it takes time to fully appreciate it. In fact, like much of the Pacific Northwest, it's best experienced on an itinerary that puts as much emphasis on nature hikes, neighborhood strolls, and ferry rides as it does on gung-ho sightseeing and untamed nights out.

Contrary to its soggy reputation, the town ranks 44th among US cities for **rainfall**. Still, the rap is mostly deserved: what gets to people is not necessarily the quantity of the rain but its regularity – in the fall and winter, drizzly days can pile upon one another endlessly, and when it's not raining it's often overcast. Despite this, Seattle is never that cold, even in the middle of winter. Summers are lovely – the average monthly rainfall in July and August hovers around just one inch, and the skies are often sunny but almost never scorching.

Some history

This Northwest colossus had a rather humble genesis, beginning when a dozen white settlers from the East Coast arrived during an 1851 rainstorm on **Alki Beach** (now in West Seattle), only to relocate their townsite along the more desirable eastern shore of Elliott Bay soon after. The early settlement, an assortment of houses on stilts over the porous ground of what's now Pioneer Square, was named Seattle in honor of Chief Sealth (see p.360), a Suquamish/Duwamish tribal leader who helped arrange treaties in lieu of armed fighting when white arrivals began to claim some of the most desirable land. Clashes could not be staved off indefinitely, however, and the **Puget Sound War** of 1855–56 resulted in local natives being consigned to reservations. Sealth himself was living on a reservation when he died of a heart attack in 1866.

As the surrounding forest was gradually felled and shipped to back to the East Coast and abroad, Seattle became a key timber town and port, but it wasn't

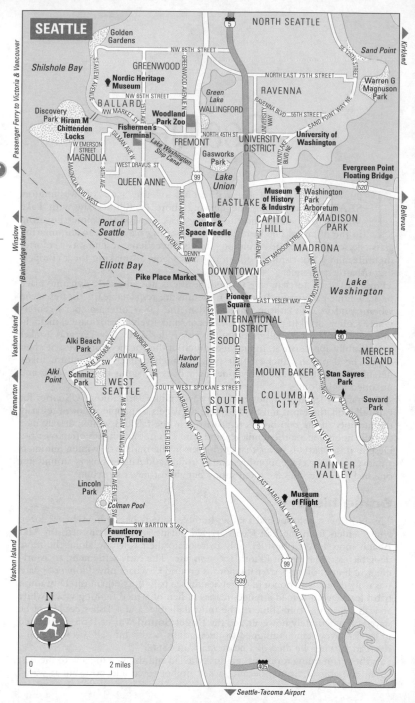

SEATTLE

North Seattle

Golden Gardens

NW 85TH STREET

GREENWOOD

Shilshole Bay

Nordic Heritage Museum

NW 65TH STREET

Green Lake

RAVENNA

NORTH EAST 75TH STREET

Warren G Magnuson Park

Sand Point

SE 125TH STREET

Kirkland

BALLARD

NW MARKET ST

Woodland Park Zoo

WALLINGFORD

RAVENNA BLVD—55TH STREET

Sand Point Way NE

Discovery Park

Hiram M Chittenden Locks

Fishermen's Terminal

GILMAN AVE W

Lake Washington Ship Canal

NORTH 45TH ST

FREMONT

UNIVERSITY DISTRICT

University of Washington

W EMERSON STREET

MAGNOLIA

WEST DRAVUS ST

Gasworks Park

Evergreen Point Floating Bridge

QUEEN ANNE

Lake Union

MAGNOLIA BLVD WEST

QUEEN ANNE AVENUE N

EASTLAKE

Museum of History & Industry

Washington Park Arboretum

Port of Seattle

ELLIOTT AVENUE

Seattle Center & Space Needle

CAPITOL HILL

12TH AVENUE

EAST MADISON STREET

MADISON PARK

MADRONA

DENNY WAY

Elliott Bay

Pike Place Market

DOWNTOWN

Lake Washington

Pioneer Square

EAST YESLER WAY

LAKE WASHINGTON BLVD S

INTERNATIONAL DISTRICT

Lake Washington

ALASKAN WAY VIADUCT

4TH AVENUE S

SODO

MERCER ISLAND

Alki Beach Park

HARBOR AVENUE SW

ADMIRAL WAY

Harbor Island

MOUNT BAKER

Stan Sayres Park

Alki Point

Schmitz Park

WEST SEATTLE

SOUTH WEST SPOKANE STREET

COLUMBIA CITY

Seward Park

BEACH DRIVE SW

CALIFORNIA AVENUE SW

DELRIDGE WAY SW

MARGINAL WAY SOUTH

SOUTH SEATTLE

RAINIER AVENUE S

RAINIER VALLEY

47TH AVENUE SW

Lincoln Park

Colman Pool

SW BARTON STREET

Fauntleroy Ferry Terminal

EAST MARGINAL WAY SOUTH

Museum of Flight

Seattle-Tacoma Airport

N

0   2 miles

until the **Klondike Gold Rush** of 1897 that the city was put firmly on the national map, boosting its trade in shipbuilding and sales of goods and mining equipment to prospectors heading north. Its rise as a major Pacific Coast port sparked its development as a large industrial center, as well as the site of the country's first general strike in 1919, engineered by the Industrial Workers of the World, or "Wobblies."

World War II brought more growth through the rise of the defense industry and air giant Boeing, and the following decades saw Seattle thrive as the economic center of the Pacific Northwest, highlighted by the **Century 21 Exposition** of 1962, the World's Fair that gave the city even greater prominence, along with its most familiar icon, the Space Needle. By the 1990s Seattle was among the most prosperous cities in the US, fueled by the high-tech industry built up around local titan Microsoft and increased Pacific Rim trade, and rich with new museums, a healthy performing-arts scene, and countless small businesses. The good times came to an end in 2000, though, when the high-tech bubble burst, and in short order Washington and Oregon became the national leaders in unemployment.

Nowadays the region's economic fortunes have rebounded, and Seattle is one of the most attractive US cities to live in for young, enterprising workers – or, as media reports have dubbed them, the "**creative class**." Even though such migrants have to cope with a housing stock that has doubled or tripled in price in less than a decade, terrible traffic congestion, a disappearing manufacturing base, and a dismal winter climate, they continue to come in droves. They're lured, no doubt, by the **dynamic aura** that surrounds the city – a glow that has as much or more to do with independent rock, funky art galleries, and freewheeling culture as it does with Microsoft, Boeing, and Starbucks.

Arrival

Unless you happen to live on the West Coast, the quickest and best way of getting to Seattle is **by plane**. A distant second to flying is **rail travel**, with few options save for Amtrak, the ailing US train system. The cheapest and most cost-effective way is to go by **bus**, but it's also the least comfortable and the most time-consuming. Similarly lengthy, a **car** ride to Seattle will devour your travel time unless you live nearby.

By air

Seattle-Tacoma International Airport, almost always known as **Sea-Tac** (☏206/433-5388 or 1-800/544-1965, ⓦwww.portseattle.org/seatac), is fourteen miles south of downtown Seattle, and there's a small **visitor information booth** in front of baggage carousel 8. The **Gray Line Airport Express** bus (daily 5.30am–11pm every 30min; $10.25, $17 round-trip; ☏206/626-6088 or 1-800/426-7532, ⓦwww.graylineofseattle.com) drops off at eight major hotels Downtown, with connector services to other hotels in the area from 5.30am to 9pm, for $2.50 extra; reserve at least one hour in advance for these connections at ☏206/255-7159. Shuttle Express has door-to-door service (daily 4am–midnight; ☏206/622-1424 or 1-800/487-RIDE, ⓦwww.shuttleexpress.com) for $28–30 to Downtown. **Taxis** charge $35–40 for the Downtown route and leave from the third floor of the parking garage; call ☏206/246-9999 for pickup once you arrive.

From Sea-Tac, there's a handful of options for **ground transportation** to Seattle. Several **car rental** firms (see p.30 for contact info) have counters in the baggage claim area, with pickup and dropoff on the first floor of the garage across from the main terminal; other companies with off-airport branches provide courtesy van service to their pickup points. **Buses** to Seattle leave from the north end of the baggage claim area. The cheapest option is Metro bus #194 ($1.25, $2 during peak hours Mon–Fri 6–9am & 3–6pm), a 30min trip which deposits you Downtown at the convention center, 7th Ave at Pike St; bus #174 plies a similar route for the same cost, but takes an extra 15min.

By car

If you're **driving**, you'll probably approach Seattle on **I-5**, the main north-south highway between Canada and California. Major north- and south-bound exits include Seneca Street (for central Downtown), Mercer Street (Seattle Center complex), and Dearborn/James streets (Capitol Hill). Coming in from the east, you'll likely arrive via **I-90**, which runs from Seattle to central Washington. I-90's Downtown exits (164–167) come quickly from both sides of the freeway; keep alert for off-ramps onto Stewart or Union streets for Downtown.

By train and bus

Trains arrive at the **Amtrak** terminal in unlovely King Street Station at Third Avenue and Jackson Street, near the International District (T206/382-4125 or 1-800/872-7245, Wwww.amtrak.com). It's about a dozen blocks from here to Downtown; just to the east along Jackson Street, the International District Station is a hub for frequent Metro buses going Downtown. Also nearby is the southern terminus of the **waterfront streetcar** (see p.288), which takes a tourist-friendly route along the bay – though it's not much fun if you're loaded down with luggage and want to reach your accommodation quickly.

    Greyhound buses (T206/628-5526 or 1-800/231-2222, Wwww.greyhound .com) arrive at Eighth Avenue and Stewart Street, on the eastern edge of Downtown, as well as at King Street Station, at Third Avenue and Jackson Street, near the International District – convenient if you need to connect to an Amtrak train.

By ferry

Puget Sound **ferries** (T206/464-6400 or 1-800/84-FERRY; Wwww.wsdot .wa.gov/ferries) dock at Pier 52 (Colman Dock) on Downtown's waterfront, with a couple of passenger-only routes using Pier 50. Other ferry routes connect at Fauntleroy in West Seattle (for a list of routes, see box in "Puget Sound" chapter, p.356).

Information

Located inside the Washington State Convention and Trade Center, Seventh Ave at Pike St (daily 9am–1pm & 2–5pm; T206/461-5840, Wwww.seeseattle.org), the Seattle Convention and Visitors Bureau's **Citywide Concierge Center** has a friendly staff that can provide directions, information, bus schedules, and help with finding accommodation. Still, it's best to arrange where you'll stay for the first night or two in advance instead of just turning up. The free official travelers' brochure, *Washington State Visitors' Guide* (call ☎1-800/544-1800 for a copy, or visit ⓦwww.experiencewashington.com), has a comprehensive list of hotels, motels, B&Bs, and the like.

City transportation

There are a number of options for **getting around** Seattle. Downtown is easy enough to cover by walking alone. Beyond this, the buses are frequent and well run, and most of the more interesting neighborhoods are pretty close to one another. However, steep hills can challenge weak knees both Downtown and elsewhere, and some areas are not well served by public transportation, especially at night. Thus, although traffic can be horrendous at peak hours, for some places you may well need to take a car or, in some cases, even a ferry.

Metro

Seattle's mass transit system, known as the **Metro** (☎206/553-3000, ⓦtransit.metrokc.gov), runs bus routes throughout the city and King County, extending into the Eastside suburbs across Lake Washington, and south to the airport. **Customer service stations** are available at Westlake Station, 5th Ave and Pine St (Mon–Fri 9am–5.30pm), and at King Street Station, 201 S Jackson St (Mon–Fri 8am–5pm); both offer maps and schedules and are the most reliable places to buy daily passes on weekdays. You can also purchase passes

Major bus routes

From Downtown

#1, 2, 3, 4 Seattle Center and Queen Anne

#5, 26, 28 Fremont

#7 International District

#10, 12 Capitol Hill

#15, 18 Ballard, via Seattle Center and Queen Anne

#16, 26 Wallingford

#17 Ballard and Fishermen's Terminal

#19, 24, 33 Magnolia and Discovery Park

#25 University District

#37 Alki Beach, West Seattle

#43, 71, 72, 73 University District

#51, 55, 56, 57 West Seattle

#256, 261, 550 Bellevue

Other routes

#7, 9 University District to Capitol Hill

#8 Capitol Hill to Seattle Center and Queen Anne

#31 Magnolia to University District, via Fremont and Wallingford

#44 Ballard Locks to University District, via Wallingford

#45 Seattle Center to University District, via Queen Anne

#167 University District to Bellevue

#174, 194 Sea-Tac Airport to Downtown (Museum of Flight en route)

online at ⓦbuypass.metrokc.gov. The Metro's best feature is its **Downtown Ride Free Area**, bounded by Battery Street, South Jackson Street, 6th Avenue, and the waterfront. From 6am to 7pm daily, bus trips beginning and ending within this zone are free; cross out of the free zone – to the University District, for example – and you pay the driver as you get off; come back in and you pay as you enter. Buses generally run weekdays from 5am or 5.30am to midnight or 1am, though some less-frequented routes may end service as early as 7pm; typically, weekend hours start an hour or two later and end an hour earlier.

Outside of the Ride Free Area, adult **fares** are $1.25, or $1.50–2 during peak hours (Mon–Fri 6–9am & 3–6pm), and kids' fares are 50¢; all tickets are valid for one hour's transit, with unlimited transfers in that time frame. **Day passes** ($5) are available for weekend and holiday travel from the Citywide Concierge Center (see p.286) or in King Street Center, 201 S Jackson St. Bus **maps** or **schedules** are available at the visitor's bureau, libraries, shopping centers, and Metro Tunnel stations. Customer service offices also dispense free copies of the large *Metro Transit System Map*, although this is such a densely packed grid that you're better off picking up the pocket-size schedules of the routes you plan to travel frequently.

The monorail and waterfront streetcar

Built for the World's Fair in the early 1960s, the **Seattle monorail** (daily 11am–9pm; $4, kids $1.50; ⓦwww.seattlemonorail.com) connects Seattle Center with the Westlake Center shopping mall and is not of much use unless you need to get from Downtown to Seattle Center. Those gearing up for a thrilling or particularly scenic high-tech ride will be disappointed: with no stops on the route, the uneventful journey takes just two minutes or so from start to finish.

Built in 1927, the charming **waterfront streetcar** (daily 6.30am–7pm; $1.25, $1.50 peak; ⓦtransit.metrokc.gov) begins its 20min route at Jackson Street in the International District, proceeds through Pioneer Square, and then runs up Alaskan Way from Pier 48 to Pier 70/Broad Street. Known as Metro route 99, the streetcar will be replaced with buses through 2007 to accommodate ongoing waterfront construction.

Taxis

Taxis can be hard to find, and have somewhat high fares. Nonetheless, there are times when you'll want to use them, particularly if you're out clubbing in Downtown areas that can get a bit dicey after midnight, or in a neighborhood where bus service becomes infrequent or nonexistent after the early evening. The more reliable companies include Graytop Cab (☎206/282-8222) and Yellow Cab (☎206/622-6500). Fares have standardized at $2.50 for the meter drop, and $2 for each mile or 50¢ per minute. Be wary of unmarked, unregulated private cabs, which can rip you off.

Accommodation

In most of its neighborhoods, Seattle has plenty of choices for **accommodation**; the problem is not so much getting a room as finding good mid-range deals, achieving a balance between decent amenities and affordable rates. Seattle's **hotels** are mostly geared toward the business traveler, with many four-star

Seattle offers a few dozen walking, boating, flying, and biking tours of the region, sometimes organized according to a specific theme. While not exactly a tour, the Seattle CityPass ($36, kids $22; good for nine days; ⓦcitypass.com) can act as a useful sort of "self-guided" option. It covers admission to the Seattle Aquarium, Pacific Science Center, Museum of Flight, and Woodland Park Zoo, and includes a harbor tour as well, costing half of what it would to visit all five attractions at regular prices. The CityPass can be purchased at any participating attraction.

Argosy Cruises ⓣ206/623-4252, ⓦwww.argosycruises.com. Offering year-round tours through most local waters, including the harbor cruise of Elliott Bay covered by Seattle CityPass (1hr; $15–19 by season), a lake cruise in Lake Washington and Lake Union (2hr; $21–28), and a locks cruise (2hr 30min; $28–36).

Gray Line ⓣ206/626-5208 or 1-800/426-7532, ⓦwww.graylineofseattle.com. One-to three-hour narrated bus tours of Seattle's best-known attractions ($19–35), with a six-hour Land & Water Tour ($58), on buses and ships, on offer from spring to summer. Also has trips to the Boeing plant ($47), Mount Rainier ($59), and Mount St Helens ($79).

Ride the Ducks ⓣ206/441-3825 or 1-800/817-1116, ⓦwww.ridetheducksofseattle .com. Land-and-sea tours in a conspicuous World War II amphibious landing craft, starting at the Space Needle, then going into Lake Union for a ride around Portage Bay (Apr–Dec leaves every half-hour 10am–6pm; 90min; $23, kids $13).

Seattle Seaplanes ⓣ206/329-9638 or 1-800/637-5553, ⓦwww.seattleseaplanes .com. Twenty-minute flights of various routes over Seattle, for $67.50/person, including options for hydroplane and dinner rides.

See Seattle ⓣ425/226-7641, ⓦwww.see-seattle.com. Half-day walking tours of Downtown for $20 (minimum six people per group), strolling by the major sights from Pike Place Market to the International District, as well as specialized tours for prearranged groups.

Victoria Clipper ⓣ206/448-5000, ⓦwww.victoriaclipper.com. Eye-opening trips to Friday Harbor on San Juan Island (May–Sept only; $60–65 round-trip, kids $30–40) or to Vancouver Island in Canada (year-round; $117–140 round-trip, kids $58–70), leaving on the high-speed, passenger-only Victoria Clipper from Seattle's Pier 69.

accommodations downtown that easily run $175 or more a night. There are few good mid-level options, and if you want a room for less than $60 a night, the level of service and cleanliness tends to drop dramatically, as does the desirability of the location. Bear in mind that Seattle imposes a steep **hotel room tax** of 15.6 percent. Farther out, the chain **motels** on Aurora Avenue (Highway 99) and around Sea-Tac airport are all rather bland, grungy, or otherwise inhospitable.

Seattle's **B&Bs** offer a good balance of comfort and value: the often-stylish rooms are almost always bigger and nicer than hotel units that go for the same rates, and many are in converted early-twentieth-century mansions – mostly grand **Capitol Hill** homes – with period decor and antiques. Reservations are a necessity during peak travel times (June–Aug), and there's often a two-night minimum stay. Specialist B&B agencies that provide lodging through the area include A Pacific Reservation Service (ⓣ206/439-7677 or 1-800/684-2932, ⓦwww.seattlebedandbreakfast.com) and the Seattle Bed and Breakfast Association (ⓣ206/547-1020 or 1-800/348-5630, ⓦwww.lodginginseattle.com).

Hostels, unsurprisingly, offer the best deals for the budget traveler, with dorm beds going for around $25 a night. Memberships are also useful in a few of them for procuring space or getting reduced rates but are not necessary to qualify for a bed in most cases. Most hostels offer **private rooms** for couples and single travelers, although you'll be paying about two or three times the dorm rate. **Campsites** are predictably few and far between in the city but are in abundance in the outlying areas around Puget Sound.

Hotels and motels

Downtown

Alexis 1007 First Ave ☎206/624-4844 or 1-800/426-7033, ⊛www.alexishotel.com. Plush decor at this top-notch hotel, as well as a spa, a steam room, and restaurant. Nearly half the rooms are suites that, at their largest, have luxurious touches like fireplaces and dining rooms. ❾

Edgewater Inn Pier 67, 2411 Alaskan Way ☎206/728-7000 or 1-800/624-0670, ⊛www .edgewaterhotel.com. Seattle's top waterfront hotel has a central location and nice rooms, the best of which have windows right on the bay – though for those you'll need to both pay about $50 more and reserve well in advance. ❽

Elliott Grand Hyatt 721 Pine St ☎206/219-6916, ⊛www.grandseattle.hyatt.com. Chic and modern digs not far from I-5. Excellent for business and upscale travelers, with great views from rooms and suites stuffed with pricey designer furnishings. ❾

Inn at Harbor Steps 1221 1st Ave at University St ☎206/748-0793 or 1-888/728-8910, ⊛www .foursisters.com. Intimate rooms in an upscale hotel near the market and the Seattle Art Museum. Each room has a fireplace, fridge, complimentary breakfast, WiFi Internet access, and a balcony overlooking an interior garden courtyard; some have spa tubs. ❼

Hotel Max 620 Stewart St ☎206/441-4200 or 1-800/426-0670, ⊛www.hotelmaxseattle.com. Located in a renovated 1920s building a block from the monorail, with 165 stylish rooms kitted out with vaguely "artistic" themes – with different photographers showcased on each floor and original art in each room. ❽

Pioneer Square 77 Yesler Way ☎206/340-1234 or 1-800/800-5514, ⊛www.pioneersquare.com. Restored 1914 brick hotel (now a Best Western), and one of the few good Pioneer Square choices for accommodation with adequate comfort. There's a juice bar on the lobby floor, as well as a saloon with microbrews on tap. ❻

Roosevelt 1531 7th Ave ☎206/621-1200, ⊛www.roosevelthotel.com. Renovated high-rise dating from 1929, with basic but comfortable rooms and fancier suites with whirlpool tubs; centrally located near Westlake Center. ❼

Hotel Vintage Park 1100 Fifth Ave ☎206/624-8000, ⊛www.hotelvintagepark.com. Offering splashy upscale decor without any accompanying attitude, a stylish boutique hotel with rooms themed around wine-drinking and vineyards; amenities include fireplaces, Jacuzzis, stereos, and of course, nightly tastings of vino. ❾

🏃 **W Seattle** 1112 4th Ave ☎206/264-6000, ⊛www.whotels.com. Stylish modern tower in the Financial District, with a staff of beautiful people and smart, cozy rooms with standard luxury amenities. Chic lobby bar has often-packed "cocktail couches," and the adjoining Northwest Cuisine restaurant, *Earth and Ocean* (see p.322), is one of the city's best. ❾

Westin Seattle 1900 Fifth Ave ☎206/728-1000 or 1-800/WESTIN-1, ⊛www.westin.com. Expansive, gorgeous views from the higher of the 865 rooms in these twin cylindrical towers – one from 1969, the other from the 1980s – with spacious rooms and good amenities including indoor swimming pool, health club, and spa. ❽

Belltown

🏃 **Ace** 2423 1st Ave at Wall St ☎206/448-4721, ⊛www.theacehotel.com. Slightly arty, modern rooms in a hotel above the *Cyclops* restaurant, in the heart of Belltown. Hardwood floors, lofty ceilings, and shared bathrooms in the rooms; add $50 for more comfortable and well-appointed suites. ❺

Hotel Andra 2000 Fourth Ave ☎206/448-8600 or 1-877/448-8601, ⊛www.hotelandra.com. An intimate, boutique hotel with 120 chic, modern units – more than half of them suites. Onsite gym and restaurant and high-speed Internet access. An abundance of style for steep rates. ❽

Inn at El Gaucho 2505 1st Ave ☎206/728-1133, ⊛inn.elgaucho.com. At the heart of Belltown's gentrified First Avenue, a former merchant-marine quarters now converted into an 18-suite boutique hotel. Units have smart, stylish furnishings, if a bit cramped for the price, and there's a free continental breakfast. Located above a chain steakhouse. ❽

Moore 1926 2nd Ave at Virginia St ☎206/448-4851 or 1-800/421-5508, ⊛www.moorehotel.com.

Ancient-feeling 1908 structure (part of a theater building) with drab decor and bland rooms, though it's well placed to take advantage of downtown sightseeing and Belltown nightlife. Extra $15 for private bathroom, otherwise ❸

Sixth Avenue Inn 2000 6th Ave ☎ 206/441-8300, Ⓦ www.sixthavenueinn.com. Although a bit east of the main attractions, a practical choice if you really need to save money, with gym and Internet access and spartan but clean rooms. ❺

Seattle Center and Queen Anne

Hampton Inn 700 Fifth Ave N ☎ 206/282-7700 or 1-800/HAMPTON, Ⓦ www.hamptoninnseattle.com. A reasonable choice for the Seattle Center area, this modern chain hotel has around two hundred rooms and suites offering fridges, microwaves, kitchenettes, and fireplaces; onsite amenities include an exercise room with Jacuzzi. ❻

Inn at Queen Anne 505 1st Ave N at N Republican St ☎ 206/282-7357 or 1-800/952-5043, Ⓦ www .innatqueenanne.com. Small but comfortable lodging on the edge of Seattle Center, with rooms offering queen-size beds, kitchenettes, and microwaves, plus complimentary breakfast and Downtown shuttle service. ❺

MarQueen 600 Queen Ave N ☎ 206/282-7407 or 1-800/445-3076, Ⓦ www.marqueen.com. A refurbished, classically styled 1918 building with 56 rooms and suites, featuring period antiques and pluses like hardwood floors, kitchenettes, microwaves, and fridges, as well as an onsite spa. ❻

Capitol Hill

Eastlake Inn 2215 Eastlake Ave E ☎ 206/322-7726. Average motor lodge, but more conveniently situated than most – it's a few blocks from Lake Union's houseboats – and cheaper than the ones around Seattle Center; some units are mini-suites with kitchens. ❹

Silver Cloud Inn 1150 Fairview Ave N ☎ 206/447-9500, Ⓦ www.scinns.com. A few blocks west of I-5 near Lake Union, with simple, clean, and modern rooms; amenities include fridges and microwaves,

and most rooms feature a view of the lake as well. There's another location near the University of Washington at 5036 25th Ave NE (☎ 206/526-5200 or 1-800/205-6940). ❻

Sorrento 900 Madison St ☎ 206/622-4400 or 1-800/426-1265, Ⓦ www.hotelsorrento.com. Just east of the I-5 freeway in First Hill, a modernized, 76-room edifice with a European flair, stylish decor, and posh onsite restaurant *The Hunt Club*. The regal 1908 exterior surrounds a circular courtyard with palm trees; some rooms have views of Puget Sound. ❾

University District

University Inn 4140 Roosevelt Way NE at NE 42nd St ☎ 206/632-5055 or 1-800/733-3855, Ⓦ www .universityinnseattle.com. Plain-looking business-oriented hotel off University Way. Some rooms have kitchens, and your stay comes with complimentary continental breakfast; there's also an onsite pool and spa, and high-speed Internet access. ❺

Watertown 4242 Roosevelt Way NE ☎ 206/826-4242, Ⓦ www.watertownseattle.com. Nice, semi-upscale hotel with gym and boutique-flavored rooms with microwaves and refrigerators, plus rentable bikes and central location just north of the main action. ❻

The suburbs

Bellevue Club 11200 SE 6th Ave, Bellevue ☎ 425/454-4424, Ⓦ www.bellevueclubhotel.com. Maximum-chic spa hotel in the suburbs with in-room soaking tubs, elegant decor, fitness complex, swimming pool, basketball and tennis courts, and a guest list of well-tanned yuppies with perfect teeth. ❽

Woodmark 1200 Carillon Point, Kirkland ☎ 206/822-3700 or 1-800/822-3700, Ⓦ www .thewoodmark.com. Located in the wealthy suburb of Kirkland, seven miles east of downtown on the shores of Lake Washington, this splendid modern hotel is the height of luxury for its swanky furnishings, but it's only worth the price if you're in one of the lakeside rooms (or suites), which typically run $50 more. ❾

Bed-and-breakfasts

11th Avenue Inn 121 11th Ave E, Capitol Hill ☎ 206/69-4373, Ⓦ www.11thavenueinn.com. Eight units named after gems, with mild chintz, retro decor, and WiFi Internet access. Shared bathrooms bring down the cost to $75 in low season, otherwise ❺–❻

Bacon Mansion 959 Broadway E, Capitol Hill ☎ 206/329-1864 or 1-800/240-1864,

Ⓦ www.baconmansion.com. Eleven elegant rooms and spacious suites in a grand 1909 Tudor Revival structure, just north of Broadway. Well decorated if a bit small, the least expensive rooms are cheap for the area, although the price is more than double at the high end. Two-night minimum stay on weekends. ❺

Chambered Nautilus 5005 22nd Ave NE, University District ☏206/522-2536 or 1-800/545-8459, ⓦwww.chamberednautilus.com. Six tasteful rooms bearing names like "Crow's Nest" and "Scallop Chamber." Four rooms have porches, and four adjoining suites are furnished with more recent, if more drab, decor. Reservations a month or two ahead of time are advisable in the summer months. ⑤

Gaslight Inn 1727 15th Ave, Capitol Hill ☏206/325-3654, ⓦwww.gaslight-inn.com. Fifteen rooms with large common areas; some units with fireplaces, small gardens, and decks; and more expensive suites for longer-term stays. Also a swimming pool, a hot tub, and a prime location – not to mention the contemporary decor and colorful modern art on view. ⑤

Mildred's 1202 15th Ave E, Capitol Hill ☏206/325-6072, ⓦwww.mildredsbnb.com. Four rooms – the Green, with southern and eastern views, the Blue, with a sitting alcove, the Lace, with a skylight in the bath, and the Rose, with a private deck – in an 1890 Victorian with a wraparound veranda near Volunteer Park. All units have TVs and VCRs. ⑤

Pensione Nichols 1923 1st Ave, Belltown ☏206/441-7125, ⓦwww.pensionenichols.com. Considering the pricey area it's in, this classy little B&B is a great deal, with small but clean rooms, shared baths, and simple, tasteful decor in a classic 1904 building. Suites with kitchenettes add about $100 per night to the price, but they can be shared by four people. Basic units with shared bath ⑤

Salisbury House 750 16th Ave E, Capitol Hill ☏206/328-8682, ⓦwww.salisburyhouse.com. Four smart doubles and an attractive suite (with hot tub and fireplace) in a mansion with maple floors, high ceilings, and a quiet yet convenient location. Ask for the Blue Room if you want morning sun, or the Lavender Room if you want the biggest space. ⑤

Shafer-Baillie Mansion 907 14th Ave E, Capitol Hill ☏206/322-4654, ⓦshaferbaillie.tripod.com. Always a popular site for weddings and receptions, this mansion offers three period-furnished rooms and two suites, and its oak-paneled walls and late-Victorian decor echo its 1914 construction. ⑥

Hostels

Green Tortoise 1525 2nd Ave between Pike and Pine sts, Downtown ☏206/340-1222 or 1-888/424-6783, ⓦwww.greentortoise.net. Old-style hotel now functioning as a hostel, with four-to-eight-to-a-room dorms ($23–27) and some private doubles ($60). Free breakfast, Internet access, and pickups at Amtrak, Greyhound, or ferries; they also do summer walking tours of the city.

The City

Seattle has roughly an hourglass shape, skinny in its central section and widening to the north and south, with **Elliott Bay** – an extension of Puget Sound – providing Downtown's western border. The city is separated from its eastern suburbs by **Lake Washington**, which is connected to the sound by the **Lake Washington Ship Canal**, a narrow waterway that, at various points, widens into Portage Bay, Union Bay, and **Lake Union**. Boats – and salmon – exit the canal into Puget Sound through the Ballard Locks, at the western edge of Salmon Bay.

Downtown contains many of the city's top attractions, particularly Pike Place Market, a busy, crowded agora of stalls and cafés; the waterfront, where ferries depart for destinations throughout the Sound; and the worthwhile Seattle Art Museum. Just south of Downtown is **Pioneer Square**, Seattle's oldest area, where the restored brick and stone-faced buildings host vivacious clubs and taverns, and the **International District**, aka Chinatown, which is also home to significant numbers of Japanese and Vietnamese immigrants. North of Downtown lies the increasingly upscale **Belltown**, with the vestiges of a hip

Navigating the city

Whatever your mode of transportation, it's essential to familiarize yourself with a few basics of Seattle's confusing street plan. To begin with, most addresses are preceded or followed by a direction (eg, NW 67th St, or 13th Ave E). These tags do not indicate the directional position of an address on a street, as they do in many American cities, but rather the position the entire street holds in relationship to the city's plan. Consequently, 2nd Avenue W and 2nd Avenue S are two different streets, and the location of something on 2nd Avenue W might be a good five miles or so from an address on 2nd Avenue S.

Think of Downtown as the center of a compass used to plot out the city's coordinates. Thoroughfares running east-west are usually designated as streets, with the section of the city in which it lies placed at the beginning of the address (eg, 500 N 36th St, since this part of 36th St is north of Downtown), while those running north-south are usually designated avenues, with the section of the city in which it lies following the address (eg, 5000 22nd Ave NE, since this part of 22nd Ave is northeast of Downtown). Be careful when you ask directions, too: natives have a habit of casually referring to a street address without directionals, so the 15th Avenue address you were heading to in Capitol Hill may actually be in the University District, depending on if it's 15th Ave E or 15th Ave NE.

edge, and the nearby **Seattle Center**, a large complex of theaters, sports arenas, and museums, dominated by the iconic Space Needle. Further northwest are the quaint neighborhoods of **Queen Anne** and **Magnolia**, the latter holding one of the finest patches of urban greenery in the US, **Discovery Park**. Across the canal north from the district, industrial **Ballard** is known primarily for its locks and a strip of historic architecture and old-time diners and taverns. To the southeast, the Woodland Park Zoo makes for an excellent family outing, while farther east is **Fremont**, the city's most unpretentiously bohemian corner, highlighted by excellent public artwork. Neighboring **Wallingford** has a liberal, middle-class air and the curious industrial playground of Gasworks Park. Across the I-5 lies the **University District**, or U District, as it's known, dominated by the campus of the University of Washington and its main thoroughfare of student life, University Way, or "the Ave." Bridges across the ship canal lead back toward Downtown and **Capitol Hill**, the nexus of Seattle's best cafés, shops, and nightlife.

On the eastern side of Lake Washington are the bulk of Seattle's suburbs, notably **Bellevue**, home to a few worthwhile sights. South of Seattle is the first-rate **Museum of Flight**, charting the development of air travel, while historic **Alki Beach** is in West Seattle, separated from Downtown by the industrial zone of Elliott Bay's Harbor Island.

Downtown

Downtown Seattle is the commercial and financial hub of the Pacific Northwest and one of the West Coast's densest urban cores. Predictably, it's also the place where most tourists drop anchor when arriving in town, even though it's not Seattle's most exciting quarter. It does, however, present a formidable **skyline** – best appreciated from the water – and the cityscape is nicely romanticized by views of Puget Sound and its steady traffic of ferries, boats, and commercial vessels.

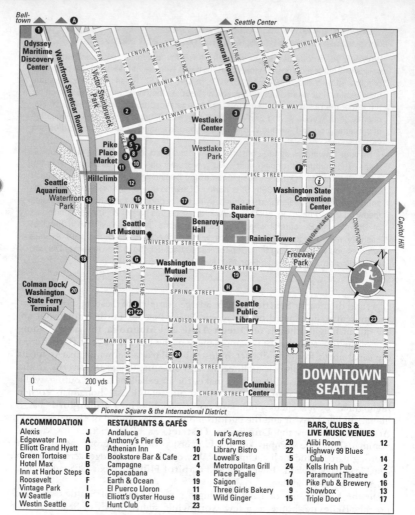

ACCOMMODATION		RESTAURANTS & CAFÉS				BARS, CLUBS & LIVE MUSIC VENUES	
Alexis	J	Andaluca	3	Ivar's Acres		Alibi Room	12
Edgewater Inn	A	Anthony's Pier 66	1	of Clams	20	Highway 99 Blues	
Elliott Grand Hyatt	D	Athenian Inn	10	Library Bistro	22	Club	14
Green Tortoise	E	Bookstore Bar & Cafe	21	Lowell's	5	Kells Irish Pub	2
Hotel Max	B	Campagne	4	Metropolitan Grill	24	Paramount Theatre	6
Inn at Harbor Steps	G	Copacabana	8	Place Pigalle	7	Pike Pub & Brewery	16
Roosevelt	F	Earth & Ocean	19	Saigon	10	Showbox	13
Vintage Park	I	El Puerco Lloron	11	Three Girls Bakery	9	Triple Door	17
W Seattle	H	Elliott's Oyster House	18	Wild Ginger	15		
Westin Seattle	C	Hunt Club	23				

The old favorite **Pike Place Market** alone merits a trip downtown, as do the **waterfront**'s scattered museums and nautical attractions. The sizable **Seattle Art Museum** and **Benaroya Hall** (home to the Seattle Symphony), having bolstered the city's cultural reputation considerably, are further enticements. Elsewhere, the staid **Business District** holds scattered appeal only for architecture enthusiasts, mainly for the eye-popping **Seattle Public Library**, the Northwest's most important modern building, and the 76-story **Columbia Center**, its tallest.

Pike Place Market

The hectic center of downtown Seattle's pedestrian life, **Pike Place Market** (daily Mon–Sat 10am–6pm, Sun 11am–5pm; ☎206/682-7453, Ⓦwww.pikeplacemarket.org) is a vibrant bazaar whose splendid retro-neon clock and sign make it one of the most recognizable places in America. With its official entrance at First Avenue and Pike Street, the market is huge – thirteen buildings on a triangular lot covering nine acres, holding three hundred produce and fish vendors, bakeries, craft stalls, and small retailers, many of whom grow or make what they sell.

Established in 1907 as a way for local farmers to sell their products directly to the city's consumers, the market was slated for demolition in the 1960s. A "Keep the Market" initiative was approved by voters in 1971, paving the way for its renovation with the establishment of a **Market Historical District** in 1974. The market has been the city's cultural and social hub ever since.

The best action centers around the ground level of the **Main Arcade**, with its dozens of produce stalls and proprietors hawking orchard-fresh fruit juice and berries. Here you can guzzle java with the locals, nosh on bread and pastries, and watch fishmongers hurl the morning catch. The weekly **Organic Wednesdays** (June–Oct 10am–4pm) and **Summer Sundays** (June–Sept 10am-4pm) give you the opportunity to buy organic produce under canopies set up on the cobblestones of Pike Place itself. There's an **information booth** on the traffic island at the First Avenue entrance, and stacks of the free monthly *Pike Place Market News* (Ⓦ www.pikeplacemarketnews .com), which includes a decent map, are piled liberally throughout the buildings. A favorite meeting place is the **brass pig** in front of the Public Market Center sign – an actual piggy bank, with receipts going to charity. One-hour historical tours of the complex begin at the **Market Heritage Center**, 1531 Western Ave (Wed–Sun 11am & 2pm, winter 11am only; $8; reserve 24hr in advance, or by Fri 4pm for weekend tours, at Ⓣ206/774-5249), though the best way to experience the place is to wander through it at your own pace.

On the south end of Pike Place Market, **Economy Row** features the Italian and Mediterranean delicacies of DeLaurenti Specialty Foods, plus an enormous newsstand, and to the north is the **Corner Market**, home to countless produce vendors. This area and the nearby **Sanitary Market** have most of the market's top bakeries, too, among them the oldest vendor at the site, the *Three Girls Bakery*, serving up baked goodies since 1912. Farther north the larger structures are separated by **Pike Place** proper and **Post Alley**, known for its street musicians and sidewalk cafés, as well as better restaurants such as *Café Campagne*. The crowds can get particularly dense as you head to the narrower, arts-and-crafts-dominated **North Arcade**, thick with dealers in jewelry, silk-screened shirts, and wooden carvings, while directly across Pike Place, at no. 1912 in the **Stewart House** building, you'll find the original seed of the *Starbucks* chain (Ⓣ206/448-8762). Just northwest of the market, **Victor Steinbrueck Park** is worth a look for its pleasantly modest, hilly patches overlooking Puget Sound, which are jammed on sunny days with tourists, office workers, and transients.

The waterfront

Heading west from the market's brass pig, you descend the **Hillclimb**, a formidable staircase that leads down from the market's lower levels, under the Alaskan Way Viaduct, and terminates at the **waterfront**, whose old wooden jetties have been colonized by tourism, offering a busy stretch of ferry landings, trinket stalls, and boutiques. Almost opposite the Hillclimb, **Pier 59** now houses Seattle's **Aquarium** (daily: June–Aug 9.30am–7pm; rest of year 10am–5pm; $12.50, kids $8.50, included in CityPass, see p.289;

www.seattleaquarium.org), with hundreds of species of fish, birds, plants, and mammals in a spacious, easily navigable layout. Along with a 400,000-gallon underwater dome that re-creates life in Puget Sound, the highlights include black-tip sharks; electric eels; octopi; a functional salmon hatchery and fish ladder, which displays the life cycle of the threatened Pacific salmon; and a hands-on **Discovery Lab**, which allows visitors to touch tide-pool specimens.

South of Pier 59, the waterfront is lined with souvenir shops, restaurants, and fish-and-chip stands, of which the most famous is *Ivar's Acres of Clams*, at Pier 54 (☎206/624-6852, www.ivars.net), well deserving of its own special stop ("Clam Central Station") on the **waterfront streetcar** (see p.288). At Pier 55 you can hop aboard the **water taxi** (May–Sept; $3 one-way) that takes visitors twelve miles across Elliott Bay to the Seacrest Park dock on the eastern side of the West Seattle peninsula. It's an attractive journey, but most of West Seattle's sights are on the other side of the peninsula, making for a very lengthy hike, though Metro bus #53 and shuttle #773 provide easy access. South at Pier 52, **Colman Dock** is the terminal for Washington State Ferries (see p.356), taking you to spots like West Seattle and Bainbridge Island; Pier 50, farther south, handles foot passengers between Seattle and Vashon Island.

North of the Aquarium, the platform above Pier 66 offers good bay watching, with free telescopes for up-close views of the ships cruising the water. At Pier 66 itself, also known as Bell Street Pier, the **Odyssey Maritime Discovery Center** (Wed & Thurs 10am–3pm, Fri 10am–4pm, Sat & Sun 11am–5pm; $7, kids $5; www.ody.org) presents fifty interactive exhibits devoted to trade and transport in Puget Sound, with many heroic displays of maritime equipment. Although kids might get a kick out of the simulated sea kayak journey, the working models of shipping boats and propellers, and the computer game that lets you play crane operator, adults may find the experience interminable.

A bit north of the last streetcar stop along the waterfront sits the 8.5-acre **Olympic Sculpture Park** (daily 7am–6pm; summer 6am–9pm; free; www .seattleartmuseum.org/visit/osp), whose modern artworks and greenery are set around a zigzagging pathway that passes over road and railway before leading down to the water's edge. At the top is the glassy, cantilevered PACCAR Pavilion, which has a cafe and lecture and performance spaces. On the way down are showpieces like Alexander Calder's 39ft *Eagle*, a jagged array of red steel arcs; Louise Bourgeois' disembodied granite *Eye Benches*; Richard Serra's undulating rusty-steel *Wake* slabs; and a Claes Oldenburg typewriter eraser, among other arch-modern pieces – they're all fine and worthy, but the greatest piece of abstract sculpture may be the park itself, a bravura example of landscape art that has quickly made this newly opened attraction one of Seattle's essential sights.

Extending north from the OSP is **Myrtle Edwards Park**, with bike and pedestrian paths winding along the shore for a couple of miles and continuing through the adjoining Elliott Bay Park before terminating near the Magnolia Bridge.

Seattle Art Museum

Close to Pike Place Market along First Avenue, the **Seattle Art Museum** (usually Tues–Sun 10am–5pm, Thurs until 9pm; $7, free first Thurs of month; ☎206/654-3100, www.seattleartmuseum.org), is one of the top cultural institutions in the Pacific Northwest. Designed by Robert Venturi, the museum is visually unmistakable for the giant, inset letters on its south façade. It's also well known for artist Jonathan Borofsky's **Hammering Man** kinetic sculpture, a 48ft black-steel and aluminum marvel pounding away below the letters. The museum has undergone dramatic remodeling and expansion in the past several years and reopened in May 2007, with a new main entrance on First Avenue at Union Street. On the first floor, visitors can take a look at the various temporary works arrayed in **Sarkowsky Hall**, or proceed up to the second level to the **Brotman Forum**, which has numerous, rotating large-scale installations, conceptual and sculptural pieces by modern artists spread across 5000 square feet.

On the third floor are the **Wright Galleries for Modern and Contemporary Art**, where you may see regional **modern art** from budding Northwest talents. However, the main attractions are the monumental **nineteenth-century American** paintings by landscape masters Frederic Church and Albert Bierstadt and **twentieth-century works** like Andy Warhol's *Double Elvis*, the sixteen photographic tunnels of Gilbert & George's *Coloured Shouting*, Bruce Nauman's neon wall-piece *Double Poke in the Eye II*, Roy Lichtenstein's cartoonish *Study for Vicki!*, and Robert Arneson's provocative pun *John With Art*. There are also **textile** pieces from a variety of eras and styles, and **international art** from Japan, China, Korea, Indonesia, the Andes, and the Near East, with a large section of indigenous art from the Northwest Coast. Especially notable are the **Native American** totem poles, rattles, and canoes, along with colorful headdresses, masks, baskets, and woven fabrics.

The top (fourth) floor is the place for **special exhibitions** – everything from retrospectives of modern masters to the big-ticket traveling shows that feature mummies, Chinese dynasty art, ancient scrolls, and the like. Two rooms showcase Italian ceramics and European porcelain. Most of the eighteenth- and nineteenth-century European works, pre-modern pieces, and antiquities on display here are minor works, though the contemporary and traditional **African art** includes surprising pieces like *Mercedes-Benz Shaped Coffin* by Ghana's Kane Kwei, a jarring blend of postmodern style and traditional design.

The museum also hosts a full schedule of concerts, films, lectures, and other special programs, detailed in the program guides available in the lobby; a fine arts **bookstore** sits just inside the entrance.

The Business District

Between Second and Seventh avenues, most of Downtown is dominated by the steel-and-glass office towers of Seattle's **Business District**. While some large, local enterprises do have their flagship stores here, including REI and Nordstrom, the resident cultural attractions are mostly limited to a few arts complexes and a handful of distinctive buildings.

The heart of the commercial center is the giant **Westlake Center**, 400 Pine St (daily 10am–9pm; ☏206/287-0762), a multi-story enclosed mall that offers the standard retail experience; it is most notable for being the southern terminus of the 1.3-mile **monorail** (see p.288). The adjacent, diagonal **Westlake Park**, on Fourth Avenue between Pike and Pine, hosts occasional lunchtime concerts and the odd political rally near its distinctive water-wall fountain. Two blocks south of the mall, at Fifth Avenue and University, the **Rainier Tower** is a familiar presence on any list of big-name Seattle skyscrapers, notable for its narrowly tapering base, which gives the structure an uneasy, top-heavy appearance.

A block west, **Benaroya Hall**, the home of the **Seattle Symphony** (see p.333), occupies an entire city block, its massive, curving glass-curtain wall in the Grand Lobby affording views of Elliott Bay, while the chandeliers by glass titan Dale Chihuly are just a few of the decorative highlights. Heading south, you'll come across a handful of the city's most noteworthy pieces of modern architecture, starting with the postmodern **Washington Mutual Tower**, 1201 3rd Ave, a 1988 landmark presenting an array of glittering, convex glass paneling and gradual setbacks, and rising up to a striped triangular roof. Seattle's highest building is the darkly looming **Columbia Center**, at 701 Fifth Ave, which has had in its twenty-year history no fewer than three name changes; three concave walls give the structure an oddly curving silhouette. Nearly a thousand feet high, the tower has more stories – 76 – than any other building west of the Mississippi River. As you might expect, the **observation deck** (Mon–Fri 8.30am–4.30pm; $5, kids $3) on the 73rd floor provides a superb panoramic view of the surrounding area.

The best modern building in the city, though, is the new central branch of the **Seattle Public Library**, 1000 4th Ave (Mon–Thurs 10am–8pm, Fri–Sat 10am–6pm, Sun noon–6pm; ☎206/386-4636, ⓦwww.spl.org), a colossal Rem Koolhaas creation that resembles few other libraries in America. With a façade composed of brilliantly reflective glass panels, unexpected angles, and cantilevered stories looming high above, the library amazes even at street level, long before you enter. Inside, the **concourse level** resembles a huge greenhouse for books, with a pitched ceiling, windows on a massive triangular grid, and sunlight cutting through to create arch shadows among the stacks. The upper levels, collectively known as the **Spiral**, are a bit harder to navigate, with their myriad ramps, escalators, and cramped geometry. Don't miss the bizarre corridor where the **conference rooms** are located, north of the concourse, an eerie, blood-red tunnel that looks more like something out of *The Shining* than a hallway in a public institution.

Pioneer Square and around

Seattle's oldest district is **Pioneer Square**, whose rough-hewn, stone-clad architecture harkens back to the glory days of late-nineteenth-century Romanesque Revival design. **Occidental Park** and tours of the **Seattle Underground** draw a steady stream of visitors, and unlike the sanitized historical zones of some cities, Seattle's variety hasn't lost all its old-time grime and squalor, so be careful at night. After dark, rock music spills out from a group of lively taverns (see "Nightlife," p.329), with blues, rock, and jazz bands on the bill at a handful of top-notch clubs. There are plenty of fine **restaurants**, **bars**, and **galleries** here, too, and smart **boutiques**, **bars**, and **bookstores** – most housed in elegant brick, terracotta, and stone edifices from the 1880s and 90s.

Pioneer Square Park and Smith Tower

A good place to start your wanderings is at the triangular block of **Pioneer Square Park**, between James Street and First Avenue, which marks the place where Henry Yesler's **sawmill** first processed logs in the 1850s. Decades later, the site was to come under the shadow of the adjacent **Pioneer Building**, a massive pile of stone cladding, chunky columns, and rough-hewn arches and towers, highlighted inside by an elegant atrium and vintage gated elevators.

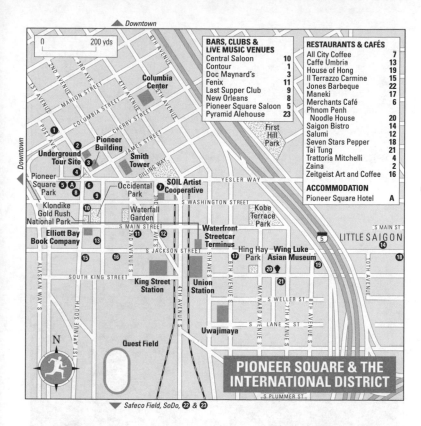

▲ Downtown

| 0   200 yds |

BARS, CLUBS & LIVE MUSIC VENUES
Central Saloon   10
Contour   1
Doc Maynard's   3
Fenix   11
Last Supper Club   9
New Orleans   8
Pioneer Square Saloon   5
Pyramid Alehouse   23

RESTAURANTS & CAFÉS
All City Coffee   7
Caffe Umbria   13
House of Hong   19
Il Terrazzo Carmine   15
Jones Barbeque   22
Maneki   17
Merchants Café   6
Phnom Penh
  Noodle House   20
Saigon Bistro   14
Salumi   12
Seven Stars Pepper   18
Tai Tung   21
Trattoria Mitchelli   4
Zaina   2
Zeitgeist Art and Coffee 16

ACCOMMODATION
Pioneer Square Hotel   A

Columbia Center

Pioneer Building

Underground Tour Site

Smith Tower

First Hill Park

Pioneer Square Park

SOIL Artist Cooperative

Occidental Park

YESLER WAY

Klondike Gold Rush National Park

Waterfall Garden

S WASHINGTON STREET

Kobe Terrace Park

Elliott Bay Book Company

S MAIN STREET

Waterfront Streetcar Terminus

S MAIN ST

LITTLE SAIGON

S JACKSON STREET

Hing Hay Park

Wing Luke Asian Museum

SOUTH KING STREET

King Street Station

Union Station

S WELLER ST

S LANE ST

Uwajimaya

N

Quest Field

PIONEER SQUARE & THE INTERNATIONAL DISTRICT

S PLUMMER ST

▼ Safeco Field, SoDo, 22 & 23

Outside the building, at First Avenue and Yesler Way, a glass and iron **pergola** has long been a local landmark (and a national one since 1977), while on its north side, another official landmark, the **Tlingit totem pole**, was acquired in 1899 after local members of the Chamber of Commerce broke into an Alaskan Indian village and stole it without apology or recompense. Although the men were fined $500 for their actions by a judge, the city kept its booty.

A block east of the park is Seattle's first major skyscraper, the white terracotta-trimmed **Smith Tower**, at Yesler Way and Second Avenue. Built in 1914 by New York gun and typewriter mogul L.C. Smith, the 42-floor tower was long the tallest building west of the Mississippi. It's worth looking in on the elegant lobby, decked out with marble and carved Native American busts. Eight old-fashioned brass elevators, still manually operated after ninety years, serve the 35th-floor **observation deck** (April–Oct 10am–dusk; Nov–March 10am–3.30pm; $7.50).

The Seattle Underground

Adjacent to the park, **Bill Speidel's Underground Tour** (hours vary by month, usually leaving daily on the hour 11am–4pm, sometimes until 6pm; $11, kids $5; ℡206/682-4646, ⓦwww.undergroundtour.com) is the most popular way of touring the **Seattle Underground**. Departing from *Doc Maynard's* pub, 610 1st Ave, the tour offers a bewitching ninety-minute look at the subterranean history of the former streets of Pioneer Square. After

△ Smith Tower

The Great Seattle Fire

The **Great Seattle Fire**, which caused more than $15 million worth of damage to downtown, was in many ways an unexpected blessing: the city was forced to rebuild the area with a safer infrastructure, which helped to modernize its Business District and gave rise to many of the buildings that lend Pioneer Square its historic character today. The fire occurred June 6, 1889, when one John Back was melting glue on a stove in a basement carpentry shop. The glue pot overheated, starting a blaze that quickly spread to the streets and ignited about fifty tons of ammunition in nearby hardware stores. More than ninety percent of the buildings in the central business district were wooden – with both streets and buildings on stilts to keep them out of the mud – and, though no lives were lost, much of Seattle was wiped out overnight. During rebuilding, businesses operated from makeshift tents as the wooden structures were replaced by brick ones and streets were straightened and widened to make them friendlier for commerce. As a result, Seattle gained 17,000 residents over the next year alone. For an informative exhibit on the fire, visit the Museum of History and Industry, p.316.

rising tides repeatedly backed up sewage drains and caused flooding, street levels were elevated by an entire story (ten feet) in the 1890s, and the original storefronts soon became underground businesses in several ways. Accessible via subterranean corridors and narrow passageways, creaky ladders and dark stairways, some legitimate merchants continued to hawk their wares underground until 1907, when the subsurface zone was officially closed, though some truly "underground" businesses, like speakeasies, burlesque joints, and brothels, continued to operate into the 1930s.

Klondike Gold Rush National Park and Elliott Bay Book Company

A few blocks south from Pioneer Square Park, at 117 S Main St, **Klondike Gold Rush National Park** (daily 9am–5pm; free; ⓦ www.nps.gov/klse) is not a park at all, but rather a simple but informative museum where free films and a few artifacts portray the 1897 rush, kick-started by the discovery of the precious ore in the Klondike region of Canada. As soon as the first ship carrying Klondike gold docked in the city, Seattle's sharp-eyed capitalists envisioned massive trading potential in selling groceries, clothing, sledges, and even ships to the gold-seekers. Hastily they launched a formidable publicity campaign, bombarding inland cities with propaganda billing Seattle above all other ports as the gateway to Yukon gold. It worked: prospectors streamed in, merchants (and con men) scented easy profit, the population escalated, and traders made a quick fortune.

A block west of Klondike Park, one of the neighborhood's other top attractions is the famed **Elliott Bay Book Company**, 101 S Main St (Mon–Sat 9.30am–10pm, Sun 11am–7pm; ☎206/624-6600, ⓦ www.elliottbaybook.com), with a selection of 150,000 volumes on three levels. The store is an essential spot for browsing, meeting literary-minded friends, or listening to readings, which take place nightly in the underground section.

Occidental Park and around

Just north of the bookstore, the 1889 **Grand Central Arcade**, 214 1st Ave S, is a prime location for restaurants and boutiques, its glassy, subterranean arcade leading to **Occidental Park**, a tree-lined, cobblestone plaza ringed by shops and cafés (and inhabited by homeless people) that prominently displays four of native artist Duane Pasco's **totem poles**, carved with various figures from regional Native American legends. The park's other striking figures include the four masked, bronze figures of the **Seattle Fallen Firefighters Memorial**, honoring the 31 local firemen who have lost their lives in the line of duty since 1889, the memorial's strewn granite slabs symbolizing the job's difficult conditions (such as chaos and collapsed buildings). A block east on Main is the **Waterfall Garden**, whose 22ft cascade was built in 1907 with rough boulders and surrounding foliage; it's maintained by a foundation associated with the delivery company UPS, which opened its first location here in the early twentieth century.

South of Occidental Park, **S Occidental Avenue** (pedestrians only between S Washington and S Jackson streets) holds the greatest concentration of Seattle's **galleries**, mostly showcases for safe, modern abstractions and glassworks; those with a taste for edgy, postmodern pursuits can walk one long block east of the Waterfall Garden and drop in on the **SOIL Artist Cooperative**, 112 Third Ave S (Thurs–Sun noon–5pm; free; T206/264-8061, W www.soilart.org), which is well regarded for its compelling, sometimes shocking displays of contemporary artworks, among them elegant porcelain sculptures of snub-nosed revolvers and a "Last Supper" featuring Ronald McDonald.

The International District and SoDo

Like many neighborhoods named by municipal bureaucracies, the so-called **International District** is a charmless moniker for what is in fact a broad collection of thriving Asian communities. Once known as Chinatown, this vivacious urban zone just southeast of Pioneer Square has in recent years welcomed immigrants from the Philippines, Laos, South Korea, and especially Vietnam. Bordered by Second and Twelfth avenues (west–east) and Washington and Weller streets (north–south), the dozen or so blocks that make up the district can be covered on foot in an hour or so. One great place to sample the district's flavor is at the huge pan-Asian supermarket/variety store **Uwajimaya**, 600 5th Ave S (daily 9am–10pm, Sun until 9pm; T206/624-6248, W www.uwajimaya.com). Acting as a busy community center as much as a retail outlet, it offers not only a giant array of foodstuffs, from spicy seasonings to the prized geoduck ("gooey-duck") clam, but also a wide range of Asian gifts and hand-crafted items, scented candles, and origami paper, and even classes on making sushi.

At the southern edge of the International District lies impressive **Safeco Field**, home to Seattle's Major League Baseball team, the Mariners, and a bit farther north, **Qwest Field**, home to the Seattle Seahawks football team (see p.56). Farther south, **SoDo**, or "South of Downtown," is the bleeding edge of gentrification in Seattle, with new condos, galleries, boutiques, and upper-end restaurants appearing by the week. There are no other major sights, though, aside from the (private) corporate headquarters of the **Starbucks** empire, a mile south at 2401 Utah Ave S, based in a 1915 brick complex with two million square feet of space, crowned with the eyes of the familiar green mermaid in a manner reminiscent of George Orwell's *1984*.

Union and King Street stations

On the west side of the International District, the unmistakable focal point is a pair of rail centers that, at one time or another, served as the city's transportation hubs. The first, **Union Station**, Fourth Ave at Jackson St (Mon–Sat 9am–5pm; free), is a sparkling, restored complex that has maintained the allure of old-fashioned railroad transit – it was originally built by a Union Pacific subsidiary in 1911 – while changing step for a new era. The building's splendid centerpiece is the **Great Hall**, a barrel-vaulted Beaux Arts jewel whose ceiling rises to 80ft and whose walls feature ornate glass windows and trompe l'oeil detailing that gives the impression of classical stone construction. By contrast, a block west at 303 S Jackson St, **King Street Station** was the Northern Pacific Railroad's 1906 entry into the rail transit scene. Now serving Amtrak trains, the dreary and somewhat dilapidated interior isn't much to look at, especially compared with Union Station.

Wing Luke Asian Museum

Three blocks east of Union Station, the main cultural institution of note in the area is the **Wing Luke Asian Museum**, 407 7th Ave S (Tues–Fri 11am–4.30pm, Sat–Sun noon–4pm; $4, kids $2; ⓦwww.wingluke.org), whose namesake was the first Asian-American elected official in the Northwest when he won a seat on the Seattle City Council in 1962. Portraying two hundred years of Asian and Pacific Island immigration, from the first Hawaiian settlers to more recent newcomers from Southeast Asia, its several small rooms are easily covered within an hour or two. The museum holds old photographs, ceremonial garments, oral and written histories of individual immigrants, and various compelling displays, including a walk-through replica that simulates the assembly center of "**Camp Harmony**" in Puyallup, Washington, where thousands of American-born Japanese from Seattle were incarcerated during World War II.

Hing Hay and Kobe Terrace parks

Just across from the museum, **Hing Hay Park**, at the corner of King and Maynard streets, is the nominal center of the International District, with its ornate pagoda made in Taiwan and its large, somewhat faded dragon mural. Although it's pleasant enough, you're better off heading three blocks north, taking a steep hike up to the top of Washington Street to enter the far greener **Kobe Terrace Park**, named after Seattle's Japanese sister city, where a two-hundred-year-old, eight-thousand-pound stone lantern graces the entrance. Narrow paths wind down through community gardens built into the park's slope, quaint cherry trees add to the splendor, and the sweeping views of the region can be inspiring – even though the rush of traffic on nearby I-5 does prove to be something of a distraction to one's reverie.

Belltown

Starting just above Pike Place Market and extending a mile north toward Seattle Center, **Belltown** has recently undergone a remarkable fifteen-year transformation from decaying inner-city wasteland to the desired address of would-be

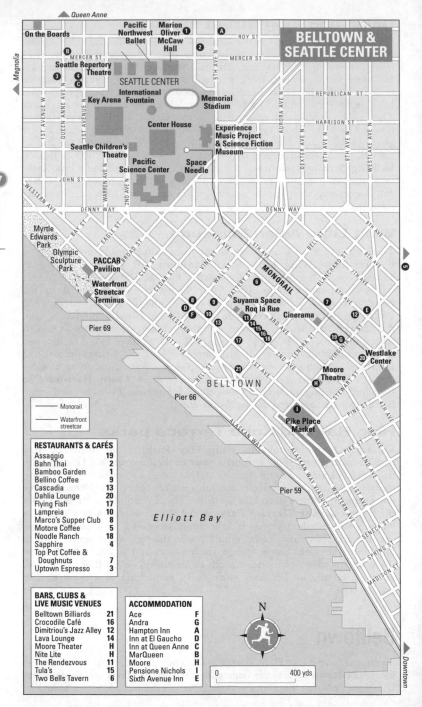

BELLTOWN & SEATTLE CENTER

Queen Anne

On the Boards

Pacific Northwest Ballet

Marion Oliver McCaw Hall ❶

ⓐ ROY ST

❷

Magnolia

ⓑ

Seattle Repertory Theatre

MERCER ST

MERCER ST

❸

❹

ⓒ

SEATTLE CENTER

REPUBLICAN ST

International Fountain

Key Arena

Memorial Stadium

HARRISON ST

Center House

Experience Music Project & Science Fiction Museum

Seattle Children's Theatre

Pacific Science Center

Space Needle

JOHN ST

WESTERN AVE

DENNY WAY

DENNY WAY

Myrtle Edwards Park

Olympic Sculpture Park

PACCAR Pavilion

Waterfront Streetcar Terminus

Pier 69

MONORAIL

Suyama Space Roq la Rue

Cinerama

❻

ⓓ ❽
ⓕ ❾
❿
⓭
⓫
⓮
⓯
⓰ ⓮
⓱ ⓲

❼

⓬ ⓔ

⓳ ⓖ

⓴

Westlake Center

Pier 66

⓴

BELLTOWN

Moore Theatre

ⓗ

ⓘ

Pike Place Market

Elliott Bay

Pier 59

Monorail

Waterfront streetcar

RESTAURANTS & CAFÉS

Assaggio	19
Bahn Thai	2
Bamboo Garden	1
Bellino Coffee	9
Cascadia	13
Dahlia Lounge	20
Flying Fish	17
Lampreia	10
Marco's Supper Club	8
Motore Coffee	5
Noodle Ranch	18
Sapphire	4
Top Pot Coffee & Doughnuts	7
Uptown Espresso	3

BARS, CLUBS & LIVE MUSIC VENUES

Belltown Billiards	21
Crocodile Café	16
Dimitriou's Jazz Alley	12
Lava Lounge	14
Moore Theater	H
Nite Lite	H
The Rendezvous	11
Tula's	15
Two Bells Tavern	6

ACCOMMODATION

Ace	F
Andra	G
Hampton Inn	A
Inn at El Gaucho	D
Inn at Queen Anne	B
MarQueen	C
Moore	H
Pensione Nichols	I
Sixth Avenue Inn	E

N

0   400 yds

SEATTLE

7

Pier 66

Sub Pop Records

No Seattle label has had a greater impact on rock music and popular culture than **Sub Pop Records**, which grew out of DJ, rock critic, and record-store owner Bruce Pavitt's fanzine on the burgeoning Seattle alternative rock scene in the early 1980s. By mid-decade, local musician and club booker Jonathan Poneman had joined the Sub Pop team, and the label quickly became recognized for recording and promoting a distinct style of music that fused punk with metal. Characterized by sludgy guitars, dirge-like riffs, and an attitude, particularly evident in the lyrics, that was even more sour and cynical than either metal or punk, this sometimes-incendiary mix became loosely known as **grunge** – though it was also inspired by such non-grunge artists as the Pixies, Sonic Youth, and My Bloody Valentine. Green River, Tad, Mudhoney, Soundgarden, and Nirvana, all Sub Pop labelmates, were some of the leaders of the movement, and their album covers, with their viciously satirical graphics, were as easily recognized as their sound. Though Nirvana left for major label Geffen before Nevermind propelled them to stardom, Sub Pop garnered a small percentage of the profits from that album's sales as part of Geffen's contract buyout deal, helping to keep the financially troubled label afloat in the early 1990s. A few years later, Sub Pop sold off part ownership to Warner Brothers for a reported $20 million, though its heyday had already passed.

hipsters. Shiny high-rise housing sits next to funky brick flophouses, upscale restaurants are pushing out low-rent diners, grungy thrift stores compete with overpriced boutiques for visitors' attention and wallets, and the downtrodden presence of the homeless receives scant eye contact from self-styled fashion mavens in knockoff designer clothes.

Belltown became a focus of Seattle's music and arts scene in the latter part of the 1980s, with **Sub Pop Records** (see box above) famously promoting the alternative-rock scene. Nowadays, the hip core of Belltown is confined to a three-block area of **Second Avenue** between Lenora and Battery streets, where the strip's remaining cafés, bars, secondhand clothing outlets, record stores, and galleries cater to those local students and artists who haven't yet been priced out of the area. For a glimpse of the remaining color and quirkiness of the area, visit the **Crocodile Café**, 2200 2nd Ave (℡206/441-5611, ⓦwww.thecrocodile.com), a club and diner presenting both unknowns and underground-rock royalty, along with poetry, theater, art, and "circus side shows."

The hub of Belltown's **gallery scene** can be found along a similar stretch of Second Avenue. **Suyama Space**, no. 2324 (Mon–Fri 9am–5pm; ℡206/256-0809), is well regarded for its challenging avant-garde and conceptual installations, while close by is the much lighter-hearted **Roq La Rue**, no. 2316 (Wed–Thurs & Sat 1–6pm, Fri 1–7pm; ℡206/374-8977, ⓦwww.roqlarue.com), presenting a flashy parade of brightly colored, often bizarre works with themes taken from pop culture and mass entertainment.

The Seattle Center

The **Seattle Center** campus (ⓦwww.seattlecenter.com), along with the **monorail** route that leads to it (see p.288), grew out of the 1962 World's Fair. Since then, it's transformed itself into a busy sports and culture hub, highlighted

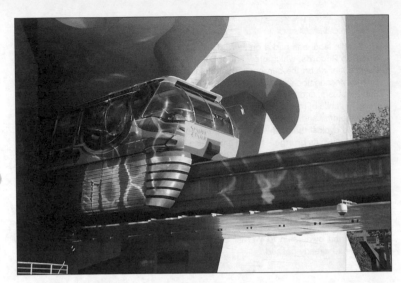

△ Monorail at The Seattle Center

by such varied institutions as the **Pacific Science Center**, **Seattle Children's Theatre** and **Children's Museum**, the **Experience Music Project**, and the iconic **Space Needle**. In addition, it features public plazas and venues for music, dance and drama. For sports fans, **Key Arena** is the home of professional basketball and minor-league hockey teams (for ticket info), and the other large onsite facilities, **Memorial Stadium**, **Marion Oliver McCaw Hall**, and **Mural Amphitheatre**, are mainly used for amateur sports, opera and dance performances, and concert events, respectively. The amphitheatre also features some of the Northwest's largest festivals (see p.334), which take place as well in the Center House, near the middle of the complex. Don't miss the **International Fountain** nearby, a hemispheric dome set in its own concrete crater that regularly pulses and blasts streams of water high in the air. The fun is watching the water spray up into the sky, then waiting as the torrent crashes down on you.

The Space Needle

The most prominent relic of the World's Fair is the **Space Needle** (Sun–Thurs 9am–11pm, Fri–Sat 9am–midnight; $14, two trips in 24hr $17; Ⓦwww .spaceneedle.com). With a shaft rising 605ft to support the flying-saucer-shaped floors near its crown, the tower was built to symbolize the future – though it more resembles an oversize prop from a vintage sci-fi flick. Whatever its architectural value, the Needle has become so inextricably linked to the skyline of the city that it now all but symbolizes the city itself. The 43-second elevator ride to the **observation deck** is a pricey but obligatory experience for the first-time visitor. Any cynicism sparked by the mobs of tourists and overpriced admission tends to disappear on arriving at the top: the striking panorama of the region encompasses neighboring lakes, the Downtown skyline, Puget Sound, Queen Anne, and distant peaks like Mount Rainier – provided the skies are clear, of course.

Seattle Children's Theatre and Children's Museum

The intriguing **Seattle Children's Theatre**, 201 Thomas St (kids $12–25, adults $20–32; ☎206/441-3322, ⓦwww.sct.org), presents local works created specifically for kids, as well as dramatic and musical adaptations of everything from Dr Seuss books to *The Devil and Daniel Webster*, in two spaces, the shows geared to different age levels. Shows run Fridays through Sundays, with matinees. Tickets tend to disappear quickly, so showing up an hour before showtime is definitely not recommended. Meanwhile, the **Children's Museum**, in the Center House (Mon–Fri 10am–5pm, Sat & Sun 10am–6pm; $7.50 for all ages; ☎206/441-1768, ⓦwww.thechildrensmuseum.org), offers tot-friendly attractions like the **Mountain Forest**, which lets kids crawl through logs or simulate a rock climb. The **Discovery Bay** section has exhibits geared for children two and a half years old or younger, and the **Global Village** is an earnest attempt to create multicultural awareness with international clothing, food, and toys.

Pacific Science Center

Close to the Children's Theatre, the ever popular **Pacific Science Center** (summer daily 10am–6pm, rest of the year Mon–Fri 10am–5pm, Sat–Sun 10am–6pm; $10, kids $7; ☎206/443-2001, ⓦwww.pacsci.org) comprises five interconnected buildings, the emphasis firmly on hands-on interactive exhibits, some computer-oriented but most simple enough for preadolescents to operate. It makes for a lively environment, full of bright, innovative, and often noisy exhibits, from robotic dinosaurs to machines that let you measure your grip strength, peripheral vision, sense of smell, and other traits in a highly tactile manner that's more akin to operating pinball machines than getting tested at the doctor's office. Fans of giant-screen, nature-oriented **IMAX films** have a chance to see such curiosities for the price of a combo museum/film ticket ($15, kids $12; IMAX only $8).

The Experience Music Project

A more recent highlight of the Seattle Center is the Frank Gehry–designed **Experience Music Project** (Wed–Mon 10am–5pm, summer closes 6pm; $20, kids $15; ☎206/367-5483, ⓦwww.emplive.org), a giant burst of colored aluminum – into which the monorail passes – that houses an 80,000-piece collection of rock memorabilia divided up into exhibits on different phases of popular music history, as well as rotating exhibits on subjects from Bob Dylan to Brooklyn hip-hop. Highlights include the **Guitar Gallery**, with its dozens of acoustic and electric guitars and basses, such as the intriguing 1933 Dobro all-electric with built-in speakers, and the 1957 Gibson "Flying V," used by ace pickers Lonnie Mack and Albert King. **Northwest Passage** traces the local rock scene from instrumental pioneers the Ventures through the grunge era to modern rockers like Sleater-Kinney and Modest Mouse, with an entire case devoted to rock anthem "Louie Louie." The large **Sound Lab** enables visitors to play guitar, bass, keyboards, drums, and DJ turntables, with a bit of help from the staff and interactive computer terminals, while the **Hendrix Gallery** traces Jimi's career from his days as a sideman with the Isley Brothers to his short-lived psychedelic funk group Band of Gypsies. Topping it all off is the monumental **Roots and Branches** sculpture, six hundred guitars tied together in a monster tree looming above the gallery floor.

Also on the site, the newer **Science Fiction Museum and Hall of Fame** is supposedly a separate institution, but you'll have to purchase a combined ticket with the EMP ($27, kids $20) to see it. Pop sci-fi fans will delight to the toy spaceships, futuristic sets, and alien attire on display – including sleek costumes from *Blade Runner*, weapons from a simple phaser to a light saber to Jane Fonda's *Barbarella* crossbow, and the iconic captain's chair from *Star Trek*.

Queen Anne

Spreading out northwest from the Seattle Center is the charming, well-heeled hillside district of **Queen Anne**. At the time of its construction, it was rarefied place where the city's upscale citizens lived in historic-revival mansions towering above the city; the only neighborhood access, other than walking, was by streetcars tugged by counterweights up a sheer incline. These days it still appeals for its architecture, some of the swells continue to live here, and you can now take a bus (#1, 2, 3, and 4) to the top of the slope.

By foot or wheel, the best route into the neighborhood is still by the steeply sloped Queen Anne Avenue, which heads northwest from the Seattle Center and connects the commercially oriented **Lower Queen Anne**, home to many decent bars and nightspots, to the loftier precinct of **Upper Queen Anne**, where the main activity takes place between Galer and McGraw streets, a six-block strip of fancy eateries and yuppie-oriented coffeehouses. Running east-west between the upper and lower parts of the district, **Highland Drive** features multimillion-dollar estates and somewhat smaller mansions, most with awe-inspiring views of the metropolis and Puget Sound. Amid this collection of Neoclassical, Georgian, Italianate and Colonial Revival dwellings you can enjoy your own view from **Kerry Park**, on Highland at 2nd Ave W, where the Space Needle and Business District are well placed for shutterbugs and the entire city spreads out before your eyes.

Magnolia

Even though it's only a few miles along the curve of Elliott Bay northwest from Downtown, affluent **Magnolia** feels much farther away, with pleasant tree-lined slopes and an aura of isolation. The neighborhood is most notable for Seattle's green jewel, **Discovery Park**. With more than five hundred acres of meadows, rustic fields, woods, and walking trails, it's that rare urban park that, on its best days, feels like a genuine slice of wilderness. The **visitor center** (Tues–Sun 8.30am–5pm; ☎206/386-4236), just inside the east entrance at 36th Ave W and W Government Way, organizes weekend walks spotlighting the park's abundant bird and plant life – from herons and owls to wildflowers. A 2.8-mile **loop trail** can be entered here that winds among much of the park's most densely forested regions. At the **south entrance**, on W Emerson St near Magnolia Blvd, a trail leads across the windswept meadows between the parking lot and the nearby bluffs. From this vantage point, the view is one of the area's best, taking in Puget Sound ships, Bainbridge Island, and, on a clear day, the snowcapped Mount Rainier. Follow the path at the edge of the bluff north until you reach the **South Beach trail**, from which a long wooden staircase winds down to the narrow, rocky, unswimmable beach to the south and the **West Point Lighthouse** to the north – a squat 1881 structure that's the city's oldest, with a vaguely New England feel.

In the park's southwestern corner, there are still vestiges of the military's presence in the old buildings of **Fort Lawton**, where the **history tours** (on periodic Saturdays 2–4pm; free; call visitor center for details) take you inside the guardhouse where drunk or misbehaving soldiers were jailed in three solitary confinement cells, each measuring just four feet by eight feet.

The Lake Washington Ship Canal

Eight miles long, the **Lake Washington Ship Canal** separates Downtown from the northern districts and connects Elliott Bay to **Lake Union** and farther east to larger **Lake Washington**. Built around 1900 to carry ships to safe harbors on the inland lakes, the canal is known for its sizable community of **houseboats** along Lake Union's eastern shore, around the residential community of **Eastlake**, and there are a few sights along the canal that are among the city's top attractions. If you want to get a look at this part of Lake Union from the water, take one of the hourly **Sunday cruises** on the *Fremont Avenue* ferry, which departs nearby from under the Aurora Bridge, 801 N Northlake Way (June–Sept 11.45am, 1pm & 2.15pm; $14, kids $6; ☎206-713-8446, ⓦwww.seattleferryservice.com), and include close-up perspectives on Seattle's canals and lakes and views of notable houseboats.

Near the western mouth of the canal, a procession of boats passes from saltwater to freshwater through the **Hiram M. Chittenden Locks** (bus #17 from downtown; daily 7.30am–9pm; ⓦwww.nws.usace.army.mil). Migrating salmon bypass the locks via the **fish ladder**, which enables the fish to lay and fertilize their eggs, tasks that must be completed in freshwater. The ladder's 21 "steps," or weirs, are best viewed between July and September, when chinook, sockeye, and coho salmon jump around the ladder at the peak of their upstream migration. The visitor center (Oct–April Thurs–Mon 10am–4pm; summer daily 10am–6pm; free), on the north side of the locks, has interesting exhibits on the history of the canal and the locks' construction, and free guided **tours** of the locks leave from here (March–Nov, hours vary; details at ☎206/783-7059).

East of the locks spreads Salmon Bay, on the south side of which, beside the Ballard Bridge at 15th Avenue NW, lies **Fishermen's Terminal**, 3919 18th Ave W (daily 7am–4.30pm; ☎206/728-3395, ⓦwww.portseattle.org/seaport), a leading home port for West Coast commercial fishing, providing moorage for about seven hundred vessels; during weekdays, you may catch their operators unloading their crab and salmon hauls. Near the dock is the striking **Fishermen's Memorial**, a towering granite pillar topped by a fisherman hauling in his catch, featuring a copper frieze of swarms of fish around the base.

Ballard

North across the ship canal from Magnolia, formerly blue-collar **Ballard** has become a rather hip scene in places, loaded with rugged, historic buildings housing grassroots galleries, alternative clubs, old-style dive bars, and scruffy diners. Begin your exploration on and around **Ballard Avenue** between 17th and 22nd avenues NW. Area highlights include the old **Fire House no. 18**,

5429 Russell Ave NW, an eye-catching brick structure from 1911 with wooden roof brackets, looming tower, and quaint red gates that used to open for the station's horse-drawn fire engines; the **Ballard Library**, 5614 22nd Ave NW (☎206/684-4089, ⓦwww.spl.org), most notable for its "**green roof**" equipped with solar panels and 18,000 hardy plants to soak up wastewater; and, on the second Saturday night of the month, the district's groovy **Art Walks** (6–9pm), where you can immerse yourself in the trendy local art scene at the late-closing galleries.

For a hint of Ballard's old-time character, the **Nordic Heritage Museum**, 3014 NW 67th St (Mon–Sat 10am-4pm, Sun noon–4pm; $4; ☎206/789-5707, ⓦwww.nordicmuseum.org), takes you through the immigrant experience from 1840 to 1920, spotlighting the region's Scandinavian American communities. The **Ballard Story** display re-creates the early days with photographs and historical narratives, while the second floor hosts the **Heritage Rooms**, devoted to fishing and logging, along with artifacts from five Nordic groups, including traditional clothing, tapestries, and household items decorated with folk art, such as a Danish flax beater and a Finnish birdhouse designed to look like a church. On the top floor, the highlight is the **Iceland Room**, a replica of the interior of a chilly rural farmhouse from the early twentieth century.

Fremont and Wallingford

The northern Seattle districts of **Fremont** and **Wallingford** are vigorous, spirited communities that, thanks to their quirky appeal and unpretentious bohemian vibe, are being forced to cope with an influx of newcomers and a potential tidal wave of new development. What makes these places so engaging has little to do with their location (isolated from much of the city) or their conventional attractions (few), but their laid-back attitudes and preservation of

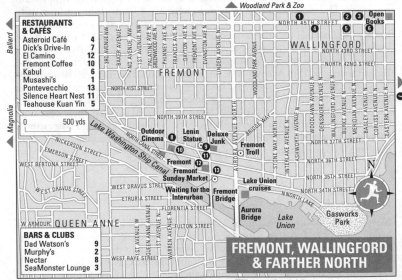

RESTAURANTS & CAFÉS
Asteroid Café	4
Dick's Drive-In	7
El Camino	12
Fremont Coffee	10
Kabul	6
Musashi's	1
Pontevecchio	13
Silence Heart Nest	11
Teahouse Kuan Yin	5

BARS & CLUBS
Dad Watson's	9
Murphy's	2
Nectar	8
SeaMonster Lounge	3

▲ Woodland Park & Zoo

FREMONT, WALLINGFORD & FARTHER NORTH

▼ Seattle Center & Downtown

Public art in Fremont

Fremont's indigenous **public art** embodies its playful sense of surrealism. Start your tour of the art scene at the **Rocket at the Center of the Universe**, a 53ft monument at the corner of N 35th Street and Evanston Avenue that looks more like a giant toy model than a space-traveling vessel, even though it's alleged to be an actual rocket fuselage taken from the facade of an Army surplus store. A block north, at the triangular corner of N 36th Street and Fremont Place, a colossal statue of **Vladimir Lenin** stands thrusting forth toward passing motorists, surrounded by blocky flames. This sculpture from Poprad, Slovakia, by Slavic artist Emil Venkov, is situated "temporarily" at this busy corner, on sale for a mere $150,000 – ironically, offers to buy the Communist Party stalwart are now entertained by the Fremont Chamber of Commerce (℡206/632-1500, ⓦwww.fremontseattle.com).

Down the road at N 34th Street, a much less aggressive artwork can be seen just east of Fremont Bridge, Richard Beyer's brilliant late-1970s sculpture **Waiting for the Interurban**, lifelike aluminum statues of five dour commuters waiting for the bus – supplemented by a small child and a dog – regularly adorned with football helmets, Hawaiian leis, and other offbeat accessories by locals. The undeniable highlight of the entire district, though, is the 18ft ferro-concrete **Fremont Troll** that lurks underneath Aurora Bridge, a five-minute walk from the Interurban at N 36th Street and Aurora Avenue N. Its left hand eternally crushing a real Volkswagen Bug between the concrete bridge pilings, the beast really does seem to preside over his own gloomy lair. The sculpture also serves as an inspiration for Fremont's Luminary Procession on October 31, dubbed "Trolloween." Starting here, a parade of masqueraders – some wearing jester outfits and wielding torches – moves through Fremont, putting on lively street performances and making cacophonous music along the way.

a certain old-fashioned, oddball Seattle style. Even with the new condos sprouting, Fremont and Wallingford retain their eccentric liberal charm.

Fremont

As you cross into the hub of Fremont from Ballard along Leary Way NW, signs proclaim "Welcome to Fremont, Center of the Universe. Turn your watch back 5 minutes." Another reads, "Welcome to Fremont, Center of the Universe. Throw your watch away." Both offer fair warning that the self-described **Artists Republic of Fremont** is not for those who take themselves too seriously. The district's core is the stretch of **Fremont Avenue N** that runs from the comparatively tiny Fremont Bridge at N 34th Street to N 37th Street, an array of coffeehouses, restaurants, microbreweries, and boutiques. One of the quirkier merchants is **Deluxe Junk**, 3518 Fremont Place N, showcasing a strange assortment of antiques, memorabilia, and flat-out garbage in a (former) funeral parlor. Just off Fremont Avenue, the **Fremont Sunday Market** (April–Oct 10am–5pm; Nov–Mar 10am–4pm; free; ⓦwww.fremontmarket.com/fremont) is a spirited flea market that highlights the city's bargain sellers of secondhand jewelry, furniture, clothing, trinkets, music, and other items, the merchants' stalls teeming with regional buyers as well as wide-eyed browsers. One long block west of the market site, Seattle's most unusual summer movie venue, the **Fremont Outdoor Cinema** (late June to Aug; $5; ℡206/781-4230, ⓦfremontoutdoormovies.com), runs a colorful variety of Hollywood blockbusters, cult films, and sing-along musicals every Saturday night at dusk during the summer. And amid everything else, Fremont is best regarded for its eye-catching, often outlandish public art (see box above).

Wallingford

Like Fremont to the southwest, **Wallingford** has a friendly, relaxed air, with an excellent assortment of restaurants, bars, antique stores, vintage clothing dealers, and cinemas. The district's axis lies along **N 45th Street** from Woodlawn to Bagley avenues; the very center of the strip is marked with giant capital letters atop a supermarket at no. 1801, spelling out "WALLINGFORD" in eye-catching blue-and-white neon. Among the more notable merchants here is **Open Books**, no. 2414 (T 206/633-0811, W www.openpoetrybooks .com), a self-described "poem emporium" located below a wine bar, flush with mainstream and alternative poetry and periodically hosting readings by notable local and national authors. An excellent pair of movie theaters, the older auditorium from 1919, is known as the **Guild 45th**, no. 2115 (T 206/633-3353, W www.landmarktheatres.com), a draw for its mainstream and independent fare.

Gasworks Park

On the southern edge of Wallingford, along the shores of **Lake Union**, twenty-acre **Gasworks Park**, 2101 N Northlake Way (daily 6am–11.30pm; T 206/684-4075), is one of the best places to get an expansive view of the city. The grounds were, until the mid-1950s, occupied by a massive industrial plant that converted coal and oil into gas. Several gigantic, ugly brown oxygen gas-generator towers still remain, the clash between the rotting dark structures and the surrounding green hills lending the site a strange aesthetic dissonance. The park's small hills and windy site on the banks of the lake make it a favorite spot for kite flyers, and its excellent location makes it Seattle's prime vantage point for Fourth of July fireworks, with Downtown and the Space Needle looming to the south.

Woodland Park Zoo and Woodland Park

North of Fremont and Wallingford, off Aurora Avenue, more than 250 species reside in the **Woodland Park Zoo**, N 55th St and Phinney Ave N (daily 9.30am–4pm, summer closes at 6pm; $10.50, kids $7.50; W www.zoo.org), a sleek facility whose spacious layout, humane enclosures, and botanical garden–quality trees and plants make it attractive to anyone with a love of nature. Most of the exhibits are thematically arranged to reflect different climates and terrains – Northern Trail, Tropical Asia, Tropical Forest, Temperate Forest, and so on – and this verisimilitude gives Woodland Park an engaging, bucolic feel, unlike the hemmed-in concrete bunkers of some big-city zoos.

The zoo is surrounded by the nearly two hundred acres of **Woodland Park** (daily 6am–11.30pm; T 206/684-4075), a nice refuge from the city and a natural preserve that's home to hiking trails, picnic tables, athletic facilities for tennis and lawn bowling, and a worthwhile **rose garden** (daily 7am–dusk; free), where you can sniff and gaze at nearly three hundred varieties of flowers in five thousand plantings – both old-fashioned red and pink roses as well as modern, multi-hued varieties.

The University District

East of I-5 sits the **University District**, or **U District**, centered on the **University of Washington**, home to 35,000 or so students. The 639-acre campus houses the **Henry Art Gallery**, one of the finest art museums in the city, and the **Burke Memorial Museum**, rich in its exhibits on Native Americans in the Pacific Northwest. But as with Capitol Hill, the U District's chief draw is its main drag, **University Way**, known as "**The Ave**," with its dozen or so blocks of student-centric establishments that stretch northward from NE 41st Street. It's always jam-packed with students and shoppers, who frequent the strip's cheap restaurants, secondhand music stores, and funky and vintage clothing boutiques.

The University of Washington campus

The **University of Washington** (ⓦ www.washington.edu) – or UW (pronounced U-dub), as it's known – is the most prominent educational institution in the Northwest, with sixteen schools and colleges. Before your wanderings, stop in at the **Visitors Information Center**, 4014 University Way NE (Mon–Fri 8am–5pm; ⓣ 206/543-9198, ⓦ depts.washington.edu/visitors), to pick up a free self-guided tour booklet of the university's highlights. Foremost among them is the botany greenhouse of the **medicinal herb garden** (Mon–Fri 8am–5pm; free; ⓦ depts.washington.edu/biology/greenhouse), which holds one of the largest collections of its kind in the US, with more than two thousand species. Particularly intriguing are the long ghostly fingers, huge green leaves, and luridly erect stalk of the *Amorphophallus titanium* – also known as corpse flower. Further along, the Gothic Revival **Suzzallo Library** (Mon–Thurs 7.30am–10pm, Fri 7.30am–6pm, Sat 9am–5pm, Sun noon–10pm; ⓦ www.lib.washington.edu/Suzzallo) has a reading room resembling the nave of a medieval church, and faces **Central Plaza**, a major student hot spot for socializing. At the edge of Union Bay, the **Waterfront Activities Center** (daily 10am–7pm; ⓦ depts.washington.edu/ima/IMA_wac.php) out rents rowboats or canoes for $7.50 an hour, providing a great way to take in the nearby lakes.

Henry Art Gallery

The university's **Henry Art Gallery**, west of Central Plaza at 15th Ave NE at NE 41st St (Tues–Sun 11am–5pm, Thurs until 8pm; $10, all students free; ⓣ 206/543-2280, ⓦ www.henryart.org), presents some of the most imaginative exhibits found in any of Seattle's art museums. Selections from the **permanent collection** include late-nineteenth- and early-twentieth-century landscapes by Winslow Homer and Ralph Blakelock, figurative paintings by Jacob Lawrence, prints by Rembrandt and Whistler, and photographs by Ansel Adams and Imogen Cunningham. By contrast, the **lower level** is full of changing contemporary exhibits, with three galleries largely devoted to risk-taking art, sometimes incorporating multiscreen projections and high technology, as well as barn-size installations combining sculpture, sound design, and architecture. The small outdoor **sculpture court** hosts James Turrell's **Skyscape** installation, an oval room with benches and a skylight hole in the roof, which allows sunlight to flit around the room at different angles depending on the hour and season.

The Burke Museum

A few blocks north of the Henry Art Gallery, the **Burke Museum**, 17th Ave NE at NE 45th St (daily 10am–5pm; $8; ⓦ www.washington.edu/burkemuseum), is UW's other top cultural attraction, focusing mostly on the natural and cultural history of Washington, the Pacific Northwest, and the Pacific Rim. On the upper floor, **The Life and Times of Washington State** is a kid-oriented time line of geological history offering the likes of volcanic crystals, a 140-million-year-old allosaurus, and a giant Ice Age-era sloth found during construction of a Sea-Tac airport runway. On the lower floor, **Pacific Voices** is a broad series of exhibits covering the cultures of Pacific Island and coastal communities, highlighted by an assemblage of masks used in the potlatch ceremonies of the Kwakwaka'wakw tribe of the Northwest Coast – including ones that change from one creature into another at the pull of a string. Also look for the "**grizzly bear house posts**" carved by Tlingit tribal artists Nathan and Stephen Jackson, which present modern carvings of the native legend of the hunter who married a bear – Nathan's is the more traditional, in wood, while Stephen's is more stylized and bizarre, in mixed-media.

Capitol Hill and around

South across Portage Bay from the U District lies **Capitol Hill**, which appeals for its easygoing vibe and liberal atmosphere, as well as its location not far from the city center. It has also, since the 1960s, been a center for the city's left-leaning political and cultural forces, an influence apparent in the area's alternative-minded shops and nightlife, its political canvassers who offer petitions to sign on the street corners, and its status as the undisputed center of the **gay and lesbian community**. Never is that more in evidence than during the annual Gay Pride parade down **Broadway** in June, now one of the city's most popular celebrations.

Volunteer Park

The northern end of the Capitol Hill district radiates old money, complete with gold-rush-era mansions sitting sedately around the shrubs and trees of **Volunteer Park**, 1247 15th Ave (daily 6am–11pm; ☎206/684-4075), named in honor of those who volunteered for the Spanish-American War of 1898. The lovely 1912 glass **Conservatory** here (daily: summer 10am–7pm; rest of year 10am–4pm; free) is divided into galleries simulating different climates (jungle, desert, rain forest, and so on). There's also a wealth of ferns and cacti, plus olive trees, orchids, and yuccas, along with bromeliads that crawl over rocks, shrubs, and trees.

Also located within the park is the **Seattle Asian Art Museum** (Tues–Sun 10am–5pm, Thurs until 9pm; ☎206/654-3100, ⓦ www.seattleartmuseum.org; $5), home to one of the most extensive collections of Asian art outside that continent. The single floor of exhibits encompasses Japanese, Korean, Vietnamese, Chinese, and Southeast Asian art, spread across many centuries and dynasties. Among the more interesting pieces are the meticulously crafted Japanese **landscape scrolls** and the theatrically grim **statues** of tomb guardians, court attendants, and warriors in the early Chinese art wing. Also in the park, the old **water tower** is, at 75ft, Capitol Hill's highest structure. At the top is the budget alternative to the Space Needle's observation deck: a free panoramic view of Seattle, although the wire mesh covering the small windows may well remind you why it's free.

Broadway and around

Despite recent commercialization, **Broadway** remains *the* place to hang out in Capitol Hill, whether you're browsing for trinkets, taking in the scene at

CAPITOL HILL

0 — 500 yds

ACCOMMODATION

11th Avenue Inn	H
Bacon Mansion	E
Eastlake Inn	A
Gaslight Inn	B
Mildred's	C
Salisbury House	G
Shafer-Baillie Mansion	F
Silver Cloud Inn	D
Sorrento	I

RESTAURANTS & CAFÉS

611 Supreme	15	Kingfish Café	3
Bauhaus	18	Machiavelli	17
Byzantion	4	Monsoon	1
Café Dilettante	7	Online Coffee Co.	14
Café Flora	5	Piecora's	25
Café Septieme	10	Siam on Broadway	2
Caffe Vita	22	Than Brothers	6
Coastal Kitchen	9	Victrola Coffee and Art	11
Globe Café	24	Vivace Espresso	12

BARS, CLUBS & LIVE MUSIC VENUES

Bad Juju Lounge	20	Neumo's	19
Century Ballroom	29	Vogue	23
Chop Suey	28	The War Room	26
Comet Tavern	21		
El Corazon	13		
Elysian Brewing Co.	27		
Linda's Tavern	16		
Lo-Fi Performance Gallery	8		

a bar or club, popping into one of the many boutiques, or sitting at one of the sidewalk cafés watching the crowds. On the northern end of Broadway, between E Roy Street and E Highland Drive, the **Harvard-Belmont Historic District**, along with adjacent Millionaires Row, is rich with huge Neoclassical mansions and sprawling period-revival homes; for a tour, contact the Seattle Architectural Foundation ($10–25; ☎206/667-9186, Ⓦwww.seattlearchitecture.org).

Many Capitol Hill attractions are located on streets just off Broadway, such as **Olive Way**, offering a good concentration of cafés, or farther south around **Pike** and **Pine streets**, featuring funky clubs, coffee houses, record stores, and boutiques. Back on Broadway, just north of Pine, the striking, life-size statue of **Jimi Hendrix** was modeled on his famous pose from the 1967 Monterey Pop Festival, in which the guitar wizard kneeled down before the crowd to set his axe ablaze.

A few blocks south is the campus of Seattle University, meriting a visit only for the unusual **Chapel of St Ignatius**, next to the parking lot at E Marion St and 12th Ave (Mon–Thurs 7am–10pm, Fri 7am–7pm, Sat 9am–5pm, Sun 9am–10pm; free; Ⓦwww.seattleu.edu/chapel), whose interior offers hanging baffles and multihued windows, many of them thin rectangular slits, which combine to cast moving patterns of colored light throughout the church, each hue representing a different sacrament or theme.

Frye Art Museum

Southwest of Capitol Hill, the **Frye Art Museum**, 704 Terry Ave (Tues–Wed & Fri–Sat 10am–5pm, Thurs 10am–8pm, Sun noon–5pm; free; ☎206/622-9250, Ⓦfryeart.org), holds works by Winslow Homer, John Singer Sargent, Thomas Eakins, and (anti)modern artists like Andrew Wyeth. Look for Eakins's *Maybelle*, a stern portrait of a pudgy matron with pinched lips, and Homer's *The Wheat Gatherer*, a painting of a European farm laborer that's more in keeping with a French Realist like Courbet than an American known for his nautically inspired pieces. The building also holds one of the most important concentrations of the **Munich school** of painting in the US, focusing on the Belle Epoque between 1870 and 1900, when Munich was one of Europe's foremost cultural centers. Recent exhibits have broadened the museum's focus to include more contemporary work, including an array of multimedia, performance, and installation pieces.

Museum of History and Industry

Northeast of Capitol Hill, across Montlake Bridge from the university, the **Museum of History and Industry**, 2700 24th Ave E (daily 10am–5pm; $10; ☎206/324-1126, Ⓦwww.seattlehistory.org), provides a detailed history of the Puget Sound region, including displays on cannery work, the timber industry, the Klondike Gold Rush, aviation pioneers, nautical life, and discarded neon signs. The museum's highlight is the well-executed **Great Seattle Fire** exhibit, with an interactive terminal featuring graphics that let you see how the fire started (see p.301) and engulfed Downtown; nearby is the small glue pot believed to have started the blaze. The permanent displays also include a full-scale replica of a Seattle street in the 1880s and a section devoted to the salmon industry, but better are the temporary exhibits covering a wide range of subjects, from intricate dollhouses to experimental hydroplanes.

△ Washington Park Arboretum

Washington Park Arboretum

With 230 acres and more than five thousand kinds of plants, the **Washington Park Arboretum** (daily 7am–dusk; free; ℡ 206/543-8800, ⓦ depts.washington.edu/wpa) – best visited on uncrowded weekdays – is a lush showcase for regional vegetation, and a beautiful place to stroll and observe the magnolias, camellias, witch hazels, and more exotic specimens. The **Graham visitors center**, at the north end of Arboretum Drive near Foster Island Road (daily 10am–4pm), has free trail maps. Especially good is the **Arboretum Waterfront Trail**, which leads through the largest remaining wetland in Seattle to Marsh Island and the much larger **Foster Island**, an appealing wildlife habitat whose marshes are crowded with birch, oak, and pine trees, as well as dragonflies, marsh wrens, and redwing blackbirds. The most popular destination is the **Japanese Garden**, just off the large parking lot on Lake Washington Boulevard near the Madison Street entrance (10am–6pm: summer daily, rest of the year Tues–Sat; $5; ℡ 206/684-4725, ⓦ www.seattlejapanesegarden.org). Constructed with more than five hundred granite boulders taken from the Cascade Mountains, it's a lovely spot, particularly at the bridges near Emperor's Gate, where exotically colored carp swim in the pond and terrapins sun themselves on nearby Turtle Island.

Along Lake Washington Boulevard

East of Capitol Hill and south of the Washington Park Arboretum, **Lake Washington Boulevard** meanders through the ritzy confines of Madison Park for a mile or so before reaching the shores of **Lake Washington**, where it hugs the water's edge for another five miles. It's Seattle's most scenic drive, passing some of the city's more elegant neighborhoods in the north, through middle- and working-class Mount Baker and Rainier Valley, then terminating at **Seward Park**.

Highlights along the way include the stone-walled former residence of **Kurt Cobain**, at 171 Lake Washington Blvd E, sitting next to cozy **Viretta Park** (most parks below daily 6am–11.30pm) and best viewed from there; in April 1994 the house became the site of Cobain's suicide. Farther south, **Leschi Park** features pleasant nature walks amid trees and flower gardens, and adjacent **Frink Park** offers wooded hiking terrain built around a steep ravine and the curve of the boulevard.

After another ten blocks, Lake Washington Boulevard reaches the engaging trails and woods of **Colman Park**, and from here the boulevard continues on its winding, lakeside route through **Mount Baker Park** and down to Seward Park. The entire three-mile stretch is set up as a linear parkway, and it's best on the occasional weekend days (May–Sept second Sat & third Sun 10am–6pm) when it's closed to traffic and its tree-lined concourse fills with cyclists and joggers.

At the southern terminus of Lake Washington Boulevard, peninsular **Seward Park** (ⓦ www.sewardpark.org) is a serene turnaround point for cyclists, pedestrians, and rollerbladers. Encircled by a two-and-a-half-mile loop path, the park offers an even more secluded forest preserve at its hilly center, replete with stately trees, and is home to a fish hatchery, Greek amphitheater, and bathhouse. A couple miles south of Seward Park is **Kubota Garden**, at Renton Ave and 55th Ave S (daily dawn–dusk; free; ⓦ www .kubota.org). Established in 1927, this quaint garden is traversed by paths constructed on a 65ft hillside and has twenty acres of tranquil ponds, pines, cypresses, bamboos, and carved stones, and a waterfall.

The Seattle suburbs

Until it was bridged, Lake Washington isolated Seattle from the countryside and small farms to the east. All this changed when two long, floating bridges, one built in the 1940s, the second in the 1960s, turned the onetime hamlets of **Bellevue, Kirkland**, and **Redmond** into affluent **suburbs**. Redmond became the world headquarters of software giant Microsoft; Kirkland built plush businesses and accommodations along its waterfront; and Bellevue – the only one now worth visiting – quickly outgrew its suburban status to become the state's fourth-largest city, with its own smart business district and shopping area. Elsewhere, appealing sights in the Seattle outskirts are few and far between, even though some of them – notably the **Museum of Flight** – more than merit the trip. Other diverting destinations include the **Boeing** airplane-assembly tours in northerly Everett and the city's original townsite of **Alki Beach** in West Seattle.

Bellevue

Complete with downtown skyscrapers and thriving local businesses, **BELLEVUE** is one of the hottest real-estate markets in the US, its center dominated by the **Bellevue Square** mall and the **Bellevue Arts Museum**, 510 Bellevue Way NE (Tues–Sat 10am–5.30pm, Thurs until 9pm, Sun 11am–5pm; $7; ⓣ 425/519-0770, ⓦ www.bellevuearts.org). Often spotlighting Pacific Northwest artists, it's devoted exclusively to rotating exhibits of contemporary work and has far more cutting-edge stuff than you'd expect from its suburban location: you might see conceptual art, comic-book and pop-art designs, postmodern puppetry, inflatable pieces, and glasswork from master sculptor Dale Chihuly and his acolytes.

A few blocks north, the unusual **Museum of Doll Art**, 1116 108th Ave NE (Mon–Sat 10am–5pm, Sun 1–5pm; $7; ☏425/455-1116, Ⓦwww .dollart.com), will appeal to both adults and children. The facility's two floors contain more than 1200 dolls of all sizes and nationalities from the last few centuries; among the most intriguing are Peruvian burial dolls, African fertility dolls, and Mexican Day of the Dead ceremonial figures. There are also exquisitely crafted miniatures – look for the Japanese boy made from ground oyster shells – and unexpected tableaux like a seventeenth-century Russian Orthodox wedding.

About a mile east past the I-405 freeway, another appealing detour can be found at the **Bellevue Botanical Garden**, 12001 Main St (daily dawn–dusk; free; ☏425/452-2750, Ⓦwww.bellevuebotanical.org), located in Wilburton Hill Park. The garden features a nice range of themed sections on almost forty acres, including plots for the **Yao Japanese Garden**, with its mix of Asian and Pacific Northwestern plants; the colorful array of blooms found in the Perennial Border Garden; a water-conservation zone filled with hardy specimens; and an Alpine Rock Garden with imported plants from northern elevations growing in soil usually found at high elevations.

Jimi Hendrix gravesite

Beyond the southeastern edge of Lake Washington lies the charmless burg of **RENTON**, notable only for **Greenwood Cemetery**, 350 Monroe Ave NE at NE 4th St (Mon–Sat 8am–5pm, Sun by appointment), where **Jimi Hendrix**, the most inventive, and perhaps the greatest, guitarist in rock history, was buried in 1970 at the age of 27. The gravesite, just off I-405, is quite a trek from Seattle (it's accessible by the #101 or #106 buses from Downtown, transferring to the #105 in Renton), but still draws about 14,000 visitors a year. Formerly, there wasn't much to see here – basically a simple, faded headstone engraved with a guitar – but in 2004 Hendrix's surviving relatives re-interred the body of the rock god (along with other family members) in a much larger **memorial** in the southwest part of the cemetery (Ⓦwww.jimihendrixmemorial.com). Now featuring a 30ft-high dome with shimmering granite columns, this new, more garish memorial is obviously designed to draw the crowds – though the long-promised, life-size bronze sculpture of the guitar wizard has yet to be erected.

The Museum of Flight

The biggest of Seattle's museums, the **Museum of Flight**, a 20min bus ride (#174) south of Downtown at 9404 E Marginal Way (daily 10am–5pm; $14, kids $7.50; ☏206/764-5720, Ⓦwww.museumofflight.org), is partly housed in the restored 1909 "**Red Barn**" that was the original Boeing manufacturing plant. It now displays relics from the early days of flight, including the nearly decrepit 1914 *Caproni Ca 20*, the world's first fighter plane; the first presidential jet (used by Eisenhower in 1959); as well as commercial planes and bizarre manifestations of aviation design such as the *Aerocar III*, a flying red sports car that can be converted from automobile to aircraft in ten minutes. The **Great Gallery** features more than fifty full-size airplanes, from ancient prototypes to a replica of John Glenn's 1962 Mercury space capsule, to an SR-71 Blackbird spy plane, which once flew 80,000 feet above the jungles of Vietnam. More

Alki Beach: A Pacific Northwest Plymouth

Alki Beach is where the first party of Seattle's white settlers landed in November 1851. Ten adults and twelve children were met by advance scout and fellow pioneer **David Denny**, who helped them ashore in the midst of heavy rain. The settlement – a mere four cabins – was optimistically named New York in honor of settler Charles Terry's home state. This was quickly amended with the addition of the Chinook slang word *alki* to the sardonic New York-Alki, which roughly translates to "New York eventually" or "New York by and by." The one aspect of Gotham that did get replicated was the **Statue of Liberty**, a miniature rendition of which now occupies the beachfront across from 60th Avenue SW, holding its bronze torch out to surfers and boaters on Elliott Bay. In any case, the settlers soon determined that the deepwater harbor farther north in Elliott Bay would be far more suitable for settlement, as ships could not dock at Alki, and the pioneers began staking claims around what is now Pioneer Square.

Near 63rd and Alki avenues, a small **commemorative column** in Alki Beach Park, inscribed with the names of the settlers, identifies the spot of the 1851 landing, and its base also features a stone from an even more famous landing site – Plymouth Rock in Massachusetts. Two blocks inland, the whole tale is recounted in depth at the **Log House Museum**, 3003 61st Ave SW (Thurs–Sun noon–4pm; $2; ☎206/938-5293, ⦿www.loghousemuseum.org), which has exhibits about the settlement of the early city, the history of Native Americans in the region, and the less interesting development of West Seattle. The house itself is not one of the original Alki cabins but the renovated carriage house of a local soap magnate, built around 1903 in an agreeable Arts and Crafts style.

icons are on display outside in the museum's expansive **Airpark** (daily: summer 11am–4.30pm; rest of the year 11am–3.30pm; free with museum admission), which has a walk-in collection of models that include the 727, 737, and jumbo-jet 747, as well as the supersonic, but now discontinued, Concorde.

Everett and the Boeing Tour Center

Thirty miles north of Seattle, the last major suburb along I-5, **Everett**, is home to the manufacturing plant for **Boeing**, site of an ever popular program of hour-long tours at the **Boeing Tour Center**, whose entrance is on Hwy 526, a few miles west of Exit 189 off I-5 (tours Mon–Fri 9am–3pm on the hour; $15 for same-day tickets, $17.50 in advance; tickets at ☎1-800/464-1476, ⦿www.boeing.com/companyoffices/aboutus/tours). It's a good idea to arrive early, as the first-come, first-served tickets often run out quickly, with waits of an hour or more not uncommon once you've gotten your time slot. Not surprisingly, the tour is a smoothly executed PR exercise, focusing on Boeing's impressive technological accomplishments, including the 98-acre **factory** that's listed in the *Guinness Book of World Records* as the largest building in the world by volume (472 million cubic feet). Overhead platforms afford views of much of the floor space, cluttered by new planes in various phases of gestation, and the tour concludes with a bus ride on the "flight line," where finished 747, 767, and 777 models are tested – and the planned 787 will be tested – giving you a glimpse of the newest jets to hit the skies.

West Seattle and Alki Beach

The isolated neighborhood of **West Seattle**, separated from Downtown by the industrial piers and waterways of Harbor Island, has few attractions other than the narrow strip of **Alki Beach** (daily dawn–dusk), located on the peninsula's northwestern edge and around its northern tip of Duwamish Head. It's the city's most popular beach, crowded on warm days with sunbathers, volleyball players, and other outdoorsy types, and from the Head the view across the bay is impressive, taking in the Space Needle, Magnolia, and Queen Anne.

You can reach West Seattle by water taxi from Downtown, but if you're out this way in a car, it's worth taking a few extra minutes to follow Alki Avenue as it curves south around Alki Point and turns into **Beach Drive**, a scenic coastal route with views of Puget Sound and the Olympic Mountains. A few miles south down the road, **Lincoln Park** (daily 6am–11.30pm) offers a narrow beach with a paved promenade, picnic tables, and the **Colman Pool**, 8603 Fauntleroy Way SW (mid-June to Aug daily 1.30–7pm; ☎206/684-7494), a heated outdoor saltwater swimming pool. True park lovers and avid hikers might also want to wander through the rugged **Schmitz Park** (daily 6am–11.30pm; ⓦwww.schmitzpark.org), about ten blocks from Alki Point (enter at SW Admiral Way and SW Stevens St), a fifty-acre old-growth forest with Douglas fir, western red cedar, and western hemlock. Just south of Lincoln Park, at 4829 SW Barton St, ferries (see "Basics," p.36, for details) regularly leave from the Fauntleroy terminal for Vashon Island.

Eating

Seattle's **restaurants** are surprisingly broad in scope and encompass a wide range of international foodways, styles of cooking, and regional twists on familiar flavors. The term **Northwest Cuisine** refers to a regional variation on California Cuisine that combines fresh, high-quality ingredients from local farms and waters – such as in-season produce and locally caught **seafood**, especially trout and salmon – in creative ways, often with Asian or French inflections. To give an example, you might order beef from a grass-fed, Eastern Oregon–raised steer or marionberry-glazed pork loin with a side of Willapa Bay oysters, followed by a Willamette Valley hazelnut *crème brûlée*. The International District has countless inexpensive East Asian spots, particularly strong on **Chinese**, **Japanese**, and **Vietnamese** offerings, while **pan-Asian** food, which fuses different kinds of Asian dishes into the same menu, or mixes Asian and North American styles, has become trendy here in recent years as well. Although there are several quality **steakhouses** in town, **vegetarians** will not have a problem in Seattle, which has a wealth of meatless alternatives.

Downtown

With its broad assortment of low-end diners, chic eateries, and chain restaurants, **Downtown**'s eating choices are as numerous as anywhere in the city. Keep in mind, though, that since the majority of visitors are based here, they are often packed during peak hours – whether or not their cuisine merits the attention.

Overall, whether dining in an upscale establishment by the bay or a hamburger joint in a shambling dive, you're apt to find something that suits both your palate and your wallet.

Pike Place Market

Athenian Inn main floor of Main Arcade ☎206/624-7166. Offers breakfast and a good spot to check out views of Puget Sound and do a bit of people-watching; try the seafood platter and munch on haddock, herring, or halibut if you're coming for a proper meal.

Campagne 86 Pine St ☎206/728-2800. The top restaurant in the market area, offering delicacies like potato-wrapped striped bass fillet and foie gras parfait in a puff pastry with shallots and turnips. Leans heavily toward seafood specialties, though there are excellent pan-roasted beef entrees and the ever-tasty pomme frites, fried in duck fat. The less expensive Café Campagne has similar dinner hours, as well as a good lunch and weekend brunch.

Copacabana Triangle Building ☎206/622-6359. A Bolivian restaurant that's one of Pike Place's most offbeat eateries, with a concentration on stuffed pies (such as *huminta*, or corn pie) and fish soups. The outdoor balcony seating has a good view of the foot traffic on Pike Place below.

El Puerco Lloron 1501 Western Ave ☎206/624-0541. "The Crying Pig," a rare authentic Mexican restaurant in Seattle – including traditional decor – serving tamales, tostadas, and excellent *chiles rellenos* in a cafeteria-style setting. Located on the Hillclimb behind the market.

Lowell's 1519 Pike Place, main floor of Main Arcade ☎206/622-2036. One of the most popular restaurants with waterfront views, renowned for its breakfasts, coffee, and seafood.

Place Pigalle 81 Pike St, Main Arcade ☎206/624-1756. Upper-end French bistro boasting high-quality seafood like mussels, crab, halibut, and regionally caught sturgeon – not to mention scrumptious desserts. Patio open in warm weather.

Saigon 1916 Pike Place, ☎206/448-1089. One of the best inexpensive places to eat in Pike Place, with a menu of Vietnamese seafood and vegetarian dishes featuring some sweat-inducing curries; try the curry tofu soup or the lemongrass squid.

Three Girls Bakery lower floor of Sanitary Market ☎206/622-1045. Endure the long lines at this well-loved haunt for the large, tasty sandwiches, available at either the takeout counter or the small adjoining café.

Waterfront and Business District

Andaluca 407 Olive Way in the *Mayflower Park* hotel ☎206/382-6999. An elegant, top-shelf Spanish restaurant, affordable for its breakfasts of citrus pancakes and salmon scrambles but better for its delicious dishes of paella, beef tenderloin, spicy lamb chops, and even a grilled halibut sandwich; expect to pay twice as much for supper as for lunch.

Anthony's Pier 66 2201 Alaskan Way ☎206/448-6688. Good, expensive seafood, such as shellfish, mahi mahi, and oysters, served in a waterfront restaurant (part of a local chain) with one of the best views of Puget Sound in town. The restaurant also runs the takeout-oriented *Anthony's Fish Bar* in the same building.

Earth & Ocean 1112 4th Ave, in the *W Seattle Hotel* ☎206/264-6060. A marvelous spot for Northwest Cuisine, highlighted by the likes of ahi tuna, crab, octopus, and salmon fillets – the "ocean" part of the equation – but also good for its pasta and steaks. The so-called Quickie menu is a three-course dinner for $22: cheap compared to everything else.

Elliott's Oyster House 1201 Alaskan Way ☎206/623-4340. As the name suggests, succulent bivalves and other seafood dishes like crab and lobster are the main attraction at this popular waterfront spot, whose dark, handsome interior has nice views of the bay.

Hunt Club 900 Madison St, inside the *Sorrento* hotel (p.291) ☎206/343-6156. A swank hotel's even swankier restaurant, where you can delight in venison, braised Sonoma duck, and filet mignon for tip-top prices.

Library Bistro 92 Madison St ☎206/624-3646. In the *Alexis* hotel (see review p.290), a delicious but affordable spot where you can get a helping of French toast or frittatas for breakfast or wait until lunchtime for the pulled pork sandwich with Dr Pepper–infused barbecue sauce.

Metropolitan Grill 820 2nd Ave between Columbia and Marion ☎206/624-3287. The beef lover's best bet in town, with a good choice of top cuts of steak, in a place that's heavy on power suits and has one of the longest bars in Seattle.

Wild Ginger 1401 3rd Ave ☎206/623-4450. Ever popular pan-Asian restaurant with extensive daily specials to supplement the already lengthy, ambitious menu, including memorable items like *pok wok* lamb, emerald prawns, and fragrant duck.

Pioneer Square

Il Terrazzo Carmine 411 1st Ave S ☏ 206/467-7797. The height of Italian chic in the area, perhaps the entire city, offering splendid risottos, rack of lamb, gnocchi, and a fine range of pastas for exquisitely steep prices.

Jones Barbeque 2454 Occidental Ave S ☏ 206/625-1339. One of the region's top barbecue joints, just a few blocks south of Safeco Field. Dine on superior ribs, sausages, brisket – all with the requisite lip-smacking sauce – and polish it off with a slice of sweet-potato pie. Adjust your belt a notch when you finish.

🏃 **Salumi** 309 3rd Ave S ☏ 206/621-8772. A local institution making sausages the old-fashioned way – with succulent ingredients like oxtail, prosciutto, and lamb – and serving them up in cheap, delicious, piping-hot sandwiches with homemade bread. Open Tues–Fri 11am–4pm.

Trattoria Mitchelli 84 Yesler Way ☏ 206/623-3883. Another fine Italian eatery in Pioneer Square (much cheaper than *Il Terrazzo Carmine*), it offers a toothsome range of thin-crust pizzas and filling portions of pasta. Open until the wee hours to accommodate late-night revelers.

Zaina 108 Cherry St ☏ 206/624-5687. Straightforward, well-crafted Mediterranean fare for cheap prices, including savory gyros, shawarma, and couscous, along with other staples.

International District

House of Hong 409 8th Ave S ☏ 206/622-7997. Tasty and simple Chinese food in a large restaurant open relatively late on weekends, making it a good option for dining after events in the Pioneer Square/Safeco Field area. Also offers dim sum until 3pm daily.

Maneki 304 6th Ave ☏ 206/622-2631. One of the last holdouts from the old days of the International District, when Japanese diners were much thicker on the ground. These days, this hundred-year-old favorite more than suffices, with its tasty sushi platters, soups, and handcrafted rolls, all for around $8–15.

Phnom Penh Noodle House 660 S King St ☏ 206/748-9825. Like the name says, an honest-to-God Cambodian noodle joint that doles out rich helpings of noodles in various sauces, as well as traditional favorites like spicy soups and fish cakes.

Saigon Bistro 1032 S Jackson St ☏ 206/329-4939. Vietnamese favorites – hot seafood soups, spicy salads, rice pancakes, and various noodle dishes – available for budget prices.

Seven Stars Pepper 1207 S Jackson St ☏ 206/568-6446. A knockout choice for hot and spicy Szechuan fixings in the traditional style, with great wontons, seafood hot pots, and noodle dishes that make you want to cheer. Don't let the uninspiring strip-mall site deter you.

Tai Tung 655 S King St ☏ 206/622-7372. One of the district's oldest Cantonese restaurants, with an incredibly extensive menu of traditional staples, some better than others; to get a dose of a few things at once, opt for one of the combo meals, which run around $10.

Belltown

Assaggio 2010 4th Ave ☏ 206/441-1399. Pleasant, mid-priced Italian restaurant with a friendly ambience and a menu featuring such items as pan-seared scallops and potato dumplings with Gorgonzola, among the expected pizzas, pastas, and veal.

Cascadia 2328 1st Ave ☏ 206/448-8884. Superb Northwest Cuisine at sky-high prices. Rotating fixed-price menus offer specialties of the region, often including such items as green-curry lamb and whiskey-smoked salmon, matched with top-notch local wines.

Dahlia Lounge 1904 4th Ave ☏ 206/682-4142. One of Seattle's most established upscale restaurants, and most famed for its seafood, of which the crabcakes are a specialty. If you can't afford to drop a wad on dinner, try the adjoining, excellent Dahlia Bakery.

Flying Fish 2234 1st Ave ☏ 206/728-8595. Though lacking the eponymous fish on the menu, this is a fine choice for all other kinds of seafood, serving up anything from familiar fare like ahi tuna to more adventurous entrees like monkfish and escolar.

Lampreia 2400 1st Ave at Battery St ☏ 206/443-3301. Very pricey Northwest Cuisine spot specializing in beef and fish, augmented with über-trendy items like grilled organic polenta and poached veal. Expect plenty of attitude if you're not wearing the right clothes – suits and ties for men, formal dresses for women.

Marco's Supper Club 2510 First Ave ☏ 206/441-7801. A local hot spot, and for good reason, with a colorful, eclectic assortment of tasty, upmarket platters like duck confit ravioli, seafood stew rich with mussels, and roasted-garlic custard, among other rotating curiosities.

Noodle Ranch 2228 2nd Ave ☏ 206/728-0463. Delicious pan-Asian cuisine starting at $10, offering imaginative noodle-based dishes and other creations in a casual atmosphere. The green curry and shrimp spring rolls are the specialty.

Seattle Center and Queen Anne

The 5 Spot 1502 Queen Anne Ave N ☏ 206/285-SPOT. The most colorful of Queen Anne's cheap eateries, a Southern-style diner with "Melting Pot Meals" that include Pumpkin Show Pasta (ravioli in pumpkin cream sauce), Honey Stung Fried Chicken (dipped in buttermilk and honey), and the Just So Brisket (with a Coca-Cola and onion marinade).

Bahn Thai 409 Roy St ☏ 206/283-0444. Relaxed Thai spot with a decorous atmosphere and a long menu of well-spiced dishes – the seafood selection is especially varied and good, with imaginative salmon and squid options.

Bamboo Garden 364 Roy St ☏ 206/282-6616. Enticing lists of beef-fried rice, Szechuan chicken, and sweet-and-sour pork. However, all the "meat" dishes are made from vegetable-protein products and 100 percent vegetable oil. It's all quite good, especially when finished off with a peanut pudding dessert.

Chinoise 12 Boston St ☏ 206/219-6911. Popular pan-Asian eatery with an diverse range of choices, from pad Thai to tempura platters and udon noodles, though best for its sushi and sashimi. Adventurous diners might try a bite of *unaju* – broiled eel to the uninitiated. One of several citywide branches.

Sapphire 1625 Queen Anne Ave N ☏ 206/281-1931. A pan-Mediterranean eatery, strong on familiar staples like North African stews, smoked fish, and shawarma. It has something of a cocktail-oriented hipster scene as well, thus the high prices.

Magnolia

Kinnaree 3311 W McGraw St ☏ 206/285-4460. Fine, inexpensive Thai restaurant whose menu allows you to order any item in vegetarian, meat, or seafood versions. The green coconut-milk curry and basil rice are both particularly tasty.

Palisade 2601 W Marina Place, in the Elliott Bay Marina ☏ 206/285-1000. The sea views and quaint atmosphere of this pricey eatery are a big draw, but the core menu items, drawing from Northwest and Italian cuisines, aren't too shabby, either. Indulge in a great prawn platter or Australian rock lobster, or sink your maw into the hearty prime rib.

Szmania's 3321 W McGraw St ☏ 206/284-7305. One of the few reasons to journey to Magnolia Village, this is one of the finest restaurants in the city, mixing German, Continental, and Northwest Cuisine. An expensive, rotating menu with many

inventive and tasty entrees, from prosciutto di parma to jagerschnitzel.

Ballard

Hattie's Hat 5231 Ballard Ave NW ☏ 206/784-0175. Long-standing favorite for its hefty slabs of meatloaf and hamburgers, 2am nightly bar closing time, and colorful mix of hard-bitten old-timers and grungy hipsters.

Madame K's 5327 Ballard Ave NW ☏ 206/783-9710. Onetime bordello–turned–pizza joint, turning out deep-dish meat pies and richly flavored pastas in hefty portions. Not subtle, but satisfying after a day prowling the antique stores.

Ray's Cafe 6049 Seaview Ave ☏ 206/789-4130. Always popular seafood haunt that offers high-priced cuisine such as sablefish and King salmon in its *Boathouse* restaurant below, and more afford-able items like salmon burgers and coconut prawns in the cafe above. Great waterside views add to the appeal.

Vera's 5417 22nd Ave ☏ 206/782-9966. Old-time Ballard on display: the cheap breakfasts and lunches are solid and cheap, but the scene inside – it's stuffed with old junk and a set from the movie *The Sting*, plus grizzled old-timers and newbies – gives the place a strange allure.

Fremont and Wallingford

Asteroid Café 3601 Fremont Ave, Fremont ☏ 206/547-9000. Groovy Italian spot dishing out primo calamari, salads, and pasta, as well as more unexpected items like shiitake-mushroom risotto cakes.

Dick's Drive-In 111 NE 45th St, Wallingford ☏ 206/632-5125. Fifty-year-old fast-food institution serving up sloppy but lip-smacking burgers, rich shakes, and fries with just the right crunch. One of several citywide locations.

El Camino 607 N 35th St, Fremont ☏ 206/632-7303. Mid- to high-priced Mexican fare with a nouvelle twist, offering elaborate dishes and homemade sodas. The rock shrimp quesadilla is a nice start; the tamarind-glazed salmon and coconut flan are also worth a go.

Kabul 2301 N 45th St, Wallingford ☏ 206/545-9000. An inexpensive Afghan establishment with a menu of moderately priced kebabs and both veggie and meat entrees, as well as live sitar music on Tues and Thurs. Try the *qorma-i tarkari*, an Indian-like stew of cauliflower, carrots, potatoes, and rice.

 Musashi's 1400 N 45th St ☏ 206/633-0212. A sushi joint where you can get full for $10 or less on tuna or salmon rolls, grilled vegetable skewers, and much more. As it seats only 25 customers, there's almost always a line out the door; be prepared to wait.

Pontevecchio 710 N 34th St, Fremont ☎206/633-3989. Dark, cozy eight-tabled Italian bistro near the Fremont Bridge serving light but authentic meals of panini and pasta, served with exuberance. Occasional guitar and flamenco dance performances. Moderately priced.

Silence Heart Nest 3510 Fremont Place N, Fremont ☎206/633-5169. Indian-leaning vegetarian spot that offers dishes like meatloaf, scrambles, omelets, and sausage – all made without the offending meat. Try the *masala dosa* – crepes stuffed with spicy potatoes.

The University District

Agua Verde Paddle Club 1303 NE Boat St ☎206/545-8570. Excellent bayside spot with convivial atmosphere and nice waterside views. A good choice for inexpensive Mexican fare, serving spicy prawns, fish and pork tacos, peppery salads, and barbecued pork ribs.

Flowers 4247 University Way NE ☎206/633-1903. A bar and affordable restaurant that attracts students and would-be bohemians for its quirky decor and reputation as a hangout. For food, it leans toward a mishmash of international fare (samosas to pasta to curry noodles), but it also offers a solid lunchtime vegan buffet.

Saigon Deli 4142 Brooklyn Ave NE between NE 41st and NE 42nd sts ☎206/634-2866. Hole-in-the-wall diner whipping out fine Vietnamese soups and vermicelli noodle dishes for eat-in or takeout. Most of the dishes are under $5; you won't go away hungry.

Tandoor 5024 University Way NE ☎206/523-7477. Amid numerous Indian joints offering all-you-care-to-eat buffet lunches, Tandoor stands out for having the lowest prices for well-executed standards like curry, tandoori, and vindaloo dishes.

Union Bay Cafe 3515 NE 45th St ☎206/527-8364. A local hot spot with refreshing, if expensive, takes on regional Northwest fare, including good traditional pasta with seafood, lip-smacking items like roasted duck and ostrich, and a mean Kobe steak.

Capitol Hill

611 Supreme 611 E Pine St ☎206/328-0292. French creperie with many savory and sweet crepes, the best of which are the *saumon-chèvre*,

with smoked salmon and goat cheese, and the *épinard*, with spinach, roasted peppers, Cambozola cheese, and walnuts.

Byzantion 601 E Broadway at E Mercer St ☎206/325-7580. The best Greek food in town, reasonably priced, and served with enough pita bread to make the prospect of dessert unthinkable; notably good spinach pie and souvlaki.

Café Flora 2901 E Madison St at 29th Ave E ☎206/325-9100. Offers creatively crafted soups, salads, and entrees like curry burgers and Oaxaca tacos. The setting is pleasant, especially the stone patio wing, complete with trees and a fountain under a pyramid skylight.

Coastal Kitchen 429 15th Ave E ☎206/322-1145. One of the most popular mid-priced breakfast and brunch spots in Capitol Hill; for dinner, the menu somewhat approximates Gulf Coast–style cuisine, with grilled prawns, crab cakes, red-pepper ravioli, and cod-and-chips.

Globe Cafe 1531 14th Ave ☎206/324-8815. Hard to beat for a Seattle experience, with a tasty all-vegan menu of full meals, drinks, and desserts, and a goofy decor of globes, oddly shaped painted salt shakers, and blackboards for patrons to doodle on.

Kingfish Cafe 602 19th Ave E between E Mercer and E Roy sts ☎206/320-8757. Affordable Southern-style food like griddle cakes, grilled catfish, and beans and rice, with terrific vintage soul and R&B music playing as you munch beneath large sepia-toned photos.

Machiavelli 1215 Pine St at 12th Ave ☎206/621-7941. Good Italian food served in somewhat small portions and featuring tangy and creative pasta sauces.

Monsoon 615 19th Ave E ☎206/325-2111. Nationally regarded pan-Asian restaurant that draws the crowds for its scrumptious drunken crispy chicken, braised short ribs, caramelized Idaho catfish, and ginger pork ribs.

Piecora's 1401 E Madison St at E Pike St ☎206/322-9411. The best pizza parlor in a city not known for its pizza joints, with satisfyingly rich, flavorful, and gooey pies and a friendly neighborhood atmosphere.

Siam on Broadway 616 Broadway E at E Roy St ☎206/324-0892. Perennially crowded and reasonably priced, an open-kitchen Thai restaurant with both counter and table seating; good for digging into familiar noodle and curry dishes that rank among the spiciest in the city.

Than Brothers 516 Broadway E ☎206/568-7218. The specialty here is pho, a spicy Vietnamese rice noodle soup served in a huge bowl for cheap prices. Other selections are heavy on beef, and the complimentary *banh choux à la crème*, a sweet custard puff dessert, is a nice treat. One of several local locations.

The Seattle suburbs

BisonMain 10213 Main St, Bellevue ☎ 425/455-2033. A local hot spot that serves up good and affordable ribs, pasta, and sandwiches for lunch, then turns around and feeds you succulent, upper-end items like duck breast and acorn-squash risotto for dinner.

Herbfarm 14590 NE 145th St, Woodinville ☎ 206/784-2222. Internationally renowned eatery specializing in elaborate dinners made with fresh ingredients and herbs of the region. Each day's menu is finalized just hours before the meal, but

seafood figures prominently in these nine-course, five-hour affairs. The prix-fixe menu ranges from $179 to $199 per person.

I Love Sushi 11818 NE Eighth St, Bellevue ☎ 425/454-5706. You'll share the sentiment of this place's name after you finish dining on its wide range of affordable Japanese delicacies, among them fresh salmon, eel, mussels, quail eggs, and geoduck clams. There's another location closer to Downtown, at 1001 Fairview Ave N on Lake Union (☎ 206/625-9604).

Salvadorian Bakery 1719 SW Roxbury St, West Seattle ☎ 206/762-4064. More than just a place to snack on bread and desserts, this is a terrific Latin eatery that offers spicy, very tasty pupusas – corn cakes stuffed with anything from pork to peppers – and solid staples like plantains and yucca.

Cafés

In Seattle **coffee** is consumed in vaster quantities, and with more gusto, than in any other metropolis in North America. Its numerous **cafés** function as much as local pubs or bars as centers for low-key unwinding: many are multimedia spaces, offering Internet terminals, poetry readings, galleries, and alternative music along with the expected coffee, tea, snacks, and pastries.

△ Vivace Espresso, Capitol Hill

Whatever your preference – solitude, art, socializing, or a strong buzz – there's a cafe for you.

The best spot to begin your sampling of cafe culture is unquestionably **Capitol Hill**, but there are alternatives: for a taste of the semi-bohemian scene, check out **Fremont**; for a mix of alternative-chic and yuppie hauteur, **Belltown**; for boisterous chat, the **University District**; for a blend of hipsters and the working class, **Pioneer Square**.

Downtown and Pioneer Square

All City Coffee 125 Prefontaine Place S, Pioneer Square ☎206/652-8331. Hip Pioneer Square cafe with local artworks, tasty cupcakes, soups, and sandwiches, and particularly good coffee. The Luna and Del Sol varieties are well worth a gulp.

Bookstore Bar & Cafe 1007 1st Ave, Downtown ☎206/582-1506. Off the lobby of the *Alexis* hotel, a cozy, upscale spot for light lunches and dinners, but most notable for its books and international magazines and newspapers for browsing, as well as for its bourbons, ports, cognacs, and malt scotches.

Caffe Umbria 320 Occidental Ave S at S Jackson St, Pioneer Square ☎206/624-5847. Pleasant space that prepares espresso and other gourmet concoctions *al modo italiano*, as well as panini, gelato, and pastries, and wine imported from the Boot.

Zeitgeist Art and Coffee 171 S Jackson St, Pioneer Square ☎206/583-0497. Mostly coffee, a few sandwiches and pastries, and modern art at this haunt at the heart of Pioneer Square's gallery scene. Also offers periodic showings of local and independent films.

Belltown

Bellino 2421 2nd Ave ☎206/956-4237. In a stretch awash in chain coffeehouses, this independent is worth seeking out for its carefully crafted organic brews and savory espresso drinks, along with pastries and desserts and a splash of arty color on the walls.

Motore Coffee 1904 9th Ave, a few blocks east of Belltown ☎206/388-2803. Along with a Vespa-inspired vibe and iMacs for Web-browsing, this joint's coffee (Caffe Vita) is supreme, as are the delicious sandwiches and the entire coffee-tea-chocolate drink menu.

🚶 **Top Pot Coffee & Doughnuts** 2124 5th Ave ☎206/728-1966. Nationally renowned java-and-doughnut haunt with hip decor, WiFi Net access, and a few offbeat selections like pink-vanilla and pink-feather-boa doughnuts. Also in Capitol Hill at 609 Summit Ave E (☎206/323-7841).

Seattle Center and Queen Anne

Caffè Ladro 2205 Queen Anne Ave N ☎206/282-5313. A groovy mix of industrial and organic designs at this enjoyable neighborhood coffee-house – the name translates to "coffee thief" – with an arty flair, hearty coffees, and a range of light meals (some veggie options). Nine other branches in the city.

El Diablo Coffee Company 1811 Queen Anne Ave N ☎206/285-0693. Famed for its colorful artwork and furnishings, and for its powerful, eye-opening blends of Cuban-roasted java, but equally regarded for its sandwiches and pastries, and delicious fruit and chocolate desserts.

Uptown Espresso 525 Queen Anne Ave N ☎206/285-3757. Despite the name, the Uptown is located in *Lower* Queen Anne, and caters to morning regulars and late-night revelers – come here to sip quality coffee and munch on buttery pastries. One of several area locations.

Magnolia and Ballard

Q Cafe 3223 15th Ave W ☎206/352-2525. The quintessential Seattle cafe: underground art on the walls, open mic and live-music shows, excellent coffee and snacks, and a nonprofit mission to help out the homeless and support progressive causes. The only challenge is finding it, in the community of Interbay, east of Magnolia.

Vérité Coffee 2052 NW Market St ☎206/709-4497. Fun and prominent coffee shop along the main drag of downtown Ballard, with excellent coffee and – notably – flavorful cupcakes with offbeat toppings like gummy fish and candy flowers.

Fremont and Wallingford

Fremont Coffee 459 N 36th St, Fremont ☎206/632-3633. An actual house with art and cozy furniture, plus excellent coffee (Lighthouse and Vivace), handcrafted sodas, and free wireless Internet.

Teahouse Kuan Yin 1911 N 45th St, Wallingford ☎206/632-2055. A necessary antidote in coffee-happy Seattle, serving several dozen varieties of black, oolong, green, and herbal tea, as well as light snacks and occasional live music shows (traditional koto and guitar).

Zoka 2200 N 56th St, Wallingford ☏ 206/545-4277. Classic coffeehouse in a comfortable setting; not as weird as the ones in the trendier districts, but fine for brews and relaxation.

University District

Allegro Espresso Bar 4214 University Way NE ☏ 206/633-3030. One of the favorite haunts of coffee connoisseurs. There are also computer terminals with free Internet access (available only if you order something at the cafe).

Grand Illusion Espresso and Pastry 1405 NE 50th St at University Way ☏ 206/729-3542. Connected to the Grand Illusion cinema, this is the homiest and most popular of the U District's cafés, with a living-room feel and good snacks, as well as basic light meals and some outdoor seating.

Capitol Hill

Bauhaus Books & Coffee 301 E Pine at Melrose Ave E ☏ 206/625-1600. Busy hangout dispensing coffee and some teas in a self-consciously somber atmosphere, with high chairs at the window counter. You can access books on the wall with a ladder.

Café Dilettante 416 E Broadway ☏ 206/329-6463. Though this pleasant cafe on the busiest stretch of Broadway in Capitol Hill does serve coffee, people come here more for the chocolate treats, the best in town. One of several area locations.

Caffe Vita 1005 E Pike St ☏ 206/709-4440. *The* place on Capitol Hill for folks into both drinking serious coffee – this brand is one of the city's best – and hanging out with a predominantly bohemian-style crowd. Two other city locations.

Online Coffee Company 1720 E Olive Way ☏ 206/328-3731. Spacious and relaxed Internet café with coffee, beer, wine, and baked goods to go along with the $6/hr high-speed Internet access (first 30min free with purchase); the outside patio has a view of Puget Sound.

Victrola Coffee and Art 411 15th Ave E ☏ 206/325-6520. A good choice for looking at modern art, taking in a musical show, savoring rich brews – single-origin beans from Rwanda and other countries – and devouring healthy snacks and light fare, some of it vegan.

Vivace Espresso 901 E Denny Way at Broadway ☏ 206/860-5869. A lodestone for Capitol Hill's serious coffee-drinkers; more fun is Vivace's sidewalk cafe at 321 Broadway E (same phone), the prime people-watching perch in the area.

Nightlife

When you consider the city's hip reputation, Seattle's **nightlife** is a little more low-key than you might expect. Still, there's plenty going on here most nights, with any number of good bars, clubs, and live-music venues to occupy your time. The drinking scene is spirited and (usually) nonthreatening, music and dancing are staged in friendly and comfortable settings, cover charges are low, and dress codes only enforced in snooty, self-important places that aren't worth entering to begin with. You can find the broadest range of listings in the *Seattle Weekly* or *The Stranger*, free weeklies you can find in boxes on the streets and in numerous cafés and stores.

Bars

Though there are plenty of typically raucous, hell-for-leather joints and sedate local hangouts, the **bar** scene in Seattle is generally quite varied. The most interesting bars are typically found in the more bohemian or culturally diverse zones, such as **Pioneer Square**, **Capitol Hill**, and **Belltown**. Some Seattle bars bear at least a passing resemblance to British pubs or to cafés that serve alcohol, complete with singer–songwriter performances, art displays, and DJs on occasion. Others cater to discriminating palates by specializing in cigars, wines, whiskeys, or bourbons. **Microbreweries** are big here, as elsewhere in the Northwest, and some of them run their own onsite bars.

Downtown

Alibi Room 85 Pike St, #410 ☎ 206/623-3180. On the lower part of the Pike Place Market, a tightly packed magnet for trendy poseurs and interloping tourists, with dance beats on the speakers, modish decor, an onsite script library, and independent-film showings.

Kells Irish Pub 1916 Post Alley, Pike Place Market ☎ 206/728-1916. Free-spirited Irish bar and restaurant in a central location, with patio seating and nightly performances by Irish-oriented folk and rock groups.

Pike Pub & Brewery 1415 1st Ave ☎ 206/622-6044. Small craft brewery serving its own beers, among them a mean stout and porter. Has a large wine list and an extensive fish- and pizza-heavy menu. The sprawling, multileveled premises are slick but unpretentious.

Pioneer Square

Central Saloon 207 1st Ave S ☎ 206/622-0209. Billing itself as "Seattle's oldest saloon" (established 1892), it's often crowded owing to its location at the epicenter of the tourist district. The live music ranges from alt-rock and eclectic acoustic to punk to metal.

Doc Maynard's 610 1st Ave S ☎ 206/682-4649. This meeting point for Bill Speidel's Underground Tours (see p.299) is a good early-1900s-style bar, and a rollicking spot to hear music on weekend nights; at other times, it mainly serves those waiting to take the tour.

Pioneer Square Saloon 73 Yesler Way ☎ 206/628-6444. Part of a restored 1914 brick hotel, a classic watering hole featuring fifteen microbrews and an amiable crowd of boozy regulars.

Pyramid Alehouse 1201 First Ave S ☎ 206/682-3377. Across from Safeco Field, an excellent regional brewery with a warehouse-like space that serves a dozen Pyramid brands, including some fruit-flavored varieties and an extra-special bitter (ESB).

Belltown

Belltown Billiards 90 Blanchard St ☎ 206/448-6779. The best hangout for those who like to play pool and drink beer. A dozen pool tables are available, plus nightly live music, DJs, or special events.

Lava Lounge 2226 2nd Ave ☎ 206/441-5660. Revival of 1950s tiki-lounge kitsch, with a South Pacific–inspired decor of lava lamps and darkly tropical murals. There's eclectic live music and DJs at night, happy hour from 3 to 7pm, and shuffleboard to pass the time.

Nite Lite 1926 2nd Ave ☎ 206/443-0899. An essential nexus for young and old, where grizzled regulars rub shoulders with black-clad newbies, amid true dive decor like vinyl walls and neon lights that look at least thirty years out of date. The main attraction, of course, is the liquor – strong, dark, and authentic.

Two Bells Tavern 2313 4th Ave between Bell and Battery ☎ 206/441-3050. A Belltown institution, still drawing arty types – though not as many as it once did. Has microbrews on tap and serves burgers on French rolls.

Ballard

Hale's Ales 4301 Leary Way NW ☎ 206/782-0737. Handcrafted English-styled ales from the third-oldest microbrewery in the Northwest, highlighted by the hearty Troll Porter, as well as a decent menu of pub-style food.

People's Pub 5429 Ballard Ave NW ☎ 206/783-6521. Belt-breaking German cuisine mixed with belly-filling draughts straight out of Deutschland, including the likes of smoky Aecht Schlenkerla Rauchbier, plus wine, scotch, and curious bar fare like deep-fried pickles.

Fremont and Wallingford

Dad Watson's 3601 Fremont Ave N, Fremont ☎ 206/632-6505. Seattle outpost of an Oregon microbrewery chain, featuring excellent craft beers like Hammerhead and Terminator Stout. Other branches are *Six Arms* in Capitol Hill, 300 E Pike St (☎ 206/223-1698), and *McMenamins Queen Anne Hill*, 300 Roy St, #105 (☎ 206/285-4722).

Murphy's 1928 N 45th St at Meridian Ave N, Wallingford ☎ 206/634-2110. Often featuring live Irish music on Friday and Saturday nights, Murphy's pours a nice Guinness, has good Irish coffee, and offers a wide selection of Northwest beers.

SeaMonster Lounge 2202 N 45th St ☎ 206/633-1824. At this fixture on the Wallingford bar scene, the cocktails are inventive and curious (the Oatmeal Nipple for one), but the quirky decor and artworks really stand out – not to mention the nightly selection of oddball music, where you're apt to hear anything from organ jams to "boomBAP jazz at its best."

University District
Big Time Brewery and Alehouse 4133 University Way NE ⊕206/545-4509. Long-standing microbrewery whose ales are the stock in trade – try the Bhagwan's Best IPA – served in a large space with hardwood decor and a shuffleboard in the back room.
Galway Arms 5257 University Way NE ⊕206/527-0404. Straightforward Irish pub that offers hearty stout beers alongside rich stews and other traditional fare; there's also folk and contemporary Irish live music.

Capitol Hill
Bad Juju Lounge 1518 11th Ave ⊕206/709-9951. Dark, swirling techno beats and eerie artworks (nerve-jangling portraits and snake

skeletons) are the main draws to this stylish, often-packed hangout, which attracts both slummers and scenesters for its hip ambience and bracing cocktails.
Comet Tavern 922 E Pike St just off Broadway ⊕206/323-9853. A smoky, rocker's-dive hangout, this sixty-year-old bar is the oldest in Capitol Hill – a place where authentic axe-wielders and bleary-eyed burnouts mix with youthful hangers-on.
🏃 **Elysian Brewing Co** 1221 E Pike St ⊕206/860-1920. Brewpub of one of the better local microbreweries, with warehouse-type decor that fits in well with the area vibe, and flavorful oddities like Zepyrus Pilsner and Dragonstooth Stout. The menu is pretty good, too, offering sandwiches, bangers and mash, and mahi mahi tacos.
Linda's Tavern 707 E Pike St at Harvard Ave E ⊕206/325-1220. One of Capitol Hill's most happening bars attracts an alternative/underground rock crowd that gets more crowded and intense as the night wears on.

Live music

Seattle's **live music** scene got a lot of notice in the early 1990s, and today there's still plenty of **alternative rock** to hear. The best spots are concentrated Downtown, in Capitol Hill, and still in Belltown – though gentrification has undercut the band scene there to a large degree. Pioneer Square is the place for **blues** and, to a lesser extent, **jazz**. The Pioneer Square **joint cover night** scheme allows you into a bunch of bars and clubs – *Bohemian Café*, *Central Saloon*, *Doc Maynard's*, *Fenix*, *Larry's Nightclub*, and *New Orleans*, among others – for one blanket fee ($5 weekdays, $12 weekends). **Folk** and **acoustic** singer-songwriters are easy to find throughout the city in cafés and the more genteel bars. **Reggae** and **world music** bands play with less frequency but are scattered here and there.

Rock and pop
Crocodile Café 2200 2nd Ave, Belltown ⊕206/441-5611. By day a diner, by night a hip and intimate rock club, one of the best Seattle spots to see most any kind of performance, from jazz, rock, and R&B to poetry readings and grunge. Usual cover $6–15.
El Corazon 109 Eastlake Ave E, Eastlake, near I-5 ⊕206/381-3094. A fiery dive for rock, punk, hardcore, metal, and milder variations like emo and shoe-gazer pop. The emphasis is on the harder stuff, though, with plenty of all-ages shows. $7–20.
Fenix 315 2nd Ave S, Pioneer Square ⊕206/467-1111. A popular venue where it's hard to predict what you'll hear, from rockabilly and punk to burlesque and 1980s cover

bands; the cover charge/ticket price is usually $10–25. There's also a dance club on the same premises.
Moore Theater 1932 2nd Ave, Belltown ⊕206/443-1744. This 1907 former vaudeville auditorium sometimes hosts exciting up-and-coming bands, but more often you'll find established names in pop and rock, along with comedians, dancers, kids' shows, and so on. $20–50.
Nuemo's 925 E Pike St, Capitol Hill ⊕206/709-9467. A hard-thrashing venue that has quickly clawed its way to the top of the indie-rock heap. Here, the murals and wall art is splashy and irreverent (themed by a creepy clown), the bands are both regional and national (of the punk, goth, rock, and alt-anything variety), and the crowd is lively but not rabid. $7–25.

Paramount 911 Pine St, Downtown ☎ 206/682-1414. On the eastern edge of Downtown, this large movie palace, built in 1928 for vaudeville shows and silent films, now seats around three thousand, often hosting well-known rock 'n' roll bands, as well as lectures, classic film programs, comedians, assorted concerts, and more. $25–100.

Showbox 1426 1st Ave, Downtown ☎ 206/628-3151. This 1000-person hall across from Pike Place Market is the best place to catch touring acts that have yet to make the bigger arenas, along with well-regarded regional bands, usually with an indie slant. $10–25.

Sunset Tavern 5433 Ballard Ave NW, Ballard ☎ 206/784-4880. Along with being a colorful bar and karaoke spot, the Sunset Tavern's also a good venue for catching aggressive young rockers and various eclectic acts in nightly performances. $5–10.

Jazz

Dimitriou's Jazz Alley 2033 6th Ave, Belltown ☎ 206/441-9729. The best of the jazz venues in Seattle, if a bit mainstream, presenting a steady march of notable out-of-towners. Heavy on established veterans, with the occasional blues or R&B act. $20–35.

Paragon 2125 Queen Anne Ave N, Queen Anne ☎ 206/283-4548. Northwest Cuisine restaurant that features performers Tues–Sat in an intimate, upscale setting. Jazz, soul, and R&B hold sway most of the time. No cover.

Tula's 2214 2nd Ave, Belltown ☎ 206/443-4221. Jazz of all stripes every evening, mostly from regional unknowns, with live jams Monday evenings. Also open for food and drink starting at 3pm. $5–15.

Blues, country, and folk

Conor Byrne Pub 5140 Ballard Ave NW, Ballard ☎ 206/784-3640. You can quaff Guinness at this top-notch Irish pub, but you should really come for the tunes: blues and bluegrass jams, alt-country and

Irish rock, and roots fiddlers and strummers make this spot an excellent choice both during the week (when it's free) or on the weekend ($3–7 cover).

Highway 99 Blues Club 1414 Alaskan Way, Downtown ☎ 206/382-2171. Any nightspot that names itself after a grim overhead viaduct must be a place worth a visit, and this rootsy joint certainly is, showcasing regional and national performers in a bare-bones space that's all about the music. Cover $5–10, unless a big name's in town, which will boost it to $15–20.

New Orleans 114 1st Ave S at Yesler Way, Pioneer Square ☎ 206/622-2563. A decent spot to catch jazz, Dixieland, and blues, with roots rock, Cajun, and zydeco thrown in on occasion. The house bands are free, but bigger names cost anywhere from $5 to $20.

Tractor Tavern 5213 Ballard Ave NW, Ballard ☎ 206/789-3599. Roots music of all kinds – zydeco, Irish, blues, bluegrass – also featuring the occasional high-profile act in rock, jazz, and blues. Often a better choice than similar spots in Pioneer Square. $7–20.

Triple Door 216 Union St, Downtown ☎ 206/838-4333. The apogee of the folk, roots, alt-country, and blues scene in Seattle: the Mainstage has major players in a moody, dramatic site ($15–25), while the Musicquarium has DJs and more experimental fare – it's also free.

World-beat and reggae

Century Ballroom 915 E Pine, 2nd Floor, Capitol Hill ☎ 206/324-7263. Major world-music acts from all over the globe swing through this spacious ballroom with a huge wooden dancefloor. It also hosts swing, salsa, and tango nights. Concerts $10–30.

Nectar 412 N 36th St, Fremont ☎ 206/632-2020. A happening, two-story club that features a mix of DJs and live performers, both of the international variety. You might hear anything from Latin drumming to Indonesian gamelan, and it's all pretty inexpensive, too. free–$10.

Clubs

Most of Seattle's **clubs** are very relaxed, with minimal dress codes, and all musical tastes and sexual orientations are welcomed. Most of the noteworthy clubs are situated in Pioneer Square or Capitol Hill, specializing in varied music and/or DJs on a nightly basis, and it's not at all unusual for the same venue to feature gothic, New Wave, and electronica the same week. **Cover charges** are usually in the $5–15 range, with prices varying according to the night of the week. Additionally, some clubs have regular free or ultra-cheap nights, and the cover can vary according to the time of the night; early in the evening it may be free, then $5 after 9pm, and ultimately $10 that same night for the peak crowd.

Chop Suey 1325 E Madison St, Capitol Hill ☎206/324-8000. An intentionally kitschy dance club and live-music venue decorated with leopard-print designs and Chinese lanterns, presenting an array of DJs on some nights (hip-hop, house, funk), dance bands on others, and a chaotic mix of instruments and turntables on occasion. $5–20.

Contour 807 1st Ave, Pioneer Square ☎206/447-7704. Fairly cramped space for grooving to house and techno, but fun if you don't mind bumping elbows with your neighbors on the small dance floor. Features a range of DJs and "open decks." free–$10.

Last Supper Club 124 S Washington St, Pioneer Square ☎206/748-9975. Moody brick walls give way to three levels and two dancefloors alive with computerized lighting effects. This chic spot varies the DJ attack from night to night – trance, acid house, Latin, salsa, and even erotic cabaret. Sometimes it's free, sometimes up to $15.

 Lo-Fi Performance Gallery 429B Eastlake Ave E, Eastlake ☎206/254-2824. One of the city's best spots to see enterprising DJs (jungle, experimental, anything creative) in a friendly environment. There are also occasional retro-rock shows, karaoke nights, and art shows. $4–15.

The Rendezvous 2322 2nd Ave, Belltown ☎206/441-5823. A converted speakeasy from the Prohibition era that now connects to a performing-arts space, offers nightly eclectic music, serves primo bar fare, and whips up potent cocktails. $5–15.

Vogue 1516 11th Ave, Capitol Hill ☎206/324-5778. One of the older Seattle club scene institutions, Vogue still packs in youthful, edgy crowds to sounds that vary from New Wave and gothic to kinkier fare like a vamp drag show and talent contest. $5–10.

The War Room 722 E Pike St, Capitol Hill ☎206/328-7666. Playing the latest hip-hop sounds and showcasing DJ culture, a multileveled venue for house and techno that offers nightly music (and rap on Sat with Yo! Son) and shows with major-name performers. $5–10.

Gay bars and clubs

The Cuff 1533 13th Ave, Capitol Hill ☎206/323-1525. Oriented toward the leather-and-Levi's crowd, a spot that can get downright boisterous at times, with a restaurant, patio, several bars, and two DJs spinning bass-heavy sounds in the club rooms.

Neighbours 1509 Broadway E, Capitol Hill ☎206/324-5358. Broadway's most popular gay disco, and the place to go if you want to dance yourself into delirium to loud, beat-heavy sounds. Increasingly straight in recent years.

R Place 619 E Pine St, Capitol Hill ☎206/322-8828. Three-floor bar with pool tables, dance floors, and dartboards; a prime cruising spot for young, professional gay men. Funky retro-DJs alternate with events like underwear contests, amateur strip shows, and karaoke.

Re-Bar 1114 Howell St, First Hill ☎206/233-9873. Draws big crowds with acid jazz, hip-hop, funk, soul, and of course, electronica from house to techno. Also some live music from bands you might have heard of, and occasional theatrical and spoken-word shows.

Sonya's Bar & Grill 1919 1st Ave, Downtown ☎206/441-7996. Friendly neighborhood bar in a gentrifying part of town, with a good menu and nice views of Elliott Bay and a central location near Pike Place Market.

Wild Rose 1021 E Pike St, Capitol Hill ☎206/324-9210. Seattle's most popular lesbian bar, and a comfortable mixing point for having a bite, playing pool or darts, or just hanging out. If you want something livelier, show up for weekend dance nights.

Performing arts and film

Seattle's **performing arts** scene is strong and vibrant in many ways: the area has one of the most active **theater** communities of any similar-size region in the US, both for big-budget and fringe productions, and offers a handful of major **opera**, **classical**, and **ballet** companies. Lesser-known **dance** and **chamber music** organizations stage noteworthy performances as well. There's also a fair demand for art-house and classic **movies**, shown in a fine collection of small, atmospheric cinemas.

Two alternative weeklies, the *Seattle Weekly* and *The Stranger*, are free from boxes on the streets and numerous cafés and stores, and are good for arts **listings**, as are the Friday editions of the *Seattle Post Intelligencer* and *Seattle Times*. TicketMaster (ⓦ www.ticketmaster.com) is the main **ticket** vendor for many of the shows and goings-on listed in this chapter; otherwise, check with the venue. Ticket Window (Ⓣ 206/325-6500, ⓦ www.ticketwindowonline .com) sells day-of-show theater and concert tickets at half-price; call or check website for outlets.

Classical music, dance, and opera

Seattle's main options for **classical music**, **dance**, and **opera** are all worthwhile institutions that often put on compelling productions. Most performance take place at venues located in the **Seattle Center**, though a few alternative sites can be found scattered throughout the city. **Ticket prices** are all over the place; as a rule, Benaroya Hall and Seattle Center performances cost the most, running anywhere from $15 to $100, while alternative performances may cost just a fraction of this.

Classical music and opera

The Esoterics rotating venues Ⓣ 206/935-7779, ⓦ www.theesoterics.org. The most ambitious and colorful of the city's classical groups, the Esoterics are a renowned *a cappella* society that performs eerie settings of Biblical texts and Latin masses, as well as avant-garde contemporary pieces and works drawing on Islam and Hinduism, among other influences.

Meany Studio Theater near the intersection of 15th Ave NE and NE 40th St Ⓣ 206/543-4880 or 1-800/859-5342, ⓦ www.meany.org. On the University of Washington campus, the 1200-seat theater stages classical music, world dance, opera, world music, and theatrical events, many featuring performers of international renown.

Seattle Opera Ⓣ 206/389-7676, ⓦ www .seattleopera.org. Plays at Seattle Center's McCaw Hall, whose dramatic modernist design and enhanced acoustics promise quite the spectacle. The operatic fare, however, is less surprising – mainly the usual Italian and German heavyweights, though there's a much-heralded Ring Cycle every four years – the next in summer 2009.

Seattle Symphony at Benaroya Hall, 200 University St, Downtown Ⓣ 206/215-4747, ⓦ www.seattlesymphony.org. Under the talented direction of conductor Gerard Schwarz, with light pops fare and odes to Hollywood film music sprinkled in to increase the subscriber base. Located in a hall whose acoustics are said to be among the finest in the world.

Dance

On the Boards 100 W Roy St, Queen Anne Ⓣ 206/217-9888, ⓦ www.ontheboards.org. In addition to its fine theater program, this performing arts organization also stages cutting-edge dance events, often of a multidisciplinary nature; these are usually held in its own space, though occasionally the group rents out bigger venues such as the Moore Theater.

Pacific Northwest Ballet Marion Oliver McCaw Hall, Seattle Center Ⓣ 206/441-2424, ⓦ www.pnb .org. When not touring internationally, the ballet puts on around seven programs per year, with the most popular being a December staging of Tchaikovsky's *Nutcracker*, with sets and costumes by Maurice Sendak.

Spectrum Dance Theater at Madrona Dance Studio, 800 Lake Washington Blvd Ⓣ 206/325-4161, ⓦ www.spectrumdance.org. One of the more prominent jazz dance companies in the US, the Seattle group performs around town – at such spots as the Moore and Paramount theaters – when not touring internationally.

Theater

Theater is one of Seattle's strongest suits, and there's never a shortage of dramatic options, from tiny experimental works to sweeping reinterpretations of the classics and big-budget musical spectaculars. **Tickets** for prestigious performances at the Seattle Center can cost more than $50, whereas many smaller shows elsewhere often cost $10 or less. You might even take in a show at a coffee house, bar, or club – Seattle is well known for serving up culture fare in unusual places.

A Contemporary Theatre (ACT) Kreielsheimer Place, 700 Union St, Downtown ☏ 206/292-7676, Ⓦ www.acttheatre.org. One of the heavyweights in town, with a broad array of works presented. There are four theaters from 99 to 387 seats; tickets are $40–60 for most shows, though at least once during a show's run you can get in for as little as $5 on "pay what you will" nights.

Annex Theatre 1122 E Pike St, Capitol Hill ☏ 206/728-0933, Ⓦ www.annextheatre.org. One of Seattle's most established companies for alternative/fringe works. It's unpredictable what you'll see here – anything from musical versions of Shakespeare to multimedia meditations on sex. Has occasional outlandish cabaret shows, too. Most tickets $10–15.

Fifth Avenue Theatre 1308 5th Ave, Downtown ☏ 206/625-1418, Ⓦ www.5thavenuetheatre.org. Seattle theater at its glitziest, located in a gigantic 1926 vaudeville house that replicates the throne room of China's Forbidden City, presenting mainstream musicals with big-name stars. $20–75.

Intiman Theatre Seattle Center ☏ 206/269-1900, Ⓦ www.intiman.org. Because it's a respectable institution housed in the Seattle Center, you're rarely going to see anything at the Intiman beyond the tried-and-true classics and modern reinterpretations of classics. There's usually one (noncontroversial) new or recent work per season. $20–50.

Northwest Actors Studio 1100 E Pike St, Capitol Hill ☏ 206/324-6328, Ⓦ www.nwactorsstudio.com. A theater center with two stages that, in addition to offering acting courses, puts on performances with a wide scope: comedy, classics, and the avant-garde are all fair game, and you can also see one-actor-shows and improv. $10–15.

On the Boards 100 W Roy St, Queen Anne ☏ 206/217-9888, Ⓦ www.ontheboards.org. In addition to its contemporary dance program, the group also sponsors challenging contemporary theater, often mixing dance and drama in the same production. $12–25.

Open Circle 429 Boren Ave N, Downtown ☏ 206/382-4250, Ⓦ www.octheater.com. A fifty-seater that's one of the city's more intimate playhouses; its house company puts on several

Festivals in Seattle

Seattle has several outstanding **festivals**, many of them based at the Seattle Center. For four days at the beginning of September, **Bumbershoot** (☏ 206/281-7788, Ⓦ www .bumbershoot.org) is a mammoth multi-event extravaganza that's one of the city's best parties. Musical acts range from the famous to the obscure, with plenty of film, comedy, and theater, too, with five hundred acts performing at twenty venues around town. Less well known outside of Seattle, but just as popular, the **Northwest Folk Festival** (☏ 206/684-7300, Ⓦ www.nwfolklife.org), on Memorial Day weekend, attracts 200,000 visitors and six thousand participants for all types of traditional music, including bluegrass, Celtic, and world music, along with crafts, ethnic food, dance, and storytelling. **Seafair** (☏ 206/728-0123, Ⓦ www.seafair.com), in July, is a three-week celebration of Northwest maritime culture, held at various locations and including maneuvers by the Navy's Blue Angels squad, hydroplane races on Lake Washington, and milk-carton races on Green Lake. Finally, the **Fremont Fair & Solstice Parade** (☏ 206/633-4409, Ⓦ www.fremontfair.com), in mid-June, is Seattle's jolliest neighborhood celebration, with hundreds of food stalls and arts vendors, plus a parade of naked bicyclists and human-powered floats, and followed by a pageant at the end of the route in Gasworks Park.

shows and workshop productions each year, everything from classic revivals to rock musicals. $10–15.

Printer's Devil Theatre various locations ☎206/860-7163, ⓦwww.printersdevil.org. Devoted to cutting-edge new work, and mounting shows at conventional theaters as well as untraditional spaces like garages, airplane hangars, and actual IKEA showrooms in Renton.

Seattle Repertory Theatre 155 Mercer St, Seattle Center ☎206/443-2222, ⓦwww.seattlerep.org. The oldest and most established company in town,

performing popular contemporary material, with a dash of the classics, at Bagley Wright Theatre. A second stage in the same facility, the Leo K. Theatre, has smaller-scaled works. Oct–May; tickets $10–45.

Theater Schmeater 1500 Summit Ave, First Hill ☎206/324-5801, ⓦwww.schmeater.org. Although its late-night dramatizations of *Twilight Zone* episodes have received most of the attention, the main focus here is on contemporary fringe theater, though classics are often added to the mix. $15–20, kids free.

Film

Seattle's abundance of quality **movie** venues means that you can enjoy foreign films, art-house fare, oddball independent cinema, or mainstream Hollywood blockbusters in a variety of different settings. The most interesting and atmospheric are the **repertory theaters** in Capitol Hill and the U District, many of which are housed in classic buildings that are either comfortably dilapidated or pleasantly spruced up. There are also several **film festivals** in Seattle, highlighted by the Seattle International Film Festival in late spring (☎206/464-5830, ⓦwww.seattlefilm.com).

Cinerama 2100 4th Ave, Belltown ☎206/441-3080, ⓦwww.seattlecinerama.com. Massive facility with state-of-the-art sound and picture quality. Features a modern 70mm screen for showing the latest blockbusters and a 90-by-30-foot screen with two thousand vertical panels for experiencing epics old and new.

Egyptian 801 E Pine St, Capitol Hill ☎206/323-4978. Housed in an old Masonic Temple, this is the Art Deco headquarters of the Seattle International Film Festival. The regular program matches the high standards of the architecture, focusing on offbeat releases and indie films.

Grand Illusion 1403 NE 50th St, University District ☎206/523-3935, ⓦwww.grandillusioncinema.org. Fine old venue for foreign films, cult movies, protest films, and Hollywood classics – though the screening room is a bit on the small side, with just a few dozen seats.

Harvard Exit 807 E Roy St, Capitol Hill ☎206/323-8986. At the northern edge of Broadway, this 1925 building – originally the Women's Century Club and featuring a fireplace and chandelier in the lobby – shows a consistent program of arty and indie releases.

Neptune 1303 NE 45th St, University District ☎206/633-5545. Lovely little curiosity with aquatic decor inspired by the eponymous Roman god, whose stern visage makes an appearance here and there on the walls. Mainly art and independent films.

Northwest Film Forum 1515 12th Ave, Capitol Hill ☎206/267-5380, ⓦwww .nwfilmforum.org. Perhaps the city's most prominent film organization, putting on nightly screenings and retrospectives of international, classic, art-house, and documentary films, and providing a springboard for up-and-coming visual artists in film and other media.

Seven Gables 911 NE 50th St at Roosevelt Way ☎206/632-8820. Very cozy and attractive 1925 two-story home and former dance hall at the edge of the U District, easily missed if you're not looking for it. Shows mainly independent fare.

Varsity 4329 University Way NE, University District ☎206/632-3131. A trio of theaters from 1940, stacked on top of each other and running one or two art-house movies every day, including old classics, documentaries, foreign films, and newly released independents.

Outdoor activities

With temperatures that seldom dip below freezing and a close proximity to some of the most scenic mountains and waterways of North America, Seattle is well suited for year-round **outdoor activities**. The ubiquitous rain hardly stops the pace of hiking, climbing, and biking, even during the colder months, and most weekend campers and sailors find plenty of opportunities to explore the outdoors, regardless of the weather. See Basics (p.55) for information on Seattle's range of spectator **sports**.

Biking

Despite its rainy climate, hilly topography, and crowded roads, Seattle has a great number of **bicyclists**, and for good reason: there are thirty miles of bike/pedestrian trails and nearly one hundred miles of marked bike routes. Although you'll have a hard time finding level routes unless you stick close to the lakes, the semi-mountainous terrain guarantees a good workout, and the scenery is often magnificent.

The most popular route is the twelve-mile **Burke–Gilman Trail**, which starts near Eighth Avenue NW and NW 43rd Street in Ballard and follows the banks of the Lake Washington Ship Canal, Lake Union, and western Lake Washington, passing through such areas as central Fremont, Gasworks Park, and the U District. The path is also open to joggers and walkers; at its northern end, it connects to the ten-mile Sammamish River Trail, which brings riders over to Redmond in the Eastside. Another good route is the stretch of **Lake Washington Boulevard** that starts at the Washington Park Arboretum (see p.317) and skirts the lake's edge for a few miles before terminating at Seward Park. The southern end of the route is closed to auto traffic from 10am to 6pm on the second Saturday and third Sunday of the month between May and September. Far more challenging, and quite stunning, is the **Elliott Bay Trail** along Magnolia Boulevard, which climbs a steep hill from the Magnolia Bridge to Discovery Park, passing gorgeous cliffside views of Puget Sound en route. Another good stretch, if a bit easier, is the **Alki Trail**, which takes you around the northern end of the peninsula at West Seattle, terminating along the sands at Alki Beach.

Bikes can be **rented** at Aaron's Bicycle Repair, 6521 California Ave SW, West Seattle (☎206/938-9795, ⓦwww.rideyourbike.com); Gregg's, 7007 Woodlawn Ave NE, Green Lake (☎206/523-1822, ⓦwww.greggscycles.com); Bicycle Center, 4529 Sandpoint Way NE, Sand Point (☎206/523-8300, ⓦwww.bicyclecenterseattle.com); and All About Bike & Ski, 3615 NE 45th St, University District (☎206/524-2642, ⓦwww.allaboutbikeandski.com). Rental rates tend to fluctuate from $5 to $12 per hour, or $20–45 per day, depending on the proximity of the bike shop to major attractions. Call the bicycle division of the city's transportation department at ☎206/684-7583 (ⓦwww.cityofseattle.net/transportation) and they'll send you the free and very handy Seattle Bicycling Map, which outlines bicycle routes and lists cycling regulations.

Running

Running is big in Seattle in all kinds of weather, and the city's many parks and waterside lanes offer many choices for the fitness enthusiast. Some of the better routes are multipurpose biking/running/walking paths, such as the Burke-Gilman Trail (see opposite) and routes along Green Lake, Lake Washington, the Washington Park Arboretum, and Myrtle Edwards Park; Discovery Park has a challenging 2.8-mile loop trail that goes through dense forest and along bluffs with great views of Puget Sound. For more on the various footpaths and jogging routes through the city's parks, the Department of Parks and Recreation offers online information, as well as downloadable brochures you can also order through the mail (☎206/684-4075, ⓦwww .cityofseattle.net/parks).

Competitive **races** are held in town throughout the year, highlighted by late November's Seattle Marathon/Half-Marathon (☎206/729-3660 or 729-3661, ⓦwww.seattlemarathon.org), partly following attractive Lake Washington Boulevard and featuring an option to do the full 26.2-mile route or just half of it. *Northwest Runner* (ⓦwww.nwrunner.com), a local periodical available at sporting goods outlets, has a calendar of races in Seattle and the entire Northwest.

Hiking and climbing

Hiking is integral to the Northwest lifestyle, with the best places being a few hours outside of town at **Mount Rainier** and the **Cascade Mountains** (see Chapter 10, p.415). A closer option is **Mount Si**, only about a half-hour's drive east of Seattle, near Snoqualmie Falls. Here, a four-mile climb ascends about 4000ft to take in glorious panoramas of the surrounding mountains; see p.432 for further details.

Within the urban boundaries, your options are considerably fewer, with most parks simply not designed to provide a vigorous hike. Two of the exceptions are **Frink Park**, off Lake Washington Boulevard in Madrona (daily 6am–11.30pm; ☎206/684-4075), which offers nicely wooded terrain built around a steep ravine, and West Seattle's **Schmitz Park**, 5551 SW Admiral Way (daily 6am–11.30pm; ⓦwww.schmitzpark.org), a rugged swath of wilderness that's been kept that way by the will of the donor who provided it to the city.

Trail maps are found in all good bookstores and outdoors shops; particularly good outlets in Seattle include Metsker Maps, 1511 1st Ave, Downtown (☎206/623-8747, ⓦwww.metskers.com), Wide World Books & Maps, 4411 Wallingford Ave N, Wallingford (☎206/634-3453, ⓦwww .travelbooksandmaps.com), and the outdoors superstore REI, 222 Yale Ave N, between Downtown and Capitol Hill (☎206/223-1944, ⓦwww .rei.com/stores/seattle).

REI is also a good place to get hiking gear, or to practice your **climbing** on its 65ft indoor rock "pinnacle," which you can ascend with guidance from the store staff ($15, or $5 for REI members). More serious climbs are offered by Vertical World, 2123 W Elmore St in Fishermen's Terminal, though you have to sign up to be a member ($89 initiation fee) to use the expansive facility (day passes $15; ☎206/283-4497, ⓦwww.verticalworld.com), which has almost 15,000 square feet of space and more than a hundred routes of various degrees of difficulty.

Water activities

There are several **swimming, windsurfing**, and **boating** centers in Seattle that enable you to get out on the lakes and bays. Foremost among these is the **Waterfront Activities Center** on the UW campus (☎206/543-9433,

△ Lake Union

Ⓦdepts.washington.edu/ima/IMA_wac.php), which rents out rowboats or canoes for $7.50 an hour; the marshes of Foster Island are just a few minutes of rowing away. Located between Mount Baker and Seward Park, the peninsula of Stan Sayres Park, 3808 Lake Washington Blvd S, holds a **Rowing and Sailing Center** (☏206/386-1913, Ⓦwww.cityofseattle.net/parks /boats), where you can launch anything from a dinghy to a sailboat and take classes on sailing, too.

On **Lake Union**, the **Center for Wooden Boats**, on Lake Union at 1010 Valley St (☏206/382-2628, Ⓦwww.cwb.org), rents out sailboats and rowboats for $15–45/hr, depending upon the size of the boat and day of the week; while the **Northwest Outdoor Center**, 2100 Westlake Ave N (☏206/281-9694 or 1-800/683-0637, Ⓦwww.nwoc.com), rents out kayaks by the hour ($12 single, $17 double) and the day ($60 single, $80 double). Similar hourly rates are also offered by the **Agua Verde Paddle Club**, on Lake Union's Portage Bay at 1303 NE Boat St ($15–18/hr; ☏206/545-8570 Ⓦwww.aguaverde.com).

Outdoor swimming is usually not a comfortable proposition in Seattle without a wetsuit, but the hardy do take to the waves at the city's two most popular beaches, **Alki Beach** (p.320) and **Golden Gardens** in Ballard – although the water temperatures are actually warmer, and the crowds thinner, around **Lake Washington**.

Listings

Banks Hours vary, but most banks are open at least Monday to Friday 10am–5pm, sometimes with Saturday hours. Central Downtown branches include Bank of America, 701 2nd Ave ☏ 206/358-0500; KeyBank, 700 5th Ave ☏ 206/684-6507; Union Bank of California, 900 4th Ave ☏ 206/587-6100; US Bank, 1301 5th Ave ☏ 206/344-2395; Washington Mutual, 1201 3rd Ave ☏ 206/461-6475; Wells Fargo, Westlake Center, 1620 4th Ave ☏ 206/287-0039. Also Umpqua Bank at 11100 NE 8th St, Suite 200, Bellevue ☏ 425/732-6016.

Bookstores University Bookstore, 4326 University Way, University District (☏ 206/634-3400, ⊛ www.bookstore.washington.edu), and Elliott Bay Book Company, 101 S Main St, Pioneer Square (☏ 206/624-6600, ⊛ www.elliottbaybook.com), are the city's biggest booksellers. The collectively run Left Bank Books, Pike Place Market at 92 Pike St (☏ 206/622-1095, ⊛ www.leftbankbooks.com), is a formidable left-wing bookshop. Bulldog News, 4208 University Way NE, University District (☏ 206/632-NEWS, ⊛ www.bulldognews.com), is one of the best of Seattle's newsstands, as is First & Pike News, 93 Pike St in Pike Place Market (☏ 206/624-0140).

Coast Guard Search-and-rescue emergencies ☏ 206/217-6001.

Crisis Clinic For resources and support for emotional crisis and trauma, disabilities, and other services, contact ☏ 206/461-3222, ⊛ www .crisisclinic.org.

Currency exchange Most large Downtown banks will change foreign currency and travelers' checks. Cash American Express checks at its Downtown office at Azumano Travel, 600 Stewart St (Mon–Fri 9am–5pm; ☏ 206/441-8622, ⊛ travel.americanexpress.com). Travelex changes money at Sea-Tac Airport, in the Main Terminal (daily 6am–9.30pm; ☏ 206/248-0401, ⊛ www .travelex.com), and in Bellevue at 10630 NE 8th St (Mon–Fri 8.30am–6pm; ☏ 425/462-2817).

Dentist The Seattle/King County Dental Society, 2201 6th Avenue, Suite 1210 (☏ 206/443-7607, ⊛ www.skcds.org), provides a referral service to low-cost dental clinics around town.

Emergencies ☏ 911.

Hospital The best overall choice is Northwest Hospital, 1550 N 115th St, North Seattle (☏ 206/364-0500, ⊛ www.nwhospital.org); for minor injuries, Country Doctor Community Clinic, 500 19th Ave E, Capitol Hill (☏ 206/299-1600, ⊛ www.cdchc.org).

Internet access Available from cyber-oriented coffee shops and city libraries. Except for libraries (free), expect to pay around 10¢ per minute to browse the Web.

Laundromats 12th Avenue Maytag Laundry, 1807 12th Ave, Capitol Hill ☏ 206/328-4610; Fremont Avenue Laundromat, 4237 Fremont Ave N, Fremont ☏ 206/632-8924; Seattle's Nicest Laundry, 5020 Roosevelt Way NE, University District ☏ 206/524-7855, and 333 NW 85th St ☏ 206/784-9020. Also check in the Yellow Pages for each neighborhood.

Left luggage You can leave luggage for up to two months at Sea-Tac Airport at Ken's Baggage, under the escalator between baggage-claim carousels 9 and 13 (daily 5.30am–12.30am; ☏ 206/433-5333), or for up to 24hr in storage lockers at Greyhound, 811 Stewart St (☏ 206/628-5526).

Legal advice Seattle King County Bar Association Lawyer Referral & Information Service (☏ 206/267-7010 or 623-2551, ⊛ www.kcba.org) does pro bono work.

Library The main, newly rebuilt branch of the Seattle Public Library is Downtown at 1000 4th Ave (Mon–Thurs 10am–8pm, Fri–Sat 10am–6pm, Sun noon–6pm; ☏ 206/386-4636, ⊛ www.spl.org). The same phone number is also a handy general information line for all library policies.

Pharmacies The prescription department is open 24hr a day at Bartell Drugs, 600 1st Ave N, Queen Anne (☏ 206/284-1353, ⊛ www.bartelldrugs.com). Check website for many other Seattle locations, with regular business hours.

Police stations West Precinct, 810 Virginia St, Downtown ☏ 206/684-8917; East Precinct, 1519 12th Ave, Capitol Hill ☏ 206/684-4300; North Precinct, 10049 College Way N, North Seattle ☏ 206/684-0850; South Precinct, 3001 S Myrtle St, Rainier Valley ☏ 206/386-1850; Southwest Precinct, 2300 SW Webster St, West Seattle ☏ 206/733-9800. See ⊛ www.cityofseattle.net /Police/contact.htm for more information.

Post office The main post office is Downtown at 301 Union St; the zip code is 98101 (Mon–Fri 7.30am–5.30pm; ☏ 206/748-5417 or 1-800/275-8777).

Rape Crisis Line 24hr ☏ 206/632-7273.

Tax Sales tax in Seattle is 8.8 percent, applied to everything except groceries, though a food and beverage tax (mainly for restaurants) bumps the total up to 9.3 percent; it's similar throughout the rest of the metropolitan area. There's also a steep hotel tax of 15.6 percent.

Weather 24hr report provided by the *Seattle Times* (T 206/464-2000, ext. 9900).

Women's resources The Women's Information Center at University of Washington, Imogen Cunningham Hall AJ50 (T 206/685-1090, W depts .washington.edu/womenctr), has information and referral services for a variety of needs; the Seattle Women's Commission (T 206/684-4537, W www .cityofseattle.net/womenscommission) maintains a large online list of women-oriented social and civic organizations; and Planned Parenthood of Western Washington, 2001 E Madison, Capitol Hill (T 206/328-7734, W www.ppww.org), has clinical services and reproductive health education.

8

Puget Sound

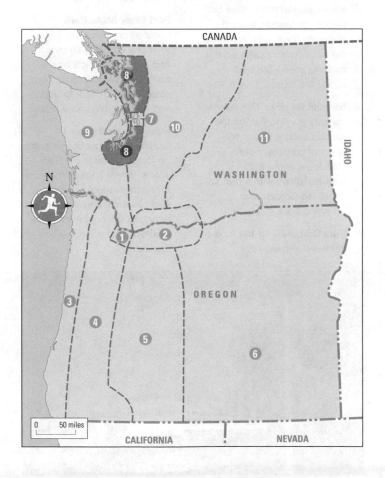

Highlights

✳ **Museum of Glass** In down-town Tacoma, a sparkling new institution devoted to the art of glass, with the work of favorite son Dale Chihuly prominently on display. See p.348

✳ **Puget Sound ferry rides** Sail past small islands, around sheltered bays, and alongside majestic creatures like whales and sea lions – the best way to see the Sound. See p.356

✳ **Bloedel Reserve** This natural conservatory on Bainbridge Island contains nearly 150 acres of gardens, ponds, meadows, and wildlife habitats, along with a tranquil Japanese Garden and reflecting pool. See p.359

✳ **Port Gamble** Visit the former lumber-company town on the edge of the Kitsap Peninsula that resembles a slice of New England – white clapboard houses, elm trees, quaint churches – transported to the Pacific Northwest. See p.360

✳ **Fort Ebey State Park** Located on massive Whidbey Island, a strange and evocative place where hiking trails lead into an eerie atmosphere of dark forests and military ruins. See p.364

✳ **Mount Constitution** The highest and most scenic point on Orcas Island in the San Juans, where a steep four-mile trail overlooks streams and pastures, and leads up to a rugged tower resembling a medieval stone fortress. See p.371

△ Washington State Ferry

8

Puget Sound

M easuring about a hundred miles from north to south, the grand waterway of **PUGET SOUND** is the lined with some of the state's major cities and dotted by hundreds of islands ranging in size from the largest in the continental US to tiny, remote refuges. Heading south on I-5 from Seattle – itself situated on the Sound inlet of Elliott Bay – the notable cities of **Tacoma** and **Olympia** together boast renovated historical architecture, engaging museums, and untrammeled parks. West of Seattle, ferries provide easy access to two of the most popular and easily reached of the Sound's islands: **Vashon** and **Bainbridge**, both offering a handful of sights along with appealing cycling routes and hiking trails. From Bainbridge Island, it's a quick trip over the Sound to the sizable **Kitsap Peninsula**, where villages like **Suquamish** and **Port Gamble** stand out for their rich heritage and architecture. Farther north along the waterway, **Whidbey Island** is a gargantuan stretch of land worth exploring for its pleasant townships, verdant state parks, and preserved military ruins. Along the mainland coast east of Whidbey, artsy **La Conner** makes for an enjoyable waterside diversion. From Anacortes, just north, the most distant – and perhaps the most spectacular – destinations in the Sound are the idyllic **San Juan Islands**, home to striking vistas, craggy coastlines, tranquil countryside, and the appealing burg of **Friday Harbor**. Finally, nestled in a bay along the Sound just below the Canadian border, **Bellingham** rewards a visit north with its nicely preserved Victorian buildings and lively college-town atmosphere.

South of Seattle

Located adjacent to the Sound thirty and sixty miles **south of Seattle**, respectively, **Tacoma** and **Olympia** are independent cities that have been almost completely enveloped by metropolitan sprawl, which has made its way south from Seattle along the Interstate 5 highway corridor. As a result, the entire stretch now resembles one long, linear suburb. If you're in Seattle for a week or so, the cities together merit at least a day-trip, though there's little else in the vicinity to distract you, aside from the curious preserve of **Wolf Haven**

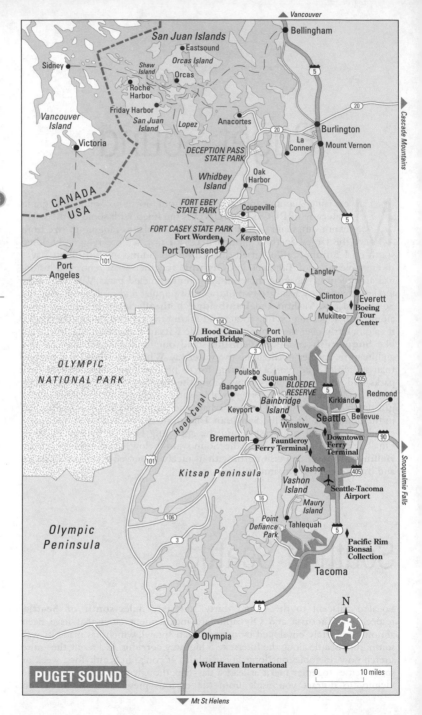

PUGET SOUND

International. South of Olympia, I-5 chugs through one of the less remarkable stretches of the state, on the way down to Portland, while northbound from town, Highway 101 begins its lengthy route around the edge of the Olympic Peninsula (see p.385). Near the beginning of this journey, the Kitsap Peninsula (see p.359) is within reach along Route 3 – though its most compelling attractions are on its north end, and best accessed from Bainbridge Island.

Tacoma

Sitting on the Seattle–Portland axis of I-5, **TACOMA** is an old industrial town that's recently experienced a resurgence with a slew of new museums, theaters, and restaurants. In fact, Washington's second-largest city has undergone such an extensive revitalization that it has now actually become something of a tourist magnet – to the shock and amazement of old-time Northwesterners.

Arrival and information

Coming in on I-5 from the north, you'll pass the enormous blue-gray roof of the **Tacoma Dome** (2727 East D St; information at ☎253/272-3663, ⓦ www.tacomadome.org), a major sports and concert venue, on your way to the city center. The downtown area is perched above Puget Sound at **Commencement Bay**, a deep harbor whose geographical appeal led railroad planners to choose Tacoma over Seattle as the western terminus for the Northern Pacific Railroad's transcontinental route in 1873 (Seattle had to wait until 1906 for its own rail station).

Tacoma is easily accessed by local and regional **mass transit**: Amtrak **trains** (☎1-800/USA-RAIL, ⓦ www.amtrak.com) pull in at Freighthouse Square, 1001 Puyallup Ave. Pierce Transit (☎253/581-8000, ⓦ www.ptbus.pierce.wa .us) runs frequent Seattle Express **bus** service between the two cities (lines #586 and 590, $3), as well as local routes ($1.50), while Sound Transit (☎1-800/201-4900, ⓦ www.soundtransit.org) offers Seattle-bound express buses (lines #590–594; $3) and the Sounder commuter rail, from a station at the Tacoma Dome (rush hour only; $4), which you can reach on the free Tacoma Link light rail from downtown Tacoma.

The **Tacoma Visitors Center**, at the *Marriott Hotel*, 1516 Pacific Ave (Mon–Sat 9am–5pm, Sun noon–5pm; ☎253/627-2836, ⓦ www.traveltacoma .com), has maps and literature about the history and attractions of the area, along with walking guides, which can prove especially helpful when exploring local architecture.

Accommodation

For **accommodation**, the usual chain hotels can be found downtown, functional motels just off the freeway, and an array of interesting **B&Bs** in rather far-flung locations. A Travelers' Reservation Service (☎206/364-5900) can put you in touch with B&Bs here and throughout the Northwest.

Devoe Mansion 203 133rd St E ☎253/539-3991, ⓦ www.devoemansion.com. Four elegant B&B rooms in a 1911 Colonial Revival estate named after a locally famous women's-rights pioneer, with savory breakfasts and several parklike acres of grounds. Located south of downtown Tacoma. ⑤

Geiger Victorian 912 North I St ☎253/383-3504, ⓦ www.geigervictorian.com. The quintessential B&B, in this case an Eastlake Victorian from 1889, loaded with all the chintz and antiques you'd expect, plus a fireplace, claw-foot tubs in the rooms, and a hand-painted

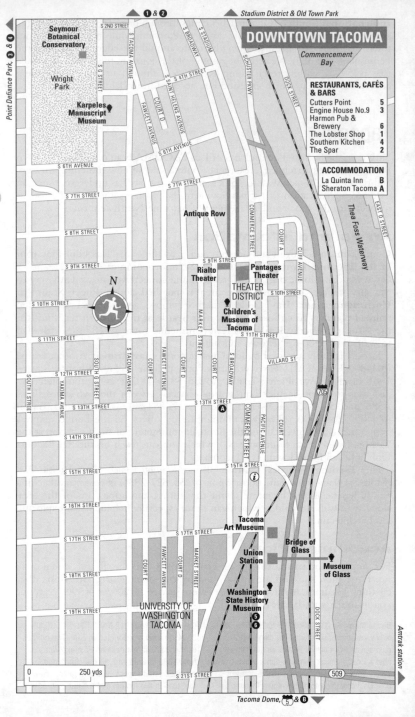

DOWNTOWN TACOMA

Commencement Bay

S 2ND STREET
S TACOMA AVENUE
S BROADWAY
S STADIUM
SCHUSTER PKWY
DOCK STREET

Seymour Botanical Conservatory

Wright Park

Karpeles Manuscript Museum

S G STREET
S 4TH STREET
SAINT HELENS AVENUE
COURT D
FAWCETT AVENUE

S 6TH AVENUE
S 6TH AVENUE

S 7TH STREET
S 7TH STREET

Antique Row

S 8TH STREET
S 8TH STREET

COMMERCE STREET

S 9TH STREET
S 9TH STREET

Rialto Theater

Pantages Theater

THEATER DISTRICT

COURT A
CLIFF AVENUE
EAST D STREET

Thea Foss Waterway

S 10TH STREET
S 10TH STREET

Children's Museum of Tacoma

S 11TH STREET
S 11TH STREET

MARKET STREET
S BROADWAY
VILLARD ST

S 12TH STREET
SOUTH G STREET
S TACOMA AVENUE
COURT E
FAWCETT AVENUE
COURT D
COURT C

S 13TH STREET

705

SOUTH I STREET
YAKIMA AVENUE

S 14TH STREET

COMMERCE STREET
PACIFIC AVENUE
COURT A

S 15TH STREET

S 16TH STREET

S 17TH STREET
S 17TH STREET

Tacoma Art Museum

Union Station

Bridge of Glass

Museum of Glass

S 18TH STREET

COURT E
FAWCETT AVENUE
COURT D
MARKET STREET

UNIVERSITY OF WASHINGTON TACOMA

S 19TH STREET

Washington State History Museum

DOCK STREET

5
6

S 21ST STREET

509

RESTAURANTS, CAFÉS & BARS

Cutters Point	5
Engine House No.9	3
Harmon Pub & Brewery	6
The Lobster Shop	1
Southern Kitchen	4
The Spar	2

ACCOMMODATION

La Quinta Inn	B
Sheraton Tacoma	A

N

0   250 yds

① & ②

Stadium District & Old Town Park

Point Defiance Park, ③ & ④

Amtrak station

Tacoma Dome, ⑤ & ⑧

ceiling in the Virginia Mason suite – by far the most unique room. ⑥

La Quinta Inn 1425 E 27th St ☎253/383-0146, ⓦwww.laquinta.com. Just a few blocks from the Tacoma Dome, a basic and clean chain motel with a heated pool, complimentary breakfast, and high-speed Internet access. The least expensive, but still more than adequate, chain accommodation close to downtown. ⑤

Sheraton Tacoma 1320 Broadway Plaza ☎253/572-3200 or 1-800/845-9466, ⓦwww .sheratontacoma.com. The best chain option in

town, next to an enormous convention center. Ask for a room with a view over Commencement Bay. Suites with parlors also available for a bit more money. ⑥

The Villa 705 N 5th St ☎253/572-1157 or 1-888/572-1157, ⓦwww.villabb.com. About a mile northeast of downtown, this Renaissance Revival mansion, surrounded by luxurious gardens, has been converted into a B&B with plenty of creature comforts. Some of the rooms (named after Italian towns) have private verandas with views of Commencement Bay and the Olympic Mountains. ⑥

The City

Tacoma is an easy city to get around, with many of its chief sights either lying on **Pacific Avenue** or around the **Theater District**. A stroll farther north takes you takes you to pleasant **Wright Park**, while the extensive acreage of **Point Defiance Park** marks the northern end of the city's worthwhile destinations. From here, the state ferry service can take you to Vashon Island, and from there on to the rest of the Sound.

Along Pacific Avenue

From the freeway, Exit 133 leads toward **Pacific Avenue**, the main cultural drag of downtown Tacoma. On the west end of the bridge across the 705 freeway, you'll see the earliest and most visible example of Tacoma's revival, **Union Station**, 1717 Pacific Ave (Mon–Fri 10am–4pm; ☎253/572-9310), a 1911 Baroque Revival treasure with a copper dome and marble lobby. Graced with colorful glassworks by world-renowned artist and native son Dale Chihuly – especially beautiful are the 27 orange- and henna-hued glass butterfly shapes in the **Monarch Window** – this elegant old station hasn't hosted an arriving train in twenty years. Instead, it's been renovated and reborn as a federal courthouse and as a station on the **Tacoma Link trolley** (Mon–Fri 5.30am–8pm, Sat 8am–10pm, Sun 10am–8pm; free), connecting the Tacoma Dome with the Theater District – a good way to get around town if you don't feel like walking. More of Chihuly's works are on display at the adjacent **Tacoma Art Museum**, 1701 Pacific Ave (Tues–Sat 10am–5pm, Sun noon–5pm; $7.50; ⓦwww .tacomaartmuseum.org). Though the minor pieces by Picasso, Degas, Renoir, and Frederic Remington aren't too inspiring, the building itself is quite a marvel, a gleaming steel-and-glass creation by Antoine Predock. The temporary exhibits are fairly wide-ranging, anything from native tribal works to classic photography to installation art.

Another vivid example of historic preservation lies across Pacific Avenue at the **University of Washington Tacoma** (ⓦwww.tacoma.washington.edu), where a handful of old grain and grocery warehouses have been cleverly converted into classrooms and offices, including the stately 1891 Romanesque Revival Garretson Woodruff Pratt Building, 1754 Pacific Avenue, and the triangular 1908 Mattress Factory Building, at Commerce and C streets. Across Pacific Avenue from the Pratt Building, the excellent **Washington State History Museum**, 1911 Pacific Ave (Mon–Wed & Fri–Sat 10am–5pm, Thurs 10am–8pm, Sun noon–5pm; $8, free Thurs 5–8pm; ⓦwww.wshs.org/wshm), has a huge array of exhibits on regional history in its **Great Hall of Washington History**, nicely re-creating the milieu of frontier towns and early logging industries, as well as a replica general store and native plank house.

△ Dale Chihuly glass art, Bridge of Glass

The Bridge and Museum of Glass

Stretching east over the 705 freeway from Union Station, Dale Chihuly's **Bridge of Glass** (ⓦwww.chihuly.com/bridgeofglass) is a colorful pedestrian overpass that displays the sculptor's talents in their full glory: an overhead skylight, the **Seaform Pavilion**, is filled with glass shapes resembling shells, urchins, and the like; a pair of crystalline **blue spires** look like rock-candy towers as they sit directly over the freeway; and the **Venetian Wall** is a series of glass vases and sculptures in viewing boxes, best seen in the morning when the rising sun illuminates the back of the glassworks to great effect.

The bridge leads to the **Museum of Glass**, 1801 East Dock St (summer Mon–Sat 10am–5pm, Sun noon–5pm; rest of the year Wed–Sat 10am–5pm, Sun noon–5pm; $10; ☏253/284-4750, ⓦwww.museumofglass.org), whose main identifying feature is a towering, metal-shingled cone that vaguely resembles an antiquated smokestack. Presenting a mix of glassworks, mixed-media assemblages, installation art, and conceptual art, the museum specializes in abstract, contemporary work, much of it focusing on Chihuly's vivid designs – swirling, sea-green vases and hypnotic sunburst chandeliers, and the like. Inside the museum's "Hot Shop," in fact, you might find Chihuly himself or another glass artist creating a piece before an amphitheater of gaping visitors.

The Theater District

Seven blocks north and two blocks west of Pacific Avenue, along South Broadway, lies the centerpiece of the **Theater District**, a complex of three major performance houses collectively known as the **Broadway Center for the Performing Arts**, 901 Broadway (☏253/591-5894, ⓦwww .broadwaycenter.org). Here you can see an array of plays as well as symphonic music, opera, and pop concerts. The highlights are two appealing landmark moviehouses – the **Pantages** and the **Rialto** – with terracotta façades and copious historic-revival decor.

A short distance away is **Antique Row**, on Broadway between S Seventh and S Ninth streets, a popular strip where fifteen dealers in historic collectibles, old-fashioned curiosities, and worn-out junk have set up shop. If the tots don't want to cooperate with your retro shopping plans, take them nearby to the **Children's Museum of Tacoma**, 936 Broadway (Tues–Sat 10am–5pm, Sun noon–5pm; kids and adults $6; ☎253/627-6031, ⊛www .childrensmuseumoftacoma.org), where the wee ones can play puppeteer, gardener, or artist – with all the requisite kid-friendly props.

Wright Park and around

About five blocks north and three blocks west of the Theater District, stately **Wright Park**, at Sixth Avenue and South G Street, occupies about ten city blocks. With more than a hundred varieties of outdoor plants, the park is an excellent spot in which to stroll, pitch horseshoes, or try your hand at a little lawn bowling. Especially compelling is the park's **Seymour Botanical Conservatory**, 316 S G St (Tues–Sun 10am–4.30pm; free; ☎253/591-5330), a 1908 glass and steel structure that holds some two hundred species, from lilies to ferns and bromeliads, including some two hundred varieties of orchids. Across the street, the often overlooked **Karpeles Manuscript Museum**, 407 South G St (Tues–Sun 10am–4pm; free; ☎253/383-2575, ⊛www.karpeles .com), is a grand Neoclassical affair, one of nine museums established by scientist and collector David Karpeles throughout the US to showcase his immense collection of manuscripts. Among its holdings are the concluding page of Darwin's *Origin of Species* and a study page for Karl Marx's *Das Kapital*. However, what you'll see will vary: all the exhibits are temporary. Typically on view for three months, they have covered everything from diplomatic records and famous proclamations to literary first editions and animation-production drawings of Mickey Mouse and Snow White.

The Stadium District and Old Town Park

Immediately north of Division Avenue from Wright Park begins the **Stadium District**, a neighborhood of Victorian architecture whose centerpiece is the stunning **Stadium High School**, 111 North E St, a monumental three-story French chateau – originally built in 1891 as a hotel, though it never opened – that would seem borrowed from a fairy tale if it weren't still swarming with teenagers.

If you have a particular zeal for nineteenth-century history, head farther west to **Old Town Park**, 30th Street at Carr Street, whose surrounding **Old Town** has a smattering of restaurants and stores. The park offers a good account of Tacoma's past at the **Job Carr Cabin Museum**, 2350 N 30th St (Wed–Sat: summer noon–4pm; rest of the year 1–4pm; free; ☎253/627-5405, ⊛www .jobcarrmuseum.org). Housed in an 1864 log home that was built in the first decade of the area's settlement, the museum displays old documents and antiques from the town's pre-industrial days.

Point Defiance Park

About four miles north of downtown, at Pearl Street off Ruston Way, lies picturesque **Point Defiance Park**. At 700 acres, it's one of the largest urban parks in the USA, with some fine gardens containing everything from Japanese plantings to dahlias, fuchsias, irises, and roses; a model pagoda with a waterfall; and a replica Shinto shrine with a Torii gate carved in cypress. There's also ferry access just outside the park up to Tahlequah on Vashon Island (see p.356 for ferry information).

The park's **Five Mile Drive** loop has nice vistas of Puget Sound and various points from which you can lose yourself on the numerous trails that weave their way through the park. Signs along the drive direct you to **Fort Nisqually** (April & May Wed–Sun 11am–5pm; June–Aug daily 11am–5pm; Sept–Mar Wed–Sun 11am–4pm; $4; ☎253/591-5339, ⓦwww.fortnisqually.org), a reconstruction of the fur-trading post Hudson's Bay Company set up in 1833, with homes and storehouses that illustrate the stark lifestyles of residents of the original fort. Near the fort, on the southern boundary of the park, **Camp Six Logging Museum** (grounds daily dawn–dusk; interior exhibits Apr–Oct Wed–Sun 10am–4pm; free; ☎253/752-0047, ⓦwww.camp-6-museum.org) is a reconstructed logging camp with antique equipment and photos, as well as vivid displays of the crude bunkhouses, dangerous-looking tools, and Industrial Age railcars that figured in the working life of loggers; the museum is best on spring and summer weekends, when the steam locomotive rides are running ($4). There's also a worthwhile **zoo** and **aquarium** in the park at 5400 N Pearl St (hours vary, generally daily 9.30am–5pm; $10; ☎253/591-5337, ⓦwww .pdza.org), with displays of arctic creatures like polar bears, plus red wolves, sharks, and a beluga whale.

Pacific Rim Bonsai and Rhododendron Species collections

For a very different sort of experience, head eight miles north of Tacoma, just off I-5 at a marked exit, to the **Pacific Rim Bonsai Collection** (Mar–Sept Fri–Wed 10am–4pm; Oct–Feb Sat–Wed 11am–4pm; free; ☎253/924-5206), whose fascinating selection of sixty-odd specimens includes the **pale-pink** weeping branches of the Tamarisk, the elegantly gnarled branches and horizontally splayed greenery of the Formosan Juniper – a quintessential bonsai look – and, as one of the most unusual items, the Sumac's single thin black trunk, twisted up to support a few vivid red and green sprigs at the top. Next to the bonsai collection is a more familiar selection of blooms, at the **Rhododendron Species Collection** (Mar–May Fri–Wed 10am–4pm; June–Feb Sat–Wed 11am–4pm; $3.50; ☎253/838-4646, ⓦwww.rsf.citymax .com), where you can get a glimpse of some ten thousand of the flowers spread over 22 acres in a pleasant wooded setting.

Eating and drinking

While **dining** out in Tacoma is not, by and large, a terribly adventurous culinary proposition, there are several dependable options to be found.

Antique Sandwich Company 5102 N Pearl St ☎253/752-4069. The budget sandwiches are just okay here, but the ambience at Point Defiance Park is inviting, and it's a good place to catch an occasional acoustic concert by a local performer.

Cutters Point 1936 Pacific Ave ☎253/272-7101. Central branch of a good local chain that serves up prime coffees in a cozy environment and has tasty baked goods and snacks. Convenient to the major sights in the area, too. Also at 6th Ave and Orchard St (☎253/761-3113).

Engine House No. 9 611 N Pine St ☎253/272-3435. This convivial tavern with fire-station decor is a better place for drinking local microbrews or hearing live music than for eating. The menu is heavy on the usual burgers and pizza.

Harmon Pub & Brewery 1938 Pacific Ave ☎253/383-2739. Located near the university, another solid choice for quaffing primo microbrews – among them Pinnacle Peak Pale Ale and Point Defiance IPA – that also has serviceable burgers, salads, and pizza.

The Lobster Shop 4013 Ruston Way ☎253/759-2165. If you feel like sampling some top-notch local seafood, this is the place to do it – a mid-to-upscale diner located in Old Town highlighted by its Hood Canal oysters, Alaskan scallops, and rock-lobster tail.

Southern Kitchen 1716 6th Ave ☏ 253/627-4282. Gumbo, catfish, hush puppies, candied yams, and fried okra are just a few of the things you can stuff your gut with at this award-winning local favorite – about as close to Dixie as you're going to find in the Pacific Northwest.

The Spar 2121 North 30th St ☏ 253/627-8215. Classic brick diner and watering hole near the waterfront in Old Town Tacoma, serving up burgers, seafood, and microbrewskis, plus blues on Sunday nights.

Olympia

Unlike most small-town state capitals, Washington State's **OLYMPIA** has more to offer than just legislative buildings and run-of-the-mill bars and diners catering to politicians and lobbyists. In fact, thanks to its quality nightlife scene and proximity to Seattle – just an hour north on the I-5 freeway – the town doesn't shut down on the weekends, either, and makes a good base for exploring the Washington Cascades and Mount Rainier.

Olympia became the capital of the Washington territory in 1853, and though it was quickly superseded commercially when railways were placed elsewhere, it became state capital in 1889 when Washington entered the Union. Today, the city has a regal **capitol building** and a surrounding **Capitol Campus**, but it also has an eccentric streak, due in part to the presence just outside town of

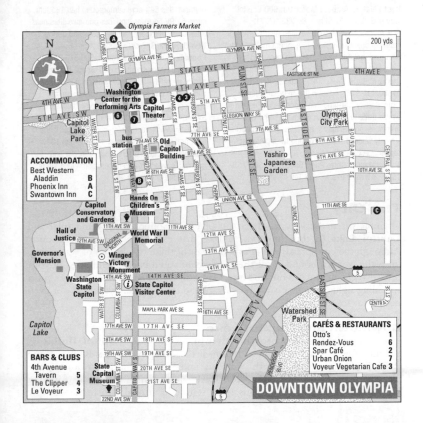

DOWNTOWN OLYMPIA

Evergreen State College, an untraditional school that allows students to design their own courses of study. Cartoonist Matt Groening (creator of *The Simpsons*) went to Evergreen, as did Sub Pop Records cofounder Bruce Pavitt and numerous indie rockers. Kurt Cobain lived in Olympia for several years before his rise to fame with Nirvana, and there are more than a few decent rock bands still making the town their home.

Arrival, information, and getting around

Olympia is on I-5 and easily accessible by **car** or bus. The Greyhound station is located in the town center at 107 7th Ave SE (☎360/357-5541, ⓦwww .greyhound.com), just north of the Capitol Campus, and runs **buses** from Seattle to Olympia several times a day (2hr). Intercity Transit (☎360/786-1881, ⓦwww.intercitytransit.com) serves the Olympia area (75¢ per bus ride, $1.50 for daily pass). The Capitol Campus's **visitor center**, Capitol Way at 14th Ave (Mon–Fri 8am–5pm; ☎360/586-3460, ⓦwww.ga.wa.gov/visitor), is stocked with maps and brochures to set you on your way.

Accommodation

For **accommodation**, Olympia has the standard assortment of chain motels, which are typically clean and comfortable, as well as some interesting B&Bs.

Best Western Aladdin Motor Inn 900 Capitol Way ☎360/352-7200 or 1-800/367-7771, ⓦwww.bestwestern.com. Located near Olympia's center, a predictably clean (if generic) motor lodge with gym, hot tub, heated outdoor pool, and breakfast buffet. ❹

Inn at Mallard Cove 5025 Meridian Road NE ☎360/491-9795, ⓦwww.theinnatmallardcove .com. Stately half-timbered Tudor Revival estate whose three lovely rooms variously come with fireplaces, private decks, and Jacuzzis. Located in a nicely wooded setting, making for a pleasant romantic escape. ❻

Millersylvania State Park Tilley Rd ☎360/753-1519, ⓦwww.parks.wa.gov. Ten miles south of

Olympia, this 840-acre campground has 135 tent sites, 52 RV hookups, and four primitive sites near a beach, with rugged facilities designed during the New Deal era. $17–22.

Phoenix Inn 415 Capitol Way ☎360/570-0555, ⓦwww.phoenixinnsuites.com. Perhaps the best choice overall for affordable luxury and convenience, with fridges and microwaves in each room and onsite pool, Jacuzzi, gym, and Internet access. ❻

Swantown Inn 1431 11th Ave SE ☎1-360/753-9123, ⓦwww.swantowninn.com. Four pleasant, if a bit precious, B&B rooms in a remodeled 1889 Victorian structure. Offers onsite gardens and gazebo, fairly affordable prices, and a location not far from the city center. ❺

The City

Olympia sits at the very southern tip of Puget Sound, along Budd Inlet and **Capitol Lake**, a thin finger of a lake that extends a mile farther south. Although the city spreads out south and east of these two bodies of water, they form the western boundary of the area where you'll likely spend most of your time – the downtown core and the **Capitol Campus**. Home to city's most appealing sights, this area is easily walkable, so much so that you may not even need a car to get around.

Downtown and Capitol Lake

The centerpiece of **downtown Olympia** is the **Old Capitol Building**, Washington at Seventh Avenue (Mon–Fri 8am–5pm; free), a Romanesque Revival jewel featuring Gothic turrets and stone arches overlooking the pleasant green square of **Sylvester Park**, named after Olympia's founder. Nowadays this early capitol houses the state educational bureaucracy. A few blocks east, the **Yashiro Japanese Garden**, Ninth Ave at Plum St (daily dawn–dusk; free; ☎ 360/753-8447), is a small refuge with a pagoda, fish pond, and waterfall that provides a brief respite on your travels, while two blocks north of the Old Capitol, the stylish, classic **Capitol Theater**, 206 E 5th Ave (☎ 360/754-3635, ⓦ www.olyfilm.org), is home to the Olympia Film Festival in early November, and regularly hosts rock bands and other acts on weekends. A block away, along **East Fourth Avenue**, are several of Olympia's best live music venues: Le Voyeur, no. 404 (☎ 360/943-5710); The Clipper, no. 402 (☎ 360-943-6300); and the 4th Avenue Tavern, no. 210 (☎ 360/786-1444). If rock isn't your thing, check out the **Washington Center for the Performing Arts**, 512 Washington St SE (☎ 360/753-8586, ⓦ www .washingtoncenter.org), which has a full schedule of classical and world music, drama, and ballet.

Three blocks west from here is **Capitol Lake**, home to the waterfront **Olympia Farmers Market**, 700 N Capitol Way (Apr–Oct Thurs–Sun 10am–3pm; Nov–Dec Sat & Sun only; ⓦ www.farmers-market.org). It has a nice selection of fruits, vegetables, herbs, pastries, and baked goods on offer, as well as items like handcrafted soaps and puzzles.

The Capitol Campus

Just south of downtown lies Olympia's impressive, thirty-acre **Capitol Campus** and its unequivocal focal point, the grand **Legislative Building** (tours daily on the hour 10am–3pm; self-guided visits daily 10am–4pm; ☎ 360/753-2580, ⓦ www.ga.wa.gov/visitor). Constructed as an imposing Romanesque Revival edifice, it was finally completed in 1928 after 34 years in the making; at 287ft, it is the tallest all-masonry domed building in the US, and the sixth-tallest in the world. The unabashedly opulent interior is highlighted by the rotunda's Tiffany chandelier, six bronze entry doors weighing five tons each, and the base of the large, circular Russian Circassian walnut table in the State Reception Room – carved from a single tree trunk in the shape of eagles' legs.

Across from the Capitol, the Neoclassical **Hall of Justice** (Mon–Fri 8am–5pm; same information as above), with its elegant colonnade clad in sandstone, echoes the architectural grandeur of its neighbor; it contains the state supreme court. The two buildings are accessible via Capitol Way, which, at 14th Avenue, hosts the Capitol Campus's **visitor center** as well as **Winged Victory**, a striking bronze memorial commemorating Washington's fallen soldiers in World War I with the winged figure herself, several soldiers, and a nurse. Memorial Day and other events typically take place around this 1938 statue, no doubt because the **World War II Memorial**, at Capitol Way and 11th Avenue, is a much more abstract bronze and granite affair, albeit one that's poignantly engraved with the names of six thousand deceased soldiers from the state.

Next to the capitol, the **governor's mansion** (Wed, by reservation only at ☎ 360/902-8880) is a red-brick Georgian Revival house that was erected as a temporary structure in 1908 and slated for demolition soon after. Surprisingly, the building has lasted nearly a century and has even been renovated and expanded several times. Its current resident is Christine Gregoire. On the northern side of the campus, the **Capitol Conservatory and Gardens**, 11th Avenue at Water Street (Mon–Fri 8am–3pm; free; ☎ 360/586-3460), is worth a look for its eclectic selection of plants from tropical to northern regions, many of which are grown here to decorate other gardens on the campus site.

Around the campus

Across from the campus at 11th Avenue and Capitol Way, the **Hands On Children's Museum** (Mon–Sat 10am–5pm, Sun noon–5pm; $8; ☎360/956-0818, ext 0, ⓦwww.hocm.org), with its art studio and science-oriented games and puzzles, offers solace for the tots who've seen too many Greek columns and statues for one day. Eight blocks south of the campus, the **State Capital Museum**, in the Renaissance Revival–style Lord Mansion at 211 W 21st Ave (Wed–Sat 11am–3pm; $2; ☎1-888/238-4373, ⓦwww.wshs .org/wscm), houses two floors of marginally interesting exhibits. The detailed but dry overview about the history of Olympia on the ground floor is typically outshone by the Native American displays and temporary exhibits on state politics and the Puget Sound region upstairs.

Eating

There is a good – albeit small – selection of worthwhile **dining** options in Olympia, with most clustered just north of downtown.

Otto's 111 N Washington St NE ☎360/352-8640. Popular and reliable bagel bakery that offers cheap and healthy breakfast and lunch dishes.

Saigon Rendez-Vous 117 5th Ave SW ☎360/352-1989. Good mix of Chinese and Vietnamese food – favorites like pad Thai, *pho*, and curry dishes – that's reasonably priced and well portioned, right in the city center.

Spar Café 114 4th Ave E ☎360/357-6444. Old-time American diner cuisine in a funky 1935-era setting, with long, curving counter, menu thick with steak and burgers, old photos of Olympia on the wall, and backroom lounge for smokers and drinkers.

Urban Onion 116 Legion Way SE ☎360/943-9242. Cafe that serves up delicious burgers for the vegetarian and carnivore alike.

Voyeur Vegetarian Cafe 404 E 4th Ave ☎360/943-5710. A reliable choice for veggie fare, with a tasty range of soups, sandwiches, and sweets, as well as cocktails and a few meat items on the menu.

Wolf Haven International

About ten miles south of Olympia, **Wolf Haven International** (April–Sept Mon & Wed–Sat 10am–3pm, Sun noon–3pm; Oct–Jan & March Sat 10am–3pm, Sun noon–3pm; $8; ☎1-800/448-9653, ⓦwww.wolfhaven.org), reached by following Capitol Way as it turns into Old Highway 99, then taking a left on Offut Lake Road, was established in 1982 to provide a safe breeding ground for the threatened North American timber wolf, as well as a sanctuary and open-air hospital for wolves shot or poisoned by livestock ranchers. Since then the refuge has grown into an 80-acre facility that's now home to more than forty wolves.

On-the-hour guided walking tours (last tour one hour before closing) take you within yards of the unexpectedly friendly animals. Don't be surprised if your tour guide happens to let loose with full-throated imitation wolf howls, encouraging a blood-curdling frenzy of mournful baying among the resident lupines. If you're moved to participate, come to a "**Howl-In**" (June–Sept Sat 6–9pm; $15; reserve tickets at ☎360/264-4695). Here, storytellers evoke various wolf-related myths and legends, especially those of the Native Americans, and when darkness falls a sort of call-and-response kicks off between the audience and the nearby wolves, baying at the rising moon.

The legend of D.B. Cooper

Before the airlines clamped down on security in the 1970s, plane hijackings, or skyjackings, were surprisingly common – there were no fewer than 150 between 1967 and 1972. Far from acting like (or actually being) box-cutter-wielding fanatics, though, these skyjackers sometimes played the part of dashing rogues and colorful rascals. Few caught the popular imagination as much as **D.B. Cooper**, who boarded a Portland-to-Seattle flight on Thanksgiving evening in 1971. As soon as the plane took off, Dan Cooper – or at least the man who had bought his ticket under that name – gave a stewardess a note saying he was carrying a bomb. The stewardess thought he was trying to chat her up, so she pocketed the note without examining it, obliging him to ask her to read it. After getting over this initial hurdle, Cooper forced the plane to land in Seattle and, in return for releasing all the other passengers, was given four parachutes and $200,000. He ordered the pilot to take off again heading south, then at cruising altitude forced the entire crew into the cockpit, opened the rear exit, and jumped – never to be seen again. He was likely killed by the freezing cold or upon landing in the dense forests east of the Washington city of Vancouver, but neither his body nor his parachutes have ever been discovered, fueling speculation that he was an expert survivalist and army veteran who survived to live a wealthy life abroad. The FBI looked for Cooper for years without success, the only discovery coming in 1980, when one bag of his loot washed up the banks of the Columbia River.

West of Seattle

Accessed by ferry, the sylvan islands **west of Seattle** are a top weekend getaway for that city's denizens, and consequently home to sizable second homes, bucolic country lanes, and a smattering of the types of businesses you find everywhere in the Emerald City – coffeehouses, boutiques, bike-rental shops, and the like. From Downtown and West Seattle, regular ferry routes take visitors on a quick trip over Puget Sound to sample the windswept scenery of these preserves. **Vashon Island** and adjacent **Maury Island**, best suited for unhurried biking and hiking, are less developed than **Bainbridge Island**, which has a few more sights worth closer inspection – notably the elegant grounds of the **Bloedel Reserve** and the quaint shops in the island's main hamlet of **Winslow**. From here, you can return by water to Seattle or take a highway bridge across to the main attractions of the **Kitsap Peninsula**, which offers its own historic appeal in places like **Suquamish** and **Port Gamble**.

Vashon and Maury islands

A half-hour from Seattle by ferry, **Vashon Island** is the most accessible bucolic getaway from the city, and the place where urbanites go to ride bikes, stroll the beach, and take in a few galleries or boutiques. There are hardly any major attractions, but if it's R&R you seek, the island makes for a fine day-trip. Spreading over 48 square miles, it's home to picturesque scenery like

If you do any traveling outside the city during your visit, particularly into Puget Sound, you'll likely be using ferries quite often; access points are listed where applicable throughout this guide. Most routes are run by Washington State Ferries (T206/464-6400 or 1-800/84-FERRY, W www.wsdot.wa.gov/ferries); tickets are available on Seattle's Downtown waterfront from Pier 52, Colman Dock, or the passenger launch site at Pier 50, as well as from Fauntleroy in West Seattle. Timetables and fares vary by season, and sailing times differ between weekdays and weekends, so it's best to pick up sailing/fare schedules before making plans. Note that fares have been increasing annually, so the fees below should be considered minimum rates, with fee hikes usually planned for late spring. Costs refer to travel on days between Wednesday and Saturday; Sunday to Tuesday travel is usually a dollar or two less.

Anacortes to San Juan Islands To Lopez (45–55min), Orcas (1hr 5min–1hr 25min), and Friday Harbor on San Juan Island (1hr 5min–2hr 5min). Round-trip fares are $10.65 for foot passengers, $12.80 peak. With car: mid-May to mid-Oct $35 to Lopez, $42 to Orcas, $50 to San Juan Island; mid-Oct to mid-May $26 to Lopez, $31 to Orcas, $37 to San Juan Island. There's a $2–4 surcharge for bicycles, and fares are free for inter-island passenger trips ($15.45 for cars, $19.35 peak season).

Downtown Seattle to Bainbridge Island Departs from Pier 52 approximately hourly 5.30am–1.35am; 35min journey length; foot passengers $6.50 round-trip, vehicle and driver $11.25 round-trip, $14 peak season.

Downtown Seattle to Bremerton (Kitsap Peninsula) 14 sailings daily 6am–12.50am; 60min; foot passengers $6.50 round-trip, vehicle and driver $11.25, $14 peak season.

Downtown Seattle to Vashon Island Three passenger-only ferries per day Mon–Fri 7am–6pm, no weekend service; 25min; $8.50 round-trip.

Fauntleroy (West Seattle) to Vashon Island Around 35 sailings daily 5.30am–2am; 15min; foot passengers $4.20 round-trip, vehicle and driver $14.40 round-trip, $18 peak season.

Mukilteo to Clinton, Whidbey Island Departs Mukilteo, about thirty miles north of Seattle; around 40 sailings daily 5am–12.30am; 20min; foot passengers $3.85 round-trip, vehicle and driver $6.65 one-way, $8.35 peak season.

Point Defiance to Tahlequah (Tacoma to Vashon Island) Around 20 sailings daily 6am–10pm; 15min; foot passengers $4.20 round-trip, vehicle and driver $14.40 round-trip, $18 peak season.

Port Townsend to Keystone, Whidbey Island Ten sailings daily, 6.30am–8.30pm; 30min; foot passengers $2.50 one-way, vehicle and driver $8.70 one-way, $10.90 peak season.

open fields, a rocky shoreline, and rural roads. The main highway runs the length of the narrow island, while a sliver of sandbar and fill connects it to adjoining **Maury Island**, less than half the size of its neighbor, with much of the same scenery, though no major towns. Maury's lone spot worth seeking out, for its striking views of downtown Seattle and Mount Rainier, is the beachside setting of the **Point Robinson Lighthouse** (Sun 12.30–4pm; free; tours by reservation only at T206/463-9602). Located on the eastern end of Maury Island off Point Robinson Road, this tiny beacon has been shining for ninety years; if you're really into the setting, you can stay for a week at the adjacent **lighthouse keeper's quarters** (May–Sept $950; Oct–April $800, or two-night off-season rental $175; T206-463-9602).

Vashon Island is well connected to the Seattle metro region, the Kitsap Peninsula, and Tacoma. You can bring over a **car** via West Seattle's Fauntleroy ferry terminal, but the best way to explore Vashon Island is either to ride the Metro bus (see p.287 for more details) along the length of the island via route #118 or over to Maury Island on #119, or to take a **bike** on the ferry that leaves from the downtown Seattle terminal (Pier 50; see opposite). The ferry connections to Tacoma and the Kitsap Peninsula take you to Point Defiance Park (see p.249) and Southworth, respectively.

Vashon Island is worth cycling for its gentle country lanes and eye-catching vistas of the city, though it's obviously not for thrill-seekers. You can rent a **bike** from Vashon Island Bicycles, in the north-central part of the island at 9925 SW 178th St (☎206/463-6225) – they go for $5 an hour or $20 a day. For an entirely different view of the two islands, you can rent a **boat** at Puget Sound Kayak, on an inlet on the island's east shore, at 8900 SW Harbor Drive ($14–25 per hour, $52–80 per day; ☎206/463-9257), and explore the beaches and coves in a single- or double-seat kayak, canoe or rowboat.

Vashon

A sleepy hamlet for most of Seattle's history, Vashon Island's main town of **VASHON** is a preserve both for Seattle yuppies and for longtime urban refugees. The little burg is mainly useful to visitors as a base for exploring the rest of the two islands. If you happen to be here during mid-July, you can check out the **Strawberry Festival**, an annual event showcasing natural foods (highlighted by the eponymous berry) and featuring spirited parades, upbeat music, and locals garbed in all manner of colorful costumes.

The one way in which bucolic Vashon would seem to defy the usual small-town stereotypes is with its engaging **gallery** scene – there are a number of good art spaces here, some of them run by current or former Seattlites, and you're apt to see more than the anodyne landscapes you might expect. Anything from performance to functional to installation art, as well as painting, sculpture, and photography, is likely to be on view at galleries in or around downtown along Vashon Highway SW. During the first two weeks of May and December, **studio tours** let you peek inside the studios of forty area artists, while the **Gallery Cruise** (first Fri of month; free) is another public event with food, music, and showings of the area's latest artwork (information for both at ⊛ www.vashonalliedarts.org).

Accommodation

Artist's Studio Loft 16529 91st Ave SW ☎206/463-2583, ⊛ www.asl-bnb.com. This B&B offers five swanky rooms and cottages with tasteful modern furnishings, fireplaces, and kitchenettes, as well as onsite gardens and a hot tub in a tranquil natural setting. ❺

AYH Ranch Hostel 12119 SW Cove Rd ☎206/463-2592, ⊛ www.vashonhostel.com. Offers hostel dorm beds in pseudo-historic log cabins, tepees, and covered wagons ($20) or private hostel rooms ($65) or tent sites ($11).

Lavender Duck 16503 Vashon Hwy SW ☎206/463-2592, ⊛ www.vashonhostel.com. Run by the hostel, this 1896 farmhouse has four serviceable, if rather basic, rooms decorated in shades of purple. ❹

Swallow's Nest Guest Cottages 6030 SW 248th St ☎206/463-2646, ⊛ www.vashonislandcottages .com. Eight bird-themed cottage units with varying amenities, from utilitarian to elegant Victorian decor; located in four separate sites throughout Vashon, including an entire house ($125 per floor). Rooms ❺

Eating and drinking

Casa Bonita 17623 100th Ave SW ☎206/463-6452. A good Mexican restaurant – a rarity in the area – with large, inexpensive portions of enchiladas, fajitas, and the like.
Hardware Store 17601 Vashon Highway SW ☎206/463-1800. A former hardware vendor now converted into a dining spot for nouveau American cuisine, with espresso bar, local art on display, and wine, furniture, and other items for sale.

Rock Island Pub & Pizza 17322 Vashon Hwy SW ☎206/463-6814. Gourmet pizzas and microbrews for moderate prices.
Sound Food 20312 Vashon Hwy SW ☎206/463-3565. Straightforward, inexpensive veggie and vegan sandwiches, salads, and pastries in an agreeable setting.

Bainbridge Island

The ferry ride to green and rural **Bainbridge Island**, gliding by the Magnolia bluffs on the outward journey across Elliott Bay and offering a panoramic view of the Seattle skyline on the return, is so delightful that it more than justifies a trip to Bainbridge Island for its own sake. Despite the island's touristy shops and galleries near the ferry dock, it's not entirely welcoming to outsiders: public transit is sparse, there are no budget accommodations (other than the state-park campsite in the north), and the narrow roads aren't great for biking. That said, there are some artsy stores and comfortable diners in the small harborside town of **Winslow**, and the **Bloedel Reserve** provides some interest for its floral blooms. The island also serves as a gateway to the north part of the Kitsap Peninsula (see opposite). Bainbridge Island's **visitor center** is located in Winslow at 590 Winslow Way E (Mon–Thurs 9am–5pm, Fri 9am–6pm, Sat 10am–3pm; ☎206/842-3700, ⓦwww.bainbridgechamber.com).

Accommodation

Bainbridge Vacation Rentals PO Box 10573, ☎206/855-9763, ⓦwww
.bainbridgevacationrentals.com. The island is loaded with one- and two-bedroom units, detached cottages, and the like for rent, and this company provides the rundown on them: anything from a simple studio to a several-story house, from one night to a month, anywhere from $110 per night to several thousand a week.
Fay Bainbridge State Park off Sunrise Dr NE ☎206/842-3931, ⓦwww.parks.wa.gov. Seventeen-acre campground on the northeast tip of Bainbridge Island, with 36 very basic sites and a beach with good views of the surrounding area. Closed mid-Oct to mid-April (but open for day use

year-round). Camp sites $17–22.
Furin-Oka 12580 Vista Dr NE, 3mi north of Winslow ☎206/842-4916, ⓦwww
.futonandbreakfast.com. Stylish Japanese guest house with traditional Japanese amenities like soaking tub, kimonos, and shoji screens, located in a bamboo grove. Japanese or American breakfasts available. ❼
Waterfall Gardens 7269 NE Bergman Rd ☎206/842-1434, ⓦwww
.waterfall-gardens.com. This inn's rambling, parklike setting offers a nice touch of nature – ponds, trails, waterfalls, and campfire rings complement four suites with kitchens, jetted tubs, refrigerators, and other amenities. ❺–❼

The Island

Bainbridge's one noteworthy town, **WINSLOW**, features restaurants, boutiques, and antique shops on its main block of **Winslow Way**. There are galleries here, too, though the work therein is not quite as interesting or adventurous as that of Vashon Island. Still, Bainbridge Arts and Crafts, 151 Winslow Way E (☎206/842-3132, ⓦwww.bainbridgeartscrafts.org), and the Island Gallery, 106

Madison Ave (℡206/780-9500, Ⓦwww.theislandgallery.net), display inventive pottery, jewelry, sculpture, and such. On the plaza behind City Hall (which is on Madison Avenue), the **farmers market** sells produce and crafts on Saturday mornings (9am–1pm) from mid-April to mid-October.

A car is necessary to reach Bainbridge Island's only official attraction, the **Bloedel Reserve**, 7571 NE Dolphin Drive, off the Agatewood Road exit of Hwy 305 (Wed–Sun 10am–4pm; $10; by reservation only at ℡206/842-7631 or Ⓦwww.bloedelreserve.org). Sited on the former grounds of a lumberman's estate, this conservatory contains nearly 150 acres of gardens, ponds, meadows, and wildlife habitats, including 84 acres of second-growth forest and rhododendrons, along with 300 varieties of trees and 15,000 cyclamen plants. It's often perfectly quiet except for the birds (there's a refuge with swans, blue herons, and other species), while the geometric Japanese garden and forest-enclosed reflecting pool add to the ethereal aura.

To sample the more woodsy essence of Bainbridge Island, try strolling through the whimsically named **Grand Forest**, a 240-acre park with second-growth forests and wetlands, about seven miles south of the Bloedel Reserve. Park on the roadside near the signs on Miller Road, just south of Koura Road.

Eating and drinking

Café Nola 101 Winslow Way ℡206/842.3822. A pleasantly decorated, popular bistro that's worthwhile for its tasty pastries, vegetarian fare, and agreeable Sunday brunch.

Harbour Public House 231 Parfitt Way SW, Winslow ℡206/842-0969, Ⓦwww.harbourpub.com. Renovated 1881 house now used for serving up the usual range of seafood, salads, burgers, and beer – most of it quite good.

Pegasus Coffee House 131 Parfitt Way SW ℡206/842-6725. Brick-and-ivy coffee joint with a fine selection of coffee and tea, light meals like quiche and soup, and a convivial atmosphere. An area fixture for 25 years.

Sawatdy Thai Cuisine 8770 Fletcher Bay Rd NE ℡206/780-2429. On the opposite side of the island from Winslow, an excellent, inexpensive Thai restaurant; try its traditional staples like spicy soup and noodle dishes.

Winslow Way Café 122 Winslow Way, Winslow ℡206/842-0517. One of the pricier local restaurants, but also the best; worth it for the gourmet pizza, pasta, and seafood.

The Kitsap Peninsula

From the northern part of Bainbridge Island, you can cross over on the Agate Pass Bridge to the **Kitsap Peninsula**. While not too far from Seattle itself, Kitsap feels a world away, with all the small-town charms of other parts of the Olympic Peninsula – of which this peninsula is an extension. You could almost mistake it for another large island, so irregular is its shoreline. However, unless you're camping at one of the remote state parks (check Ⓦwww.parks.wa.gov for the rundown), there's little reason to stay overnight here, and Kitsap's sights are best explored on a day-trip leading up to Port Townsend (see p.387). These are spread out along **Hwy 305**, which merges into Hwy 3 to form the handiest route from Seattle to the Olympic Peninsula (see p.385). A less appealing option is to take one of the limited Kitsap Transit bus routes ($1.25; ℡360/373-2877 or 1-800/501-RIDE, Ⓦwww.kitsaptransit.org) around the peninsula.

Suquamish and around

The tiny burg of **SUQUAMISH** offers little in the way of atmosphere, though it does sit among some of the more compelling historical sights on the peninsula. Just beyond the Agate Passage Bridge, a signed right turn leads a couple of miles off the highway to quiet **St Peter's Churchyard**, 7076 NE South St (daily dawn–dusk), which holds the **grave of Chief Sealth**, Seattle's namesake, who was the tribal leader of the Suquamish people when the first whites arrived. Two painted canoes stand above the headstone and the plaque proclaims him "the firm friend of the whites" – something of a dubious accolade, considering how things turned out (see below). Nearby, surrounded by modern housing, **Old Man House Park** (daily 8am–dusk) was where the Suquamish people's 500ft-by-50ft **longhouse** stood. The longest one ever constructed on Puget Sound, it was burned down by the government in 1870. Today, the park is a pleasant little spot that provides a nice respite with its picnic tables and good views of the Sound.

Back on Hwy 305, it's a couple of minutes' drive to the turnoff that twists down to the **Suquamish Museum**, 15838 Sandy Hook Rd (May–Sept daily 10am–5pm; Oct–April Fri–Sun 11am–4pm; $4; ☎360/598-3311, ext 422, ⓦwww.suquamish.nsn.us/museum). The museum traces the history of the Suquamish tribe, which occupied much of the Kitsap Peninsula until American settlers arrived. Chief Sealth chose to avoid conflict with his new neighbors, but it didn't do much good, and his people received an appallingly bad deal in the carving up of their land. Formerly based throughout Puget Sound, they have, since that 1855 treaty, been stuck on the 7500-acre **Port Madison Indian Reservation**. The museum movingly recounts the tribe's forced Americanization after whites established dominance in Puget Sound, and presents exhibits on their games, craftwork, and culture, along with a selection of vintage photographs of its members from the early twentieth century.

Poulsbo and around

As you continue north, you'll come to **POULSBO**, a bizarre sort of tourist trap that has exploited its Norwegian heritage by revamping the gabled cafes and souvenir shops along its main route, Front Street, in "little Oslo" kitsch, including Viking signs. Needless to say, locals take every opportunity to dress up in fancy Nordic duds, especially during mid-May's **Viking Fest** (☎360-779-3378, ⓦwww.vikingfest.org). Heading north, you soon rejoin the main road – Hwy 3 – and reach the **Hood Canal Floating Bridge**, which crosses over to the Olympic Peninsula (see p.385). It's mainly known for its traffic, which can be hellish if you're coming back to Seattle at the end of a weekend or holiday, when an endless procession of freighters along the canal keeps the drawbridge raised.

North from Poulsbo, you can turn right off Hwy 305 just north of town onto Hwy 307 and, after about four hundred yards, take a left down **Big Valley Road**. Drifting through a river valley of antique wooden farmhouses, rolling farmland, and forested hills, this lovely country lane passes by the delightful *Manor Farm Inn*, 26069 Big Valley Rd (☎360/779-4628, ⓦwww .manorfarminn.com; ⑥). Here, a working farm surrounds a charming picket-fenced farmhouse of 1890 that's been tastefully converted into a plush inn.

Port Gamble

Draped above a tiny bay just a mile or so beyond the Hood Canal Floating Bridge is the Kitsap's prettiest settlement, **PORT GAMBLE**, a pocket-size hamlet whose entrepreneurial founders, Andrew Pope and William Talbot, made a killing in Puget Sound timber. Pope and Talbot carefully maintained the port's late-nineteenth-century appearance, and all might have been well if they hadn't closed the mill down in 1995. As a result, Port Gamble is presently a very pretty town but one without much of a purpose – though it does make for a pleasant wander amid its agreeable coffeehouses, antique stores, and homespun boutiques.

In this tranquil, leafy setting, the **Port Gamble Historical Museum**, directly facing the bay (May–Oct daily 10.30am–5pm; $2.50; T 360/297-8074, W www.ptgamble.com), traces the development of the town and its lumber trade, and is well worth a quick look. Also mildly interesting is the adjoining **General Store**, whose cast-iron pillars and wooden floors accommodate the **Of Sea and Shore** museum on the upper floor (daily 9am–5pm; free), a voluminous collection of seashells. Not far away sits the charming, Carpenter Gothic–style **St Paul's Episcopal Church** and the town's finest home, the **Walker–Ames House**, a stately, multicolored gem built in 1889, poised on a hill overlooking the Sound and, unfortunately, off-limits to interlopers.

For more information on the town, call or drop by the Kitsap Peninsula Visitor and Convention Bureau, in Port Gamble at 2 Rainier Ave (T 360/297-8200, W www.visitkitsap.com).

Keyport and Bremerton

Once you reach Highway 3 from Poulsbo, there are two main reasons for heading south toward Olympia – either to complete a grand loop of the Puget Sound region or to hop the ferry back to Seattle from Bremerton, a magnificent ride (see "Basics," p.358) that lasts an hour and takes you past the verdant, craggy bays and inlets around the Kitsap Peninsula and Bainbridge Island. On the highway down to Bremerton, military enthusiasts will be keen to visit **KEYPORT**, site of the **Naval Undersea Museum**, just east of Hwy 3 on Hwy 308 (June–Sept daily 10am–4pm; Oct–May closed Tues; free; T 360/396-4148, W www.keyportmuseum.cnrnw.navy.mil). Operated by the US Navy, it displays an imposing array of nautical weaponry, from torpedoes to depth charges to aquatic mines and various other bombs and destructive

---

Nuclear weapons in Washington State

While the town of **Bangor** hardly ranks on the list of major Washington tourist attractions, it is the only site harboring active **nuclear weapons** in the Pacific Northwest. Being one of two US naval bases hosting the country's formidable fleet of ballistic missile submarines, unlikely little Bangor is therefore a prime target in the event of a nuclear war. Armed with approximately half of all the warheads in the American arsenal, these "submarine-launched ballistic missiles" form one leg of America's triad of nuclear weapons systems, the others being long-range bombers and ICBMs, and are poised at the ready on the eighteen Trident subs that patrol the world's oceans. Eleven of these submarines are based out of Bangor, and according to some estimates each carries two dozen missiles fitted with eight warheads apiece. That means there are some 2000 hydrogen-based bombs in Bangor, with a destructive power of 800 megatons – enough to destroy life on Earth several times over.

Needless to say, you can forget about taking a tour of one of these high-powered ships. While the US Navy is happy to have you look over the array of outmoded Civil War mines and disused warships in Bremerton, it has no patience with interlopers when nuclear weapons are involved, and trespassing at the base will surely get you a harsh interrogation and even jail time. Stick to the more anodyne military attractions on the peninsula or buy a Tom Clancy novel.

gadgets – though it avoids mentioning too many details about the local presence of nuclear submarines in nearby Bangor (see box, p.361).

Ten miles south along Hwy 3, **BREMERTON** is a rough-edged shipyard town that, apart from its ferry terminal, is home to the **Bremerton Naval Memorial Museum**, 402 Pacific Ave (Mon–Sat 10am–4pm, Sun 1–4pm; donation; ☎360/479-SHIP), which presents a somewhat diverting assortment of historic weaponry and model ships, topped by a medieval Korean wooden cannon wrapped in bamboo. If you're still in need of a military fix, you can tour the warship **USS Turner Joy**, 300 Washington Beach Ave (May–Sept daily 10am–5pm, Oct–April Fri–Sun 10am–4pm; $8; ☎360/792-2457, ⓦwww.ussturnerjoy.org). This 1959 destroyer is most notable for being involved in the 1965 Gulf of Tonkin incident, which became President Lyndon Johnson's main excuse for Congress to escalate the war in Vietnam dramatically.

Whidbey Island

The longest island in the continental US, **WHIDBEY ISLAND** is the first spot in Puget Sound to feel like a world unto itself. Nearly fifty miles in length, it has a network of narrow country roads that wind through farmland and small villages and are ideal for cycling. Its small towns of **Langley** and **Coupeville** are both pleasant getaways, while **Fort Casey**, **Fort Ebey**, and **Deception Pass state parks** are more enticing with their remote wooded trails and stark cliffside vistas – certainly preferable to Oak Harbor, Whidbey's largest (and dullest) town, with a slew of drab motels. Once considered a key stronghold in the defense of the Sound, the island also carries martial relics from various eras: nineteenth-century blockhouses built against Native American attack, concrete bunkers from a century ago, and a large naval base housing modern air and naval defense systems. Plan to stay at least a full day – if not more – to appreciate the island's diverse qualities.

Arrival and information

Coming from Seattle, the quickest route onto Whidbey Island is via the Mukilteo **ferry** (see box, p.356, for schedule and fares), whose landing is about thirty miles north of Seattle, adjacent to Everett. The 20min ride terminates at **Clinton**, a tiny town near Whidbey's southern edge. From here, Hwy 525 snakes through the middle of the island to Deception Pass at the top, turning into Hwy 20 halfway into the journey. A second ferry leaves Port Townsend on the Olympic Peninsula for the half-hour trip to Whidbey's Keystone, halfway up the island near Fort Casey State Park. Bringing a car is advisable, although Island Transit has a **free bus service** running the length of the island on eleven different routes – you'll need to take routes #1 and 4 to go the full distance (Mon–Sat; ☎360/678-7771, 360/321-6688 or 1-800/240-8747, ⓦwww.islandtransit.org). You can rent a bike at Half Link Bikes, in Langley at 5603 Bayview Rd (☎360/331-7980), for $20–30 a day.

The Central Whidbey Chamber of Commerce runs a **visitor center** in Coupeville, 107 S Main St (Mon–Fri 10am–5pm; ☎360/678-5434, ⓦwww.centralwhidbeychamber.com), with all the requisite brochures, though a free visitor's guide, with a detailed map of the island, can also be picked up on the ferry.

Accommodation

As far as **accommodation** goes, Whidbey isn't much for fancy hotels, and its Oak Harbor motels are unexceptional. However, many of the island's old villas, especially in Coupeville, have been turned into lavish (and sometimes quite expensive) **B&Bs**.

Anchorage Inn 807 N Main St, Coupeville ☎360/678-5581, ⓦwww.anchorage-inn.com. One of the better deals around – seven affordable B&B rooms, decorated in a mild Victorian style, in a pleasant setting with a view of the Sound. Adjacent cottage ($170 per night) is an 1883 charmer with two bedrooms. Special discounts for art students and ministers. Rooms ⑤

Captain Whidbey Inn 2072 W Captain Whidbey Inn Rd, Coupeville ☎360/678-4097 or 1-800/366-4097, ⓦwww.captainwhidbey .com. Out of the way but worth it, with quiet rooms overlooking Penn Cove, cottages and chalets in the forest, and a restaurant renowned for its seafood. Four- to six-day package trips include cruises on the inn's *Cutty Sark* ship ($1950 and up). Rooms ⑤, cabins ⑦, cottages ⑨

Country Cottage of Langley 215 6th St, Langley ☎360/221-8709 or 1-800/718-3860, ⓦwww .acountrycottage.com. Five rooms in a restored 1920s farmhouse, on a bluff above Langley and Puget Sound. All rooms have CD players and fridges, while higher-end suites have Jacuzzi tubs and fireplaces. ⑥

Deception Pass State Park 5175 N Hwy-20 ☎360/657-2417, ⓦwww.parks.wa.gov. One of the most popular state parks in the region, spread over 4000 acres with around 250 tent sites, as well as primitive grounds. It fills up quickly in the summer months, so call ahead. $17–22.

Ebey's Landing National Historic Reserve north of Keystone ☎360/678-4636, ⓦwww.parks.wa .gov. An interesting place to camp, the reserve comprises Fort Casey and Fort Ebey state parks, both built around old defense installations, with good hiking trails and a mix of trailer, tent, and primitive campsites. Reservations taken at Fort Ebey; closed Nov–Feb. $17–22.

The Inn at Langley 400 First St, Langley ☎360/221-3033, ⓦwww.innatlangley.com. One of the poshest stopovers on Puget Sound, built into a bluff overlooking the water; starting around $265, all 26 rooms have jetted tubs and porches with waterfront views, with suites and private cottages costing about two and three times as much. ⑨

Langley and Coupeville

The Mukilteo ferry lands at sleepy, unexceptional **Clinton**, but a more interesting first stop is **LANGLEY**, a well-heeled seaside village just a few miles away off Hwy 525, with a stretch of wooden storefronts set on a picturesque bluff overlooking the water. Quaint and appealing, **First Street** is lined with antique stores and galleries such as the **Artists Cooperative of Whidbey Island**, no. 314 (☎360/221-7675), and the various artisans at the **Hellebore Glass Studio**, no. 308 (☎360/221-2067, ⓦwww.helleboreglass.com), where you can pick up handmade art and crafts.

In the island's center, **COUPEVILLE** is Washington's second-oldest city and home to Whidbey's most historic district, with several dozen buildings dating back to the late nineteenth and early twentieth centuries, and neighborhoods dotted with vintage Victorian homes. Once a flourishing seaport, it was settled back in the 1850s by sea captains and merchants attracted by the protected harbor in **Penn Cove**, and by the plentiful oak and pine trees. The several blocks of waterfront on **Front Street**, between Main Street and the pier, feature most of Coupeville's top shops and eateries, while the area around **Main Street** offers a selection of attractive homes and other classic structures along a half-mile south from the shoreline. The 1886 **Loers House**, Eighth St at Grace St, is especially worth a look for its mix of traditional Victorian architecture with an onion-domed turret.

The **Island County Historical Museum**, 908 NW Alexander St (summer Wed–Mon 10am–5pm; rest of year Sat & Sun 10am–4pm; $3; ☏360/678-3310, ⓦwww.islandhistory.org), can give you the lowdown on the local heritage, though one of the most historic buildings, **Alexander's Blockhouse**, just outside the museum, can be toured on its own for free. This creaky wooden structure was built by settlers in 1855 to defend themselves from attack by Skagit Indians – which never occurred.

Fort Casey and Fort Ebey state parks

Coupeville is actually part of **Ebey's Landing National Historical Reserve** (☏360/678-3310, ⓦwww.nps.gov/ebla), an officially protected series of farms, forests, and privately owned land named after one of the island's first white settlers, **Colonel Isaac Ebey**. In 1851 the colonel penned a letter to his brother describing his new home as "almost a paradise of nature . . . I think I could live and die here content." Ebey did get part of his wish: in 1857 he was slain by Alaskan Tlingit in revenge for the killing of one of the tribe's chieftains.

On the western side of the island are the reserve's two state parks, each of which has several miles of shoreline on the Strait of Juan de Fuca. The smaller of the two, **Fort Casey State Park** (daily 8am–dusk), was built at the beginning of the twentieth century to guard the entrance to Puget Sound, though it was soon obsolete. Check out the grim cluster of dark **gun batteries**, whose artillery emplacements can be freely explored, along with the eerie, bomb-shelter-like **bunkers** underneath. Much cheerier is the squat but charming **Admiralty Head Lighthouse** nearby (April & Oct Sat–Sun 11am–5pm; May & Sept Fri–Mon 11am–5pm; June–Aug daily 11am–5pm; late Nov & Dec most weekends noon–4pm; closed Jan and Feb; donation; ⓦwww.admiraltyhead.wsu.edu), one of several lighthouses on Whidbey Island. A half-mile southeast of the fort, the **Keystone ferry landing** allows you to make the short trip to Port Townsend (see p.387), just across Admiralty Inlet to the southwest.

Seven miles north along the beach from Fort Casey, the aesthetically pleasing **Fort Ebey State Park** (summer 6.30am–dusk; rest of the year 8am–dusk; ☏360/678-4636) offers an attractive shoreline and plenty of opportunities for hiking, biking, and fishing. An abandoned gun and bunker emplacement also remains here, built in 1942 to defend against possible attack from the Pacific; the eerie atmosphere is enhanced by the remote location and heavy forest cover. If time or energy don't permit the beachside trek to the park, a small parking area between the forts at Ebey's Landing (at the southern end of Ebey Road) puts you right next to a gorgeous trail. Rising and dipping for a mile or two along a ridge that overlooks the bluff and Admiralty Inlet, it yields some of the most striking views to be found anywhere on Puget Sound.

Deception Pass State Park

Beyond Ebey's Reserve, contemporary military matters dominate the economy of **Oak Harbor**, Whidbey's largest – and most unappealing – town. You'd do much better to continue north to **Deception Pass State Park**, 5175 N Hwy 20 (daily 8am–dusk; ☎360/675-2417), where a steel bridge arches gracefully over the narrow Deception Pass gorge between Whidbey and Fidalgo islands, a connecting point (via Anacortes) for the San Juan Islands. With excellent hiking trails and campsites, the park occupies land on both islands, sprawling over four thousand acres of rugged land and sea that's great for hiking, fishing, bird-watching, scuba diving, and so on. The turbulent waters of the pass were originally thought to have been a small bay when charted by the Spanish. Even the intrepid George Vancouver was wary of them, initially deceived (hence the name) into believing he had charted part of the Whidbey "peninsula," rather than the strait that makes it an island.

Grab a map from the Whidbey-side park office and head to the **Lighthouse Point Trail** that begins near the **interpretive center** (summer 8am–5pm; free), meanders along beach and forest for nearly a mile, and eventually leads to rocky bluffs with good views of the pass. The center has a small but interesting exhibit and video on the creation and history of the Civilian Conservation Corps (CCC), one of the programs initiated by President Franklin D. Roosevelt in the 1930s to create employment, at the same time helping to conserve the nation's natural resources. Most of the 2.5 million men who enrolled were young, hungry, and in need of the steady meals (and $30-per-month pay) the organization provided. In Washington State, the CCC built most of the structures in about a dozen state parks, including the trails and facilities in Deception Pass State Park.

△ Deception Pass

Eating and drinking

As you might expect, most of the good **eating** and **drinking** options on Whidbey Island are located in either Coupeville or Langley.

The Braeburn 197D 2nd Street, Langley ☎360/221-3211. A favorite local place for breakfast, as well as old-fashioned lunches with meatloaf and coleslaw, and pot roast and apple dumplings for dinner.
Christopher's 23 Front St, Coupeville ☎360/678-5480. Fine lunches, dinners, and microbrews; the place strikes a good balance between basic diner food and ritzier cuisine with its panini, seafood, pastas, and steaks.
Knead & Feed 4 Front St, Coupeville ☎360/678-5431. Offering inexpensive home-made breads, pies, and cinnamon rolls at its bakery, plus an onsite espresso bar for tasty gourmet coffee.

Neil's Clover Patch Cafe 2850 SR 525, Langley ☎360/321-4120. Buffet spot with gut-busting weekly specials of fish 'n' chips and pork ribs, with hefty staples like eggs and steak the rest of the time.
Toby's Tavern 8 Front St, Coupeville ☎360/678-4222. Surprisingly tasty seafood, burgers, and microbrews at this divey-looking wharfside joint, plus solid, gut-stuffing pastrami sandwiches and French dips.
Village Pizzeria 108 First St, Langley ☎360/221-3363. Well-regarded pizza joint that serves up piping hot slices of pepperoni-and-cheese, as well as more exotic offerings with clams and pesto. No credit cards.

The San Juan Islands

Northwest of Whidbey Island, midway between the Washington coast and Canada, the **San Juan Islands** scatter across the eastern reaches of the Strait of Juan de Fuca and, for many people, entirely upstage the rest of Puget Sound. Tailor-made for strolling, cycling, and nature-watching, the idyllic San Juans act as breeding grounds of rare birds and sea creatures: white-headed bald eagles circle over treetops, and Orca ("killer") whale pods pass close to shore. A convoluted maze of green islands, with myriad bluffs and bays, the archipelago has 743 islands, but only about 170 of them are actually visible during high tide and only sixty of those are populated. The best of them are exceptionally scenic getaways, but unless you've got your own boat or quite a bit of money, your visits will be restricted to the four major islands served by Washington State Ferries – **San Juan**, the largest, offers historic state parks and a thriving port, Friday Harbor; **Orcas** is the most scenic, especially in the mountainous interior of Moran State Park; **Lopez** is the most sedate and quiet, its flat and largely empty roads a haven for cyclists; and **Shaw** has barely anything – or anyone – to see.

The islands were first spotted by Europeans in 1592 when explorer **Juan de Fuca**, now believed to be a Greek sailing for the Spanish, claimed to have found an inlet at 47 degrees north latitude while searching for the mythical Northwest Passage connecting the Pacific and Atlantic oceans. This discovery went unacknowledged until 1787, when Englishman **Charles Barkley** found a strait at the approximate location and named it in honor of de Fuca. It was the Spanish, though, who first fully explored the strait in 1790 under **Manuel Quimper**, accounting for the Spanish names that grace several of the islands today.

Around the time the Europeans got their toehold on the islands the native Salish population was, as elsewhere, decimated by a smallpox epidemic brought by the foreign adventurers. Subsequently, the white population of English and

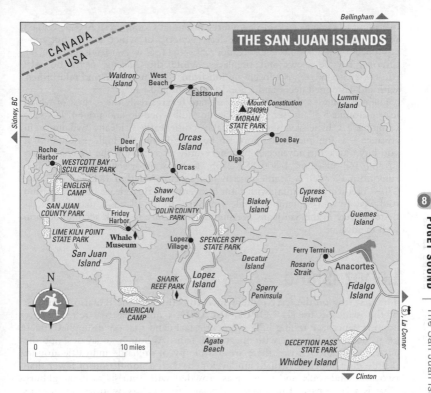

Bellingham ▲

CANADA
USA

Sidney, BC

Waldron Island
West Beach
Eastsound
Mount Constitution (2409ft)
MORAN STATE PARK
Lummi Island

Roche Harbor
Deer Harbor
Orcas Island
Doe Bay

WESTCOTT BAY SCULPTURE PARK
Olga
Orcas

ENGLISH CAMP
Shaw Island
Cypress Island

SAN JUAN COUNTY PARK
Friday Harbor
ODLIN COUNTY PARK
Blakely Island
Guemes Island

LIME KILN POINT STATE PARK
Whale Museum
Lopez Village
SPENCER SPIT STATE PARK
Ferry Terminal

San Juan Island
Decatur Island
Rosario Strait
Anacortes

N

SHARK REEF PARK
Lopez Island
Sperry Peninsula
Fidalgo Island

La Conner

AMERICAN CAMP

Agate Beach
DECEPTION PASS STATE PARK

0 ————— 10 miles

Whidbey Island

▼ Clinton

American residents grew, especially the latter after the mid-nineteenth century, and nowadays the islands' farming and fishing communities are jostled by escapees from the cities. Indeed, in summer there are more visitors than the islands can accommodate, and you'll definitely need to book somewhere to stay in advance: during high-season weekends dozens of disappointed travelers end up spending the night at the ferry terminal, something all the tourist authorities work hard to avoid. However, even in July and August, peaceful corners away from the crowds are easy to find.

Getting to the islands

Washington State Ferries runs boats bound for the San Juans from the small port of **ANACORTES**, just west of La Conner on Hwy 20. The town is reachable via **Airporter Shuttle** (6am–11.30pm; 3hr trip; $33 one-way, $61 round-trip; ☎1-866/235-5247, ⓦwww.airporter.com), which runs twelve buses daily from Sea-Tac Airport and two from downtown Seattle, with a westbound connection in Mount Vernon. Anacortes has several decent places to **eat** before getting on the boat: try *Geppetto's*, 3320 Commercial Ave (☎360/293-5033), with good Italian takeout food and baked goods, or *La Vie En Rose*, 418 Commercial Ave (☎360/299-9546, ⓦwww.laviebakery.com), serving tasty deli sandwiches, desserts, and breads. It's also worth a stop to visit the *Rockfish Grill*, 320 Commercial Ave (☎360/588-1720), which has serviceable wood-fired pizzas, steak, and pasta but is best for its handcrafted microbrews, from pilsners and porters to barleywines. If you need to **stay** overnight to catch a crack-of-dawn ferry, note that Commercial Avenue is lined with numerous budget hotels, the least generic of which is the hot tub–equipped *Islands Inn*, no. 3401 (☎360/293-4644, ⓦwww.islandsinn.com; ❸), offering bayside views and fireplaces, while the *Majestic Hotel*, no. 419 (☎360/293-3355; ❺), is a lovely option from 1889, reopened and refurbished, with old-fashioned decor and a good restaurant and bar.

There are about a dozen Washington State **ferries** daily, the earliest of which leaves around 5.30am (see box, p.356, for full schedule and prices). If you're bringing a vehicle, you should probably come early – ideally two hours in advance – as the lines at the port can be long during the high season, even if you buy a ticket in advance. A passenger-only alternative is the *Victoria Clipper* (☎360/448-5000 or 1-800/888-2535, ⓦwww.victoriaclipper.com), which runs from Pier 69 in Seattle to San Juan's Friday Harbor ($42–47 one-way, $70–75 return; 3hr 30min), with a 4hr layover there. Boats leave once daily from mid-May to mid-September. While a day-trip to the islands is manageable, it's better to stay in the San Juans overnight; just be sure to book accommodation well in advance.

Lopez Island

The first stop on the ferry route, which runs through the Rosario Strait east of the islands, is usually **LOPEZ ISLAND**, a quiet, pastoral retreat where country lanes lace rolling hills and gentle farmland that once supplied much of western Washington with meat and fruit. Although today it's not the agricultural power it was, there are still plenty of orchards and cattle around, if little else: Lopez is virtually undeveloped, with a population of fewer than two thousand souls, and is never as crowded with tourists as its neighbors. That is a large part of its appeal, especially for cyclists, who can explore its bucolic roads without much intrusion from cars. In as much as the island has a base, it's the little stop of **Lopez Village**, down Fisherman Bay Road about five miles from the ferry terminal.

Arrival and information

The best way to explore small, mostly flat Lopez is by **bicycle**. Rentals are available from Lopez Bicycle Works, 2847 Fisherman Bay Rd (May–Sept; ☎360/468-2847, ⓦwww.lopezbicycleworks.com), which charges $5/hour or $25/day. At the same location, Lopez Kayaks (May–Oct only; ☎360/468-2847, ⓦwww.lopezkayaks.com) arranges **sea trips** ($35/2hr tour, $75/3hr 30min tour) and rents **kayaks** ($15–35/hr or $40–80/day).

Accommodation

For such an untrammeled island, Lopez offers a surprisingly nice range of **places to stay**.

Hotels and B&Bs

Blue Fjord Cabins 862 Elliott Rd ☎1-888/633-0401, ⓦwww.interisland.net/bluefjord. A quiet retreat in the woods, offering two cozy, secluded cabins at reasonable rates. Closed Nov–Mar. ❺

Inn at Swifts Bay 856 Port Stanley Rd ☎360/468-3636, ⓦwww.swiftsbay.com. The most luxurious B&B on Lopez, nestled at the bottom of a little-traveled road near the ferry; turn left one mile south of the dock and you'll find it on the right, just

past the fire station. Only a few minutes' walk from the beach, the inn has five units (three of them suites) with hot tubs and fireplaces, and an onsite sauna. ⑤–⑧
Lopez Islander 2847 Fisherman Bay Rd ☎360/468-2233 or 1-800/736-3434,

Ⓦwww.lopezislander.com. The only luxury hotel on Lopez, sited on Fisherman Bay, has spacious rooms (most with sunset views), Internet access, swimming pool, and hot tub; Lopez Bicycle Works and Lopez Kayaks are also located here. ⑥

Campgrounds

Lopez Farm Cottages & Camping Fisherman Bay Rd south of Military Rd ☎1-800/440-3556, Ⓦwww.lopezfarmcottages.com. For about twice the price of the more basic campgrounds on Lopez (see below), these campsites have a few more modern amenities, for $33 (open April–Sept). Comfortable cottages – each with fireplace, porch, deck, and Jacuzzi access – are available year-round, varying from $100 to $160 according to season.
Odlin County Park North side of Lopez, south of Upright Head ☎360/378-1842,

Ⓦwww.co.san-juan.wa.us/parks. By the beach, just a mile from the ferry; charges $17 for campsites ($20 for premium sites on the beach), or $13 for those without a vehicle; rates about $5–7 less Nov–March.
Spencer Spit State Park Baker View Rd ☎360/468-2251, Ⓦwww.parks.wa.gov. Thirty-four tent sites (along with three primitive ones) at an isolated park with good hiking, crabbing, and clamming nearby. This is the best place to camp on Lopez, so reserve ahead in peak season. Campsites $17–24.

The Island

In Lopez Village, there are few traditional sights except for the **Lopez Island Historical Museum**, 28 Washburn Place (May–Sept Wed–Sun noon–4pm; donation; Ⓦwww.rockisland.com/~lopezmuseum), which has an interesting selection of bric-a-brac from the past – old gillnets, hand-carved canoes, stuffed birds – and will give you an introduction to the native tribes and early pioneers who populated the Lopez, as well as an overview of the island's limited attractions. You can pick up a useful map of a **driving tour** of the area's historic sites and homes here.

The top destination on Lopez Island is **Shark Reef Park** (☎360/378-8420), at the island's southwest tip on Shark Reef Road, accessible via Fisherman Bay and Airport roads. A ten- to fifteen-minute walk through dense forest is rewarded by beautiful rocky vistas at the water's edge, from where you can spot the occasional sea lion (and rare shark) past the tide pools. Also on the island's southern end is **Agate Beach**, whose shoreline is strewn with fat little pebbles that make a memorable sound at high tide. Back on the northeast side of the island, **Spencer Spit State Park** offers good camping (see "Accommodation," above), hiking, clamming, and picnicking, as well as sunbathing on a slender strand of sand that juts out from the shore.

Eating and drinking

By default, the island's best **eating** and **drinking** options can be found in Lopez Village.

Bay Cafe 9 Old Post Rd, Lopez Village ☎360/468-3700. The only spot in Lopez for elegant dining, and the eclectic seafood entrees – seafood curry and risotto cakes, in the $17–20 range – are worth it. Reserve in advance; live jazz on Sun nights.

Holly B's Bakery 165 Cherry Tree Lane, Lopez Village ☎360/468-2133. Small but worthwhile stop for tasty cinnamon buns, breads, pastries, pizza, and light snacks. Open April–Nov.
Isabel's Espresso 308 Lopez Rd, Village House Building, Lopez Village ☎360/468-4114. One of

the better spots to have your coffee in town, with juice drinks, tea, sweets, and some lunch items, too. A good place to fuel up on espresso or cool down with herbal tea.

Love Dog Cafe 1 Village Center, Lopez Village ☎360/468-2150. Deli sandwiches, seafood, and pasta are the main draw at this unassuming spot with a relaxed patio.

Orcas Island

The most alluring destination in the San Juans, horseshoe-shaped **ORCAS ISLAND** teems with rugged hills and leafy timber that tower over its leisurely roads, craggy beaches, and abundant wildlife – enviable qualities that have not escaped the notice of the larger world. While there are only 4400 full-time island residents, there are three times as many property owners. Yet, despite being much busier than Lopez, Orcas still offers the possibility of finding tranquillity and seclusion – the island's holiday resorts are so well tucked into distant coves that the island's peace and quiet is hardly disturbed.

Arrival and information

Ferries dock in tiny **Orcas**, and ten miles down the main road of Horseshoe Highway is the slightly larger town of **Eastsound**. Maps and island **information** are available from a small visitor center near the ferry dock or through the **Chamber of Commerce**, PO Box 252, Eastsound 98245 (☎360/376-2273, ⓦwww.orcasislandchamber.com). In the summer you can get around the island on the **Orcas Island Shuttle** (June–Aug; $5 per ride; ☎360/376-RIDE, ⓦwww.orcasislandshuttle.com), which connects the ferry dock with Eastsound, Rosario, and Moran State Park, and whose parent company also offers rental cars ($60–100 per day). You can rent **bikes** (for $30 per day) in Orcas from Dolphin Bay Bicycles, just up from the dock (☎360/376-4157, ⓦwww .rockisland.com/~dolphin), or in Eastsound from Wildlife Cycles, 350 N Beach Rd at A Street (☎360/376-4708, ⓦwww.wildlifecycles.com), and cycle north through the island's fetching farm country – the onetime heart of the state's apple orchards, until Eastern Washington was irrigated and commercialized.

Accommodation

Accommodation choices on Orcas Island are plentiful, but, as with the other major San Juan Islands, advance **reservations** are advised, especially during summer months.

Hotels and B&Bs

Beach Haven Resort 684 Beach Haven Rd ☎360/376-2288, ⓦwww.beach-haven .com. An appealing refuge three miles west of Eastsound, with beachfront log cabins, cottages, and a lodge amid wooded grounds. While remote, it's not undiscovered: reservations for summer stays (one-week minimum) are needed a year in advance. ⑥

Orcas Hotel at the ferry landing in Orcas ☎360/376-4300, ⓦwww.orcashotel.com. A restored Victorian inn whose plushest rooms have Jacuzzis, balconies, and harbor views; the rooms on the sides and in the back don't, though they're considerably less expensive. ⑤–⑧

Outlook Inn 171 Main St, Eastsound ☎360/376-2200, ⓦwww.outlook-inn.com. Pleasant late-Victorian complex spread over three buildings and offering waterside rooms (④–⑦ by season) and suites with hot tubs, fireplaces, and balconies (⑦–⑨), plus onsite restaurant and lounge. The shared-bath rooms are cheapest (④–⑤).

Rosario Resort & Spa 1 Rosario Way ☎1-800/562-8820, ⓦwww.rosario-resort.com.

Former Seattle mayor and wealthy shipbuilder Robert Moran built this elegant waterside mansion that now serves as a luxury resort. Prices dip dramatically in the low season. ⑤–⑧ by season.

Campgrounds

Doe Bay Village & Resort Doe Bay Rd ☎360/376-2291, ⓦwww.doebay.com. Reachable by turning right at the sign for Doe Bay Natural Foods Cafe & General Store, the resort has eight hostel dorm beds for $20–30/night by season (private rooms $50–75), plus yurts ($60–85) and various cabins ($65–95 for primitive facilities, $100–210 for deluxe). Hot tub and sauna use included (except for hostelers); $30–35 campsites cover a single tent for two persons.

Moran State Park off Horseshoe Hwy southeast of Eastsound ☎1-800/452-5687, ⓦwww.orcasisle .com/~elc or ⓦwww.parks.wa.gov. Nicely rugged park with plenty of wooded terrain, lakes, and thirty miles of hiking trails, topped by the imposing sight of Mount Constitution. Campsites $17–22.

The Island

While **Orcas** will most likely be your first stop on the island, it's really just a street with a few simple shops. **Eastsound**, ten miles in on the main road, is slightly larger with more amenities, including a handful of decent restaurants. Here you can also find the **Orcas Island Historical Society & Museum**, 181 N Beach Rd (Tues–Sun 10am–3pm, Fri 1–6pm; $3; ⓦwww.orcasisland.org/~history), which illuminates the island's Native American and pioneer history. The museum is most noteworthy, though, for its layout – it's spread over six interconnected log cabins from the 1880s and 1890s, originally constructed by homesteaders carving out a space on the isolated terrain.

Past Eastsound, it's a few miles to the gates of **Moran State Park** (camping reservations at ☎1-800/452-5687, ⓦwww.orcasisle.com/~elc), with five thousand acres of forest and lakes and thirty miles of trails. The toughest is the 4.3-mile trek on the **Cold Springs Trail** that uses switchbacks to ascend to **Mount Constitution**, at 2409ft the highest point on the San Juans (also accessible by car via a five-mile paved road). The steep path twists around creeks, fields, and thick foliage, and there's a fair chance of spotting some of the nearly two hundred species of birds on Orcas. At the summit, the stone **Mount Constitution Tower** has an intriguingly rugged design, resembling a medieval fortress from the Crusades. The panoramic views here are as good as you'd expect, looking out as far as Vancouver Island, and back toward snowcapped Mount Baker and Mount Rainier.

If you've had your fill of hiking, the best place to unwind on Orcas is at **Doe Bay Village & Resort** (see "Accommodation," above). Perched at one of the calmest spots in the San Juans, it's a lovely place, built on a secluded bay, with echoes of its previous incarnation as a New Age–flavored "human potential center" still hanging around its cabins, cottages, and hostel dorms. Its open-air, spring-fed hot tubs are available for day use by non-guests for $10. A more adventurous dip into the water can be had from Shearwater Adventures, on kayak trips that leave from Doe Bay, Deer Harbor Marina, and *Rosario Resort* ($55/3hr trip, $85/full day; ☎360/376-4699, ⓦwww .shearwaterkayaks.com), yielding closer views of the island's population of bald eagles, seals, and whales.

Eating and drinking

While serviceable food is available in most places throughout the island, the better spots for **eating** and **drinking** are in Eastsound.

Bilbo's Festivo North Beach Rd and A St, Eastsound ⓣ360/376-4728. Inexpensive Mexican food dished out in an affable setting; reservations are advised, as this is a popular spot.

Café Olga Eastsound Square, Eastsound ⓣ360/376-5862. Succulent soups and sandwiches, along with seafood and pasta, served in an arty environment. Especially good are the home-made cinnamon rolls and blackberry pies.

Christina's 310 Main St, Eastsound ⓣ360/376-4904, ⓦwww.christinas.net. Well-regarded local favorite that offers some of the chicest dining in the San Juans, serving up Northwest Cuisine and seafood for around $30 an entree.

The Kitchen 249 Prune Alley, Eastsound ⓣ360/376-6958. Appetizing pan-Asian fare, such as seared salmon, chicken teriyaki, and spring-roll wraps; most everything's cheap and tasty.

Portofino Pizzeria 274 A St, Eastsound ⓣ360/376-2085. Handcrafted pizza and calzone, made mostly with thin crusts and using fresh local ingredients, including sun-dried tomatoes, mushrooms, and the like.

Rose's Cafe 382 Prune Alley, Eastsound ⓣ360/376-4292. Top-notch morning fare like pastries, home-made bread, coffee, and egg dishes, as well as lunchtime sandwiches and soups.

San Juan Island

Ever-popular **SAN JUAN ISLAND** holds the San Juans' only incorporated town, **Friday Harbor**, whose wharfside blocks seem more commercially active than the rest of the islands put together. That said, the rest of San Juan Island is rural and sparsely populated, with plenty of good scenery, hiking, and even a few cultural sights – most notably, a **whale museum** and two national historic parks, **American Camp** and **English Camp**, that were military bases during a land dispute in the mid-1800s and are located on the south and northeast sides of the island, respectively.

Arrival and information

Ferries arrive at **Friday Harbor**, where San Juan Transit provides **information** in the Cannery Building, next to the terminal at 91 Front St (Mon–Fri 9am–4.30pm; ⓣ360/378-8887, ⓦwww.sanjuantransit.com). You can also pick up information and **maps** of the island's irregular main roads at the **chamber of commerce** at 135 Spring St (Mon–Fri 10am–4.30pm, Sat & Sun 10am–4pm; ⓣ360/378-5240, ⓦwww.sanjuanisland.org).

The best way to check out the scattered points of interest on San Juan is by **car**; you can either bring one over by ferry or rent one in Friday Harbor. M&W, 725 Spring St (ⓣ1-800/323-6037, ⓦwww.sanjuanauto.com), is a local outfit renting vehicles for $40–80 a day, depending on the season. From April to Sept, though, the **San Juan Shuttle** stops at most of the island's principal attractions ($5/one-way, $8/round-trip, $15/day pass, $25/two-day pass, or $17 for 25min guided bus tour; ⓣ360/378-8887 or 1-800/887-8387, ⓦwww.sanjuantransit.com). **Bikes** ($7–9/hr, $35/day, $150/week) can be rented at Island Bicycles, 380 Argyle St (Wed–Sat only; ⓣ360/378-4941, ⓦwww.islandbicycles.com), while **mopeds** are available from Susie's Mopeds, corner of First and A streets, across from the ferry departure lanes ($25/hour or $62/day; ⓣ360/378-5244 or 1-800/532-0087, ⓦwww.susiesmopeds.com).

To get on the water, San Juan Safaris (ⓣ360/378-1323 or 1-800/450-6858, ⓦwww.sanjuansafaris.com) runs **sea kayak treks** and **whale-watching cruises** ($65 each) from Friday and Roche harbors. Crystal Seas Kayaking (ⓣ360/378-4223, ⓦwww.crystalseas.com) and Sea Quest Kayak Expeditions (ⓣ360/378-5767, ⓦwww.sea-quest-kayak.com) run trips ranging from basic 3hr outings ($59) to multi-day tours (starting at $300). Island Dive

& Watersports (☎360/378-2772, ☻www.divesanjuan.com) has half-day scuba-diving charters ($79 per person).

Accommodation

Bed and breakfasts are the most prevalent form of **accommodation** on the island, though you'll also find the odd hotel and a range of worthwhile **campgrounds** – none of which, unfortunately, are sited in the national parks. It's essential to book ahead in summer for rooms in Friday Harbor, especially during the popular **San Juan Island Jazz Festival** (☎360/378-5509), held the last weekend in July.

Hotels and B&Bs

Blair House 345 Blair Ave, Friday Harbor ☎360/378-5907, ☻www.fridayharborlodging .com. Up from the ferry off Spring Street, one of the island's less pretentious B&Bs, with four units nearly enclosed by trees and a big front porch and hot tub. Add $50 for weekend rates. ❻

Friday's 35 First St, Friday Harbor ☎360/378-5848 or 1-800/352-2632, ☻www.friday-harbor .com. Renovated 1891 hotel, convenient to the ferry, with agreeable ambience and a range of rooms from economy (❸) to suites (❼). Rates jump by $40 in the high season.

Harrison House 235 C St, Friday Harbor ☎360/378-3587, ☻www.harrisonhousesuites .com. Popular B&B in a verdant setting, with kayaks and mountain bikes for island use, and four sizable suites (❺–❻) with Jacuzzis, kitchens, fireplaces, and one to three bedrooms each. Add $50–100 more in high season.

Hotel de Haro 248 Reuben Memorial Drive, Roche Harbor ☎1-800/451-8910,

☻www.rocheharbor.com. Located in the Roche Harbor Resort, an elegant 1886 complex with standard rooms with shared bathrooms (❹), as well as four upscale suites and quaint cottages with antique decor (❻). Add $25 (for basic rooms) to $100 (for cottages) in the high season.

Wharfside slip K-13, port of Friday Harbor ☎360/378 5661, ☻www.slowseason.com. Two private staterooms on a 60ft sailboat in the harbor make for an interesting change of pace from the usual B&B. Offers morning breakfast cruises around the harbor in summer, though this can raise the cost up to $265. ❼–❾ by season

Wildwood Manor 5335 Roche Harbor Rd, Roche Harbor ☎360/378-3447 or 1-877/298-1144, ☻www.wildwoodmanor.com. Old-fashioned Victorian estate with four tastefully decorated rooms and the standard B&B amenities, in an appealing forested location with fine views of the island and strait. ❼–❽ by season

Campgrounds and hostels

Lakedale Resort 4313 Roche Harbor Rd, between Roche Harbor and Friday Harbor ☎360/378-0944 or 1-800/617-2267, ☻www.lakedale.com. Offering guest-only lake activities like swimming, fishing, and kayaking, and a range of accommodation, including simple campsites ($21–26), tasteful lodge rooms with decks, fireplaces, and jetted tubs (❼–❽), and individual log cabins with kitchens and fireplaces (❾).

San Juan County Park 380 West Side Rd ☎360/378-1842, ☻www.co.san-juan.wa.us /parks. Appealing for its rugged bluffs and rocky

beaches, this park offers campsites with fire rings and picnic tables, as well as a boat launch for $25–35 if you have a vehicle. Come by foot, bike, or kayak and they're only $6. Reserve ahead in high season.

Wayfarer's Rest 35 Malcolm St, Friday Harbor ☎360/378-6428, ☻www.rockisland .com/~wayfarersrest. The island's only hostel, reachable on foot from the ferry, with bunk rooms for $30/night or private rooms for $60/night. Full kitchen facilities and herb garden; advance booking is advised.

Friday Harbor

When **FRIDAY HARBOR** became the county seat in 1873, it had a population of no more than three. Thanks in part to a protected harbor and good anchorage, by the turn of the century the town's residents numbered up to four hundred, and it continued to grow through the first half of the 1900s until a postwar decline refocused the town toward tourism and real estate. Now, with a population of nearly two thousand, Friday Harbor is by far the biggest town in the San Juans.

With its numerous cafes and restaurants, the **waterfront** area is the handiest place to eat before touring the island. To dig into local history, the **San Juan Historical Museum**, 405 Price St (May–Sept Thurs–Sat 10am–4pm, Sun 1–4pm; Mar–April & Oct Sat 1–4pm; $2; ☎360/378-3949, ⓦ www.sjmuseum .org), has the expected antiques and relics; a 2000-piece collection of photos from the days of farming, fishing, and lime quarrying; and a small collection of old buildings, a rickety log cabin, and municipal jail among them.

The area's main highlight is the modest but enjoyable **Whale Museum**, 62 1st St N (daily: June–Aug 9am–6pm; rest of year 10am–5pm; $6; ☎360/378-4710, ⓦ www.whalemuseum.org), which has a small set of whale skeletons and displays explaining their migration and growth cycles, as well as a listening booth for seven different kinds of whale songs, along with walrus, seal, and dolphin soundtracks. Short documentaries detail research expeditions, and the museum also monitors whale activities on a **"whale hotline"** (☎1-800/562-8832), to which you can report any sightings. The local orca whales are protected by a ban on their capture, which was instituted in 1976, but they're still threatened by pollution. The museum promotes an "Adopt an Orca" program to help the eighty or so left in Puget Sound; about twenty of them remain in the Sound year-round, while the others return only for about four or five months a year, starting in May.

One good place to spot the whales is at **Lime Kiln Point State Park** (daily 8am–dusk), known to some as "whale-watcher park," on the island's western side at 6158 Lighthouse Rd. Named after the site's former lime quarry, this is where orcas come in summer to gorge on migrating salmon, and there's usually at least one sighting a day. If you're really interested in seeing the whales up close, contact San Juan Safaris (see p.372), which runs good cetacean-oriented tours.

American Camp and English Camp

At San Juan's southern tip is **American Camp** (dawn–11pm; free; ☎360/378-2902, ⓦ www.nps.gov/sajh), a national park that played a role in the infamous Pig War (see box, opposite). Morale among the US troops once stationed here was quite low, and it's not hard to see why: the windswept, rabbit hole–strewn fields are bleak and largely shorn of vegetation. A self-guided, one-mile **trail** begins from the parking lot, passing the camp's few remaining buildings and what's left of a gun emplacement. Costumed volunteers reenact life in both camps during the summer; for details, drop in at the **visitor center** (summer daily 8.30am–5pm; rest of year Wed–Sun 8.30am–4.30pm; free), which also has relics dug up from the camps and historic photos.

On the island's western side is **ENGLISH CAMP** (same information as American Camp), the site of the only foreign flag officially flown by its itself on American soil. Here, forests line pleasant green fields and big-leafed maple trees dot the shoreline, where four military buildings from the 1860s and a small formal garden have been restored. A slide show in the barracks (summer daily

The Pig War

Both English Camp and American Camp were established on San Juan Island as a result of the **Pig War**, a dispute in which not a single shot was fired at a human being, the lone casualty being a swine that belonged to the British. Its death, however, ultimately sparked the resolution of a long-simmering border conflict between the US and the UK (which still ruled Canada).

The **Oregon Treaty of 1846** had given the United States possession of the Pacific Northwest south of the 49th parallel, extending the boundary "to the middle of the channel which separates the continent from Vancouver's Island." As there were two channels – Haro and Rosario straits – between Vancouver Island and the mainland, and San Juan Island lay between them, both the British and the Americans claimed the island and began settling it in the 1850s.

In 1859, short-tempered American settler **Lyman Cutlar** shot a wayward British-owned pig that was munching on his garden vegetables. When the British threatened to arrest him, 66 American troops were sent in by rash US General William Harney, who considered the "hog crap" an "outrage." The governor of British Columbia responded by sending three warships, and Harney then posted fifty troops with Gen. George Pickett – soon to become infamous for his ill-fated Gettysburg "Pickett's Charge" (resulting in the deaths of 2600 Confederate troops). Eventually, US President James Buchanan sent Winfield Scott, commanding general of the US Army, to cool things down. An agreement was reached allowing for joint occupation of the island until the dispute could be settled (or more important, in the case of the US, until the Civil War came to an end). This co-ownership ultimately lasted for twelve years, until the matter was finally referred to Kaiser Wilhelm I of Germany in 1871, who ruled in favor of the US the following year.

9am–5pm; free) explains the Pig War – a tale that you will no doubt have fully memorized over the course of your visit. From here you can hike an easy loop to **Bell Point**, a promontory with expansive waterside views, or retreat to the parking lot to mount the short but steep one-mile wooded trail to **Young Hill**, passing a small **cemetery** on the way. The 650ft summit has views over much of the island, and looks out to the shore of British Columbia, not more than ten miles away. The English Camp **visitor center** (summer daily 9am–5pm; free) has guided walks, historic reenactments, and nature exhibits.

Roche Harbor

At San Juan's northwest tip is **ROCHE HARBOR**, established in the 1880s to serve the limestone trade and highlighted by the gracious, white **Hotel de Haro** (see "Accommodation," p.373) and a few scattered remnants of the lime operation. The hotel's part of the *Roche Harbor Resort*, but unless you're staying here, there's not much in town to do aside from taking a peek at the building and a stroll around the small wharf and general area.

When you head back up to Roche Harbor Road, veer off to the left just before the arch welcoming visitors to town and park at the small lot marked "Mausoleum Parking." A few yards farther down the road, you'll find a small footpath leading into the **Roche Harbor Cemetery** (daily dawn–dusk); signs from here direct you to the haunting mausoleum of **John Stafford McMillin**, founder of the Hotel de Haro. Set far back from the street in the woods, with seven stately pillars surrounding a chipped round table and chairs honoring various members of the McMillin clan, the monument is the creepiest sight on the island; one expects wolves to start howling at any moment. For an explanation of all the weird, complicated Masonic symbolism behind the design of the site, check out Ⓦwww.rocheharbor.com/walkingtour.html, which informs us that the site is still unfinished, perhaps thankfully, because Mr. McMillin "did not see fit to install the bronze dome with its Maltese Cross."

For another peculiar, if less ominous, sight, drop by the **Westcott Bay Sculpture Park**, 8607 Cattle Point Rd, just outside town (daily dawn–dusk; donation; ℡360/370-5050, Ⓦwww.wbay.org), a surprisingly extensive nineteen-acre site built around a pond and marsh that features a number of paths leading past a hundred or so pieces of regionally produced sculpture. The artworks – most of them made of steel, bronze, stone, and marble – tend to be modern and abstract and are of varying quality, but the site makes for a harmonious whole. Expect to see all manner of hawks, eagles, woodpeckers, kingfishers, owls, and sandpipers – or at least the results of their presence atop some of the sculptures. The institute that runs the park also operates a **museum** in town, at 314 Spring St (Tues–Sat 11am–5pm; donation suggested; ℡360/370-5050), showcasing various regional artists in painting, sculpture, and multimedia, though in a rather less enticing setting.

Eating and drinking

Most appealing **eating** and **drinking** options on the island can be found in Friday Harbor, and while this isn't exactly prime dining turf, there are enough decent entries to make a culinary stop worthwhile.

Bella Luna 175 1st St, Friday Harbor ℡360/378-4118. Hefty Italian and American fare, best for pizzas, pastas, and breakfasts that include frittatas and English muffins smothered with veggies, eggs, and hollandaise sauce.

Downriggers 10 Front St, Friday ℡360/378-2700. A long-standing presence for its seafood – everything from lobster quesadillas to crab griddle cakes – along with more familiar salads, burgers, and fish and chips. Only a few entrees are more than $20.

Friday Harbor House 130 West St, Friday Harbor ℡360/378-8455. Swank, elegant spot for dining on Northwest Cuisine, but particularly good for its sizable wine list, hard ciders, and well-made cocktails.

The Place 1 Spring St, Friday Harbor ℡360/378-8707. Crab cakes, oysters, and all types of seafood, as well as savory pasta, are the reasons to visit this pleasant, upscale waterfront restaurant, whose regional fare is among the best on the island.

Roche Harbor Restaurant 248 Reuben Memorial Drive, Roche Harbor ℡360/378-5757. The finest of several eateries at Roche Harbor Resort. It's pricey, but the prime rib and crab are worth it, and the place offers pleasing waterside vistas.

Steps Wine Bar and Cafe First St at Friday Harbor Center ℡360/370-5959. Highly regarded spot for vino whose Northwest Cuisine menu is also quite tempting, with inventive starters like apple parsnip soup and risotto balls and larger plates that may include sausage tamales and calamari steak. Desserts like apple fritters and squash *crème brûlée* are also worth a try.

North of Seattle

North of Seattle, the urban sprawl drifts up the coast on either side of I-5, sweeping around Everett to stretch out toward the pancake-flat floodplain of the Skagit River, whose waters are straddled by the twin towns of Mount Vernon and Burlington. There's little here to catch the eye – the exception being the attractive town of **La Conner**, near the mouth of the Skagit. North of here, farther along I-5, is **Bellingham**, part bustling student town, part outdoor base, from where it's just a short hop over the border to Vancouver.

La Conner

Located near the Skagit Bay section of Puget Sound, across from the north-eastern corner of Whidbey Island, quaint **LA CONNER** offers touristy, yet amiable, souvenir shops and cafes. Its downtown is situated along the waterfront of the **Swinomish Channel**, a sheltered inlet between the San Juan Islands and Puget Sound. Before the area was diked and drained, the surrounding landscape of the **Skagit delta** was a marsh prone to flooding; the original trading post here was built on a hill to avoid the soggier ground; it was named by the town's leading landowner after his wife, Louisa Ann Conner. When the railroads reached the Pacific Northwest in the 1880s, La Conner was all but abandoned – though in the 1930s, the artist Morris Graves became attracted by its isolation, cheap land, and scenic landscapes. Kindred spirits such as fellow painter Guy Anderson followed Graves's lead, and the backwater town became both an artists' colony and a hangout for oddballs and counterculture types. Since the 1970s, though, when the waterfront was spruced up with new shops and amenities, the town has traded on its offbeat reputation to pull in the tourist dollar. As such, it's hard to get a glimpse of anything vaguely "alternative" here nowadays, unless you count the town's several **art galleries**, though even they offer mostly safe, unadventurous pieces aimed at visiting urbanites.

Arrival and accommodation

La Conner is located about an hour's drive north of Seattle off Hwy 20, or by bridge from Whidbey Island along the same highway. La Conner's **visitor center**, a short walk from the waterfront at 606 Morris St (Mon–Fri 10am–4pm, Sat 11am–3pm; summer also Sun 11am–3pm; ☎360/466-4778, ⓦwww.laconnerchamber.com), issues free maps and has a comprehensive list of local **accommodation**. Lodgings can get scarce during the month-long **Skagit Valley Tulip Festival** (ⓦwww.tulipfestival.org) in April, when it's best to book ahead.

Heron Inn 117 Maple Ave ☎360/466-4626, ⓦwww.theheron.com. A mix between a familiar B&B and a boutique hotel, offering twelve units (⑤–⑥) with swanky modern furnishings, fireplaces, and Jacuzzis, nice mountainside views, and suites for about $30 more.
Hotel Planter 715 S 1st St ☎360/466-4710 or 1-800/488-5409. Plush, modern queen beds and doubles in a stylish Victorian inn, complete with antique decor and a hot tub. ⑤
Katy's Inn 503 S 3rd St ☎360/466-3366 or 1-800/914-7767, ⓦwww.katysinn.com. Attractive old B&B with wraparound porch, antique pump organ, two standard rooms, and two slightly more expensive suites. ④–⑥ by season

La Conner Channel Lodge 205 N 1st St ☎360/466-1500, ⓦwww.laconnerlodging.com. Lavish waterside doubles with fireplaces and balconies, featuring an adjacent dock (⑥). Also operates the *La Conner Country Inn*, 107 S 2nd St (☎1-888/466-4113), offering 28 mostly double rooms with fireplaces, at cheaper rates (⑤).
Wild Iris Inn 121 Maple Ave ☎360-466-1400 or 1-800/477-1400, ⓦwww.wildiris.com. Fancy suites (⑦) with DVD players, hot tubs, fireplaces, and decks, along with several smaller, but still comfortable, rooms that sport fewer amenities (⑤).

The Town

Lined by pleasant boutiques and eateries, La Conner has an artistic flavor and puts on occasional outdoor sculpture exhibitions in the winter, often near S First Street. The highlight of its attractive waterfront is the town's excellent **Museum of Northwest Art** (**MoNA**), 121 S 1st St (daily 10am–5pm; $5;

$\textcircled{T}$360/466-4446, $\textcircled{W}$www.museumofnwart.org), which showcases the work of the region's painters. The first floor is given over to temporary displays, while the second holds the permanent collection – a bold and challenging sampling of modern art, including work by the likes of Morris Graves, William Morris, Dale Chihuly, and especially Guy Anderson, whose paintings are of particular note for their naked human figures adrift against somber landscapes.

A few blocks away, at 703 S 2nd St, the Gaches Mansion – the MoNA's former home – now holds the **La Conner Quilt Museum** (Feb–Nov Wed–Sat 11am–4pm, Sun noon–4pm; Dec Fri–Sat 11am–4pm, Sun noon–4pm; Jan closed; $5; $\textcircled{T}$360/466-4288, $\textcircled{W}$www.laconnerquilts.com), which presents a rotating display of quilts from around the world, with antique, handwoven items mixed with more bizarre modern creations. If anything, the museum's grand edifice is just as interesting as its collection, an odd mix of Eastlake and other Victorian architecture styles, with a touch of Tudor Revival in its half-timbered dormers and fairy-tale tower.

Eating and drinking

Being a rather small place, La Conner has limited choices for **eating** and **drinking**, though occasionally a European expat chef or Seattle culinary refugee will open a new restaurant with some fanfare.

Cafe Culture 109 E Commercial St $\textcircled{T}$360/421-0985. Well-regarded coffee house and art gallery that serves up solid espresso but is best for its regular exhibitions of international artwork and compelling local pieces.

Calico Cupboard Café and Bakery 720 S 1st St $\textcircled{T}$360/466-4451. Affordable breakfasts and lunches in a tearoom-like atmosphere in a classic 1887 structure. If available, try the banana-coconut griddlecakes, a savory omelet, or a fudge pie from the takeout bakery.

Kerstin's 505 S 1st St $\textcircled{T}$360/466-9111. Worthwhile mid-priced lunch and dinner spot serving a broad range of regional cuisine, including seafood, pasta, steak, and lamb, with nice views and comfortable atmosphere.

La Conner Seafood & Prime Rib House 614 S 1st St $\textcircled{T}$360/466-4014. Seafood (crab cakes, salmon 'n' chips, and fresh clams and oysters) is the focus of the menu here, but burgers and steaks are also available. Outdoor seating and waterside vistas, too.

The Next Chapter 721 S 1st St $\textcircled{T}$360/466-2665. This bookstore and coffeehouse is a reasonable place to sip an espresso or herbal tea as you browse the eclectic assortment of titles.

Bellingham

A successful blend of industry, Victorian architecture, and college-town liveliness, **BELLINGHAM** runs ten miles along a broad curve of wedge-shaped Bellingham Bay, 85 miles north of Seattle and just eighteen miles south of the Canadian border. It's actually the sum of four smaller communities, whose separate street patterns make a disjointed, hard-to-navigate whole – though orientation isn't too difficult if you use I-5 to get your bearings.

Arrival and information

Greyhound **buses** and Amtrak **trains** pull in at the **Bellingham Cruise Terminal**, in the Fairhaven district at 401 Harris St ($\textcircled{W}$www.portofbellingham .com), which is also the starting point of the Alaska Marine Highway (see box, p.382). Victoria–San Juan Cruises ($\textcircled{T}$360/738-8099 or 1-800/443-4552, $\textcircled{W}$www.whales.com) operates a passenger-only summer service to San Juan Island ($49 one-way, $59 round-trip) and Victoria in British Columbia ($50–55

△ La Conner Quilt Museum

one-way, $89–99 round-trip), though it's primarily aimed at whale watchers. Other companies based at the terminal operate agreeable sightseeing and whale-watching cruises. Local Whatcom Transit **buses** (☎360/676-RIDE, ⓦwww.ridewta.com) ply 33 routes for a fare of 75¢. The **visitor center** is at 904 Potter St, off I-5 Exit 253 (☎360/671-3990 or 1-800/487-2032, ⓦwww.bellingham.org), and provides maps and information on the town as well as the surrounding Whatcom County.

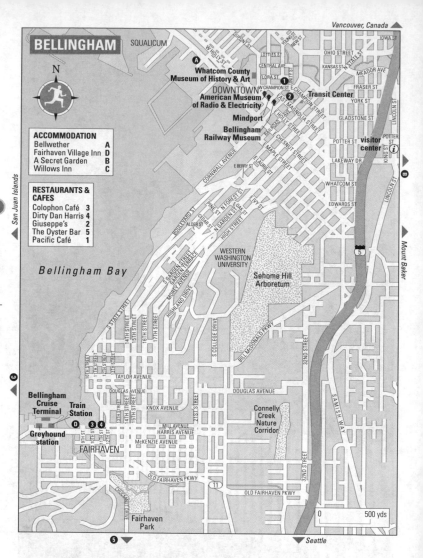

BELLINGHAM

SQUALICUM

Vancouver, Canada

N

Whatcom County
Museum of History & Art

DOWNTOWN
American Museum
of Radio & Electricity

Mindport
Bellingham
Railway Museum

Transit Center

visitor center

ACCOMMODATION
Bellwether   A
Fairhaven Village Inn   D
A Secret Garden   B
Willows Inn   C

RESTAURANTS & CAFES
Colophon Café   3
Dirty Dan Harris   4
Giuseppe's   2
The Oyster Bar   5
Pacific Café   1

Bellingham Bay

San Juan Islands

WESTERN
WASHINGTON
UNIVERSITY

Sehome Hill
Arboretum

Mount Baker

Bellingham
Cruise
Terminal   Train
Station

Greyhound
station

FAIRHAVEN

Connelly
Creek
Nature
Corridor

Fairhaven
Park

0   500 yds

Seattle

Accommodation

From the cruise terminal, it's only five hundred yards to the center of Fairhaven along Harris Avenue, where you'll find several good places to **stay**, including pleasant **B&Bs** and reasonable hotel chains. The town's chain **motels** are strung along Lakeway Drive, off I-5 at Exit 253.

Bellwether near Roeder Ave and F Street ☎ 1-877/411-1200, ⓦ www.hotelbellwether.com. Large resort, looking oddly like a big, fancy motel, that has the usual range of upscale amenities: spacious suites with modern

furnishings, onsite spa, gym, and salon, and private boat dock for your finest yacht. ❺–❼ by season

Fairhaven Village Inn 1200 10th St ☎ 360/733-1311, ⓦ www.fairhavenvillageinn.com. One of the more conveniently sited hotels, whose upscale rooms have fireplaces, balconies, and plush furnishings, with bayside views bumping up rates by about $30. ⑦

Larrabee State Park seven miles south of Bellingham on Hwy 11 ☏1-888/226-7688, ⓦwww.parks.wa.gov. Peppered with idyllic lakes and beachside coves, this 2700-acre site is the best place to camp in the vicinity, though there are other campgrounds along the road heading eastbound to Mount Baker as well. $17–22; Feb–Nov only.

A Secret Garden 1807 Lakeway Dr ☏360/650-9473, ⓦwww.secretgardenbb.com. Century-old Victorian with four rooms and suites, some of which have bayside views, jetted tubs, assorted artworks, and themes from "tropical" to "multicultural." ⑤

🏃 **Willows Inn** 2579 West Shore Dr ☏360/758-2620, ⓦwww.willows-inn .com. Located on Lummi Island, a 5min ferry ride south of town, a terrifically warm and atmospheric B&B with five rooms (two of them with fireplaces; ⑤) and a more elaborate guest house (⑦) and cottage (⑨). Another draw is the restaurant, which serves "slow food" – locally raised and produced meat and produce, with a range of creative, rotating entrees.

The Town

The late-nineteenth-century brick and sandstone buildings that constitute central **Fairhaven** – the most southerly (and easily the most diverting) of the town's districts – occupy a four-block square between 10th and 12th streets to either side of Harris Avenue. These commercial structures witnessed two brief booms – the first in the 1870s when the town was touted as the Pacific terminus of the Great Northern Railroad, the second twenty years later during the Klondike Gold Rush. Nowadays, Fairhaven is noted for its laid-back cafes and bars, which have an arty flavor that's very refreshing, especially if you've been hiking the great outdoors. Moving north on I-5, Exit 253 leads **downtown**, where a routine gridiron of high-rises congregate on the bluff above the industrial harbor.

Make sure to drop by the old **City Hall**, a grandiose 1892 red-brick Victorian that is now the main part of the **Whatcom County Museum of History and Art**, 121 Prospect St (Tues–Sun noon–5pm; free; ⓦwww .whatcommuseum.org), displaying antiques, clothing, and a fair smattering of doodads and trinkets. In an annex, the ARCO Exhibits Building, across the street, there's more Victoriana on view, including period dioramas with quaint clothing and furniture, plus exhibits touching on aspects of Native American history and culture. Both spaces regularly have temporary exhibits from regional artists, too. A little over a block south, one of the region's more unusual institutions is the **American Museum of Radio and Electricity**, 1312 Bay St (Wed–Sat 11am–4pm; $5; ☏360/738-3886, ⓦwww .americanradiomuseum.org), which, along with a working radio station that broadcasts classics from the "golden age of radio" (the 1920s to the 1950s), has dioramas re-creating a seventeenth-century electricity lab and *Titanic*'s wireless room, from which the doomed ship's distress signals were sent. There are also plenty of old radios and phones for telecom buffs, topped by a theremin from 1929, whose eerie frequencies you can attempt to "play." Nearby, one of the more oddball manifestations of the local art scene is **Mindport**, 210 W Holly St (Wed–Fri noon–6pm, Sat 10am–5pm, Sun noon–4pm; $2; ⓦwww.mindport.org), which, along with the usual mixed-media pieces from area artists, is known for its eye-popping interactive pieces – miniature tornados, magnetic turntables, and various other spheres, planes, and complex devices and gizmos that you can manipulate with sufficient patience and effort. A more conventional attraction is also nearby, the **Bellingham Railway Museum**, 1320 Commercial St (Tues & Thurs–Sat noon–5pm; $3; ☏360/393-7540, ⓦwww.bellinghamrailwaymuseum.org),

The **Alaska Marine Highway** (☏1-800/382-9229, ✆www.akmhs.com; one-way passenger fares $316 and up, depending on season; vehicles one-way $716–1100) is a three-day ferry ride that winds between wooded islands and hard, craggy coast from Washington's Bellingham to Alaska's Skagway, with stops along the way at Ketchikan, Wrangell, Petersburg, Juneau, and Haines. Ferries leave the Bellingham Cruise Terminal every Friday early in the evening from May to September (less frequently in the winter) and arrive in Skagway the following Monday night. The round-trip takes about a week. Vehicles and cabins have to be reserved months in advance and even walk-on passage requires at least a couple of weeks' notice. You can, however, try to get a ticket at the Bellingham terminal on the day of departure – but don't bank on success. For further details, contact Alaska Ferry Adventures, 4667 Homer Spit Rd, Suite 1, Homer, AK 99603.

whose kid-friendly exhibits detail the glory days of rail transport with model trains, simulators, and castoffs like lanterns, equipment, and other antiques.

Beyond all this, however, Bellingham's chief attraction is its access to a wide range of excellent **parks**, set among the bluffs and forests in and around the city, with myriad hiking trails and inspiring vistas. **Sehome Hill Arboretum**, off McDonald Parkway (daily 6am–dusk; free; ✆www.ac.wwu.edu/~sha), is a splendid 180-acre preserve that overlooks the city (and includes an 80ft observation tower for this purpose) but is best for its six miles of nature walks and abundant views of wildlife such as native birds, deer, and even the odd mountain lion. Also worthwhile is **Connelly Creek Nature Corridor**, Donovan Ave at 30th St, where you can pick up an easy, half-hour-long trail that leads around varied natural scenery like forest groves, meadows, and a swamp, and is mostly aimed at casual sightseers of nature.

Eating and drinking

If you've come to Bellingham to **eat** and **drink**, you're probably going to end up in **Fairhaven**, where most of the notable restaurants, bars, and other night-spots can be found

Colophon Café 1208 11th St ☏360/647-0092. Serves delicious vegetarian food, with good soups – among them a mean African peanut soup and clam chowder – and salads and great desserts. Located inside Village Books in Fairhaven.

Dirty Dan Harris 1211 11th St, Fairhaven ☏360/676-1011. Mostly all-American fare like solid prime rib and steaks, but some seafood, too, including savory choices like gulf prawns, regional oysters, and king salmon. A healthy wine list to boot.

Giuseppe's 1414 Cornwall Ave ☏360/714-9100. One of the few decent entries for Italian fare in northern Washington, and worth a visit for its savory pastas, cioppino, rack of lamb, and other pricey but delicious choices.

The Oyster Bar 2578 Chuckanut Dr ☏360/766-6185. If you want a nice meal out, this mid-priced spot is as good as any, with a tantalizing collection of local bivalves (the Kumamoto and Penn Cove varieties are among the best), as well as simpler items like fish and chips. The excellent location has expansive views.

Pacific Cafe 100 N Commercial St ☏360/647-0800. Adjacent to the Mount Baker Theatre is this upscale bistro that has a fine array of regional offerings, especially strong on seafood, as well as beef and lamb, and unexpected offerings like Punjabi chicken curry. Among the better choices in the vicinity.

9

The Olympic Peninsula and SW Washington

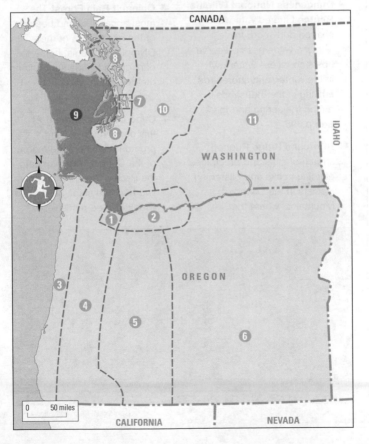

CHAPTER 9

Highlights

* **Port Townsend** See the September Wooden Boat Festival in this nicely preserved Victorian hamlet from the late nineteenth century, peppered with elegant mansions, quaint restaurants, and charming boutiques. See p.387

* **Dungeness National Wildlife Refuge** Littered with weirdly shaped driftwood, this fetching wilderness preserve hosts countless waterfowl in the winter, and shorebirds arriving in the thousands during the spring and fall. See p.395

* **Hurricane Ridge** Rugged stretch of cliffs and precipices, piercing peaks and glistening glaciers in the Olympic Mountains, where the snowcapped peak of Mount Olympus rises before you. See p.400

* **Sol Duc Hot Springs** Relax at this peaceful spot in the Olympic range, in which mineral water bubbles out of the earth to be channeled into three pools. See p.401

* **Quinault Rain Forest** The most accessible and beautiful of the rain forests of the Olympic Peninsula, home to dark green foliage surrounding the deep blue waters of Quinault Lake. See p.404

* **Cape Disappointment** At this dangerous, striking promontory where the mouth of the Columbia River meets the Pacific Ocean, more than two hundred ships have been wrecked. See p.409

△ Rain forest, Olympic National Park

The Olympic Peninsula and SW Washington

West of Seattle, rugged peaks dominate the core of the **Olympic Peninsula**, rising high above the lush subalpine vegetation, which gives way to the tangled rain forests of the western valleys, and the wild beaches of the Pacific edge. Fringed with logging communities and encircled by US-101, the peninsula's most magnificent parts are protected within **Olympic National Park**, complete with scores of superb hiking trails, numerous campsites, and several fine old lodges. You can also stay just outside of the park in **Sequim**, the most likable of the surrounding towns. Closer to Puget Sound, another possible base for visiting the national park is **Port Townsend**, a lively little town that is worth a visit in itself for its fancy Victorian architecture and sociable nightlife.

The sheltered bays that punctuate the **southwest corner** of the state along the **Pacific Coast** are protected from the open sea by elongated sand spits. While the shoreline stretches out for miles, the scenery is mostly flat and monotonous, though resorts like Ocean Shores and Long Beach do have their fans. However, it's best to head for the scenic pleasures – if not the military remains – of **Cape Disappointment State Park** at the mouth of the Columbia River in the very southwestern tip of the state. As an alternative, farther east you can access I-5 south of Olympia (see p.351) to reach Washington's own **Vancouver**, site of a reconstructed Hudson's Bay Company fur-trapping outpost. Beyond is Portland, Oregon, 170 miles from Seattle.

The Olympic Peninsula

Projecting west from Puget Sound, the **OLYMPIC PENINSULA** is a broad mass where dense temperate rain forests nestle between imposing, glacier-draped mountains and the rocky and remote Pacific coastline. Small towns

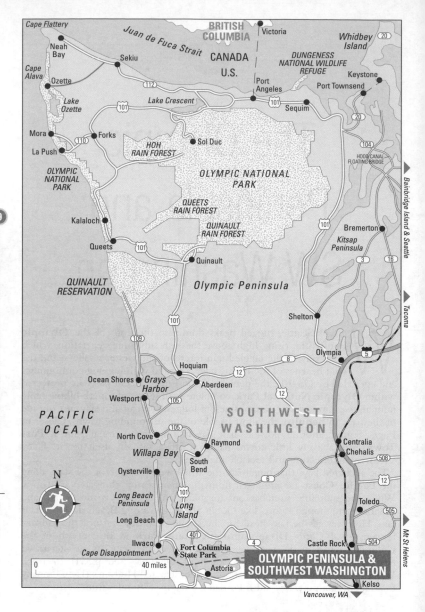

The Olympic Peninsula

sprinkle the peninsula's edges, and at its center the mighty Olympic Mountains thrust upward, shredding the clouds that drift in from the Pacific and causing the peninsula's western side to be constantly drenched by rain. These moist conditions have led to the peninsula's being carpeted with a thick blanket of forest, and in the western river valleys the dense vegetation thickens into **temperate rain forest**, primarily composed of Sitka spruce, western hemlock,

Douglas fir, alder, and maple – a rare and remarkable environment. The peninsula's wild and lonely Pacific shore offers some extraordinary scenery, and both the forests and the coast provide habitat for a variety of wildlife.

It was partly to ensure the survival of a rare elk subspecies that Franklin D. Roosevelt created **Olympic National Park** here in 1939, where, appropriately, the largest herd of Roosevelt elk in the US roams. The park also protects the heart of the peninsula, though large tracts of forest surrounding it are heavily logged. The issue of economy versus ecology is debated with particular intensity here, since it was the timber trade that lured settlers in the first place, and the logging industry still provides many local jobs. Environmentalists reluctantly favor tourism as the lesser ecological evil, though the balance between industry and amusement is uneasy in places.

Graced by its charming waterside setting and ornate old mansions, northerly **Port Townsend** is easily the most appealing town on the peninsula and, handily enough, the logical first stop if you're arriving from the east: ferries arrive here from Keystone on Whidbey Island (see p.362), and a short drive will get you here from Seattle via Bainbridge Island (see p.358). The rest of the peninsula's settlements are rather nondescript: only **Sequim**, a pleasant little town in the rain shadow of the Olympic Mountains, offers much incentive to hang around, though **Port Angeles** is useful for its ferry links with Victoria in Canada and as the location of the Olympic National Park Visitor Center. Otherwise, you're well advised to make straight for the wilderness, either to camp at the national park or stay in one of its excellent lodges.

Getting around

The peninsula's main highway, **US-101**, loops around the coast, but no roads run across the peninsula's mountainous core. However, several paved and/or gravel-topped arteries do nudge into the interior, exploring the peripheries of the national park. Two local **bus** companies provide a limited and slow Monday-through-Saturday service across the northern part of the peninsula. Clallam Transit buses (75¢–$2; ☏360/452-4511 or 1-800/858-3747, ⓦwww .clallamtransit.com) go west from Port Angeles around the peninsula to Lake Crescent, Neah Bay, and Forks, and east to Sequim – from there connecting with Jefferson Transit buses to Port Townsend ($1.25; ☏360/385-4777, ⓦwww .jeffersontransit.com). That said, if you want to do any walking, you'll have problems reaching trailheads without your own vehicle – and a **car** is by far the best bet; on a **bike**, you're most likely to get soaked time and again, and sharp corners and hurtling logging trucks represent considerable hazards.

Port Townsend and around

Located at the tip of the Quimper Peninsula, a stumpy northeast adjunct to the adjoining mass of the Olympic Peninsula, **PORT TOWNSEND** is alive with brightly painted Victorian mansions, convivial cafes, and a vigorous cultural (and countercultural) scene. A would-be San Francisco since the mid-nineteenth century, it was poised for local supremacy in the 1890s, when confident predictions of a railway terminus lured rich settlers, who set about building extravagant Neo-Gothic homes on the bluff above the port. Unfortunately for the investors, the railway petered out before it reached Port Townsend, the hoped-for boom never happened, and the town was left with a glut of stylish residences and a small business district.

This combination turned out to be Port Townsend's salvation. Ever since the old mansions were bought up and restored in the 1960s, the town has mellowed

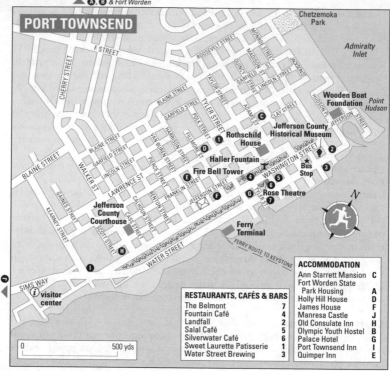

PORT TOWNSEND

Chetzemoka
Park

Admiralty
Inlet

Wooden Boat
Foundation   Point
Hudson

Jefferson County
Historical Museum

Rothschild
House

Haller Fountain

Fire Bell Tower

Bus
Stop

Rose Theatre

Jefferson
County
Courthouse

Ferry
Terminal

FERRY ROUTE TO KEYSTONE

SIMS WAY

i visitor
center

0   500 yds

RESTAURANTS, CAFÉS & BARS	
The Belmont	7
Fountain Café	4
Landfall	2
Salal Café	5
Silverwater Café	6
Sweet Laurette Patisserie	1
Water Street Brewing	3

ACCOMMODATION	
Ann Starrett Mansion	C
Fort Worden State	
Park Housing	A
Holly Hill House	D
James House	F
Manresa Castle	J
Old Consulate Inn	H
Olympic Youth Hostel	B
Palace Hotel	G
Port Townsend Inn	I
Quimper Inn	E

into an artsy community with hippie undertones and a good degree of charm.
Tourists in search of Victoriana fill plush B&Bs, while jazz and blues fans flock
to the annual music festivals, and nearby, nineteenth-century **Fort Worden**
provides ample camping and youth hostel facilities.

Arrival and information

Port Townsend is easy to reach, either by a half-hour **ferry** ride from Keystone
on Whidbey Island or by **road** over the Hood Canal Bridge from the Kitsap
Peninsula or up along US-101 from Olympia. To get here by **bus**, take the
Olympic Bus Lines (☎360/417-0700, ⓦwww.olympicbuslines.com) coach
from the Amtrak or Greyhound stations in Seattle ($39) or from Sea-Tac
Airport ($49). From the Bremerton ferry terminal, you can also pick up the
Kitsap Transit bus ($1.25; ☎360/373-2877 or 1-800/501-RIDE, ⓦwww
.kitsaptransit.org) to Poulsbo for the connection with Jefferson Transit ($1.25,
good bus travel all day; ☎360/385-4777, ⓦwww.jeffersontransit.com) to Port
Townsend. The town can also be reached by passenger **boat** from Friday
Harbor, on San Juan Island, with Puget Sound Express (May–Sept, one boat
daily; 3hr 30min; $49.50–52.50 one-way, $62.50–72.50 return; ☎360/385-
5288, ⓦwww.pugetsoundexpress.com).

Port Townsend's compact center occupies a triangle of land jutting out into
the sea. The **ferry terminal** is just south of downtown, off the main drag, Water
Street, which is dotted with stops for the Jefferson Transit bus. Pick up
information at the helpful **visitor center**, 2437 E Sims Way (daily 9am–5pm;

T 360/385-2722, W www.ptguide.com), half a mile south of the center on Hwy 20. To get around, **rent a bike** from PT Cyclery, 252 Tyler St (Mon–Sat 9am–6pm; T 360/385-6470), for $7 an hour or $25 per day. Port Townsend is also a major launching point for **kayaking** in Puget Sound. PT Outdoors, 1071 Water St at Tyler (T 360/379-3608, W www.ptoutdoors.com), offers competitive kayak rentals ($20–45/hr, $40–85/half-day) and harbor tours lasting from two to three hours ($55) to a full day ($110).

Accommodation

Port Townsend is **B&B** central, with more than a dozen moderately expensive establishments sprinkled among the old villas of the uptown area. At B&Bs, advance **reservations** are strongly advised throughout the summer; prices fluctuate considerably with demand and with the room – some B&Bs have smaller rooms for as little as $60, as well as suites for upward of $200. A few miles north of town, the old military compound at **Fort Worden State Park** has two **campsites** (Fort Worden, off Cherry St; T 360/344-4431, W www.fortworden.org; $25–31, plus $7 reservation fee): one's near the conference center, while the other is in a more enticing location by the seashore; the park also offers vacation units, dorms, and a youth hostel (see below).

Ann Starrett Mansion 744 Clay St at Adams T 360/385-3205 or 1-800/321-0644, W www.starrettmansion.com. With its high gables and precocious tower, this 1889 Queen Anne is one of the town's most imposing Victorian mansions. The antique-filled interior features ceiling frescoes, a splendid spiral staircase, and ornate and extremely comfortable doubles (⑥). Also offers a pair of two-room suites in a downtown cottage (⑥).

Fort Worden State Park Housing 200 Battery Way, Fort Worden T 360/344-4431, W www.fortworden.org. Thirty-three old officers lodgings have been refurbished as fully furnished houses, with fireplaces and kitchens, starting at $125–140 for a double and rising to $275–323 for six people. Also on the compound, spartan dorms with wood and linoleum floors house one to eight people for $15–18.50 apiece. Advance reservations essential.

Holly Hill House 611 Polk St at Clay T 360/385-5619 or 1-800/435-1454, W www.hollyhillhouse.com. Enticing, well-run B&B in an appealing late-nineteenth-century structure with high gables, a nice garden, and a relaxing veranda. Each of the five guest rooms – four with private baths – is adorned with lavish period decor. ⑤

James House 1238 Washington St at Harrison T 360/385-1238 or 1-800/385-1238, W www.jameshouse.com. This appealing old pile with high brick chimneys and a handsome front terrace sits on the edge of the bluff overlooking the harbor. Ten tastefully decorated rooms, plus two off-site private bungalows for $60 more. ⑥

Manresa Castle 7th and Sheridan sts T 360/385-5750 or 1-800/732-1281, W www.manresacastle.com. A bit south of downtown, this quasi-French castle from 1892 is now an elegant hotel with thirty rooms that range from cozy single units (⑤) to swanky suites in the tower (⑧). Also with a surprisingly good, if pricey, Northwest Cuisine restaurant on the premises.

Old Consulate Inn 313 Walker St at Washington T 360/385-6753 or 1-800/300-6753, W www.oldconsulateinn.com. This elegant 1889 villa, with its spiky tower and wraparound veranda, has seven plush suites (plus one rather small room), as well as a grand piano and an old organ. It takes its name from the days when the German consul lodged here. Suites ⑥, room ⑤

▽ Old Consulate Inn

Olympic Youth Hostel 272 Battery Way, Fort Worden State Park ℡360/385-0655. Up the hill from the Parade Ground, this HI-affiliated hostel has dorm beds as well as private rooms ($28) and a kitchen. Beds $17 for members, $20 non-members. Check-in 5–10pm; checkout 9.30am. Access by Jefferson Transit bus #12 from downtown.

🏃 Palace Hotel 1004 Water St at Tyler ℡360/385-0773 or 1-800/962-0741, Ⓦwww.palacehotelpt.com. The best bet for staying downtown, a refurbished Victorian charmer with elegant lobby and in-room antique decor, claw-footed tubs, and excellent views of the

sound. The basic rooms are ultra-cheap (❸), with shared bath), and even the two-room suites are affordable (❺–❻).

Port Townsend Inn 2020 Washington St ℡360/385-2211 or 1-800/216-4985, Ⓦwww .porttownsendinn.com. Comfortable motel at south end of town center, with continental breakfast, microwaves and fridges in the rooms, indoor heated pool, and spa. ❹

Quimper Inn 1306 Franklin St at Harrison ℡360/385-1060 or 1-800/557-1060, Ⓦwww .quimperinn.com. Delightful 1888 B&B decked out in Colonial Revival style and furnished with period decor; has five comfortable guest rooms. ❺

The Town

Port Townsend's physical split – half on a bluff, half at sea level – reflects Victorian-era social divisions, when wealthy merchants built their homes uptown and the working class were stuck amid the noise and ruckus of the port below. **Downtown** is the commercial center of Port Townsend, its shops and cafes are located on and around **Water Street**. The main route into town, Sims Way, leads right to this historic stretch, and the ferry pulls in just a few blocks south as well. Above downtown is the **uptown** bluff, which is accessible by road on its north and south ends and also by staircase off Taylor Street, which leads past the incongruous **Haller Fountain**, decorated with a sculpture of a nude Venus rising from the sea.

Downtown

Downtown sports an attractive medley of 1890s brick and stonework buildings centered on **Water Street**. To the business folk of the late nineteenth century, these structures were important status symbols: timber is the obvious building material in the area, and owning a sizable brick building was quite a coup. Today, many of these structures are occupied by stylish restaurants, boutiques, and, especially, **art galleries**. The latter are particularly concentrated on Water and Washington street, from Quincy to Tyler streets, and sell all manner of locally crafted items – from the masks, dolls, and textiles of native tribes (at Pacific Traditions, 637 Water St; ℡360/385-4770) to cedar and myrtle-wood sculptures and carvings (Forest Gems, 807 Washington St; ℡360/379-1713) to vintage beads and handcrafted jewelry (Wynwood's, 940 Water St; ℡1-888/311-6131). Also not to be missed is the splendid little **Rose Theatre**, near the fountain at 235 Taylor St (Ⓦwww.rosetheatre.com), a restored 1907 gem that plays independent and art films. Just two blocks away along the wharf, you can take a break at any of the **landings** to watch the ferries, fishing trawlers, and pleasure cruisers go about their business in Puget Sound.

The most prominent edifice downtown is the **City Hall**, at Water and Madison streets, a robust red-brick assertion of civic dignity that manages to incorporate a wide mixture of architectural styles – with Gothic, Roman-esque, and even Neoclassical features. The interior held the firehouse and courthouse and has been recently restored as the **Jefferson County Histor-ical Society Museum** (March–Dec daily 11am–4pm; $2; ℡360/385-1003, Ⓦwww.jchsmuseum.org). Look for the photographer's chair draped with bear and buffalo skins, which were intended to add luster to the picture-portraits of the late nineteenth century, and the unusual late-nineteenth- and early-twentieth-century two-necked harp guitars by local musician and instrument-builder Chris Knutsen. There are also displays on native peoples in the area, nautical activities, and the port's appearance (along with Fort Worden's) in such Hollywood films as *An Officer and a Gentleman*. Prison cells that were actually used as the city jail occupy part of the basement, and keep an eye out for the excellent section devoted to the history of local prostitution and VD, a common hazard in port towns a hundred years ago.

From the museum, it's just a short walk northwest to the waterfront bluff of **Chetzemoka Park**, named after a native chief who was extremely helpful to the first white settlers. It's a particularly pretty park with banks of rhododendrons, pine trees, manicured lawns, a trim bandstand, and a narrow slice of beach.

The upper town

Upper Port Townsend is conspicuously marked by the **Fire Bell Tower**, which looms above downtown on a bluff, its wooden red frame rising 75ft in a picturesque, but no longer purposeful, manner. It was built in 1890 to summon volunteer firemen during powerful blazes with a 1500-pound brass ringer, but it's been nearly eighty years since it stopped working. Still, it's relevant enough to Port Townsend's image to have been architecturally restored in 2004. In the blocks around the tower are some of the big wooden mansions it was no doubt put there to save, including the 1889 icon of Port Townsend's boom period, the **Ann Starrett Mansion** (see "Accommodation," p.389), at Adams and Clay streets, which swarms with gables and boasts an octagonal tower and an impressively ornate elliptical staircase that has to be seen to be believed. By contrast, the 1868 **Rothschild House**, at nearby Franklin and Taylor streets (May–Sept daily 11am–4pm; $4; T 360/385-1003), predates the high times, its plank frame and simple columns resembling a sedate Colonial Revival farmhouse. The house was built for a local merchant, one D.C.H. Rothschild, a German immigrant who was related to the famous banking family "enough to get the name, but not the money," as he put it. More impressive than either house, though – or practically anything else in town – is the grand **Jefferson County Courthouse**, Walker and Jefferson streets (Mon–Fri 9am–5pm; W www.co.jefferson.wa.us), a towering red Romanesque Revival edifice with a clock tower that looks like a medieval Italian version of Big Ben.

Fort Worden

Fort Worden, two miles north of downtown Port Townsend (Jefferson Transit bus #12 from downtown; T 360/344-4400, W www.fortworden.org), was part of a trio of coastal fortifications built at the beginning of the twentieth century, designed to protect Puget Sound from attack by the new breeds of steam-powered battleships then being developed by all the great powers. Used by the army until 1953, then converted into a juvenile detention center for the next twenty years, Worden is now designated as a 443-acre state park. Just beyond the main gates is a large, green **Parade Ground** lined on one side by the soldiers' barracks, a series of plain wooden buildings that are rented as vacation accommodation (see p.389); the *Olympic Youth Hostel* and the **visitor center**, 200 Battery Way (summer daily 10am–4pm; March–April & Nov Sat & Sun only; T 360/344-4458), are also found here. Another barracks contains the **Coastal Artillery Museum** (summer daily 11am–4pm; $2), which gives the military lowdown on the site and has a scale model of the Kinzie Battery (see below). Lining the south side of the Parade Ground is the century-old **Officers' Row**, which culminates in the sedate **Commanding Officers'**

House (March–May & Sept–Oct hours vary, generally Sat & Sun noon–4pm; June–Aug Wed–Fri noon–5pm, Sat–Mon 10am–5pm; $2), a 1904 Colonial Revival home whose interior has been carefully decked out in full Victorian style, its upper story adorned with stern-looking portraits of most of the 33 commanders who called the place home.

Beyond the Parade Ground, old bunkers and gun batteries radiate out across the park – though the most diverting are down along the seashore, where you can scramble around the massive concrete gun emplacements of the 1890s **Kinzie Battery**. If you're really intrigued by these deadly relics, you can take a trail and go poking around **Artillery Hill**, where the guns sit silently under heavy tree cover. Also along the shore – but much nearer to the Parade Ground, at the end of the wharf – the small **Marine Science Center**, 532 Battery Way (April–Oct hours vary, generally Fri–Sun noon–4pm; $5; ⓦwww.ptmsc.org), has large tanks in which you can touch tide-pool creatures and observe local animals and plants.

Don't leave the area before you've had a chance to see one of Port Townsend's visual icons, the **Point Wilson Lighthouse**, a 1913 column at the end of Quimper Peninsula off Harbor Defense Way, just beyond Fort Worden (grounds tours Wed 11am–4pm; donation). Even though the light's been automated for thirty years, the isolated beacon guides ships through the Admiralty Inlet of Puget Sound, giving you a sense of the rugged maritime atmosphere of a century ago.

Eating, drinking, and entertainment

Port Townsend has a good supply of plain, inexpensive **cafes**, many of which offer light meals and snacks with a vegetarian or health-food slant, and pricier **restaurants** serving a wider-than-expected mix of cuisines. Uptown, *Aldrich's*, 940 Lawrence St (ⓣ360/385-0500, ⓦwww.aldrichs.com), is a pleasantly traditional general store with great coffee and sandwiches; it is also supposedly the oldest business in town, though it's been rebuilt after a 2003 fire. Nearby, the hippie-oriented *Food Co-op*, 414 Kearney St (ⓣ360/385-2883), sells organic products and local produce in comfortable digs.

The Belmont 925 Water St ⓣ360/385-3007. A smart, bistro-style restaurant featuring a range of delicious entrees, mostly steaks, seafood, pasta and salads, with main courses averaging $15.

Fountain Café 920 Washington St ⓣ360/385-1364. Seafood and pasta specialties like oyster stew and wild mushroom risotto in a small spot a short distance from the waterfront.

Landfall 412 Water St ⓣ360/385-5814. Pleasant dining on the Point Hudson waterfront, with an imaginative menu of vegetarian, seafood, and meat dishes – from fish tacos to caramelized onion burgers – as well as fresh salmon for summer barbecue specials.

Salal Café 634 Water at Taylor ⓣ360/385-6532. Renowned for its breakfasts – blintzes, omelets, frittatas, and crepes – and also good for its solid lunchtime burgers and pastas. Serves up a mean tofu stroganoff, too.

Silverwater Café 237 Taylor St ⓣ360/385-6448. Best for its seafood dishes – such as ahi tuna, cioppino, and pan-fried oysters – the cafe also has decent pasta and vegetarian selections.

Sweet Laurette Patisserie 1029 Lawrence St ⓣ360/385-4886. One of the best bets for French-style baked goods in town, with elaborate (and expensive) cakes that resemble artworks, and more affordable scones, pies, and pastries with a range of fresh local ingredients.

Water Street Brewing 639 Water St ⓣ360/379-6438. Funky live music joint showcasing blues and rock bands, and boasting great microbrews, solid staples like fish 'n' chips, and a wonderful old wooden bar with an enormous mirror to boot.

Port Townsend puts on several big **music festivals** throughout the year, most notably the **Country Blues Festival** in early August, the **Festival of American Fiddle Tunes** in early July, and the **Jazz Port Townsend Festival** in late July. The programs are organized by a nonprofit arts organization, Centrum, based in Fort Worden, 223 Battery Way (☎360/385-5320 or 1-800/733-3608, ⓦwww .centrum.org). Perhaps the town's most celebrated festival, however, is the annual **Wooden Boat Festival** (☎360/385-4742, ⓦwww.woodenboat.org), a three-day weekend event in early September put on by the prestigious **Wooden Boat Foundation** at Point Hudson, with more than 150 wooden boats of all shapes and vintages on display.

Along the northern coast

South of Port Townsend, Hwy 20 rounds Discovery Bay to meet **US-101** at the start of its journey west along the **northern Olympic Peninsula**'s narrow coastal plain, with the national park on one side and the **Juan de Fuca Strait** on the other. The most immediate sights are **Sequim** and the **Dungeness National Wildlife Refuge** and, just beyond, the Olympic National Park gateway of **Port Angeles**. Farther west the major attractions are much more scarce, until you reach the remote and windswept settlement of **Neah Bay**, at the very northwestern tip of the peninsula – and the continental US.

Sequim

Eighteen miles from the junction of Hwy 20 and US-101 lies **SEQUIM** (pronounced "Skwim"), the only town on the rain-soaked peninsula to hold an annual irrigation festival (ⓦwww.irrigationfestival.com), a century-old early-May event with a beauty pageant, car show, food and crafts displays, and parade. While drenching everything else, the Olympic Mountains cast a rain shadow over this area, depositing just 17in of rainfall per year, and the sunshine has attracted droves of retirees to live here. The result is a cozy little town whose neat bungalows line the sides of the long main drag, **Washington Avenue**, which runs just to the north of the US-101 bypass and divides into West and East at Sequim Avenue, the town's main intersection. There's nothing remarkable here, but it's close enough to Olympic National Park to use as a base. For a quick glimpse a local heritage – ancient and modern – drop by the **Museum and Arts Center**, 175 W Cedar St (Tues–Sat 8am–4pm; donation suggested; ☎360/683-8110, ⓦwww.sequimmuseum.org), whose collection encompasses an assortment of regional antiques, early automobiles and buggies, and even the bones of an Ice Age mastodon.

Sequim's **visitor center**, on the east edge of town at 1192 E Washington Ave (☎360/683-6197, ⓦwww.visitsun.com), has free local maps and a list of all the available accommodation. Monday through Saturday, Jefferson Transit (route #8; $1.25; ☎360/385-4777, ⓦwww.jeffersontransit.com) runs several **buses** daily from Port Townsend to Sequim, and Clallam Transit ($1.25; ☎360/452-4511 or 1-800/858-3747, ⓦwww.clallamtransit.com) links Sequim with Port Angeles. Sequim's main **bus stop** and transfer point is one block north of Washington at North 2nd Avenue and West Cedar Street.

Several adequate motels are strung along West Washington Avenue, though distinctive **accommodation** is much thinner on the ground. By far the best is the ☂ *Lost Mountain Lodge*, 303 Sunny View Drive (☎1-888/683-2431,

The **Juan de Fuca Strait**, linking the Pacific Ocean with Puget Sound, was once thought to be the fabled Northwest Passage on the basis of a chance meeting, famous among early-seventeenth-century mariners, between an English merchant and one **Apostolos Valerianos** in Venice in 1596. The Greek Valerianos claimed to be an exiled Spanish sea captain by the name of Juan de Fuca and, for good measure, added that he had sailed from the Pacific to the Arctic Ocean via the strait that bears his (assumed) name. The gullible explorers sought to follow in his nautical footsteps, and the name stuck to the strait. More recently it has also, curiously enough, been appended by geologists to the triangular crustal plate just to the west, which, thanks to continental drift, has been colliding with the North American Plate for many millions of years. The **Juan de Fuca Plate** is just a fragment of what it once was, but as it subducts into the earth's mantle is continues to build up the mountains in western Washington and western Oregon, leading to volcanic eruptions and the occasional earthquake as well – all in all, a rather impressive legacy for a minor historical charlatan.

Ⓦwww.lostmountainlodge.com), located in an expansive natural setting, which features a main lodge with three European-style suites (❼–❾ by season) with fireplaces, plush amenities, widescreen HDTVs and DVD players, with an onsite spa and waterfall. There also rentable vacation cottages (❾) with similar features and well-provisioned kitchens on the grounds. Alternately, the *Red Caboose Getaway*, 24 Old Coyote Way (☎360/683-7350, Ⓦwww.redcaboosegetaway .com; ❻), has four units built into actual train cabooses, which variously come with fridges, Net access, bunks, jetted baths and fireplaces. It's an overgrown kid's delight, though ironically, no children are allowed.

Sequim has the usual range of cheap all-American **restaurants**. Among the better choices, the *Old Mill Cafe*, 721 Carlsborg Rd (☎360/582-1583), is a reasonable mid-priced eatery with nice seafood and pasta dishes, and *El Cazador*, 531 W Washington St (☎360/683-4788), has better-than-average Mexican staples like burritos and enchiladas, as well as filling soups and salads. **Dungeness crabs**, the ultimate in crabmeat, are a local specialty: a good place to try them is *Three Crabs*, 11 Three Crabs Rd (☎360/683-4264), located on the coast about five miles north of Sequim. To get there, turn off Washington Avenue along Sequim Avenue and keep going – you'll see the signs.

Dungeness River Audubon Center and Dungeness National Wildlife Refuge

Two miles west of Sequim, at 2151 West Hendrickson Rd, the **Dungeness River Audubon Center** (March–Nov Tues–Sat 10am–4pm, Sun noon–4pm; Dec–Feb Tues–Fri 10am–4pm, Sat noon–4pm; free; ☎360/681-4076, Ⓦwww .dungenessrivercenter.org) is built around a decommissioned railroad bridge, part of **Railroad Bridge Park**, which features a pleasant hiking and cycling trail on and around its craggy iron span. The center itself is dedicated to profiling the animals and plants of the Dungeness River watershed, and nature enthusiasts will want to check out its periodic lectures, guided walks, workshops, and other activities ($10–15). Among the local residents for birdwatchers to gape at are woodpeckers, swans, pelicans, loons, and kingfishers.

The triangular chunk of farmland north of Sequim ends with **Dungeness Spit**, a long and slender sandbar that curves out into the Juan de Fuca Strait for almost six miles. On its exposed northern edge, the surf-pounded stretch is littered with rocks and weirdly shaped driftwood, but its sheltered side – where the attached Graveyard Spit cuts back toward the shore, providing even more protection – is entirely different. Here waterfowl rest and feed among the rich tidal flats during winter, and shorebirds – typically the likes of murres, oystercatchers, and shovelers – arrive by the thousands during spring and fall migrations, with fewer numbers of threatened or endangered species such as snowy plovers, marbeled murrelets, and bald eagles. The area is now protected as the **Dungeness National Wildlife Refuge** (daily dawn–dusk; $3; Ⓦwww .dungeness.com/refuge). Although sections are not open to the public, a lovely hiking trail leads from the parking lot at the base of Dungeness Spit through a patch of coastal forest to a bluff, and then out along the beach to the squat historic **lighthouse** built in 1857 – a round-trip of ten miles. Although the hike isn't difficult – you can easily complete it in a half-day – be sure to take enough drinking water.

There are several ways to reach the refuge, but the most straightforward is to head west out of Sequim along US-101 and then, four miles from the town center, take the signposted right turn along Kitchen Dick Lane. From the turn, follow the signs for the five-mile drive to the parking lot. Incidentally, don't get confused by the separate Dungeness Recreation Area, which you drive through as you near your destination. (See the lighthouse website, Ⓦwww.newdungenesslighthouse.com, for the most complete directions.)

Port Angeles

Founded by the Spanish in 1791, and named Puerto de Nuestra Señora de los Angeles (Port of Our Lady of the Angels) until postal clerks insisted that one Los Angeles on the West Coast was enough, **PORT ANGELES**, seventeen miles west of Sequim, is the peninsula's main town and the most popular point of entry for those heading for Olympic National Park. Although new small businesses have taken root in recent years – from quaint boutiques to trinket shops – the place is still mostly a working town; its main strip of motels and commercial buildings – on Front and First streets – is rather drab. Still, the surrounding scenery and ferry connections with Victoria, BC, make this a useful base for outdoor explorations.

Arrival and information

Port Angeles has the peninsula's best transportation connections. The **bus** depot is beside the waterfront at W Front and Oak streets, and from there it's only a couple of minutes' walk to the main **ferry** terminal. Olympic Bus Lines (Ⓣ360/417-0700, Ⓦwww.olympicbuslines.com) offers daily trips to Amtrak and Greyhound stations in Seattle ($39) and to Sea-Tac Airport ($49), while Clallam Transit buses ($1.25; Ⓣ360/452-4511 or 1-800/858-3747, Ⓦwww .clallamtransit.com) go west from Port Angeles around the peninsula to Lake Crescent, Neah Bay, and Forks, and east to Sequim – from there connecting with Jefferson Transit ($1.25; Ⓣ360/385-4777, Ⓦwww.jeffersontransit.com) buses to Port Townsend.

Black Ball Transport (Ⓣ360/457-4491, Ⓦwww.cohoferry.com) **car ferries** arrive from – and shuttle over to –Victoria, British Columbia (March–Dec two to four ferries daily; 1 hr 45min trip; one-way fares $11.50 walk-on, $44 per car and driver), but note that peak-season delays are common for those taking a vehicle and reservations are not accepted. Arriving at a neighboring pier at the foot of Lincoln Street, the **passenger ferries** of Victoria Express (Ⓣ360/452-8088 or 1-800/633-1589, Ⓦwww.victoriaexpress.com) operate a faster service (2–3 daily) for $25 round-trip. Finally, local **car rental** firms offer reasonable rates for one- and two-day rentals. Budget, 111 E Front St (℡ 360/452-4774 or 1-800/345-8038), is as competitive as any.

The town's **visitor center**, right by the main ferry terminal at 121 E Railroad Ave (summer daily 8am–6pm; rest of year Mon–Fri 10am–4pm; ℡ 360/452-2363, Ⓦ www.portangeles.org), has information on the entire peninsula and can put you in touch with local river-rafting and sea-kayaking operators. Port Angeles also houses the **Olympic National Park Visitor Center**, 600 E Park Ave (April–Oct daily 9am–4pm; summer closes 6pm; ℡ 360/452-0330 or 565-3100, Ⓦ www.nps.gov/olym), an excellent source for the maps and information you'll need if you're planning to do any hiking. Next door, the **Wilderness Information Center**, 3002 Mount Angeles Rd (hours vary by season; ℡ 360/565-3100), specializes in backcountry hiking and camping and can answer questions about reservations, permits, and trail conditions.

The Town

The **town** harbor has its own gritty beauty: sheltered by the long arm of the Ediz Hook sand spit, mammoth freighters are backdropped by mountains, and out in the bay cormorants hover over fishing boats. For a better look, there's an enticing 6.5-mile **Waterfront Trail** that begins at the Coast Guard station's entry gate and makes a scenic circuit for biking, walking, and jogging.

You can also spend a few minutes wandering the town's compact downtown core, just behind the waterfront between Oak and Chase streets. Here, some 24 pieces of quirky outdoor sculpture pepper the sidewalks, including a craggy iron seahorse and oddball combination weathervane and wind chime, among other curiosities. To find out more, drop by the Downtown Association, 208 Laurel St (℡ 360/457-9614, Ⓦ www.portangelesdowntown.com), for a free walking-tour guide, or get a guided tour on the second Saturday of the month at 11am. There's also a smattering of estimable brick buildings here, highlighted by the stately Federal-style pile of the **Clallam County Courthouse**, 223 E 4th St at Lincoln (Mon–Fri 9am–4pm; ℡ 360/417-2279), a little slice of the East Coast dropped into the Pacific Northwest. A few blocks north, the **Feiro Marine Life Center**, 315 N Lincoln St (June–Sept Tues–Sun 10am–5pm; Oct–May Sat & Sun noon–4pm; $3; ℡ 360/417-6254, Ⓦ www.olypen.com /feirolab), has the usual marine-biology exhibits and a "touch tank" enabling you to take a poke at tide-pool creatures, but more compelling is the **Port Angeles Fine Arts Center**, 1203 E Lauridsen Blvd (Mar–Nov Thurs–Sun 11am–5pm, Dec–Feb Thurs–Sun 10am–4pm; free; ℡ 360/417-4590, Ⓦ www .portangelesartscenter.com), a cut above the typical provincial art gallery, with a good array of regional, often abstract art on display in painting, sculpture, multimedia, and other forms. The center is best for its adjacent **Webster's Woods Art Park**, where, amid a five-acre outdoor setting, some eighty sculptures are arrayed on the grounds, hiding in the trees and in the foliage, making for a nice blend of art and nature.

Port Angeles is a good place to get properly equipped: Sound Bikes and Kayaks, 120 E Front St (℡ 360/457-1240), rents out **mountain bikes** and has half-day **kayak tours** (Mon–Sat 8.30am & 1pm; $70 per person) that lead you into the Strait of Juan de Fuca and around the area bays and inlets, as well as much more intensive trips up to Victoria ($100) or even Alaska ($2200). For **hiking** and climbing, if you want to go charging up Mount Olympus, outfitters like Brown's camping, 112 W Front St (℡ 360/457-4150, Ⓦ www.brownsoutdoor.com), can fix you up with tents, snowshoes, poles, and portable stoves for reasonable rates.

Although it's preferable to stay inside the national park, Port Angeles has a number of inexpensive chain **motels** near its main drags, 1st Street and Front Street. The best of these is the *Best Western Olympic Lodge,* 140 Del Guzzi Dr (℡1-800/600-2993, Ⓦwww.portangeleshotelmotel.com; ❺), with a pool and spa, and rooms with Internet access, fridges, and microwaves. For more upscale accommodation, try ⚑ *Domaine Madeleine,* eight miles east of downtown at 146 Wildflower Lane (℡360/457-4174, Ⓦwww.domainemadeleine.com; ❼), an elegant B&B with a lovely five-acre garden and five art-themed rooms, which variously come with jetted tubs, fireplaces, and balconies; or *The 5 Seasuns,* 1006 S Lincoln St (℡360/452-8248, Ⓦwww.seasuns.com; ❺), which occupies a handsome 1920s villa, with extensive gardens, one carriage-house suite, and four guest rooms, some of which come with Jacuzzis and balconies. If you're staying inside the park at any of the sixteen excellent **campgrounds** ($10–18; ℡360/565-3130, Ⓦwww.nps.gov/olym), you'll need your own vehicle. Try **Heart o' the Hills**, six miles south of Port Angeles, along Hurricane Ridge Road (see p.400), or, farther west, **Elwah** and **Altaire** (closed in winter), which are equally good with access to the numerous hiking trails; these three campgrounds are all $12 per night.

For **eating**, *Michael's Divine Dining,* 117-B E 1st St (℡360/417-6929), is the best you're going to do in this area, a fine-dining spot that has paella, oysters, pasta, and especially steak for prices ranging from $15 to $30; almost as good, the mid-to-upscale *Bella Italia,* 118 E 1st St (℡360/457-5442), has prime seafood, pasta, pizza, and traditional Italian cuisine; while for something a little more basic, the *Olympic Bagel Company*, 802 E 1st St (℡360/452-9100), appeals for its range of tasty bagels, omelets, panini, burgers, and pizza.

Neah Bay and Cape Alava

West of Port Angeles, US-101 cuts inland to begin its circuitous journey round the flanks of Olympic National Park. This is the obvious route to follow, but it's also possible to take **Hwy 112** right along the coast, a seventy-mile drive that becomes increasingly solitary the farther you go. Eventually, the road passes the graveled turnoff that bumps down to Lake Ozette before clinging precariously to the cliffs as it approaches end-of-the-world **NEAH BAY**, the small village of the **Makah** tribe. At the northern corner of the Makah Reservation ($7 entry fee) is **Cape Flattery**, the continental US's northwesternmost point, a remote headland accessible by an unpaved road from Neah Bay. A half-mile hike from the road through the rain forest leads to the cape that once "flattered" Captain Cook with the hope of finding a harbor. Below the cape, the waves have worn caves into the sheer rock of the cliff face, while opposite, on **Tatoosh Island**, the Coast Guard runs a remote lighthouse (closed to public view).

In 1970, a mudslide at an old village site on **CAPE ALAVA**, several miles south of their present reservation, revealed part of the tribe's ancient settlement – buried, Pompeii-like, by a previous mudslide some five hundred years before and perfectly preserved. The first people to uncover the remains encountered bizarre scenes of instantaneous aging – green alder leaves, lying on the floor where they fell centuries ago, shriveled almost as soon as they were exposed, but more important were the archaeological finds: throughout eleven years of careful excavation, the **Ozette Dig** revealed thousands of artifacts, including harpoons, intricately carved seal clubs, watertight boxes made without metal, strangely designed bowls, and toys, all belonging to a period before trade began with Europeans. Rather than being carted off to the depths of a government museum, these artifacts have remained in Makah hands. A number are now

The Makah people

Like that of many tribes in the Western US, the **Makah**'s bitter history is typical: a seagoing people, they once lived by fishing, moving from camp to camp across the western part of the peninsula. Like most Native Americans, they were happy to trade with passing European ships, and even when the Spanish built a stockade here in 1792 (abandoned four months later) the relationship remained cordial and mutually beneficial. However, when whites began to settle in the 1840s, bringing smallpox with them, Makah social structures were decimated by an epidemic of savage proportions. Samuel Hancock, who had built a trading post at Neah Bay in 1850, recorded the tragedy: "The beach for a distance of eight miles was literally strewn with the dead bodies . . . still they continue to die in such numbers that I finally hauled them down the beach at low tide, so they would drift away." Other indignities were to follow with American territorial and state governments: treaties restricted their freedom of movement, white settlers were given vast chunks of their land, and they were forced to speak English at white-run schools, as missionaries set about changing their religion.

In more recent years, the Makah have become notable in the media as **whale hunters**. Tribe members have always been skilled at fishing for salmon, cod, and the like, but in the 1990s they sought and were granted permission to hunt gray whales, reviving a tradition suspended for seventy years due to the oceanic depletion of the creatures. Lawsuits and public debate ensued, pitting the tribe's right to preserve its traditional practices against environmentalists' desire to preserve cetacean life. Ironically, the tribal whalers were criticized for using a rifle in lieu of the traditional harpoon to hunt, though they only did so because the International Whaling Commission recommended rifles to limit the suffering of the hunted animal. At present, the tribe is bound by the US Marine Mammal Protection Act, which requires a waiver to be given for any future kills.

displayed at Neah Bay's **Makah Cultural and Research Center**, Hwy 112 at Bayview Ave (daily 10am–5pm; $5; ☎360/645-2711, ⓦwww.makah.com), a well-curated museum displaying marine dioramas, dugout cedar canoes, fishing gear, a life-size replica of a fifteenth-century longhouse, and poignant nineteenth-century photographs of the Makah people. The site of the ancient village was, however, reburied in 1981 to preserve it.

You can get to Neah Bay on Clallam Transit (see p.395), though there are few good options for **accommodation**, aside from a few drab motels. To find anything special you'll have to head seventeen miles east to **Sekiu**, a sportsfishing town, to reach *Van Riper's Resort*, 280 Front St (☎360/963-2334, ⓦwww.vanripersresort.com; ❸–❻), which has a range of simple motel rooms and campsites, and more elaborate lodge units and waterfront suites, along with beach access and boat rentals.

Olympic National Park

Magnificent **OLYMPIC NATIONAL PARK** (☎360/452-0330, ⓦwww.nps.gov/olym), consisting of the colossal Olympic Mountains in the heart of the peninsula plus a separate, fairly isolated sixty-mile strip of Pacific coast farther west, is one of Washington's prime wilderness destinations, with boundless opportunities for spectacular hiking and wildlife watching. Although the park is best known as the location of the only **temperate rain forests** in North America, the special conditions responsible for producing such zones prevail only at lower altitudes, and into its 1.5 million acres are crammed an extraordinarily diverse assortment of landscapes and climates. About sixty percent of the

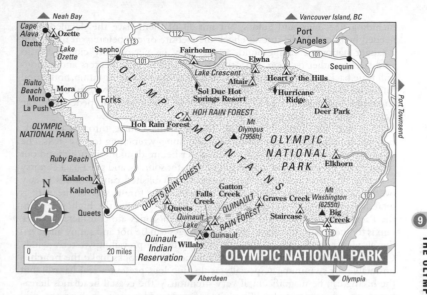

Neah Bay   Vancouver Island, BC

Cape Alava
Ozette
Ozette
Neah Bay
Lake Ozette   Sappho   Fairholme   Port Angeles
(113)   (112)
Rialto Beach   Mora   101   Lake Crescent   Elwha   101   Sequim
Mora   Altair   Heart o' the Hills
La Push   (110)   Forks   Sol Duc Hot Springs Resort   Hurricane Ridge
HOH RAIN FOREST   Deer Park
Hoh Rain Forest   Mt Olympus (7956ft)
OLYMPIC NATIONAL PARK   OLYMPIC
101   NATIONAL
Ruby Beach   PARK   Elkhorn

N   Kalaloch
Kalaloch   QUEETS RAIN FOREST   Gatton Creek   Mt Washington (6255ft)
Falls Creek   Graves Creek   101
Queets   Queets   QUINAULT   Big Creek
Quinault Lake   RAIN FOREST   Staircase
Quinault   Quinault   (119)
Quinault Indian Reservation   Willaby

0   20 miles   OLYMPIC NATIONAL PARK

Aberdeen   Olympia

park – the areas between 2000ft and 4000ft – is **montane forest**, dominated by Pacific silver fir and Douglas fir. At higher elevations, these trees give way to a **subalpine forest** of mountain hemlock, Alaska cedar, and fir, the forest broken up by lush meadows. Higher up still, the mountain slopes and summits constitute a forbidding **alpine zone** where windborne ice crystals can feel like flying shards of glass, and hardy mosses and lichens are nearly the only vegetation. Here, the hiking trails are free of snow only for about two months a year (late June–Aug). The **coast** is different again: the wild and lonely Pacific beaches that stretch down the peninsula's west side are studded with black rocks that point dramatically out of a gray sea, inhabited mostly by loons, grebes, puffins, and cormorants – and federally protected as the **Flattery Rocks National Wildlife Refuge**.

No roads cross the central segment of the park from one side to the other, but many run into it from separate directions, and only parts of the coastal strip are accessible by road. The text that follows reflects the most logical itinerary, working **counterclockwise on US-101** around the park and making forays into different sections from the access points along the way. As noted, some parts of the park can be reached only on gravel-topped roads that may not be manageable in an ordinary vehicle, particularly in wet or foggy weather. If you're planning to do a lot of backcountry driving, equip yourself with a four-wheel-drive vehicle and carry the necessary equipment in case of emergency (see "Basics," p.37).

Park practicalities

Before heading into the park, load up on information at the **Olympic National Park Visitor Center** and the **Wilderness Information Center**, both back in Port Angeles. There are other, smaller NPS visitor centers at **Hurricane Ridge** and **Hoh Rain Forest**, supplemented by a string of seasonal **ranger stations** – at Lake Crescent, Ozette, Mora, Kalaloch, Lake Quinault, and elsewhere – as well as the occasional US Forest Service station in the adjoining Olympic National Forest. Most have a wealth of literature, including free maps and guides, but not all of them have the detailed maps needed by hikers. Make sure to check the website or call before you turn up at a ranger station or campground, as sites may be periodically closed due to landslides, weather damage, and other hazards. Most NPS centers and stations will issue backcountry permits ($5 to register, $2 per person to camp, both good for fourteen days), but don't assume this to be the case, and always phone ahead. **Entrance** to the park costs $15 per vehicle, $5 for cyclists and pedestrians; the ticket is valid for seven consecutive days.

More than six hundred miles of **hiking trails** course through the park, ranging from the gentlest of Sunday strolls to lung-wrenching torture treks. The usual backcountry rules apply: treat the water before drinking it, store food out of the reach of bears, avoid defecating near water sources, and get a backcountry permit if you're venturing beyond the park's established campgrounds to stay overnight. Naturally, the weather on the west (rain forest) side of the park is incredibly wet – the average annual precipitation is 140in, the highest level in the Pacific Northwest – and though the eastern slopes are considerably drier, rain is frequent here, too. That said, summer days can be hot and sunny, and even the heaviest rain clouds are often swept away by the prevailing westerly winds. On the coast, strong currents, cold water, and hidden rocks make the **beaches** unsuitable for swimming (especially as floating logs present a real hazard), but the hiking can be magnificent, if very strenuous – the coastal headlands hereabouts are often extremely difficult to negotiate. Also, you do hear the odd horror story about hikers cut off by the tide, so carry a tide table, printed in the *Peninsula Daily News* (Ⓦ www.peninsuladailynews.com), or copy down such times at a ranger station or visitor center, and err on the side of caution. Lastly, wherever you go, don't forget the insect repellent.

The one-horse communities dotting the park's perimeter offer **motel** accommodation, but generally speaking, you're better off staying inside the park. Here you can either **camp** – there are sixteen established campgrounds ($10–18), ten open all year and operating on a first-come, first-served basis, and around ninety backcountry sites ($2) – or stay in one of the **lodges** (④–⑦), among which there are three of note: at Lake Crescent, Lake Quinault, and Kaloch. The *Sol Duc Hot Springs Resort* (see opposite), deep within the park, is another excellent choice. At all four establishments, book your room well in advance.

The park is best accessed by car, but Clallam Transit of Port Angeles (see p.395) does provide a reasonably frequent weekday **bus** service to *Lake Crescent Lodge* and Forks, where you can change for La Push.

Hurricane Ridge and the Olympic Mountains

On the southern edge of Port Angeles, the Olympic National Park Visitor Center (see p.399) is the starting point for the seventeen-mile haul up to **Hurricane Ridge**, passing (after about five miles) the **Heart o' the Hills** campground. It's a formidable drive, the road wrapping itself around cliffs and precipices until the piercing peaks and glistening glaciers of the **Olympic Mountains** spread out before you, a huge, thick band of snowcapped peaks with mighty Mount Olympus the tallest of all at nearly eight thousand feet. **Hiking trails** lead off to more isolated spots, through meadows filled with wildflowers in early summer.

The most popular trek is the **Hurricane Hill Trail**, a three-mile round-trip to the top of the eponymous hill, where there are great views out across the Juan de Fuca Strait. A longer alternative is the strenuous eight-mile (one-way) hike west, over the mountains through classic alpine and subalpine scenery. Both trails start at the Hurricane Ridge visitor center. East from Hurricane Ridge, a

Extraordinary as it may seem in cool Washington, climatic factors in the river valleys on the western side of the Olympic Peninsula produce an environment akin to a jungle. Such **temperate rain forests** are extremely rare – the only others are located in Patagonia and New Zealand. Here an average annual rainfall of 140in, mixing with river water running down from the mountains, creates conditions wet enough to produce a density of foliage normally associated with much warmer climes. Sitka spruce and maple flourish, all but overwhelmed by the thick, trailing tendrils of club mosses and lichens, epiphytes whose roots gather nourishment from the drizzly air. On the ground, some three hundred species of plants jostle for space to grow, crowding the ground with ferns, mushrooms, and wood sorrel oozing out of the dense, moist soil. The rain forests intermingle with the montane forests of western hemlock and Douglas fir, among which are the park's largest trees – in fact the world's biggest Douglas fir stretches skyward in the Queets Valley.

Several rain-forest areas can be visited, notably those in the valleys of the Hoh and Quinault rivers. The only way to get through the rain forest is on the specially cleared, intermittently paved **trails**, though these tend to get slippery as moss grows back again – wear boots or shoes that grip well. You'll need a **vehicle** to reach any of the trailheads, but there are campgrounds in both valleys and lodging beside Quinault Lake.

difficult and steep nine-mile dirt road heads to **Obstruction Peak**, noted for its views of Mount Olympus, several trails venture from the end of the road into the valley beyond, with one leading to the campground at **Deer Park**.

Lake Crescent and the Sol Duc River Valley

West of Port Angeles, US-101 slips through low-lying forest on its fifteen-mile journey to glacier-cut **Lake Crescent**, a handsome fishing lake known throughout the region for its fine Beardslee trout. Just off the highway, beside the lake's southern shore, the 1930s *Lake Crescent Lodge* (May to mid-Oct; ☎360/928-3211, ⓦwww.lakecrescentlodge.com) occupies a beautiful, densely wooded headland, offering simple rooms (❸–❹ by season), more spacious rooms with lake and mountain views (❺–❻), and elegant cottages with fireplaces and other amenities (❼–❽). Nearby, the one-mile **Marymere Falls Trail** leads through old-growth forest to a 90ft waterfall, and continues up the forested mountain slope, as the two-mile Mount Storm King Trail, to Happy Lake Ridge, where there are magnificent views back over the lake. If you're staying at the lodge, they're only too pleased to provide further hiking (and boating) suggestions.

Just beyond the western tip of Lake Crescent, a paved turnoff branches south off US-101 to thread up through the densely forested **Sol Duc River Valley**, a fascinating part of the transitional zone between the rain forests to the west and the drier lowland forest to the east. After twelve miles the road reaches the 🍴 *Sol Duc Hot Springs Resort* (late March to Oct; ☎360/327-3583, ⓦwww .visitsolduc.com; ❻), whose 26 basic cabins come with spartan but adequate amenities, though the six pricier ones have kitchens for just $20–30 more. There's also a three-bedroom suite with kitchen and outdoor deck. The restaurant, **The Springs**, is outstanding, serving fine Northwest Cuisine, and splendid hiking trails nudge into the surrounding mountains. Also, bathing in the resort's **hot springs** (late-March to Oct Fri–Sun 9am–7pm; summer daily 9am–9pm) is nicely relaxing, with the mineral water bubbling out of the earth to be channeled into three outside pools – from 100 to 108°F (38 to 42°C).

Overnight guests can use the pools for free, but visitors – including those using the resort's **RV campground** ($22) – have to pay $11.

From the end of the road, a couple of miles beyond the resort, you can hike further along the river to **Sol Duc Falls**, from where a steep path heads south along Canyon Creek into the mountains to the **Seven Lakes Basin**. More ambitious souls can hike across the Bogachiel Peak, past Hoh Lake and down into the Hoh River Valley – the site of one of the most visited rain forest areas (see opposite).

Forks

Back on US-101, it's about fourteen miles west from the Sol Duc turnoff to Hwy 113, which cuts off north for the lengthy journey to Neah Bay (see p.397), and another fourteen miles to the small blue-collar burg of **FORKS**, located between the main mountainous section and the coastal portion of Olympic National Park. Despite half-hearted attempts to catch the peninsula's tourist trade, Forks remains a timber town, and it's been hit hard by the decline of the industry. Nonetheless, heavy trucks still rumble through, unloading logs at local sawmills and hauling sawn lumber away to be shipped out of Port Angeles or Grays Harbor. It is decidedly not visitor friendly, but it can act as a sort of base if you're focusing your travel on this side of the park.

If you're sufficiently inspired by the timber trade, the history of logging is on vivid display at the **Forks Timber Museum**, about a mile south of town on US-101 (mid-April to Oct daily 10am–4pm; donation). Various exhibits depict life in the lumber camps of the 1920s and 1930s, when men were based in the forest, sleeping in bunkhouses and hitting the towns for only a few days each month. Cheaply built roads between towns and timber ended the camps after World War II, and in recent years mechanized devices (some on display) have made logging less hazardous, though it remains a dangerous occupation.

For an up-close view of the Northwest lumber scene, or if you have an interest in the town's world-class river fishing, drop by the Forks **visitor center** at 1411 S Forks Ave (℡360/374-2531 or 1-800/44-FORKS, ⓦwww.forkswa .com). Here you can inquire about seasonal logging tours (May–Sept Mon, Wed & Fri 9am; 3hr; free; reserve at ℡1-800/443-6757), in which an old-time timberman (or, very occasionally, timberwoman) leads you on a jaunt through the cutting and milling sites in the region, with lots of talk of timber lore and history, though scant regard for anyone piping up about environmental concerns. There's also a **ranger station** administered by the US Forest Service in town, 427 Tillicum Lane (℡360/374-6522, ⓦwww.fs.fed.us/r6/olympic), where you can get the usual maps and brochures as well as learn the status of trails and other conditions in this part of the national park.

Decent **accommodation** is available at *Miller Tree Inn*, 654 E Division St (℡360/374-6806, ⓦwww.millertreeinn.com; ❺–❼), with Victorian-style suites and pleasant guest rooms, and at *Olympic Suites*, 800 Olympic Dr (℡360/374-5400 or 1-800/262-3433, ⓦwww.olympicsuitesinn.com; ❸), with inexpensive one- and two-bedroom suites that have balconies and/or decks, as well as fridges and microwaves, in rather basically designed units. Alternatively, the *Manitou Lodge*, 813 Kilmer Rd (℡360/374-6295, ⓦwww .manitoulodge.com; ❺–❻ by season), offers seven B&B rooms with colorful quilts and old-fashioned decor, as well as summer-only cabins with minimal amenities (❸). Clallam Transit (see p.395) runs **buses** from Port Angeles to Forks, with connections on to the coast at La Push. Forks is hardly prime turf for **eating**, but the *Forks Coffee Shop*, 241 Forks Ave (℡360/374-6769), does serve decent all-American burgers and sandwiches for lunch, and more expensive steaks and seafood for dinner, while good old-fashioned *Sully's Drive-In*, 220 N Forks Ave (T 360/374-5075), whips up burgers, pizza, and fountain favorites like sundaes and banana splits.

The Pacific coastline

A couple of miles north of Forks, Hwy 110 cuts west off US-101 for the half-hour drive west to the park's **coastline**. About eight miles along the turnoff the road splits into two branches – one above, the other below the Quillayute River: the southern branch meanders round to the down-at-heel village of **La Push**, on the small Quillayute Indian Reservation, while the northern fork continues on into the national park's coastal strip at **Mora**, site of an attractive **campground** ($12) sitting amid old-growth forest, and a ranger station (T 360/374-5460). Close by, a mile or two farther down the road, lies **Rialto Beach**, a driftwood-cluttered strand from where it's possible to hike north along the shoreline, passing beneath the wooded bluffs to the sound of the booming surf. Most visitors are content with a manageable hike along the coast, but others opt for the longer, extremely arduous twenty-mile trek north to **Ozette**, where the seasonal ranger station (T 360/963-2725) and all-year **campground** ($12) are a little inland beside Lake Ozette. This longer hike takes three to four days, and you should arrange transportation at both ends; as always, take good care not to get cut off by the tide and be prepared for strenuous climbs over steep coastal headlands. A comparatively easy 3.3-mile trail – part of the Indian Village Nature Trail – runs from Ozette Ranger Station to the coast at Cape Alava, the site of the **Ozette Dig**, a prehistoric Makah village revealed (and subsequently reburied) after a 1970 mudslide (see p.397).

South of Forks beyond the Hoh turnoff (see below), US-101 dips down to the park's wild **southern beaches**, where black rocks jut out of the tumultuous sea, and the strong undertow, floating tree trunks, and dramatic tides make the waters striking to watch, if rather unsuitable for swimming. The hiking can be magnificent, though, and a series of short, appealing trails head down to and along the seashore – **Ruby Beach**, named for its red-and-black-pebbled sand, is the unmistakable highlight. Near the end of the park's coastal stretch, **Kalaloch** has a few **campgrounds** ($14–18; reserve at T 1-800/365-CAMP, W reservations.nps.gov), while the impressive *Kalaloch Lodge* (T 360/962-2271, W visitkalaloch.com) has basic lodge rooms and suites (⑥–⑦ by season) and more upscale cabins (⑥–⑧), variously featuring kitchenettes, fireplaces, and microwaves, as well as a good onsite restaurant. The **ranger station** here also provides information and suggestions for hiking trips (T 360/962-2283).

The Hoh and Queets rain forests

South of Forks, US-101 threads through logging country to pass, after about fourteen miles, the paved turnoff that leads deep into the **Hoh Rain Forest**. This is the most popular of the Olympic rain forests, principally because of the excellent **visitor center**, located nineteen miles from US-101 (9am–4pm: June–Sept daily; rest of year Fri–Sun only; T 360/374-6925), where you can examine various displays on the unusual habitat and pick up all sorts of explanatory pamphlets. Afterward, explore the rain forest along two short trails, the three-quarter-mile **Hall of Mosses Trail** or the slightly longer **Spruce Trail**, which reaches the Hoh River on a circuit through the forest. More energetic hikers can follow the 36-mile round-trip **Hoh River Trail** right up to the base of Mount Olympus; climbing the ice-covered peak is a major undertaking, so even if you just want to camp out along the route, be sure to check in with the rangers and get a backcountry permit. There's also a ninety-site, year-round **campground** ($12) next to the visitor center, but keep in mind that cougars and other beasts are very much present in the park, and in winter Roosevelt elk from higher elevations gather here.

Farther to the southwest, the next rain forest over is accessible only via US-101 south of the park's southern beaches (see above). Here, just beyond Kalaloch, the highway loops awkwardly inland to skirt the sizable **Quinault Indian Reservation**, an infertile chunk of wilderness wedged against the shoreline. It's home to several Salish-speaking tribes who were stuck here in the 1850s during the aggressive treaty-making period that followed Washington's incorporation as a US territory. The highway runs along the northern edge of the reservation, passing, after about ten miles, the fourteen-mile-long dirt road which heads inland to the **Queets Rain Forest**, the least visited of the three main rain forest areas but worthwhile for its rustic, accessible trails, which take you through a rare coniferous rain forest populated by the likes of western hemlock and cedar trees. It's also the site of the world's **largest Douglas fir** – 220ft tall and 45ft around. Note that in 2006, parts of the Queets Rain Forest (including the campground) were closed and access restricted due to mudslides; contact the main visitor center for updates (☏360/452-0330, ⓦwww.nps.gov/olym).

Quinault Lake and rain forest

Farther inland from the turnoff to the Queets Rain Forest, US-101 reaches, in short succession, the two side roads that lead the couple of miles off the highway to **Quinault Lake**, whose dark blue waters are surrounded by the deep greens of the **Quinault Rain Forest**, the most accessible and most beautiful of all the peninsula's rain forests. The lake was already a popular resort area when Teddy Roosevelt visited in the 1900s and proclaimed it part of an expanded Olympic National Park: you only have to glimpse the lake and its idyllic setting to see why Roosevelt was so impressed.

Of the two **access roads** leading off US-101, one travels the length of the lake's north shore, the other the south, but they don't connect until you're well past the lake and farther up the river valley – a thirty-mile loop. Dense overgrowth crimps the narrow road as it enters the deeper recesses of the forest, but it perseveres (as a rough gravel track), and the loop is negotiable by vehicle – though you should check conditions before you set off: floods have on occasion wrecked the more remote portions of the road.

A variety of **hiking trails** lead off from the road; the longer and more strenuous is through the rain forest of the **Quinault River Valley** and on up to the alpine meadows and glaciated peaks at the center of the national park. Others serve as easy introductions to the rain forest: the half-mile **Maple Glade Trail** is one of the best short hikes, clambering along a small stream through signature rain-forest vegetation, while the four-mile **Quinault Loop Trail** snakes through a wonderful old-growth forest dominated by colossal Douglas firs. Backcountry permits, hiking maps, weather forecasts, details of all the trails, and information on the five **campgrounds** ($12–18) dotted around the lakeshore are available at the US Forest Service **ranger station** at 353 S Shore Rd (late June to mid-Sept Thurs–Mon 9am–4.30pm; ☏360/288-2525, ⓦwww .fs.fed.us/r6/olympic). A few yards away, occupying a fine lakeshore location, the high timber gables and stone chimneys of *Lake Quinault Lodge* (☏360/288-2900 or 1-800/562-6672, ⓦwww.visitlakequinault.com; ❹–❼ by season) date from the 1920s, though the interior has been revamped in a comfortable modern style. It's a justifiably popular spot, so reservations are essential. There's less expensive accommodation in the vicinity, too – try the *Lochaerie Resort*, 638

North Shore Rd (☎360/288-2215, ⓦwww.lochaerie.com; ❺), which has five comfortable cabins also dating from the 1930s.

Southwest Washington

Compared to the glories of Seattle, Puget Sound, and the Olympic Peninsula, **southwest Washington**'s offerings are rather thin. Although the southern stretch of I-5 is almost unavoidable if you're heading down to Portland, you're unlikely to find much here that can't be found in bigger, glossier, and more scenic form elsewhere in western Washington or northwestern Oregon. That said, there are a number of scattered points of interest, and a handful of decent choices for accommodation. And clearly, if you want to get a true sense of the region and appreciate the region's nineteenth-century commercial and pioneer background, you can't miss historic spots like **Grays Harbor**, **Cape Disappointment**, and **Fort Vancouver**. Nonetheless, with almost nothing of interest between **Vancouver**, at the state's southern edge, and **Centralia**, midway between Portland and Seattle, it's perhaps not surprising that transit links to the region – except of course along the I-5 corridor, an essential route for Amtrak **trains** and Greyhound **buses** – are spotty at best.

The southern Pacific coast

As you leave the Olympic Peninsula's western half for the state's **southern Pacific coast**, the scenery gradually grows tamer and less desolate and the national forests are replaced by privately owned timberland. The coastline cuts deeply into the mainland at two points: the bay of **Grays Harbor**, at the apex of which lie the twin industrial cities of Hoquiam and **Aberdeen**, and muddy **Willapa Bay**, dotted with oyster beds and wildlife sanctuaries. The sand spit sheltering Willapa Bay – **Long Beach Peninsula** – was formed from sediment

△ Cape Disappointment

carried here by the ocean from the churning mouth of the Columbia River near its base. The beach is very long, but the straggling resorts behind it are bland, modern places without much appeal. The lower coast's saving grace is right at its southern tip just beyond tiny **Ilwaco**, where the ruggedly handsome headland that pokes out into the mouth of the Columbia River is protected as **Cape Disappointment State Park** – and here you can camp or stay in the old lighthouse-keeper's quarters.

Grays Harbor and Aberdeen

South of Olympic National Park's Quinault Rain Forest (see p.404), US-101 cuts across logging country, whizzing through the forested hills until it hits gritty Hoquiam, beside the bay of **GRAYS HARBOR**, which takes a big triangular bite out of the coastline. The loggers who settled here in the mid-nineteenth century originally meant to stay only until the dense forest within easy reach of the waterfront had been cut down and the area was "logged out." But railways soon made it possible to transport lumber from deeper in the forest, and a combination of this and the plentiful fishing – canneries soon joined the sawmills along the waterfront – led to the development of Hoquiam and its larger neighbor **ABERDEEN** – the (reviled) hometown of grunge icons and Nirvana bandmates Kurt Cobain and Krist Novoselic.

Now hit by a seemingly endless recession in both the fishing and forestry industries, these twin towns are not obvious places for a visit, though Aberdeen is making a plucky attempt at catching passing tourists with its **Grays Harbor Historical Seaport** (☎360/532-8611 or 1-800/200-2359, ⊛www .ladywashington.org). In these unpromising surroundings, this harbor reinvigoration project has painstakingly reconstructed the *Lady Washington*, the eighteenth-century brig of Captain Robert Gray, the American trader who discovered Grays Harbor. Built to conform both to original designs and modern Coast Guard safety regulations, the ship is now a floating museum with a crew dressed in period costume. A more recent arrival is the *Hawaiian Chieftain*, a reconstruction of a topsail ketch that used to sail off the West Coast in the 1790s. Both are open for guided tours ($8–10) or 3hr sailing trips ($35–50) that concentrate on ship history or involve pretend "battles" of the sort seen during the ships' heyday – call for schedules and reservations, as the ships sometimes sail to different ports for months at a time.

US-101 slices through Aberdeen's town center, which is located on the north bank of the Chehalis River as it flows into the bay. The historical seaport is just to the east across the Wishkah River, a tributary of the Chehalis – just follow the signs. In the unlikely event you want to **stay** in Aberdeen, the Grays Harbor **visitor center**, off US-101 at 506 Duffy St (☎360/532-1924, ⊛www .graysharbor.org), is on the strip connecting Hoquiam and Aberdeen and has a comprehensive list of local lodgings.

Willapa National Wildlife Refuge and Ilwaco

US-101 leads south out of Aberdeen over the hills to **Raymond**, a pocket-size lumber town where the highway turns west to skirt the flat and tedious shoreline of **Willapa Bay**. Too shallow to be used as a commercial port, the bay is much less developed than Grays Harbor, though its muddy depths support a profitable underworld of oysters – you'll spot the bivalve beds from the highway. Several parts of the bay have been incorporated into the 15,000-acre **Willapa National Wildlife Refuge**, whose various dunes, forests, marshes, and mudflats shelter some two hundred species of migrating shorebirds. The highlight is the marvellous 5600-acre preserve of **Long Island**, one of the last preserved slices of coastal old-growth forest in the region and home to bear, elk, otter, and flying squirrels, among other species. Though one of its sections – Leadbetter Point at the tip of Long Beach Peninsula – can be reached by car, most of the refuge is accessible only by boat, keeping the more casual tourist traffic away and leaving some ten miles of hiking trails relatively untrammelled. You can **camp** here at any of five designated sites (24 sites total), on a first-come, first-served basis, though you'll have to float your supplies over. Advice on what wildlife to see and where, and the most immediate vendors for boat travel, can be obtained from the refuge's **visitor center** (T 360/484-3482, W www.fws.gov/willapa), at 3888 US-101 across from Long Island, about 35 miles south of Raymond.

Named after a Chinook chief, the fishing port of **ILWACO**, ten miles southwest of Willapa Bay, achieved some notoriety at the start of the twentieth century when competition between fishermen with nets and those with traps broke into a series of street battles, the **gillnet wars**, fought with knives and rifles – and only finally resolved when fish traps were banned on the Columbia River in 1935. Nowadays, Ilwaco is an unassuming little place, where everyone knows the times of the tides and where to dig for clams. There's nothing much to see, though you could take a **sea-fishing trip** – there are several operators down along the harborfront – or drop by the **Ilwaco Heritage Museum**, 115 SE Lake St (Mon–Sat 10am–4pm, Sun 1–5pm; $5; T 360/642-3446, W www .ilwacoheritagemuseum.org), which has displays on Chinook culture, pioneer artifacts, and the myths and realities of the Lewis and Clark Expedition. From the town marina, you can take the eight-mile **Discovery Trail**, a nature path that winds westward through forest and over wetlands to the coast south of Long Beach – it's quite a slog, but worth it when you get to the ocean overlook and its fine, expansive views.

There are more interesting places to stay nearby – namely in Cape Disappointment and Fort Columbia state parks (see p.410) – but Ilwaco does have a reasonable supply of **accommodation**. The pick of the bunch is the ﹡ *Inn at Harbour Village*, 120 Williams Ave NE (T 360/642-7044 or 1-888/642-0087, W www.innatharbourvillage.com; ❻–❼ by season), whose nine small but comfortable rooms occupy the renovated parsonage and vestry of the Presbyterian church on a wooded rise just above the town. The *Shaman Motel*, 115 3rd St SW (T 360/642-3714 or 1-800/753-3750, W shamanmotel.com; ❹–❺), is a second, much cheaper choice, offering some units equipped with kitchenettes and fireplaces.

Long Beach Peninsula
Lined by 28 miles of uninterrupted beach, and less prone to fog than other parts of Washington's coast, the **Long Beach Peninsula**, separating the Pacific Ocean and Willapa Bay, has been a holiday destination since steamboats ferried vacationing Portlanders here in the 1890s. Today it's something of a low-rent resort area, offering chain motels and a smattering of tourists, who come to browse the kite shops, gnaw on saltwater taffy, and pick up kitschy souvenirs. One of the peninsula's few attractions, the **Pacific Coast Cranberry Museum**, 2907 Pioneer Rd in the town of Long Beach (April–Dec 10am–5pm; T 360/642-5553, W www.cranberrymuseum.com), gives you the opportunity to wander through a cranberry bog and pick up berry-flavored treats; peak growing and harvesting season is the end of summer and early autumn.

Willapa Bay is widely known as one of the nation's – and the world's – top producers of **oysters**, bringing in some forty million pounds or so per year. In the old days, almost all of the bivalves were shucked, since shellfish-eaters didn't

The Chinook

Although there's not much evidence of them today, the area around the mouth of the **Columbia River** was once populated by the **Chinook** people. Their "Chinook jargon," a mix of their own language with French and English, was widely used for trading and, later, for treaty-making. By all accounts, it was extremely easy to learn: Paul Kane, an Irish-Canadian explorer and painter who passed this way in the mid-1840s, wrote that it took only a few days before he could "converse with most of the chiefs with tolerable ease; their common salutation is *Clak-hoh-ah-yah*, originating . . . in their having heard in the early days of the fur trade . . . *Clark, how are you*?"

The Chinook also caught white nineteenth-century imaginations with their supposedly **flattened skulls**, as depicted in careful sketches brought back to a curious East by both Kane and explorers Lewis and Clark, who spent the winter of 1805–06 quartered at Fort Clatsop, on the south side of the river (see p.148). The skull-flattening was achieved by pressing a piece of bark firmly to a baby's (padded) forehead every time it went to bed for about a year, the end result being seen as a sign of noble distinction.

Although this practice died out by the twentieth century, and the Chinook had to deal with threats from white encroachment and exploitation, the tribe has survived on its ancestral lands and puts on festivals, craftwork displays, and other events several times a year around the southwest Washington region. To get a sense of tribal culture, check out ⓦ www.chinooknation.org, which provides information on the remaining Chinook's various festivities and details their history, lore, and legends, as well as offering a photographic glimpse of what people looked like with their skulls flattened.

want to get their hands dirty with prying out the creatures; these days, sales of whole oysters are on the rise, and they're definitely what you should sample if you want to indulge in the succulent, slurpy meat. The **Willapa Bay Interpretive Center**, at 273rd Place in the town of Nahcotta (June–Aug Fri–Sun; free; ⓣ 360/665-4547), is built around a replica of an old-fashioned oyster production facility and has the skinny on the rise of the shellfish industry. Better, though, is to drive up Hwy 103 to **Oysterville**, about sixteen miles north of Ilwaco and five miles from the peninsula's tip. Companies here made a killing in the 1860s and 1870s by shipping oysters to San Francisco and selling them to the big names of the gold rush, at up to $40 a plate. Then, in an all-too-familiar pattern, increasing demand fueled overharvesting; with the oysters soon decimated, the town slipped into a long decline. There are still growers here, but little more than a tiny **historic district** remains, with Victorian houses of shingles and scrollwork set behind trim picket fences. Once you've strolled around town, you can sample the local delicacy at the bayside **Oysterville Sea Farms** (ⓣ 360/665-6585, ⓦ www.oysterville.net), recognizable by its bayside piles of discarded shells, whose specialty is freshly packaged smoked oysters ($6.50 per unit). The other attractions at the north tip of the peninsula are the dunes and marshes of **Leadbetter Point**, which form one section of the Willapa National Wildlife Refuge (see p.406). Several vague footpaths meander over the point, but wet conditions soon flood them out and there are no set hiking trails. Before you set out, get advice from the refuge's headquarters.

If you want to **stay** on the peninsula, note that the town of Long Beach is the most central, though most of your choices will be of the roadside chain motel variety. There are a few exceptions, though: the *Lighthouse Oceanfront Resort*, 12417 Pacific Way, Long Beach (ⓦ 1-877/220-7555, ⓦ lighthouseresort.net), has an onsite pool, spa, and gym as well as a wide range of accommodation, from oceanfront town houses with kitchens, fireplaces, decks, and oceanside views (⑥) to more rustic 1950s motel-cottages with kitchens, fireplaces, and beach access (❹). Rates can vary dramatically by season. Also good is the *Boreas B&B*, 607 N Ocean Beach Blvd (☎360/642-8069, ⓦwww.boreasinn.com; ⑥), which has excellent breakfasts and five comfortable rooms and suites, along with a nineteenth-century beach house with slightly cheaper rates.

Cape Disappointment State Park

A few miles southwest of Ilwaco, a heavily forested promontory pokes out into the Columbia River, sheltering the town from the full force of the Pacific. Scenic, 2000-acre **Cape Disappointment State Park** (daily: summer 6.30am–9.30pm; rest of year 6.30am–4pm; ☎360/642-3078, ⓦwww.lewisandclarknationalpark.com) is one of several sites around the mouth of the river (including those in Oregon near Astoria) that has a significant legacy of exploration, encampment, and exhaustion by the explorers Meriwether Lewis and William Clark. The park covers the whole of the headland, based around fortifications constructed here in the 1860s. **Fort Canby** was one of a chain of military installations whose batteries guarded the Pacific Coast from the middle of the nineteenth century through both world wars. Little remains of the fort today – just a few weather-beaten gun emplacements – but there are two interesting lighthouses. The first – reached down a side road as you approach the park – is **North Head Lighthouse** (same hours as park; $1), built in 1898 in a magnificent spot high above Dead Man's Hollow, named after the unfortunate victims of an earlier shipwreck.

Doubling back, the main park road pushes on to the **Lewis and Clark Interpretive Center** (daily 10am–5pm; winter closes 4pm; $3), which has displays dealing with the hazards of navigating the Columbia River mouth, as well as murals, paintings, journal entries, and multimedia displays that outline the expedition's journey to the Pacific. From the center, a steep, three-quarter-mile trail leads down to the more southerly of the two beacons, **Cape Disappointment Lighthouse** (no public access), perched on **Cape Disappointment** itself, a short finger of land stuck at a right angle to the rest of the promontory. In operation for 150 years, the lighthouse is supposedly the oldest on the West Coast. The cape got its name when a British fur trader, John Meares, beached his ship on the dangerous sandbar at the river's entrance in 1788. In fact, Meares was lucky – more than two hundred ships were later wrecked on the sandbar, and although dredges, automated lights, and a pair of long jetties have now made the river mouth much safer, the Coast Guard still trains its sailors off the cape; you can sometimes see their small boats facing massive waves.

From the interpretive center there are a number of **trails** ultimately leading into thick groves of forest and over sand dunes, including one that links up with the Discovery Trail (see p.407) from Ilwaco to Long Beach. There's a large **campground** ($17–22) in the park between the interpretive center and North Head Lighthouse that has regular tent sites as well as cabins and yurts. Even better, two old North Head **lighthouse-keeper's houses** have been revamped to accommodate tourists, with three bedrooms, a living room, a kitchen, and a dining room in each (Nov to mid-May Mon–Thurs $130–185, Fri–Sun $200–280; mid-May to Oct $260–370; two-night minimum except Mon–Thurs in off-season; reservations at ☎1-888/226-7688). Although one house is a bit larger, they both hold a maximum of six people.

Fort Columbia State Park

Heading east from Ilwaco on US-101, it's eight miles to **Fort Columbia State Park** (daily: summer 6.30am–9.30pm; rest of year 8am–5pm; Ⓦwww.parks .wa.gov), which occupies a hilly, wooded headland that was purchased from the Chinook in 1867. The headland was developed as a military installation in the 1890s, acting as a second line of nautical defense behind Fort Canby (see above) and Fort Stevens (see p.149). Several gun emplacements dot the park: grim concrete affairs built largely underground with their seaward-facing sides flush to the land to mitigate the effects of incoming shells – which in any case they never encountered. Behind, just up the hill, are several rows of regulation army houses with wide verandas and neat columns. One of them, the former enlisted men's barracks, houses an **interpretive center** (June–Sept 10am–5pm; $3, includes museum) with several period rooms; the former commander's quarters, Columbia House, holds a modest **museum** (June–Sept 11am–4pm) with yet more of them. Fort Columbia has a few trails worth taking, including the **Scarborough Hill Trail**, a rugged mile-long jaunt up to the hill summit, and the 1.5-mile **Concomly Trail**, an easier route that leads you through the park's dense groves of coastal forest.

The park itself has a fine seashore setting, and you can stay here either in the former hospital, now **Scarborough House** (Nov to mid-May Mon–Thurs $200, Fri–Sun $295; mid-May to Oct $400), which accommodates up to twelve and is fully furnished with five bedrooms, or in the **Steward's House** (Nov to mid-May Mon–Thurs ❹, Fri–Sun ❻; mid-May to Oct ❼), which has two bedrooms with full amenities like a kitchen and antique-furnished living room. Linen for both is provided, and there's a minimum stay of two nights. Reservations are strongly recommended at ☎1-888/CAMPOUT.

From Fort Columbia, it's two miles to the huge, four-mile-long 1966 bridge that spans the Columbia River over to Oregon's Astoria (see p.141).

South on I-5: Centralia to Vancouver

The only other places of interest in southwest Washington are peppered along **I-5 south** from Olympia, from where it only takes about ninety minutes to cover the one hundred miles to Portland. The workaday lumber town of **CENTRALIA**, 23 miles from Olympia, is of passing interest for its old-fashioned architecture and assorted antique shops. It was also the site of one of the nastiest incidents in the history of Washington's Wobblies (see p.478). During the Armistice Day parade of 1919, several members of the American Legion attacked the town's union building (807 N Tower St) and, in the fight that followed, four Legionnaires were shot. Local Wobblies were promptly rounded up and thrown into jail, but vigilantes broke in that night to seize, mutilate, and then lynch one of their number, a certain Wesley Everest. To make sure the others took the point, the police laid the body out on the jail floor.

Beyond this bit of history, a few odd visitors stop here to drop in on the 🕺 **Olympic Club** (☎360/736-5164, Ⓦwww.mcmenamins.com; ❸), a restored hotel, restaurant, and brewpub that showcases nightly movies, quirky artwork, and flavorful microbrewed beer in Art Nouveau-style surroundings. The hotel once operated as a union stronghold, speakeasy (repeatedly raided by federal "revenuers"), and hangout for all kinds of unsavory characters, including gentlemen with names like Tacoma Iron Mike and One-Eyed Tony, some of whom are commemorated with pictures in the hotel's basic but tasteful rooms (with shared bath); bunks go for as little as $40 a night. The club has the advantage of being a mere block from the **Amtrak** station at

210 Railroad Ave, making it a convenient stopover on train journeys between Seattle and Portland.

A bit farther south on I-5, the most obvious detour is east to **Mount St Helens** (see p.439), where the scarred, volcanic landscape, witness to the massive eruption of 1980, constitutes one of the region's most remarkable attractions. Several turnoffs lead to the volcano, but the easiest (and busiest) is located about halfway between Olympia and Portland: coming from the north, turn down Hwy 505 near Toledo, or approaching from the south, take Hwy 504 at Castle Rock; Hwy 505 joins Hwy 504 about fifteen miles east of I-5.

Vancouver

At the southern edge of the state, Washington's **VANCOUVER**, much more modest than its Canadian counterpart, lies just across the Columbia River from Portland, Oregon. Dwarfed by its larger and more prosperous neighbor, Vancouver is a drab sort of place – half bedroom community, half small town. The only real sight worth seeing, **Fort Vancouver National Historic Site** (daily 9am–4pm; summer closes 5pm; $3 for seven-day pass; ☎360/816-6200, ⓦ www.nps.gov/fova), serves as a credible reconstruction of the Pacific Northwest's first substantial European settlement, located just east of I-5 (Exit 1C, Mill Plain Blvd). Dating from the 1820s, this stockaded outpost of the British-owned Hudson's Bay Company was for more than twenty years a remote but prosperous station dedicated to the fur trade. The British cited its early occupation as grounds for including present-day Washington in their empire, but as American colonists poured into the Willamette Valley, the British claim lost all weight. At last, when the 49th Parallel became the official border between the US and Canada, Fort Vancouver was left stranded in US territory. By 1860, the Hudson's Bay Company had moved out, and the fort and buildings disappeared, only to be mapped and rebuilt by archaeologists in the 1960s.

These days, rangers give interpretive tours of the site – five one-story log structures protected within a rectangular palisade – throughout the day; it certainly merits a look, as does nearby Officers' Row, elegant villas built for US Army personnel between 1850 and 1906. If you're here on Independence Day, try to drop in on the formidable display of **fireworks**, supposedly the biggest such spectacle in the Pacific Northwest, on the West Coast, or west of the Mississippi, depending on whom you ask. Whatever the case, it's a remarkably popular affair, with the crowds arriving as early as dawn to stake out the best seats.

⑩

The Washington Cascades

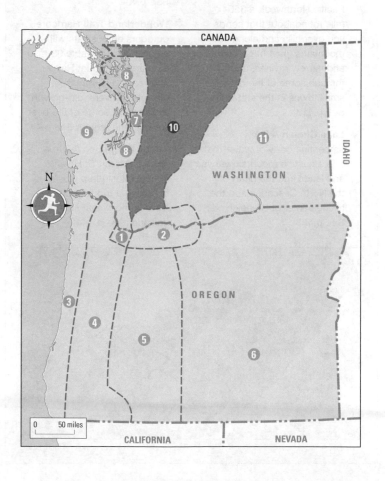

CHAPTER 10

Highlights

* **Mount Baker** Climb up and ski down this grand snowy peak offering pristine slopes about an hour's drive east of Bellingham. See p.417

* **The Cascade Loop** Perhaps the best driving circuit in the Pacific Northwest, a 350-mile roundabout that sends you over hills and alongside mountains, past huge dams and narrow ravines, and through some of the quirkiest small towns in the state. See p.418

* **Lake Chelan** A thin, serpentine body of water that offers pristine mountain views and leads into the heart of the North Cascades and the hiking center of Stehekin. See p.423

* **Snoqualmie Falls** A 270ft waterfall that flows from the heights of a solid-bedrock gorge, located near the opulent wooden Salish Lodge – both sights familiar from the cult TV show Twin Peaks. See p.432

* **Wonderland Trail** Hardcore outdoors enthusiasts will enjoy this memorable 93-mile loop around Mount Rainier, showcasing idyllic lakes, glacier-fed rivers, old-growth forests, and some of the best views in the region. See p.437

* **Windy Ridge** See the true force of Mount St Helens' 1980 explosion up close by taking a trip to the less-traveled northeast side of the volcano. See p.444

△ Ice climbing on Mount Baker

The Washington Cascades

S eparating the wet, forested regions of western Washington from the parched prairies and canyonlands of the east, the snowcapped and pine-covered **Washington Cascades** extend northeast-southwest across the state toward Oregon, where they are gashed by the grand Columbia River Gorge. Yet for all their outwardly serene beauty, the peaks conceal a colossal and dangerous geothermal power – as Mount St Helens proved when it exploded in 1980, annihilating wildlife over a massive area and covering the region with ash. Protected by a series of national parks and national forests stretching across the state, the Washington Cascades feature mile upon mile of dense wilderness, traversed by a skein of beautiful trails and ample opportunities for camping, fishing, skiing, and other activities.

Best accessed by state highways from the populous communities lining Puget Sound, the mountains sit along a rough axis stretching from Canada to California, part of a volcanic chain that's been uplifted over millions of years due to the subduction of the Juan de Fuca Plate offshore in the Pacific Ocean. From north to south, the first of the major peaks is **Mount Baker**, a short drive east from Bellingham along Highway 542 and a lovely destination often overshadowed by the state's other big mountains. Farther south, the **North Cascades** and the **Cascade Loop**, reached by several eastbound freeways from Mount Vernon to Seattle, are a remote but fascinating array of rugged peaks, glacial lakes, sheltered valleys, and small resort towns – the most agreeable of which are **Chelan** and **Leavenworth** – that eagerly await summer tourist traffic.

Another eastbound route, I-90, leads from Seattle past the incomparable spray of **Snoqualmie Falls** and over the mountains into dusty towns on the edge of eastern Washington before finally continuing south, via US-97, toward the Columbia Gorge (see p.117). South on I-5 from Seattle, several exits lead toward the two most prominent mountains in the entire Cascade chain – **Mount Rainier**, an imposing peak set in its own national park and readily accessible from Tacoma and Olympia, and the blasted terrain of **Mount St Helens**, a National Volcanic Monument whose dramatically scarred landscape is a potent reminder of its 1980 eruption. The last major peak, **Mount Adams**, on the same longitude as St Helens but forty miles farther east, is more remote and less visited but has its own charm for hikers and outdoors enthusiasts.

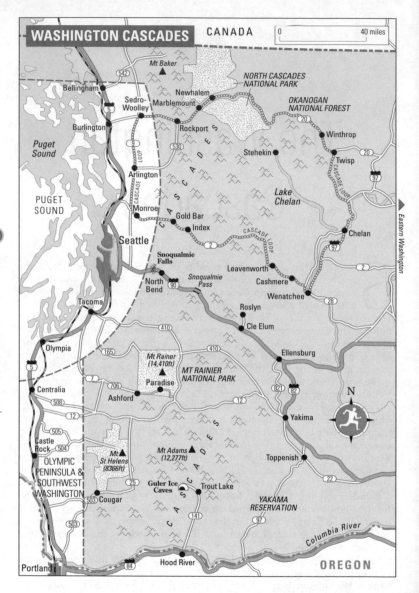

The **climate** here, as elsewhere in western Washington, is rainy or snowy for much of the year, with just a brief respite from late June to early September. Don't let this put you off, though: even seen through a haze of fine gray drizzle, the scenery is incredibly beautiful, and you should try to tackle at least a few hiking trails, which are well laid-out and come in manageably short varieties.

Getting around

Public transportation throughout the region is quite limited. Other than its route through the Columbia River Gorge, **Amtrak**'s sole passage through the Washington Cascades is from Everett to Wenatchee on its once-daily Empire Builder line. **Greyhound buses** (☎1-800/231-2222, ⓦwww.greyhound.com) run east from Seattle along I-90 to Ellensburg and then either continue on that highway to Spokane or take a southern turn on I-82 to Yakima and down to Oregon. From Seattle, Northwestern Trailways (☎1-800/366-3830, ⓦwww .northwesterntrailways.com) buses run across the mountains on US-2 to Leavenworth, Cashmere, and Wenatchee and on to Spokane. **Local buses** are uncommon, but the LINK network (☎1-800/851-LINK, ⓦwww.linktransit .com) connects some of the towns of the eastern foothills in the vicinity of Chelan, Leavenworth, and Wenatchee.

Mount Baker and around

With its seven-month ski season stretching from early November to mid-May, **Mount Baker**, sixty-odd miles east of Bellingham (see p.378), is one of Washington's premier resorts (daily lift tickets $40 on weekends, $32 midweek; ☎360/734-6771, ski reports on ☎360/671-0211, ⓦwww.mtbaker.us). Lifts and runs are dotted over several lower slopes in the shadow of the great mountain itself, and in 1999 the mountain set a world snowfall record for 95ft of precipitation recorded over the season. At 10,778 feet, Mount Baker is the highest peak for miles around and the Cascade volcano boasting the most acreage covered by **glaciers**, though like most peaks in the region its ice sheets are retreating, likely due in some measure to global warming. This volcanic behemoth, while not as regularly active as its neighbors to the south, does hiss great clouds of steam during periods of geothermal activity – the last significant time was in 1975. Not surprisingly, it has played a leading role in native folklore: the local Lummi saw it as a sort of Ararat, the one peak that survived the Great Flood to provide sanctuary for a Lummi "Noah" in his giant canoe. It was also here in 1947 that a US Air Force pilot saw the unidentified flying objects that he creatively christened "flying saucers."

The main approach road from Bellingham, Hwy 542, loops around the mountain's northern foothills, passing three US Forest Service campgrounds, which are among the dozens of mostly fee-based campsites in the mountain region ($12–18). Beyond this you pass the village of **Glacier** before making a final, nail-biting fling up through the ski area to **Artist Point**, where you can get an appropriately painterly and evocative view of Mount Baker and the rest of the region. From here, a stiff 1.5-mile trail leads up lava cliffs to flat-topped Table Mountain, with Baker soaring high above. There are lots of other trails, but this is the basic starter with several possible extensions, such as the difficult trek south along Ptarmigan Ridge to Coleman Pinnacle.

In Bellingham, information and hiking maps are available in the town's better bookshops. Thirty-four miles east of town on the Mount Baker Highway, you can get more data, as well as a required Northwest Forest Pass ($5), at the **Glacier Public Service Center** (mid-June to mid-Oct daily 9am–4pm; rest of year Sat & Sun 9am–3pm; ☎360/599-2714, ⓦwww.fs.fed.us/r6/mbs), located in tiny Glacier, about 25 miles from Mount Baker. **Ski equipment** can be rented at the resort ski shop and in Bellingham at – among several places – Fairhaven Bike and Mountain Sports, 1108 11th St (☎360/733-4433,

ⓦfairhavenbike.com), which has cross-country ski-rental packages starting at $25 per day or snowshoes at $14, and also rents out bikes for $20–40 per day.

The **American Alpine Institute**, in Bellingham at 1515 12th St (ⓣ360/671-1505, ⓦwww.mtnguide.com), offers a variety of hiking and climbing programs for Mount Baker and the North Cascades from May to October, covering everything from simple two-day treks in the hills to gut-wrenching two-week alpine ice climbs. Naturally, the cost varies widely depending on the number of days for your outing, level of training required, and the skills you need to learn; prices range from $95 to $1050, though costlier programs (in the $2000–2500 range) are given for training expedition leaders in the wilderness.

The Cascade Loop

When Hwy 20 opened up the rugged **North Cascades** in 1972, the towns of the eastern foothills got together and came up with the 350-mile **CASCADE LOOP** (information at ⓣ509/662-3888, ⓦwww.cascadeloop.com), which channels tourist traffic from the highway through several small villages before sending it south along US-97 and finally back west over US-2. As one of the state's scenic highlights, it's a magnificent trip, with long stretches of the road shadowed by the wet western forests and, at higher elevations, jagged, glacier-studded mountains. But unless you've three or four days to spare – maybe more – you won't be able to appreciate just how fascinating the scenery is, with its lonesome byways, quirky small towns, and off-the-beaten-path attractions. With less time, you're better off focusing on the pick of the scenery, which straddles Hwy 20 – try **camping** in the mountains or staying as near to the mountains as you can: **Marblemount**, on the west side of the range, is the handiest spot, though it only has a handful of inns and motels. If you're traveling during the summer, the **Mountain Loop Highway** is perhaps the best day-trip up from Seattle, a miniature version of the larger loop, beginning in Granite Falls and continuing on to Barlow Pass.

On the main loop, the towns of the eastern foothills offer a good choice of accommodation, the most amenable being **Chelan**, an easygoing lakeshore resort that's the starting point for boat (or seaplane) trips up Lake Chelan to the remote village of **Stehekin**, at the heart of good hiking country. Two other towns have made heroic efforts to rise from the ruins of their industrial past: **Winthrop** dresses itself up in Wild West regalia, and **Leavenworth** in ersatz Bavarian, though both have the taint of tourist traps and are better considered as bases for mountain exploration rather than as destinations by themselves.

Though the Cascade Loop is best traveled from spring to early fall, when the hiking trails are usually free of snow, the highway is for the most part open year-round, a notable exception being a small but significant 50-mile stretch from Mazama to Newhalem on Hwy 20, which closes from mid-November to mid-April. For the latest details on highway conditions, contact the state department of transportation (ⓣ1-800/695-7623, ⓦwww.wsdot.wa.gov) or the Winter Mountain Pass Report agency (ⓣ1-888/766-4636). There's no **bus** service on Hwy 20, but Northwestern Trailways (ⓣ1-800/366-3830, ⓦwww.northwesterntrailways.com) runs buses across the mountains on US-2 from Seattle to Leavenworth (for Spokane), and LINK (ⓣ1-800/851-LINK, ⓦwww.linktransit.com) provides a frequent minibus service between the towns of the eastern foothills, including Chelan, Wenatchee, and Leavenworth.

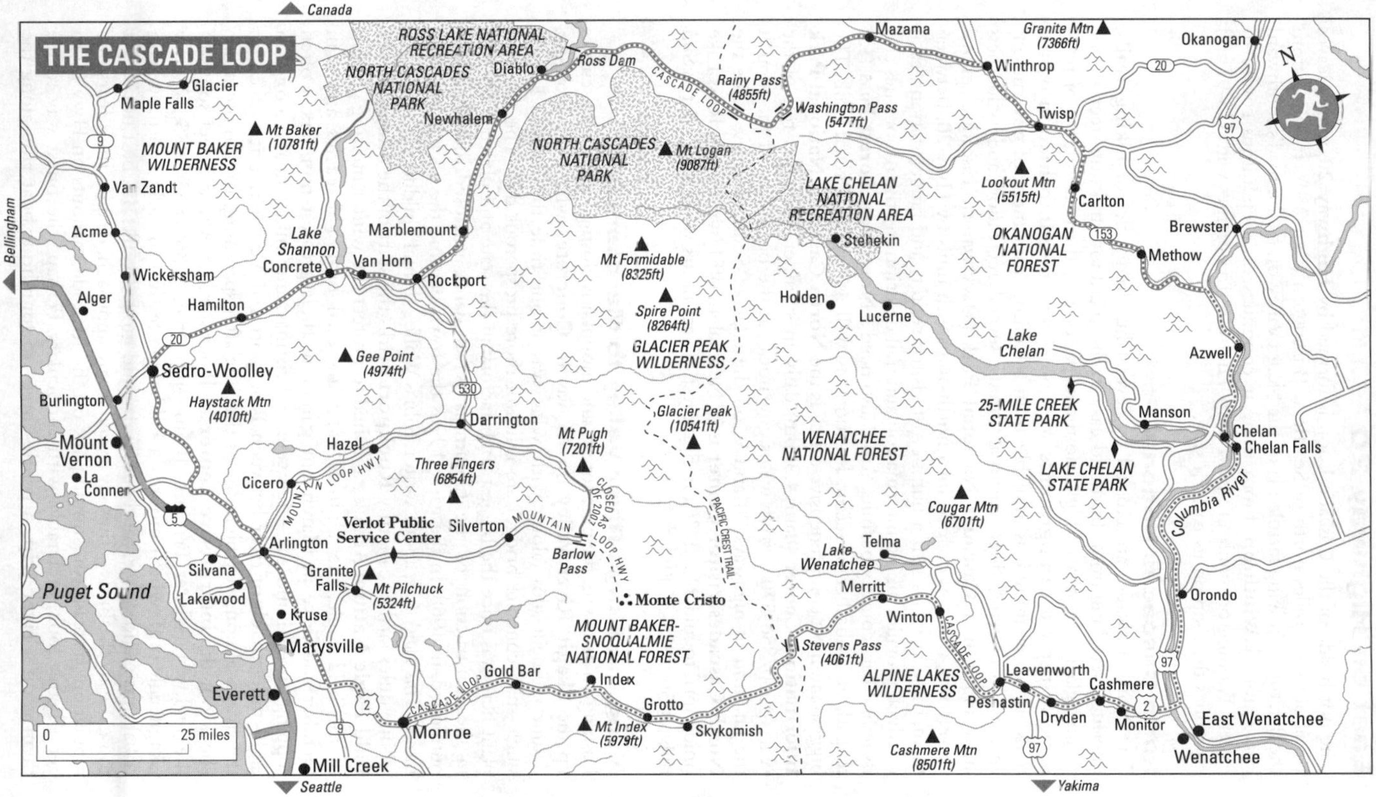

THE CASCADE LOOP
Canada
Bellingham
Seattle
Yakima
ROSS LAKE NATIONAL RECREATION AREA
NORTH CASCADES NATIONAL PARK
NORTH CASCADES NATIONAL PARK
LAKE CHELAN NATIONAL RECREATION AREA
OKANOGAN NATIONAL FOREST
MOUNT BAKER WILDERNESS
GLACIER PEAK WILDERNESS
WENATCHEE NATIONAL FOREST
MOUNT BAKER-SNOQUALMIE NATIONAL FOREST
ALPINE LAKES WILDERNESS
25-MILE CREEK STATE PARK
LAKE CHELAN STATE PARK
Puget Sound
Lake Shannon
Lake Chelan
Lake Wenatchee
Columbia River
Glacier
Maple Falls
Van Zandt
Acme
Wickersham
Alger
Hamilton
Sedro-Woolley
Burlington
Mount Vernon
La Conner
Concrete
Van Horn
Rockport
Marblemount
Newhalem
Diablo
Ross Dam
Rainy Pass (4855ft)
Washington Pass (5477ft)
Mazama
Winthrop
Twisp
Carlton
Methow
Brewster
Okanogan
Azwell
Manson
Chelan
Chelan Falls
Orondo
East Wenatchee
Wenatchee
Monitor
Cashmere
Dryden
Peshastin
Leavenworth
Winton
Merritt
Telma
Stevens Pass (4061ft)
Skykomish
Grotto
Index
Gold Bar
Monroe
Mill Creek
Everett
Marysville
Kruse
Lakewood
Silvana
Arlington
Granite Falls
Verlot Public Service Center
Silverton
Barlow Pass
Monte Cristo
Cicero
Hazel
Darrington
Stehekin
Holden
Lucerne
Mt Baker (10781ft)
Mt Logan (9087ft)
Mt Formidable (8325ft)
Spire Point (8264ft)
Glacier Peak (10541ft)
Mt Pugh (7201ft)
Three Fingers (6854ft)
Gee Point (4974ft)
Haystack Mtn (4010ft)
Mt Pilchuck (5324ft)
Mt Index (5979ft)
Cashmere Mtn (8501ft)
Cougar Mtn (6701ft)
Lookout Mtn (5515ft)
Granite Mtn (7366ft)
CASCADE LOOP
MOUNTAIN LOOP HWY
CLOSED AS OF 2007
PACIFIC CREST TRAIL
20
9
153
97
530
5
2
N
0
25 miles

East on Highway 20

The north side of the Cascade Loop is formed by **Highway 20**, which leaves I-5 about sixty miles north of Seattle at Burlington (Exit 230), traveling from the flat, tulip-growing farmlands of the Skagit Valley on to the road's southward curve around **Winthrop**. From there it continues on a circuitous course to eastern Washington, while at tiny **Twisp**, Highway 153 merges with US-97 and continues the loop on its eastern side.

North Cascades National Park

The North Cascades are crossed by several hundred miles of **hiking trails**, offering everything from short and easy strolls to arduous treks up steep slopes, around glaciers, and over high mountain passes, and there are plenty of first-come, first-served **campgrounds** to choose from, too. **Information** on the trails and campgrounds is available from a baffling assortment of government agencies overseeing three national forests, several recreation and wilderness areas, and **North Cascades National Park** (Ⓦ www.north.cascades.national -park.com), which is divided into north and south units by Hwy 20. Between them, these agencies staff a number of visitor centers and ranger stations, each of which provides hiking information and trail descriptions; the major ones also issue free backcountry permits. You'll also need a **Northwest Forest Pass** ($5) to park at a number of scenic locations as well as to use selected trails. The biggest and most comprehensive office is the **North Cascades National Park Information Center** (8am–4.30pm: daily in summer; Mon–Fri rest of the year; Ⓣ 360/856-5700, Ⓦ www.nps.gov/noca), at the beginning of the loop at the junction of highways 20 and 9, on the edge of Sedro-Wooley, while the **North Cascades Visitor Center** is in Newhalem off Hwy 20 near Ross Lake (mid-April to mid-Nov 8.30am–5pm; rest of year hours vary, usually Sat & Sun only; Ⓣ 360/856-5700).

Along the Skagit River Valley to Marblemount

Pushing on east, with the pine forests and mountains closing in, Hwy 20 scuttles up the **Skagit River Valley** on its way to **Concrete**, where the looming, defunct cement silos (along with what was at one time the nation's longest single-span concrete bridge) are relics of more prosperous days. The concrete plant here was once the biggest such factory in the state and played a key role in the construction of the Columbia River dams; it closed, outdated and outmoded, in 1968. In the early 1990s the town became the backdrop to the movie *This Boy's Life*, about writer Tobias Wolfe's dismal childhood.

Nine miles farther east, tiny **Rockport** marks the start of the **Skagit River Bald Eagle Natural Area**, established to protect the winter hunting ground of the bald eagle, the United States' national bird. The eagles arrive in October and leave in March but gather in their greatest numbers – often topping three hundred – between Christmas and mid-January along an eight-mile stretch of river between Rockport and Marblemount to feed on the river's salmon, easy pickings, as they die after spawning. To find out more, check out the **interpretive center** in Rockport, on Alfred Street south of the highway (winter Fri–Sun 10am–4pm; free; Ⓣ 360/853-7283, Ⓦ www .skagiteagle.org), which mounts a bald eagle festival in early February, with tribal music and dance, food and crafts, and guided walks. It's best not to get too close to the birds – they fly away at any approach, despite their fearsome reputation. Instead, you should park on the roadside turnouts on Hwy 20 to get a better look, preferably with binoculars. Perhaps the finest way to see them is on a **river trip**, a gentle three- to four-hour boat ride along the

Skagit with any one of several companies, notably Chinook Expeditions (☎1-800/241-3451, ⓦwww.chinookexpeditions.com), based in Index (see p.430). There are also daily boat trips from November to March (one-day trip $85, two-day $285) leaving from the jetty just east of and across the river from minuscule **MARBLEMOUNT**. Ten miles east of Rockport, the town was founded in the 1860s as a supply center for the gold diggers ferreting through the surrounding hills, with only limited success. Today, it provides the last regularly open gas station you'll see for ninety miles if you're headed east, as well as an opportunity to get a roof over your head. The *Skagit River Resort*, three miles west of Marblemount along Hwy 20 (☎360/873-2250 or 1-800/273-2606, ⓦwww.northcascades.com), offers the best **lodgings** in the area, with chalets and rustic cabins (❹) and as well as sites for RVs and tents ($15–25) and a simple but friendly four-room B&B (d–e). The ⚞ *Buffalo Run Inn*, 58179 Hwy 20 (☎1-877/828-6652, ⓦwww.buffaloruninn .com; ❹), has fifteen units with kitchenettes, plus a bunkhouse, in a sizable, though modernized, 1889 log cabin. You can register for the hotel across the street at the *Buffalo Run Restaurant* (☎360/873-2461), which specializes in the likes of elk, ostrich, and, of course, buffalo, as well as wine and microbrews. Also worth a stop is the *Good Food Drive-In*, 59924 Hwy 20 (☎360/873-9309), an old-fashioned all-American diner with solid burgers, fries, and shakes. Wilderness permits and hiking maps are available at the seasonal **Marblemount Wilderness Information Center**, 7820 Ranger Station Rd (July–Aug Sun–Thurs 8am–6pm, Fri–Sat 8am–7pm; June & Sept daily 8am–5pm; ☎360/873-4500).

Ross Lake National Recreation Area

Just beyond Marblemount, Hwy 20 enters **Ross Lake National Recreation Area**, a narrow, elongated slice of river valley that divides North Cascades National Park into two sections. The first town you reach is **Newhalem**, owned by Seattle City Light, whose electrical generators lie a little to the east in a chain of three dams spanning the Skagit River. The town is the site of a useful **North Cascades National Park Information Center**, milepost 120 on Hwy 20 (May–Oct daily 9am–5pm, plus winter weekends; ☎206/386-4495). From the end of Main Street you reach a suspension bridge that leads to the half-mile **Trail of the Cedars**, a memorable trek through a grove of western red cedar that ends at the dam powerhouse. From here other trails branch off into the green hillside, past some fine gardens for endemic plants with charming wooden bridges, and end at Ladder Creek Falls. From Newhalem, it's not far to the reservoir of the first dam, **Gorge**, and a few more miles to the second, **Diablo**, built at a dangerous bend in the river called "Devil's Corner," its name translated into Spanish so as not to offend local sensibilities. Here the highway offers views across the dam and its little blue-green lake; the dam's parking lot is where you catch the water taxi to *Ross Lake Resort* (see p.422).

A couple miles east of Diablo Dam on Hwy 20 lies the first-come, first-served **Colonial Creek campground** ($12; ☎360/856-5700, ext. 515). Boasting an attractive location along the lakeshore, the campground serves as the starting point for several particularly fine hikes, including those along Thunder Creek and the longer Fourth of July Trail to Panther Creek – invigorating jaunts through stands of forest and watershed, overseen by the glaciated, rugged Colonial Peak to the west. A few minutes away are the fabulous mountain views of the overlook for **Diablo Lake**, which is tourable by boat through Seattle City Light (June–Sept Sat & Sun 12.30pm;

2hr 30min; $25; reserve at ☎206/684-3030). More imposing, farther east off Hwy 20, **Ross Dam** is the largest dam of the three and the one that created **Ross Lake** (Ⓦwww.nps.gov/rola), which stretches north for 25 pine-rimmed miles into Canada, flanked by hiking trails and campgrounds – but no roads. Reached by boat ($20 round-trip) from Diablo Dam and then by truck ($7 round-trip), or along a two-mile hiking trail from Ross Dam, the *Ross Lake Resort* (mid-June to Oct; ☎206/386-4437, Ⓦwww .rosslakeresort.com) provides some of the region's most distinctive lodgings. Built for City Light workers, the resort literally floats on its log supports and has various **cabins** with simple 1950s designs, boasting kitchens and wood stoves (❺); bunkhouse versions holding up to ten guests (❼); and a chic, two-story model with full amenities, for up to ten people (❽). The resort has no telephones in the cabins and you have to bring your own food, but it does operate a water-taxi service ($35–110 one-way per person) to the remote trailheads farther up Ross Lake.

Okanogan National Forest

Hwy 20 bypasses Ross Lake, veering southeast after Ross Dam to leave the national park for the remote wilds of the 1.7-million-acre **Okanogan National Forest** (Ⓦwww.fs.fed.us/r6/oka), then running up Ruby and Granite creeks to **Rainy Pass**, where it crosses the Pacific Crest Trail (see p.51). To the north the long-distance trail heads off into depths of the Okanogan, while to the south it slips along Bridge Creek and curves round the flanks of McGregor Mountain to meet the rough dirt road that leads to Stehekin at the tip of Lake Chelan. Beyond Rainy Pass, Hwy 20 has an abundance of stopping points, each providing remarkable views over the Cascades. One of the most magnificent is at **Washington Pass Overlook**, about thirty miles east of Ross Dam, where a short paved trail from the roadside parking lot leads to a spectacular mountain panorama featuring the craggy, rocky peak of **Liberty Bell Mountain**. Afterward, there's a final flurry of mountain scenery before the road reaches the tamer landscapes of the **Methow Valley** and descends to Winthrop.

Winthrop

Beyond the mountains Hwy 20 turns south, leading into tiny **WINTHROP**, where wooden false fronts, boardwalks, swinging saloon doors, and other western trappings bedeck the main drag of **Riverside Avenue**, a somewhat kitschy assemblage that nonetheless saved the town from becoming a high-altitude ghost town after the Great Depression. Winthrop was founded by an East Coast entrepreneur, Guy Waring, who turned up in 1891 with a wagonload of merchandise and diplomatically named the settlement after John Winthrop, the Puritan governor of his native Massachusetts, the state that provided his backing. Waring was visited by an old Harvard classmate, Owen Wister, whose novel *The Virginian* – widely acclaimed as the first Western novel – was clearly (in the town's opinion) based on Winthrop. Waring's log-cabin home, set on a hill behind the main street at 285 Castle Ave, is now part of the **Shafer Museum** (June–Sept Thurs–Mon 10am–5pm; donation), whose assortment of old buildings – such as a print shop, schoolhouse, milliner's shop, and assay office – is crammed with pioneer antiques. It is, however, Waring's cabin, with its heavy-duty logs, that most catches the eye – just as it was meant to: he labored away for months building this structure to entice his wife to come West, away from the more familiar creature comforts of New England.

Practicalities

Winthrop's handy **visitor center**, 202 Riverside Ave (late April–Sept daily 10am–5pm; ☎509/996-2125, Ⓦwww.winthropwashington.com), is well stocked with brochures on outdoor activities from horse riding and whitewater rafting to fishing – both in the valley and the neighboring mountains; there's a USFS **ranger station** (☎509/996-4003, Ⓦwww.fs.fed.us/r6/oka) downtown at 24 W Chewuch St, and the town also has a few arts-and-crafts boutiques that are worth a look for a taste of the regional art scene.

Winthrop has a reasonable range of **accommodation**, including a clutch of serviceable motels that provide a good base for your mountain excursions if you don't want to camp. Try the *Hotel Rio Vista*, 285 Riverside Ave (☎509/996-3535 or 1-800/398-0911, Ⓦwww.hotelriovista.com; ❹–❺ by season), whose facade resembles something out of an old Hollywood Western and offers nice suites with hot tubs, kitchenettes, and DVD players; the hotel also operates a lofted cabin ten miles west of town (❺–❻) that has a kitchen, fireplace, and deck, and goes for only about $40 more. In town, an even better value is the ⚜ *River Run Inn*, on Rader Rd off Hwy 20 (☎509/996-2173, Ⓦwww.riverrun-inn.com), which has one- and two-bedroom cabins (❻–❼ by season) that feature fireplaces, kitchens, and decks, as well as rooms (❹–❺) with decks, patios, and kitchenettes, and an onsite pool and hot tub. Prices jump $10–30 on weekends. The luxurious *Sun Mountain Lodge* (☎509/996-2211 or 1-800/572-0493, Ⓦwww.sunmountainlodge.com; ❽–❾) has cabins and lodge rooms in a grand setting on the edge of the Cascades, nine miles southwest of town along Twin Lakes and then Patterson Lake Road. As for **eating** options, the *Duck Brand Cantina*, 248 Riverside Ave (☎509/996-2192, Ⓦwww.methownet.com/duck), serves up cheap and tasty Mexican fare, plus some serviceable ribs and steaks, and has six simple, Western-themed rooms in its onsite B&B (❸), while *Winthrop Brewing Company*, 155 Riverside Ave (☎509/996 3183), offers solid microbrews like the excellent Outlaw Pale Ale and Grizzly Paw Honey Rye.

Continuing south along the Methow Valley, it's eleven miles to uneventful **Twisp**, where Hwy 20 begins its long and circuitous journey through the remote national forests that fill out the northeastern corner of Washington; Highway 153, merging with US-97, forms the eastern edge of the Cascade Loop before making the lengthy trip south to Oregon's Columbia River Gorge (see p.117).

Lake Chelan and around

US-97 follows the Columbia River as it curves south to the short turnoff (US-97Alt) that leads over the hills to the glacially carved finger of **LAKE CHELAN**. Framed by wooded hills and mountains, the long, thin lake's southern reaches are laced with fine **hiking trails**, many of which are fairly easy to reach from the town of **Chelan** along a patchwork of rutted forest roads. Alternatively, several of Chelan's sports shops rent out mountain bikes and kayaks (be aware of the sudden squalls on the lake). If you have time, a ferry trip to the lake's remote northern outpost of **Stehekin** can be a fun excursion, and for many visitors makes a worthy trip just by itself.

Chelan

Tucked in between the lake's southeastern shore and the Chelan River is pocket-size **CHELAN**, not much more than a simple grid of modest buildings and a base for visitors who want to explore the lake and its mountainous surroundings. Your first stop should be the **visitor center**, near the waterfront at 102 E Johnson Ave (Mon–Fri 9am–5pm, Sat 10am–4pm; summer also open Sun; ☎509/682-3503 or 1-800/4-CHELAN, ⊛www.lakechelan.com), which has free information about the region and can provide maps and general hiking advice. For more detailed trail guidance, the **ranger station**, at 428 W Woodin Ave (7.45am–4.30pm: winter Mon–Fri, rest of the year daily; ☎509/682-2576), is a five-minute walk over the bridge and along the waterfront from the visitor center. Monday through Saturday, local LINK (☎1-800/851-LINK, ⊛www.linktransit.com) **buses** connect Chelan with several nearby towns, including Leavenworth.

You can **rent** watercraft like Jet Skis and boats from vendors around the lakeshore, but the best option for exploration is to get out on a **kayak**. *Clear Water Kayaking*, seven miles up the eastern shore in the burg of Manson (June–Aug; ☎509/630-7615, ⊛www.kayaklakechelan.com), has singles for $30 per two hours up to $60 for a full day and doubles for about half again as much, as well as half-day training courses ($59–89) and guided tours in the morning or evening ($49) or all day ($85). Some of the better **hikes** in the vicinity of Chelan include the Chelan Gorge Road, a 4.5-mile dirt concourse with stunning river and mountain vistas; the North Fork trail from **25-Mile State Park**, about a third of the way up the western lake shore ($5 Northwest Forest Pass required), which lazily follows a creek bed for its initial climb, then takes a steep lunge upward as it continues; and the simpler jaunt up Chelan Butte, off Butte Road from Lakeside Park, a nice overlook that encompasses some pretty alpine views. If you're really intent on plowing into the outback, you can rent cross-country **skis** and **showshoes** from Lake Chelan Sports, 132 E Woodin Ave (☎509/682-2629), for only $12 per day, or from Uncle Tim's Toys, two miles north of town (☎509/687-TIMS), which also has snowmobile and **mountain bike** rentals and can provide information on the most rugged courses in the lake area.

Chelan has lots of **places to stay**, but in the height of the summer rooms can be hard to find, so book ahead. The town's major hotel, *Campbell's Resort*, 104 W Woodin Ave (☎509/682-2561 or 1-800/553-8225, ⊛www.campbellsresort .com; ❹–❽), has lakeside rooms and suites – some of which come with fireplaces, kitchenettes, and balconies; rates vary but can get very expensive in the summer. Less pricey, ⚓*Darnell's Lake Resort*, 901 Spader Bay Rd (April–Oct; ☎1-800/967-8149, ⊛www.darnellsresort.com; ❸–❻ by season), has a pool, tennis courts, a boat launch, and other amenities, as well as affordable rooms that variously come with kitchenettes, kitchens, fridges, and/or microwaves. The cheapest decent choice is the clean and simple *Apple Inn Motel*, 1002 E Woodin Ave (☎509/682-4044; ❷–❸), which has some units with kitchenettes and an onsite hot tub. The best **restaurant** in town is at *Campbell's Resort*, known for its steak, pasta, and salmon, as well as its English-style fish 'n' chips and beef Burgundy pie. A more recent addition to the dining scene is the *Bonfire Grill*, 229 Woodin Ave (☎509/682-2101), which has hearty steaks and seafood, outdoor fire pits, and regular live music.

Stehekin

Accessible only by trail, seaplane, or boat, **STEHEKIN**, at Lake Chelan's mountainous northern tip, makes an excellent base for hiking in the North Cascades. In every direction, trails lead into the mountains, nudging up along bubbling creeks through the thinning alpine forest, with easier trails along the lakeshore. In the village, a few yards from the jetty, the *Stehekin Landing Resort* (see opposite) rents out bikes and boats and also runs daily bus

The Lake Chelan Boat Company, 1418 W Woodin Ave (℡509/682-2224 info, ℡509/682-4584 reservations, Ⓦwww.ladyofthelake.com), provides one of the area's highlights in the form of its **Lady of the Lake** passenger ferry. Sailing the 55 miles from Chelan up the lake to Stehekin, the ferry usually stops at Lucerne, where it drops supplies for **Holden**, a Lutheran retreat that occupies the site of an old copper mine in a remote valley to the west, where the spiritually inclined can find inspiration in the rugged mountain environment (information at Ⓦwww.holdenvillage.org). The scenery becomes even more impressive the farther you go, with the forested hills of the south giving way to the austere, glaciated peaks that circle in on the northern-most part of the lake, which juts into the very heart of the North Cascades.

Leaving from the jetty a mile west of town along Woodin Avenue, the ferry makes the 4hr trip once daily (May to mid-Oct leaves 8.30am, returns by 6pm; $22.50 one-way, $38 round-trip) with a 90min stopover at Stehekin. The faster **Lady Express** (May to mid-Oct $34.50 one-way, $57 round-trip; mid-Oct to April $38 round-trip) departs at 8.30am or 10am and takes just over 2hr to complete the same trip. You can go up on the *Lady Express* and return on the *Lady of the Lake* (or vice versa), and if you do so you can give yourself three hours in Stehekin (round trip $57). With the cost of gas rising in recent years, there are also fuel surcharges of $1–5 per round-trip ticket.

Finally, if you're flush, you can take a **seaplane** to Stehekin on Chelan Airways ($89 one-way, $149 round-trip; ℡509/682-5555, Ⓦwww.chelanairways.com), which also offers airborne **tours** of the region ($59–229)

trips up to **Rainbow Falls**, a mist-shrouded, 312ft waterfall flanked by red cedars just four miles north of the village; times of departure are fixed to coincide with the arrival of the ferry. Alternatively, the **Golden West Visitor Center** (April–Oct daily 8.30am–5pm; Nov–Mar Wed–Mon 12.30–2pm; ℡360/856-5700), also a short walk from the jetty, has maps, brochures, and trail information (as well as free backcountry permits), and can connect you with seasonal **shuttle buses** ($5–7 per person) that travel up along the Stehekin River Valley. It's an exhilarating trip that accesses trailheads and campgrounds and follows a small portion of the Pacific Crest Trail (see p.51); advance booking is advised. If you want to hoof it to Stehekin from Chelan or southbound from Hwy 20, it's quite a hike across dramatically varying terrain, and you should verify current conditions and get advice from any of the North Cascades visitor centers (Ⓦwww.nps.gov/noca). Discovery Bikes, a five-minute walk from the boat landing, can get you on a **mountain bike** ($3.50/hr, $25/day, or $12.50/day for older models) for your alpine adventures, and offers a breakfast ride that includes an early meal and shuttle transport nine miles up the valley ($25 per person).

For **accommodation**, the pleasant *Stehekin Landing Resort* (℡509/682-4494, Ⓦwww.stehekinlanding.com; ④–⑥ by season) offers lakeside rooms that are a bit pricier than standard units; reservations are usually necessary here, as they are for the handful of cabin-lodges farther up the Stehekin Valley. One such option is *Stehekin Valley Ranch* (℡509/682-4677, Ⓦwww.courtneycountry.com; ④–⑤), which has basic tent cabins without bathrooms and more spacious and functional log cabins with bathrooms (and a few with kitchenettes), and the same company's *Cascade Corrals* (℡509/682-7742, Ⓦwww.cascadecorrals.com; ⑥), which has furnished log cabins with kitchens and linens, though you must book a month in advance. Get directions for both of these sites from the proprietors.

Wenatchee

South of Chelan, the Columbia River weaves its way through prime apple-growing country, tracked by US-97 on its east bank and US-97Alt on its west bank. Both roads lead the forty-odd miles to **WENATCHEE**, named for a Yakama tribal word for either "canyon river" or "rainbow robe." The town straddles the Columbia River and has long been Washington's **apple capital**, the center of an industry that fills the valleys of the eastern foothills with orchards and grows nearly half the country's supply. Despite increased competition from China, fruit is still big business here, and **apple stalls** dot the roadsides in the fall, piled with the expected sweet, outsize Red Delicious (the most popular kind in the US), the enormous Golden Delicious, the red Winesap, and the tart, green Granny Smith. There are also selected "heritage" varieties that have become popular in recent years through sales at organic markets – the mildly sweet-and-tart Cameo, the pearlike Gingergold, and, perhaps the best, the Pink Lady, a crisp and zesty New Zealand import with nice complexity.

One worthwhile option is the **Apple Capital Loop Trail**, a nonmotorized ten-mile path that leads you past a series of city parks and over three bridges – following the railway and a pipeline – that cross the Columbia and Wenatchee rivers. Despite its industrial air, the trail is a good spot for running, biking, and Rollerblading. Another type of stroll is available at **Ohme Gardens**, a few miles from town at 3327 Ohme Rd (mid-April to mid-Oct 9am–6pm; summer closes 7pm; $7; ⓦ www.ohmegardens.com), where over the course of an hour you can take in a pleasant series of sloping lawns, paths, ponds, and pockets of foliage, along with quaint touches such as wishing wells and waterfalls.

Apart from these outlying attractions, the town itself has a rather drab, workaday air, and it's unlikely you'll want to hang around long. Apple fanatics

△ Wenatchee Valley apple orchard

can learn about the history of the industry at the **Wenatchee Valley Museum**, 127 S Mission St (Tues–Sat 10am–4pm; $5; ☎509/664-3340, ⓦ www.wenatcheevalleymuseum.com), which has exhibits on the history and lore of the Columbia River and dioramas that replicate a nineteenth-century agricultural tool shop, Victorian-era house, and, in miniature, the Great Northern Railway, along with a grab bag of old cars and artifacts from the native tribes of the region. There's more information on the industry at the **Washington Apple Commission Visitor Center**, on the northern edge of town at 2900 Euclid Ave (Mon–Fri 8am–5pm; free; ☎509/663-9600, ⓦ www.bestapples.com), where you can munch away on various varieties and guzzle apple juice as well. Fittingly, Wenatchee's big annual celebration, the ten-day all-American **Apple Blossom Festival** (ⓦ www.appleblossom.org), features carnival floats and marching bands in late April, with one lucky girl crowned Apple Blossom Queen.

Practicalities

Wenatchee's Columbia Station, downtown at Wenatchee Avenue and Kittitas Street, is something of a public **transit** hub for the immediate area. Northwestern Trailways **buses** (☎1-800/366-3830, ⓦ www.northwesterntrailways.com) pull in here, bound for Seattle or Spokane, and so do Amtrak **trains** (☎1-800/872-7245, ⓦ www.amtrak.com) connecting Wenatchee with Portland, Seattle, Leavenworth, and Spokane. In addition, local LINK **buses** (☎1-800/851-LINK, ⓦ www.linktransit.com) depart Wenatchee for several nearby towns – most usefully Chelan and Leavenworth. Wenatchee isn't the most distinctive place to **stay**, mostly populated with the usual chain motels. Of these, the best value is the *La Quinta*, 1905 N Wenatchee Ave (☎509/664-6565, ⓦ www.lq.com; ④–⑤), which has clean, basic rooms and an onsite pool, gym, hot tub, and sauna, along with Internet access. Alternately, the *Warm Springs Inn*, 1611 Love Lane (☎509/662-8365, ⓦ www.warmspringsinn.com; ⑥), is a solid B&B whose six rooms and suites have agreeable decor, DVD players, and views of the adjacent Wenatchee River. Your best bet for **dining** is ⌘ *McGlinn's Public House*, 111 Orondo Ave (☎509/663-9073), which is good not only for its regional microbrews but for its tasty wood-fired pizzas, burgers, fish, and signature beer bread.

West on Highway 2

Heading **west on Highway 2** from Wenatchee, the last, southerly section of the Cascade Loop (if proceeding clockwise around it) provides a good access route into the Washington Cascades from Seattle and is peppered with worthwhile campgrounds, hikes, and mountain lakes. Undoubtedly, the highlights along this stretch include the Bavarian theme town of **Leavenworth** and the lovely preserve of the **Alpine Lakes Wilderness**. There are also several ski resorts, the first of which, from Wenatchee, is **Mission Ridge Ski and Board Resort**, 7500 Mission Ridge Rd, best accessed southbound from Hwy 2 off US-97 (☎509/663-6543, ⓦ www.missionridge.com), which has dozens of routes for mostly mid-level skiers, four chairlifts – the longest and steepest leading up to the 6800ft summit – and night-skiing lift-ticket rates ($12) that are good value, much cheaper than the regular day rates ($46).

At the practical end of the Cascade Loop, you reach **Monroe**, a neon-lit sprawl heralding Seattle, just thirty miles away. From here you can proceed southwest to the Emerald City or continue north onto Highway 9 to access yet another interesting circuit, the **Mountain Loop Highway** – a smaller route contained within the bounds of the Cascade Loop, and compelling for its intriguing blend of rustic scenery and historic ruins.

Cashmere

Just north of Wenatchee, Highway 2, in combination with US-97, heads west into the mountains toward the themed village of **CASHMERE**. Showcasing a tasteful late-nineteenth-century main street and a small, outdoor **Pioneer Village**, the town comprises about twenty restored and relocated buildings such as a school, hotel, saddle shop, and general store, looking like a Hollywood Wild West backlot transported up into the mountains. These architectural antiques form part of the **Chelan County Historical Museum**, 600 Cotlets Way (March–Dec daily 9.30am–4.30pm; $10), whose main building holds a large and wide-ranging collection focused on the Northwest. Among the Native American artifacts displayed on the upper floor are archaeological treasures such as petroglyphs and early tools, as well as baskets and headdresses, weapons, and Hudson's Bay Company trading trinkets.

Cashmere is also somewhat famous for its sugary "aplets" and "cotlets" (as in apricot) – available at **Liberty Orchards**, 117 Mission St (April–Dec Mon–Fri 8am–5.30pm, Sat & Sun 10am–4pm; Jan–March Mon–Fri 8.30am–4.30pm; free; ℡509/782-4088). Made of boiled-down fruit juices and walnuts coated with corn starch and powdered sugar, these popular confections were launched by two immigrant Armenian farmers at the beginning of the twentieth century to dispose of the fruit they could not sell. Naturally, the sweets made them a fortune. Finally, although you'll have to go five miles west to Leavenworth to rent a mountain bike, it's worth doing so to take in the stunning **Devil's Gulch trail**, a 13-mile route that begins with a marvelous overlook of the North Cascades and takes you on a smooth, fast dirt course that can send you flying downhill at a hell-bent-for-leather speed – though be careful not to get injured out here, as the location, nine miles south of Cashmere, is fairly isolated. Check in at the historical museum for maps and other information on this and other excellent rides, as well as memorable hikes in the same area.

Leavenworth

Farther west, **LEAVENWORTH** is a former timber and railroad town that warded off economic death thirty years ago by going Bavarian. Local motels and stores now sport steeply roofed half-timbered, ski chalet–style facades, complete with wooden balconies and quaint window boxes. Wiener schnitzel, sauerkraut, and strudel feature on local menus and gift shops sell musical boxes that play "authentic" alpine folk music. This can be fun if you're in the right mood, and even if you're not, you can always escape into the surrounding gorgeous mountain scenery.

No longer combined with US-97 (which darts south toward the Columbia River Gorge), Hwy 2 heads westbound into Leavenworth and forms the northern perimeter of the town center, which slopes south to fill out a small loop in the Wenatchee River. Leavenworth's main drag, **Front Street**, runs parallel to – and one block south of – Hwy 2, and Northwestern Trailways **buses** (℡1-800/366-3830, ⓦwww.northwesterntrailways.com) from Seattle and Spokane stop a five-minute walk from downtown. The municipal **visitor center**, 940 Hwy 2 (℡509/548-5807, ⓦwww.leavenworth.org), has copious listings of places to stay and eat, as well as the lowdown on the many local companies that organize **outdoor activities** – everything from horse-drawn wagon rides, treks on snowmobiles and snowshoes, and dog sledding to skiing, fishing, and hunting. Leavenworth is a particularly convenient spot if you want to get out on a river in an inner tube or take a chance with whitewater rafting. River Rider (℡1-800/448-RAFT, ⓦwww.riverrider.com) is one of the more prominent guides offering tubing on the Wenatchee River ($10 per person) and kayaking and rafting excursions ($45–75) on a range of Cascade rivers, including the Methow, Skyhomish, Toutle, and Yakima. The town also has a **ranger station**, off the highway at 600 Sherbourne St (daily 7.45am–4.30pm; ℡509/782-1413), where you can pick up hiking maps and trail descriptions. Leavenworth Mountain Sports, 220 Hwy 2 (℡509/548-7864), rents out skis, canoes, mountain bikes, and climbing gear.

Practicalities

There are plenty of places to stay in Leavenworth, but you're still advised to book ahead in the summer. Downtown **accommodation** includes the excellent *Hotel Pension Anna*, 926 Commercial St (℡509/548-6273 or 1-800/509-2662, ⓦwww.pensionanna.com; ❺–❻), a pseudo-Austrian lodge that also has some suites (❽) with fireplaces and Jacuzzis in the onion-domed chapel across the street, and *Mrs Anderson's Lodging House*, 917 Commercial St (℡509/548-6173 or 1-800/253-8990, ⓦwww.quiltersheaven.com; ❸), offering ten comfortable rooms with antique furnishings in the style of Grandma Moses – there's even an onsite quilt shop. Another mock-Teutonic spot, the *Enzian Motor Inn*, just west of the center at 590 Hwy 2 (℡509/548-5269 or 1-800/223-8511, ⓦwww.enzianinn.com; ❺), is a grand motel-lodge that offers commodious rooms done out in full alpine style; suites (❻) that may have fireplaces, balconies, and hot tubs; and regular alphorn concerts.

Leavenworth has more than its share of undistinguished **restaurants** geared up for the passing tourist trade, but you can still find some tasty surprises. *Los Camperos*, upstairs on The Alley at 200 8th St (℡509/548-3314), dishes up surprisingly decent Mexican fare. *Andreas Keller*, 829 Front St (℡509/548-6000), doles out hefty helpings of gut-busting German cuisine, while upstairs *Café Mozart* (same phone) has more expensive takes on the same cuisine, with fine desserts as well. Best of all, ⅄ *King Ludwig's*, 921 Front St (℡509/548-6625), features lively Bavarian dancing, hearty pork schnitzel, and beer-bearing barmaids – bring your Tyrolean hat.

Alpine Lakes Wilderness

The real point of visiting Leavenworth is to **hike** the surrounding mountains, a small portion of the colossal 2.2-million-acre **Wenatchee National Forest** (ⓦwww.fs.fed.us/r6/wenatchee), which extends north as far as Lake Chelan and south to I-90. Among these striking wilderness areas, the **Alpine Lakes Wilderness**, west of Leavenworth, boasts some of the region's finest scenery, with plunging valleys and scores of crystal-clear mountain lakes set beneath a string of spiraling peaks. You'll need a Northwest Forest Pass ($5) to park your vehicle and, between mid-May and mid-October, a free wilderness permit to get into the outback; both are available from any ranger station.

From Leavenworth, the most straightforward approach into the Alpine Lakes is along **Icicle Road**, which weaves south and then west through thick forest and past cascading waterfalls to a series of trailheads and busy **campgrounds** ($5–10). The nine-mile-long **Enchantment Lake Trail** is a particularly popular route, with hikers heading south up Mountaineer Creek for the beautiful lakes that pepper the mountains above; the trailhead is about eight miles out of town. For something less strenuous, stick to the forested footpath running beside Icicle Road. For more **information** on the area, contact the

ranger station in Leavenworth or inquire at ☎509/674-4411, ⓦwww.fs.fed
.us/r6/wenatchee/cle-elum-wilderness.

West from Leavenworth

Heading **west from Leavenworth** toward Puget Sound, Hwy 2 scrambles
over the Cascade Mountains at **Stevens Pass**, named after the Great Northern
Railroad's surveyor John Stevens, who chose to route trains this way in 1892.
You can ski and snowboard at **Stevens Pass Ski Area**, 37 miles from
Leavenworth off Hwy 2 (☎206/634-1645, ⓦwww.stevenspass.com), one of
the premier resorts in the state, with ten chairlifts and three dozen runs, though
the prices (lift tickets $52–57) reflect its popularity. Five miles away on the
highway, the area's Nordic Center (seasonally Thurs–Sun 9am–4pm) is open to
snowshoers and cross-country skiers, and has passes significantly cheaper ($17)
than lift rates at the resort. Beyond, the highway loops down to the Skykomish
River Valley, where tiny **Index**, an old mining and quarrying settlement a mile
or so from the highway, is worth a pit stop for its antique **general store**, selling
everything from sandwiches to fertilizer. The sheer, 400ft granite cliff towering
over Index, the so-called **Town Wall**, is a favorite with Seattle rock climbers,
and there are a few pleasant hikes along the banks of the north fork of the
Skyhomish River.

Eight miles farther west lies **Gold Bar**, one of the last sights of any interest
before the Cascade Loop reaches its end at Monroe. Once a hard-edged mining
town and railroad settlement where, as anti-Chinese sentiment reached a
boiling point in the 1890s, a railway engineer shipped terrified Chinese locals
out in purpose-built "coffins," Gold Bar is best known today for its proximity
to **Wallace Falls State Park** (closed winter Mon & Tues; ⓦwww.parks.wa
.gov). Two miles northeast of town, the relaxing park boasts **campgrounds**
($17–24) and two trails – one three miles long, the other four – leading to a
265ft waterfall.

The Mountain Loop Highway

Although hardly one of the best-known routes into the Cascades, the
Mountain Loop Highway – basically a small circle within the much larger
Cascade Loop – represents one of the better day-trips from the north Seattle
area, a hundred-mile "**National Scenic Byway**" taking you through some
striking landscapes and past the preserved ruins of the region's early-
twentieth-century heyday. To access the start of the loop, take Hwy 2 east
from I-5 in the suburb of Everett, then pick up highways 204 and 9 (both
northbound) until you reach Hwy 92. Continue on 92 for some ten miles
until the road ends in the little burg of **Granite Falls** – the Mountain Loop
Highway's start. The town itself is a quaint holdover from the late nineteenth
century, with a few old-fashioned storefronts recalling the glory days when it
served as the western terminus of a mining railroad that transported gold from
the area around the **Stillaguamish River** canyon.

The railroad eventually closed in 1936 due to various persistent obstacles, one
of which was the river's frequent **flooding**, whose impact is vividly on display
six miles from Granite Falls along the three-mile **Old Robe Trail** (watch for
turnout signs on the highway). The hike itself is one of the most eye-catching
in the Cascades, a winding concourse along the long-disused rock cuts of the
rail bed, down narrow switchbacks and passes, and through two large tunnels
carved out of the hillsides. Most conspicuous, though, is the presence of the
Stillaguamish River alongside the trail – in winter the heaving churn of dark

gray current is notorious for spilling over its banks, tearing out trees, and causing massive rockslides, one of which marks the trail's abrupt end. Before the Loop Highway begins from Granite Falls, an equally fascinating route follows the south bank of the Stillaguamish (follow Pioneer Road out of town to a left on Waite Mill Road to the trailhead), where the recently constructed **Lime Kiln Trail** wends its way through forest groves along an old rail bed, past various antique castoffs such as tools and saw blades, to a long-abandoned lime kiln sitting amid the foliage, its 30ft apparatus now overgrown with ferns. Here, from the 1890s to the 1930s, this towering relic would transform quarried limestone into powdered lime for local paper mills and smelters. It's now a fittingly romantic ruin to cap off this fascinating 3.5-mile trek.

Back on the highway at mile 12, a right-side turnout leads you seven miles up the slope of **Mount Pilchuck**, once the site of a popular winter resort (it closed in 1980) and now a 1900-acre state park. Although there's no more skiing (unless you want to carry your gear up and risk a hell-for-leather trip down), the mountain offers a fine but difficult three-mile hike up to an accessible fire lookout at the top, a 2200ft rise that affords incredible views of the surrounding terrain in the North Cascades, as well as occasional views of bear, cougars, deer, coyote, and eagles.

The disused ski area and the abandoned mining operation nearby (with its ruined dam at mile 14 and filled-in tunnels at miles 19 and 21) are not the only conspicuous failures on this section of the Mountain Loop Highway. Three miles beyond tiny Silverton, you reach the former site of the **Big Four** resort, which operated in grand fashion here with a golf course, cabins, and tennis courts from 1921 to 1949, when a mysterious fire closed it for good. Nowadays, all that remains are sidewalks leading nowhere, the vestiges of a grand fireplace, and assorted ponds active with beavers – the new denizens of the old resort site. You can, however, take an easy, one-mile hike to the area's **ice caves**, created when the winter's runoff collects in caves and forms frozen columns and the like. Keep in mind, though, that the site is officially open only from August to October – when there's no snow – so you'll be taking a risk (and disobeying the rather ominous signs) if you venture inside during the colder months, when rock- and ice-falls have injured more than a few unwary visitors.

If the highway's open – it's usually closed at, or even well before, Big Four between November and March – you can head another five miles (to mile 30) to reach **Barlow Pass**. From here, a closed section of roadway – which you'll need to travel on foot or a bike – leads some four miles away to the centerpiece of the area, the ghost town of **Monte Cristo**, which was formerly the eastern terminus of the mining railway and subsequently a small-time resort from the 1920s to the 60s. These days, little remains from either heyday, aside from a few rusty old tools, cabins, and pieces of antiquated machinery. However, the site is a great place to hike or mountain bike, and the scenery is filled with unkempt paths and road cuts, boarded-up mine entrances, and overgrown foliage.

As of 2007 the Mountain Loop Highway is closed beyond the Barlow Pass due to flooding damage. You can contact the Verlot Public Information Center (see below) for the latest information on the road's status; if it's closed, the less interesting northern part of the Loop Highway can be reached only via Darrington. Luckily, most of the highlights are densely packed into the first thirty miles of the mountain loop, and you won't miss too much simply by turning around at Barlow Pass and returning through Granite Falls.

You can get **maps** and brochures from the Forest Service's **Verlot Public International Center**, near the beginning of the loop at 33515 Mountain Loop Hwy (March–Oct Mon–Fri 8am–4.30pm; ☏360/691-7791). As for

lodging, the main place to stop is the basic *Mountain View Inn* motel, 32005 Mountain Loop Hwy, around mile 10 (☎360/691-6668; ❹), which also provides the best of a very limited selection of **restaurants** in the area – in this case, serving up steaks, seafood, and burgers, highlighted by a nice rainbow trout. If you'd prefer to rough it and **camp**, there are plenty of options on this scenic byway (most $10–16); Mount Pilchuck and Monte Cristo offer some of the most attractive choices. Finally, if you're intending to **hike**, a $5 Northwest Forest Pass is required at a number of sites along the road. Order one online or pick one up at a local ranger station; check ⓦwww .fs.fed.us/r6/mbs/passes for details.

East from Seattle

The drive **east from Seattle** – through the mountains on I-90 – is one of the prime routes for urbanites escaping the Emerald City and, in the other direction, for tourists headed toward it. Not surprisingly, it is also among the least engaging ways to see the Washington Cascades, with a smattering of major attractions here and there, and a steady stream of SUVs and RVs to crowd your path. Although **Snoqualmie Falls** is one of the most prominent sites, and deservedly a well-loved highlight of the state's natural attractions, the others are rather few and far between until you get to the eastern Washington gateway of Ellensburg (see p.451). The highway does, however, meander past some interesting, serpentine lakes and rugged mountain passes, and is good for accessing off-road hiking and skiing options, with a few good spots for lodging and dining.

Snoqualmie Falls and around

As the lowest and most traversable of the Cascade crossings, **Snoqualmie Pass** was long the regular route of traders, trappers, and Native Americans. Upon reaching the area, some 25 miles outside Seattle, turn off I-90 at Exit 31 for the five-mile detour north through North Bend along Hwy 202 to **Snoqualmie Falls** (☎425/831-5784, ⓦwww.snoqualmiefalls.com). Exceeding Niagara Falls in height by 100ft, the dreamlike vision was pictured in the opening sequence of David Lynch's cult TV show *Twin Peaks*. The flow, actually controlled by the local power company, cascades 270ft from the heights of a solid-bedrock gorge and spews out a dense, almost choking mist in places. The **observation platform** is just across from the parking lot cantilevered over the gorge to provide can't-miss shots for amateur shutterbugs. For an equally dramatic but less crowded viewpoint, take the half-mile **River Trail**, which leads from the platform to the bottom of the falls. Between the platform and the waterfall is the **Salish Lodge** (☎425/888-2556 or 1-800/826-6124, ⓦwww.salishlodge .com; ❾), the grand wooden structure that featured in many *Twin Peaks* episodes. It's wonderful for its plush guest rooms with whirlpool tubs, fireplaces, and luxurious in-room amenities, as well as an onsite spa, chic dining room for Northwest Cuisine, and similarly upscale bistro.

Several miles south of the falls, in the town of North Bend, you can grab a slice of the famous cherry pie at the legendary ⌘ **Mar-T Cafe**, now known as *Twede's*, 137 W North Bend Way (☎425/831-5511), where Twin Peaks agent Dale Cooper always took care to enjoy a "damn fine cup o' coffee." If you're not interested in TV-related tourism, you may enjoy **hiking** some of the nearby trails, the best of which are near North Bend at **Mount Si**. A good choice is the steep, four-mile climb up to Mount Si's peak, which begins on

Mount Si Road. Towering trees shade the trail most of the way to the stony area near the 4000ft summit, where great views of the surrounding mountains (including Mount Rainier) can be had. The hair-raising walk to the top of the nearby "haystack" outcropping is not advised for casual day-trippers. Another good hike is the less steep, but still challenging, route up neighboring **Little Si**, accessible from a trail that begins near the junction of Mount Si Road and 434th Avenue. The five-mile round-trip takes you up to Little Si's 1600ft peak, in the process winding its way past much striking scenery – huge Ice Age–era boulders, dark, primeval-looking forests, and, in the spring, meadows flush with wildflowers.

Mount Baker–Snoqualmie National Forest

From Snoqualmie Falls, I-90 dips, rises, and curves around the topography of the southern side of **Mount Baker–Snoqualmie National Forest**, which has agreeable trails along the way. Among them is the transcontinental Pacific Crest Trail (see p.51), which crosses the summits of Red and Silver mountains around a severe clockwise hairpin in the highway. For more information on exploring this captivating landscape, visit the **ranger station** back in North Bend, 42404 SE North Bend Way (Mon–Fri 8am–4.30pm; ☎425/888-1421, ⊛www.fs.fed .us/r6/mbs), or the one at **Snoqualmie Pass** (summer Mon–Fri 8am–4.30pm; rest of year Fri–Sun 9am–3pm; ☎425/434-6111). The pass itself is a 3000ft notch through the Cascades, around which are some good hikes, highlighted by the **Snow Lake Trail**, at Exit 52 off I-90. This is an intense, three-mile one-way trek that has a spur to Source Lake, but is most memorable for its switchbacks leading up to a mountain ridge and lake overlook, from which you can continue on to other rugged trails along Rock Creek or the High Lakes. **Skiing** is also excellent in this area, with the resort at the ⋇ **Summit at Snoqualmie** (☎425/434-7669, ⊛www.summitatsnoqualmie .com) among the best, with four separate sites around Exit 53 off I-90, daily lift tickets for $46–49, night skiing for $31, and rental packages running $29–35. Other perks include the trio of **terrain parks** and a superpipe for gung-ho snowboarders. For other pursuits, you can get a day pass for snowshoeing ($11) or inner tubing or cross-country skiing (both around $13–19). Serious adventurers, though, will want to take on the resort's **Alpental** course on the opposite side of I-90, deep-powder terrain that's full of black-diamond runs with names like "Adrenalin" and meant for the most skilled skiers and boarders. You'll even need a backcountry pass, or "card," to access this slope, since the area is prone to avalanches and there's always a possibility of getting trapped in a blizzard or other disaster and needing rescue. Drop by a ski-patrol shack to get more information and a card.

Cle Elum to Roslyn

Ten miles east, the road passes a trio of glacially carved finger lakes – **Keechelus**, **Kachess**, and **Cle Elum** – surrounded by handsome mountain scenery and lined with a number of **campgrounds** (late May to Sept; $16–20). These are places that, depending on the season, are terrific for their hiking, cross-country skiing, and especially fishing – kokanee and lake trout in particular. Just to the southeast of Cle Elum Lake, you reach little **CLE ELUM** ("Swift Water" in Salish), once a company town created by the Northern Pacific Railroad when coal deposits were found in the area, ultimately leading to two millions tons of the mineral being removed from the area every year. The **Chamber of Commerce**, 401 W 1st St (Mon–Fri 9am–4pm; ☎509/674-5958), can direct you to the town's historic high point, the fascinating **Coal Mines Trail**, a 4.7-mile course that heads to Roslyn and beyond, and leads past all manner of obscure and conspicuous relics from the old industrial era – which ended in 1963 when the last mine closed – as well as ominous signs telling of the various explosions that took the lives of miners in the early twentieth century. For **food**, you can stock up on fresh bread and cinnamon rolls at the *Cle Elum Bakery*, 501 E 1st St (℡509/674-2233). A good-value place to **stay** is the *Stewart Lodge*, 805 W 1st St (℡509/674-4548, Ⓦwww.stewartlodge.com; ❹), which has basic but clean rooms with fridges and microwaves, as well as a two-bedroom cottage with kitchen, Jacuzzi, and fireplace.

The area's main draw is, however, the town's neighbor, **ROSLYN**, a five-minute drive from the lakeshore on Hwy 903, an Appalachian look-alike of old timber houses in a forest pocked with slag heaps. Every inch a company town, no one seemed bothered about Roslyn until its unreconstructed appearance was "discovered" by TV location scouts and used as the set for *Northern Exposure*. With its fame have come the sightseers (fewer since the show's been canceled), but it's still an odd sort of place. To get the lowdown on the town's history and see memorabilia from the TV show, check out the **Roslyn Museum**, 203 Pennsylvania Ave (daily 1–4pm; ℡509/649-2776). Next door, the *Roslyn Café* (℡509/649-2763) serves delicious burgers and bagels.

Mount Rainier National Park

Set in its own national park ninety miles southeast of Seattle, glacier-clad **MOUNT RAINIER** is, at 14,410ft, the tallest and most accessible of the Cascade peaks, and a major Washington landmark – prominent in the background of countless Seattle cityscape photos. To the Native Americans living in its shadow, it spawned a complex mythology, appearing as a jealous wife who was magically metamorphosed into a giant mountain vengefully

△ Snowcapped Mount Rainier

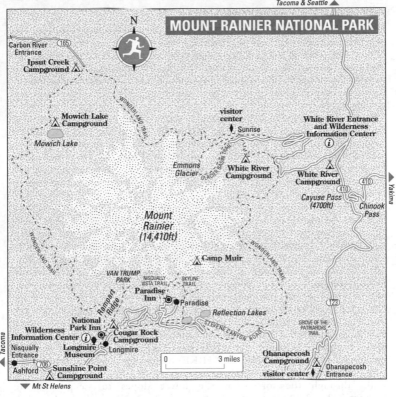

protective of its higher ridges and peaks. On no account would local **Klickitat** venture up the slopes into this hostile spirit country, where the hazards were inscrutable to human eyes – an apt conclusion, considering the summit is wreathed in clouds much of the time. The Klickitat called the mountain *Tahoma* ("snowiest peak"), and there have been moves to revive the original appellation if for no other reason than to end the dire puns about the name describing the weather (though Rainier is actually pronounced "ray-NEER"). The mountain acquired its current moniker after explorer George Vancouver named it after one of his cronies, eighteenth-century British rear admiral **Peter Rainier**, who never even saw it.

Mount Rainier sees heavy snowfall during the long winter season, and along with it a steady stream of snowshoers, snowboarders, and crosscountry skiers. There are both marked and unmarked trails on novice, intermediate, and advanced routes, varying in length from one to ten miles; check with park staff for current routes and availability, which depend on snow conditions.

As spring takes hold, the snow-line creeps up the mountain, unblocking roads and revealing a lattice of **hiking trails**, which at the higher elevations are rarely clear before mid-June. July and August are the sunniest months, when the air is crisp and clear, meadows sprout alpine flowers, and wildlife emerges, with deer, elk, and mountain goats at the forest edges and small furry marmots scuttling among their burrows.

Arrival and information

Note that in November 2006 the park closed due to extensive **flooding**, and many visitor centers, campgrounds, and facilities have still not been reopened as of press time. Parts of the park may be open by autumn of 2007, but you should check the status of any site you plan to visit by either calling or looking on the website. The contacts, hours, and prices below reflect those in place before the flooding – expect reduced hours, at a minimum, as facilities are rebuilt and operations resume.

Mount Rainier National Park is roughly square in shape, with an entrance at each corner; the nearest to Seattle, **Nisqually**, lies at the park's southwest corner. Other than this main entrance, there are two entrances on the park's eastern flank, **Ohanapecosh** to the south and **White River** in the north. **Carbon River**, the fourth and least-visited entrance, can be found in the park's more remote northwest corner (visitor center information for each of these is provided on the following pages).

If you're coming in by car, head south on I-5, taking Exit 127 onto Hwy 512 east, and after a few miles follow Hwy 7 south to Hwy 706, where you'll enter the park just short of Longmire, a small cluster of buildings that includes the **Longmire Museum** (May to mid-Oct 9am–5pm; mid-Oct to Dec 9am–4pm; closed Jan–April; ☎360/569-2211, ext. 3314). The museum offers information on area wildlife and the mountain and sells seven-day **park permits** – $15 per vehicle, or $5 each for those on foot, bike, or motorcycle – and **annual passes** to the park, covering a vehicle driver and passengers, for $30. Be aware that road access depends on weather conditions, so unless you're traveling in the height of summer, call ahead to the National Park Service (☎360/569-2211, ⓦwww.nps.gov/mora) for details. Next door to the Longmire Museum, the **Wilderness Information Center** (June to mid-Oct 7.30am–5pm; ☎360/569-HIKE) has plenty of information on the park's network of **trails**, over three hundred miles in all, ranging from easy walks through the forests of the lower slopes to steep treks to Rainier's 14,411-foot summit. Longmire's *National Park Inn* (see "Accommodation," below) is the only place in the park to rent **skis** and **snowshoes** in winter.

Tours are limited to the mountain, with many operators having gone out of business. One of those remaining, **Gray Line**, operates daily, ten-hour-long round-trips (May–Sept; $59; ☎360/624-5077 or 1-800/426-7505, ⓦwww .graylineseattle.com); reservations are required.

Accommodation

The park offers two splendid **lodges**, though the *Paradise Inn* – a stately 1917 timber hotel – will be closed for renovation until 2008. There are also six **campgrounds** ($10–15), available on a first-come, first-served basis, except for Cougar Rock, in the southwest part of the park, and Ohanapecosh, in the southeast (reserve for both at ☎1-800/365-CAMP). The only campgrounds open throughout the year, and not just in the high season, are Sunshine Point, adjacent to the Nisqually entrance, and Ipsuit Creek, five miles east of the Carbon River entrance – though they offer only eighteen and twenty-nine campsites, respectively. **Wilderness permits** (free, or $20 by reservation at ☎360/569-2211 or ⓦreservations.nps.gov) are required for heading into the backcountry with your gear. If all else fails, there's standard motel **accommodation** in Ashford, just outside the Nisqually entrance, as well as the more distinctive choices listed below.

Mountain Meadows Inn 20912 State Route 706 East, Ashford ☎360/569-2788, ⓦwww .mountainmeadowsinn.com. Six cozy, antique-laden B&B rooms with various historic themes (early Colonial, Native American, and so on), some detached from the main house and offering kitchenettes and claw-foot tubs. Onsite hot tub also available for use by all guests. ❻

Mounthaven 38210 State Route 706 East, Ashford ☎360/569-2594 or 1-800/456-9380, ⓦwww .mounthaven.com. Nine cabins, some with fireplaces, kitchenettes, fridges, wood stoves, and porches, on six acres lying between two mountain creeks. Hot tub (for a fee) and playground; minimum two-day stay on weekends. Also seventeen full-hookup RV sites for $25. ❺

National Park Inn at Longmire in Mount Rainier National Park ☎360/569-2275, ⓦwww .guestservices.com/rainier. Currently the only park lodge open. Comfortable accommodations in a classically rustic lodge, with 25 guest rooms and a restaurant. Cross-country skiing and snowshoe rentals available. Open year-round, though B&B amenities such as complimentary breakfast are included only in the winter and spring; reservations essential. Add $34 for private bath. ❻

StormKing Cabins 37311 State Route 706 East, Ashford ☎360/569-2964, ⓦwww .stormkingspa.com. Not exactly roughing it, but if you want the feel of a real-wood cabin nestled in a forest glade, then these four luxury units, with kitchenettes, hot tubs, fireplaces, and mosaic floors, will more than suffice. Two-night minimum stay. Also offers spa treatments ($50 and up), and sauna and hot tub rentals ($15 per hour) to non-guests. ❼

Whittaker's Bunkhouse 30205 State Route 706 East, Ashford ☎360/569-2439, ⓦwww .whittakersbunkhouse.com. A favorite among local climbers and hikers, this old loggers' bunkhouse offers both dorm beds (❶) and double rooms (❹) with private baths, plus an onsite hot tub, espresso bar, and Internet access.

Nisqually entrance trails

After passing through the **Nisqually entrance** and beginning at Longmire, the **Trail of the Shadows** is a popular half-hour stroll around the alpine meadow where James Longmire, a local farmer, built a now-defunct mineral-springs resort at the end of the nineteenth century. Although it's no match for the higher, steeper, and less accessible trails, it's still a pleasant walk through meadow and forest in the shadow of mountain peaks, passing an early homestead cabin along the way. Leading off from this loop are more strenuous hikes, such as the five-mile **Rampart Ridge Trail**, which takes you on a climb through thick trees to the ridge – created by an ancient lava flow – from where you'll have a good view of the mountain.

The Trail of the Shadows loop also intersects with the 93-mile **Wonderland Trail**, which encircles the mountain and is an essential route for serious nature enthusiasts in excellent physical condition; hiking the length of it will take you ten to fourteen days. A hardy but manageable hike branching off from the trail (four to five hours one-way) begins back in Longmire near the Wilderness Information Center (see opposite). From there, head two miles northeast through old-growth forest to the Cougar Rock campground; as the trail meanders to Reflection Lakes, five miles east, it crosses over the Nisqually River – with its muddy-gray, glacier-fed waters – then follows Paradise River by some lovely waterfalls.

Keep in mind that, although trails around Longmire are free from snow earlier than those at higher elevations, in midsummer you'll probably want to drive farther up the mountain, where much of the snow, still many feet deep even in June, will have melted enough to allow passage that's impossible at other times of the year.

Trails from Paradise

From Longmire, it's just eleven miles through the thinning forest, past waterfalls of glacial snowmelt, to **Paradise**, where the **Jackson visitor center** (May to mid-Oct daily 10am–6pm; mid-Oct to Dec 10am–5pm; ☎360/569-2211 ext.

2328) has films and exhibits on natural history and offers a circular observation room for viewing the mountain. From Paradise, both the 1.2-mile **Nisqually Vista Trail** loop and the five-mile **Skyline Trail** climb the mountain, providing gorgeous views of its craggy peak and glistening glaciers. The park rangers also offer a summer program of **guided walks**, and from late December to early April, two-hour guided snowshoe walks leave from the visitor center (weekends only 10.30am & 2.30pm; limited to 25 people on first-come, first-served basis; $1 for snowshoe rental, or bring your own).

Paradise is the starting-point for **climbing Mount Rainier**, a serious endeavor involving ice axes, crampons, and some degree of danger. It usually takes two days to get to the summit – with its twin craters rimmed with ice caves – and back. On the first day climbers aim for the base camp at **Camp Muir**, ready for the strenuous final assault and the descent to Paradise on the second. You have to **register** with the rangers, paying $30 per person, and an additional $20 for the climbing party (information at ☏360/569-HIKE or 360/569-2211, ext. 3314). Unless you're very experienced, the way to do it is with the Rainier Mountaineering guide service in Paradise (☏360/569-2227, ⓦwww.rmiguides.com), which offers three-day courses – one day's practice, then the two-day climb – from May to mid-October for $805. Specialist equipment rental (lug-sole climbing boots, ice axes) costs extra, and reservations with advance payment in full are required.

Other entrances

In summer, it's possible to drive about an hour from Paradise along rugged **Stevens Canyon Road** to the park's southeast corner, cruising around hillside ridges on a winding concourse with plenty of switchbacks. Here, the **Ohanapecosh entrance** and **visitor center** (July–Oct daily 9am–5pm; ☏360/569-6046) is set in deep forest near the gurgling Ohanapecosh River. Among several trails in the area, one of the most enjoyable is the **Grove of the Patriarchs**, a 1.5-mile loop along an islet in the Ohanapecosh River, where there are ancient groves of giant Douglas fir, western hemlock, and red cedar trees.

North from Ohanapecosh, in the park's northeast corner, is the **White River entrance** and the **White River Wilderness Information Center** (July–Oct daily 7.30am–4.30pm; ☏360/569-6046), which gives out trail information and issues backcountry and climbing permits. Six miles west, at the White River campground, you can reach any number of trails leading around mountain ridges and the lower reaches of glaciers, or pick up the **Wonderland Trail**, which traces the shores of the dramatic Shadow and Frozen lakes and offers astounding views of the volcanic terrain. Eleven miles farther up the mountain from the White River entrance, on another winding route full of switchbacks, the **Sunrise visitor center** (July–Sept daily 9am–5pm; ☏360/663-2425) affords wonderful views of **Emmons Glacier**, a huge tongue of ice on the mountain's northeastern side, and of the mountain summit. The hardiest hikers can get a better look on the **Glacier Basin Trail**, a seven-mile slog with striking summer views of wildflowers, craggy peaks, and mountain goats.

The last and least frequently visited of the national park's four entrances, the **Carbon River entrance** lies in the northwest corner of the park, and isn't linked by road to the other three. Hwy 165, the paved approach road, runs as far as the ranger station, which serves as the trailhead for the short and easy **Carbon River Rainforest Trail**, which nudges into Mount Rainier's one and only chunk of temperate rain forest. As visually evocative as the forest's moss-covered spruces and canopies of greenery are, it's a long way to go for a trail that's just a third of a mile long. More rugged types should consider the seven-mile round-trip **Carbon Glacier Trail**, beginning at the Ipsut Creek campground (four miles east of the Carbon River park entrance), highlighted by a suspension bridge that crosses a river below the mouth of the dirty, crumbling Carbon Glacier – the glacier of lowest elevation in the US outside of Alaska, and the source for the Carbon River itself.

Mount St Helens National Volcanic Monument

The native Klickitat knew **MOUNT ST HELENS** as *Tahonelatclah* or "fire mountain" – and, true to its name, in May of 1980 the mountain erupted, leaving a blasted landscape and scenes of almost total destruction for many miles around. Slowly but surely, though, second-growth forests are emerging, and the ash is disappearing beneath new vegetation. That said, much of the land continues to bear witness to the incredible force of the eruption, with once-pristine valleys sheared by mudflows, mangled trees ripped from their roots, and entire mountainsides resembling a post-nuclear wasteland. And recent tremors and small billows of steam and ash haven't given any relief that the mountain is finished with its violent business.

Arrival and information

Designated a National Volcanic Monument, Mount St Helens has understandably become a major attraction in the region, making a feasible **day-trip** of around two hundred miles from Olympia. While it's only half that distance from Portland, the approach from the south passes slopes that bear few traces of the eruption – the most dramatic views are almost entirely confined to its northwest side. Thus, most tourists head for the two **visitor centers** – **Coldwater Ridge** and the smaller **Johnston Ridge Observatory** – that overlook the blast area from the northwest. These are reached, traveling north on I-5, by turning off at Hwy 504 (or traveling south, via its main feeder road, Hwy 505) roughly halfway between Olympia and Portland. The other main approach road is the quieter Hwy 503, which runs to the mountain's steep and densely forested southern slopes. During the summer, the east side of the mountain can also be reached along paved forest roads from US-12 to the north and Hwy 14 in the south. These eastern access roads are connected to Hwy 503, which means it's possible to drive across the mountain's south and east flanks, though this is a time-consuming haul. Note that **flooding** in November 2006 damaged some roads in the Mount St Helens area (though not as extensively as at Mt Rainier), so call or check online if you plan on accessing any particular back road, as some may be closed due to flooding damage or seasonal weather.

If possible, visit during the week, as traffic can clog the access roads on summer weekends. Check winter and other conditions ahead of time (and for general information) by calling the **Mount St Helens Silver Lake Visitor Center**, five miles east of Castle Rock at 3029 Spirit Lake Hwy (daily 9am–4pm; summer closes 5pm; ☏360/274-0962, ⓦwww.fs.fed.us/gpnf/mshnvm). The one-day **Monument Pass** ($3 single visit, $6 multiple visits) allows entry to the Coldwater Ridge and Mount St Helens visitor centers, and the Johnston

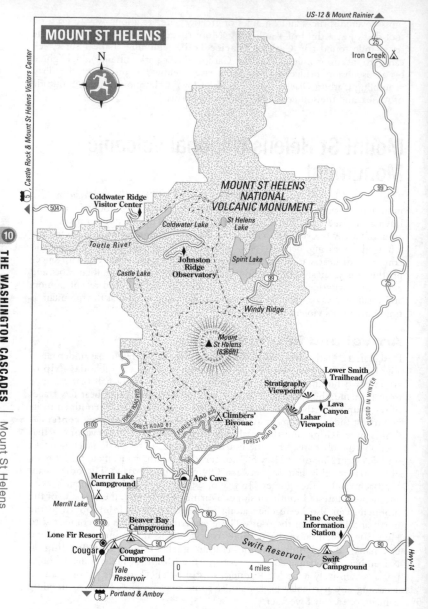

MOUNT ST HELENS

N

Iron Creek

Coldwater Ridge
Visitor Center

MOUNT ST HELENS
NATIONAL
VOLCANIC MONUMENT

Castle Rock & Mount St Helens Visitors Center

Coldwater Lake

St Helens
Lake

Toutle River

Johnston
Ridge
Observatory

Spirit Lake

Castle Lake

Windy Ridge

Mount
▲ St Helens
(8366ft)

Lower Smith
Trailhead

Stratigraphy
Viewpoint

Lava
Canyon

Climbers'
Bivouac

Lahar
Viewpoint

CLOSED IN WINTER

FOREST ROAD 83

Merrill Lake
Campground

Ape Cave

Merrill Lake

Pine Creek
Information
Station

Beaver Bay
Campground

Lone Fir Resort

Cougar

Cougar
Campground

Swift Reservoir

Swift
Campground

Yale
Reservoir

0   4 miles

Portland & Amboy

Hwy-14

Ridge Observatory, while the **Northwest Forest Pass** ($5) is good for other sites, such as the Ape Cave and Lava Canyon, and is available through putting money in drop boxes at site parking lots. You can also see the blown-out mountain on a dramatic 30min **helicopter tour** over the caldera, from Hillsboro Aviation, leaving from the Hoffstadt Bluffs Visitor Center, 27 miles east of I-5 at Exit 49 (flights June–Sept 11am–6pm; $129 per person;

Scenic hikes

One of the undisputed glories of the Pacific Northwest is its direct and immediate access to a wealth of scenic hikes in a variety of forms, for both hardcore adventurers and pleasure-seeking strollers. Oregon and Washington offer a bevy of routes in varied locations, from national, state, and local parks, to urban esplanades and promenades, to remote forests, prairies, and deserts. Obviously, for the longer hauls you should be well prepared, but part of the joy of the outdoors in the Northwest is its spontaneous appeal – an excellent hike through a dappled forest grove or along a beachside path or wetland overlook is rarely more than an hour's drive away.

Urban jaunts

The Northwest's cities hold a number of great trails in their midst. Seattle's verdant jewel in its crown of parks is the Burke-Gilman Trail, a splendid 27-mile route that lines the northern side of the ship canal from Ballard to Lake Washington. The fittest walkers can continue

▲ Wildwood Trail, Portland's Forest Park

on to the eastern suburbs on the ten-mile Sammamish River Trail, finally ending up in pleasant Marymoor Park around Bellevue. There are also easier Seattle strolls around the Washington Park Arboretum and Foster Island. In Portland, the main long-distance draw is the engaging Wildwood Trail, which offers thirty miles of trekking over forested slopes and creek beds in the city's outstanding Forest Park. Much less green is the Eastbank Esplanade, a true urban constitutional between the Willamette River and I-5 freeway, which brings you over several city bridges, past the old Eastside industrial zone, and near the roar of highway traffic. Other cities, too, have worthwhile trail systems, from the running paths of Eugene's Alton Baker Park to Spokane's Centennial Trail to Wenatchee's historic Apple Capital Loop Trail to Bend's fetching thirty-mile Deschutes River Trail.

Mountain climbs — and hikes

Mountain climbing is obviously serious business in the Cascades of the Northwest, and the leading peaks for such activity — Hood, Rainier, Olympus, and Baker — are all protected by a clutch of regulations, especially in the wake of the recent deaths of several members of climbing expeditions. Those desiring a rugged trip up a mountainside without putting their life in jeopardy might consider a **mountain hike**.

Called "climbing" by official agencies, mountain hiking isn't as dangerous as a full-scale climb up a glaciated peak because the slopes may be lower, their terrain more even, or they may not even lead to a peak at all. That's certainly the case with **Mount St Helens**, which amounts to a rugged hike up half a mountain, since the top blew away 27 years ago. Also good is the hearty hike up **Mount Adams**, which many people use as an excuse to go schussing down from the summit on skis or a snowboard. Oregon's Cascades, too, have a range of good mountain-hiking options, from the manageable journey up small, wildflower-covered peaks like **Iron Mountain** to the lengthier scrambles up **Mount McLoughlin**, with its blocky terrain and remnants of glacial moraines, and **Mount Thielsen**, whose unusually eroded, ten-foot-wide summit well rewards the eight-mile ascent. In any case, if you make a serious hike up a mountain and leave the crampons and ice axes behind, it's an easy way to tell the folks back home that you climbed up a mountain in the Cascades and lived to tell about it, without risking your life in the process.

The rugged outdoors

The Northwest's federal and state parks are among the best in the nation for hiking. Oregon's one national park, **Crater Lake**, offers nice sightseeing from the trails that follow the rim of its blown-out volcano, while Washington's **Olympic National Park** has dozens of ways to explore its signature rain forests, where the old growth is thick enough to blot out the sun. Hardier hikers may take as a challenge the steep haul up **Cape Perpetua** along Oregon's coast, or the varied scenery of the eight-mile **Discovery Trail** along Washington's. The **Cascade Mountains** of either state offer short, fascinating walks past **historic ruins** deep in the forest (the Old Robe and Coal Mines trails), **longer jaunts** that lead to good views of the surrounding terrain and seasonal flora (the Twin Tunnels route, Chelan Gorge

▲ Oregon Dunes National Recreational Area

Road), or **serious expeditions** into the outback that require plenty of preparation, time, and stamina – or a handy mountain bike (the McKenzie River Trail, Devil's Gulch Trail). If you're headed into the Cascades, though, be prepared to acquire the required passes and permits (see p.54), and register with a ranger station for any lengthy excursions.

The long haul

Oregon and Washington also feature several **long-haul trails**. The lengthiest of these treks can make for a multi-day or multi-week affair, so you'll have to carry your own water, food, a tent, maps, and other provisions, and be ready to be alone for hours or days at a time, perhaps in the company of a lone black bear, coyote, or mountain lion. The king of these trails is the **Pacific Crest Trail**, an incredible natural concourse that runs along the spine of the Cascades in both states and connects Canada and Mexico on an amazing 2650-mile run. Any section of the PCT is a major undertaking, given the remote locations of most of the trail and the difficulty of arranging transport at either end. A more manageable option is the **OC&E Woods Line** near Klamath Falls, which occupies a former railbed and runs a hundred miles across all kinds of terrain past marvelous vistas of southern Oregon. In Washington, the **Columbia Plateau Trail** is another former railbed hiking course that links the outskirts of Spokane with the Tri-Cities on a spellbinding 130-mile tour of the channeled scablands in the southeast. Although the Washington coast has a few long hikes, it has nothing to match the scenic splendor of the 360-mile **Oregon Coast Trail**, which wends past the state's many protected beaches and parks to present a picture of the shoreline in all its rugged beauty.

▼ Hikers in Washington's Tatoosh Wilderness

Hidden hiking gems

Many of the best Northwest jaunts are the least discovered, leading past lovely vistas unknown to others, or perhaps bypassed in favor of more popular excursions. What follows is a selection of some of the more intriguing places for your expeditions.

Alpine Lakes Wilderness – Thousands of acres of striking wilderness set in the Washington Cascades, and laced by fine paths like the nine-mile Enchantment Lake Trail overlooking some of the best views.

Black Crater – A little-known former volcano in the Oregon Cascades, whose 7.5-mile ascent rewards the hiker with magnificent views of the mountain scenery, including the Three Sisters and Broken Top.

Blacklock Point – The undeveloped Floras Lake State Natural Area (see p.178) along Oregon's southern coast is vivid for its volcanic columns, railway ruins, and limestone cliffs, and two enticing trails lead through the heart of the area.

Cape Flattery – An unpaved road and a short half-mile hike lead you out to this remote headland, which is well worth the journey for its views of oceanside rain forests, its sea caves, and its position at the very northwestern edge of the continental US.

Dusty Lake – One of the more accessible of Washington's intriguing "pothole lakes," carved out by Ice Age floods and surrounded by majestic, thousand-foot-high basalt mesas and good for their views, fishing, and birdwatching.

Juniper Dunes – Only recently opened to legal hiking, this sandy preserve in southeastern Washington is a remnant of the Bretz Floods (see p.462), and an unexpected place to find juniper trees and 130ft-tall sand dunes.

Kalmiopsis Wilderness – A massive, 180,000-acre swath of pure wilderness between the Rogue River Valley and southern Oregon coast, where nature is at its wildest, without any facilities or development.

Lime Kiln Trail – Evocative trek along the Stillaguamish River past the romantic ruins of a lime-quarrying complex, whose railway, saw blades, and relics are now overgrown with ferns, and its signature lime kiln an abandoned monolith.

Sky Lakes Wilderness – With more than 100,000 acres, 200 lakes, and countless pumice fields and volcanic formations, this is an undisputed highlight of southern Oregon – and surprisingly little known to Northwesterners, much less tourists.

South Breitenbush Gorge – Accessible on a National Scenic Trail, this area deserves the accolades for its splendid five-mile concourse along a riverbank that leads through a stark, steeply walled basalt canyon.

▲ Walking the Washington Coast

☎360/274-7750); this center is basically aimed at the summer tourist trade, with books, craftworks, videos, and, of course, preserved pockets of volcanic ash from the 1980 eruption.

Climbing the mountain

A network of **hiking trails** radiates out from the access roads as they near the mountain, exploring its every nook and volcanic cranny, but unless you're indifferent to clouds of dust and ash, a morning or afternoon hike is really enough. If you'd like to **climb** the mountain, you'll be ascending nearly four thousand feet within five miles up to the truncated summit at 8365 feet – a serious trek, to be sure, but with a lesser risk than the higher, more perilous climbs up mounts Rainier and Hood. The route begins at the **Climbers' Bivouac**, at the end of a hair-raising road high up the mountain, and the round-trip takes between seven and twelve hours. The climb takes you to the crater rim, but the crater itself – a jagged cauldron of rock and steam – is out of bounds (though geologists and other scientists are allowed to visit it by helicopter).

Permits are required for those interested in climbing above 4800 feet (lower-level routes don't require them), where the majority of routes up to the summit begin. From mid-May to October, only a hundred permits per day are given out, for $22 each, and you must reserve your permit ahead of time online at ⓦ www.mshinstitute.org – the process is first-come, first-served, so make your reservation as soon as possible; no refunds are allowed. From April to mid-May, the fee is still charged, but there's no limit on the number of daily permits (which still must be reserved online). The rest of the year (Nov–Mar) there's no fee or limit, but you still need a permit and cannot reserve it online. To pick up a permit, reserved or otherwise, you have to go to *Jack's Restaurant* (☎360/231-4276), five miles west of Cougar, a tiny settlement on Hwy 503.

Note that with the increased seismic activity on the mountain in 2005–06, the park service has been occasionally disallowing climbing above 4800 feet. Check or call for details on the latest conditions.

Accommodation

If you're keen to avoid a long drive – especially on summer weekends when traffic clogs the access roads – or want to have time for a decent hike, then **staying** overnight in the area is a good choice. There's motel accommodation beside the junction of I-5 and Hwy 504 in the uneventful town of **Castle Rock**, but your best bet may be to aim for the hamlet of **Cougar**, which straggles along Hwy 503 nearer the mountain.

Although there aren't any government-run **campgrounds** within the national monument, there are private ones (all $15, except Swift) operated by the PacifiCorp energy company, in the vicinity of Cougar (June–Aug only; ☎503/813-6666 for reservations): the Cougar campsite, located on Yale Reservoir just north of the village (reservations required); Beaver Bay, about a mile north on 503 (first-come, first-served); Cresap Bay, accessed by turning right at *Jack's Restaurant* while going east on Hwy 503 and continuing on for two miles south (reservations required); and Swift (first-come, first-served; $12), near the Pine Creek Information Station southeast of the mountain on Hwy 90. Inside the park, **wilderness camping** is allowed below 4800 feet, and at Climbers Bivouac – the Northwest Forest Pass is required ($5; see opposite).

Ike Kinswa State Park 14 miles east of I-5 (exit 68) on US Hwy 12, near Mossyrock ☏360/864-2643, ⓦwww.parks.wa.gov. Located north of the mountain, and spread over 450 acres. Good for its boating, fishing, and water sports, with more than a hundred campsites. $17–24.

Lone Fir Resort 16806 Lewis River Rd (Hwy 503) in Cougar ☏360/238-5210, ⓦwww.lonefirresort .com. Seventeen basic motel rooms, half with kitchens and microwaves, plus a swimming pool, and located along a central route on the south side of the mountain; ❷–❹. Also has RV and tent camping for $15–27.

Mount St Helens Motel 1340 Mount St Helens Way in Castle Rock, near the junction of I-5 and Hwy 504 ☏360/274-7721, ⓦwww.mtsthelensmotel.com. Standard motel accommodations located a bit east from the main mountain attractions, though with queen-size beds in every room. ❸

Seaquest State Park at Silver Lake about five miles east of I-5 on Hwy 504 ☏1-800/452-5687, ⓦwww.parks.wa.gov. Spread over 475 acres (and across the road from the Mount St Helens Visitor Center), an excellent, scenic choice for birdwatching, cycling, hiking, and fishing, with 55 tent sites. $17–24.

Silver Lake Motel & Resort Hwy 504 six miles east of I-5 in Silver Lake ☏360/274-6141, ⓦwww .silverlake-resort.com. Convenient for mountain access and bass fishing – you can even cast a line from your balcony – with clean, comfortable motel rooms, with kitchenettes, right on the waterfront (❺) and cabin sites with kitchens (❹). Also has RV hookups ($27) and campsites ($17).

The eruptions of Mount St Helens

From its first rumblings in March 1980, **Mount St Helens** drew the nation's attention as one of the rare examples of (recent) volcanic activity in the continental US. Residents and loggers were evacuated and roads were closed, but by April the entrances to the restricted zone around the steaming peak were jammed with reporters and sightseers. However, the mountain didn't seem to be doing much, and impatient residents demanded to be allowed back to their homes. Harry Truman, operator of the Lodge at Spirit Lake, famously refused to move out and became a national celebrity, lauded for his "common sense" by Washington's governor.

Waiting at the barriers, a convoy of homeowners was about to go and collect their possessions when the **explosion** finally came on May 18 – powered by subsurface water heated to boiling by geothermal activity, and causing a chain reaction that blew apart the peak not upward but sideways, ripping a great chunk out of the northwest side of the mountain. An avalanche of debris slid into Spirit Lake, raising it by two hundred feet and turning it into a steaming cauldron of mud, as dark clouds of ash buried Truman and suffocated loggers on a nearby slope. Altogether, 57 people died on the mountain; a few were there doing their official duties, but most had ignored the warnings. The wildlife population was harder hit: about a million and a half animals – deer, elk, mountain goats, cougars, and bears – were killed, and thousands of fish were boiled alive in sediment-filled rivers. There were dire economic effects, too, as falling ash devastated the land, and millions of feet of timber were lost.

For decades afterward the mountain remained fairly quiet, with second-growth forests and groundcover taking root, and early colonizing plants and animals taking advantage of the relative lack of competition and predation. On October 1, 2004, though, the mountain rumbled back to life with small bursts of steam and ash that continued throughout the month. Despite predictions, however, no eruption came – that is, until **March 8, 2005**, when a minor, but actual, eruption at dusk clouded the skies with ash, creating a plume that reached a jet-level height of 36,000 feet in a few minutes. Since then, seismic activity and small hiccups of ash and steam have occurred, making the US Forest Service understandably nervous about letting hikers get too close to the forbidding crater.

Even if you want to keep your distance from this fearsome giant, the mountain's presence is unmistakable in the region, and not just up-close on the forest service roads. Indeed, looking north from southwest Washington and Portland, Oregon, you can't help but notice the looming silhouette of a ruined gray mound over the horizon, the charred remains of what was once a lively and romantic winter playground.

The northwest slope

The obvious introduction to Mount St Helens is on Hwy 504 (heading east from I-5), which takes you past the most dramatic volcanic scenery on the **northwest slope** of the mountain. The road runs through dark-green forests, past **Silver Lake** and **Toutle River Valley**, until bald, spiky trees signal a sudden change: beyond, thousands of gray tree-shards still lie in uniform rows, knocked flat in different directions back in 1980 when blast waves bounced off the hillsides. It's a weird and disconcerting landscape, the matchstick-like flattened forest left to rot to regenerate the soil and provide cover for small animals and insects. There are several good vantage points as you progress up the road – notably at **Hoffstadt Bluffs**, where you can make out the path taken by the avalanche of debris that swept down the valley – to the **Coldwater Ridge Visitor Center** (May–Oct daily 10am–6pm; rest of year Thurs–Mon 10am–5pm; ☎360/274-2114), which has exhibits, interpretive programs, and a film detailing the eruption.

Eight miles farther along Hwy 504, the low-slung **Johnston Ridge Observatory** (mid-May to Oct daily 10am–6pm; ☎360/274-2140) is as close as you'll get to the mountain by car, since the observatory lies at the end of a dead-end road; the views here, over the still-steaming lava dome and pumice plain, are quite extraordinary – the site was named after David Johnston, a government geologist who died at the location when the mountain erupted. Again, interpretive displays, a video, and a fifteen-minute film give the background. Outside the center, the half-mile paved **Eruption Trail** leads to slightly higher viewpoints marked with interpretive displays; there's also a short, dusty, and in places steep hiking trail that takes you toward **Spirit Lake**, with much longer and more strenuous side trails leading up toward the edge of the crater peak.

The south and east slopes

Interstate 5 intersects Hwy 503 twice before it reaches Portland, Oregon, and either exit will do to access the fascinating **south slope** of the mountain – the side seen mainly by locals, since tourists head to Johnston Ridge and few other locations. The highway leads both to **Cougar**, where there's a good motel and a campground, and nearby **Beaver Bay**, which has only a campground. Beyond Cougar, it's ten miles farther along Forest Road 83 to the **Ape Cave**, a rocky, tubelike lava cavern – the longest in the continental US – channeled two thousand years ago by the rushing molten lava of an eruption. Despite the compelling name, there are no oversize primates lurking inside – the place was named after the St Helens Apes, an outdoors group for local youth. In the cave, there are two subterranean routes to choose from: the three-quarter-mile lower trail, which requires you to return to the entrance to get out, and the much more difficult 1.5-mile upper trail, which emerges higher up the mountain. For a less strenuous jaunt, the quarter-mile **Trail of Two Forests** elevated boardwalk, off the road shortly before Ape Cave, has a 55ft crawl through a lava tunnel; bring a flashlight.

Ranger-led **tours** (July & Aug daily 10.30am–4.30pm, on the hour), pointing out all kinds of geological oddities you'd otherwise miss, leave from **Apes Headquarters** beside the cave. Lanterns can be rented until 4pm for $4 at the headquarters. Also, keep in mind that it's much colder in the cave than outside, so bring extra clothing.

Climbers Bivouac to Lava Canyon

Farther up the mountain, **hiking trails** climb and traverse the south side of Mount St Helens, exploring its every nook and cranny. Take detailed advice

△ Ape Cave

from the rangers before you set out on all but the shortest of walks, and remember to pack plenty of water. The most popular climbing route begins at the **Climbers Bivouac** trail base, high up the mountain at the end of hair-raising US Forest Service Road 830; it takes you to the crater rim and back in seven to twelve hours. Climbing is hedged with restrictions, though (see p.441).

Farther east begins an excellent drive on Forest Road 83, leading you past the highlights of the south slope. The first of these is the **Lahar Viewpoint**, which gives you a good look at how this side of the mountain was changed by mudflows both ancient and recent – the 1980 blast carved up many landscapes in the vicinity, exposing their basaltic rocks and geologic layers. Indeed, a short distance away, the **Stratigraphy Viewpoint** provides a look at one such vivid vista, where volcanic flows are revealed in bright horizontal bands of orange and yellow tephra (hardened ash). At the end of the loop, the **Lava Canyon** has several short trails leading past harrowing drop-offs near gigantic igneous rocks, past scenic waterfalls, to dramatic, mudflow-scoured landscapes. If you want to give yourself a scare, traverse the hanging **suspension bridge** that leads over the canyon's sheer-rock gorge, your heart skipping a beat with every rickety bounce.

Windy Ridge

Simply put, the **east slope** of Mount St Helens has the most striking, almost unbelievable views of the volcano's tremendous power, yet it is also the most difficult to reach. From Hwy 503, near where Forest Road 83 branches away, you'll need to travel 53 switchbacking miles to curve around the eastern side of the mountain. You can also travel there via the northern slope, but in the end it's no quicker. Along the way, you can check conditions at **Pine Creek Information Station**, seventeen miles east of Cougar on Hwy 90 (summer daily 9am–5pm), and then head north along Forest Road 25, before making the final push up Forest Road 99 to **Windy Ridge**, a rocky outcrop with breathtaking views of the crater from the northeast. A short hike from here also leads to the long, circular trail around the summit and the somewhat easier hike down past Spirit Lake to Johnston Ridge – though check with rangers about the latest conditions, since bad weather and seismic activity can keep many trails closed for months at a time.

On Windy Ridge, the devastation wrought by the 1980 eruption is glaring: entire slopes denuded of foliage, colossal tree husks scattered like twigs, and huge dead zones where everything alive was vaporized. The former resort area of **Spirit Lake**, below the ridge, was one such area: the lake's once deep-blue water boiled away during the cataclysm even as a violent cascade of burning rock and mud filled it with dark volcanic debris. Windy Ridge can also be accessed by car from the north from **Randle** off Hwy 12, which provides access to what remains of Spirit Lake and passes through lava flows with many fine viewpoints en route.

Mount Adams

A mere forty miles east of Mount St Helens, but inaccessible from it by road, 12,326ft **MOUNT ADAMS** is one of the less-heralded peaks in the Washington Cascades, but it nevertheless attracts its own devoted flock of outdoor adventurers – indeed, the Pacific Crest Trail (see p.51) heads over its western flank. Although the Yakama Indian Reservation stretches to its eastern flanks, the mountain is best approached via Washington Hwy 14 in the Columbia River Gorge, with a northbound turn onto Hwy 141 around Oregon's Hood River (see p.128). Although about a thousand feet taller than its southern neighbor Mount Hood (see p.131) on the opposite side of the gorge, Mount Adams has a less distinctive presence in the region, no doubt because of its smoother, more rounded summit and the easier slope of the land. Nonetheless, the mountain is the second-tallest in the Northwest and offers a beguiling topography with its surrounding landscape of broken lava beds, cinder cones, and basaltic buttes – highlighted by the **Guler Ice Caves** (May–Nov daily dawn–dusk), located five miles after the point where Hwy 141 turns west and becomes southbound Route 24. A 650ft-long lava tube whose stalactites and stalagmites are coated in ice and frost much of the year, the main cave – and the only one tourable – is especially dramatic in autumn, when it is a strange and chilly world of frosty domes, sparkling walls, and spiky ice crystals. The ice on the floors and rails can be hazardous, though, so make sure to bring along a flashlight, and don't get too enthralled by the natural spectacle and take a tumble onto the beautiful, but unforgiving, rocks.

Around the bend on Highway 141, Route 80 leads north toward the upper slopes of Mount Adams, but in branching off into the narrower Route 8040 stops at the trailhead at **Cold Springs**. In this area there are countless rugged hikes and paths around natural bridges, waterfalls, and the like, but in the summer if you want to aim for the summit, or ascend past 7000ft, you'll need a **Cascades Volcano Pass** ($10 weekdays, $15 weekends, $30 annual) and the requisite gear. It's quite an intense jaunt, taking you up the slope once traversed by mules, when the crest of the mountain was used for sulfur mining, and over the upper reaches of **Suksdorf Ridge** leading to the false summit of Pikers Peak, and then the actual summit. The mountain is not just for climbing per se, and attracts a small but fervent crowd of **skiers** during the spring and summer. However, all gear must be carried up the slopes **on foot**, and the mountainside runs are for serious schussing, gliding over steep canyon walls, across ice fields, and around glaciers and other challenging elements.

For **information** on the many excellent trails around the mountain, or for attaining passes, maps, and other materials, contact the official site for **Gifford Pinchot National Forest**, of which Mount Adams is a part (☎509/395-3400, ⓦwww.fs.fed.us/gpnf). If you're not going above 7000ft, you'll still need a free wilderness permit and a Northwest Forest Pass ($5); both are available from the **Mount Adams Ranger District** station, 2455 Hwy 141, near Trout Lake about 25 miles north of the Columbia Gorge (Mon–Fri 8am–4.30pm; ☎509/395-3400), as is a climbing register you'll need to sign before going up to the higher levels.

Eastern Washington

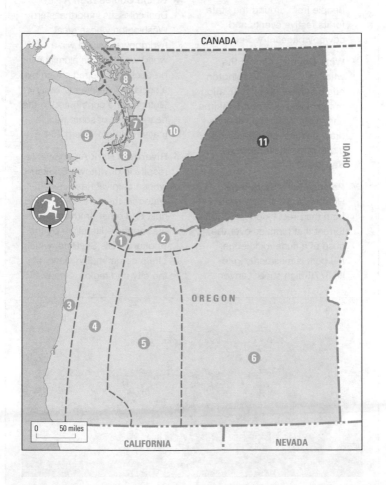

CHAPTER 11

Highlights

✳ **Ellensburg** A hardy but fetching town that offers historic architecture, some interesting museums, and a singular rodeo that draws people from around the state for its festive events and cowboy pageantry. See p.451

✳ **Wine Country** Almost the whole of eastern Washington offers some kind of cultivation of the vine, but around Yakima and Walla Walla the wineries draw national attention, and many offer onsite tastings. See p.456

✳ **Palouse Falls State Park** Home to the last large waterfall from the Bretz Floods, a 200ft torrent that tumbles over the cusp of a huge rock ledge, the park is mesmerizing for its 377ft-high sheer canyon walls and scabland features like flood-carved potholes and grand lava buttes and pinnacles. See p.463

✳ **Grand Coulee Dam** A New Deal colossus in northeastern Washington whose great hydropower helped win a world war (through aluminum production), inspired a tune by a socialist folksinger (Woody Guthrie), and contributed to the near-demise of some wildlife (native salmon). See p.464

✳ **Riverfront Park** An enjoyable respite in downtown Spokane, whose carnival rides, waterfall, theaters, ice-skating rink, and other amusements are topped – literally – by the Spokane Falls SkyRide, which offers commanding views of the city and region. See p.465

△ Palouse Falls

Eastern Washington

The parched, dusty terrain of **eastern Washington** is well off many tourists' radar screens, and with its isolation on the far side of the Cascades from the Puget Sound region, sizable farm plots, and arid climate it would seem to have little of the appeal of the rest of the state. However, while short of showcase museums, fine dining, and cultural icons, the area is nonetheless fascinating for two reasons – its wine and its geology. In short, eastern Washington has one of the most distinctive topographies in the nation, built on volcanic rocks and soil that make it perfect for natural sightseeing and wine growing.

Like eastern Oregon, eastern Washington is thinly populated and possesses only a couple of towns of any size – the compelling mix of old-time architecture and modern amusements that is **Spokane**, and the much less appealing **Tri-Cities** (Pasco, Richland, and Kennewick), once the heart of the American nuclear industry and now a rapidly expanding agricultural enclave. More enticing are **Ellensburg** and **Toppenish**, likable little Western places known for their restored architecture and rodeo, and Wild West murals, respectively. The center of the state wine industry, **Yakima** (and its surrounding valley) and **Walla Walla** are well worth a stop for a leisurely wine tour, with just a handful of attractions that don't involve grapes. Elsewhere, it's rural America without the window-dressing, a vast, empty region dotted with grain silos, 1950s diners, and battered pickup trucks, with dogs in the back and Stetsons in the front. A trip down **I-82** – connecting the eastern fringe of the Cascades with the northern rim of the Columbia River Gorge – is one way to explore the region, mainly hitting the larger towns; alternatively, you can make a beeline for Spokane on **I-90** on the way to Idaho or Montana. The most eye-opening features of the **Columbia Plateau** can be found, however, between the population centers in the **channeled scablands** – a vast, unusual terrain unlike any in the continental US, or perhaps the world, where columns of basaltic rock tower overhead, giant **"kolk"** potholes testify to ancient geological violence, and colossal lava flows have submerged the land under igneous rock up to a mile deep. Other than the **Grand Coulee Dam**, there are few brand-name attractions in this forbidding land – but that shouldn't prevent you from exploring its strange dry waterfalls, wide canyons of basalt, and sheer gorges with vigor.

Some history

Native American legends say that the thirsty people of eastern Washington once went to the Ocean to ask for water. Ocean sent his children Cloud and Rain to water the land, but the people refused to let the spirits return home:

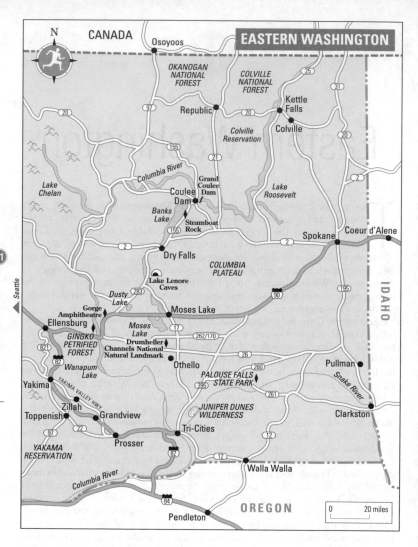

Ocean, furious, rescued his offspring and built the Cascade Mountains as a great punitive barricade between the people and the sea. Whether or not the gods had a hand in it, the great spine of the Cascades is still a crucial divide, separating the wet, forested, sea-facing regions of the west from the parched prairies and canyonlands to the east.

The vast, sagebrush-covered plains, with their exposed buttes and bluffs, conjure cowboy-movie images of the Old West, but in fact the landscape has changed considerably from early pioneer days, when all was open **rangeland** grazed by cattle and sheep. The range was later parceled up into individual ranches, and much of it was ploughed and seeded by horse and mule. In the 1920s, things changed again when machinery replaced the horses and mules, which were quickly sold off, often for hog food. Thereafter, large farms became the order of the day with wheat fields reaching horizon-filling proportions – but only where the plateau was irrigated: the land was too dry to farm without being watered, and the most ambitious **irrigation** scheme was the damming of the Columbia River, most memorably at Grand Coulee. Mechanized, irrigated **agribusiness** did not, however, require many people: by the 1940s, the great gangs of itinerant farmworkers who had roamed the region from the beginning of the century had all but disappeared, and so had most of the tenant farmers. In more recent decades, though, some towns, such as the Tri-Cities, have made a comeback with seasonal workers and undocumented labor, who have populated with grain- and fruitlands once more and given a new cultural vitality to the region – or at least the part along the interstate corridors.

Practicalities

Public **transportation** in eastern Washington is fairly rudimentary. There's a reasonable range of bus services between the larger agricultural towns but almost nothing at all to the smaller burgs and geological sites. Greyhound **buses** (T1-800/231-2222, Wwww.greyhound.com) run east from Seattle along I-90 to Ellensburg, and then on I-82 to Yakima and down to Pendleton, Oregon, with some services continuing on I-90 at Ellensburg to head northeast to Spokane. From Seattle, Northwestern Trailways (T1-800/366-6975, Wwww .northwesterntrailways.com) buses head across the mountains on US-2 to Leavenworth and Wenatchee for Spokane. **Amtrak** (T1-800/872-7245, www .amtrak.com) runs the daily Empire Builder route on two lines: the first crosses the Cascades, connecting Seattle with Wenatchee and Spokane; while the second travels the Columbia River Gorge, connecting Portland, Oregon, and Vancouver with Pasco (Tri-Cities) and Spokane, where the two lines merge on their eastward course to Chicago.

Along I-82

Most visitors to eastern Washington see the area from their car windows passing over the winding course of the interstates, with **Interstate 82** being the most heavily traveled route. Linking Oregon with the commercial nexus of the Tri-Cities and then proceeding to Yakima and Ellensburg, where it merges with I-90, the route rarely inspires (except between the latter two towns), but it does have a number of attractions around its agricultural hamlets and some pockets of roadside interest.

Ellensburg

At the northern terminus of I-82, about a hundred miles east of Seattle via I-90, the rustic country town of **ELLENSBURG** sits in the middle of the wide and fertile **Kittitas Valley**. The town began when white traders set up shop here in the 1860s, making a tidy profit from the steady stream of settlers and drovers heading over Snoqualmie Pass. As a joke, the partners called their trading post "Robbers' Roost," and the name stuck until a Seattle merchant bought them out and renamed it after his wife. The Northern Pacific Railroad reached the site in 1886, and the town boomed, its boosters even arguing it should become the state capital when the matter was put to the vote in 1889, the year of statehood. When Olympia, the old territorial capital, won, the

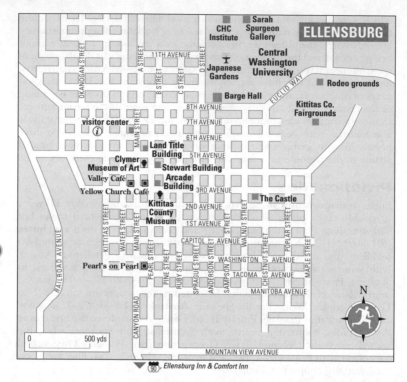

CHC Institute

Sarah Spurgeon Gallery

Central Washington University

11TH AVENUE

Japanese Gardens

Rodeo grounds

Barge Hall

EUCLID WAY

Kittitas Co. Fairgrounds

8TH AVENUE

OKANOGAN STREET

A STREET

B STREET

C STREET

D STREET

visitor center
ⓘ

7TH AVENUE

MAIN STREET

6TH AVENUE

Land Title Building

5TH AVENUE

Clymer Museum of Art

Stewart Building

Valley Café

Arcade Building

Yellow Church Café

3RD AVENUE

The Castle

Kittitas County Museum

2ND AVENUE

POPLAR STREET

WALNUT STREET

1ST AVENUE

KITTITAS STREET

WATER STREET

MAIN STREET

PEARL STREET

CAPITOL AVENUE

STREET

Pearl's on Pearl

WASHINGTON AVENUE

PINE STREET

RUBY STREET

SPRAGUE STREET

ANDERSON STREET

SAMPSON STREET

TACOMA AVENUE

CHESTNUT STREET

MAPLE STREET

MANITOBA AVENUE

RAILROAD AVENUE

CANYON ROAD

0   500 yds

N

MOUNTAIN VIEW AVENUE

90, Ellensburg Inn & Comfort Inn

editor of the local newspaper thundered: "Capital or no capital, Ellensburg will get there. No grass in her streets, no flies on her back, no lard on her tail. Whoop her up again, boys!"

Downtown

Despite its boosters' enthusiasm, Ellensburg suffered the fate of many frontier towns when its early timber buildings were razed by fire in 1889. Luckily there was enough money – and confidence – to pay for it to be rebuilt in brick and stone. Many of Ellensburg's **downtown** buildings have survived and have been restored, and are worth a closer look for their grand Victorian flourishes and lovingly rendered ornament and detailing. Start with the imposing 1911 **Land Title Building**, 5th Ave and Pearl St, with its sturdy Neoclassical pillars and columns and fetching sandstone trimmings adorned with sheaves of wheat and gargoyles. Perhaps the most beautiful structure in downtown Ellensburg, the **Davidson Building**, Pearl St at 4th Ave, is a Victorian gem of the Italianate style, with arched windows, tin detail work, and a grand turreted tower on the corner. Two blocks away, the likes of the **Arcade Building**, 308 N Main St, could only be found in the Old West, its huge arches and stone keystones gracing a strangely elegant building that first housed a saloon before, naturally, becoming an opera house (today, it serves a variety of purposes). There are many other noteworthy piles in the area, among them the delightful crenellated former mansion known as **The Castle**, 716 E 3rd Ave, built in a failed attempt to create a governor's mansion to lure the state capital here. Drop by the **visitor center**, 609 N Main St (Mon–Fri 8am–5pm, Sat 10am–2pm; also summer Sun 10am–2pm; ☎509/925-3137, ⓦwww.visitellen.com), for a comprehensive architectural walking guide.

Another eye-opener, the striking **Cadwell Building**, 114 E 3rd St at Pine St, with its quirky horseshoe arches and windows, is now home to the **Kittitas County Museum** (Mon–Sat 10am–4pm; donation; ⓦwww.kchm.org), the proud possessor of a six-pound hunk of the locally unique Ellensburg blue agate, among other interesting gemstones and minerals, Native American artifacts, and pioneer relics. More diverting is the **Clymer Museum of Art**, 416 N Pearl St at 4th Ave (Mon–Fri 10am–5pm, Sat & Sun noon–5pm; free; ⓦwww.clymermuseum.com), named after John Ford Clymer, a diligent painter of historical Western scenes and a talented illustrator who was responsible for no fewer than eighty *Saturday Evening Post* covers. Born in Ellensburg, Clymer loved the West and traveled the region extensively, painting a long series of bold, epic pictures with titles like *Narcissa Whitman Meets the Horribles*, *Hunt at Crowheart*, and *Whisky, Whisky*. The museum details Clymer's life and displays many of his paintings and illustrations alongside temporary exhibitions focused on the West – everything from patchwork quilts and wheat weaving to cowboy poetry. Ellensburg also has its share of contemporary art, and a good place to see it is in the 1889 **Stewart Building**, where **Gallery One**, 408 N Pearl St (Tues–Sat 11am–5pm; free; ☎509/925-2670, ⓦwww.gallery-one.org), a nonprofit arts center that shows works in modern media – and not just on cowboy themes – from installation and op art to conceptual and sculptural. Drop by this and other downtown sites on the **First Friday** (6–9pm) of the month, when local artists open the doors of their galleries and studios.

Nonetheless, in keeping true to the town's identity, the main event hereabouts is linked to Old West. The annual **Ellensburg Rodeo**, held over Labor Day weekend, fills the town with Stetson-wearing cowboys and cowgirls, who rope steers, ride bulls, and hold onto bucking broncos, accompanied by much pageantry and unfurling of star-spangled banners. For tickets, call the Rodeo Ticket Office ($16–23; ☎509/962-7831 or 1-800/637-2444, ⓦwww .ellensburgrodeo.com). Rodeo ticket prices include admission to the **Kittitas County Fair** (fair without rodeo $7; ⓦwww.kittitascountyfair.com), an odd combination of penned livestock and showy carnival rides that takes place at the same time.

CWU Campus

Ellensburg's **Central Washington State University**, a few blocks north of downtown, is one of the more agreeable regional colleges in the state, known for its fine music and theater-arts programs. But there are also a handful of interesting sights that are worth a look if you're staying in town for a few days. The university's signature emblem is the grand **Barge Hall**, 400 E University Way, a brick-and-white-sandstone marvel from 1894 topped with a regal tower that serves as the gateway to campus. Two blocks north, the **Japanese Gardens** (daily 6am–6pm; free) blend the traditional style of Eastern topiary, ponds, and rock gardens with the indigenous plants of the Western US, and the **Sarah Spurgeon Gallery**, three blocks farther north at Randall Hall, room 141 (Mon–Fri 8.30am–4.30pm, Sat & Sun noon–3pm; free; ⓦwww.cwu.edu/~art), features modern works from regional and student artists, including some eye-opening installations and conceptual pieces. The highlight of the university, though, is visiting the **Chimpanzee and Human Communication Institute**, a block west of Randall Hall (ⓦwww.cwu.edu/~cwuchci), whose intriguing "**chimposiums**" (1–5hr; times and dates vary; $10–100; by reservation at ☎509/963-2244) present the latest research on monkey communication. The tours and workshops focus on the sociable chimp Washoe and other family members, who talk to the researchers in sign language and give you a new perspective on what it means to be a fellow primate.

Practicalities

Connecting Seattle as well as Spokane, Greyhound **buses** stop in Ellensburg at 1512 Hwy 97. In the downtown area, north of the highway, the **visitor center** (see p.452) provides maps and has a list of local **accommodation**. Chain motels are strung along Canyon Road, the main access road into town; your best bet is the *Inn at Goose Creek*, 1720 Canyon Rd (T 509/962-8030, W www .innatgoosecreek.com; ❺), one of those B&Bs whose ten rooms are themed around ideas like hunting, sports, Christmas, the rodeo, and so on, though the most stylish – the antique and honeymoon rooms – are decorated in classic, tasteful Victorian style. Plus, every room features a Jacuzzi, digital cable TV, Internet access, and a fridge. For something more conventional, the *Best Western Lincoln Inn*, 211 W Umptanum Rd (T 509/925-4244, W www.bestwestern .com; ❺–❻ by season), is a reliable choice for its "mini-suite" rooms, which feature microwaves and fridges, plus an indoor pool, gym, and hot tub; there are similar amenities at the cheaper *Comfort Inn*, 1722 Canyon Rd (T 509/925-7037, W www.comfortinn.com; ❺). Needless to say, if you're here to see the rodeo, you should book accommodation well ahead of time.

As for **eating**, the Art Deco 🍴 *Valley Café*, 103 W 3rd Ave at Main (T 509/925-3050), has a wide-ranging and imaginative menu, leaning toward seafood, while the *Yellow Church Cafe*, 111 S Pearl St (T 509/933-2233), appeals for its former Lutheran church setting, even if the serviceable seafood and pasta are a bit less inspired – the sizable breakfasts are the real draw. Two blocks away, *Pearl's on Pearl*, 311 N Pearl St (T 509/962-8899), has top-shelf regional wines and microbrews, plus a stylish setting and upscale menu featuring pasta, lamb, steak, and salmon.

Finally, Ellensburg is a good base for **outdoor activities** in the valley, or as a jumping-off point into the Cascades to the west (toward Cle Elum. There are some hundred or so hiking trails in the outlying area (contact the visitor center for maps and details), as well as good fishing and rafting on the Yakima River. For **pontoon**, **drift boat**, and **raft rental** ($60–149 per day), along with fishing permits, gear rental, and an area shuttle, drop by Red's Fly Shop, on Canyon Rd thirteen miles south of Ellensburg (T 509/929-1802, W www.redsflyshop.com). The shop also sponsors guided **fishing trips** ($300–500 per half-day or full day) down local rivers for steelhead, bass, and trout.

The Yakima River Valley

South of Ellensburg, I-82/US-97 splits from I-90 (which heads to Spokane) and dips down into the **YAKIMA RIVER VALLEY**, fruit- and vine-growing country, where apples, cherries, pears, peaches, apricots, and grapes grow prolifically in what was once forbidding desert. The best route, if you have the time, is **Highway 821**, a pleasant 25-mile link between Ellensburg and Yakima that follows the sagebrush contours of the **Yakima River Canyon** past some of the state's best areas for **trout fishing** and rafting (see Red's Fly Shop, above, for help getting out on the water); milepost 8 is a convenient place for river access. There also some nice hikes along the shore. For more information on permits, geography, and area wildlife – especially the broad array of hawks, eagles, and falcons – contact the **Bureau of Land Management**, in Wenatchee at 915 N Walla Walla St (℡ 509/665-2100, ⓦ www.blm.gov), which manages much of the area.

~a

The Yakima River cuts free of its canyon and eases out into a wide valley to absorb the Naches River, where sprawling **YAKIMA**, the region's urban hub, is one of the region's most successful commercial towns, a busy trading center with a huge agricultural hinterland and a metropolitan population of almost a quarter-million. Since the 1940s, much of the region's farm labor has been provided by migrant Mexican workers, and today Hispanics form a third of Yakima's population. Indeed, a handful of good, authentic Mexican eateries provide one of the few good reasons to drop into town. Considering its size and importance, Yakima should be a more appealing destination than it is. At present, though, it's mainly used as a base for the surrounding wine country region, and even then, you may be better off staying closer to the grapes several miles to the south.

Yakima has repeatedly tried to brighten up its **downtown** – to reach it, take I-82's Exit 33 if coming from Ellensburg – and has repeatedly failed, with the successful businesses locating away from the center and countless vendors and department stores closing in recent years. Still, Yakima's sturdy nineteenth-century piles do house a handful of antique and arts-and-crafts stores; **Track 29**, Yakima Ave at N First St, a mall that houses a collection of shops and food vendors, is a draw for its selection of brightly painted antique railroad cars on display. Perhaps the most compelling reason to stop in Yakima is the redoubtable **Yakima Valley Museum**, 2105 Tieton Drive (Tues–Sat 10am–5pm, Sun 11am–5pm; $5; ℡ 509/248-0747, ⓦ www.yakimavalleymuseum.org), one of the most curious museums in eastern Washington, a historical grab bag of neon signs, old buggies and wagons, rebuilt Victorian and Danish-modern dining rooms, a pioneer log cabin, and a "Time Tunnel" featuring scale-model replicas of the (now extinct) mastodons, mammoths, horses, and camels that used to roam this ancient valley. There's also an "exhibit" of a 1930s soda fountain that is actually one of the better places in town to grab a classic hot dog, milkshake, or sundae.

Practicalities
Greyhound **buses** stop at 602 E Yakima Ave, close to downtown, and the **visitor center**, downtown at 10 N 8th St at Yakima Ave (Mon–Fri 9am–5pm; also summer Sat & Sun; ℡ 509/575-3010 or 1-800/221-0751, ⓦ www.visityakima.com), has details about wine tastings and tours at the many vineyards of the Yakima Valley (see p.456). The wineries make Yakima a good base if you want to **stay the night**. The best of the chain options is the *Hilton Garden Inn*, 401 E Yakima Ave (℡ 509/454-1111, ⓦ www.hilton.com; ❺), centrally located with rooms offering microwaves, fridges, Net access, and an onsite pool, gym, and Jacuzzi. There are plenty of bland motels, but particularly good value is the *Cedar Suites Yakima*, 1010 East A St (℡ 509/452-8101, ⓦ www.cedarsuites.com; ❹), whose units are more like regular motel rooms but offer microwaves, fridges, Net access, and a good breakfast with omelets and waffles. More distinctive is *Birchfield Manor B&B*, 2018 Birchfield Rd (℡ 509/452-1960, ⓦ www.birchfieldmanor.com; ❻), an attractively revamped 1880s house set in its own grounds just two miles east of town off Hwy 24, with five en-suite guestrooms and six cottage units for slightly more money. There's also **camping** across the Yakima River on Hwy 24 at **Sportsman State Park** ($17–24; ℡ 509/575-2774 or 1-800/562-0990), which is good for its fishing.

For **food** and **drink**, *Santiago's*, 111 E Yakima Ave at N 1st Street (℡ 509/453-1644), serves good Mexican dishes ($15–20 per entrée) and has a convivial atmosphere; ☂ *Birchfield Manor* (see p.455; Thurs–Sat dinner only) offers a classy, imaginative menu of Continental and Northwest cuisine and excellent local wines – main courses start at $20; and *Bert's Pub*, 5110 Tieton Drive, located inside a converted fruit warehouse called Glenwood Square (℡ 509/575-2922), serves tasty pub food and handcrafted ales – amazingly, in 1982 this was the first brewpub to open in North America since Prohibition (though it's since moved from its original downtown location).

Yakima Valley wine country

Washington State boasts nearly 30,000 cultivated acres of vineyards, most of which are east of the Cascades in the area designated the **Columbia Valley**. Protected with its own AVA (American Viticultural Area) appellation, the Columbia Valley lies roughly east of the Cascades and runs to the Columbia and Snake rivers but is particularly focused around the **Yakima Valley** southeast of town, which grows a third of the state's wine grapes. This area has helped make Washington the nation's second-largest wine-producing state, behind California. As with Oregon wines, Washington's vintages show up at prestigious dealers and restaurants across the nation (and around the world), but the vineyards here are not compact and sited in a wet, green valley as they are in Oregon, but rather spread out across parched semi-arid scrublands. Of course, although the valley's volcanic soil is naturally rich and the sun shines about three hundred days of the year, copious irrigation has been needed to make the land fertile, and intricate systems of reservoirs, canals, and ditches have been built to divert water from the Yakima River to the orchards and vineyards.

The growing of Washington grapes is nothing new – it's been going on for nearly two hundred years, originally by the Hudson's Bay Company – but

△ Yakima Valley vineyards

today's vast viticultural complex had its genesis in the 1960s, with the introduction of classic European **vinifera** vines. Organized by a group of Washington vintners, the move was actually something of a gamble: many experts thought the state's winters would be too harsh for the precious vines to survive, but the plants flourished. The intense cold of winter stresses the vines and concentrates the flavor of the fruit, while in summer the hot days and comparatively cool nights give Columbia Valley wine its characteristic crispness.

Practicalities

Although the Yakima Valley lacks the profusion of charming B&Bs and delicious Northwest Cuisine eateries that define Oregon's Willamette Valley (see p.186), most of the wineries here are easy to find, being concentrated east of the Yakima River and I-82, around the **Yakima Valley Highway**, which turns into Wine Country Road farther south. From the freeway, the sites are located between exits 40 and 96, and are clustered around the hamlets of Zillah (Exit 52) and Prosser (Exit 82). Some of the more prominent and higher-rated local wineries include *Hogue*, 2800 Lee Rd, Prosser (☎1-800/565-9779); *Kestrel*, 2890 Lee Rd (☎509/786-2675); and *Covey Run*, 1500 Vintage Rd, four miles north of Zillah (☎509/829-6235). Most wineries are open Monday to Friday from 10am to 5pm, with reduced hours during the winter, and offer tastings by the glass, brief tours of the facility or vineyard, and occasionally historic exhibits.

The Yakima Valley Wine Growers Association (☎1-800/258-7270, ⓦwww .yakimavalleywine.com) helps monitor the quality of every bottle sporting the region's sub-appellation (within the larger Columbia Valley AVA) and has information on the area's vintages on its website. Worthwhile places to **stay** include the *Cozy Rose Inn*, eight miles north of Prosser in Grandview, 1220 Forsell Rd (☎509/882-4669, ⓦwww.cozyroseinn.com; ⑥), with four plush suites all offering CD players and fridges, and half with fireplaces and jetted tubs – along with breakfast delivered to each suite in the morning. The *Sunset House Wine Country Inn*, 1401 S Kinney Way, Prosser (☎509/303-0355; ⑤), has a hilltop location that's good for sweeping valley views, and features four rooms with satellite TV and radio and onsite pool and hot tub; April–Nov only. Though nothing fancy, the reliable *Comfort Inn*, 911 Vintage Valley Hwy, Zillah (☎509/829-3399, ⓦwww.comfortinn.com; ⑤), has a central location, free continental breakfast, and good, clean rooms. For **dining**, the eateries worth a stop are fairly scattered, though *El Ranchito*, 1319 1st Ave, Zillah (☎509/829-5880), is a popular spot for authentic Mexican cuisine; *Los Hernandez*, 3706 Main St, Union Gap (☎509/457-6003), is well known for its delicious, authentic tamales; and *Snipes Mountain Brewery*, 905 Yakima Valley Hwy, Sunnyside (☎509/837-2739), has adequate pub food – burgers, pasta, seafood – and good regional microbrews.

Toppenish

Twenty miles south of Yakima on I-82, **TOPPENISH** is a small, dusty burg mainly known for its **murals**. Originally, the town was a telegraph office and water tower beside the Northern Pacific Railroad. The railway employees were soon joined by horse traders, who made a handsome profit buying wild horses from the adjacent Yakama Indian Reservation and selling the animals in New York. Fortuitously, just when the horse trade began to fizzle out, a sugar company moved in, building a sugar-beet processing plant here in 1918. When the plant closed in 1980, locals looked around for an alternative moneymaker, and set about commissioning sprightly murals focusing on local characters and events. Seventy of these bright and breezy paintings now adorn the tiny town center, focused on Toppenish Avenue, and although some are rather hackneyed (cowboys by the light of the moon), others tell intriguing tales or set the scene perfectly, as in the historic buildings and peoples depicted in *The Palace Hotel, Toppenish* and *Indians' Winter Encampment*.

The **visitor center**, downtown at 5A Toppenish Ave (daily: April–Oct 10am–4pm; Nov–March 11am–3pm; ☏509/865-3262 or 1-800/569-3982), provides a free guide to the murals, with each painting described in detail. It takes only an hour or two to view them all on foot, but if you want a ride and live narration, you can take a **guided tour** by covered wagon or stagecoach (May–Sept Mon–Sat on the hour 10am–4pm; 90min; $12; ☏509/697-8995). The town also has two festivals: the annual **Mural-in-a-Day** extravaganza, usually held in early June, which sees Toppenish stuffed with tourists who come to watch a team of artists put up a brand-new mural, and the four-day **Toppenish Pow Wow and Rodeo** (tickets from $13; ☏509/865-5566, ⓦwww.toppenishrodeo.com), held every Fourth of July weekend. Also diverting, the **Northern Pacific Railway Museum**, sited in a stylishly renovated depot at 10 S Asotin Ave (May–Oct Wed–Sat 10am–4pm, Sun noon–4pm; $3; ☏509/865-1911, ⓦwww.nprymuseum.org), tells the story of the Iron Horse in eastern Washington, with various antiques and restored rail cars. Finally, just as the Yakima Valley is known for growing grapes for wine, Toppenish is known for raising hops for beer, and the **American Hop Museum**, 22 South B St (May–Sept Wed–Sat 10am–4pm, Sun 11am–4pm; $3; ☏509/865-4677, ⓦwww.americanhopmuseum.org), offers a mildly interesting selection of old photos and antiques to illustrate the agricultural history of this overlooked but essential vine.

Since Toppenish's choice of lodging and restaurants is fairly limited, you're better off using Yakima or the rest of the valley as a base.

Yakama Nation Cultural Center

East of Yakima, the Yakima River marks the thirty-mile-long northern boundary of the **Yakama Indian Reservation** – the tribal council having changed the *i* to an *a* – a great slab of dry and rugged land that stretches down toward the Columbia River. Here, set beside US-97 just northwest of Toppenish, the large **Yakama Nation Cultural Center** holds a variety of community facilities and, in a 76ft-tall replica wigwam, a **museum** (daily 8am–5pm; $4; ☏509/865-2800, ⓦwww.yakamamuseum.com) outlining Yakama traditions by means of dioramas and wall displays. One of the most unusual exhibits is a time-ball, a sort of macramé diary kept by married women as a record of their lives; in old age, major events were recalled by unraveling the sequence of knots and beads. Several exhibits are devoted to Yakama religious practices involving **Spilyay** – the local version of the godlike coyote figure that crops up in many Native American legends – and to the series of brutal skirmishes in the 1850s known as the **Yakima War**, in which the tribe was forcibly ejected from its traditional lands along the Columbia and Yakima rivers and consigned to this largely infertile reservation. You can find out more about this grim chapter in local history at **Fort Simcoe**, a state park inside the reservation, west of Toppenish via Fort Road. Here, an **interpretive center** (April–Sept Wed–Sun 9.30am–4.30pm; ☏509/874-2372) provides an overview of white–native relations in that troubled era and features five original military buildings (amid other modern replicas), from a blockhouse to the commander's house, used by the government to keep its thumb on the tribe.

The Tri-Cities

About eighty miles east of Yakima, the cluster of three towns known as the **Tri-Cities** straddles the Columbia River as it executes a dramatic change of direction west to the Pacific. All three towns – **Pasco**, **Richland**, and **Kennewick** – were once reliant on the now-defunct **Hanford Site**, a massive nuclear energy and research area immediately to the north that, during World War II, housed a top-secret plant to produce plutonium. That site closed in 1988 and is now mostly known for being contaminated. You can't visit it in any case, and the Tri-Cities themselves mainly make up a large agricultural complex that offers little cause for a visit – your most memorable experience will likely involve being stuck in endless traffic. From here, you can push south twenty miles on I-82 to the eastern end of Oregon's Columbia Gorge or dip 45 miles southeast on Hwy 12 to the comfortable college town of Walla Walla.

Walla Walla

Named after a tribal word for "little river" and surrounded by wheat fields, **WALLA WALLA** is home to Whitman University and famous for its eponymous **onion** – a large, round, and sweet treat that is grown in plots around the area (see Ⓦ www.sweetonions.org for a list of growers and shippers). Walla Walla has been known for its signature onion for nearly a century, but more recently the wine grape (see below) has become nearly as lucrative. Indeed, with the rise of the tourist trade coming to sample the vino, Walla Walla's modest downtown has seen new galleries and cafes open, and old hotels restored, making for a strange hybrid of boutique town, college town, and old-time Western burg. You'll find the pick of the art scene at the **Walla Walla Foundry**, 405 Woodland Ave (Mon–Fri 7am–4.30pm; free; ☎509/522-2114, Ⓦ www.wallawallafoundry.com), which has a range of mixed-media works, some of them by nationally recognized artists like Jim Dine, and has drawn other major sculptors to cast works here, such as Louise Bourgeois, Robert Arneson, Nancy Graves, and Ed Kienholz.

The town is also known for a pair of historical attractions. The first, the **Whitman Mission** site (daily: mid-June to Aug 8am–6pm; Sept to mid-June 8am–4.30pm; $3; ☎509/522-6360, Ⓦ www.nps.gov/whmi), is located in a lovely little dell seven miles west of Walla Walla off US-12. The mission itself was razed by the Cayuse after the massacre (see box, p.460); simple marks on the ground, plus interpretive plaques, show its original layout and the places where Marcus and Narcissa Whitman were murdered. A visitor center shows a film on Whitman's work and the massacre, and is well stocked with books on the subject, including Narcissa Whitman's diary. The second attraction is the **Fort Walla Walla Museum**, 755 Myra Rd (Apr–Oct daily 10am–5pm; Ⓦ www.fortwallawallamuseum.org; $7), a curious mock-up of a pioneer village, with seventeen shacks loaded with antiques and Old West dioramas, and historical interpreters doing old-fashioned tasks like blacksmithing, making beer, reaping, working a foundry, and telling tall tales.

Unquestionably, though, in recent years most out-of-towners come to Walla Walla for its wineries. The area has its own wine appellation and sixty or so **vineyards** – not as many growers as other parts of the state, but its finest vintages consistently finish near the top of the list of the state's – and the nation's – best wines. So, like Oregon's Willamette Valley and the Yakima Valley to the northwest, Walla Walla is an essential stop for the American wine enthusiast. Among the many brands that regularly make the pages of *Wine Spectator* and other magazines are *Cougar Crest*, 202 A St (☎509/529-5980); *Russell Creek*,

The Whitmans and the Cayuse

In 1836, at the site that became Walla Walla, Dr **Marcus Whitman**, a key figure in the settling of the Northwest, arrived from the East Coast as a missionary, hoping with his wife, Narcissa, to convert the local **Cayuse** people from their nomadic ways into church-going, crop-growing Christians. They had little success with the Cayuse, however, so, like other Western missionaries, they turned their attention instead to the settlers who soon followed in their pioneering footsteps. Within a few years the Whitmans' mission became a refuge along the Oregon Trail for sick and orphaned travelers.

The Cayuse eyed the increasing numbers of settlers very warily, and when a measles epidemic decimated the tribe, suspicions grew that they were being poisoned to make way for the whites. Their uneasiness was reinforced by Dr Whitman's ability to help (some) whites but hardly any of the Indians, who had no natural immunity to the disease. Whitman sensed the growing tension, and he must have known of the native belief that medicine men were directly liable for the deaths of their patients, but he continued to take on even hopeless cases. In November 1847 a band of Cayuse arrived at the mission and **murdered** Whitman, Narcissa, and several others and destroyed the mission. Fifty more people, mostly children, were taken captive, and although they were later released, angry settlers raised volunteer bands against the Cayuse.

When the story hit the newspapers back East, it generated such a tide of fear about native uprisings that the government finally declared the Oregon (then including Washington) an official US territory, which meant the army could be sent in to protect the settlers, with drastic implications for the original inhabitants. For the next seven years, the **Cayuse War** raged – an early, ugly conflict between whites and natives that would only get worse in later decades with further **Indian Wars** – until the Cayuse lost the battle and were forced onto Oregon's Umatilla Indian Reservation, their ancient tribal lands confiscated to make way for white farmers and property speculators.

301 Aeronca Ave (℡509/386-4401); *Tamarack*, 700 C St (℡509/526-3533); *L'Ecole*, 41 Lowden School Rd (℡509/525-0940); *Seven Hills*, 212 N 3rd Ave (℡509/529-7198); *Whitman*, 1015 W Pine St (℡509/1142); and *K*, 820 Mill Creek Rd (℡509/526-5230). Contact the **Walla Walla Wine Alliance**, 128 N 2nd Ave, #219 (℡509/526-3117, ⊛www.wallawallawine.com), for the locations and opening hours of most area facilities, as well as driving maps.

Practicalities

The Walla Walla **visitor center**, 29 E Sumach at Colville (Mon–Fri 9am–5pm; ℡509/525-0850, ⊛www.wwvchamber.com), can provide you with information on area vintners, town maps, and brochures. The most prominent place to **stay** is the hulking 1927 tower of the Marcus Whitman Hotel, 6 W Rose St (℡509/525-2200, ⊛www.marcuswhitmanhotel.com; ⑥), which after being vacant for decades has been renovated into a boutique property with a grand lobby, hotel-sponsored wine-tasting tours, and stylish, if small, rooms that come with a savory complimentary breakfast. The best **B&B** choices are the *Inn at Blackberry Creek*, 1126 Pleasant St (℡509/520-7372, ⊛www.innatblackberrycreek .com; ⑤–⑥ by season), whose three, artist-themed rooms (Cézanne, Monet, Renoir) have pleasant antique decor, flat-screen TVs, DVD players, and, in selected rooms, a fireplace, wood stove, and/or Jacuzzi; and *Green Gables Inn*, 922 Bonsella St (℡509/525-5501, ⊛www.greengablesinn.com; ⑥), occupying an impressively restored 1909 Craftsman mansion and hosting rooms with claw-foot tubs, antiques, and Victorian (but not Arts and Crafts) decoration.

Among the more enjoyable **dining** choices are *The Marc*, in the *Marcus Whitman Hotel* (see opposite), which has a broad, if pricey, menu that includes sushi, pasta, lobster, steak, and osso buco; the *Destination Grill*, 416 N 2nd Ave (☎509/529-3800), solid for its prime rib, cocktails, and microbrews; and *CreekTown Cafe*, 1129 S 2nd Ave (☎509/522-4777), with tasty sandwiches, pasta, and burgers for lunch, and for twice as much money, top-shelf oysters, salmon, and duck for dinner – plus a good selection of Walla Walla wine.

The Columbia Plateau

Like that of Oregon, Washington's eastern side is geologically one of the most interesting and expressive terrains in the country. No one really knows what this huge swath of country looked like before 14–17 million years ago, when 170,000 cubic kilometers of **molten lava** erupted from the earth and submerged the land under basaltic flows more than a mile deep. Most of Washington and north-central Oregon was buried under the magma, and this curious rock formation – the **Columbia Plateau** – defines the land east of the Cascades. However, unlike eastern Oregon, eastern Washington underwent a second geological trauma during the last Ice Age, when colossal torrents of water swept across the land and scoured much of it clean of sedimentary rock and soil, leaving bare patches of igneous rock and creating the Columbia River Gorge in the process. No event even remotely like the **Bretz Floods** (see box, p.124) has been seen on earth since then, and eastern Washington's topography – known as the **channeled scablands** – testifies to the event's unique characteristics: sheer walls of basalt towering above the landscape, unexpected "pothole" lakes carved out by underwater vortexes, great dry waterfalls transformed into perilous cliffs, and desolate coulees outlining the course of flood channels from thousands of years ago.

Needless to say, since most of this area is rural or undeveloped, transportation links outside the I-90 corridor (which Greyhound travels) are nonexistent. You'll need a **car**, or a bike if you're looking for a spring or fall adventure tour, and **camping** gear if you really want to explore the terrain. Decent accommodation outside of a state park is few and far between, mostly consisting of dreary roadside motels removed from the sites of greatest interest. Note that vendors and outfitters in Wenatchee, Ellensburg, and Yakima also offer **kayaking** or **river rafting** on selected rivers in the area; contact those cities' visitor centers for details.

Around I-90

The easiest route into the **channeled scablands** is I-90, which connects Ellensburg and Spokane on a lengthy course that occasionally passes worthwhile sights but more often plods through farm- and scrubland, especially as you draw near to the Idaho border. As you head out of Ellensburg, the first stop you'll come to is the **Gingko Petrified Forest State Park**, Exit 136 at Vantage (summer 6.30am–dusk; rest of year 8am–dusk); a natural wonder that preserves some fifty different types of trees, mostly conifers, that have been petrified into stone logs. The process began fifteen million years ago, when wood in what was then a humid, swampy environment was submerged by mudflows and then by lava eruptions. The combination of mud and magma resulted in the trees' structure being mineralized until it was turned to rock, only to be re-exposed during the Bretz Floods. The park's name refers to the handful of rare fossilized **gingko** trees that are on display here, and the site also preserves some sixty Wanapum tribal **petroglyphs**, rescued from canyon walls before they were inundated by the adjacent dam and reservoir. Along with its natural appeal, the park is very popular during summer months for **camping** ($17–24; reserve at ℡1-888/226-7688), so make sure to reserve ahead. Though the campground is prone to wind gusts, it's far better to camp here than in the nearby car-camping lot (a nonstop college party zone) surrounding the **Gorge Amphitheatre**, eastbound Exit 143 or westbound Exit 149 at the town of George (℡206/628-0888, Ⓦwww.hob .com/venues/concerts/gorge). This beautiful concert site is the home of summer concerts by a variety of major acts in pop and rock, but is best for its **Sasquatch Festival** (tickets $56–60), one of the nation's top indie-rock events, where musicians from Beck to Modest Mouse perform on a stage that overlooks a particularly stunning turn of the Columbia River through bare canyon walls.

Also in the vicinity, off Hwy 281 southwest of Quincy, the Quincy Wildlife Area is a favorite fishing and bridwatching spot whose so-called **pothole lakes** were carved out by the violent waters of the Bretz Floods; they sit amid huge lava cliffs, benches, and canyons, and are best seen on the 3.5-mile hike to **Dusty Lake**, itself a pothole surrounded by thousand-foot-high basalt mesas. For information on directions, fishing permits ($11), and primitive camping, contact the Washington Department of Fish and Wildlife, 1550 Alder St NW, just north in Ephrata (℡509/754-4624, Ⓦwww.wdfw.wa.gov). Also ask for information and directions to the popular **Frenchman's Coulee**, near Vantage, a trio of lava columns that provide a great opportunity for crack and chimney climbing.

The pothole lakes are not to be confused with **Potholes State Park** (summer 6.30am–dusk; rest of year 8am–dusk), a dam reservoir 25 miles east on I-90 that provides good opportunities for fishing, swimming, and kayaking, as well as **camping** ($17–24; reserve at ℡1-888/226-7688). From here, unless you're going to Spokane, it's best to take Hwy 17 north- or southbound, which leads on to further sites of great natural appeal.

Southeast Washington

The landscape south of I-90 in the **southeast** corner of the state just gets more intriguing and jaw-dropping. As you follow Hwy 17 to Hwy 262, you reach – five miles northeast of Othello – the **Columbia National Wildlife Refuge**, a 23,000-acre preserve for ducks, hawks, owls, and other birds that offers pleasant hiking, fishing, and **camping** (at Soda Lake Campground; $5; first-come, first-served), but is best for its astounding **Drumheller Channels National Natural Landmark**. The landmark's huge basaltic buttes were dramatically sculpted by the Bretz Floods over the course of repeated torrents, leaving behind towering sheer cliffs separated by a dense network of small and large channels, which are now almost all dry. At their height, the waters were 160ft deep and some twelve miles across, and they have left behind a strangely beautiful, almost surreal topography. For more information, contact the refuge office at 735 E Main St, Othello (Mon–Fri 7am–4.30pm; ℡509/488-2668). Thirty miles south, on Hwy 17 connecting to Hwy 395, another compelling sight takes a bit more effort to reach. Near Eltopia, Hwy 12 leads east to a two-mile-long footpath that brings you to the **Juniper Dunes Wilderness**, largely unknown to outsiders since it just became publicly accessible in 2007. It's quite a sight – seven thousand acres of **sand dunes**, some up to 130ft tall, deposited by the Ice Age floodwaters and peppered with twenty- to sixty-foot-tall juniper trees. You can hike, ride horses, or charge around on dune buggies – usually with locals who've been trespassing here for decades – but there are no facilities like water stations or campgrounds, and you'll have to bring any provisions with you – an important note since the sun, reflecting off the sand, can make summer temperatures unbearable. For information on how to reach the wilderness, contact the Bureau of Land Management's area office, 1103 N Fancher St, Spokane (☎509/536-1200, ⓦwww.blm.gov).

A more accessible, and even more striking, natural monument is accessible sixty miles northeast off Hwy 261, or just south of Hwy 26, where **Palouse Falls State Park** is home to the last large waterfall from the Bretz Floods, a 200ft torrent that tumbles over the cusp of a huge rock ledge, visible on an easy quarter-mile walk. It's worth **camping** here ($17–24; first-come, first-served) to explore the area more in depth, which is mesmerizing for its 377ft-high sheer canyon walls and scabland features like flood-carved potholes and grand lava buttes and pinnacles. From Palouse Falls, you can continue east on Hwy 261 to Hwy 12 – a course that crosses the lower reaches of the **Snake River**, which curves south at the Washington–Idaho border to enter its most fascinating stretch, at **Hells Canyon** (see p.268), reachable by taking Hwy 12 to Hwy 129 south, which leads to Oregon Hwy 3.

Grand Coulee and around

Less than an hour's drive north on Hwy 17 from I-90 will put you at the southern end of the **Grand Coulee** at Banks Lake, one of several huge reservoirs that filled in this colossal natural chasm after the last Ice Age. Before you reach the coulee, though, it's worth taking a side trip to the **Lake Lenore Caves**, 33 miles north of I-90 and signposted east of Hwy 17 (open daylight hours; free), a publicly protected site hosting seven shallow, basaltic caves in the coulee walls where native tribes would temporarily store food and find shelter. The formations were created when the ancient floodwaters gouged out hollows in the softer rock of the coulee walls, leaving behind a pockmarked appearance. Narrow trails lead up to the caves, which you can enter, and look out at Alkali Lake and the dry flood channels below. You can camp at **Sun Lakes State Park** just north (daily 6.30am–dusk; $17–24; reserve at ☎1-888/226-7688), which has boating, fishing, and swimming, though its main draw is the sight that some call the most spectacular in eastern Washington – **Dry Falls**. Another relic from the floods, this gargantuan formation is almost beyond description: three and a half miles across, 400ft high, ten times as large as Niagara Falls, and allegedly the biggest waterfall in measurable human or geologic history. Although it's now desiccated, its size is still impressive, and it's up to the viewer to imagine how, at the height of the floods, water poured over the crescent-shaped cliff at a speed of 65 miles per hour and with ten times the force of all of today's rivers combined. The park **visitor center** (mid-May to Sept 10am–6pm) has the full story of this natural marvel, as well as guides to hikes near the falls' rim and the pocket lakes in the shadow of the falls.

Just north, **Dry Falls Dam** forms the southern tip of man-made **Banks Lake**, a serpentine reservoir whose most compelling feature is **Steamboat Rock**, a 600-acre monolith that stands 800ft above the lakeshore fifteen miles north of Hwy 2 along Hwy 155 in **Steamboat Rock State Park** (daily 6.30am–dusk; camping $17–24; ☎1-888/226-7688). The rock was at one point an island in the ancestral course of the Columbia River – a more impressive image in itself than the vaguely steamboat shape that provides its moniker. Before the river was dammed, the lake site made up the southern stretch of the amazing **Grand Coulee**, a great slash in the landscape created when Ice Age glaciers carved up the basalt of ancient lava flows and subsequent floodwaters ripped away the bedrock and deepened the gouge. Of course, you can't see any of this today, since the coulee has been dammed to create Banks Lake and spindly **Lake Roosevelt** (℡509/633-9188, Ⓦwww.nps.gov/laro), which stretches 150 miles all the way to the Canadian border.

The Grand Coulee Dam

The Columbia Plateau reaches a dramatic climax at the **Grand Coulee Dam**, one of the few human works to rival the natural ones in the area. Around ninety miles west of Spokane and separating Banks and Roosevelt lakes, the dam, begun in 1933, is the kingpin of the Columbia River dams and was as much a political icon as an engineering feat. The most ambitious of FDR's New Deal schemes to lift America out of the Depression, it symbolized hope for the Northwest, promising abundant energy and water for irrigation. It also provided jobs for thousands of workers from all over the country, notably the dust-bowl regions to the southeast, whose unemployed agricultural laborers were then migrating west. As **Woody Guthrie** had it, "Columbia's waters taste like sparklin' wine / Dustbowl waters taste like picklin' brine." Guthrie worked on the Bonneville Dam lower down the river and was commissioned to write some twenty songs about the Columbia project – one of which, "Roll On, Columbia," you'll probably hear in the visitor center (see opposite).

The dam is now the world's biggest single producer of **hydroelectricity**, and has certainly controlled flooding lower down the Columbia. Its heyday was during World War II, when its waterpower was harnessed to make the aluminum that became essential to the production of war materiel. However, there's been ecological criticism of the Columbia project, too: salmon migration along the river has been reduced to a fraction of its pre-dam level, though schemes have since been set up to increase stocks of fish.

△ The Grand Coulee Dam

Heroic tales of power production are detailed in the **visitor center** (daily 9am–5pm; summer 8.30am–10pm; free; Ⓦ www.grandcouleedam.org), on Hwy 155 just north of the dam. There are lots of photographs, information, and a free film touching on everything from the dangerous working conditions of the 1930s to how the turbines operate. Free **guided tours** (daily every two hours 10am–4pm) of the dam and its generating plants are available, but while views of the churning water are quite exciting, you'll need a fair amount of enthusiasm for things mechanical to appreciate the intricacies of power generation. The outdoor **laser light show**, free every evening in the summer after dark, is perhaps more appealing – and attracts visitors in the hundreds.

Practicalities

Set against the surrounding scrubland, the leafy streets and shady lawns of the little town of **Coulee Dam**, just north of the dam, provide a good advertisement for the difference the Grand Coulee's irrigation schemes have made. Otherwise, the town and its two tiny neighbours, **Grand Coulee** and **Electric City**, just to the south along Hwy 155, provide little reason to hang around. But if you'd like to explore the larger area, they muster up a handful of **motels**: Coulee Dam's *Columbia River Inn*, 10 Lincoln Ave (Ⓣ 509/633-2100 or 1-800/633-6421, Ⓦ www.columbiariverinn.com; Ⓑ), has a gym and sauna and overlooks the dam, as does the nearby *Coulee House Motel*, 110 Roosevelt Way (Ⓣ 509/633-1101 or 1-800/715-7767; Ⓞ, dam views $20 extra). Both have outdoor pools and hot tubs. Alternatively, *Spring Canyon Campground*, a few miles east of the dam off Hwy 174, is one of 35 campsites that dot Lake Roosevelt's long, curving shore ($10; Ⓣ 509/633-9188, Ⓦ www.nps.gov/laro) and is excellent for its boating and swimming in the thin, deep reservoir. For true relaxation and isolation, ten of the more remote campsites are boat-in only; contact the park for locations and information.

Good **food** is not the area's strong suit, but the *Melody Restaurant*, near the dam at 512 River Drive (Ⓣ 509/633-1151), can set you up with fine and filling seafood and pasta dishes for a fair price.

Spokane

The wide-open spaces of the Columbia Plateau don't prepare you for **SPOKANE**. Just a few miles from the Idaho border, it's eastern Washington's only major city, boasting a metropolitan population of nearly 600,000, and its scattering of grandiose c.1900 buildings – built on the spoils of the Coeur d'Alene silver mines, across the state divide – sport some unexpectedly elegant touches. That said, Spokane has taken something of an economic battering since its late-nineteenth-century heyday and, although it was revamped in preparation for the World's Fair held here in 1974, shades of industrial shabbiness still haunt the modern city. Spokane has one real claim to fame, however: it was here in 1910 that a certain Mrs Dodd specified a special day on which she honored her father who had raised his kids on his own after the death of his wife; the idea caught on – hence Father's Day.

Downtown and around

Spokane's long and narrow **downtown** squeezes into the seven blocks between I-90 and the Spokane River. The place to make for is **Riverfront Park** – a one-hundred-acre park straddling the river that in summer, at least,

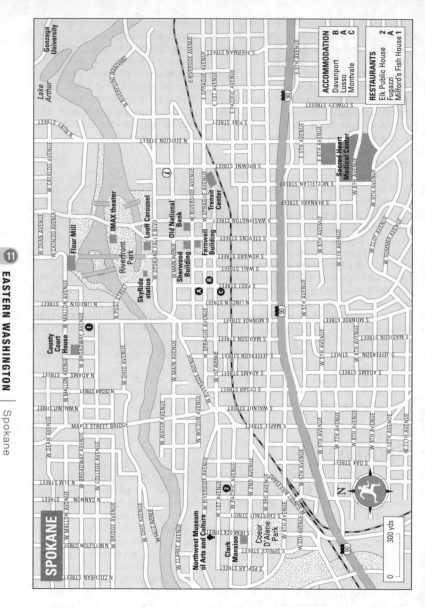

SPOKANE

Gonzaga
University

Lake
Arthur

ACCOMMODATION
Davenport — B
Lusso — A
Montvale — C

RESTAURANTS
Elk Public House — 2
Fugazzi — A
Milford's Fish House — 1

Sacred Heart
Medical Center

IMAX theater

Looff Carousel

Old National
Bank

Transit
Center

Flour Mill

Fernwell
Building

Riverfront
Park

Sherwood
Building

SkyRide
station

County
Court
House

Maple Street Bridge

Northwest Museum
of Arts and Culture

Clark
Mansion

Coeur
D'Alene
Park

N

300 yds

0

is the town's main venue for strolling, picnicking, and hanging out. It was designed by Frederick Law Olmsted, creator of New York's Central Park. The **attractions** (June–Aug Sun–Thurs 11am–8pm, Fri & Sat 11am–10pm; day passes $15; Ⓦ www.spokaneriverfrontpark.com) include assorted carnival rides, plus an **ice-skating rink** (Oct–March; $4.25), **IMAX theater** (tickets $8), and the charming hand-carved **Looff Carousel** (Feb–Sept; $2). As it slices through the park, the river tumbles down the rocky ledges of **Spokane Falls**, once a fishing site for the Spokane tribe and later the settlement of the first white pioneers. Early settlers harnessed the churning water to power their mills, and on the far side of the river the **Flour Mill** was an economic cornerstone when it opened in 1896, though it's now been converted to house cutesy shops. The **Spokane Falls SkyRide** ($7) runs across the river from the park's west end, offering commanding city and river views. Park day-passes cover all attractions except IMAX and the SkyRide.

The architectural relics of Spokane's early grandeur are sprinkled all over town, from the monumental flamboyance of the **Davenport Hotel**, downtown at Sprague and Post (see p.468), to the extravagant **County Court House**, built in the style of a French chateau on the north side of the river at 1116 W Broadway, to the **Clark Mansion**, 2208 W Second Ave, an 1897 marvel of lovely classical arcades and red-tiled roofs. West Riverside Avenue, between Washington and Howard, gets into the act, too, with several first-rate examples of late-nineteenth-century American commercial architecture. The **Fernwell Building**, for example, at no. 503, dates from 1890 and is typical of the cast-iron frame structures that were popular until steel frames were developed. Steel was a stronger and more flexible building material, and the fifteen-story, terracotta-clad 1910 **Old National Bank** (now U.S. Bank Building), at no. 422, illustrates the point. Kirtland Cutter was Spokane's leading designer, and his **Sherwood Building**, at no. 510, is adorned with Gothic icons, from lions and griffins through to terracotta gargoyles.

The city's most noteworthy institution is the **Northwest Museum of Arts and Culture**, a mile west of the city center at 2316 W 1st Ave (Tues–Sun 11am–5pm; $7; ☎509/456-3931, Ⓦwww.northwestmuseum.org), focusing on historic and modern art, pop culture, regional heritage, and international art from as far away as nineteenth-century Japan and seventeenth-century Holland. The museum also owns an outstanding assortment of Native American artifacts from the tribes of the Columbia Plateau. Included are a number of tableaux showing excruciating-looking initiation ceremonies with the candidates suspended from hooks embedded in their chests as a test of manhood. Make sure to drop by the adjacent **Campbell House** (Tues–Sun 11am–5pm; free with museum admission), a restored Tudor Revival confection dreamed up for a silver baron by Kirtland Cutter in 1898.

Also of interest is the **Bing Crosby Memorabilia Room** (Mon–Fri 7.30am–midnight, plus Sept–May Sat & Sun 11am–midnight; free), located in the Crosby Student Center on the campus of Gonzaga University, northeast of and across the river from downtown. Harry Lillis Crosby is easily the university's most famous alumna, and was awarded an honorary doctorate in 1937. Crosby proved a generous benefactor, giving the college this hoard of memorabilia, everything from gold records and sporting awards to Crosby-endorsed products, pipes, and slippers. He was a little less forthcoming with his original sheet music, but some of his most famous numbers are here, notably "Moonlight Becomes You" and "White Christmas."

Outdoor activities

Spokane is a good base for a number of **outdoor activities** that encompass the surrounding region. Among the best options, the **Centennial Trail** (Ⓦwww.spokanecentennialtrail.org) leads 37 miles from Nine Mile Falls northwest of town to the Idaho border. You can access the trail at milepost 17 at Riverfront Park, where you can rent bikes; the trail loosely follows the course of the Spokane River and makes for a very enjoyable ride, run, or walk. Much more intensive, and aimed at the most gung-ho adventurers, is the **Columbia Plateau Trail**, which you can access ten miles west of town at Cheney (I-90 Exit 270, then eight miles south to the Fish Lake Trailhead), which leads 130 miles along a hundred-year-old rail bed to the Tri-Cities, covering the plateau's parched terrain and passing some eye-opening vistas of the channeled scablands, as well as an enthralling passage over a rail trestle at Burr Canyon. Along the way, signs point out the highlights of ecological, geological, and human history – just make sure to bring sufficient provisions, as this can be very desolate country. Back in town, River City Runners (☏509/884-5934, ⓦwww.rivercityriverrunners.com) can get you out on the water with guided **rafting tours** from seven to fourteen miles along the Spokane River ($45–70 per person).

Practicalities

As you drive into Spokane from the southwest, I-90 skirts the southern edge of downtown, which is best accessed from Exit 281; US-2 (from Coulee Dam,) feeds into I-90 west of the city. Amtrak **trains** as well as Northwestern Trailways and Greyhound **buses** share the same transit terminal, downtown at W 221 1st Ave and Bernard Street; if you arrive after dark, be warned that the surrounding streets aren't safe – take a taxi. **Local buses**, operated by Spokane Transit Authority (tickets $1; ☏509/328-7433, ⓦwww.spokanetransit.com), cover the city and its suburbs. Well stocked with city and regional information, the **visitor center** is three blocks north of the transit terminal – and five minutes' walk from Riverside Park – at 201 W Main Ave and Browne (Mon–Fri 9am–5pm, plus May–Sept Sat 8am–4pm & Sun 9am–2pm; ☏509/747-3230 or 1-888/776-5263, ⓦwww.visitspokane.com).

Spokane has plenty of chain hotels and motels for those who want to save money, but the best **accommodation** is in structures from a century ago that have been restored into chic boutique or business hotels. These include the 1914 ⚘ *Davenport Hotel*, 10 S Post St (☏1-800/899-1482, ⓦwww .thedavenporthotel.com; ➐), a stately 1914 pile that's been renovated to showcase its wildly ornate lobby and has spacious, well-designed suites; the lush and stylish *Hotel Lusso*, N One Post St (☏509/747-9750, ⓦwww .hotellusso.com; ➐), whose rooms have nice amenities and Internet access, and whose suites are rich with designer furnishings, CD players, and fireplaces; and the *Montvale*, W 1005 1st Ave (☏509/747-1919, ⓦwww .montvalehotel.com; ➏), a pile from 1899 that's been stylishly transformed into a sleek boutique property, with rooms boasting Internet access and flat-screen TVs. There's also **camping** in Riverside State Park ($17–24; ☏509/456-3964), six miles northwest off Hwy 291.

Eating out well in Spokane is easy. *Fugazzi*, in the *Hotel Lusso* (see above), offers affordable pasta and sandwiches for lunch, and upscale salmon, sea bass, steak, and rack of lamb for dinner. *Milford's Fish House*, 719 N Monroe St (☏509/326-7251), is a favorite local spot for its chic seafood like pan-fried oysters, lobster tail, tuna cakes, and manila clams, while ⚘ *Luna*, 5620 S Perry St (inquire at the visitor center for directions; ☏509/448-2383), is well worth seeking out for its smart, elegant Northwest cuisine that may encompass dishes from beef carpaccio to lobster bisque. To have a **drink**, head for the *Elk Public House*, 1931 W Pacific Ave (☏509/363-1973), which presents a fine and wide array of area microbrews and tasty pub food from catfish to pork chops to lamb sandwiches.

Contexts

Contexts

A brief history of Oregon and Washington

History is never far away in Oregon and Washington. Not only is the rugged, verdant landscape much the same as it's been throughout human existence, but the marks of civilization remain as well. Across an arid plain you might find the dusty ruts of wagon-wheel tracks, while settler cabins and homesteads still dot the inland valleys. Even in the cities stand the proud red-brick citadels of nineteenth-century commerce. There are, of course, the weary stretches of strip malls and fast-food joints you'll find in every corner of the US, but the past in the Pacific Northwest often lies just a short distance away – a sturdy lighthouse beacon here, a wooden fort there, Victorian mansions everywhere. Even when this history has been dark or violent – as with native genocide, racist upheavals, and natural catastrophes – residents have often kept a considerable record of it, building museums to explore the conflicts, erecting memorials to commemorate them, and sometimes just leaving a historic site untouched, as with the ghost towns of eastern Oregon or the geological wreckage of Mount St Helens, so it can speak for itself.

Geologic beginnings

Some fifty million years ago, what was the West Coast of the North American landmass (or something that vaguely resembled it) lay just west of the current border with Idaho; Oregon and Washington, for all practical purposes, simply did not exist. In the coming millennia, however, the actions of **plate tectonics** – through which the earth's crustal plates are forever moving, disappearing, and re-emerging on a geological conveyor belt known as **continental drift** – caused the rupture and eastward drift of an oceanic plate to the immediate west, with profound consequences for the future. When this plate crashed into the North American plate, the coastal lowland was crumpled, deformed, and eventually raised to become the **North Cascades** mountain range. At the same time, distant **tropical island arcs** were moved up toward the expanding edge of North America and welded against the coastline. Much of the area, then, became a hodgepodge of discordant layers of land and rock from different eras, with some mountain chains like the **Klamath** in southern Oregon and California among the oldest, and colossal peaks like today's **High Cascades** among the newest. Indeed, the High Cascades – a volcanic chain with most of the region's familiar peaks, including **Mount Rainier** and **Mount St Helens** – is generally less than five million years old, with some mountains emerging only in the last 200,000 years, a blip by geological standards. Other major changes – the demise of the old **Western Cascades**, the lava floods of central Oregon, and the spectacular formation of the **Columbia River Gorge** by the Bretz Floods – have had an equally impressive effect on the region (discussed further in their respective chapters), showing just how powerfully – and violently – the earth's dynamism has shaped the region's landscape.

Native peoples

The ancestors of the **native peoples** of the Pacific Northwest first entered the region twelve thousand to eighteen thousand years ago, when vast glaciers covered most of the North American continent, keeping the sea level far below that of today. These first human inhabitants to cross the land bridge linking Asia with present-day Alaska were likely **Siberian hunter-nomads** in pursuit of mammoths, hairy rhinos, bison, wild horses, and giant ground sloths, the Ice Age animals that were a major part of their diet and culture. These people left very little evidence of their passing, apart from some simple graves and the grooved, chipped stone spearheads that earned them the anthropological name **Fluted Point People**. In successive waves they moved down through North America, across the isthmus of Panama, until they reached the southernmost tip of South America. As they settled, so they slowly developed ever more distinctive cultures and languages.

Numbering perhaps 150,000, the peoples that settled along the Pacific Northwest spoke many languages. The most prominent language groups were the **Plateau Panutian** family, including subgroupings like Chinook, Tsimshian, Siuslaw, Coos, Klamath, and Cayuse, and the **Salishan** family, including Salish, Duwamish-Suquamish, Nisqually, Siletz, Columbian, Okanagan, and Spokane. The wheel was unknown to these early inhabitants, and most were reliant on the canoe, though the plains and plateau peoples east of the coastal mountains used draft animals – the largest of which was initially the dog. Over the centuries, each of the tribes developed techniques that enabled them to cope with the problems of survival posed by their particular environments.

Coastal peoples, for example, took advantage of an agreeable climate and fertile environment to create a sophisticated culture that stretched from southeast Alaska to Oregon. Here, a multitude of groups such as the **Salish, Chinook, Suquamish**, and **Makah** depended on the ocean to provide them with a

△ Tlingit totem pole, Pioneer Square, Seattle

plentiful supply of food. Living a comparatively settled life, they moved only from established winter villages to summer fishing sites, and occupied giant cedar lodges, clan dwellings dominated by a hereditary chief. There was, however, little cohesion within tribes, and people from different villages – even though of the same tribe – would at times be at war with one another. Surplus food, especially **salmon**, was traded, and the sizable profits underpinned a competitive culture revolving around an intricate system of ranks and titles, which culminated in the winter **potlatch**, a giant feast where the generosity of the giver – and the eloquence of the speeches – measured the clan's success. Prestige was also conferred upon clans according to the excellence of their woodcarvings, the most conspicuous manifestation being totem poles (new and old versions of which you can see in Seattle's Pioneer Square and Occidental parks).

Other tribes, living south of the northern forests and east of the Pacific Coast, also developed cultures in response to climatic conditions. The nomadic hunter-gatherers of the inland valleys and prairies, like the **Nez Percé**, foraged for nuts and roots and mixed seasonal fishing with hunting, while the **Modoc** and **Klamath** tribes of the arid basin surrounding today's Upper Klamath Lake in southern Oregon subsisted on plants and waterfowl and lived in semi-subterranean, earthen-domed lodges. Farther inland, the culture of the plateau tribes of the east, such as the **Palouse** and **Spokane**, echoed that of their more famous bison-dependent cousins, such as the Sioux, on the prairies east of the Rockies. In the late seventeenth century, the hunting techniques of these prairie-plateau peoples were transformed by the rearrival of the **horse** – long extinct in North America, it made its return from Mexico, where it had been introduced by the Spanish *conquistadors*. On the prairies, the horse made the bison easy prey, and this ready food supply spawned a militaristic society centered on the prowess of the tribes' young braves.

The arrival of the Europeans

Europeans first spied the Pacific Northwest coast in 1542, when a Spanish expedition sailing from Mexico dropped anchor at the mouth of the Rogue River in southern Oregon. Stormy weather and treacherous currents prevented a landing, just as adverse conditions were later to hinder a succession of early explorers, most famously **Sir Francis Drake**, whose *Golden Hind* was buffeted up and down the Oregon coast in 1579. The Spaniards, fresh from conquering Mexico, were looking to extend their American empire, whereas Drake was searching for the fabled **Northwest Passage** from the Atlantic to the Pacific – and hence Asia. (By finding the passage, the English hoped to break free of the trading restrictions imposed by the Portuguese at Africa's Cape of Good Hope and the Spanish at South America's Cape Horn.) There was indeed a Northwest Passage, but it was so blocked by Arctic ice as to be an impossible commercial route; not until the end of the nineteenth century did a (steel-hulled) ship finally manage to sail it. Consequently, the Pacific Northwest coast remained a Spanish preserve well into the eighteenth century, with only the gossip of Mediterranean sea captains remaining to excite English nautical interest. The most famous rumor was put about by **Juan de Fuca**, who insisted he had discovered the (ice-free) Northwest Passage – a shameful lie that nevertheless helped him get a key strait named after him.

The British, still searching for the Northwest Passage, dispatched the illustrious **Captain Cook** to the Pacific Northwest in 1776. Cook took the easterly route, sailing round the Cape of Good Hope and across the Pacific Ocean to land on Vancouver Island after a year at sea. He hunted in vain for both the Northwest and Northeast (Siberian) Passage and while wintering in the Sandwich Islands (present-day Hawaii) was murdered by Polynesians. On the way home, Cook's ships dropped by Canton, where the sailors found, much to their surprise, that the Chinese were keen to buy the **sea otter skins** they had procured from the Native Americans for next to nothing. News of the expedition's fortuitous discovery – and its commercial potential – spread quickly, and by 1790 around thirty merchants from various countries were shuttling back and forth between China and the Pacific Coast.

The British Admiralty were, however, still preoccupied with the Northwest Passage. In 1791, they sent **George Vancouver** out to have another look. Although his ultimate aim was unachievable, Vancouver did chart a long stretch of coastline, including the island that bears his name. He named dozens of other features too, some in honor of bigwigs at home, others after his subordinates – Whidbey, Puget, Baker, and Rainier to name but a few. Vancouver failed to notice the mouth of the Columbia River – a mistake remedied by the American **Robert Gray** shortly afterward.

All this colonial activity did not lead to any fighting among Russia (which had claims to Alaska), Spain, and Britain. Needless to say, no one bothered to consult the indigenous peoples. Although the Native Americans had benefited by trading furs for metal goods, and relations between them and the newcomers were often cordial, they could hardly have guessed at the catastrophe that was soon to overwhelm them.

British ascendancy

In 1670, Charles II of England established the **Hudson's Bay Company** – a royally chartered private corporation that was the oldest in North America and is still in business after 337 years. It was awarded control of a million and a half square miles adjacent to Hudson Bay, a vast inland sea about 1500 miles east of the Pacific Coast. The king's two main objectives were to consolidate the British fur trade and to encircle New France (broadly Québec). In 1760, at the height of the struggle known here as the **French and Indian War**, and in Europe as the Seven Years War, the British captured Montréal, marking the beginning of the end of the French North American empire. But with French knowledge of the interior too valuable to jettison, British merchants employed many of the "voyageur" fur traders in the newly formed **North West Company**, which merged with and enlarged the Hudson's Bay Company in 1821.

For the purposes of the Pacific Northwest, the company ruled the region as a virtual fiefdom until almost the middle of the nineteenth century, discouraging immigration in order to protect its fur trade. It did, however, exercise its powers in the name of the British Crown and consequently, after the **War of American Independence**, was used to aggressively counter American territorial aspirations.

American settlement

Under the terms of the **Louisiana Purchase** of 1803, the US paid just $15 million – or $203 million in 2007 dollars – for the French territory that blocked its path west, a huge chunk of land stretching from Canada to Mexico between

From the 1830s onward, the **Native Americans of the Pacific Northwest** were simply overwhelmed by the pace of events and the rise of the United States. Lacking any political or social organization beyond the immediate level of the tribe, they found it difficult to act against the organized legions of white colonists arriving – though admittedly European-borne diseases did much of the damage, with epidemics of measles and smallpox decimating the region's indigenous population by up to seventy percent.

In the Oregon Country, the US government initially tried to move willing tribes onto fairly large reservations, but as more settlers came and made political demands for land, the tribes were forced onto smaller and smaller parcels. Some groups chose to resist – the **Cayuse** slaughtered the Whitmans, the **Nez Percé** killed a handful of white settlers, and most determined of all, the **Modocs** from the California-Oregon border fought a long-running guerrilla war against the US Army. For the most part, though, the native peoples were simply swept aside by the tide of guns, disease, and immigration. By 1880, the survivors had been consigned to **Indian reservations**, which mostly comprised the infertile land no one else wanted. Further damage was inflicted by the **Dawes Severalty Act** of 1887, which required Native Americans to select individual 160-acre reservation landholdings (lands had traditionally been held communally). Land ownership was an alien concept to most of the tribes, and it obliged their children to attend government or mission schools. Deprived of their traditions and independence, many lapsed into poverty, alcoholism, and apathy.

In recent years, the US government has (somewhat intermittently) attempted to right historic wrongs, but socioeconomic indicators demonstrate that native peoples remain at a significant disadvantage compared with the rest of the population. More positively, native peoples have begun to assert their culture and campaign for self-determination. Starting in the 1960s, the rise of **ethnic identity** movements (spurred by the civil rights marchers of the 1950s and the later Black Power movement) emboldened some native groups to demand more favorable treatment. Nowadays, although some compacts have been renegotiated with tribes, and the situation isn't quite as dismal as it once was, the future is still troubled. While the so-called Indian casinos have been touted as the solution to the economic malaise of the reservations, other native critics see little potential in a dubious enterprise such as organized gambling to solve the entrenched problems.

the Mississippi River and the Rockies. With the sale, France dropped its last major colonial claim to North America, leaving the US and Britain to sort matters out between themselves. Perhaps the only US politician to realize the full importance of the purchase was President Thomas Jefferson, who both engineered the deal and bankrolled the **Lewis and Clark Expedition** the following year, with the expectation that the two explorers would open up the interior for American fur traders. At that time the tribes of the Missouri basin carried their furs to Hudson's Bay Company posts in Canada, and Jefferson believed, quite rightly, that they would find it far easier to dispatch the pelts downriver to American buyers. Indeed, Jefferson's dream was to displace the British entirely – his sentiments were considerably more pro-French – thereby securing economic control of a continent whose potential he foresaw. With this in mind, his two protégés, Meriwether Lewis and William Clark, were dispatched to the Pacific with instructions to collect every scrap of information they could find.

Setting out on May 14, 1804, the expedition comprised forty-eight men, three boats, four horses, twenty-one bales of trade goods and presents to buy goodwill, and, in case that failed, rifles, a blunderbuss, and a cannon. The party ascended the Missouri, crossed the Rockies, and descended the Columbia River to reach the Pacific eighteen months later. It was a well-led expedition and the two leaders dealt tactfully with the tribes they encountered, hiring local guides wherever possible and dispatching emissaries ahead to reassure the next tribe down the line of their peaceful intentions before they arrived. Ultimately, they steered clear of any real conflict and suffered only one casualty (from appendicitis), though they did endure all sorts of hardships – treacherous whitewater rapids, dangerous trails, and just plain discomfort: they were all, for example, infested with fleas in their winter base on the West Coast, **Fort Clatsop**. They covered about four thousand miles on the outbound trip, carefully mapping and describing the country and its people in their **journals** (see p.496), which provide intriguing glimpses of Native American cultures just before they were decimated by war and disease.

Lewis and Clark also laid the basis for American competition with British fur traders: Clark founded the **Missouri Fur Company** on his return, and **John Jacob Astor** was sufficiently encouraged to establish an American fur trading post, Astoria, at the mouth of the Columbia River in 1811. In the next twenty years, several factors combined to accelerate the pace of the American move westward, one of the most important of which was the dispatch of missionaries – most notably **Dr Marcus Whitman**, who set about Christianizing the Cayuse from his farm near the present-day city of Walla Walla, Washington. The Whitmans wrote home extolling the virtues of the **Oregon Country** (as both Washington State and Oregon were then known), firing the interest of relatives and friends. Perhaps more important, the Whitmans had made their long journey west by ordinary farm wagon: if they could do it, then so, it was argued, could other settlers.

The Oregon Trail

It was Whitman himself who, in 1843, guided the first sizable wagon train (of a thousand souls) along the **Oregon Trail** – a pioneering journey that became known to later generations as the **Great Migration**. The migrants sweated their way across the plains, chopped through forests, and hauled their wagons over fast-flowing streams behind oxen that traveled at around 2mph. It was a long and hard trip, but impressions of the trail varied enormously. To some who encountered hostile natives, grizzlies, cholera, or bitter weather, it was hell on earth; to others it was exhilarating – "a long picnic," wrote one. Each succeeding year a couple of thousand more emigrants followed, and soon American farmers – who were the vast majority of migrants heading for Oregon – were all over the **Willamette Valley**, much to the consternation of the Hudson's Bay Company. Later groups forged their own paths, whether settling in the dusty lands of eastern Oregon or trekking farther afield. Most notably, Jesse Applegate led a bedraggled group of settlers down to southern Oregon along the soon-to-be-infamous **Applegate Trail**, sending wagons tumbling down hillsides and pioneers into fits of disease, anger, and frustration. In the end, though, this smaller trail had the same effect as its more famous sibling – despite the hardships, it brought settlers to new lands far from their original homes. The totality of this mass movement made Oregon an American community and was to ensure its future lay within the USA.

Fixing the frontiers

Tying up the inconclusive War of 1812, Britain and the United States signed the **Treaty of Ghent** in 1814 to formalize American recognition of the legitimacy of British North America. The latter's border was established along the 49th Parallel west from Lake of the Woods in Ontario to the Rockies. Less clear was the arrangement concerning present-day Oregon and Washington: the treaty deferred the issue of sovereignty until the indefinite future, while promising the nationals of both regions free access to the whole area.

Initially, events on the ground went in Britain's favor. Astor was so irritated by the failure of the Americans to trounce the English in the war that he lost all interest in Astoria, selling his trading post to the Hudson's Bay Company, which promptly relocated its western headquarters to **Vancouver, Washington**, near what would become Portland. But soon the dominant position of the company was undermined by the influx of American farmers along the Oregon Trail. In the presidential campaign of 1844, under the jingoistic slogan of "**54-40 or fight**" (54 degrees and 40 minutes latitude), James Polk agitated for American control over the region up to central British Columbia – a jarring demand. However, in due course the present international frontier was fixed in 1846, following a sensible westward extension of the original 49th Parallel.

The **Oregon Territory** came into being the following year and Washington was sliced off it in 1853. Oregon's subsequent application for US statehood was, however, delayed by the issue of slavery, with neither the existing free states nor the rival slave states eager to refight the drama of California's admission as a free state in 1850. Oregon was finally accepted as a free state in 1859, though with an appalling state constitution that forbade free blacks from living there at all; this was rescinded after the Civil War. Thinly populated **Washington** didn't manage to assemble enough settlers to qualify for statehood until 1889.

Economic booms

In 1848, **gold** was discovered in California's Sierra Nevada range. Guessing the effect the news would have in Oregon, a certain **Captain Newell** sailed up the Willamette River buying every spade, pick, and shovel he could get his hands on. He then informed locals of the gold strike and promptly sold their own tools back to them – at a substantial markup. It was quite a scam, and in the ensuing California Gold Rush more than two-thirds of able-bodied Oregonians hightailed it south. Yet despite the exodus, the gold rush turned out to be a boon for Oregon. For the first time there was a ready market for the farmers of the Willamette Valley – and an even closer one when gold was found at **Jacksonville** in 1850 – while Oregon lumber towns like Ashland and Roseburg boomed supplying building materials, and Portland flourished from the dramatic upturn in trade.

In the early 1860s, the story was repeated when gold was unearthed in the Oregon interior, in the hills around John Day and Baker City. Both strikes had a dramatic impact, opening up the area east of the Cascade Range – and displacing the native population, who had previously been assured they'd be allowed to stay there. To feed the miners, thousands of cattle were driven over the mountains and, once they'd reached the interior, drovers found their animals thrived on the meadow grass of the valley bottoms and the plentiful supply of bunchgrass. This marked the beginning of the great **cattle empires** of eastern Oregon, though the ranchers' success was short-lived: the railroad reached the west in the 1880s and at a stroke overturned local economics. Railroad transportation meant that more money could be made from an acre sown than an acre grazed, and the cattle barons soon gave way to farmers.

Washington followed a similar pattern, with the eastern towns of Spokane and Walla Walla prospering as supply depots for the gold and silver mines of Idaho

The Wobblies

In 1905, enthusiastic delegates to a labor congress in Chicago founded the **Industrial Workers of the World** (the IWW), the most successful revolutionary labor movement in US history. It was born out of frustration with the dominant union organization of the day, the American Federation of Labor (AFL), both for its failure to organize successful strikes and its ideological conservatism: the AFL had no political strategy and its main objective was to protect the interests of skilled workers. IWW members became known as **Wobblies** as a result of mispronunciation of the movement's acronym by the Chinese immigrants, who constituted a sizable number of its members. Dedicated to the overthrow of capitalism by means of agitation and strikes, their flyers proclaimed, "The working class and the employing class have nothing in common." The IWW's goal was to unite the workers of individual industries – such as mining, construction, and logging – within brotherhoods that would eventually be combined into the so-called **One Big Union**.

IWW membership was never large – it reached a peak of around 100,000 in 1912 – but the Wobblies managed to exercise an influence out of all proportion to their numbers. They inspired thousands of workers to actively struggle against harsh anti-strike laws, low pay, and dreadful conditions. The IWW was particularly strong in Washington and Oregon, calling a series of strikes against the lumber companies. The employers frequently resorted to violence to defeat the union's causes, and in 1916, in one of several bloody incidents, seven IWW organizers were shot, and many others drowned, when the sheriff of Everett, Washington, tried to stop them from leaving the steamboat that had brought them from Seattle.

Three years later, a (peaceful) general strike mobilized 60,000 workers and paralyzed Seattle. IWW organizers fed strikers at labor-run cafeterias, handled emergency services, and delivered milk to babies so effectively that many employers feared they were witnessing the beginnings of a Bolshevik-style revolution. But in fact the Wobblies had never devised a coherent political program, nor did they want to seize power, and the strike simply faded away. Indeed, the IWW was by then deeply split between radical revolutionary factions and elements that favored democratic reform.

In the later 1910s and 1920s, the IWW began to fragment and its influence waned, due to a combination of internal conflict, demoralizing attacks by right-wing vigilante mobs (some paid for by the Wobblies' corporate adversaries), and, most of all, **government repression** in reaction to the rise of Soviet Russia. The Red Scare enabled the government to prosecute and imprison many leftist "subversive elements" in the country, using the tool of the Espionage Act of 1917 to slap long jail terms – up to twenty years – on union leaders for organizing, picketing, and protesting against the Great War in Europe. The IWW soon disappeared from the Pacific Northwest, even though it continued to maintain a lingering presence in the industrial Midwest for another thirty years. Its biggest influence, though, was on the large industrial unions to come, who were now wary enough of government reaction to act as patriotic friends of the working man and, after the presidency of Franklin Roosevelt, loyal financial and organizing supporters of the Democratic Party.

and Montana. Here, too, cattle grazed the rolling grasslands of the interior until the appearance of the railroad (and the savage winter of 1881) precipitated the shift from livestock to grain production. The Washington seaboard got in on the act during the **Klondike Gold Rush** of the 1890s, when Seattle became the jumping-off point for Alaska-bound miners, and grew to rival San Francisco. The town was inundated with fortune-seekers, their dreams fired by tales of those who had found unimaginable wealth up north. To keep the gold-diggers coming, the Seattle Chamber of Commerce placed ads in papers and magazines across the nation extolling the Seattle–Klondike connection. Eventually, even one of Seattle's mayors caught gold fever, quitting his job to take part in the frenzy up north. Few of the fortune hunters who set off from Seattle returned with their pots of gold, but with the massive influx of traffic through the town, business boomed in banking, retail, shipbuilding, and real estate.

The twentieth century

At the beginning of the **twentieth century**, the region's economy was largely reliant on primary products and raw goods, principally timber, grain, and fish, but there were also pockets of manufacturing, especially in and around Seattle and Tacoma. The shipping and timber industries were hit hard by the **Great Depression**, but **World War II** reinvigorated Seattle and Portland, boosting the cities' small black populations as African Americans moved here to work in war-related industries. Simultaneously, though, the **Japanese American** population, previously the largest minority in Seattle, was persecuted and depleted as a result of President Roosevelt's **Executive Order 9066**, which interned them in **detention camps**.

World War II also accelerated the pace of **industrialization** and **urbanization**, and the Pacific Northwest played a prominent part in the war effort, its factories churning out aircraft and munitions, its shipyards building warships, and its huge Columbia River dams supplying the hydropower for aluminum manufacturing. This trend toward industrialization continued after the war, further alleviating dependence on logging, fishing, and farming, but was not enough to insulate the Pacific Northwest from the wearisome cycle of boom and bust, with prices determined by Eastern stock markets far beyond local control.

The aerospace company **Boeing** had been around in Seattle since 1916, but only with government orders for wartime bombers did the company really begin its outsize growth. The Cold War added to its success, as the company employed countless engineers and technicians to design the latest in missile technology and, of course, build the transcontinental jets for which it is best known. The area's marriage of industry and technology was celebrated by the **Century 21 Exposition** (also known as the World's Fair) in 1962, for which Seattle's most recognizable symbol, the **Space Needle**, was built. In short order, though, the political movements sweeping much of America in the 1960s were mirrored here. There were the requisite **Vietnam War** protests on the campuses of the universities of Oregon and Washington, and the subsequent trials of radicals such as the so-called **Seattle Seven**. Eugene, Oregon, became something of a hippie center as well, attracting great numbers of people practicing alternate lifestyles, among them writer **Ken Kesey**, who took his "Merry Pranksters" here to escape the chaos of the Bay Area.

Within the next decade, Oregon made headlines for the anti–urban sprawl and pro-environmental policies championed by Governor **Tom McCall**, while Portland, too, shook off the torpor of its decaying timber-town image and emerged as a leader in the urban **"quality of life"** movement. Guided by mayors like Neil Goldschmidt, the city took such steps as dismantling a waterfront freeway to create a park, closing off traffic lanes to make a newfangled bus mall, and stopping unrestrained development by setting up its own **"urban growth boundary"** – all fairly revolutionary for the time. Seattle, however, showed little interest in such thinking, and through its business initiatives and

△ Seattle's Space Needle

aggressive development emerged as the showcase city of the Pacific Northwest – to the chagrin of some old-timers.

The turn of the 1980s was marked by two dramatic events: the colossal **explosion of Mount St Helens** on May 18, 1980, coating the region in ash and blowing apart one of the region's signature postcard images, and the later, rapid emergence of **high-tech companies**, many of which rooted themselves along the Pacific seaboard, the biggest being Microsoft, based in Seattle. At the same time, the logging and fishing industries found their activities significantly curtailed by federal lawsuits against **overfishing** and timber **clear-cutting**, and a region that had once been thoroughly blue collar was suddenly flooded with white-collar computer and service workers. This structural change underpinned the newfound chic that washed over Seattle and, to a lesser extent, Portland in the 1990s: the new information technology (IT) companies were renowned for laid-back work practices and informal dressing; coffeehouses proliferated; and a slew of bright new museums, skyscrapers, and civic institutions resculpted the cities' horizons. The transformation was essentially an urban one, though, as the small towns that once characterized the region were firmly excluded. However, while Portland and Seattle could complacently view the struggles of the port villages and mill towns with a certain distance, the new millennium brought a fresh understanding of what economic struggle really meant.

A new era

At the end of 2000, the **high-tech bubble** abruptly burst, and the national economy, key to so much local success, soured. Countless firms went out of business or suffered through their toughest years yet. Even Boeing – still one of the region's largest employers – began laying off thousands of workers, moving its corporate headquarters to Chicago in the process, and long-standing resource companies like Willamette and Louisiana-Pacific, both timber outfits, also packed up shop for good. Ultimately, what started as a national recession became something closer to a regional depression for some industries, making Washington and Oregon national leaders in **unemployment**.

Washington's February 2001 **earthquake** made things still more dismal, adding to the dreary outlook with a slew of damaged or closed businesses, including many old structures in Pioneer Square. The combination of a weakened local economy, steep decreases in public revenue through reduced taxes, and unconscionable slash-and-burn ballot measures caused **widespread cutbacks** in state funding for health care, education, the arts, parks, social programs, and business development.

However, despite all of their problems, the more sizable Northwest cities – Seattle and Portland, but also such places as Eugene and Olympia – began attracting young, enterprising people to live and work in them – a group the media have dubbed "**creative class.**" Even though such migrants have had to cope with a housing stock that has doubled in price in five years (even as real wages have increased by only half that amount), terrible traffic congestion, a disappearing manufacturing base, and a climate that in autumn and winter is gloomy at best, they continue to come in droves – often taking a pay cut in the process, going from being a mid-level manager in, say, Cincinnati to pulling espresso shots in Seattle. The contradiction is one that has puzzled economists, some of whom chalk it up to the **dynamic aura** that still surrounds the region – a glow that has as much or more to do with independent rock, funky art galleries, and freewheeling culture as it does with any particular industry.

Indeed, it's not surprising that the previous addresses of many arrivals are not, as you'd expect, in Idaho or Montana, but in New York and California. You can see the results of the new immigration in districts like Seattle's Belltown and Fremont, Portland's Pearl District and South Waterfront, and in towns like Tacoma and Bend. And with the rise of the **wine industry**, even smaller burgs have gotten in on the act, with such previously obscure spots like Newberg, Dundee, Yakima, and Walla Walla now drawing a steady stream of vino lovers from around the country and world. Still, for those rural communities that aren't blessed with a trendy aura, the future continues to be bleak, with many logging towns and fishing ports dying with each passing year, hoping only for the next new trend – golfing in Bandon, murals in Toppenish, windsurfing in Hood River – to give them a fresh breath of life.

Northwest wildlife

The Pacific Northwest boasts a wide range of **natural habitats**, from glaciers on Cascade mountainsides to parched deserts in central Oregon. Between these extremes the region's hills, forests, and grasslands support an incredible variety and profusion of **wildlife** – any brief account can only scratch the surface of what you can expect to see. National, state, and local parks offer the best starting points, and we've listed some of the outstanding sites for spotting particular species. Don't expect to see the big attractions like bears, mountain lions, and wolves easily, however; despite the enthusiasm of guides and tourist offices, these are encountered only rarely – perhaps for the better.

The ocean

The **Pacific Ocean** largely determines the climate of the Northwest, keeping the coastal temperatures moderate all year round. In spring and summer, cold, nutrient-rich waters rise to the surface, producing banks of cooling fog and abundant phytoplankton (microscopic algae). The algae nourish creatures such as krill (small shrimp), which provide baby food for juvenile fish. This food chain sustains millions of nesting seabirds, as well as elephant seals, sea lions, and whales.

Gray whales, the most common species of whale viewed from land, were almost hunted to the point of extinction, but have returned to the coast in large numbers. During their southward migration to breeding grounds off Mexico, from December to January, they are easy to spot from prominent headlands all along the coast, and many towns have charter services offering whale-watching tours. On their way back to the Arctic Sea, in February and March, the newborn whale calves can sometimes be seen playfully leaping out of the water, or "breaching." Look for the whale's white-plumed spout – once at the surface, it usually blows several times in succession.

Humpback whales are also frequently seen, largely because they're curious and follow sightseeing boats, but also because of their surface acrobatics. They too were hunted to near-extinction, and though they have been protected by international agreement since 1966, their population is less than ten percent of what it once was.

Another Northwest resident, **sea otters** differ from most marine mammals in that they keep themselves warm with a thick soft coat of fur rather than with blubber. This brought them to the attention of early Russian and British fur traders, and by the beginning of the twentieth century they were virtually extinct. They were reintroduced in 1969 to the Northwest coast, where they are now breeding successfully at the heart of their original range. With binoculars, it's often easy to spot these charming creatures lolling on their backs, using rocks to crack open sea urchins or mussels and eating them off their stomachs; they often lie bobbing asleep, entwined in kelp to keep from floating away. If all else fails, you can see them in resigned captivity in a space like the Oregon Coast Aquarium in Newport.

Lovable scamps who are sure to draw a crowd, northern **sea lions** – "eared seals" that can manage rudimentary shuffling on land thanks to short rear limbs, and swim by making strokes with their front flippers – are year-round residents that can be spotted on the rocks and wharves around Newport, Oregon, and other coastal towns.

Tide pools

The Pacific Northwest's shorelines are composed of three primary ecosystems: **tide pools**, sandy beaches, and estuaries. You can explore tide pools at the twice-daily low tides (consult local newspapers for times), so long as you watch out for freak waves and take care not to get stranded by the incoming tide. You should also tread carefully – there are many small lives underfoot. Of the miles of beaches with tide pools, one of the best is at Yaquina Head on the central Oregon coast. Here you will find sea anemones (which look like green zinnias), hermit crabs, purple and green shore crabs, red sponges, purple sea urchins, starfish ranging from the size of a dime to the size of a hub cap, mussels, abalone, and Chinese-hat limpets – to name a few. Black oystercatchers, noisily heard over the surf, may be seen foraging for an unwary, lips-agape mussel. Gulls and black turnstones are also common, and during summer brown pelicans dive for fish just offshore.

The most famous resident of the tide pools is the **hermit crab**, which protects its soft and vulnerable hindquarters with scavenged shells, usually those of the aptly named black turban snail. Hermit crabs scurry busily around in search of a detritus snack, or scuffle with other hermit crabs over the ownership of vacant snail shells.

Much of the **seaweed** you see growing from the rocks is edible. As one would expect from a Pacific beachfront, there are also **palms** – sea palms, that is, with three-inch-long rubbery stems and flagella-like fronds. Their thick, root-like tethers provide shelter for small crabs. You will also find giant **kelp** washed up on shore – harvested commercially for use in thickening ice cream.

Sandy beaches

Long, golden **sandy beaches** may look sterile from a distance, but observe the margin of sand exposed as a gentle wave recedes, and you will see jet streams of small bubbles emerge from numerous clams and mole crabs. Small shorebirds called sanderlings race among the waves in search of these morsels, and sand dollars are often easy to find along the high-tide line. Humans, too, can be found on the lookout for **crabs**, **clams**, and **oysters** near the beach, with the most intrepid hunters on the prowl for the famed **geoduck clam**, a sizable creature that burrows deep into the sand and has a long, phallic siphon that sticks far out of its shell – making this bivalved beast weigh up to fifteen pounds in some cases (though usually one to three pounds).

Just as unusual, **northern elephant seals** will tolerate rocky beaches, but prefer soft sand mattresses for their rotund torsos. The males, or bulls, can reach lengths of over 20ft and weigh upward of four tons; the females, or cows, are petite by comparison – 13ft long, and averaging a mere one ton in weight. They have large eyes, adapted for catching fish in deep or murky waters; indeed, elephant seals are the deepest diving mammals, capable of staying underwater for up to twenty minutes and reaching depths of more than half a mile, where the pressure is ninety times that at the surface.

As the otter population was depleted by fur traders, so the elephant seals were decimated by commercial whalers in the mid-nineteenth century for their blubber and hides. By the late nineteenth century fewer than a hundred remained, but careful protection has partially restored the population in many of their native Northwest habitats.

Elephant seals emerge from the ocean only to breed or molt, most of which occurs off the California coast. They do, however, travel seasonally between the Golden State and Alaska, and may on occasion be spotted near the Oregon and Washington coasts. Their name comes from the male's long, trunk-like **proboscis**, through which they produce a resonant pinging sound that biologists call "trumpeting," done to attract a mate.

Estuaries

Throughout much of the Northwest, especially in the more developed southern part of the region, many **estuary** or river-mouth habitats have been filled, diked, drained, "improved" with marinas, or contaminated by pollutants. Those wetlands that survive consist of a mixture of **mudflats**, exposed only at low tide, and **salt marsh**, together forming a critical wildlife area that provides nurseries for invertebrates and fish, and nesting and wintering grounds for birds. Cordgrass, a dominant wetlands plant, produces five to ten times as much oxygen and nutrients per acre as does wheat.

Many interesting creatures live in the thick organic ooze, including the fat "innkeeper," a revolting pink hot dog of a worm that sociably shares its burrow with a small crab and a fish, polychaete worms, clams, and other such critters. Most prominent of estuary birds are great blue herons and egrets. Estuaries are the best places to see wintering shorebirds such as dunlins, dowitchers, western sandpipers, and yellowlegs. Eagles, hawks, falcons, and osprey are also found here.

Coastal bluffs

Along the shore, **coastal meadows** are bright with pink and yellow sand verbena, lupine, sea rocket, sea fig, and the bright orange California poppy – which, despite its name, is also found in Washington and Oregon. Slightly inland, the hills are covered with coastal scrub, consisting largely of coyote brush. Coastal canyons contain broadleaf trees such as the California laurel (known as myrtlewood in Oregon), alder, buckeye, and oak, and a tangle of sword ferns, horsetail, and cow parsnips.

Common rainy-season canyon inhabitants include four-inch-long banana slugs and rough-skinned newts. Coastal thickets also provide homes for weasels, bobcats, gray foxes, raccoons, black-tailed deer, quail, and garter snakes, together with the reintroduced **tule elk**, a once common member of the deer family. You can also spot majestic **Roosevelt elk** in certain viewing corridors just inland from the shore.

River valleys

Like many fertile **river valleys**, the large river systems of the Northwest – near cities at least – have been affected by agriculture. Riparian (streamside) vegetation has been logged, wetlands drained, and streams contaminated by agricultural runoff. Despite this, the riparian environment that does remain is a prime wildlife habitat, especially in the mountain parks, where conditions in many respects are still pristine. Wood ducks, kingfishers, swallows, and warblers are common, as are gray foxes, raccoons, and striped skunks. Common winter migrants include Canadian geese, green-winged and cinnamon teals, pintail, shovelers, and widgeon, and their refuges are well worth visiting. Don't be alarmed by the large numbers of duck-hunters – the term "refuge" is something of a misnomer, although many such areas do have places where hunting is prohibited.

Mountain forests

Mountain forests cover much of the Pacific Northwest and, depending on their location and elevation, fall into one of four categories: West Coast, Columbia, montane, and subalpine.

Some of the creatures common to most of these forests include **beavers** – Oregon is, of course, the Beaver State – which you may see at dawn or dusk, heads just above the water as they glide across lakes and rivers. Signs of their legendary activity include logjams across streams and ponds, stumps of felled saplings resembling sharpened pencils, and dens that look like domed piles of mud and sticks. Forest **wetlands** also offer refuge for **ducks** and **geese**, with loons, grebes, and songbirds attracted to their undergrowth. Three species of ptarmigan – willow, rock, and white-tailed – are common, and you'll see plenty of big raptors, including the great **gray owl**, the Northwest's largest owl. In certain wilderness preserves, you may even spot grand creatures like the **bald eagle** or a variety of **hawks** and **osprey** – such rich habitats are often prominently highlighted by local preservation groups.

West Coast forest

West Coast forests are the Northwest's most impressive woods, their huge trees a product of the Northwest's torrential rainfall, mild maritime climate, deep soil, and long growing season. Swaths of luxuriant temperate **rain forest** cover the Olympic Peninsula, dominated by Sitka spruce, western red cedar, Pacific silver fir, western hemlock, western yew, and, biggest of all, **Douglas fir**, some of which tower 300ft and are 1200 years old. However, these conifers make valuable timber, and much of this forest is under severe threat from logging.

Below the dripping canopy of the big trees lies an **undergrowth** teeming with life. Shrubs and bushes like salal, huckleberry, bunchberry, salmonberry, and twinberry thrive alongside mosses, ferns, lichens, liverworts, skunk cabbage, and orchids. Birds are legion, and include a wealth of woodland species such as the Townsend's warbler, Wilson's warbler, orange-crowned warbler, junco, Swainson's thrush, and golden-crowned kinglet. Rarer birds include the rufous hummingbird, which migrates from its wintering grounds in Mexico to feed on the forest's numerous nectar-bearing flowers.

Columbia forest

The **Columbia forest** covers the lower slopes (1300–4500ft) of the Cascades. Trees here are similar to those of the warmer and wetter rain forest – western red cedar, western hemlock, and Douglas fir – with Sitka spruce, which rarely thrives away from the coast, as the notable exception. The undercover, too, is similar, with lots of devil's club (a particularly vicious thorn), azaleas, black and

△ Bald eagle in Skagit River Valley, Washington

red twinberry, salmonberry, and redberry alder. Mountain lily, columbine, bunchberry, and heart-leaf arnica are among the common flowers.

Few mammals live exclusively in the forests, with the exception of the **red squirrel**, which makes a meal of conifer seeds and is in turn preyed on by hawks, owls, coyotes, and weasels, among others. Bigger predators roam the mountain forest, however, most notably the **brown bear**, a western variant of the ubiquitous black bear. Aside from the coyote, the tough, agile **black bear** is one of the continent's most successful carnivores and the one you're most likely to see around campgrounds and garbage dumps. Black bears have adapted to a wide range of habitats and food sources, and their only natural enemies – save wolves, which may attack young cubs – are hunters, who bag some 30,000 annually in North America. Almost extinct in the Northwest is the famous **grizzly bear**, a far larger and potentially dangerous creature distinguished by its silver-tipped, brownish fur and the ridged hump on its back. It feeds mainly on berries and salmon. More than other bears, grizzlies are unpredictable and readily provoked.

Montane forest

Montane forest covers the more southerly and sheltered reaches of Washington and Oregon, featuring Douglas fir, western larch, ponderosa pine, and **lodgepole pine**. The lodgepole requires intense heat before releasing its seeds, and huge stands of these trees grew in the aftermath of the forest fires that accompanied the building and operation of the railways.

Plentiful voles and small rodents attract **coyotes**, whose yapping – an announcement of territorial claims – you'll often hear at night close to small towns. Few predators have the speed to keep up with coyotes – only the stealthy **mountain lion**, or wolves hunting in tandem, can successfully bring them down. Among the biggest and most beautiful of the carnivores, mountain lions seem to arouse the greatest bloodlust in hunters. **Wolves**, too, have been significantly hunted and are thin on the ground, and your best bet for spotting or hearing them may be to attend a "howl-in" at Wolf Haven International (see p.354) outside Olympia, Washington.

Ponderosa and lodgepole pines provide fine cover for **birds** like goshawks, Swainson's hawks, and lesser species like ruby-crowned kinglets, warblers, pileated woodpeckers, nuthatches, and chickadees. In the forest's lowest reaches the vegetation and birds are those of the southern prairies – semi-arid regions of sagebrush, prickly pear, and bunchgrasses, dotted with lakes full of common ducks like mallards, shovelers, and wigeon. You might also see the cinnamon teal, a red version of the more common green-winged teal, a bird whose limited distribution lures birdwatchers to British Columbia.

Subalpine forest

Subalpine forests cover mountain slopes from 4200ft to 7200ft throughout the Northwest, supporting lodgepole, white-bark and timber pines, alpine fir, and Engelmann spruce. They also contain a preponderance of subalpine larch, a deciduous conifer whose vivid yellow needles dot the Cascade mountainsides in the fall to beautiful effect.

One of the more common animals of this zone is the elk, or **wapiti**, a powerful member of the deer family that can often be seen in large herds above the tree line in the summer. Elk court and mate during the fall, making a thin nasal sound called "bugling." Make sure to respect their privacy, as rutting elk have notoriously unpredictable temperaments.

Small herds of **mule deer** migrate between forests and alpine meadows, using glands between their hooves to leave a scent for other members of the herd to follow. They're named after their distinctive ears, designed to provide early warning of predators. Other smaller animals that are also attracted to the subalpine forest include the golden-mantled ground squirrel and birds such as Clark's nutcracker – both are tame and curious creatures that often gather around campgrounds in search of scraps.

Alpine zones

Alpine zones occur in mountains above the tree line in parts of the Cascades. Plant and animal life varies hugely between summer and winter, and according to terrain and exposure to the elements.

In spring, alpine meadows are carpeted with breathtaking displays of **wildflowers**: clumps of Parnassus grass, lilies, anemones, Indian paintbrushes, lupine, and a wealth of yellow flowers such as arnica, cinquefoil, glacier lily, and wood betony. Especially appealing are the slopes of Iron Mountain (see p.242) in Oregon's Western Cascades. Alpine meadows make excellent pasture, attracting **elk** and **mule deer** in summer, as well as full-time residents like **Dall** and **bighorn sheep**. **Marmots**, resembling hugely overstuffed squirrels, hibernate through the worst of the winter and beyond. In a good year they can sleep for eight months, prey only to grizzly bears, which are strong enough and have the claws to dig down into their dens. In their waking periods they can be tame and friendly, often nibbling contentedly in the sunnier corners of campgrounds. When threatened, however, they produce a piercing and unearthly whistle. (They can also do a lot of damage: some specialize in chewing the radiator hoses of parked cars.) The strange little **pika**, a relative of the rabbit, is more elusive but keeps itself busy throughout the year, living off a miniature haystack of fodder that it accumulates during the summer.

Birds are numerous in summer, and include rosy finches, pipits, and blue grouse, but few manage to live in the alpine zone year-round. One that does is the **white-tailed ptarmigan**, a plump, partridge-like bird that, thanks to its heavily feathered feet and legs, is able to snowshoe around deep drifts of snow; its white winter plumage provides camouflage. Unfortunately, ptarmigans can be as slow-moving and stupid as barnyard chickens, making them easy targets for hunters and predators.

Oregon and Washington on film

Despite being one of the most photogenic regions of North America, Oregon and Washington's presence on **film** is less stellar than you might expect. Hollywood, especially during the first fifty years of its history, often opted for the mountains of its own backyard rather than trekking all the way north. Even a movie as distinctly Northwestern as Stanley Donen's boisterous Oregon musical *Seven Brides for Seven Brothers* (1955) was shot on studio lots against backdrops so fake they might as well have been left over from *Bambi*. The situation has improved since then. In the early 1970s the mists and gloomy skies that are a staple of the Northwest climate – the same that had scared off many a film crew in the past – suddenly became popular among the European-influenced auteurs of the American New Wave. Moreover, Hollywood movies are now regularly filmed on location in the Northwest, and there's an actual homegrown filmmaking industry here to boot.

Portland

Drugstore Cowboy (Gus Van Sant 1989). Grim tale of pharmacy bandits who prowl Portland hunting for prescription-drug highs, starring Matt Dillon in one of his better early roles.

Elephant (Gus Van Sant 2003). Stark, desaturated take on the Columbine killings, set in a Portland high school. Well-made, disturbing portrait of teen angst and subsequent violence, though with little empathy for any of the characters.

The Hunted (William Friedkin 2003). Formulaic Vietnam-vet-turned-psycho-killer plot is enlivened by countless views of the city, including a climactic chase on a fictional train running over the Hawthorne Bridge – which seems to span for miles.

Jackass – The Movie (Jeff Tremaine 2002). MTV staple and now cult-film franchise that staged many of its nauseating escapades and jaw-dropping stunts on the streets of Portland.

Mala Noche (Gus Van Sant 1985). Depressing tale of drugs and street hustlers set in a grim slice of mid-1980s Portland. The film that first won its director his indie acclaim.

My Own Private Idaho (Gus Van Sant 1991). Somewhat overlooked curiosity with River Phoenix and Keanu Reeves as two acting out their own psychosexual drama with allusion to the works of Shakespeare.

Thumbsucker (Mike Mills 2005). Lou Pucci is the eponymous character, a man-child who comes of age in the suburbs of Portland under the tutelage of Keanu Reeves and Vince Vaughn.

What the #$*! Do We Know? (William Arntz 2004). Perhaps the ultimate cult documentary, largely filmed in town and involving all manner of iffy speculation about quantum physics, the nature of existence, magic, and psychology – and lots of computer imagery.

Elsewhere in Oregon

Animal House (John Landis 1978). The archetypal frat-house movie, with John Belushi and a cast of lesser-knowns as drunken college students in the 1960s, causing all manner of destruction. Eugene's University of Oregon and other Willamette Valley locations pose as the grounds of the fictional Faber College.

Bend of the River (Anthony Mann 1952). Jimmy Stewart adventure set around the Columbia River Gorge, in which reformed lawbreaker Jimmy Stewart's smiling new attitude is severely tested when he's abandoned by a greedy bunch of wagoneers on Mount Hood.

Emperor of the North (Robert Aldrich 1973). Uniquely Northwestern Depression-era showdown in which a sadistic Ernest Borgnine battles freeloading hobo Lee Marvin on the rails of Oregon.

Free Willy (Simon Wincer 1993). Family-oriented flick about a boy and his killer whale. Filmed in Astoria, and the main reason why an orca named Keiko ended up in the Oregon Coast Aquarium for several years.

The Goonies (Richard Donner 1985) Another Astoria-filmed kids adventure, this one involving buried treasure, pirates, and skeletons that would be forgettable as a pint-size Indiana Jones ripoff if it hadn't developed a cult of its own, mostly in Oregon.

One Flew Over the Cuckoo's Nest (Milos Forman 1975). Ken Kesey novel filmed at the Oregon State Hospital in Salem, and memorable for Jack Nicholson being lobotomized and resident Native American "Chief Bromden" smashing his way to freedom.

Paint Your Wagon (Joshua Logan 1969). Groan-a-minute spectacular filmed in eastern Oregon that has gold prospectors Lee Marvin and Clint Eastwood belting out a bevy of B-grade show tunes. Often cited as a key reason for the demise of the Hollywood musical.

The Postman (Kevin Costner 1985). Shot in central Oregon, a legendary bomb about post-apocalyptic America that, with *Waterworld*, has been held responsible for permanently derailing the actor-director's career.

Rooster Cogburn (Stuart Miller 1975). A far better film shot in central Oregon, including Smith Rock to nice effect, involving John Wayne playing a half-blind Wild West marshal who tangles with Katharine Hepburn. The sequel to *True Grit*.

The Shining (Stanley Kubrick 1980). Liberal adaptation of the Stephen King novel, with exteriors filmed at Mount Hood's Timberline Lodge. Unfortunately, the grand horror sets were shot in a British soundstage.

Short Circuit (John Badham 1986). Another kids' film shot in Astoria, involving a sentient, cringe-inducing robot who escapes from government clutches with the aid of 1980s teen queen Ally Sheedy.

Sometimes a Great Notion (Paul Newman 1971). Quintessential Northwest movie providing a stark look at the fallout from a lumbermill strike in a small Oregon town. Based on the Ken Kesey book and starring the director.

Stand By Me (Rob Reiner 1986). The director's soft-focus paean to lost youth, with River Phoenix as a bad little boy and based on the Stephen King tale "The Body." Memorably filmed in Brownsville, Oregon.

Without Limits (Robert Towne 1998). Biopic about the legend of Steve Prefontaine, who was coached to glory by Eugene track coach and Nike cofounder Bill Bowerman, only to die in a car accident at age 24.

Seattle

Cinderella Liberty (Mark Rydell 1973). James Caan is a sailor on leave, and Marsha Mason his love interest, in a film with many location shots of a pre-gentrified, down-at-the-heel Belltown. Not great cinema, but interesting as a period piece.

House of Games (David Mamet 1987). Modern film noir about a psychologist who gets drawn into a ring of con men, making effective use of dark, gritty Seattle locations.

Hype (Doug Pray 1996). Nostalgic grunge documentary chronicling the old days of the alt-rock scene in places like Seattle's Belltown, which has changed markedly since then. Has interviews with most of the major musicians and scenesters and live footage of all the knowns and unknowns.

It Happened at the World's Fair (Norman Taurog 1963). Typically dispensable Elvis Presley film – flimsy plot, mediocre music, and a spectacular location, in this case the Century 21 Exposition.

Kurt and Courtney (Nick Broomfield 1998). Controversial, sometimes hilarious guerrilla documentary on real and imagined mysteries surrounding the death of Kurt Cobain.

The Last Days (Gus Van Sant 2005). Revolving around the middling, suicidal end of Seattle rock-star "Blake," this thinly veiled portrait of Kurt Cobain's demise is strikingly well acted, visually evocative, and amazingly tedious.

Little Buddha (Bernardo Bertolucci 1994). Uneven flick (with Keanu Reeves as Siddhartha) about a Seattle boy thought by local Tibetan monks to be the reincarnation of a lama. Less than half is set in Seattle, but Bertolucci wanted the city for its architecture and overcast light.

The Parallax View (Alan Pakula 1974). Stunning paranoid thriller – the epitome of 1970s conspiracy filmmaking – that begins with a memorable assassination at the top of Seattle's Space Needle.

Singles (Cameron Crowe 1992). Romantic, very early-nineties look at young Seattlites living in a Capitol Hill apartment building, with cameos by members of Pearl Jam and Soundgarden. Also interesting for Matt Dillon's turn as a goateed grunge wanna-be.

Sleepless in Seattle (Nora Ephron 1993). Sappy smash in which a widowed Tom Hanks falls for reporter Meg Ryan, with help from his son and talk radio. Great location scenes, and a long comic exchange with Rob Reiner in Pike Place Market's Athenian Inn.

Streetwise (Martin Bell 1984). Poignant documentary about homeless kids on Seattle's Pike Street, one of the grittiest views of any Northwest city.

Triumph of the Nerds (Robert X. Cringely 1996). Involving three-hour TV documentary about the rise of Bill Gates, Steve Jobs, and the other techno-nerds who created modern computing. Followed two years later by a sequel, *Nerds 2.0.1: A Brief History of the Internet.*

Trouble in Mind (Alan Rudolph 1986). Odd, self-consciously arty film of murky crime schemes and romantic tangles that makes good use of the grayest aspects of Seattle (called "Rain City" here).

Elsewhere in Washington

The Deer Hunter (Michael Cimino 1978). Vietnam War–era epic ostensibly set in the mountains of Pennsylvania, but actually shot three thousand miles across the country in the Cascade Mountains.

Fire Walk with Me (David Lynch 1992). Less-inspired movie prequel to the director's classic TV series *Twin Peaks*, which really put the snowcapped mountains and logging towns of Washington on the media map. You can still visit the Double R Diner (aka Twede's Cafe) in North Bend and order a damn fine slice of cherry pie.

Five Easy Pieces (Bob Rafelson 1970). Classic "dismal Northwest" piece that takes middle-class piano-prodigy manqué Jack Nicholson from the sunbaked oilfields of Texas north to visit his family in Washington's San Juan Islands – the change of scenery and climate perfectly conveying his cruel malaise.

McCabe & Mrs Miller (Robert Altman 1971). Perhaps the greatest film ever made about the Northwest, starring Warren Beatty and Julie Christie. Set in the Washington frontier town of "Presbyterian Church" at the beginning of the twentieth century, where an unexpected three-day blizzard provided Altman with an unforgettable cinematic climax.

An Officer and a Gentleman (Taylor Hackford 1982). Debra Winger and Richard Gere military melodrama filmed in Port Townsend, though Louis Gossett, Jr, has the best role as a tough-as-nails drill sergeant.

The Ring (Gore Verbinski 2002). Formulaic remake of a popular Japanese horror film, in this case concerning a reporter who visits western Washington to investigate a mysterious videotape that causes death to those who watch it. More sequels on the way.

Snow Falling on Cedars (Scott Hicks 1999). Based on the novel about a 1954 murder on a fictional Puget Sound island and the ensuing trial, which digs up wounds dating back to the internment of the community's Japanese Americans during World War II.

This Boy's Life (Michael Caton-Jones 1993). Based on Tobias Wolff's book (see p.500) and set in the small North Cascades town of Concrete, Washington. Stars Leonardo DiCaprio as the victim of abusive patriarch Robert De Niro.

The Vanishing (George Sluizer 1993). American remake of a better Dutch original by the same director. Set in wilderness Washington and involving a particularly eerie and creepy abduction – though this version slaps on a mindless happy ending.

Books on Oregon and Washington

M any, though not all, of these **books** are readily available in the UK and US. Publishers for each title are listed in the form US/UK publisher, unless the book is published in one country only; o/p means out of print. Out-of-print books can usually be found quite readily on the Internet and, unless truly rare, typically cost the same as or less than their original retail prices. Titles marked with 🏃 are especially recommended.

Travel

Peter Alden *National Audubon Society Field Guide to the Pacific Northwest* (Knopf, US). Excellent, all-purpose guide to the region covering all the flora and fauna you might see and where you'll see it. Superbly illustrated.

David D. Alt and Donald W. Hyndman *Roadside Geology of Washington, Roadside Geology of Oregon* (Mountain Press, US). Excellent volumes in the series, pointing out and analyzing everything from the rock visible at highway roadcuts to the reasons for the area's earthquakes.

🏃 **Ralph Friedman** *In Search of Western Oregon* (Caxton, US). A fine aid for exploring the western half of the state in depth, loaded with observations and anecdotes about even the smallest of towns and arranged by journeys on major and minor roads. Now a bit out of date (1990 pub.), but still good for the author's musings.

Ruth Kirk and Carmela Alexander *Exploring Washington's Past: A Road Guide to History* (University of Washington Press, US). Every nook and cranny of the state is explored in detail in this comprehensive book. Jam-packed with intriguing information.

🏃 **Tom Kirkendall and Vicky Spring** *Bicycling the Pacific Coast* (Mountaineers Books, US). Detailed

guide to the bike routes all the way along the coast from Mexico up to Canada, with many fine avenues to explore along the Oregon Coast. Also good is the authors' *100 Best Cross-Country Ski Trails in Washington*, from the same publisher.

Cathy McDonald and Stephen R. Whitney *Nature Walks in and Around Seattle* (Mountaineers Books, o/p). Guides to several dozen walks in parks, forests, and wetlands in Seattle and environs, from favorites like the Discovery Park loop trail to obscurities like West Hylebos Wetlands State Park.

Christina Melander *Pacific Northwest: The Ultimate Winery Guide* (Chronicle, US/UK). The very latest (2007) overview of the region's wineries, which you'll need to keep up with the burgeoning vineyards of the Willamette Valley and Columbia Plateau.

Marge and Ted Mueller *The San Juan Islands Afoot & Afloat* (Mountaineers Books, US). Trails, parks, campgrounds, and water activities in the San Juans, by authors who have done similar guides to the North, Middle, and South Puget Sound areas.

🏃 **Rhonda and George Ostertag** *100 Hikes in Oregon* (Mountaineer Books, o/p). Excellent volume with many fine, detailed suggestions for wandering the outback of the state. If you can't find this volume, try the authors' in-print *50 Hikes in Hells Canyon and Oregon's Wallowas* and *Best Short Hikes in Northwest Oregon* (same publisher).

Chuck Palahniuk *Fugitives and Refugees* (Crown/Vintage). In one of the most offbeat tours of any city you're likely to find, cult-fiction author (see below) directs you to Portland's quirkiest and most disturbing spots – from a vacuum-cleaner museum and a four-story sex club to junk emporia and haunted moviehouses.

Robert Schnelle *Valley Walking* (Washington State University Press, US). The author, who lives in the Kittitas Valley, explores its remoter reaches on foot with this book of 33 essays – meditative hikes laced with thought-provoking comments on the environment.

William L. Sullivan *100 Hikes in Northwest Oregon* (Mountaineers Books, US). Detailed guide to the trails within an easy day-trip of Portland. One of several of Sullivan's outdoor guides to Oregon.

Native American

🔆 **Dee Brown** *Bury My Heart at Wounded Knee* (Owl Books, US/UK). Seminal 1970 work that played a leading role in the rewriting of Native American history: a grim story that details the brutal campaigns that punctuated the American drive west. Of particular relevance are the chapters on the Nez Percé and the Modoc.

Ella C. Clark *Indian Legends of the Pacific Northwest* (University of California Press, US). Good selection of tales from several tribes, organized into thematic sections and linked by useful critical passages.

Peter Cozzens *The Wars for the Pacific Northwest: 1865–1890* (Stackpole, US). A fascinating presentation of both native and white views of the major conflicts – the Nez Percé and Modoc wars – and minor ones – the Bannock War and Sheepeater campaign – that shaped the region, drawn from contemporary accounts.

Christian F. Feest *Native Arts of North America* (Thames & Hudson, o/p). Comprehensive, lavishly illustrated survey of the development of North American native arts with

chapters devoted to painting and engraving, textiles, and sculpture.

🔆 **Jan Halliday and Gail Chehak** *Native Peoples of the Northwest: A Traveler's Guide to Land, Art and Culture* (Sasquatch, US). Comprehensive, visually rich overview of the culture of native peoples – from Alaska to Oregon and Washington to Montana – as reflected in their monuments, sacred sites, rodeos, museums, and festivals.

Warren Jefferson *The World of Chief Seattle: How Can One Sell the Air?* (Native Voice, US). Fine historical portrait of the city's namesake and his Duwamish–Suquamish tribe, from the injustice visited on them by white settlers to their modern society and lifestyle.

Francis Parkman *The Oregon Trail/ The Conspiracy of Pontiac* (Library of America/Oxford). Memorable nineteenth-century studies by one of the country's greatest historians. In these volumes, the author, who spent considerable time among native tribes, argued that the end of the French empire in North America would inevitably lead to British and American domination and the demise of Native Americans.

Explorers

Ron Anglin *Forgotten Trails: Historical Sources of the Columbia's Big Bend Country* (Washington State University Press, US). Enjoyable book that brings together samples from the best of early pioneer and explorer travel accounts of the Grand Coulee area.

Derek Hayes *Historical Atlas of the Pacific Northwest: Maps of Exploration and Discovery* (Sasquatch, US). An engaging look at the great powers' rivalries and explorers of the Northwest, from Oregon to Alaska, as seen through its antique maps and historic documents.

Meriwether Lewis and William Clark *The Journals of the Lewis and Clark Expedition, 1804–1806* (University of Nebraska, US). Six volumes of meticulous jottings by some of the Northwest's first inland explorers, who scrupulously recorded every detail of flora, fauna, and native inhabitants. Edited versions, such as Bernard DeVoto's classic *The Journals of Lewis & Clark* (Mariner, US), are of more use to the casual reader.

Axel Madsen *John Jacob Astor: America's First Multimillionaire* (Wiley, US). Ostensibly a biography taking a look at the New York magnate's whole life but most focused – and most lively – in describing his troubled Pacific Fur Company, and those who toiled for him in the wilds of the Northwest a continent away.

Stephanie Ambrose Tubbs and Clay Jenkinson *The Lewis and Clark Companion: An Encyclopedic Guide to the Voyage of Discovery* (Owl Books, US). An essential guide to the famous expedition, covering everything from munitions to draft animals to barter, including incisive portraits of the group members.

Natural environment

John Eliot Allen et al. *Cataclysms on the Columbia* (Timber Press, US). Excellent introduction to the colossal Ice Age floods that created the modern landscape of the Columbia River Gorge and the Willamette Valley, and how the floods were discovered through the efforts of a pioneering researcher facing a tidal wave of scientific hostility.

Charles A. Blakeslee *Crater Lake National Park: Wild and Beautiful* (Farcountry Press, US). Splendid coffee-table book full of vivid, detailed photos of the magnificent former Mount Mazama, which, since blowing its top, has become the deepest lake in North America.

Rob Carson *Mount St Helens: The Eruption and Recovery of a Volcano* (Sasquatch, US). Fine narrative and photographs of the devastation wrought by the mountain in May 1980, as well as the rebirth of its surrounding landscape over the next twenty years.

Timothy Egan *The Good Rain: Across Time and Terrain in the Pacific Northwest* (Vintage, US & UK). One of the key books about the region, focusing on its beleaguered ecology and social and environmental leaders, as well as the industries that have done much to reshape the landscape.

Stephen L. Harris *Fire Mountains of the West: The Cascade and Mono Lake Volcanoes* (Mountain Press, US). Easily the best introduction to the geology, history, and lore of the Cascades, also providing information on visiting and climbing these majestic peaks.

Philip Jackson and A. Jon Kimerling *Atlas of the Pacific Northwest* (Oregon State University Press, US). Shows every imaginable aspect of Washington and Oregon in graphs or maps – from geology, history and land ownership to hunting and fishing.

Sallie Tisdale *Stepping Westward: The Long Search for Home in the Pacific Northwest* (Perennial, o/p). Personal stories and observations of the ongoing conflict between man and nature throughout the region – clear-cut logging, dam building, and other human threats.

History

Kurt E. Armbruster *Orphan Road: The Railroad Comes to Seattle 1853–1911* (Washington State University Press, US). History of the long, tortuous process of bringing railways to the region, including how Tacoma was initially chosen as a rail terminus instead of Seattle.

Gordon DeMarco *A Short History of Portland* (Lexicos o/p). Thorough and charmingly written account of the city's development, with a wry tone and pointed perspective missing from booster accounts of the city's history. Well worth seeking out a copy if you can find one.

Robert L. Friedheim *The Seattle General Strike* (University of Washington Press, o/p). The most complete documentation of this 1919 event, though perhaps a bit dry and detailed for the casual reader.

Stewart Holbrook *Wildmen, Wobblies & Whistle Punks* (Oregon State University Press, US). Entertaining tales written by one of the region's most popular journalist-writers. About thirty short stories appear here, a small part of Holbrook's enormous output. Each tale delves into a colorful historical event in a laconic, folkloric style.

Washington Irving *Astoria* (Kegan Paul International, UK/US). Originally published in 1839, this account of Oregon's first American fur-trading colony offers fascinating insights into contemporary attitudes to the then still-unsettled Northwest.

Frank McLynn *Wagons West: The Epic Story of America's Overland Trails* (Grove/Pimlico). A grand history of the great migrations of the 1840s, with particular focus of the travails of the pioneers on the Oregon Trail and troubled offshoots like the Applegate Trail.

Dorothy Nafus Morrison *Outpost: John McLoughlin & the Far Northwest* (Oregon Historical Society, US). An employee of Canada's Hudson's Bay Company, McLoughlin disobeyed orders and sheltered incoming American settlers reaching the Willamette Valley from the Oregon Trail.

National Park Service *The Overland Migrations* (National Park Service, US). Short but useful guide to the trails that led pioneers west from the Missouri Valley in the middle of the nineteenth century.

Peter C. Newman *Caesars of the Wilderness* (Penguin, o/p). Highly acclaimed and readable three-volume account of the rise and fall of the Hudson's Bay Company.

Carlos Schwantes *The Pacific Northwest: An Interpretive History* (University of Nebraska, US). A leading Northwest historian explores every aspect of Oregon and Washington's history (along with Idaho's), from prehistoric to modern times, in a thoughtful and perceptive manner. Well illustrated and highly recommended.

Jean M. Ward and Elaine A. Maveety (eds.) *Pacific Northwest Women 1815–1925; Lives, Memories and Writings* (Oregon State University Press, US). Potent collection of writing from Northwest women of the era, touching on marriage, racism, women's rights, and family life, and highlighted with poems and photographs.

Biography

Charles R. Cross *Room Full of Mirrors: A Biography of Jimi Hendrix* (Hyperion, US). A lengthy bio that may well end up being the defining tome about Seattle's legendary guitarist, with especially good info on the early years about Jimi's myriad struggles in Seattle.

Walt Crowley *Rites of Passage* (University of Washington Press, US). Memoir of left-wing activism and counterculture in 1960s Seattle by the editor of an underground newspaper, who went on to become one of the city's most renowned journalists.

Ron Strickland *River Pigs and Cayuses: Oral Histories from the Pacific Northwest* (Oregon State University Press, US). Fascinating tales of the long-lost professions and people that shaped the region, from cowboys and lumbermen to pirates and blacksmiths.

John E. Tuhy *Sam Hill, the Prince of Castle Nowhere* (Timber Press, o/p). Detailed biography of the life and times of the amazingly energetic and eccentric Sam Hill, the tycoon who built Washington's Maryhill Art Museum.

Brent Walth *Fire at Eden's Gate: Tom McCall and the Oregon Story* (Oregon Historical Society, US). Well-written biography of Oregon's most important politician, a liberal Republican whose favorite causes – beach protection, the bottle bill, anti-sprawl policies – would influence civic planners nationwide.

Art, music, and architecture

Ginny Allen *Oregon Painters – The First 100 Years, 1859–1959* (Oregon Historical Society, o/p). Thoroughly researched and well-presented account of its subject, but given the variable quality of most of the painters, the tome is most useful as a reference guide.

Gideon Bosker and Lena Lencek *Frozen Music: A History of Portland Architecture* (Oregon Historical Society, US). Now a bit out of date, but still the definitive saga of the city's structures and the social landscape that produced them, from Victorian terracotta wonders to modern steel boxes.

James Bush *Encyclopedia of Northwest Music* (Sasquatch, US). Biographical entries and discographies of numerous Northwest musicians of all styles, as well as essays on major regional musical movements.

Kurt Cobain *Journals* (Riverhead Trade, US). Controversial reproduction of the diaries of the Nirvana frontman, complete with random thoughts, creative ideas, and various doodles, plus brickbats for more aged rockers like Pete Townsend and other targets.

William Goetzmann *Looking at the Land of Promise: Pioneer Images of the Pacific Northwest* (Washington State University Press, o/p). Beautiful book covering early artists' and then photographers' impressions of Washington and Oregon. The text is illuminating, though most of the painters are second-rate.

Clark Humphrey *Loser* (Abrams, US). The definitive account of Seattle rock, starting from its pre-rock origins in jazz and R&B, but focusing mainly on the punk and postpunk periods of the 1970s to the 1990s.

Bart King *An Architectural Guidebook to Portland* (Gibbs Smith, o/p). Long-overdue guide to the city's finest buildings, along with some of its more unfortunate modern debacles.

Jeffrey Carl Ochsner and Dennis Alan Andersen *Distant Corner: Seattle Architects and the Legacy of H.H. Richardson* (University of Washington Press, US). Penetrating look at the architecture of Pioneer Square, and how a brief historical opportunity – rebuilding after a massive fire and the rise of a Romanesque Revivalist – could reshape an entire district in one architect's image, from an entire continent away.

Tina Oldknow *Pilchuck: A Glass School* (University of Washington Press, US). Illustrated history of the founding and evolution of the most influential art institution in Washington State in the past 25 years, overseen by the imposing figure of Dale Chihuly.

Lara Swimmer *Process: Seattle Central Library* (Documentary Media, US). A fine photographic overview and history of what may be Seattle's most important building, Rem Koolhaas's strange and beautiful geometry of glass and steel, which also happens to be stuffed with books.

Fiction and literature

Sherman Alexie *Indian Killer* (Minerva/Atlantic). Acclaimed story of a Seattle serial murderer and the community reaction to the crimes. On a broader level it serves as a framework for reflections on inter-racial relations. One of several fine volumes by this native writer.

Lynda Barry *Cruddy* (Simon & Schuster, US). Affecting, sometimes shocking tale of a teenage girl in early-1970s Seattle, told with copious dark humor and vivid descriptions, enhanced further by the author's own lurid, striking illustrations.

Richard Brautigan *Trout Fishing in America, The Pill Versus the Springhill Mine Disaster*, and *In Watermelon Sugar* (Mariner/Houghton Mifflin). Associated with the West Coast Beat writers of the 1950s and 1960s, this Tacoma-born writer and poet wrote surreal fables overlaid with cultural references that question, and often attack, the social and political drift of the US.

Charles Burns *Black Hole* (Pantheon, US). An essential graphic novel of the region, a dark, mesmerizing view of Seattle in the 1970s as suburban teens are terrorized and transformed in unexpected ways by a particularly surreal disease.

Ernest Callenbach *Ecotopia* (Bantam, US). Highly influential fantasy of the Pacific Northwest breaking away from the US and establishing a progressive, ecologically friendly utopia. Has served as inspiration to countless local nature-lovers and environmental activists.

Raymond Carver *What We Talk About When We Talk About Love* (Harvill/Vintage), *Cathedral* (Panther/Vintage), *Fires* (Vintage, US), *Elephant* (Harvill, UK), *Where I'm Calling From* (Harvill/Vintage). Northwest-born and -raised writer whose short stories (many set locally) are superbly written, terse, and melancholic tales of everyday life and disintegrating family relationships. His best-known poetry volume is *A New Path to the Waterfall* (Atlantic Monthly Print, US).

Robin Cody *Ricochet River* (Ooligan, US). Affecting coming-of-age novel set in a declining mill town in the Oregon Cascades, focusing on love and loss and the elusive search for community in the modern age.

Douglas Coupland *Microserfs* (Regan/Flamingo). Curious novel/journal, by the coiner of the "Generation X" concept, which focuses on six Microsoft workers who also all live together, trying to make it in the shadow of Bill.

Katherine Dunn *Geek Love* (Vintage US/UK). Bizarre, influential cult novel set in Portland about a family of traveling circus geeks and sideshow freaks, narrated by a dwarf albino and strangely compelling for its colorful characters and energetic, experimental style.

G.M. Ford *Black River* (Avon/Eos). Gripping thriller about Seattle-based reporter and crime novelist Frank Corso, who becomes immersed in tracking down an evasive and thoroughly dangerous mobster in the Emerald City.

David Guterson *Snow Falling on Cedars* (Vintage US/UK). Highly regarded, but long-winded and repetitive, tale of life and death on a rural Puget Sound island. The central plot deals with a Japanese-American fisherman accused of murder. Many people swear by the book – as they do by the same author's moody short stories, *The Country Ahead of Us, the Country Behind* (Vintage US/UK).

Ken Kesey *Sometimes a Great Notion* (Penguin, US/UK). A stark evocation of Oregon's declining timber industry provides the background for a tale of psychological complexity. More famous for his *One Flew Over the Cuckoo's Nest* (Penguin, US/UK), where a psychiatric ward serves as a metaphor for a fascistic US culture, though his *Demon Box* (Penguin, US) is an

equally compelling selection of quasi-autobiographical short stories.

Craig Lesley *Winterkill* (Picador, US). Nez Percé drifter and failed rodeo star attempts to reconnect with his son after the death of his wife. The Portland writer returned with the same protagonist five years later in *River Song* (Picador, US). Another novel, *The Sky Fisherman* (Picador, US), is set in small-town Oregon and deals with the coming of age of a white youngster in a bigoted society.

Glen A. Love (ed.) *The World Begins Here: An Anthology of Oregon Fiction* (Oregon State University Press, US). No lightweights here (Ken Kesey, Raymond Carver, and Ursula K. Le Guin), but it's the other writers (Molly Gloss, Juan Armando Epple) who bring home the real nature of locality and roots.

Chuck Palahniuk Increasingly Portland's signatur e author, with a huge international cult following. His debut novel, *Fight Club* (Norton, US/UK), concerns bare-knuckle, illicit fighting as a metaphor for social rot; *Invisible Monsters* (Norton/Vintage) deals with a model whose looks are destroyed in a car accident; and *Diary* (Anchor/Vintage) is a surreal horror tale set on an island resort.

Lee Williams *After Nirvana* (Harper Perennial, US). Dark portrait of the lives of four homeless street kids living in the Seattle demimonde, where drugs and prostitution are commonplace and a morbid humor often creeps into the grimmest predicaments.

Tobias Wolff *This Boy's Life* (Grove/Bloomsbury). Set in 1950s Washington State, this forceful memoir relates a brutal upbringing, though a sharp, self-deprecating humor infuses the book, as it does Wolff's *In Pharaoh's Army* (Vintage US/UK), culled from his Vietnam War experiences.

Travel store

UK & Ireland
Britain
Devon & Cornwall
Dublin **D**
Edinburgh **D**
England
Ireland
The Lake District
London
London **D**
London Mini Guide
Scotland
Scottish Highlands & Islands
Wales

Europe
Algarve **D**
Amsterdam
Amsterdam **D**
Andalucía
Athens **D**
Austria
Baltic States
Barcelona
Barcelona **D**
Belgium & Luxembourg
Berlin
Brittany & Normandy
Bruges **D**
Brussels
Budapest
Bulgaria
Copenhagen
Corfu
Corsica
Costa Brava **D**
Crete
Croatia
Cyprus
Czech & Slovak Republics
Denmark
Dodecanese & East Aegean Islands
Dordogne & The Lot
Europe
Florence & Siena
Florence **D**
France
Germany
Gran Canaria **D**
Greece
Greek Islands
Hungary
Ibiza & Formentera **D**
Iceland
Ionian Islands
Italy
The Italian Lakes
Languedoc & Roussillon
Lanzarote & Fuerteventura **D**
Lisbon **D**
The Loire Valley
Madeira **D**
Madrid **D**
Mallorca **D**
Mallorca & Menorca
Malta & Gozo **D**
Menorca
Moscow
The Netherlands
Norway
Paris
Paris **D**
Paris Mini Guide
Poland
Portugal
Prague
Prague **D**
Provence & the Côte D'Azur
Pyrenees
Romania
Rome
Rome **D**
Sardinia
Scandinavia
Sicily
Slovenia
Spain
St Petersburg
Sweden
Switzerland
Tenerife & La Gomera **D**
Turkey
Tuscany & Umbria
Venice & The Veneto
Venice **D**
Vienna

Asia
Bali & Lombok
Bangkok
Beijing
Cambodia
China
Goa
Hong Kong & Macau
Hong Kong & Macau **D**
India
Indonesia
Japan
Kerala
Laos
Malaysia, Singapore & Brunei
Nepal
The Philippines
Rajasthan, Dehli & Agra
Singapore
Singapore **D**
South India
Southeast Asia
Sri Lanka
Taiwan
Thailand
Thailand's Beaches & Islands
Tokyo
Vietnam

Australasia
Australia
Melbourne
New Zealand
Sydney

North America
Alaska
Baja California
Boston
California
Canada
Chicago
Colorado
Florida
The Grand Canyon
Hawaii
Honolulu **D**
Las Vegas **D**
Los Angeles
Maui **D**
Miami & South Florida
Montréal
New England
New Orleans **D**
New York City
New York City **D**
New York City Mini Guide
Orlando & Walt Disney World® **D**
Pacific Northwest
San Francisco
San Francisco **D**
Seattle
Southwest USA
Toronto
USA
Vancouver
Washington DC
Washington DC **D**
Yellowstone & The Grand Tetons
Yosemite

Caribbean & Latin America
Antigua & Barbuda **D**
Argentina
Bahamas
Barbados **D**
Belize
Bolivia
Brazil
Cancùn & Cozumel **D**
Caribbean
Central America
Chile
Costa Rica
Cuba
Dominican Republic
Dominican Republic **D**
Ecuador
Guatemala
Jamaica
Mexico
Peru
St Lucia **D**
South America
Trinidad & Tobago
Yúcatan

Africa & Middle East
Cape Town & the Garden Route
Dubai **D**
Egypt
Gambia
Jordan

D: Rough Guide **DIRECTIONS** for short breaks

Available from all good bookstores

Information on over 25,000 destinations around the world

- **Read** Rough Guides' trusted travel info
- **Access** exclusive articles from Rough Guides authors
- **Update** yourself on new books, maps, CDs and other products
- **Enter** our competitions and win travel prizes
- **Share** ideas, journals, photos & travel advice with other users
- **Earn** points every time you contribute to the Rough Guide
  community and get rewards

ROUGH GUIDES

BROADEN YOUR HORIZONS

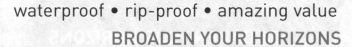

Small print and Index

A Rough Guide to Rough Guides

Published in 1982, the first Rough Guide – to Greece – was a student scheme that became a publishing phenomenon. Mark Ellingham, a recent graduate in English from Bristol University, had been traveling in Greece the previous summer and couldn't find the right guidebook. With a small group of friends he wrote his own guide, combining a highly contemporary, journalistic style with a thoroughly practical approach to travelers' needs.

The immediate success of the book spawned a series that rapidly covered dozens of destinations. And, in addition to impecunious backpackers, Rough Guides soon acquired a much broader and older readership that relished the guides' wit and inquisitiveness as much as their enthusiastic, critical approach and value-for-money ethos.

These days, Rough Guides include recommendations from shoestring to luxury and cover more than 200 destinations around the globe, including almost every country in the Americas and Europe, more than half of Africa and most of Asia and Australasia. Our ever-growing team of authors and photographers is spread all over the world, particularly in Europe, the USA and Australia.

In the early 1990s, Rough Guides branched out of travel, with the publication of Rough Guides to World Music, Classical Music and the Internet. All three have become benchmark titles in their fields, spearheading the publication of a wide range of books under the Rough Guide name.

Including the travel series, Rough Guides now number more than 350 titles, covering: phrasebooks, waterproof maps, music guides from Opera to Heavy Metal, reference works as diverse as Conspiracy Theories and Shakespeare, and popular culture books from iPods to Poker. Rough Guides also produce a series of more than 120 World Music CDs in partnership with World Music Network.

Visit www.roughguides.com to see our latest publications.

Rough Guide travel images are available for commercial licensing at www.roughguidespictures.com

SMALL PRINT

Rough Guide credits

Text editor: Shea Dean
Layout: Anita Singh
Cartography: Jasbir Sandhu
Picture editors: Sarah Smithies, Roland Smithies
Production: Aimee Hampson
Proofreader: Susannah Wight
Cover design: Chloë Roberts
Photographer: JD Dickey
Editorial: **London** Kate Berens, Claire
Saunders, Ruth Blackmore, Polly Thomas,
Alison Murchie, Karoline Densley, Andy
Turner, Keith Drew, Edward Aves, Nikki Birrell,
Alice Park, Sarah Eno, Lucy White, Jo Kirby,
Samantha Cook, James Smart, Natasha Foges,
Roísín Cameron, Emma Traynor, Emma Gibbs,
Joe Staines, Duncan Clark, Peter Buckley,
Matthew Milton, Tracy Hopkins, Ruth Tidball;
New York Andrew Rosenberg, Steven Horak,
AnneLise Sorensen, Amy Hegarty, April Isaacs,
Ella Steim, Anna Owens, Joseph Petta, Sean
Mahoney; **Delhi** Madhavi Singh, Karen D'Souza
Design & Pictures: **London** Scott Stickland,
Dan May, Diana Jarvis, Mark Thomas, Jj Luck,
Chloë Roberts, Nicole Newman, Sarah Cummins;
Delhi Umesh Aggarwal, Ajay Verma, Jessica

Subramanian, Ankur Guha, Pradeep Thapliyal,
Sachin Tanwar, Nikhil Agarwal
Production: Vicky Baldwin
Cartography: **London** Maxine Repath, Ed
Wright, Katie Lloyd-Jones; **Delhi** Jai Prakash
Mishra, Rajesh Chhibber, Ashutosh Bharti,
Rajesh Mishra, Animesh Pathak, Karobi Gogoi,
Amod Singh, Alakananda Bhattacharya, Swati
Handoo
Online: **New York** Jennifer Gold, Kristin
Mingrone; **Delhi** Manik Chauhan, Narender
Kumar, Rakesh Kumar, Amit Verma, Rahul Kumar,
Ganesh Sharma, Debojit Borah
Marketing & Publicity: **London** Liz Statham,
Niki Hanmer, Louise Maher, Jess Carter, Vanessa
Godden, Vivienne Watton, Anna Paynton, Rachel
Sprackett; **New York** Geoff Colquitt, Megan
Kennedy, Katy Ball; **Delhi** Reem Khokhar
Manager India: Punita Singh
Series Editor: Mark Ellingham
Reference Director: Andrew Lockett
Publishing Coordinator: Helen Phillips
Publishing Director: Martin Dunford
Commercial Manager: Gino Magnotta
Managing Director: John Duhigg

Publishing information

This first edition published November 2007 by
Rough Guides Ltd,
80 Strand, London WC2R 0RL
345 Hudson St, 4th Floor,
New York, NY 10014, USA
14 Local Shopping Centre, Panchsheel Park,
New Delhi 110017, India
Distributed by the Penguin Group
Penguin Books Ltd,
80 Strand, London WC2R 0Rl
Penguin Group (USA)
375 Hudson Street, NY 10014, USA
Penguin Group (Australia)
250 Camberwell Road, Camberwell,
Victoria 3124, Australia
Penguin Books Canada Ltd,
10 Alcorn Avenue, Toronto, Ontario,
Canada M4V 1E4
Penguin Group (NZ)
67 Apollo Drive, Mairangi Bay, Auckland 1310,
New Zealand
Cover concept by Peter Dyer.

Typeset in Bembo and Helvetica to an original
design by Henry Iles.

Printed and bound in China

© JD Dickey and Phil Lee 2007

No part of this book may be reproduced in any
form without permission from the publisher except
for the quotation of brief passages in reviews.

520pp includes index

A catalogue record for this book is available from
the British Library

ISBN: 978-1-84353-849-3

The publishers and authors have done their
best to ensure the accuracy and currency of
all the information in **The Rough Guide to
Oregon and Washington**, however, they can
accept no responsibility for any loss, injury, or
inconvenience sustained by any traveler as a
result of information or advice contained in the
guide.

1   3   5   7   9   8   6   4   2

Help us update

We've gone to a lot of effort to ensure that
the first edition of **The Rough Guide to
Oregon and Washington** is accurate and up
to date. However, things change – places get
"discovered", opening hours are notoriously
fickle, restaurants and rooms raise prices or lower
standards. If you feel we've got it wrong or left
something out, we'd like to know, and if you can
remember the address, the price, the time, the
phone number, so much the better.
We'll credit all contributions, and send a copy
of the next edition (or any other Rough Guide

if you prefer) for the best letters. Everyone who
writes to us and isn't already a subscriber will
receive a copy of our full-color thrice-yearly
newsletter. Please mark letters: "**Rough Guide
Oregon and Washington Update**" and send
to: Rough Guides, 80 Strand, London WC2R
0RL, or Rough Guides, 345 Hudson St, 4th
Floor, New York, NY 10014. Or send an email to
mail@roughguides.com.
Have your questions answered and tell others
about your trip at
www.roughguides.atinfopop.com.

SMALL PRINT

Acknowledgements

First, **JD** would like to thank his editor, Shea Dean, whose own skill and artistry contributed much to this book, and made it into the ass-kicking travel guide it was always meant to be. Also valuable were other colleagues and esteemed figures at Rough Guides, including Steven Horak and Andrew Rosenberg, and all JD's friends and associates throughout the Northwest, who made useful suggestions, provided illuminating insight, and otherwise made this book worth writing.

The **editor** thanks the author, whose sharp observations, pop-off-the-page writing, and sense of humor made editing this book an unexpected pleasure. She would also like to thank photo editors Sarah and Roland Smithies, who showed diligence and creativity in finding just the right images to illustrate this gorgeous and funky region, the excellent cartographers in Delhi for their precision and artistry and Anita Singh for putting it all together with such style. Finally, thanks to Rough Guides editors Andrew Rosenberg and Steven Horak for their continued guidance and support.

Photo credits

All photos © Rough Guides except the following:

Title page
Haystack Rock at Cannon Beach, Oregon
© Stuart Westmorland/Corbis

Full page
Mount Bachelor ski area © George and Monserrate Schwartz/Alamy

Introduction
Oregon Shakespeare Festival, Ashland © Greg Oregon Shakespeare Festival © Greg Vaughn/Alamy
Farmers market, Eugene, Oregon © Greg Vaughn/Alamy
Hikers in Columbia River Gorge © Jonathan Ley (www.leyphotography.com)
Edmonds–Kingston ferry, Washington © picturedimensions/Alamy
Isaac Brock of Modest Mouse © Tim Mosenfelder/ABACA/PA Photos
Mount St Helens © Jonathan Ley (www.leyphotography.com)
Historic Columbia River Highway © Jonathan Ley (www.leyphotography.com)

Things not to miss
01 Olympic National Park © Jonathan Ley (www.leyphotography.com)
02 Bumbershoot © WorldFoto/Alamy
03 Appetizer at Vinny's in Friday Harbor © Catherine Karnow/Corbis
04 Rafting on the Skykomish River © Michael O'Leary/Getty
05 Mount St Helens © Jonathan Ley (www.leyphotography.com)
06 Pike Place Market, Seattle © Kim Karpeles/Alamy
07 Historic Columbia River Highway © Danita Delimont/Alamy
08 Multnomah Falls © Brad Mitchell/Alamy
09 Pendleton Round-Up © Gary Brettnacher/Getty
10 Lake Chelan © age fotostock/SuperStock
12 Hells Canyon National Scenic Area © Dennis Frates/Alamy
13 Ecola Beach © Jonathan Ley (www.leyphotography.com)
14 Rose Festival Parade, Portland © Danita Delimont/Alamy
15 Snoqualmie Falls © Salish Lodge & Spa
16 Fins Coastal Cuisine in Port Townsend, Washington © Macduff Everton/Corbis
17 Erath Vineyards, Dundee © Cephas Picture Library/Alamy
18 John Day Fossil Beds © Jonathan Ley (www.leyphotography.com)
19 Snowboarder on Mount Hood © Stock Connection/Alamy
20 Crater Lake © Jonathan Ley (www.leyphotography.com)
21 Windsurfing at the Hatchery, Hood River © Richard Hallman/Photolibrary
23 Fremont Troll under Aurora Bridge, Seattle © Stephen Finn/Alamy
24 Oregon Caves National Monument © Peter Chapman/Photolibrary
25 Wildwood Trail, Portland © Jonathan Ley (www.leyphotography.com)
26 Oregon Shakespeare Festival © Oregon Shakespeare Festival/T. Charles Erickson

SMALL PRINT

SMALL PRINT

Index

Map entries are in color.

INDEX

INDEX

517

W

Y

Map symbols

maps are listed in the full index using colored text

-----	International boundary	♜	Castle/fort
---···	Province/territory border	⬇	Viewpoint
-----	Chapter boundary	⚊	Campsite
🛣	Interstate	⚲	Lighthouse
⬡	US highway	◆	Place of interest
⬡	Province/state highway	⊙	Statue
	Pedestrianized street	⚕	Gardens
	Unpaved road	◉	Accommodation
-----	Path/track	▣	Restaurant
	Railway	ⓘ	Information office
—T—	Tram	⊠	Post office
— —	Ferry route	⊞	Hospital
	Waterway	✈	Airport
‿	Bridge	Ⓜ	Metro
I	Dam	♦	Museum
⁂	Crater		Building
⋀	Mountains	—+—	Church
▲	Peak	⬭	Stadium
⇗	Pass		Park
⚲	Waterfall	+⁎	Cemetery
⋔	Spring		Forest
⌇	Gorge/rocks		Glacier
◠	Cave		

MAP SYMBOLS

We're covered. Are you?